THE PAKISTAN PARADOX

THE CERI SERIES IN COMPARATIVE POLITICS AND INTERNATIONAL STUDIES

Series editor, Christophe Jaffrelot

This series consists of translations of noteworthy manuscripts and publications in the social sciences emanating from the foremost French researchers at Sciences Po, Paris.

The focus of the series is the transformation of politics and society by transnational and domestic factors—globalisation, migration and religion. States are more permeable to external influence than ever before and this phenomenon is accelerating processes of social and political change the world over. In seeking to understand and interpret these transformations, this series gives priority to social trends from below as much as to the interventions of state and non-state actors.

CHRISTOPHE JAFFRELOT

The Pakistan Paradox

Instability and Resilience

Translated by
Cynthia Schoch

OXFORD
UNIVERSITY PRESS

Oxford University Press is a department of the
University of Oxford. It furthers the University's objective
of excellence in research, scholarship, and education
by publishing worldwide.

Oxford New York
Auckland Cape Town Dar es Salaam Hong Kong Karachi
Kuala Lumpur Madrid Melbourne Mexico City Nairobi
New Delhi Shanghai Taipei Toronto

With offices in
Argentina Austria Brazil Chile Czech Republic France Greece
Guatemala Hungary Italy Japan Poland Portugal Singapore
South Korea Switzerland Thailand Turkey Ukraine Vietnam

Oxford is a registered trade mark of Oxford University Press
in the UK and certain other countries.

Published in the United States of America by
Oxford University Press
198 Madison Avenue, New York, NY 10016

Library of Congress Cataloging-in-Publication Data is available
Jaffrelot, Christophe
The Pakistan Paradox/Instability and Resilience
ISBN 978-0-19023-518-5

Printed in India on acid-free paper

CONTENTS

v

CONTENTS

CONTENTS

LIST OF TABLES

LIST OF TABLES

PREFACE AND ACKNOWLEDGEMENTS

Pakistan focuses the concern of quite a few chancelleries and international organizations today. Not only is it a nation that possesses nuclear weapons without having a stable political system, the military having held the reins of power on a number of occasions since independence in 1947, but it is also wracked by Islamist forces, many of which have links with the Afghan Taliban, Al Qaeda and possibly the Islamic State. A serious compounding factor, the civil and especially military authorities show considerable ambivalence with regard to certain Islamist groups that they view as allies against India in Kashmir, but also in Afghanistan, where NATO, now on its way out, has been mired in war since 2001 against the Taliban and groups based in Pakistan where Al Qaeda leaders are suspected of hiding.

Western fears about Pakistan have, however, been a poor advisor for sociological and political analysis, portrayals of the country too often being oversimplified. That is not to say that certain trends are not alarming, but in attempting to explain them, it is important to discard preconceived notions and avoid culturalist conflations. The present book sets out to decipher this complexity. It is not a work of field research per se, but an essay based on over fifteen years of familiarity with Pakistan.

I am most grateful to many friends and colleagues who have helped me to improve this book over the course of time. In Pakistan (and in Europe as well as in the United States where we have met repeatedly), I have benefited from the guidance of Mohammad Waseem over the last fifteen years. I also want to thank Tariq Rehman, Saeed Shafqat and Ayesha Siddiqa for the long discussions we have had on three continents. In the United States, I have learnt from Phil Oldenburg more than from anybody else during our "seminars" near The Cloisters. I am also most grateful to Hassan Abbas,

Christine Fair, Frédéric Grare, Sana Haroon, Farah Jan, Zia Mian and Aqil Shah for their comments on conference papers and during rich conversations. In the United Kingdom, in addition to my earliest guides—Ian Talbot and Yunus Samad—I am especially indebted to Farzana Shaikh for her deep understanding of Pakistan and her generous comments on my work, and to Michael Dwyer and David Lunn for their careful editing. Last but not least, in France, Mariam Abou Zahab has been an invaluable source of information and critique based on a truly erudite knowledge of Pakistan's culture and politics. I also thank my friends Amélie Blom and Laurent Gayer for their enlightening essays, oral presentations and daily conversations. The making of this book has hugely benefited from the work of three remarkable experts: Elise Roy, from my French publishing house, Fayard, Miriam Périer, from my *alma mater*, CERI-Sciences Po/CNRS and Cynthia Schoch, my favourite translator!

Naturally, any mistakes and misinterpretations are mine.

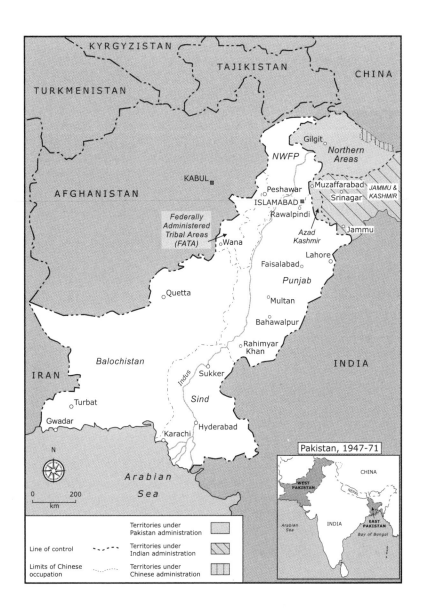

KYRGYZISTAN

TAJIKISTAN

CHINA

TURKMENISTAN

Gilgit

NWFP

Northern Areas

KABUL

AFGHANISTAN

Muzaffarabad

JAMMU & KASHMIR

Peshawar

ISLAMABAD

Srinagar

Rawalpindi

Federally Administered Tribal Areas (FATA)

Wana

Azad Kashmir

Jammu

Lahore

Faisalabad

Punjab

Quetta

Multan

Bahawalpur

Rahimyar Khan

INDIA

Balochistan

Sukker

IRAN

Indus

Sind

Turbat

Gwadar

Hyderabad

Karachi

N

Arabian Sea

0   200
km

Line of control	- - - -	Territories under Pakistan administration	
Limits of Chinese occupation	· · · · ·	Territories under Indian administration	
		Territories under Chinese administration	

Pakistan, 1947-71

CHINA

WEST PAKISTAN

NEPAL

Arabian Sea

INDIA

EAST PAKISTAN

Bay of Bengal

INTRODUCTION

The new nation was thus born with an image of India as a villain, a satan, and a monster next door, out to devour the newborn state. (Mohammad Waseem, *Politics and the State in Pakistan*, Islamabad, National Institute of Historical and Cultural Research, 1994, p. 99)

Since the beginning Pakistan has been confronted with the monumental task of formulating a national identity distinct from India. Born out of a schism of the old civilisation of India, Pakistan has debated over the construction of a culture of its own, a culture which will not only be different from that of India but one that the rest of the world can understand. (M. Ali, "In Search of Identity", *Dawn Magazine*, 7 May 2000)

As the two excerpts above indicate, Pakistan was born of a partition that overdetermined its subsequent trajectory not only because of the difficult relations it developed with India, but also because this parting of ways defined the terms of its collective quest for identity. Indeed, the 1947 Partition was the outcome of an intense struggle as well as a trauma.

It grew out of the separatist ideology which crystallised at the end of the nineteenth century among the Urdu-speaking Muslim intelligentsia of North India, whose key figure was none other than Syed Ahmad Khan, the founder, in 1877, of the Anglo-Mohammedan Oriental College in Aligarh, a little town not far from Delhi. The Aligarh movement—as it was to be remembered in history—turned to politics in the early decades of the twentieth century when it became the crucible of the Muslim League. This party, founded in 1906, was then separatist in the sense that it obtained from the British Raj a separate electorate for the Indian Muslims. The demand for a separate state emerged much later, in the 1940s, under the auspices of Muhammad Ali Jinnah, although in formulating it he did not outline the

1

contours of the future Pakistan until the last year of the Raj, nor did he fully grasp the traumatic implications Partition would have.[1]

The 1947 Partition resulted in unprecedented violence.[2] One million people died and about ten million others crossed borders.[3] The plural is in fact required here because Pakistan was then made up of two wings (and therefore had two borders with India), the two areas of the Raj where Muslims were in a majority: East Pakistan (made up of East Bengal) and West Pakistan (made up of West Punjab, Sindh, the North West Frontier Province, the area that was to become Balochistan, and a few princely states). Violence and migration were of such magnitude that this tragic episode can be regarded as the first example of ethnic cleansing in history (indeed, the word "*safai*", "cleaning" was used at that time by the local actors). Not only millions of Muslims from East Punjab and Hindus from East Bengal crossed over and settled down in the western part of "their" now truncated former province, but Muslims and Hindus of both countries took refuge in the country where their community was a majority. The circumstances in which Pakistan was born are thus largely responsible not only for the way it has related to India, but also for its complicated trajectory.

Three Wars, Three Constitutions and Three Coups

The history of Pakistan over the last sixty-seven years ;as been marked by chronic instability due to internal and external factors. In 1947, the British awarded Pakistan the status of a dominion. Under the aegis of M.A. Jinnah, the new Governor General, the 1935 Government of India Act became its interim constitution, minus its initial references to imperial control. It would take nine years for the country to give itself a constitution. In the course of this endeavour, political parties eventually lost the initiative as a result of their own internal divisions and the hunger for power of senior bureaucrats. In 1954, one of them, Ghulam Mohammad, the then governor general who had taken over from Khawaja Nazimuddin, the successor of Jinnah (who had died in September 1948), dissolved the Constituent Assembly (with the consent of the Supreme Court) and had another one

---

[1] Ian Talbot and Gurharpal Singh, *The Partition of India*, Cambridge, Cambridge University Press, 2009.

[2] Yasmin Khan, The Great Partition. *The Making of India and Pakistan*, New Haven, Yale University Press, 2007.

[3] Over the 1947–1950 period, 14 million people were involved in the population exchange.

elected. The 1956 Constitution was not particularly democratic, but it could not be fully implemented anyway since another bureaucrat, Iskander Mirza, and then the Commander-in-Chief of the army, Ayub Khan, seized power in 1958. Till 1969, the latter established a military regime that claimed to modernise Pakistan in the framework of Martial Law and then, after 1962, of a new constitution. This second constitution was authoritarian, but did not completely disregard political pluralism, especially after 1965 when Ayub Khan further liberalised his regime. But eventually, after months of unrest, he had to resign in favour of another general, the chief of the army, Yayha Khan, in 1969.

By the end of 1970, Yayha Khan, having few other options, gave Pakistan its first opportunity to vote. The Bengalis of East Pakistan seized it to win the elections by massively supporting the Awami League, a party whose nationalism had been exacerbated by years of exploitation under the thumb of West Pakistan. Its leader, Mujibur Rahman, asked for a confederal system that would give East Pakistan considerable autonomy. But almost all West Pakistanis—including the winner of the elections in Punjab and Sindh, Zulfiqar Ali Bhutto's Pakistan People's Party (PPP)—rejected this option and supported repression. Civil war ensued and resulted in the creation of Bangladesh in 1971—after the military intervention of India, New Delhi arguing that violence and the flow of refugees to West Bengal had to stop.

The arrival in power of Zulfiqar Ali Bhutto, to whom Yayha Khan handed the reins in 1971, marked the beginning of the first democratic transition. Not only was the army subjected to the civilian government, but a third, parliamentarian Constitution was promulgated in 1973. However, Bhutto displayed such authoritarian tendencies that the federal dimension of this text was stillborn and the social reforms (including land reform) that the PPP had promised were not truly implemented. Finally, Bhutto rigged the 1977 elections, a move that resulted in mass protests from the opposition. These events provided the army with an excuse to seize power once again, led by General Zia ul Haq.

This second military coup gave birth to a dictatorial regime and even a police-state: in contrast to the Ayub years, scores of politicians were sent to jail, opponents were tortured, and Bhutto was even executed in 1979. Zia also instrumentalised Islam in order to legitimise his rule. His Islamisation policy affected all areas of life: education (with the development of Qur'anic schools), law (with the setting up of sharia courts), and the fiscal system (with the transformation of *zakat* and *ushr* into compulsory, state-coordinated contributions). This policy gained momentum in the context of a new kind of war: the anti-Soviet jihad from 1979–89 in Afghanistan, its foot soldiers being mostly the Afghan mujahideen who had found refuge in Pakistan. While Zia, like Ayub Khan, resigned himself to seeking the support of the Pakistani citizens through elections, he never gave up his uniform and it was not until his mysterious death in 1988 that Pakistan's second democratic transition became possible.

This transition was not as substantial as the first one. While the generals returned to their barracks, they continued to be in charge of key policies regarding Afghanistan, Kashmir (India at large) and defence (including the nuclear programme). They were also in a position to oust prime ministers one after another between 1988 and 1999. Benazir Bhutto, who had won the 1988 elections, benefiting from the PPP political machine and her family's prestige—partly based on her father's "martyrdom"—was the first prime minister to be dismissed by President Ishaq Khan in the 1990s. She was replaced by her archenemy, Nawaz Sharif, after army-supervised elections in 1990. But Sharif alienated Ishaq Khan and the army as well. He was dismissed in 1993 and replaced by Benazir again. She herself was eased out in 1996, this time by the President Farooq Leghari, enabling Nawaz Sharif to stage a comeback. The 1997 elections were different from the three previous ones because they gave Sharif's party, the PML(N), the two-thirds majority that allows the prime minister to reform the Constitution: the thirteenth amendment re-established the parliamentary nature of the Constitution and deprived the president of the power to dismiss the prime minister and to dissolve both the national and provincial assemblies. But Sharif misused power. He did not respect either the independence of the judiciary or freedom of the press. Furthermore, he alienated the army— including the chief of the army, Pervez Musharraf—by bowing to American pressures during the "Kargil war".

In October 1999, Musharraf's coup brought the army back into power. He then militarised the state and the economy more than his predecessors. Not only were (ex-)army officers appointed to positions normally reserved for civilians, but their business activities benefited from the patronage of the state more than ever before. While Zia had profited from the anti-Soviet, US-sponsored war in Afghanistan, Musharraf exploited the fact that Pakistan had become a frontline state again during the war the US once again sponsored, this time against the Taliban and Al Qaeda after the 11 September attacks in 2001. While Musharraf—like Ayub Khan—was ousted from power in 2007–8 in the wake of street demonstrations, those who protested so effectively this time were affiliated with a specific institution, the judiciary—hence the fear of "a government of judges" expressed by supporters of parliamentarianism after democracy was restored.

The 2008 elections brought back the same parties—and the same families, the Bhuttos and the Sharifs, both freshly returned from exile—as in the 1980s–90s. Benazir was assassinated in December 2007, but her widower, Asif Ali Zardari, was elected President after the PPP won the 2008 elections. The new government, with the support of key opposition parties, restored the parliamentary nature of the 1973 Constitution that Musharraf, like Zia, had presidentialised. Not only federalism but also the independence of the judiciary were at last in a position to prevail. However, the civilians failed to reassert their authority over the Inter-Services Intelligence (ISI), the military intelligence agency that since the 1980s has become a state within the state, and the army retained the upper hand on key policies such as relations with the Taliban, the Kashmir issue and the nuclear programme. The army justified its role by arguing that the country was facing huge challenges ranging from the unleashing of ethno-nationalist violence in Balochistan and Karachi to the rise of both sectarian and jihadi Islamist movements, some of which were affiliated with Al Qaeda and attacked the Pakistani state because of its association with the US in the "global war on terror".

However, this escalation of violence did not prevent Parliament from completing its five-year term in March 2013 and citizens from voting in large numbers two months later, mostly in favour of Nawaz Sharif, who in June became prime minister for the third time.

The alternation of phases of democratisation and military rule every ten years or so is not the only source of instability in Pakistan. The recurrence of armed conflict is another cause. Some of these conflicts come under the category of civil war, such as in 1970–71 in Bengal or during the 1973–7 insurgency in Balochistan—and the war that started in the mid-2000s in that area. Others have primarily opposed Pakistan and India, overtly or covertly. As early as 1947–8, both countries fought each other in Kashmir. In 1965, Pakistan attacked India, whereas in 1971, the conflict was a sequel to the movement for Bangladesh. The most recent conflict, the 1999 "Kargil war" (named after a town in Jammu and Kashmir), was short and circumscribed.

Thus, the number of military coups (three—or four if one includes Yayha Khan's martial law episode in 1969–70) is equal to the number of wars with India (three—four if one includes the "Kargil war"). This is not just by chance. In fact, Pakistan's political instability is to some degree overdetermined by the regional context, and more especially by the sentiment of vulnerability of Pakistan vis-à-vis India.

Between India and Afghanistan: Pakistan Caught in a Pincer Movement?

In the beginning, this sentiment (which would be exploited by the army subsequently) stemmed from the conditions in which Partition took place. Pakistan resented the slow and incomplete manner in which India gave the country its share of the military equipment and the treasury of the defunct British Raj. Pakistanis also felt cheated by the way the Kashmir question was settled. On 15 August 1947, Jammu and Kashmir was one of the last princely states that was still undecided about its future. The Maharajah—a Hindu—and the main party—the All Jammu and Kashmir National Conference—were not willing to join Pakistan in spite of the fact that the state was comprised of a majority of Muslim subjects. But they did not support accession to India either, fearing Pakistani retaliation.[4] On 22 October 1947, 5,000 paramilitaries from the Pashtun tribal belt who were not in uniform but were supported by Pakistani officers infiltrated Jammu and Kashmir and established a parallel government (the government of Azad Kashmir—free Kashmir) while they were approaching Srinagar, the state capital.[5] The Maharajah turned to India and Nehru sent troops on 27 October. Three days latter, the government of Pakistan deployed its own soldiers, but India's military superiority enabled New Delhi not only to retain the Valley of Srinagar, but also to reconquer key positions such as Baramulla. Certainly, when the matter was brought before the UN Security Council, India was asked to organize a referendum in Jammu and Kashmir to let the local people decide whether they wanted to remain part of the Indian Union or not. But this referendum was supposed to take place after the withdrawal of Pakistani troops—which did not occur. In fact, the line of ceasefire that was officially agreed in the truce signed on 1 January 1949 gave Pakistan control of a fraction of the erstwhile princely state that was divided in two: Azad Kashmir[6] and the areas of Gilgit and Baltistan, which were amalgamated to form the Northern Areas. These regions were directly administered by the central government. Most Pakistanis considered that without Kashmir as part of their country, Partition remained unachieved.

---

[4] Jammu and Kashmir was largely connected to the rest of India via roads which had now become part of Pakistan.

[5] The Pakistani army "formally entered the war in April 1948" (Aqil Shah, *The Army and Democracy. Military Politics in Pakistan*, Cambridge (Mass.), Harvard University Press, 2014, p. 42).

[6] On Azad Kashmir, see Christopher Snedden, *The Untold Story of the People of Azad Kashmir*, London, Hurst, 2012.

Furthermore, some of them feared that India had not resigned itself to the very fact of Partition and that New Delhi would try to reunite with the subcontinent one day or another. Not only did Hindu nationalists dream of Akhand Bharat (undivided India), but statements made by a few Congress leaders lent themselves to a similar interpretation. The then party president, Acharya Kripalani, for instance, declared in 1947, "Neither the Congress not the nation has given up its claim of a united India." Deputy Prime Minister Vallabhbhai Patel concurred when he said, "Sooner than later, we shall again be united in common allegiance to our country."[7]

The fear of India was reinforced by an encirclement complex due to the attitude demonstrated by Afghanistan. In the early 1940s, the Kabul government had asked the British, upon their departure, to allow the Pashtun tribes of the Raj to choose between claiming independence and becoming part of Afghanistan. Pakistan was not an option. At the same time, the Muslim League was disturbed by Kabul's unwillingness to recognise the Durand Line as an international border. In 1947, this attitude prevented the Pakistanis from having distinct borders, its territory not being clearly defined (or stabilised) on the eastern side either. These difficulties harked back to the pervasiveness of Pashtun nationalism on both sides of the Durand line. Certainly, this nationalism remained fuzzy. It was not clear whether its supporters were in favour of a separate country made up of Pashtun tribes or whether they were willing to incorporate Pakistan's Pashtuns into Afghanistan. Whatever their agenda, it was bound to undermine the project of Pakistan's founders. The latter felt especially threatened because Pashtun nationalists cultivated excellent relations with India. The main architect of Pashtun nationalism under the Raj in the North West

---

[7] Cited in Muhammad Ayub Khan, *Friends not Masters. A Political Autobiography*, Karachi, Oxford University Press, 1967, p. 136. I have been unable to locate the exact source of these quotes, but the very fact that Ayub Khan cites them in his autobiography shows that one of Pakistan's most important leaders believed these words to be true and/or used them to cultivate obsessive fears in his own country. Patel, according to another minister of the Indian government, Abdul Kalam Azad, was "convinced that the new State of Pakistan was not viable and could not last"—even though, "he was the greatest supporter of partition" among Congressmen, "out of irritation and injured vanity" (Abul Kalam Azad, *India Wins Freedom*, Hyderabad, Orient Longman, 1988, p. 225). Nehru himself at one point mentioned the possibility of creating a "confederation" between India and Pakistan, something the Pakistanis found utterly unacceptable (cited in Aparna Pande, *Explaining Pakistan's Foreign Policy*, London and New York, Routledge, 2011, p. 30),

Frontier Province, Abdul Ghaffar Khan, was a staunch supporter of the Congress and was known as "Frontier Gandhi" because of his close relationship to the Mahatma.

In June 1947, Afghan Prime Minister Muhammad Hashim Khan declared, "If an independent Pukhtoonistan cannot be established, then the Frontier Province should join Afghanistan."[8] Neither of these options came about and so in September 1947, Afghanistan was the only country that voted against Pakistan's admission to the UN. The Afghan representative to the UN then declared that his country could not "recognize the North West Frontier as part of Pakistan so long as the people of the North West Frontier have not been given the opportunity free from any kind of influence—and I repeat, free from any kind of influence—to determine for themselves whether they wish to be independent or to become part of Pakistan."[9]

The leaders of Pakistan were convinced that Kabul and New Delhi tried to take their country in "a pincer movement", as Ayub Khan confided in his autobiography.[10] Indeed, in 1949, at a time when Afghanistan formally rejected the Durand line, many Indian cities celebrated "Pashtunistan Day", which Kabul had decided to celebrate every year on 31 August.[11]

The Pakistani Paradox

The fear of encirclement, and more especially of India, partly explains the role of the Pakistani army in the public sphere. Indeed, the military could project themselves as the saviours of a vulnerable country, and this argument was likely to appear even more convincing in the post-Jinnah context when the political personnel looked weak, factionalised and corrupt. But there are other factors to the democratic deficit affecting Pakistan since the 1950s. To make sense of it, one needs to understand the way civilians related to power. Pakistani politicians not only occasionally collaborated

---

[8] Abdul Sattar, *Pakistan Foreign Policy, 1947–2009*, Karachi, Oxford University Press, 2010, p. 21.

[9] Cited in Aparna Pande, *Explaining Pakistan's Foreign Policy*, op. cit., p. 64. One month later, Afghanistan softened its stance but made three demands in exchange: that the Pashtuns of Pakistan should be granted a proper province, that Pakistan should give Afghanistan access to the sea, and that both countries should sign a treaty according to which they agreed to remain neutral if one of them fought a war against a third country. None of these demands were met.

[10] Muhammad Ayub Khan, *Friends not Masters*, op. cit., p. 197.

[11] Aparna Pande, *Explaining Pakistan's Foreign Policy*, op. cit., p. 65.

with military rulers, compromising their reputation, but when they were in charge of the government of the country they also tended to display authoritarian tendencies. As mentioned above, Bhutto rigged the 1977 elections and many of his successors as prime ministers showed little respect for the independence of the judiciary and sometimes even for freedom of the press.

Pakistan's democratic deficit can also be measured by the centralisation of the state. Even when a federal constitution was (re-)introduced, the provinces were never given the autonomy they demanded, whereas almost all of them—East Bengal, West Punjab, Sindh and the NWFP—had experienced form of self-administration under the Raj and coincided by and large with an ethno-linguistic group.

Centralisation, once again, may be explained by the need for a strong, unified state to face India. However, on that front too, one should not focus mainly on this external factor. Even before Partition, Jinnah's project was that of a unitary state. Certainly, the 1940 Lahore resolution through which the Muslim League officially spelled out its separatist agenda, recognised a prominent role for the provinces of the country envisioned, but their autonomy was drastically reduced as early as 1946 in the last pre-Partition blueprint of Pakistan as Jinnah imagined it. And in 1947, the citizens of the new country were required to identify not only with one religion—Islam—but also with one language—Urdu—, an idiom that became the country's official tongue even though it was spoken only by a small minority.

These developments reflected sociological dynamics. The idea of Pakistan was primarily conceived by an Urdu-speaking upper caste elite group fearing social decline. Made up of aristocratic literati, this group embodied the legacy (and the nostalgia) of the Mughal Empire. Their ancestors had prospered thanks to land and the administrative status the emperors had given them between the sixteenth and the eighteenth centuries. But in the nineteenth century, colonisation called these privileges into question, not only because the British took over power from some of the Muslim rulers, but also because they did not trust the Muslims (who were seen as the former dominant group) as much as they did the Hindus.

Furthermore, the Hindus asserted themselves at the expense of the Muslims because of their growing role in the economy (through trade and then industrial activities), because of their adhesion to the university system, which resulted in their increasingly important role in the administration, and because of their political influence that developed parallel to the democratization of the Raj almost in proportion to their numbers. The separatism of the Urdu-speaking elite crystallised in this context in the nineteenth century and was subsequently exacerbated (especially in the 1930s–40s) in reaction to the fear of losing their traditional status—eventually prompting them to work toward obtaining a state to govern. The Muslim League leaders argued that they demanded Pakistan to protect Islam from Hinduism, but they also (and more importantly) did it to protect their interests from the growing influence of the Hindus.

The following pages will elaborate on this sociological interpretation of the Pakistani project, which is not new. Hamza Alavi developed a similar analysis in the 1970s–80s,[12] at a time when Paul Brass argued in a similar vein that the League's claim that Islam was in danger in the 1930s–40s was a political ploy used by elite groups to mobilise Muslim masses in support of their idea of Pakistan.[13] But the present book's approach is less Marxist than Alavi's reading and less instrumentalist than Brass's interpretation for the simple reason that it emphasizes the weight of the cultural and societal parameters that defined the mentality of the Muslim elite during the Raj.[14] More importantly, this book offers a reading of the Pakistani trajectory that focuses on the implications of these sociological factors for the country since its creation.

The history of Pakistan has been overdetermined by three sets of tensions all rooted in contradictions that were already apparent in the 1940s. The first one can be summarised by the equation "Pakistan = Islam + Urdu". While all the ethnic groups of Pakistan could identify with one variant or another of Islam, they could not easily give up their linguistic identity, all the more so because it often epitomized full-fledged nationalist sentiments

---

12 Hamza Alavi, "Class and State in Pakistan", in Hassan Gardezi and Jamil Rashid (eds), *Pakistan: The Roots of Dictatorship*, London, Zed Press, 1983, and Hamza Alavi, "Pakistan and Islam: Ethnicity and Ideology", in Fred Halliday and Hamza Alavi (eds), *State and Ideology in the Middle East and Pakistan*, London, Macmillan, 1987.

13 Paul Brass, *Language, Religion and Politics in North India*, Cambridge, Cambridge University Press, 1974.

14 The Brass thesis will be discussed in the first part of the book. Regarding Alavi's approach, it may be sufficient to say that his definition of the "salariat"—the key actor behind the Pakistani project in Alavi's view—is too restrictive. As will be shown in the following chapters, the idea of Pakistan was crafted by an intelligentsia that was not only motivated by vested interests, but by a specific upper caste Islamic culture. This is why an interpretation of Muslim separatism in terms of class needs to be supplemented by an analysis taking societal dimensions into account.

(or movements). Hence a first contradiction between the central(ising) government and centrifugal forces (which sometimes have given rise to separatist movements).

The second tension pertains to another form of concentration of power that the army officers and the politicians have developed over the course of time. Indeed, from the 1950s onwards, Pakistani society has been in the clutches of a civil-military establishment which has cultivated the legacy of the pre-Partition Muslim League in the sense that it was primarily interested in protecting its interests and dominant status. The elitist rationale of the Pakistan idea therefore resulted in social conservatism and the persistence of huge inequalities. Certainly, some politicians have fought for democracy, but they have never managed to dislodge from power a very well entrenched civil-military establishment and promote progressive reforms in a decisive manner—either because they were co-opted, or because they eventually turned out to be autocrats themselves. In fact, some of the main opposition forces to the system that have emerged have been the judiciary (when the Supreme Court had the courage to rise to the occasion), civil society movements (including the media) and the Islamists. In the absence of a credible political alternative within the institutional framework, the tensions that have developed have been especially radical. What has been at stake in most of the crises that Pakistan has experienced has been the regime itself, not only in political terms, but also, sometimes, in social terms.

The role of Islam in the public sphere is the root cause of the third contradiction. Jinnah looked at it as a culture and considered the Muslims of the Raj as a community that needed to be protected. They were supposed to be on a par with the members of the religious minorities in the Republic to be built. His rhetoric, therefore, had a multicultural overtone. On the contrary, clerics and fundamentalist groups wanted to create an Islamic state where the members of the minorities would be second-class citizens. Until the 1970s, the first approach tended to prevail. But in the 1970s the Islamist lobby (whose political parties never won more than one-tenth of the votes) exerted increasingly strong pressure. It could assert itself at that time partly because of circumstances. First, the trauma of the 1971 war led the country to look for a return to its ethno-religious roots. Second, the use of religion was part of Z. A. Bhutto's populist ideology, which associated socialism with Islam. Third, Zia also used religion to legitimise his power and to find allies among the Islamists.

The promotion of Islam by Bhutto and Zia was partly due to external factors as well. The former supported Afghan Islamists who were likely—so he thought—to destabilise the Pashtun nationalist government of Kabul. The latter backed the same Afghan leaders and other mujahideens (including Arab groups like Al Qaeda) against the Soviets in order to make the Pakistani army's presence felt in Afghanistan and thereby gain "strategic depth" vis-à-vis India. Zia's Islamisation policy also (re)activated the conflict between Sunnis and Shias, an opposition that was exacerbated by another external factor: the proxy war that Iran and Saudi Arabia fought in Pakistan from the 1980s onwards.

The critical implications of the legacy of Zia's Islamisation—which also resulted in the massive infiltration of jihadis in Kashmir in the 1990s— became clear after 9/11 when the US forced the Pakistani state to fight not only Al Qaeda but also the Taliban and the Islamist groups that the ISI had used so far in Indian Kashmir and elsewhere. In response, these groups turned their guns towards the Pakistani army, its former patron, and intensified their fight against their traditional targets, the Shias and non-Muslim communities, creating an atmosphere of civil war.

The three contradictions just reviewed provide a three-part structure to this book, which is therefore not organised chronologically. This thematic framework is intended to enhance our understanding of the Pakistani paradox. Indeed, so far, none of the consubstantial contradictions of Pakistan mentioned above has had the power to destroy the country. In spite of the chronic instability that they have created, Pakistan continues to show remarkable resilience. This can only be understood if one makes the effort to grasp the complexity of a country that is often caricatured. This is the reason why all sides of the three tensions around which this book is organised must be considered together: the centrifugal forces at work in Pakistan and those resisting them on behalf of Pakistani nationalism and provincial autonomy; the culture of authoritarianism and the resources of democracy; the Islamist agenda, and those who are fighting it on behalf of secularism or "Muslimhood" à la Jinnah. The final picture may result in a set, not of contradictions, but of paradoxes in which virtually antagonistic elements cohabit. But whether that is sufficient to contain instability remains to be seen.

PART ONE

NATIONALISM WITHOUT A NATION—AND EVEN WITHOUT A PEOPLE?

After sixty-one years of its existence, Pakistan has gone from a 'nation' searching for a country to a country searching for a nation (Lal Khan, *Pakistan's Other Story*, Lahore, The Struggle Publications, 2008, p. 294).

Nationalism is a modern ideology that was as yet unknown in mid-nineteenth-century British India, when the first signs of the separatist trends that would give birth to Pakistan crystallised. The Muslims were even less an exception to the rule as, despite their relatively small numbers—they made up one-fifth of the population of the Raj—, they were wracked by both religious and social divisions.

Which Islam(s)?

Regarding religion, diversity among Muslims tended to be underestimated in British India as elsewhere due to a dominant analysis of Islam in purely scriptural terms. Differences are easily levelled when the "fundamental theological and philosophical principles that can be said to constitute the core of the Islamic faith are enshrined in a single scriptural source and are supposed to be universally adhered to by all those who call themselves Muslims".[1] From such a standpoint, it is easy to define a Muslim on the

[1] Imtiaz Ahmed, "Introduction", in Imtiaz Ahmed (ed.), *Ritual and Religion among Muslims in India*, Delhi, Manohar, 1981, p. 1.

13

basis of the pillars of Islam: *shahada* (professing faith in Prophet Muhammad as enshrined in the Quran), daily prayers, fasting for Ramadan, *zakat* (almsgiving) and pilgrimage to Mecca. But this interpretation reflects a classic bias consisting of understanding a culture or civilisation through what Robert Redfield called the "great tradition".[2]

In British India more than anywhere else perhaps, the "little" Muslim tradition, that of the people and not of the clerics, was highly complex and partly syncretic.[3] All the more so as it readily made room for seemingly heterodox elements such as the cult of saints or possession rites, in which certain trances had a curative purpose akin to exorcism.[4]

This heterogeneity owed much to India's distance from the Islamic crucible in the Middle East, both from a geographic and cultural standpoint. Not only was Islam transformed on arriving in India through contact with Turkish and Iranian influences, but Indic civilisation was extremely foreign to it. Since it was unable to take over entirely, its followers and promoters were obliged to adapt—as elsewhere, like in Indonesia for instance. This adjustment resulted in various types of synthesis, the Sufi phenomenon being one of the more striking of them.

Sufism took on considerable importance in India due to its affinities with the Hindu ideal of asceticism. Its main figures attracted a number of followers, mostly from the lower strata of Indian society, and allowed a particular form of Islam to assert itself. This popular congregation-based Islam established the cult of saints and institutionalized *dargahs*—places of retreat of the holy men and later their tombs/shrines—which became places of pilgrimage. In the sixteenth century, under Akbar's reign, the *ulema* declared that the pilgrimage to Mecca was no longer an obligation, while pilgrimage to shrines of Sufi saints was spreading.[5]

Among the congregations, the Chishtis became one of the most popular. Established in India in the late twelfth century by Khwajah Muinud-din

---

[2] Redfield, Robert, *The Little Community*, Chicago, University of Chicago Press, 1956.

[3] Aziz Ahmad, *An Intellectual History of Islam in India*, Edinburgh, University of Edinburgh Press, 1969, p. 44. Back in the nineteenth century in France, Garcin de Tassy had drawn the attention to the specific nature of Indian Islam in his *Mémoires sur les particularités de la religion musulmane dans l'Inde* (1832).

[4] Imtiaz Ahmed, "Unity and Variety in South Asian Islam", in Dietmar Rothermund (ed.), *Islam in Southern Asia*, Wiesbaden, Franz Steiner Verlag, 1975.

[5] C. Shackle, "The Pilgrimage and the Extension of Sacred Geography in the Poetry of Khawaja Ghulam Farid", in Attar Singh (ed.), *Socio-Cultural Impact of Islam on India*, Chandigarh, Punjab University, 1976, pp. 159–160.

Chishti, a native of Sajistan (at the crossroads of contemporary Iran, Afghanistan and Pakistan), its epicentre soon became the Dargah of Ajmer (Rajasthan) where the founder of the Chishti order had moved and was buried. This Sufi order owed its influence—including among Hindu devotees—to the ascetic nature of the Chishti line that has come down through time. Other congregations on the contrary would become associated with the government, such as the Suhrawardis who would obtain benefits in kind (land in particular). Still others, such as the Naqshabandis, originating from Central Asia, would not only develop close relations with the authorities, but also show a sense of orthodoxy that resulted in hostile reactions to the Hindus—and the Shias.

Aside from the Sufi orders, other sects constantly developed within Indian Islam. The Muslims of the subcontinent first brought with them one of the structuring divisions of Middle Eastern Islam, the opposition between Sunnis and Shias. This schism for a long time remained latent, probably due to a strong demographic imbalance, the latter being only a small minority. But the political and social influence of this group should not be underestimated. Among them were many landowners as well as major dynasties such as the one that ruled over the Awadh kingdom in Lucknow until the mid-nineteenth century.

Among the Shias, the Ismailis mainly settled in western India, in Gujarat and the Bombay region.[6] The Bohras formed the largest group among them. They recognize Ali as successor to the Prophet, but—like other is—they diverged from the Twelvers after the death of the sixth Imam in 765, considering that his elder son, Ismail (and not his second son) should have taken over from him. Paying allegiance to the Cairo-based Fatimid Caliphate, they established their own church. Bohras experienced a schism in the sixteenth century that spawned two groups, the Dawoodi Bohras and the Sulaimani Bohras. While the latter would remain in the Middle East, the former migrated to India in 1539 and adopted a separate leader, the Syedna, to whom they paid full allegiance (and taxes). There, they attracted Hindus—including Brahmins—in relatively large numbers.[7] Bohras have adopted a dress code that makes them easily identifiable. Other Ismailis

---

[6] Asghar Ali Engineer, *The Muslim Communities of Gujarat. An Exploratory Study of Bhoras, Khojas and Memons*, New Delhi, Ajanta, 1989.

[7] Asghar Ali Engineer, *The Bohras*, Sahibabad, Vikas, 1980; Shibani Roy, *The Dawoodi Bohras: An Anthropological Perspective*, Delhi, B. R. Publishing Corporation, 1984; Jonah Blank, *Mullahs on the Mainframe. Islam and Modernity among the Daudi Bohras*, Chicago, The University of Chicago Press, 2001.

coming from the Middle East, the Khojas, followed a partly similar trajectory. While they migrated to India in the twelfth century, their leader, the Aga Khan—who claims to descend from Ali—remained in Persia till the nineteenth century, when he moved to India as well. Like the Bohras, the Khojas are mostly converts from Hinduism, but they have primarily attracted members of merchant castes such as the Bhatias (whose marriage rites they have retained).[8] Muhammad Ali Jinnah—who married a Parsi—was born in a Khoja, business family.[9]

The creation of new sects has continued into the modern era. In the late nineteenth century for instance, Mirza Ghulam Ahmad (1835–1915) founded a movement known either by his namesake, Ahmadi, or after his place of birth, Qadian, in Gurdaspur district, Punjab. This man claimed to be the new Messiah, contradicting the Muslim belief that Muhammad was the last Prophet. At his death, his disciples numbered in the hundreds of thousands.

Although Ahmadis were recruited among various castes, the Bohras and the Khojas, as mentioned above, came from Brahmin castes and merchant castes—and continued to pursue some of their caste-related activities after having left Hinduism. This coincidence of caste and sect is not rare in Indian Islam. This is the case of the Memons. Originating with the conversion of one Hindu merchant caste, the Lohanas, in Gujarat by a Sufi saint in 1400, the Memons finally settled in Bombay in the early seventeenth century, where they prospered in trade and industry while maintaining a separate religious identity. At the other end of the social scale, the Moplahs were Muslim peasants from Kerala who descended from the early Arab migrants settled on the Malabar Coast starting in the eighth century. Exploited by Hindu landowners, the Moplahs were known for their frequent uprisings—the jacquerie of 1836 being the most famous of a long series of them. An ethnic community speaking its own language, Malayalam—which gave rise to a literature written in Arabic, Mappila Pattu—the Moplahs also have their own priests, Musaliyars.

Castes and tribes

Despite the egalitarian values that Islam professes to promote, at least since the Raj which reified social categories, the Muslims of South Asia form a

---

[8] Hanna Papanek, *Leadership and Social Change in the Khoja Ismaili Community*, Cambridge (Mass.), Radcliffe College, 1962.

[9] The controversy about Jinnah's religious background is well studied in Faisal Devji, *Muslim Zion: Pakistan as a Political Idea*, London, Hurst, 2013, p. 215.

hierarchical community, be they part of caste-based milieus or of the tribal world—or even a combination of the two.[10] The fact that the mechanisms of caste and tribe overlap is not so surprising since caste implies endogamous practices that flow from relations of kinship also characteristic of tribes.

The Pashtun tribal structures are based on a segmentary lineage system, each tribe comprising clans, sub-clans and still smaller kin groups claiming that they descend from a common ancestor. Social hierarchies in this milieu have traditionally been fluid since they rely on the observance of (or disregard for) a code of honour, Pashtunwali, based on—among other things—righteousness and courage (for instance in seeking justice—a quest which has resulted in cycles of family-related vendettas).[11] Tribal chiefs were men who best complied with this life-style and displayed leadership qualities—hence the notion of "individual captaincy"[12] emphasized by Fredrick Barth. As a result, they received the title of Khan, whereas those who came under them were usually known as Maliks.[13] Yet, Khans were primus inter pares who could lose their status if their personal qualities eroded—and if rivals joined forces to dislodge them from power. The theoretically impermanent character of these hierarchies reflected the fundamentally egalitarian nature of the Pashtun social order that was evident from the modus operandi of the *jirgas*, the plenary assemblies convened when an important issue had to be sorted out collectively. Certainly, only those who had inherited land were allowed to take part in *jirgas*, but land was regularly redistributed to prevent the best plots from remaining with the same families forever. This basically egalitarian system known as *wesh* was spoiled by the British when they recognized property rights of the "big Khans". They did so to promote a group of landlords on whom they could rely to establish their authority via indirect rule. This policy, which took shape at the

---

[10] In his seminal work on the Pashtuns, Barth shows that their predominantly tribal universe allows for caste practices in the Swat valley (Fredrik Barth, *Political Leadership among Swat Pathans*, London, The Athlone Press, 1965 [first edition 1959], pp. 16–19).

[11] Abubakar Siddique, who hails from South Waziristan, points out that while "'Doing Pashto', or observing the behaviour code of the *Pashtunwali*, is closely tied to speaking the language (...) *Pashtunwali* also includes the values of forgiveness and egalitarianism, ad chivalry" (Abubakar Siddique, *The Pashtun Question. The Unresolved Key to the Future of Pakistan and Afghanistan*, London, Hurst, 2014, p. 14.).

[12] Fredrik Barth, *Political Leadership among Swat Pathans*, p. 133.

[13] However, the use of the word "Khan" has tended to become pervasive due to an inflationary expression of marks of respect. (ibid., p. 72).

expense of the "small Khans", precipitated the decline of the *jirga* culture. The big Khans henceforth exerted decisive influence in the assemblies thanks to the protection of the British, to whom they paid allegiance in return. Pashtun society had become (more) hierarchical.[14]

Baloch society was also structured along somewhat similar tribal segmentary lineages during the Raj, but in a rather more inclusive perspective.[15] Indeed, Baloch tribes were the by-products of migrations dating back to the sixteenth century. When the British Raj established authority over the Baloch area, at the confluence of today's Pakistan and Iran, these tribes had already amalgamated groups coming from Iran as well as Pashtuns, Sindhis and Punjabis. Hence their resilient multilingual character and the fact that language has never been a distinctive cultural feature of the Balochs.[16] Their unity came more from endogamous practices and their solidarity against others when they came under attack.[17] Hierarchies were also more marked than on the Pashtun side right from the beginning because of the authority of Khans and Sardars, who dominated the *jirgas*.

While tribes prevail west of the Indus, caste hierarchies play a dominant role in Punjab and Sindh, two regions more directly connected to Indian civilisation. The caste system which originated in the Hindu world is based on three complementary criteria: (1) the relation to purity and impurity, Brahmins at the top of the hierarchy embodying the first pole and untouchables, at the other extreme, representing the epitome of impurity in the social sphere; (2) professional specialisation, each caste being traditionally associated with a socio-economic activity linked to its status; and (3) caste endogamy, which perpetuates the social structure over time, each caste providing the frame of a closed marriage market.

Indian Islam softened the contours of this system without really questioning it. The most discriminating criterion of the Hindu caste hierarchy,

---

14 On this transition, see Abkar Ahmed, *Pukhtun Economy and Society: Traditional Structure and Economic Development in a Tribal Society*, London, Routledge and Kegan Paul, 1980 and Sayed Wiqar Ali Shah, *Ethnicity, Islam and Nationalism. Muslim Politics in the North Indian Frontier Province (1937–1947)*, Karachi, Oxford University Press, 1999.

15 Fredrik Barth, "Ethnic Processes on the Pathan-Baluch Boundary", in Georges Redard (ed.), *Indo-Iranica. Mélanges présentés à Georg Morgenstierne à l'occasion de son soixante-dixième anniversaire*, Wiesbaden, Otto Harrassowitz, 1964.

16 Brian Spooner, "Baluchistan", *Encyclopaedia Iranica*, vol. 3, New York, Routledge and Kegan Paul, 1988, pp. 598–632.

17 Nina Swidler, *Remotely Colonial. History and Politics in Pakistani Balochistan*, Karachi, Oxford University Press, 2012.

the relation to purity and impurity, has generally not been as preponderant among the Indian Muslims as among the Hindus. As a result, upper-caste and lower-caste Muslims could generally attend the mosque together. But the Arzals (former Untouchable converts) usually remain excluded from it unless they remain on the steps outside. Similarly, they could read the Quran, but not teach it.[18]

Although observance of the relation to purity and impurity is less systematic in Muslim circles than in Hinduism, Indian Islam has established a social stratification on the basis of geographic origin that is nearly as strict. The so-called noble (Ashraf) upper castes are made up of descendants of Muslims who (allegedly) migrated to India from abroad, whereas those who converted to Islam after it spread throughout Indian territory make up the two lower categories, the Ajlafs (lower castes) and the Arzals (formerly Untouchables).[19] The first are subdivided into three categories in which are found those of Middle Eastern extraction (the Syeds who claim descent from the Prophet and the Shaikhs who say they have roots in Mecca and Medina), those claiming a Central Asian, and particularly Afghan, lineage, the Pathans (or Pashtuns) and last, the Mughals who claim Turkic or Tatar origins.[20]

The Rajputs (a high Hindu warrior caste) are the only converts who are part of the social elite. The others are part of the Ajlafs when they are of Shudra origin, which is most usually the case. These were lower caste Hindus, primarily cultivators and artisans who converted to Islam in the vain hope of escaping an oppressive social system. Most of them are weavers (Julaha or Momins). The Arzals are the descendants of Hindu Dalits who followed the same route with the same result.[21] Among them are mainly sweepers (Bhangis in Sindh and Churas in Punjab) to whom are assigned the most thankless cleaning tasks.

Traditionally, these status groups often matched caste-specific jobs and were all the more reminiscent of the Hindu hierarchy as many Indian

---

[18] In many cases when a man of higher caste served them food or drink, it was in disposable clay vessels. See Ghaus Ansari, *Muslim Caste in Uttar Pradesh*, Lucknow, The Ethnographic and Folk Culture Society, 1960, p. 50.

[19] This rule is subject to many exceptions, some upper castes having gone from Hinduism to Islam without a drop in status. Such is the case of the Rajput castes in North India, for instance.

[20] Few in number, the Mughals are concentrated in Rohilkhand, a region on the Ganges plain.

[21] Marc Gaborieau, *Un autre islam. Inde, Pakistan, Bangladesh*, Paris, Albin Michel, 2007.

Muslims came from this religion. The Syeds and Shaikhs, like the Brahmins, were scholars occupying positions of power in the traditional state apparatus; the Pathans—reminiscent of Hindu Kshatriyas—dominate the military (all the more so since the British saw them as a "martial race" and recruited them into the army in great numbers). As for the Memons, Bohras and Khojas, they usually ran businesses. The Ajlafs have remained cultivators and artisans—a particularly high number of weavers converted by entire caste. As for the Arzals, they formed a populace that can be exploited at will—and still do.

These social divisions go together with a legacy of strong geographic contrasts. A brief comparison between the Muslims of Bengal, those of the Gangetic Plain and those of Punjab suffices to illustrate this point. The first, primarily a result of the mass conversion of castes of Hindu peasants, remained traditionally at the bottom of the social pyramid, even when the ruling dynasties were of the Islamic faith. Not only were the Muslims of Bengal less numerous in urban centers—such as Calcutta—but in the countryside they were often under the command of Hindu landowners. At the other geographic extreme of India, in Punjab—another predominantly Muslim province, like Bengal—the Muslims were also predominantly rural, Hindu merchants and intelligentsia dominating in the cities. But Punjab—which warrants particular attention because of the key role it will play in Pakistan[22]—in contrast to Bengal, experienced some radical changes under the Raj. The British, who were grateful to the Muslims of Punjab for their help during the 1857 Mutiny (see below), developed the economy of the region through the creation of a sophisticated irrigation system. The "canal colonies" would contribute to the formation of a new class of farmers in which Muslims would be over-represented since the Hindus were more over-represented in the cities, among traders and professionals.[23] The British also protected the farmers from the moneylenders by passing the Punjab Alienation of Land Act in 1900, which prevented "non-agricultural tribes" (mostly Hindu traders) from acquiring land.[24] Last but not least, the

---

[22] At the Quetta Staff Command College, the soldiers trained to become the officers of the Pakistani army learn that each country is organised around a vital province, its heartland, whose loss results in disintegration. In the case of Pakistan, Punjab is naturally this key province.

[23] Imran Ali, *The Punjab under Imperialism, 1885–1947*, Karachi, Oxford University Press, 2003.

[24] Edward Maclagan, *The Punjab Peasant in Prosperity and Debt*, London, Oxford University Press, 1928 (second edition).

British recognized *pirs* (descendants of sufi saints in charge of their dargah) as part of the cultivating groups—making their land inalienable—and other groups (including Muslim Jats and Rajputs) as a "martial race", which gave them new opportunities in the army. The Muslims of Punjab did not for all that constitute an elite as they did in Gangetic India.

The Ganges Plain from Delhi to Bihar, the true crucible of Muslim civilisation in India, was the area in which a number of Muslim political structures were experimented, from the Delhi Sultanate to the Mughal Empire—of which the capital was also Delhi for most of the time. After the gradual disintegration of the Mughal Empire, it was also in this region that many successor states ruled by Muslim dynasties, including the Kingdom of Awadh, took shape. The British, who took over most of them in the first half of the nineteenth century, baptised this region the North-Western Provinces and Oudh in 1860, later renaming it the United Provinces of Agra and Oudh in 1902 without changing its borders—which independent India would moreover keep for many years, as the northern province of Uttar Pradesh was not subdivided until 2000.

Muslim society in this area was dominated by Ashraf of four categories, the Syeds, the Shaikhs, the Mughals and the Pathans. This elite—into which Muslim Rajputs readily include themselves without being accepted by the Ashraf as regards marital unions—is clearly distinct from the long list of Ajlafs[25] and even more so from the Arzals. The Syeds and the Shaikhs have a virtual monopoly on clerical occupations, which are often handed down from father to son. At the bottom of the social pyramid, the Bhangis suffer discrimination that excludes them not only from holy places but also restricts commensality.[26] It is worth noting that in Northern Indian Muslim society there were practically no large merchants likely to go into industry.[27]

* * *

---

[25] It includes Julahas (weavers), Darzis (tailors), Qasabs (butchers), Nais or Hajjams (barbers), Kabariyas or Kunjras (greengrocers), Mirasis (musicians), Dhuniyas (cotton carders), Fakirs (beggars), Telis (oil pressers), Dhobis (launderers) and Gaddis (herdsmen and milk producers). See Ghaus Ansari, *Muslim Caste in Uttar Pradesh*, op. cit.

[26] Ibid., p. 50.

[27] Francis Robinson, *Separatism among Indian Muslims*, Cambridge, Cambridge University Press, 1974, p. 15.

From both a social and religious standpoint, Indian Islam across the territory delineated by the British Raj thus formed a mosaic that complicated the ascendancy of communal boundaries. It was a mosaic that not only fragmented the group but also made it more porous to outside, particularly Hindu, influences, as much due to forms of religious synthesis as to social ties. In fact, popular Hinduism and popular Islam have been the crucible of many syncretic practices which developed in particular around places of what thus became joint worship.[28] Yet, even if Islam's adaptation to Indian soil and its own internal tensions clearly show that this religion does not have the fine sociological unity that a scriptural approach would lead one to believe, the scale of the theological and doctrinal conflicts among Muslims of the Great Tradition should not be exaggerated. After all, Indian Islam has always been, much more than many others, overwhelmingly dominated by Sunnism and a school of law, the Hanafi school.

This overview also suggests that the Muslims of the United Provinces were in a very peculiar situation, which explains their pioneering role in the movement that was to lead to Pakistan. The Muslims of the Ganges Plain formed a small minority in the province. In the first census, which took place in 1881, there were about 6 million of them, as opposed to 38 million Hindus. But although they were less than 14 per cent of the total, they continued to be most influential, as evident from the fact that they accounted for two-fifths of the urban population. This overrepresentation in towns and cities—in stark contrast with the situation of their coreligionists of Bengal and Punjab—reflected their key position in the bureaucracy, but should not conceal their importance as a landed group as well, since the Muslim aristocracy used not to live in villages.[29] This is a legacy of their past domination and a sign of their resilience.

Although they made up an eighth of the population, the Muslims owned one-fifth of the farmland, often as large landlords. The Taluqdars in Awadh, whose ancestors under the Mughal Empire were in charge of collecting taxes and meting out justice, continued to dominate the country, as the

---

[28] Jackie Assayag, *At the Confluence of Two Rivers. Muslims and Hindus in South India*, Delhi, Mnohar, 2004 and Yoginder Sikand, "Shared Hindu-Muslim Shrines in Karnataka: challenges to liminality", in Imtiaz Ahmed and Helmut Reifield (eds), *Lived Islam in South Asia*, New Delhi, Social Science Press, 2011, pp. 166–186.

[29] Laurent Gayer and Christophe Jaffrelot, "Introduction. Muslims of the Indian city: from centrality to marginality", in Laurent Gayer and Christophe Jaffrelot (eds), *Muslims in India's Cities. Trajectories of Marginalization*, London, Hurst, 2012, pp. 1–22.

British recognised their property rights.[30] Numbering fewer than a hundred,[31] these men exerted an influence that had as much to do with their prestige as their economic clout—including as moneylenders.[32] The other pole of Muslim power came from the overrepresentation of the Ashraf elite within the administration. Civil servants, whose prominence dated back to the Mughal Empire, retained power in the successor states—particularly the Kingdom of Awadh—that was handed down from one generation to the next. In 1882—statistics not being available prior to that—the Muslims still made up 35 per cent of the civil servants in the United Provinces—and even 45 per cent of the Unconvenanted Civil Service.[33] Although they occupied two poles of power—one more rural and informal, the other more urban and administrative—these two groups, Muslim landlords and civil servants, were part of the same world, that of an elite proud of its past and cultivating the refinement of the Ashraf culture. It was within this relatively small circle—there were 2.5 million Ashraf in 1881 in the United Provinces—that Indian Muslim separatism was born in the wake of the 1857 Rebellion when the status and the interests of this elite group were challenged.

---

[30] See S.N.A. Jafri, *The History and Status of Landlords and Tenants in the United Provinces (India)*, Delhi, Usha, 1985 (1st edition, 1931), p. 159 ff.

[31] Francis Robinson counted 76 of them (*Separatism among Indian Muslims*, op. cit., p. 20).

[32] See the remarkable book by Thomas R. Metcalf, *Land, Landlords and the British Raj. Northern India in the Nineteenth Century*, Berkeley and Los Angeles, California University Press, 1979.

[33] Francis Robinson points out that Muslims occupied 55% of Tahsildar posts, highly sought after as these local officers wielded great influence over their district (*Separatism among Indian Muslims*, op. cit., p. 23).

1

THE SOCIO-ETHNIC ORIGINS
OF INDIAN MUSLIM SEPARATISM

THE REFORM PHASE (1857–1906)

The Mutiny,[34] an uprising started by British Army Indian soldiers that threw North India into a state of turmoil in 1857, marked a turning point in the Muslims' trajectory during the colonial period. Muslims, one-fifth of the population of the British Raj at the time, had lost most of their political clout, but they continued to be perceived by the colonizers as a dominant community that was heir to the Mughal Empire. That dynasty moreover continued to rule over Delhi, its historic capital. The British suspected the aristocrats who cultivated the nostalgia of "their" Empire of wanting to return to power and, therefore, held them responsible for a revolt in which, in fact, Hindus played as much a role as Muslims. Geography partly explains the British interpretation of the event since the uprising was particularly violent in the Ganges Plain, the stronghold of the Taluqdars, the landlords of Awadh. The repression visited upon this epicentre-area in 1857-8 served to catalyse community introspection among the Muslim elite.

---

[34] On this key episode in Indian history and its peasant dimension, see Eric Stokes, *The Peasant Armed. The Indian Revolt of 1857*, Oxford, Clarendon Press, 1986.

The Crushing of the 1857 Revolt and Reactions of the Muslim Elite

Despite the participation of many Hindus—including members of the princely elite such as the Rani of Jhansi—in the Sepoy mutiny, "in the British view it was Muslim intrigue and Muslim leadership that converted a sepoy [literally soldier, man in uniform] mutiny into a political conspiracy, aimed at the extinction of the British Raj."[35] The British reacted with great brutality to the challenge put to them. Not only was the last of the Mughals, an eighty-year-old man hidden away in his palace and used against his will by certain mutineers as a symbol of their combat, tried and exiled to Rangoon, but his sons and grandsons were executed on the spot and the sovereign's entourage was decimated. Delhi was the theatre of many summary executions primarily targeting the Muslim elite. Beyond that, the property of many aristocrats was confiscated. The Taluqdars of Awadh[36] were the first to be targeted due to the staunch resistance this province put up against the British.[37]

The impact of this measure should nevertheless be analyzed carefully. British historian Peter Hardy, who consulted Awadh archives, did not detect any anti-Muslim bias. He instead simply noted "a shift in landholding within the Muslim community itself with those having a Mughal past losing to those with a British future."[38] For him, the impact on North Indian Muslims of crushing the 1857–8 revolt was less socio-economic than psychological. Whereas until then the Muslims—whose Mughal Empire was already in tatters—did not pay much attention to the British whom they found uncivilized and who in any event refrained from interfering in the life of Indian communities (whether religious or social), after 1857, they were forced "to realise not only that the British were in India to stay, but

---

[35] Thomas R. Metcalf, *The Aftermath of Revolt: India 1857–1870*, Princeton, Princeton University Press, 1965, p. 298.

[36] Before the British recognized them as "landlords", the Taluqdars—like the Zamindars and Jagirdars found in other regions of India, were agents charged by the Mughal Empire with collecting taxes. After the disintegration of the Empire, many of them gained their independence by keeping their fiefs, which were to become the princely states. See Jagdish Raj, *The Mutiny and British Land Policy in North India, 1856–1868*, Bombay, Asia Publishing House, 1965.

[37] Details of decisions made by the British can be found in the official report of 1882: Rajkumar Sarvadhikari, *The Taluqdari Settlement in Oudh*, Delhi, Usah, 1985 (first edition, 1882).

[38] Peter Hardy, *The Muslims of British India*, Cambridge, Cambridge University Press, 1972, p. 78.

also that they intended to stay on their own terms."[39] And they turned out to be superior to the natives. To what did they owe this success? If it was not their virtues, then it had to be "success of a superior technique, the sources of which could no longer be ignored."[40]

Faced with overwhelming British firepower—literally in military terms as well as figuratively in terms of Christian proselytism and administrative and economic efficiency—in the early nineteenth century the Hindu elites had already adopted one of three different attitudes. Some of them fell back on their traditions and tried to restore them in their supposed pristine purity to bring about a movement of revival. Others, on the contrary, subscribed without reservation to western modernity to the extent of changing their dress and eating habits. The third attitude, which subsequently would gain prevalence, involved opting for a social-religious reformism that aimed to combine tradition and modernity. Among Muslims, the second attitude had few followers. But on the other hand, revivalism and reformism developed in the wake of the Revolt of 1857.

The Traditionalist Reaction or the Birth of Muslim Fundamentalism in India

The traditionalist or revivalist reaction was embodied in two different currents which both claimed to derive from the legacy of Shah Waliullah (1703–62) and Syed Ahmad Barelwi (1786–1831), two major figures of Indian Islam partly inspired by Wahhabism and advocating an Islam cleansed of Hindu influences.

Drawing its inspiration from these sources, the Ahl-i-Hadith movement took shape in 1864 to "looked for fundamentalist solutions in the traditions of the Prophet (*hadith*), hence the name of the school which signifies 'people of traditions'."[41] This school of thought was fundamentalist in the sense that, in reaction to Western modernity—or anything new—it turned to the words and deeds of the Prophet to guide its action. Any innovation (*bidaa*) based on sources not having been approved by the movement's theologians could moreover only be considered to go against Islam. This movement, whose spiritual master, Nadhir Husain (d.1902) was based in

---

[39] Ibid., p. 61.
[40] Ibid.
[41] Marc Gaborieau and Christophe Jaffrelot, "Socio-religious reforms and nationalism (1870–1948)", in Claude Markovits (ed.), *A History of Modern India (1480–1950)*, London, Anthem Press, 2002, p. 456

Delhi and whose financial patron, Siddiq Hasan Khan (d.1890) was a member of the princely family of Bhopal, endeavoured to develop a network of schools throughout all of Northern India.

In contrast to the Deobandis and the Barelwis—which will be discussed below—the Ahl-i-Hadith do not follow the Hanafi school of jurisprudence. In fact they do not follow any school of jurisprudence at all, viewing it as a betrayal of the Prophet. They consider that Muslims must comply only with the Quran and the *hadiths*, using their personal judgement (*ijtihad*). They therefore represent the South Asian variant of Salafism, which takes its name from the founding fathers of Islam, the al-Salaf al-Salih, whom they claim to emulate. As a result the Ahl-i-Hadith display a distinct superiority complex vis-à-vis other Muslims and openly criticise Shiism, a deviant sect in their view. Promoted originally by eminent families of the Mughal Empire's aristocracy, they form a small, elitist circle.[42]

The post-1857 traditionalist revival was also embodied in the so-called Deoband movement, named after a small city near Delhi where a Sufi by the name of Haji Muhammad Abid founded a seminary (*madrassa*) in 1867.[43] He was soon joined by survivors of the British repression such as Maulana Muhammad Qasim Nanotvi (1833–77), the descendant of a line of ulema, and Rashid Ahmed Gangohi (1829–1905). In the 1860s, these men, supported by patrons who had all been close to the Mughal rulers,[44] were keen to defend Islam by using new methods. Nanotvi, an excellent orator, thus entered into debates against Christian missionaries and Hindu activists of the Arya Samaj, a revivalist group founded in Punjab but active throughout North India. Teaching, however, was their true vocation. The Deoband seminary promoted knowledge of *hadiths*, the *sharia* (Islamic law) and *fiqh* (Islamic jurisprudence).[45] The subjects taught ranged from Arabic and Persian grammar to Greco-Arab medicine and included the history of Islam, philosophy,

---

[42] Mariam Abou Zahab, "Salafism in Pakistan: The Ahl-e Hadith Movement", in Roel Meijer (ed.), *Global Salafism: Islam's New Religious Movement*, London, Hurst, 2009, pp. 126–142.

[43] Barbara Metcalf, *Islamic Revival in British India: Deoband, 1860–1900*, Princeton, Princeton University Press, 1982.

[44] Muhammad Moj, *Deobandi Islam. Rise of a Counterculture in Pakistan*, forthcoming, p. 91.

[45] On the curriculum of Deoband, see, U. Anzar, *Islamic education. A brief history of madrassas with comments on curricula and pedagogical practices*, pp. 15–16. (http://schools.nashua.edu/myclass/fenlonm/block1/Lists/DueDates/attachments/10/madrassah-history.pdf).

medieval geometry and astronomy.[46] But the language of instruction was Urdu—more accessible than Persian or Arabic—and the Deobandis followed a British-style educational system: their institution was not attached to any mosque (to the discontent of local clerics, especially when an edifice specifically devoted to teaching was built in 1876); the seminary was divided into departments and classes; it had a permanent faculty, followed a predefined curriculum and introduced written examinations. It also had student dormitories modelled after the British universities.

Reputed for its sense of organization, the Deoband seminary soon established a vast network of educational institutions through its first graduates who, starting in 1880, mainly invested the areas of Rohilkhand and the northern Doab (the area between the Yamuna river and the Ganges). These branches, like their headquarters, trained many *ulema* who spearheaded a wave of proselytism that increasingly spread via the written word through the publication of a large body of religious literature, including a catechism in Urdu.

For the Deobandis, religious scholarship was based on the Quran, *hadiths*, *qiyas* (reasoning by analogy) and *ijma* (or consensus). But they believed that none of these four areas could be explored without the guidance of an *alim*. While they recognised Sufism as a spiritual discipline, they rejected the authority of the *pirs* who claimed sacred qualities handed down from father to son as well as the cult of saints with its pilgrimages to the shrines of *pirs* and *urs* (festivals held on the *pirs'* anniversary dates). They viewed such practices as a corruption of Islam due to Hinduism. The Deobandis established their authority by issuing *fatwas* pertaining to all aspects of Muslim life fighting popular Islam and even more Shiism.[47]

For these fundamentalist movements, both Ahl-i-Hadith and Deoband, Islam remained a universal reference. They were in direct contact with the Arab world, which their members visited regularly—particularly to make the pilgrimage to Mecca (Haj)—and which provided an increasing number of students. They did not view Indian Muslims as a separate community but as participating in the *umma*, or global body of Islam.

---

[46] Aziz Ahmad, *Islamic Modernism in India and Pakistan, 1857–1964*, Oxford, Oxford University Press, 1967, p. 105.

[47] Muhammad Moj, *Deobandi Islam*, p. 113 and p. 115.

Syed Ahmad Khan's Reformism

Syed Ahmad Khan (1817–98) reacted to the Sepoy mutiny—during which he demonstrated his loyalty to the British—in a very different way. Grandson of a *wazir* of the Grand Mughal, his background could probably not have been more aristocratic. He had studied the classics and was awash in the nostalgia of past grandeur, as attests his masterwork on Delhi's monuments, *Traces of the Great* (1847).[48] His follower, Mohsin-ul-Mulk claimed that writing up this study had "brought home to him the fact that the Muslims were now plunging into an abyss of wretchedness."[49] But he had learned English, and against the advice of his friends had joined the East India Company administration, following a career path that recalled that of another reformist, R.M. Roy. Entering at the level of deputy judge (*naib munshi*), he climbed the ranks of the judicial hierarchy as he was appointed to one district and then another throughout the North-Western Provinces (which were to become part of the United Provinces).

He had allegedly supported the British during the Revolt of 1857 because he was said to have "preferred the East India Company 'Raj' to Hindu Raj".[50] After this traumatic event, he worked to dissipate the opprobrium the British had cast upon the Muslims. He wrote a book, *Loyal Mohammedans of India*, in which figure the names of all the Muslims who had come to the aid of the British during the Revolt, and another, *Causes of the Indian Revolt*, to show that many Hindus had been involved in it as well. Beyond that, he tried to reconcile the British with the Indian Muslims by pointing out the affinities between Christianity and Islam in a book he began writing in 1862, *Commentary on the Bible*.

Beyond this effort to reconcile the British and the Muslims, Syed Ahmad Khan undertook a task of social and religious reform involving a Westernization of his coreligionists' education. Even more than the Deobandis, Syed Ahmad Khan was convinced that Indian Muslims stood much to gain by imitating their British masters in matters of education. But he did not stop at importing the mere framework—colleges, written exams, boarding schools, etc.—he also drew inspiration from Western science to show that

---

[48] C.M. Naim, "Syed Ahmad and His Two Books Called 'Asar-al-Sanadid'", *Modern Asian Studies*, 45 (3) (2011), pp. 669–708.

[49] Cited in Francis Robinson, *Separatism among Indian Muslims*, op. cit., p. 89 (note 1).

[50] Safdar Mahmood and Javaid Zafar, *Founders of Pakistan*, Lahore, Publishers United, 1968, p. 17.

it was not at all incompatible with Islam.[51] With this goal in mind, he founded the Scientific Society in 1864. However, his action did not fully begin to develop until five years later when, finally retired, he made a trip to England to visit Oxford and Cambridge in 1869–70.

He returned with a plan to modernise education that would be embodied in the "Aligarh movement", named after the city where he held his next-to-last post and where he founded a school in 1875 and then the Mohammedan Anglo-Oriental College two years later. Modelled after Cambridge, this institution—which became a university in 1920—had an English department and an "Oriental studies" department, symbolising Syed Ahmad Khan's philosophy of reform, to achieve a synthesis of knowledge that would allow his community to enter the modern era without losing its soul.[52] David Lelyveld points out that "One tendency in Sayyid Ahmad's original motivation of founding the college was to encourage individual judgment in the evaluation of the sources of Islamic revelation in the light of 'rational' and 'emprirical' criteria. But such individual judgment was subordinated to an overriding desire to create student solidarity as a basis for communal mobilization among Indian Muslims at large".[53]

From the Aligarh Movement to the Muslim League

Even if—partly through Syed Ahmad Khan's work—the British no longer distrusted the Muslims as much in the 1870s as they did in the aftermath of the Revolt of 1857, this community again felt threatened in the 1870–80s for another reason: the rise in power of the Hindu elite. This danger was particularly palpable in the United Provinces, the birthplace of the "Aligarh movement" whose College became the crucible of a political organisation at the turn of the twentieth century, the Muslim League.

[51] Considering that superstitions and other beliefs not based in reason were the product of the corruption of religions by man, Syed Ahmad Khan held that Islam "is a rational religion which can march hand in hand with the growth of knowledge. Any fear to the contrary betrays lack of faith in the truth of Islam". Syed Ahmad Khan, "Islam and Science", in K. Satchidananda Murty (ed.), *Readings in Indian History, Politics and Philosophy*, London, George Allen and Unwin Ltd., 1967, p. 322. See also Christian Troll, *Sayyid Ahmad Khan: Reinterpretation of Muslim Theology*, Delhi, Vikas, 1978.

[52] In 1877, the cornerstone of the College was laid by the Viceroy, Lord Lyton, after the British helped Syed Ahmad Khan acquire a parcel of land in Aligarh.

[53] David Lelyveld, "Disenchantment at Aligarh: Islam and the Realm of the Secular in Late Neneteenth Century India", *Die Welt des* Islams, 22 (1–2), 1982, p. 99.

A Muslim Elite under a Hindu Threat

In the last decades of the nineteenth century, North Indian Muslims underwent a relative decline vis-à-vis Hindus. In the west of the United Provinces and the Doab, urban growth due as much to industry as to commerce mainly benefited the Hindu traders and moneylenders who found themselves in a position to buy land from landowners, including from some Muslim Taluqdars. In the area of Kanpur, these businessmen owned over 40 per cent of the land at the turn of the twentieth century.[54] The Muslims also lost ground to the Hindus in the administration, over which they previously had absolute control, provoking growing opposition which crystallised around the language issue.

For decades, the distinction between Hindu and Muslim elite groups of North India had remained confined to the private sphere. In the public sphere, men of power from these two groups worked together closely, sharing the same culture of government.[55] The language spoken by this ruling class was first Persian and then Urdu when in 1837 the British replaced the former with the latter as the official language. Urdu, however, remained associated with the Indian Muslims since they had arrived in the country. Evolved even before the Delhi Sultanate—but established then—by the Central Asian and Middle Eastern invaders to communicate with the natives, this new idiom borrowed from the syntax of the Hindi dialects used in North India (particularly the Khari Boli spoken around Delhi) and infused it with Persian, Arabic and Turkish vocabulary. Although Urdu and

---

[54] Francis Robinson, "Municipal Government and Muslim Separatism in the United Provinces, 1880 to 1916", *Modern Asian Studies*, 7 (3), 1973, p. 402. And Francis Robinson, *Separatism among Indian Muslims*, op. cit., p. 31.

[55] "In the second half of the nineteenth century, Kashmiris [known as the Pandits, Brahmans, who, like the Nehru family, served the Muslim rulers one dynasty after another], Kayasths [Hindu caste of scribes, shudra by status, but very competent scholars], Rajputs, Muslims, Banias [Hindu merchants] and Khattris [Hindu and Sikh merchants claiming Kshatriya status], whose ancestors had served, or who were now serving, the government of northern India, were in the main the men with power. They may be defined as a group, almost a class, by their adherence to a government-bred culture, the culture of those whose lives revolved around government service and the towns. Its external forms were Muslim: the sherwani, Muslim food, mushairas, nautch parties and conspicuous extravagance. Its strongest expression was literary, and membership of this class is best defined by the use of the changing languages of government." Francis Robinson, *Separatism among Indian Muslims*, op. cit., p. 31.

Hindi sound very much alike, Urdu is written in Persian script whereas Hindi has inherited the "Devanagari" or "Nagari" script from Sanskrit. That at the end of the nineteenth century Urdu was the language used by all the elite—Hindus and Muslims alike—is evident in the number of books printed in that language. In the 1880s, 4,380 books had used that idiom, as opposed to 2,793 in Hindi, 1,022 in Persian and only 531 in English. But things started to change by the turn of the twentieth century. In the 1910s, the number of books published in Urdu and Persian fell to 3,547 and 281 respectively, whereas the number of books published in Hindi and English jumped to 5,063 and 923 respectively.[56]

Indeed, the last decades of the nineteenth century were marked by the growing assertion of a new Hindi-speaking as well as English-speaking Hindu middle class. That was largely the result of the post-1857 policy of the British who had decided to train a larger number of young Indians the modern way in order to rely more on an indigenous, educated elite (the subtext for "middle class" in South Asia) sharing their world view. They established universities to this end in Calcutta, Bombay and Madras—and then in smaller cities. Beyond higher education, but partly because such education was now available, Indian families who could afford to increasingly sent their children to government schools.

In the United Provinces, Hindus were more determined than Muslims to play this game. In 1880, 44 per cent of the pupils educated in private institutions were still Muslim children (compared to fewer than 20 per cent Hindus). Most of these were Quranic schools.[57] Learning the Quran remained an absolute obligation for all good families, the remainder of children's education being secondary and a modern curriculum causing constant concern among a community that was more wary than the Hindus of public education. Called to testify before the Education Commission in 1882, Syed Ahmad Khan declared regarding his coreligionists, "Their antipathy was carried so far indeed that they began to look upon the study of English by a Mussalman as little less than the embracing of Christianity".[58]

The reluctance of Muslims in the United Provinces vis-à-vis modern education did them all the more harm since starting in the 1860s, still in the aftermath of the Revolt of 1857, the British set about modernising the administration by raising their requirements for civil service candidates. In

56 Ibid., p. 77.
57 Ibid., p. 39.
58 Ibid., p. 38.

1860, those who wished to join the police force had to take a literacy test and, starting in 1874, the Tahsildars had to take an administrative exam. A further aggravating factor, MacDonnell, appointed Lieutenant-Governor of the province and thus the local strongman in 1895, considered Muslims to be fanatics who were hostile to the British government and whose influence in the administration had to be curbed at all costs. He introduced a recruitment ratio stipulating that for every three Muslims in the UP, five Hindus were to be recruited.

But it was of course the change in status of the Urdu language that was the real turning point at the end of the nineteenth century. In 1868, Babu Shiva Prasad, who was an official in the Education Department, had submitted to the British a "Memorandum on Court Character" arguing that the use of Urdu in Persian script in the administration put the Hindu majority at a disadvantage given that they had to learn an alphabet that was only natural for the community elite.[59] This line of argument boiled down to legitimating the aspirations of a middle class undergoing social advancement in the name of the democratisation of education. In 1881, these arguments convinced the government of neighbouring Bihar to replace Urdu in Persian script with Hindi in Devanagari as its official language, which restored hope among Hindi-speaking activists in the United Provinces. Their new leader, Madan Mohan Malaviya, known for his Hindu nationalist tendencies,[60] took up this issue in a very incisive pamphlet, *Court Character and Primary Education in the N.-W. Provinces and Oudh*. In it, Malaviya "claimed that this highly Persianized Urdu not only separated the urban, educated elite, brought up in an atmosphere of Indo-Persian culture, from the rural masses, but it served to perpetuate the dominance of a narrow class of people trained in the official jargon in the position of employment open to Indians trained in the courts and government offices of the time."[61]

The terms of a long debate to come were posed. They can be summarised by an opposition: democratic Hindus vs. aristocratic, even autocratic Muslims. At first, Syed Ahmad Khan—adopting a class-based strategy which will be discussed further on in greater detail—managed to mobilise Hindu personalities of the old Urdu-speaking elite, including the Maharajah

---

[59] Alok Rai, *Hindi nationalism*, Hyderabad, Orient Longman, 2002, p. 39.

[60] For further detail on M.M. Malaviya, see Christophe Jaffrelot, *India's Silent Revolution. The Rise of the Lower Castes in North Indian Politics*, London, Hurst, 2003, pp. 55–58.

[61] Paul Brass, *Language, Religion and Politics in North India*, Cambridge, Cambridge University Press, 1974, p. 131.

of Benares, within a United Indian Patriotic Association, against the replacement of Urdu in Persian script. But gradually the religious divide won out over linguistic ties that were slackening faster than ever, to such an extent that the above-mentioned Association was replaced in 1893 by the Mohammedan Anglo-Oriental Defence Association of Upper India. This initiative did not prevent MacDonnell from granting a request from Hindi-speaking activists to recognise Hindi in Devanagari on an equal footing with Urdu in Persian script as the language of the administration in 1899.[62] This measure hastened the rise of a new Hindu elite to the Muslims' detriment, while the latter were already losing civil service positions.[63] While Hindus and Muslims represented respectively 24.1 per cent and 63.9 per cent of the clerks in the subordinate executive and judicial services in the United Provinces in 1857, the share of the former rose to 50.3 per cent in 1886–87 and 60 per cent in 1913 while that of the latter fell to 45.1 and 34.7 per cent over the same period.[64]

Alongside the challenges to their status in the administration and to what had become their language, the Muslim elite in the United Provinces were the first victims of the (still very tentative) democratisation of politics intended by the British. This process, related to the efforts of a government seriously in debt to transfer over to local government bodies certain functions that had become too costly, was first deployed at the municipal level.[65] The famous Local Self-Government Act of 1882 thus placed the administration of education, public works and health care into the hands of the largest towns and the "district boards", which operated at just above the municipal level.

Democratisation occurred at the expense of the Muslim elites for two reasons. First, their community was almost everywhere in a minority; it

---

[62] Concretely, that meant that a citizen could henceforth petition the civil service in either language, implying that officials also had a command of both languages. Hindus who could speak and write Urdu were far more numerous than the Muslims who had a command of Devanagari. On this point, see Tariq Rahman, *Language and Politics in Pakistan*, Karachi, Oxford University Press, 1998, p. 69.

[63] Beyond the decline of Muslims in the administration, Urdu was beginning a slow descent into hell as the cultured written language in North India. Not only was there a decrease in the number of books published in this language, the Hindi press also proved more dynamic (Francis Robinson, *Separatism among Indian Muslims*, op. cit., p. 78).

[64] Ibid., p. 46. The 1857 figures refer to the North-West Provinces only.

[65] Hugh Tinker, *The Foundation of Local Self-Government in India, Pakistan and Burma*, London, 1968.

stood to lose from the introduction of a system that, *in fine*, was based on the law of numbers. Even if this effect was mitigated by voter eligibility criteria, ultimately, the logic of "one man, one vote" was likely to apply and already exercised its influence. Second, the relative economic decline of the Muslims in the United Provinces, compared to the Hindus who were growing rich from commerce and industry, penalised them even in areas where they had a majority. Thus in the west of the province and the Doab, whereas Muslims were a majority in eighteen cities, there were only eleven Muslim mayors there, due to the fact that Muslims voters were a majority in only six of them.[66] Throughout the United Provinces, the share of Muslims in municipal councils dropped from 34.1 per cent in 1884–5 to 30.1 per cent in 1907–8.[67]

The Muslims suffered all the more from this loss of power since it was translated into vexations—or what they interpreted as such—from Hindu politicians who were sometimes overcome by ideological hostility toward Islam. For instance in Moradabad (a majority Muslim town), the municipal authorities obliged Muslim butchers to tan the hides of their animals outside the city after the elections. In Chandpur, slaughtering of cows was simply banned. In Bijnor, Muslims butchers were thrashed for selling beef on the market.[68]

The Birth of a Separatist Movement—and a Syndrome

In view of the accelerating decline of Muslims in the United Provinces, the first reaction of the Aligarh reformers and their followers was to further intensify their efforts in education, including in English (Table 1.1.).

Table 1.1. illustrates the amplification of the educational strategy Syed Ahmad Khan developed in the post-1857 Revolt context. An ever-increasing

[66] Francis Robinson, "Municipal Government and Muslim Separatism in the United Provinces, 1883–1916", in John Gallagher et alii (eds), *Locality, Province and Nation. Essays on Indian Politics, 1870–1947*, Cambridge, Cambridge University Press, 1973, p. 92 and Francis Robinson, *Separatism among Indian Muslims*, op. cit., p. 81.

[67] Ibid., p. 82. The situation was even more problematic for the Muslims in Punjab (Gerald Barrier, "The Punjab Government and Communal Politics, 1870–1908", *Journal of Asian Studies*, 27 (3), 1968, p. 536). In Bengal, the share of the Muslims in the legislative council declined from 50 to 13% between 1895 and 1906. Farzana Shaikh, *Community and Consensus in Islam. Muslim Representation in Colonial India, 1860–1947*, Delhi, Imprint One, 2012 (1989), p. 131.

[68] Francis Robinson, *Separatism among Indian Muslims*, op. cit., p. 82.

Table 1.1: Male literacy by religion, 1891–1931 (in thousands and in %)

Literacy	In general			In English			Urban			Urban, in English		
Year	Total	Hind.	Mus.	Total	H	M	Total	H	M	Total	H	M
1931	2,043	79.8	15.2	240	63.7	19.9	364	63.2	28.4	118	58.1	22.3
1921	1,556	80.2	14.3	156	60.6	17.4	258	62	26.5	87	56.5	18.4
1911	1,505	80.6	13.6	121	52.5	17.2	221	60	23.6	65	47.8	18
1901	1,422	82.9	12.8	87	54.5	14.8	174	73	20.6	36	66	18
1891	1,257	84.4	11.7	43	40.3	9.7	–	–	–	–	–	–

Source: Paul Brass, Language, Religion and Politics in North India, Cambridge, Cambridge University Press, 1974, p. 149.

number of Muslims, mostly from the Ashraf elite, attended university and learned English. Between 1891 and 1901, the number of Muslims having a command of this language multiplied by more than three, going from 4,189 to 12,919, whereas among Hindus it only multiplied by 2.7. Aligarh College contributed significantly to this success. Between 1898 and 1902, it educated three-fifths of the Muslim graduates in the United Provinces (and a quarter of them in all of India).[69] This effort spawned a new elite. But the newly educated youth was enlightened enough to realize that education would not be capable of preserving Muslim minority interests. Although there were 12,919 English-speaking Muslims in 1901, the Hindus were 47,739, nearly four times as many.

Syed Ahmad Khan was the first to supplement—even substitute—his approach in the 1870s by another as of the following decade, in particular after the Self Government Act of 1882. The aim was to resist the democratisation process to avoid subjecting the Muslims to Hindu domination. With remarkable clear-sightedness, he explained in 1883 that resorting to elections in a society bound by religious and caste communities of very different sizes rather than individual citizens could not help but produce tensions:

So long as differences of race, and creed, and the distinctions of caste form an important element in the socio-political life of India, and influence her inhabitants in matters connected with the administration and welfare of the country at large, the system of election pure and simple cannot safely be adopted. The larger community would totally override the interests of the smaller community, and the ignorant public would hold Government responsible for introducing measures which might make the differences of race and creed more violent than ever.[70]

Syed Ahmad Khan develops not one but two arguments here. First, he was against democracy because it meant that the plebeians would take over from the elite group he belonged to. Hence his attempt to make an alliance with Hindus of a similarly high, aristocratic status against the rising middle class that he identified the Bengalis with and who, indeed, were making rapid progress in the administration through education. In a speech of 1888 in Meerut, he asks, "In your opinion, can the Rajput or fiery Pathan, who do not fear the noose, the police or the army, live peacefully under the Bengali?"[71]

[69] Ibid., p. 110.

[70] C.H. Phillips (ed.), *The Evolution of India and Pakistan, 1858–1947: Select Documents*, London, 1962, p. 185.

[71] Cited in Faisal Devji, *Muslim Zion: Pakistan as a Political Idea*, op. cit., p. 54.

Secondly, he was against democracy because the Muslims were in a minority—or more exactly had become a minority because of the growing divide between Muslims and Hindus, differentiating the erstwhile syncretic Hindustani elite. Syed Ahmad Khan admitted that this trend was developing quickly when he realised that the Hindus of Northern India (and elsewhere) were getting closer and distanced themselves from the North India Muslims:

Our Hindu brothers in this country are leaving us and joining hands with the Bengalis [sic!—aren't some Bengalis Hindus too?] So we should join the people whom we can associate with [...] We can befriend the English socially. We can eat with them. Whatever expectations of improvement we have, we have from the English. The Bengalis can do nothing good for our community.[72]

Syed Ahmad Khan therefore was against democracy for two reasons that he sometimes combined, as evident from his assessment of what for him would be the worse scenario: universal franchise,

Let us suppose first of all that we have universal suffrage as in America and that everybody, chamars [a Dalit caste] and all, have votes. And first suppose that all the Mahomedan electors vote for a Mahomedan member and all Hindu electors for a Hindu member... It is certain that the Hindu member will have four times as many because their population will have four times as many... and now how can the Mahomedan guard his interests? It would be like a game of dice in which one man had four dice and the other only one.[73]

By the mid-1880s, Syed Ahmad Khan was inclined to move closer to the British because he shared a common enemy with them: the Bengali-dominated Indian National Congress. Founded in 1885, the Congress party was the brainchild of the Hindu intelligentsia (Muslims represented only 6.5 per cent of the delegates to the movement's annual sessions from 1892 to 1906—combined figures).[74] It pressured the British to Indianise the administration and democratise political life in order to empower this group. In answer to the Congress' demand for democratisation of the political system and greater accessibility to civil service posts for Indians, Syed Ahmad Khan retorted that the movement had created the conditions for "a civil war without arms. The object of civil war is to determine in whose hands the rule of the country shall rest. The object of the promoters of the National Congress is that the Government of India should be English

---

[72] Cited in ibid.

[73] Cited in Peter Hardy, *The Muslims of British India*, op. cit., p. 130.

[74] P.C. Ghosh, *The Development of the Indian National Congress, 1892–1909*, Calcutta, 1960, p. 23.

in name only, and that the internal rule of the country should be entirely in their own hands."[75] Without saying so, Syed Ahmad Khan accused the Congress of being the mouthpiece of the Hindus and chose to appeal to the British to protect the Muslims from this majority, true in this regard to the loyalist stance he had taken in 1857.[76] Beyond that, he conjured up in scarcely veiled terms the risks of conflict between Hindus and Muslims that pursuing a transfer of power partly divesting the latter of their prerogatives was likely to engender. Elsewhere, he was more explicit:

I consider the experiment which the Indian National Congress wishes to make is fraught with danger and suffering for all the nationalities of India, especially Muslims. The Muslims are a minority but a highly united minority. At least traditionally they are prone to take the sword in hand when the majority oppresses them. If this happens it will bring about disasters greater than the ones which came in the wake of the happenings of 1857.[77]

Here Syed Ahmad Khan was using the threat of violence as a kind of bargaining chip.

To obtain special protection from the British, the Aligarh movement people, however, combined two other very different arguments. They first leaped into the breach opened by W.W. Hunter. In 1871, Viceroy Mayo had asked Hunter, at the time a member of the British administration in Bengal, to answer a question that had worried many British administrators since the Revolt of 1857: "Are Mussalmans bound by their religion to rebel against the Queen?" Hunter answered in the negative and even suggested that they could become loyal subjects to her Majesty as long as they were treated with respect. In parallel, he explained the anti-British bias of some Muslims by the fact that the modernisation of the educational system, if it served Hindu interests, had penalised the Muslims, who were already poorer than the average Indian before. He thus produced a bleak portrait of Indian Muslims that owed much to Hunter's experience in Bengal but that the British would tend to take as an overall reference.[78] The elite that graduated from Aligarh College managed to exploit this myth to attract

[75] Cited in Francis Robinson, *Separatism among Indian Muslims*, op. cit., p. 119.

[76] He collected 40,000 signatures—for a petition he presented to the House of Commons—against the extension of the franchise.

[77] Cited in Safdar Mahmood and Javaid Zafar, *Founders of Pakistan*, Lahore, Publishers United 1968, pp. 53–54.

[78] William Wilson Hunter, *The Indian Musalmans*, London, Trübner and company, 1876. Available online at: http://www.apnaorg.com/books/english/indian-musalmans/book.php?fldr=book (Accessed on September 15, 2013).

British sympathies. Thus in 1882 the National Muhammedan Association handed Lord Ripon a Memorandum describing "the depressed and desperate condition of the Muhammedans"[79] in order to support a request for special treatment.

In the Aligarh Muslim repertoire that was taking shape at the end of the nineteenth century, this argument was connected with another totally different one claiming that if the Muslims had to be protected from the Hindus, it was due to their "importance" (the word was often conjoined with the adjectives "political", "social" or "historical"). Spokesmen for the Muslim elite invited the British to weigh quantitative criteria against qualitative aspects that could only argue in favour of the heirs to the Mughal Empire. This rhetoric in defence of Muslims was coupled with a sort of thinly veiled threat: not only were the Muslims superior in quality and heirs to a rich history, but they also wielded an influence that they could use against the British if necessary. In 1900, a pamphlet defending the status of Urdu thus stated:

the Hindus, including of course all classes of them, constitute the majority; but it cannot be said that the entire body of them can claim the same political and social importance of the Mohammedans (...) Are these two classes [Hindu and Muslims] then merely to be judged by their quantity and not quality, by their size, and not by their importance, by their bare numbers and not their influence?[80]

The political stance of the Muslim elite at the end of the nineteenth century can be explained by both socio-political interests and cultural factors. The former have been highlighted by Paul Brass and other proponents of the instrumentalist approach according to which nationalism offers a convenient repertoire to elite groups whose domination over society is threatened by upwardly mobile others and which therefore try to mobilise behind them "their" community by manipulating identity symbols (including religious and linguistic ones).[81] The culture-oriented explanation was first spelled out by Francis Robinson and other supporters of the primordiaist model. According to them, the Muslims of India were so clearly different from the Hindus in civilisational terms that they were bound to become separatists.

---

[79] Paul Brass, *Language, Religion and Politics in North India*, Cambridge, Cambridge University Press, 1974, p. 141.

[80] Cited in ibid., p. 133.

[81] Paul Brass, "Elite group, symbol manipulation and ethnic identity among the Muslims of South Asia", in David T. Taylor and Malcolm Yapp (eds), *Political Identity in South Asia*, London, Curzon Press, 1979.

To understand the dynamics of the Aligarh movement, this dichotomy has to be transcended and the two dimensions combined, as Farzana Shaikh suggests. She shows that while the socio-political decline of the Indian Muslims of North India vis-à-vis Hindus was the catalyst of their separatism, this project can only be understood "in the light of their religious traditions".[82] Among them was a conception of power and society inherited from the Mughal Empire. At that time, the plurality of potentially conflicting groups (which were divided along ethnic and sectarian lines) was such that an emphasis had been placed on the need to consider the Muslims as a collective body rallying around the Great Mughals—whose power needed to be strong to keep the group united.[83] Hence, according to Farzana Shaikh, Syed Ahmad Khan's propensity to consider the Muslim as a political unit entitled to political representation irrespective of its number—as an existential imperative.

Secondly, for those who carry the legacy of the Mughal Empire, power must remain the preserve of ascriptive elite groups claiming Arab and Turkish roots.[84] Syed Ahmad Khan in this vein declared, "Would our aristocracy like that men of low caste or insignificant origin, though he be a BA or MA, and have the requisite ability, should be in a position of authority above them and have power in making laws that affect their lives and property? Never."[85] Qualifying the nature of his superiority and that of his peer group, Syed Ahmad Khan mentions elsewhere, "I am a Muslim, an inhabitant of India and descended from the Arabs... The Arab people neither seek, nor do they desire that instead of ruling themselves, someone else should rule them."[86] In the same spirit, he added in 1887, "Our nation is of the blood of those who made not only Arabia, but Asia and Europe to tremble. It is our nation which conquered with its sword the whole of India."[87]

To these quasi-genetic qualities, Syad Ahmad Khan added one moral explanation of the Ashraf's superiority: the fact that their religion "qualified them especially for power"[88] and, on the contrary, the fact that non-

---

[82] Farzana Shaikh, "Introduction to the second edition (2012)", in Farzana Shaikh, *Community and Consensus in Islam*, op. cit., p. xxv.

[83] David Lelyveld, *Aligarh's First Generation. Muslim Solidarity in British India*, Princeton, Princeton University Press, 1978, p. 21.

[84] Farzana Shaikh, *Community and Consensus in Islam*, op. cit., p. 93

[85] Cited in ibid., p. 115.

[86] Cited in ibid., p. 116.

[87] Cited in ibid.

[88] Ibid., p. 141.

Muslims should not be endowed with the charge to rule. This idea was explicitly spelled out several years later, in 1908, by Sayyid Ali Imam (1869–1932), a lawyer from Patna who descended from the Great Mughal Aurangzeb. For him should be excluded from power "the uncivilised portion of the country classified as Hindu".[89]

In the late nineteenth to early twentieth centuries, the Muslim elite concluded from its Mughal legacy, its "racial" quality and its moral (Islam-related) superiority, that it was entitled to rule. In Syed Ahmad Khan's rhetoric, the rejection of democracy that such a stance implies relied also on a very apt use of British thinkers, including John Stuart Mill and his idea that majorities can be tyrannical.[90]

This attitude contains the harbingers of two major components of the Pakistani syndrome. One is a certain Muslim superiority complex rooted, in the case of Syed Ahmad Khan, in the Mughal legacy—with respect to the Hindus justifying recognition of a sort of parity with them. The other is a propensity to use a form of blackmail on third parties—generally Western—to achieve their aims.

This approach would gain in greater intensity in the early years of the twentieth century during the debate on separate electorates, which, however, marked some acceptance of a form of proto-democracy, an evolution Syed Ahmad Khan had already initiated. This debate was triggered by the British decision to extend the democratisation process to the provincial level.[91] In response, the Aligarh school drafted a memorandum whose authors were none other than Mohsin-ul-Mulk and another Syed from a prestigious family of the United Provinces who graduated from Aligarh, Imad-ul-Mulk. Their text restated the "political importance" of Indian Muslims, in view of "the position which they occupied in India a little more than a hundred years ago", to ask for better representation both in government service where they were losing "in the prestige and influence which are justly their due" and in elected assemblies at both the local and provincial level. As the provincial Legislative Councils were on the verge of

[89] Cited in ibid., p. 153.

[90] In Mill, Syed Ahmad Khan found a plea against the "tyranny of the majority" that democracy could lead to, which Khan was keen to translate into ethnic terms, the dreaded majority in this case being the Hindu majority. See Safdar Mahmood and Javaid Zafar, *Founders of Pakistan*, Lahore, Publishers United, 1968, p. 52.

[91] For further detail regarding this decision, see Christophe Jaffrelot, *La démocratie en Inde. Religion, caste et politique*, Paris, Fayard, 1998.

acquiring new responsibilities, the memorandum focused more particularly on these to ask that Muslims be represented separately in them according to "the numerical strength, social status, local influence and special requirements of either Community."[92]

In concrete terms, this demand would translate into a petition for a separate electorate when the viceroy, Lord Minto, received a Muslim delegation dominated by Aligarh College officials[93] and notables[94] at his Himalayan summer residence in Shimla in 1906. Minto immediately pledged his support, thus galvanising the delegation's members who in the wake of this meeting founded the Muslim League, in December 1906, to have a permanent political pressure group.[95]

The reforms conceived by Morley and Minto, promulgated in 1909, finally acceded to most of the Indian Muslim demands. They obtained a separate electorate that was generally greater than their population size, with a quota of seats in the Imperial Council of Calcutta (which was still the capital) and in provincial legislative councils. Here, the Muslims of the United Provinces were overrepresented, when the Muslims of the provinces where they were in a majority—Bengal and Punjab—were not. While the Muslims of East Bengal and Assam represented 53 per cent of the population of their province, only 23.5 per cent of the seats of the Legislative Council of their province were reserved for them, whereas 19 per cent of the seats of the UP Council were reserved for Muslims, who represented only 14 per cent of the population of the province.[96]

The system set up by the 1909 reforms was all the more favourable to Muslims as they were entitled to a second vote in order to participate along

---

[92] Cited in Francis Robinson, *Separatism among Indian Muslims*, op. cit., pp. 144–145.

[93] With 11 members, the UP Muslims were largely overrepresented in the delegation, which moreover counted only 7 Punjabis and a single Bengali. It was nevertheless in Bengal, in the city of Dhaka, that on 30 December 1906, the Mohammedan Educational Conference became the Muslim League under the auspices of the Nawab of Dhaka.

[94] "Only 11 out of 35 members of the Simla Deputation were not titled", according to Mohammad Waseem who, therefore, records a larger number of participants. Mohammad Waseem, *Politics and the State in Pakistan*, op. cit., p. 62.

[95] The government in London showed more reluctance than the viceroy to grant the Muslims of the Raj a separate electorate. The Secretary of State for India, Lord Morley, in charge of reforming Indian institutions, was particularly hostile toward such a concession. But the Muslim League stepped up its lobbying effort remarkably. It established a British branch based in London, where hundreds of Indian Muslims would stay—some of them educated at Aligarh.

[96] Francis Robinson, *Separatism among Indian Muslims*, op. cit., p. 161.

with all their eligible fellow citizens, in choosing representatives of the other, so-called general constituencies. In 1915 the Muslim League in the United Provinces obtained a similar setup at the local level.[97]

The 1909 reforms constitute the first achievement of what can be called, after Francis Robinson, "Muslim separatism", although at the time it was only a matter of a separate electorate. But, asks Robinson, what had prompted the British to "concede so much of the League's demand"?[98] He suggests that the government had acquired the conviction that the Muslims "deserved special treatment" because they "were a separate and distinct community, a potential danger to the Raj, and an important conservative force."[99] These three explanations do not take into any account the British strategy of divide and rule, which nevertheless cannot be disregarded, given how tempting it was for the government to build the Muslims into a political force loyal to the British crown to counterbalance the Congress, the leaders of which were often Hindu. The first of his explanations reflects the prevailing culturalism at the time, fed by colonial ethnography. It is hence plausible, even if the resonance of a Hindustani culture which brought Hindus and Muslims together should have led the British not to reify the religious communities in this way. The second explanation reflects the blackmailing power the Indian Muslims were able to exert on the British. It is corroborated by an entry in the diary of Dunlop Smith, an advisor to Minto who had received the Muslim delegation in Shimla in 1906: "What I want to stop is these young Mohammedans forming small societies all over India. Once they start that game they can make us really anxious."[100] This anxiety—echoed in Minto's saying, "though the Mohamedan is silent he is very strong"[101]—reflects the fear of Muslims that had taken hold among the British during and after the Revolt of 1857. Some—such as MacDonnell—had concluded that they had to be brought to heel and the Hindus should thus be relied on; others, such as Morley and Minto, had come to believe that it was better to pander to them, also driven as they were by a reverse logic of divide and rule when the Hindus got together behind the Congress. Robinson's third explanation acknowledges the social influence of conservative notables dominating the Muslim community that

---

[97] Francis Robinson, "Municipal Government and Muslim Separatism in the United Provinces, 1883–1916", op. cit.

[98] Francis Robinson, *Separatism among Indian Muslims*, op. cit., p. 163.

[99] Ibid., p. 164.

[100] Cited in ibid., p. 166.

[101] Cited in ibid., p. 168.

the British would have been quite wrong to alienate as long as they were representatives for their authority.

The British strategy nevertheless had fateful consequences in the medium and long term as it reinforced the notion among the Muslim elite that it could continue to defend its interests without modernising and playing by democratic rules, but by waving the threat of agitation (and possibly violence) as blackmail and relying on its social influence. The arbiter here, who were the British (on a checkerboard on which Hindus and Muslims confronted one another in an increasingly conflictual fashion), encouraged the Muslim elite to cultivate a certain sense of entitlement, an important dimension of the future Pakistani syndrome. Morley moreover admitted this explicitly in 1870: "the Mohammedan community is entitled to a special representation on the Governor General's and local Legislative Councils commensurate with its numbers and political and historical importance."[102] The reference to numbers here is mainly rhetorical because quantitative considerations were largely offset by the other variable mentioned. The Muslim League eventually concluded that it could play along different lines than those of democratic principles, a tendency that came naturally to it given the sociological profile of its cadres.

Muslimhood as a Communal Ideology

The fundamentalists discussed earlier—whether they were from the Ahl-i-Hadith or from Deoband—viewed Islam as a universal religious community embodied by the *umma*. The reformers who started the Aligarh school—Syed Ahmad Khan being a prototype—behaved very differently in that they placed emphasis on the Muslims as a community—rather than on Islam. The result was not only an ethnicisation and a territorialisation of religion, but also an obsession with parity with the other community, the Hindus.

Territorialisation and Ethnicisation

As mentioned above, the reform movement—particularly the Aligarh movement—first of all emanated from a declining social elite (or one threatened with decline). This elite was Muslim, but it did not suffer only from its religious identity, even if it was an important factor in the opprobrium cast

---

[102] Quoted in Stanley Wolpert, *Morley and India 1906–1910*, Berkeley and Los Angeles, California University Press, 1967, p. 191.

upon it in the aftermath of the Revolt of 1857. In the following decade, the official status of its language, Urdu, was also threatened. Though Islam may have been intended as universal, Urdu, on the other hand, was territorialised. It was an ethnic marker, although admittedly malleable—its Arabic and Persian references could be emphasised to varying degrees, for instance—but it could not easily escape its grounding in North India. Those who took up its defence in the last third of the nineteenth century to preserve the interests of a traditional elite thus defined themselves as Muslim, but even more precisely as North Indian Muslims. Faisal Devji emphasised that "Syed Ahmad Khan resisted the efforts of associates like Mahdi Ali Khan, known as Nawab Mohsin-ul-Mulk, to build a countrywide Muslim organization, despite the fact that Muslim elites in cities like Bombay were eager to do so."[103] Such territorialisation and ethnicisation of the Muslim identity at the time as the Aligarh movement likens the Indian Muslims to a politicized *millat*. A *millat* perceives itself as a subgroup of the *umma* grounded in a territory. But it does not necessarily dispose of as much power as Syed Ahmad Khan wanted for his community. He had, indeed, conceived a truly political agenda aiming to make Indian Muslims the subgroup of a nation in which they were meant to exercise power. The emphasis thus shifted from the universal (*umma*) to the national and from the religious level toward the political sphere. Syed Ahmad Khan almost never mentioned Muslim solidarity across borders and disapproved of the Caliphate of Constantinople's claim to play the role of Commander of the Faithful throughout the world.[104]

In a famous speech made in 1883, Syed Ahmad Khan declared in the same spirit,

Just as the high caste Hindus came and settled down in this land once, forgot where their earlier home was and considered India to be their own country, the Muslims also did exactly the same thing—they also left their climes hundreds of years ago and they also regard this land of India as their very own.[105]

This speech—which reflects an obsession with parity with the Hindus which will be discussed further on—should be put in perspective with Syed Ahmad Khan's tendency to emphasise the foreign—in this case Arab—lin-

---

[103] Faisal Devji, *Muslim Zion: Pakistan as a Political Idea*, op. cit., p. 54.

[104] David Lelyveld, *Aligarh's First Generation*, op. cit., p. 311.

[105] Cited in Vishwanath Prasad Varma, *Modern Indian Political Thought*, Agra, Lakshmi Narain Agarwal, 1980 (7th edition), p. 430.

eage of his family as well as most Ashraf families.[106] This is not at all contradictory: the roots of the Indian Muslim elite were certainly to be found abroad—this was one of the sources of their prestige—but the *millat* was Indian and defined by a sense of Muslimhood more than by an allegiance to the transnational religion that is Islam.

The territorialisation effect was naturally reinforced by the past legacy, particularly the history of Mughal rule. The Aligarh school in fact never missed a chance to recall that the Muslims once governed the country in which they were currently asking for a say in matters—a say which, due to their history, could not be merely proportionate to their numbers.[107]

Two Communities, One Nation? The Obsession with Parity

While the Aligarh school marked a decisive turning point toward the ethnicisation and territorialisation of Indian Islam, its ethno-religious nationalism did not lead to separatism other than in the electoral sense. Syed Ahmad Khan did not set the Muslims and the Hindus up as two separate nations, but as communities destined to work together to build the Indian nation.

In his 1883 speech, the beginning of which was quoted above, he also declared,

...my Hindu brethren and my Muslim co-religionists breathe the same air, drink the water of the sacred Ganga and the Jamuna, eat the products of the earth which God has given to this country, live and die together (...) I say with conviction that if we were to disregard for a moment our conception of Godhead, then in all matters of everyday life the Hindus and Muslims really belong to one nation (qaum)[108] (...) and the progress of the country is possible only if we have a union of hearts, mutual sympathy and love (...) I have always said that our land of India is like a newly wedded bride whose two beautiful and luminous eyes are the Hindus and the Musalmans; if the two exist in mutual concord the bride will remain for ever

[106] Farzana Shaikh, *Community and Consensus in Islam*, op. cit., pp. 93–96 and 114–118.

[107] In that sense, the Indian Muslims initial separatism is not as a-historical as Faisal Devji suggests (Faisal Devji, *Muslim Zion*, op. cit.).

[108] Elsewhere, Syed Ahmad Khan would go so far as to underline how Hindus and Muslims mingled their blood and gave rise to a new culture made of both: "the blood of both have changed, the colour of both have become similar (...) we mixed with each other so much that we produced a new language—Urdu, which was neither our language, nor theirs" (Shan Muhammad (ed.), *Writings and Speeches of Syed Ahmad Khan*, Bombay, Nachiketa Publications, 1972, p. 160).

resplendent and becoming, while if they make up their mind to see in different directions the bride is bound to become squinted and even partially blind.[109]

This speech well defined the terms of the debate on the national question as formulated by the Aligarh school. The religious communities could confine expression of their faith to the private sphere to pledge allegiance to an Indian nation[110] as long as the Muslims occupied a higher rank than that conferred by their demographic weight. This is precisely the meaning of the metaphor of the bride representing the Indian nation in which the Muslims and the Hindus are of equal worth since the two communities are each incarnated in one of her eyes. Here again is evidence of the entitlement syndrome, accompanied with the sententious tone that would come to characterise the Muslim League, threatening reprisal in the event their conditions were not met. Syed Ahmad Khan did not hesitate to suggest that in that case, India would become disfigured because—one would suppose—of Muslim retaliation.

* * *

Ernest Gellner has taught us that "nationalism is not the awakening of nations to self-consciousness: it invents nations where they do not exist—but it does need some pre-existing differentiating marks to work on."[111] The case of the Muslims of North India well illustrates this lesson—up to a point. Indeed, their nationalism was the product of a strategy of identity building that an elite group developed in order to escape the Other's domination. While religion was not an exclusive dividing line before the late nineteenth century, it became one at the turn of the twentieth century because of socio-economic, educational and political factors. This process took place, at first, in spite of the Muslim leaders who, like Syed Ahmad Khan, tried to remain close to Hindu elite members. But then it developed because of them when they realised that the Congress was the brainchild of the Hindu intelligentsia and then started to rely on this religious character to secure protection

---

[109] Cited in Vishwanath Prasad Varma, *Modern Indian Political Thought*, Agra, Lakshmi Narain Agarwal, 1980 (7th edition), p. 430.

[110] In 1884, Syed Ahmad Khan declared in this regard, "Do not forget that Hindu and Muslim are words of religious significance otherwise Hindus, Mussalmans and Christians who live in this country form one nation regardless of their faith" (Shan Muhammad (ed.), *Writings and Speeches of Syed Ahmad Khan*, Mumbai, Nachiketa Publications, 1972, p. 266).

[111] Ernest Gellner, *Thought and Change*, London, Weidenfeld and Nicholson, 1964, p. 168.

from the British—who, in fact, had been responsible for the rise of communal identities by enumerating communities and democratizing the public sphere. Gellner's approach is all the more relevant as, in his model, the separatism of elite ethnic groups fearing marginalization eventually results in the demand for a separate territory—a state to govern.[112] And, in fact, the seeds of Pakistan were contained in the Aligarh movement.

Yet, the materialistic nature of Gellner's interpretation needs to be qualified.[113] As mentioned above, this question was part of one of the most significant academic controversies to occur in Indian studies in the 1970s. On one side, Paul Brass, unknowingly applying Gellner's framework of interpretation, maintained that the Aligarh movement's nationalism was spawned by a self-interested Muslim elite which then manipulated Islamic symbols of identity to construct an identitarian ideology from the ground up and rally the masses to its cause.[114] On the other side, Francis Robinson argued that the Hindu and Muslim communities had never overcome their cultural differences and that Muslim nationalism thus largely proceeded from age-old divisions.[115] As it often occurs, both approaches contained a kernel of truth and unless the aim is to fan the controversy, both sources must be drawn on. For if the Muslim elites of North India invented a new form of ethno-religious nationalism to achieve their ends, there is little doubt that the Hindu and Muslim cultures had remained separate in spite of areas of synthesis (including in the culture of power and the linguistic domain).

On the Muslim side, as Farzana Shaikh has shown, North Indian elite groups drew from their Arab and Turkish origins (which gave them the status of Ashraf), from their aristocratic ethos harking back to the Mughal Empire and from their belief in the moral superiority of Islam, a political culture not compatible with any form of subordination to the Hindu majority. Hence the aggressive overtone of the Aligarhis' Muslim nationalism and the demand of a separate electorate as well as the creation of the Muslim League.

---

[112] Ibid., p. 165.

[113] I endeavoured to do so from a comparative perspective in "For a Theory of Nationalism", in Alain Dieckhoff and Christophe Jaffrelot (eds), *Revisiting Nationalism. Theories and Processes*, London, Hurst & Company, 2006, pp. 10–61.

[114] Paul Brass, "Elite groups, symbol manipulation and ethnic identity among the Muslims of South Asia", op. cit.

[115] Francis Robinson, "Nation formation, the Brass thesis and Muslim separatism", *Journal of Commonwealth and Comparative Politics*, 15 (3), Nov. 1977, pp. 215–230.

No matter where the focus is directed—either toward the socio-economic and political pole or toward the cultural and religious pole—the conditions under which Muslim nationalism emerged at the end of the nineteenth century held significant consequences for what was to follow. The sociological motives for Muslim separatism make the Aligarh school an elite movement. Its political culture rejected democracy out of its attachment to an aristocratic sense of entitlement and out of a refusal of majority rule, partly because the Muslims were a minority that could not stand Hindu domination and partly because of the aristocratic ethos mentioned above. In its quest for an alternative source of legitimacy, the Muslim League constantly invoked the political, historical and social importance of the elite it represented. The rejection of democracy thus went hand in hand with a culture of entitlement, a major component of the Pakistani syndrome. This conservative elitism was to be a cause of instability when it clashed with popular aspirations for greater equality and freedom.

2

AN ELITE IN SEARCH OF A STATE—AND A NATION (1906–1947)

I have no doubt that you fully realize the gravity of the situation as far as Muslim India is concerned. The League will have to finally decide whether it will remain a body representing the upper classes of Indian Muslims or the Muslim masses, who have so far, with good reasons, taken no interest in it. (Letter from Iqbal to Jinnah dated 28 May 1937, *Letters of Iqbal to Jinnah*, Lahore, 1942).[1]

Although the Aligarh school—and the Muslim League that grew out of it—can be said to mark the birth of the separatist movement that would lead to the creation of Pakistan in 1947, one should be wary of any sort of retrospective determinism. Of course, the League continued to make substantial gains in the 1910s. In 1915, separate electorates were extended to the municipalities of the United Provinces, as mentioned above. The following year, with the Lucknow Pact, the Congress party officially recognised this system at both the local and national level and even admitted that in provinces where the Muslims were a minority, they should be accorded overrepresentation in the Legislative councils.[2] In exchange, the Muslim

---

[1] Cited in G. Allana, *Pakistan Movement Historical Documents*, Karachi, Department of International Relations, University of Karachi, nd [1969]), pp. 129–133. Available at: http://www.columbia.edu/itc/mealac/pritchett/00islamlinks/txt_iqbal_tojinnah_1937.html (Accessed on September 15, 2013).

[2] According to the Lucknow Pact, 30% of the seats were to be reserved for Muslims in the United Provinces, 25% in Bihar, and 33% in the Bombay Presidency and 15% in the Madras Presidency.

League pledged to throw itself behind the freedom movement following a declaration of principle that allowed them considerable leeway.

But shortly thereafter, the Muslim League encountered an unforeseen obstacle: the resurgence of pan-Islamic sentiment that would culminate with the Caliphate Movement between 1918 and 1922. This agitation, which offered a different path by which to counter the minority status of the Indian Muslims, as will be seen see below, attested to the popular following enjoyed by the *ulema*, a social and intellectual milieu linked in particular to the Deobandis and thus very remote from the League's circles. For the "caliphatists", Islam could not be envisaged in only one specific country. Shaken by the pan-Islamist wave in the late 1910s and the early 1920s, the League afterward was faced with the salience of regional identities based on ethno-linguistic markers that were now eating away at the foundations of its nationalism rather than attacking its summit. It was not until the end of the 1930s that the League began to overcome this obstacle, but imperfectly.

Muslim Politics beyond the North Indian Elite

The prominence of pan-Islamism—and in particular allegiance sworn to the caliph, which Syed Ahmad Khan had always combated—is first of all evident in the works of many Muslim scholars at the end of the nineteenth century. In 1889, Amir Ali for instance published his *Short History of the Saracens* in praise of the first two caliphs. Shibli Numani—who will be discussed further on—wrote a biography of the second, Omar. For India's Sunni Muslims, like for the others, the Caliph was the Amir al-Muminim, i.e. the commander of the faithful, both a spiritual and worldly leader.[3] This allegiance partly reflected the influence of one man in particular, Jamaluddin al-Asadabadi, known as "al-Afghani" (1839–97), who travelled tirelessly throughout the Muslim world to promote political solidarity among all Muslims. In India, where he remained from 1857 to 1865—before returning in 1879—Afghani considered Syed Ahmad Khan his "main enemy".[4] While less influential than Sir Syed, he made a strong impression on key figures

---

[3] Tipu Sultan, the warlord in southern India who put up the most successful resistance to the British, had sent an emissary to Constantinople in 1785 requesting that he brings back a letter of investiture from the Ottoman Sultan.

[4] Mushirul Hasan, "The Khilafat Movement: A Reappraisal", in Mushirul Hasan (ed.), *Communal and Pan-Islamic Trends in Colonial India*, Delhi, Manohar, 1985, p. 4.

such as Maulana Abdul Kalam Azad (1888–1958) and Mohammed Iqbal (1873–1938) who will accompany us throughout this entire chapter.

Indian Muslim allegiance to the caliph made them particularly concerned about the fate of the Ottoman Empire as Constantinople was both the seat of the Caliphate and the empire's capital. Each time the Turkish were involved in a conflict—against the Russians in 1877–8 and against the Greeks in 1897—Indian Muslims leapt to their aid, especially to raise funds.[5]

Ulema in the Public Sphere

On such occasions, the *ulema* were the first to take up the defence of the Ottoman Empire whose Sultan, as caliph, they saw as the guardian of holy places on the Jazirat al-Arab (the Arabian peninsula). These *ulema* came from a very different social background than that of the Aligarh school. Although Islam—except in its Shia variant (along with a few minor sects)— never developed an institutionalised priesthood, a body of religious specialists had gradually taken shape in the course of history, composed mainly of scholars well versed in the Quran and the *hadiths*. Those who possess this knowledge (*ilm*) and exercise it, particularly by reciting the Quran, are recognised as *ulema* and officiate in the mosques and *dini madaris* (plural of *madrassa*). They regulate the life of their community, particularly by issuing *fatwas* in the name of the sharia.

The status of Indian *ulema* declined sharply after the British conquest and the loss of power of the Mughal Empire and subsequently of the Muslim princely families at the head of the states that succeeded it. Until then, they were advisors to the prince, living in osmosis with the aristocratic elite, all the more since they were frequently related through marriage ties. Moreover, the British establishment of a new legal framework and judicial institutions in charge of administering it proved detrimental to the ulema who until then enjoyed a pre-eminent role (if not a monopoly) as regards law enforcement, or at least anything that came under the sharia—which was increasingly in competition with the new law.

But as the case of the Deobandis shows, far from reacting to the British conquest by showing any interest in politics, the *ulema* mainly endeavoured to safeguard their traditions by placing an emphasis on education.

---

[5] In addition to the French occupation of Tunisia in 1871 and the British takeover of Egypt in 1882, Italy's capture of Tripoli in 1911 caused a considerable stir, creating the general impression of the decline and dismembering of the Muslim world.

The Deobandis may have paved the way as early as 1867, but others soon followed their initiative. In 1893, Shibli, a former professor of Arabic and Persian in Aligarh, founded the Nadwat al-Ulama to form the crucible of an Islam that would transcend forms of sectarianism—including that of the Deobandis.[6] Established in Lucknow, the Nadwat nevertheless had considerable trouble convincing the *ulema* of other schools to follow a common curriculum.[7] Though it strove to be less conservative than the Deoband seminary, the Nadwat ended up resembling it in many regards, as attests its emphasis on *taqlid*, the refusal of the exercise of individual judgment (*ijtihad*) and its basic attachment to tradition. In 1913, in Azamgarh (east UP), Shibli founded a similar institution, Dar al-Musaniffin, which illustrates the densification of a rather orthodox network of *ulema* throughout North India.

In 1919, this process culminated in the creation of an organisation aiming to federate all the *ulema* in British India, the Jamiat-e-Ulama-e-Hind (JUH), at the initiative of Abdul Bari (1878–1926), a scholar from the Farangi Mahal seminary, the foundation of which harked back to Aurangzeb.[8] The two organisations at the root of the JUH were in fact the Farangi Mahal and Deoband seminaries. At the time the JUH was formed in 1919, the All India Khilafat Conference spawned the All India Khilafat Committee. This coincidence in dates is not accidental, because the *ulema* were already in the vanguard of the Caliphate Movement.

Ismailis as Pan-Islamists and Shias as Muslim Activists

Pan Islamism was not the monopoly of the *ulema*, however. This notion attracted groups often seen in India as being at the periphery of mainstream Islam, including Ismaili communities. The leader of one of them, the Aga Khan,[9] wrote a book in 1918 called *India in Transition* that presented

---

[6] Jamal Malik, "The making of a council: the Nadwat al-'Ulama", *Zeitschrift der deutschen morenlandishen Gesellschaft*, 144 (1994), pp. 60–90.

[7] Muhammad Qasim Zaman, "Religious Education and the Rhetoric of Reform: The Madrasa in British India and Pakistan", *Comparative Studies in Society and History*, vol. 41, no. 2 (Apr., 1999), p. 305.

[8] Francis Robinson, "The Ulema of Farangi Mahall and their Adab", in Barbara Daly Metcalf (ed.), *Moral Conduct and Authority; The Place of Adab in South Asian Islam*, Berkeley and Los Angeles, California University Press, Berkeley, 1984, pp. 52–83.

[9] On this interesting character see, Siumen Mukherjee, "Being 'Ismaili' and 'Muslim': Some Observations on the Politico-Religious Career of Aga Khan III", *South Asia: Journal of South Asian Studies*, vol. 34, no. 2, July 2011, pp. 188–207.

the country as playing a pivotal role in the Muslim world. His plan for a "South Asiatic Federation" would have amalgamated the populations of western as well as eastern neighbours of the sub-continent, whether they were Muslim or not. It would have been "a vast agglomeration of states, principalities and countries in Asia extending from Aden to Mesopotamia, from the two shores of the Gulf to India proper, from India proper across Burma and including the Malay Peninsula; and then from Ceylon to the States of Bokhara, and from Tibet to Singapore".[10]

As Faisal Devji argues, this "plan" was intended to kill two birds with one stone. First, it allowed the Muslims of India to surmount their minority status by pointing out that in a larger perspective, at the regional level, Muslims were in a majority. The Aga Khan offers in this regard a very telling interpretation of his project: "If we turn from numbers to surface of territory, the Islamic provinces of South Asia will be almost as great in extent as the India of yesterday. Hence there is little danger of the Mahommedans of India being nothing but a small minority in the coming federation".[11] And this transnational approach presented them as being on a par with the other transnational power that was the British Empire—which should definitely recognise the Muslims of India as its partners. Secondly, this worldview challenged the common assumption that North Indian Muslims were the custodians of subcontinental Islam, a vision with which cosmopolitan groups like the Khojas and other trading communities spread over in the Persian Gulf and Africa could only be uncomfortable. In fact, the Aga Khan is very critical in his book of the overcentralized and tyrannical rule of the Mughal Empire, whose oppressiveness is described as the root cause for its fall.[12]

Pan-Islamism and cosmopolitanism were the two paradoxical routes that non-Sunni and non-North Indian Muslims found, at the turn of the twentieth century, to be part of the mainstream politics of their community. And some of them longed for such inclusion cum recognition. A more practical strategy in the pursuit of that goal pertained to financial support. As Faisal Devji points out, in addition to the Aga Khan—the first president of the Muslim League—many Shia leaders financed this movement, be they part of trading communities of western India like Adamjee or landlords of the North like the Raja of Mahmudabad or the Nawab of Rampur. These people

---

[10] Cited in Faisal Devji, *Muslim Zion*, op. cit., p. 71.
[11] Cited in ibid., p. 74.
[12] Ibid., p. 73.

were "largely responsible for financing the League and making it a non-sectarian as well as country-wide party during its early history, in which it is normally written about only as an unrepresentative grouping of elites".[13]

These new figures certainly made the League more national, but not less elitist since—as evident from their fortunes and their titles—they were mostly rich magnates. The Caliphate movement, however, marked not only a turning point in the dilution of the Northern orientation of Muslim politics in India, but also in its plebeianisation, according to a religious repertoire.

The Caliphate Movement

Though pan-Islamic mobilisation had already taken off with the Balkan wars in the early 1910s, the movement acquired an entirely new dimension late in the decade after the coalition the Ottoman Empire had joined was defeated in the First World War. In autumn 1918 Constantinople was occupied. One year later, as Turkey was about to lose Cyprus, Sudan and the Arab lands of its Empire, Indian Muslims who feared for the Caliphate launched a movement of the same name.[14]

Although the *ulema* played a major role in this movement, they were not the only ones involved. By their side, and even in the vanguard, stood what was called the "young party" for lack of a better appellation. These Muslims did not only have in common their youth. They also shared the same rejection of the Aligarh school's loyalty to the British, a policy they believed had done nothing for them since 1909, as attested by the annulment of the Partition of Bengal in 1911.[15] Many of them were also more eager to protect Islam, while the Aligarh school was striving to reform it. Certainly, some members of the "young party" were graduates of Aligarh, but their loyalty to Syed Ahmad Khan's reformism was waning. Already in 1910, Maulana Ubaid-Allah Sindhi (1872–1944) had founded a Jamiyat al-Ansar (mutual aid society) in Deoband for the benefit of Deoband and Aligarh alumni, and

---

[13] Ibid., p. 64.

[14] On this movement, see M. Naeem Qureshi, *Pan-Islamism in British India: the Politics of the Khilafat Movement, 1918–1924*, Karachi, Oxford University Press, 2009.

[15] In 1905, the British had drawn Muslims sympathy by cutting Bengal in two, creating a province with a very strong Muslim majority in the East on more or less the territory occupied by today's Bangladesh. This measure was very popular with Muslims among whom the British sought to curry favour, but it outraged the Hindu elite in Calcutta.

this initiative had evinced the rapprochement of the two institutions to the detriment of the latter's reformist integrity.

More radical and more Muslim, the "young party" identified with the *ulema*'s pan-Islamism, exemplified in the career of their main leaders, Muhammad and Shaukat Ali, two brothers trained in Aligarh[16] who had taken their distance from this institution. They asserted themselves for the first time during the Muslim League session of December 1912–January 1913 by vehemently denouncing the exploitative policy of the British in India. Both had been imprisoned during the war between Great Britain and the Ottoman Empire, for fear they would carry out anti-British attacks. In 1914, when the First World War broke out, Maulana Muhammad Ali published an article with the explicit title "The Choice of the Turks" in *Comrade*, his weekly publication.

Another young activist destined for a bright future, Maulana Abdul Kalam Azad, whose political career had begun with revolutionary movements in Bengal, also founded an Urdu newspaper in Calcutta. A staunch "caliphatist", he clearly expressed the pan-Islamic philosophy of the Caliphate Movement in a book *Masla-i Khilafat* (The Issue of the Caliphate) in 1920.[17] In it he explains that God had given the Earth to various communities before finally handing it over to that led by Prophet Mohammed to whom all owed obedience. According to Azad, God also instituted the Caliphate to ensure all obeyed him. Azad went on to relate the heroic deeds of the successive caliphs before admitting that the Great Mughals were probably loath to swear the allegiance they should have to the caliph. He nevertheless found this lapse understandable given that their immense power enabled them to administer Islamic law on their own. Since the dynasty had come to an end, Azad concluded, Indian Muslims could only turn to the caliph to make sure their law was enforced. He also pointed out

---

[16] Mushirul Hasan, *Mohamed Ali. Ideology and Politics*, Delhi, Manohar, 1981. Lelyveld looks at Muhammad Ali as a typical exemplar of the educated young Muslims of his generation, who had been "indoctrinated with the ideology of Sayyid Ahmad Khan: that Indian Muslims had declined and that the only hope for their regeneration was to mobilize them under the aegis of Aligarh". David Lelyveld, "Three Aligarh Students: Aftab Ahmad Khan, Ziauddin Ahmad and Muhammad Ali", *Modern Asian Studies*, vol. 9, Part 2, April 1975, p. 240.

[17] The best resource regarding its philosophy remains the book by Peter Hardy, *Partners in Freedom and True Muslims*, Lund, Studenlitteratur, 1971. See also his autobiography, Maulana Abul Kalam Azad, *India Wins Freedom*, Hyderabad, Orient Longman, 1988. This edition at long last publishes Azad's text in full.

the caliph's sacred role as protector of the holy places on Arab land: "The Jazirat al-Arab [the Arabian peninsula] must at all times be free of non-Muslim control and if it has escaped from the control of the khalifa of Islam then it must be restored to him by force, force to which all Muslims all over the world must contribute."[18]

Recourse to force might have remained the first choice of Azad and other "caliphatists" if another political calculation had not won out. Aware of their limits, these activists in fact preferred to form an alliance with the Congress, whose anti-British activism was well-known, all the more since Gandhi—who was about to assume party leadership—made overtures to them. The Mahatma was anxious to promote Hindu-Muslim unity and his religious temperament prompted him to support the "caliphatists'" demands. He took part in the November 1919 meeting that produced the All India Khilafat Committee and even agreed to become its president. He was thus in a position to enlist Muslims in the Movement of Non-Cooperation—his first non-violent agitation campaign against the British—which he launched the following year. In this context, the All India Khilafat Conference in Karachi presided over by Muhammad Ali in 1921 passed a resolution stating that it was "religiously unlawful" for Indian Muslims to serve in the British army[19] and that they would declare India independent if Great Britain attacked Turkey.

Far from reflecting a desire for rapprochement with the Hindus founded on a common identity, the cooperation undertaken by the "caliphatists" with Gandhi's Congress was entirely pragmatic. The aim was to make up the numbers before a common enemy that the Congress wanted to chase out of India and the "caliphatists" out of the Middle East. Syed Sulaiman Nadwi, one of Shibli's pupils at the Nadwat al-Ulama, thus wrote to Abdul Bari that to liberate the Ka'aba, they first had to free India.[20]

Many Hindus were aware of the limits of any convergence of the two communities. The fact that events occurring thousands of miles from India could mobilise the Muslims to such an extent left them wondering about their political identity, which for the Hindu nationalists seemed to be more transnational than nationalist. For Muslims were mobilising on a scale

---

[18] Peter Hardy, *The Muslims of British India*, op. cit., p. 192.

[19] Such a resolution merely restated the one passed by the JUH in March 1921, that it was a sin (*haram*) for a Muslim to serve in the British army. Mushirul Hasan, "Religion and Politics in India: the Ulama and the Khilafat Movement, in Mushirul Hasan (ed.), *Communal and Pan-Islamic Trends in Colonial India*, p. 31.

[20] Ibid., p. 30.

never seen before.[21] Not only did the agitation last for months, even years (1919–21), and affect all four corners of India, but also all categories of society were involved:

Many left the fields and factories to migrate to the dar al-Islam in response to a call for hijrat; students abandoned their studies and joined the swelling ranks of non-cooperators; and many others gave up their lucrative jobs and high-sounding titles. Never before did so many Muslims unite on a common platform to fight a common cause. It was a unique example of their religious solidarity.[22]

The involvement of urban and rural masses alike in the movement can largely be explained by the influence the ulema had over them. As for the sway of the notables who up until then were careful not to antagonise the British, it reflects the force of religious fervour as well as the importance they attached to their coreligionists' opinion.

Umma and *Millat* versus *Qaum*

The plan initially conceived by Syed Ahmad Khan's disciples at Aligarh was suddenly challenged by a force that came from deep within Muslim society. Those who had strived to ethnicise and territorialise Indian Islam—and won the support of the British—found themselves confronted with a new political repertoire emphasising the universal (or in any event trans-national) aspect of their religion—and confronted with the British.

This difficulty was compounded by another that may at first appear contradictory. The Caliphate Movement *ulema*, finding themselves without a commander of the faithful, came up with another model of religious authority that even further undermined the foundations on which the Muslim League had been built.

The JUH *ulema* could not resign themselves to the disappearance of the Caliphate. They advocated a struggle to re-establish it. But in the meantime, they invented a temporary system to replace it. At the annual JUH conference in December 1921, a subcommittee made up of obscure *ulema*—who were for that all the more representative or typical—agreed to elect an

---

[21] The best study on the subject remains Gail Minault's *The Khilafat Movement: Religious Symbolism and Political Mobilization in India*, New York, Columbia University Press, 1982

[22] Mushirul Hasan, "Religion and Politics in India: the Ulama and the Khilafat Movement, in Mushirul Hasan (ed.), *Communal and Pan-Islamic Trends in Colonial India*, op. cit., p. 18.

Amir-i Hind (Emir of India). This Emir, required for as long as the caliph was not reinstated, would be responsible for maintaining a vast network of Qazis and overseeing their enforcement of the sharia. This included reviving a number of rules guiding Muslim life that had fallen into disuse. This Emir, a wise man and a scholar, was to be assisted by a seven-member council that would include five *ulema*. Even if the JUH committee acknowledged the next caliph's power to dismiss and appoint the Emir of India, these changes had to be made in consultation with the JUH, which thus foresaw itself elevated to the status of parliament for Indian Islam—a parliament that the Emir, and even the caliph, would answer to.

This assertion of the *ulema*'s power—or at least their aspirations in this direction that would again manifest itself just after the creation of Pakistan—should be viewed in light of their attempts to (re)establish Islamic law during the Caliphate Movement. They thus set up sharia tribunals in certain districts of the NWFP.[23]

The *ulema*'s approach reflects a new sort of political agenda. They were not interested in reforms such as separate electorates, to which they never accorded any importance anyway, given that political representation mattered less to them than the Islamic nature of the law governing them. Nor were they interested in demanding a separate state, because Islam could not be territorialized.[24] Their aim was to ensure the *millat* an autonomy such that, if the model was systematised and extended to all denominations, India would be only a loose federation of self-administered communities.

This model, fashioned during a period of extreme pan-Islamic mobilisation, boiled down to a communitarianism that was relatively consistent with the Gandhian definition of the nation. Its roots were no less Muslim, for it is indeed the universal nature of the *umma* that makes the *millat* a more relevant and legitimate basic unit than a separate electorate (or a separate state). Therefore, most of the architects of the Caliphate Movement logically joined the Congress party once their movement came to an end. This was the case for many JUH *ulema* and for Abdul Kalam Azad. In November 1921 Azad presided over a JUH session at which a resolution was passed stating that "it was essential that Muslims should be at perfect liberty and completely independent with respect to their religious life and that no force of power should be a hindrance or restraint in the declaration

---

[23] Ibid., p. 29.
[24] On the impossibility to territorialize Islam according to Azad, see Ian Henderson Douglas, *Abul Kalam Azad: An Intellectual and Religious Biography*, Delhi, Oxford University Press, 1988, pp. 225–226.

and propagation of Islamic commandments, either social or penal". In the following resolution, the JUH "Acknowledge[d] that Muslims can and will achieve liberty and freedom in conjunction with different Indian communities subject to the provisions of the Islamic law and religion".[25]

In other words, Indian Muslims did not aim to blend into an Indian nation, but to fight within the Indian context alongside other communities to achieve the right to live freely, that is, following the rules of their religion and law (the sharia). Peter Hardy concluded from this, "In 1920–2 Abdul Kalam Azad and the Jamiyat were advocating the mental partition of India".[26] The remark is perhaps too strong but has the advantage of differentiating this new political current from the one handed down from the Aligarh school which, through the Muslim League more or less unofficially by the end of next decade—and officially in the course of the following one—would demand the geographical partition of India. For the League, the Caliphate Movement finally put up two obstacles and not one, since the ethnicisation of Indian Muslims in Syed Ahmad Khan's political perspective was confronted not only with pan-Islamism but also a form of communitarianism, the two currents not sharing the former's separatism. Sir Syed had sought to promote parity between the two potential nations, Hindu and Muslim—and India's two "eyes" to use his metaphor; the caliphatists' emblem on the other hand placed Indian Muslim allegiance to Islam as a transnational reality on equal footing with allegiance to India as a nation. Their symbol, indeed, was formed by two intersecting circles of the same size in which the Indian Muslims occupy the overlapping space.[27]

The Caliphate Movement came to a sudden end in the beginning of the 1920s. In February 1922 Mahatma Gandhi suspended the Non-Cooperation Movement following an outbreak of violence that made him fear a drift contrary to his political philosophy.[28] A few months later, in November 1922, the Turkish Assembly voted to separate the Sultanate and the Caliphate—the latter which would be officially abolished by Ataturk in 1924, and so it was Muslims themselves who did away with the issue around which their Indian coreligionists had mobilised.

---

[25] Cited in P.C. Bamford, *Histories of the Non-Cooperation and Khilafat Movements*, Delhi, Government of India, 1925 (reprinted in 1985 by K.K. Book, in Delhi), p. 178.

[26] Peter Hardy, *The Muslims of British India*, op. cit., p. 195.

[27] Mushirul Hasan, "The Khilafat Movement: A reappraisal", op. cit., p. 7.

[28] In Chauri Chaura, near Gorakhpur (east UP) demonstrators set fire to a police station, burning police officers alive.

Muslim League leader Khaliquzzaman himself admitted, "The history of the next sixteen years of Muslim India is a mass of confusion and a chapter of political benightedness. The disruption of the Khilafat organisation was like a breach in the embankment of the flowing stream of Muslim mass emotion, which diverted into several petty streams."[29] The confusion Khaliquzzaman mentioned first flowed from the Caliphate Movement itself. It had in fact brought to light the contradiction between the Muslim League's agenda and the strength of pan-Islamic and anti-British sentiments running through Indian Muslims.

The years 1918–22 also marked the birth of another current that soon became known as the "Muslim Nationalists", uniting Muslim Congress party supporters and other opponents to the League.[30] The members of this very heterogeneous group, as it included such figures as JUH *ulema* and Azad, had in common the defence of Indian Muslim interests in the name of a national agenda that would grant religious communities considerable autonomy.

Starting in the 1920s, however, the countless little streams Khaliquzzaman mentioned were less ideological than regional. Indeed, the Muslim League had to face an even more substantial problem than the transnational obstacle of pan-Islamism or the national obstacle of "Muslim Nationalists": the regionalism of Indian Muslims living in areas where they were in a majority.

Jinnah, the Congress and the Muslim-majority Provinces

In 1919 the British granted the Indians a reform of their political institutions by making the provinces the basic unit of the Raj. Provincial legislative councils not only gained some legislative autonomy from Delhi but also the prerogative of appointing (and dismissing) ministers who were now part of governments half-composed of Indians. The ministers in charge of education, agriculture, local administration, industry and public works came under the Councils and answered to them, while other portfolios (the police, justice, prisons and property taxation) remained with the lieutenant governor accountable only to Delhi. The 1919 reform thus instituted a "dyarchic" regime making the provinces the main arenas of political life for Indian political parties, as that was where they could exercise an increasing share of power.

---

[29] Choudhry Khaliquzzaman, *Pathway to Pakistan*, Lahore, Longmans, 1961, p. 74.
[30] Including, in addition to Azad, M. C. Chagla, Asaf Ali, M.A. Ansari Syed Mahmud and Rafi Ahmad Kidwai.

The last major reform initiated by the British, the Government of India Act of 1935, deepened the tendencies outlined in 1919. The most significant changes in fact came once again at the provincial level, where the diarchy was eliminated. While the governors—British subjects still appointed by the viceroy—retained only a few sovereign prerogatives that they could of course expand by resorting to emergency procedures and dismissing the provincial governments, these governments had more room to manoeuvre with respect to the central authorities. All the ministerial portfolios were now in the hands of Indians working under the authority of a chief minister and these governments were accountable to assemblies elected by a broader body of eligible voters.

This decentralisation, which became clear with the 1919 reform, had the disadvantage for the Muslim League—an already confused body—of pushing the matter of Indian Muslims into the background, the members of this community preferring to organise at the regional level.[31] Such a tendency was particularly clear in areas where Muslims were a majority. For them, the underlying rationale of the League since its creation was not the most relevant. The Aligarh movement had formed this party to defend themselves from a perceived threat of marginalisation in the United Provinces where they were a minority. But in Punjab, Bengal and the Northwest Frontier Province (NWFP),[32] Muslims were a majority. Furthermore, the British, by granting provincial governments greater autonomy, gave them even more leeway. Why should they mobilise behind the League in the service of Muslims in minority provinces? Mere religious solidarity was not a sufficient motive. Still in 1943, in his presidential address delivered at the Muslim League annual session, Mohamed Ali Jinnah was obliged again to declare:

Don't forget the Minority Provinces. It is they who have spread the light when there was darkness in the majority Provinces. It is they who were the spearheads that the Congress wanted to crush with their overwhelming majority in the Muslim minority provinces. It is they who had suffered for you in the Majority Provinces, for your sake, for your benefit and for your advantage.[33]

---

[31] This dynamic is the focus of David Page's very astute analysis in *Prelude to Partition. The Indian Muslims and the Imperial System of Control. 1920–1932*, Oxford, Oxford University Press, 1987.

[32] This province only came about in 1901 when the Pashto-speaking districts of Punjab were grouped together under the supervision of the British chief commissioner. The province did not have its own council and government until 1932.

[33] Jinnah's speech before the Muslim League session in Delhi, 24 April 1943, in Syed Sharifuddin Pirzada (ed.), *Foundations of Pakistan, 1940–1947: A Selection of*

Four years before the creation Pakistan, Jinnah was thus still seeking to rally "majority Muslims" to the League's cause. He would not obtain their backing until the last minute, on the basis of a misunderstanding.

Jinnah, the Twentieth Century's Sir Syed?

In many respects, in spite of his western Indian and Khoja background, Jinnah embodied the spirit and the sociological profile of the initial Muslim League. He came from an area where Muslims were a minority, the Bombay Presidency, which included the province of his birth, Sindh, until 1936.[34] He was a member of the liberal intelligentsia not only because he had studied law in England—like so many politicians of the era he was a lawyer—but also because as member of the small Khoja community, he carried his heterodoxy so far as to marry a Parsi.[35] He had moreover begun his political career in the shadow of a Parsi leader, D. Naoroji. Jinnah paid little heed to Islam's taboos—particularly dietary ones—to the point, it is said, of drinking alcohol.[36]

In the shadow of Naoroji, Jinnah had begun his career in the Congress Party and only joined the Muslim League in 1913 while remaining a Congress Party member. He was also an advocate of Indian national unity beyond religious divides as long as minority rights—starting with those of the Muslims—were respected. He had thus been one of the architects of the Lucknow Pact in 1916. He did not leave the party until 1920 when Gandhi launched his Non-Cooperation Movement which he deemed too radical.[37] From then on, Jinnah shared with Sir Syed a tactical loyalism that aimed to

---

Documents Presenting the Case of Pakistan, vol. 1, Karachi and Dhaka, National Publishing House, 1969, p. 407.

34 The "standard" Jinnah biography remains the one authored by Stanley Wolpert. Stanley Wolpert, *Jinnah of Pakistan*, New York, Oxford University Press, 1984, of which Francis Robinson gave an excellent review. "The Jinnah Story", in M.R. Kazimi (ed.), *M. A. Jinnah. Views and Reviews*, Karachi, Oxford University Press, 2005, pp. 91–105.

35 Although he denied his daughter the right to do the same (Roger D. Long, "Jinnah and His 'Right Hand', Liaquat Ali Khan", in M.R. Kazimi, *M. A. Jinnah. Views and Reviews*, p. 130).

36 Stanley Wolpert, *Jinnah of Pakistan*, op. cit., pp. 78–79.

37 See David Page, "Mohammed Ali Jinnah and the System of Imperial Control in India 1909–1930. A Case Study in Political Leadership and Constitutional Innovation", in M.R. Kazimi, *M. A. Jinnah. Views and Reviews*, op. cit., pp. 1–22.

make the British arbitrate in favour of the Muslims against the Congress and the Hindus. Most of all, he would gradually oppose the Congress, which he feared had become a vehicle for Hindu hegemony, being obsessed with the need for parity between Hindus and Muslims even more than Sir Syed.

Minority Muslims vs. Indian National Congress—Jinnah and the Obsession with Parity Revisited

The break between Jinnah and the Congress was complete at the end of the 1920s, following the Nehru Report, which had been commissioned from Motilal Nehru and his son Jawarharlal so that the Congress could produce a draft Constitution for India that rivalled with the one being concocted by the British in the Simon Commission (1928). Jinnah had his own proposals. He proved open to calling the separate electorates into question in exchange for a 33 per cent quota for Muslims in the parliament and concessions to Muslims in the majority provinces, a matter discussed further on.

The Congress, via the Nehru Report, largely ignored these demands by virtue of a conception of the Indian nation based more on individual citizens than on communities. It recommended the abolition of separate electorates and the maintenance of seats reserved for Muslims only in the provinces where they were in a minority.[38] Jinnah reacted with a 14-point programme (that actually contained 15) which outlined his own project for a constitution: the India he dreamed of was federal; the majority communities in a province should have the guarantee of remaining so in assemblies elected at this level; the electorates should remain separate as long as no arrangement could be found with the Congress in this regard; the Muslims should have one-third of the seats in the national assembly. This plea failed to convince Muslims leaders won over by the Nehru Report such as Azad and M. A. Ansari, who were now the two main leaders of the Muslim Nationalists within the Congress.

In 1930–31 the British organised Round Table Conferences in London which did not help to reconcile viewpoints and attested to the increasing clout that regional leaders had among Muslims owing to the 1919 reform. Jinnah concluded that he had no place in the Indian political landscape of the 1930s and decided to remain in London to exercise his profession as a lawyer. But for Muslims in the Hindu majority provinces, he remained a

---

[38] *All Parties Conference—1928: Report of the Committee Appointed by the Conference to Determine the Principles of the Constitution of India*, Allahabad, 1928.

sort of providential figure that they constantly called back to his homeland, a point worth underscoring given that Jinnah is often described as a solitary figure who acted only according to his own inclination: he actually had a considerable following and was sometimes a mere *primus inter pares* among "Minority Muslim" leaders as it would turn out.

The first to ask him to return to India was probably Liaquat Ali Khan in 1933.[39] He was Jinnah's closest lieutenant and they were to work in tandem for over a decade. While Jinnah represented the Minority Muslims of western India (the Bombay Presidency) and merchant circles as well as the professions in the League, Liaquat Ali Khan was the spokesman for the Muslims of North India and represented the agrarian, even aristocratic elites. His ancestors—who were said to descend from the Persian sovereign Nausherwan the Just—allegedly migrated to India and served the Mughal Emperor. Owning land on both banks of the Yamuna in Punjab (in Karnal)[40] and in the United Provinces (in Muzaffarnagar district), he was associated with this latter region due to his studies at Aligarh College where he matriculated in 1910 and his election to the UP Legislative council for Muzaffarnagar in 1926. Meanwhile, like Jinnah, he had studied law in England.[41] Although he joined the Muslim League in 1923, Liaquat Ali Khan was elected in 1926 under the label of a landowner's movement. He moreover used his parliamentary position to defend the interests of his corporation, convinced that "a stable rural society was essential to the well-being of the state".[42] Furthermore, when he joined Jinnah in London for the Round Table Conferences, it was to defend the landowners' as well as the Muslims' interests. It was after these conferences that he asked Jinnah to return to India, persuaded, like so many other minority Muslims, that they would not find a better leader. After becoming the Honorary Secretary of the Muslim League in 1936, Liaquat Ali Khan became Jinnah's right hand man.[43]

---

[39] The following year, the Muslims of Bombay would elect him in absentia to the central legislative assembly. See Ian Talbot, "Jinnah and the Making of Pakistan", in M.R. Kazimi, *M.A. Jinnah. Views and reviews*, op. cit., p. 83).

[40] Muhammad Reza Kazimi, *Liaquat Ali Khan. His Life and Work*, Karachi, Oxford university Press, 2003, pp. 4–5. Liaquat Ali Khan's elder brother inherited this estate as well as the title of Nawab that went with it.

[41] Like Jinnah, he also married a non-Muslim (his second marriage), a Brahman converted to Christianity, who converted to Islam to marry him (Roger D. Long, "Jinnah and His 'Right Hand'", in M.R. Kazimi, *M.A. Jinnah. Views and Reviews*, op. cit., p. 128).

[42] Ibid., p. 129.

[43] After 1947, it seems that the relations between Liaquat Ali Khan and Jinnah

The Government of India Act of 1935 finally convinced Jinnah to return to India in October 1935, driven by an ever-growing desire to gain acceptance from the Congress (which he henceforth qualified as a Hindu party) of the idea that India's two main communities and their political mouthpieces should be treated on an equal footing. Following the Congress victory in the 1937 elections, he asked the party that had just triumphed to form coalition governments with the League in some of the provinces where it had won. He expounded on this theme during the Muslim League annual session where he insisted, "an honourable settlement can only be achieved between equals". Demanding of the Congress that it acknowledge the League "on a footing of perfect equality", he declared, "I have got as much right to share in the government of this country as any Hindu", and again, "I must have equal and effective share in the power".[44] The Congress, which was in a position to govern alone in the provinces where it had won, flatly rejected Jinnah's request, even when a minority participation in provincial governments was at stake. In the United Provinces, for instance, the Congress government did not seek to form a coalition with the Muslim League of which at least two of its leaders—Chaudhury Khaliquzzaman and Ismail Khan—had expected to become ministers (the two Muslim ministers finally appointed were Congress members).[45]

The Congress rejected the parity rationale not only because it contradicted the democratic principle of "one man, one vote", but also because the Congress was gearing up more than ever to become a national party.[46] In this perspective, Nehru undertook a campaign to attract Muslims to his party.[47] However, Congress' overwhelming electoral victory in 1937 instead enhanced the Muslim League's appeal.

---

deteriorated (See the biograhy of Jinnah by Fatima Jinnah, *My Brother* cited in Nadeem Paracha, "Fatima Jinnah: a sister's sorrow", *Dawn*, 4 May 2014 (http://www.dawn.com/news/1103505).

[44] R.J. Moore, "Jinnah and the Pakistan Demand", in M.R. Kazimi (ed.), *M.A. Jinnah. Views and reviews*, p. 46.

[45] Roger D. Long, "Jinnah and His 'Right Hand'", in M.R. Kazimi (ed.), *M.A. Jinnah. Views and reviews*, op. cit., p. 132.

[46] In 1939 Congress President Rajendra Prasad in a half-incredulous, half-ironic tone, deduced from Jinnah's remarks that they implied a "division of power in equal shares between the Congress and the League or between Hindus and Muslims, irrespective of population or any other consideration" (Cited in R.J. Moore, "Jinnah and the Pakistan Demand", in M.R. Kazimi (ed.), *M.A. Jinnah. Views and reviews*, op. cit., p. 60).

[47] Mushirul Hasan, "The Muslim Mass Contact Campaign: An Attempt at Political

Majority Muslims versus Minority Muslims

For the minority Muslims who formed the core of the Muslim League's base, the main obstacle to their aspirations was not only the Congress and the Hindus, but also Muslims of the majority provinces. The distribution of the Muslim population over British India territory gave them a demographic majority in the peripheral provinces only, but these regions were large and sometimes densely populated, as evident from the profile of Bengal and Assam in the east, and Punjab, Balochistan and the NWFP in the west (Sindh was part of Bombay Presidency till 1936). The two most important regions of these were Bengal and Punjab. The Muslim League had not managed to gain a foothold in either of these areas, as their Muslim elites did not emphasise their religious identity on the political scene.

This state of affairs could be explained by the fact that the Muslims in these regions did not feel threatened: they were in a majority in provinces that enjoyed considerable autonomy and only recently, in the mid-1930s, the British had met their most significant demands: they had agreed to give the NWFP full-fledged provincial status, to separate Sindh from the Bombay Presidency and to include plans for a federation in the Government of India Act of 1935 with a parliament made up of one-third Muslim representatives and one-third representatives of the Princes; even if the Congress won the remaining seats, it would not have a majority. Fazl-i-Husain, the Punjabi leader who increasingly appeared as the spokesman for Indian Muslims, stated in 1936 that their interests were "adequately safeguarded".[48]

But the "majority Muslims" placed little emphasis on their "Muslimhood" also because they focused on other forms of allegiance. If the Muslims of the Bengali and the Punjabi elite groups did not primarily define themselves as Muslims, this was due to their attachment to a language—and more generally speaking a culture—as well as to the socioeconomic interests that they shared with the Hindus of their class in their region. Indeed they readily formed alliances with the elites of other communities because of a keen awareness of these interests.

Mobilisation", *South Asia*, vol. 7, no. 1, 1984, pp. 58–76, and James E. Dillard, "The Failure of Nehru's Mass Contacts Campaign and the Rise of Muslim Separation", *Journal of South Asian and Middle Eastern Studies*, vol. XXXI, no. 2, winter 2008, pp. 43–65.

[48] Azim Hussain, *Fazl-i-Husain: A Political Biography*, Bombay, Longman, 1946, p. 265. Available online at: http://www.apnaorg.com/books/english/fazl-i-husain-biography/book.php?fldr=book (Accessed on September 15, 2013).

Table 2.1: Muslims in the Provinces of British India, 1917

Province	% of Muslims
Assam	28.1
Bengal	52.7
Bihar and Orissa	10.6
Central Provinces	4.1
United Provinces	14.1
Bombay Presidency	20.4
Madras Presidency	6.6
Punjab	54.8
British India	*23.5*

Source: Judith Brown, *Modern India. The Origins of an Asian Democracy*, Delhi, Oxford University Press, 1985, p. 121.

In Punjab, after the 1919 reform, the Muslim and Hindu rural elites had formed a dominant coalition involving the Sikhs. In 1922, with the prospect of elections organised in the framework of the 1919 reform, their leaders established the National Union Party which, as its name implied, intended to unite Muslims, Hindus and Sikhs. It won the elections in 1923 and its Muslim leader, Fazl-i-Husain (1877–1936), prevailed; since the province was in majority Muslim, he became head of the Punjabi government. But the Hindu party leader, Chhotu Ram (1882–1945), was immediately named agriculture minister, a sign of his political clout given the importance this portfolio had for the "unionists". Husain and Ram won the elections in1926 and 1934.[49] After Husain's death, Sikander Hayat Khan (1892–1942) replaced him, retaining the same political equation with his Hindus allies and particularly Chhotu Ram. The two men led their party to victory once again in 1937, in elections that confirmed the marginalisation of the Muslim League in Punjab.

The verdict at the polls in 1937 was clear. Whereas the NUP garnered 95 seats, including 74 won in constituencies reserved for the Muslims, the League won only a single one. The NUP further confirmed its multicultural facet by forming a government coalition with a Hindu group (the Hindu Electoral Board) and a Sikh party (Khalsa National).

The situation was comparable in Bengal, even if the League made a better showing. In the 1930s, as in Punjab, it had to face not only the Congress—particularly well established among Hindus—but also an agrarian party

---

[49] Ian Talbot, *Punjab and the Raj—1849–1947*, Delhi, Manohar, 1988, p. 89.

that intended to overcome religious divides, the Krishak Proja Party (Peasant People's Party). This group in fact mainly represented the *jotedar* (tenant farmers) against the *zamindar* (landlords), the latter enjoying considerable power over the former by virtue of the Permanent Settlement that the British had imposed back in the late eighteenth century.[50] The party, whose members also included small farmers and agricultural workers (mostly Muslim), had been founded by Sher-e-Bangla (Bengal tiger) A. K. Fazlul Haq (1873–1962), in 1936. The following year, it garnered 31 per cent of the vote as opposed to 27 per cent for the League, which won no less than 39 of the 82 seats.[51] Haq was thus induced to form a coalition government with League support. This government passed a few acts in favour of the peasantry where Muslims were in a majority (the Bengal Tenancy Act Amendment, the Bengal Agricultural Debtors Act and the Bengal Money Lenders Act).

Table 2.2: Results of the 1937 elections in Punjab

Parties	Muslim Constituencies	General Constituencies	Sikh Constituencies	Total
NUP	74	13	–	95
Hindu Electoral Board	–	10	–	11
Khalsa National (Sikh)	–	–	14	14
Congress	2	11	5	18
Akali Dal	–	–	10	10
Muslim League	1	–	–	1
Other	11	10	4	25

Source: Stephen Oren, "The Sikhs, Congress and the Unionists in British Punjab, 1937–1945", *Modern Asian Studies*, 8 (3), 1974, p. 398.

But he "protested against Muslim League interference in Bengal politics",[52] despite the fact that he had moved the Lahore Resolution in 1940 (see infra). He resigned from the League the following year. He made a mistake, however, in joining hands with Hindu nationalists, including

[50] Joya Chatterji, *Bengal Divided. Hindu Communalism and Partition, 1932–1947*, Cambridge, Cambridge University Press, 1994, p. 72 ff.

[51] Although the League won 61.4% of the Muslim votes in urban constituencies, it only took 26.5% in rural areas where the KPP won 31.8%. See Shila Sen, *Muslim Politics in Bengal, 1937–47*, New Delhi, Impex India, 1976, pp. 88–97.

[52] Khalid B. Sayeed, *Pakistan, the Formative Phase, 1857–1948*, London, Oxford University Press, 1968, p. 213.

Shyam Prasad Mookerjee, in order to retain power. This move—which might have been a reflection of his cosmopolitanism—discredited his party in the eyes of his Muslim supporters. It lost all the by-elections of 1942 and in 1943 Haq had to step down in favour of Khawaja Nazimuddin. The new Chief Minister of Bengal was Jinnah's main lieutenant in the province—and, indeed, a character typical of the regional sociology of the League.[53]

In Bengal, until the 1930s at least, the party attracted mainly members of the Urdu-speaking elite—which was relatively cut off from society.[54] Indeed, the League was led by the family of the Nawab of Dhaka who had taken part in the Simla delegation in 1906 and who had convened the founding meeting of the League in his "luxurious residence, Ahsan Manzil, [which] became the centre for Muslim League activities in Bengal from the time of its foundation, and remained so throughout the Pakistani period".[55] This family descended from migrants from Kashmir who had settled in Bengal only in the eighteenth century. It owed the title of "Nawab", granted by the British, to the support it had shown the East India Company during the 1857 Mutiny. These outsiders did not speak Bengali, "nor did they feel any particular ties to Bengal".[56] The family member who played the largest role in the making of the Bengal chapter of the League was Khawaja Nazimuddin (1894–1964). Mayor of Dhaka in 1922–9, he was elected to the provincial Legislative Council in 1923 and served as education minister in 1929–34 before joining the Executive Council in 1937. The same year, he was re-elected as a Muslim League candidate to the legislative council and became Home minister.[57] This loyal follower of Jinnah was a member of the League's executive body for ten years (1937–47), a body otherwise dominated by North Indian aristocrats—who had much in common with him, including the Urdu language.

---

[53] On the role of Bengali elite members in the entourage of Syed Ahmad Khan and in the early years of the Muslim League, see Farzana Shaikh, *Community and Consensus*, op. cit., p. 85 and p. 109.

[54] In Bengal, Urdu was the idiom of the Ashraf who "never accepted Bengali as a proper language for the Muslims and always considered it a Hindu language". Rafiuddin Ahmed, *The Bengal Muslims, 1871–1906. A Quest for Identity*, Delhi, Oxford University Press, 1981, p. 23.

[55] France Bhattacharya, "East Bengal. Between Islam and a Regional Identity", in Christophe Jaffrelot (ed.), *A History of Pakistan and its Origins*, London, Anthem Press, 2002, p. 39.

[56] Ibid.

[57] "Khawaja Nazimuddin", see: http://www.cybercity-online.net/pof/khawaja_nazimuddin.html (Accessed on September 15, 2013).

The other social category from Bengal for which the League had some appeal was made up of professionals and businessmen who had in common with the aristocracy mentioned above a non-Bengali origin and often the status of Ashraf. The most famous representative of this group was Hussain Shaheed Suhrawardy who was the Chief Minister of the last Bengal government before Partition. But Suhrawardy, in contrast to Nazimuddin, was attached to Bengali as a language and to Bengal as a province. In fact, he "taught himself to speak Bengali so that he could reach the people...".[58] When he joined the League in 1936, it was less to create a separate Muslim state than to escape Hindu domination. The Muslims of Bengal, indeed, were in a very specific situation. Despite their demographic weight, they were still under the economic and cultural tutelage of the Hindus. Their separatism, therefore, was "negative"[59] and they did not adhere to Pakistan as a country that would provide them with a distinctive identity—they already had one.

The situation of the Muslim League was more precarious still in the NWFP, a region dominated by the Pashtuns where the ethnic or cultural variable played a greater role than elsewhere. While "Pathan" is the name given to the dominant group of Pashtuns living east of the Durand Line, the Pathans belong to the same tribes as those which stretch from Afghanistan across this Line. As mentioned above, in addition to its language, this group is united by an ethos reflected in a common code of conduct, Pashtunwali.[60] This customary law regulates Pathan society more systematically and to some extent more rigorously than the sharia. It is what dictates the duty of hospitality that Pashtuns practice, even toward fugitives from the law seeking asylum; it is also the basis for a particularly strong sense of individual and family honour—also giving rise to the virtually sacred notion of *badal* (revenge) leading to vendettas that extend over generations and that can only be settled by a conciliatory *jirga* (assembly) or holy men.

---

[58] Begum Shaista Suhrawardy Ikramullah, *Huseyn Shaheed Suhrawardy. A Biography*, Karachi, Oxford University Press, 1991, p. 39.

[59] Golam Wahed Chowdhury, *The Last days of united Pakistan*, Bloomington, Indiana University Press, 1974, p. 10.

[60] See Sir Olaf Caroe, *The Pathans*, Oxford, Oxford University Press, 1976; Sana Haroon, *Frontier of Faith: Islam in the Indo-Afghan Border*, London, Hurst, 2007; Magnus Marsden, *Living Islam: Muslim Religious Experience in Pakistan's North West Frontier*, Cambridge, Cambridge University Press, 2005 and James W. Spain, *The Way of the Pathans*, Oxford, Oxford University Press, 1962.

As of the 1920s, certain Pathan leaders in the NWFP moreover propounded a form of Pashtun nationalism with an irredentist tinge. They aspired to assemble the Pashto-speaking ethnic groups on either side of the border into a single Pashtunistan. In the NWFP, this ideology was codified by Abdul Ghaffar Khan. Known as Badshah Khan (Khan of Khans), this man was born in a village of Peshawar district. He belonged to a clan of "small Khans" but acquired an immense aura because of his work as a reformer and an educationist—before turning to politics. Eager to modernise the Pashtuns, in the 1920s he initiated a network of schools teaching in Pashto, not in Urdu. In 1928 he started a Pashto monthly, *Pakhtun*, and the following year developed a movement called Khudai Khidmatgar, better known by the name "red shirts" for the colour of its uniform.[61] This movement campaigned to defend Pashto against the expansion of the Punjabi language. Insensitive to the Muslim League's Islamic rhetoric, he allied with the Congress whose leader, Gandhi, he admired. He would moreover earn the nickname of "Frontier Gandhi" due to his non-violent methods of agitation. This alliance gained strength on the ground when Gandhi launched his civil disobedience movement in 1930. Such a coalition left little room for the Muslim League, which saw its influence shrink to the urban intelligentsia. In 1937, it did not even field a candidate in the elections, carried off by the Congress, which formed a government in the province with Abdul Ghaffar Khan's brother, Dr. Khan Sahib, becoming Chief Minister.

The only region in 1937 where the League could be satisfied with its electoral performance remained the United Provinces where the party had recruited a highly influential figure in the person of Choudhry Khaliquzzaman, a former Congressman. The League secured 9 of the 12 urban seats reserved for Muslims that it ran for and 20 of the 27 rural seats for which it had fielded candidates. That did not, however, prevent the Congress from forming the government in the province and not making any sort of alliance with the League (cf. supra), an additional sign for these "minority" Muslims that they could only count on their coreligionists in the majority provinces for protection.[62] Jinnah had to rally them around the League. But how?

---

[61] Mukulika Banerjee, *The Pathan Unarmed: Opposition and Memory in the Khudai Khidmatgar Movement*, Oxford, James Curey, 2000, chapter 2.

[62] Lance Brennan considers that in the United Provinces, after the 1937 elections, "for the first time since 1909, the Muslim elite seemed to have no leverage in the new institutions of government". Lance Brennan, "The Illusion of Security: The Background to Muslim Separatism in the United Provinces", *Modern Asian Studies*, 18 (1984), p. 231.

Jinnah's Strategy

Although he remained a champion of "minority Muslims", Jinnah had never turned his back on the "majority Muslims". In 1924, he campaigned within the Muslim League for greater political autonomy for the Muslim-majority provinces. In 1927, after the appointment of the Simon Commission charged with taking stock of the 1919 reform and proposing another to pursue democratisation of the regime, he indicated he was prepared to renounce separate electorates in exchange not only for reservation of one-third of central parliament seats for Muslims as mentioned above, but also for concessions to "majority Muslims": 1) creation of a new Muslim-majority province, Sindh, until then part of the Bombay Presidency; 2) conversion of the NWFP and Balochistan into full-fledged provinces (which implied setting up elected assemblies); 3) guarantee of political representation for Punjab and Bengal Muslims in proportion to their demographic weight in their respective provinces.[63] The Congress had bluntly rejected Jinnah's demands with the Nehru Report. He retaliated unsuccessfully with his 14-point plan, the federal nature of which was to the liking of the "majority Muslims".

Paradoxically, the 1937 electoral defeat of the League helped Jinnah, giving him the opportunity to return to the "majority Muslims" with new arguments, in particular a new sort of Hindu threat. The Congress having won the 1937 elections and formed a government in 7 of the 11 provinces of British India, it looked like the natural successor to the British, whose departure loomed on the horizon. As Ayesha Jalal points out:

Muslim provinces would now feel the brunt of Congress pressure. In its turn this might give the League at the centre a chance both to mediate on behalf of these Muslim provinces and perhaps in due course to help in disciplining them itself. In the meantime, the Muslim provinces would be forced to recognise their need to have a spokesman at the centre; and their own embattled provincialism had left Jinnah and his League as the only plausible candidate for this role.[64]

In her study on the strategy Jinnah developed to appear finally as "the sole spokesman"[65] for Indian Muslims, Jalal shows that 1937 marked a turning point. Congress' success at the polls, although it had boycotted all the elec-

---

[63] Mushirul Hasan, *Nationalism and Communal Politics in India, 1916–1928*, New Delhi, Manohar, 1991, chapter 9, "Illusions of Insecurity: The Nehru Report".

[64] Ayesha Jalal, *The Sole Spokesman. Jinnah, the Muslim League and the Demand for Pakistan*, Cambridge, Cambridge University Press, 1994 (first edition, 1985), p. 33.

[65] The first scholar who used this formula was Khalid B. Sayeed. See Khalid B. Sayeed, *Pakistan. The Formative Phase*, op. cit., p. 213.

tions up until that point—even if Congress members had already run under a different label—finally enabled the Muslim League to apply the strategy of fear it had used in the United Provinces to other regions. In October 1937, Sikander Hayat Khan and Fazlul Haq agreed to let their party ally with the Muslim League.[66] It was also at this time that representatives of the mostly Bombay-based Muslim business community joined Jinnah and backed him financially. Among them were important families such as the Habibs, the Valikas, the Adamjees, the Saigols, and the Isphahanis[67] who were already struggling with competition from the large Hindu and Parsi groups and could fear that it would only increase in the future—after decolonization. It was in this context that Jinnah reformed the League's leadership to make more room for leaders from Muslim majority provinces (Table 2.3.).

Table 2.3: The quotas of the British Indian Provinces in the Muslim League Council

Region	No of members	
	Prior to 1938	After 1938
Delhi	10	15
United Provinces	50	70
Punjab	50	90
Bombay Presidency	20	30
Sindh	10	25
Madras Presidency	18	20
NWFP	10	20
Balochistan	4	5
Bengal	60	100
Bihar and Orissa	30	30
Assam	12	25
Ajmer	6	5
Total	280	445

Source: Ayesha Jalal, *The Sole Spokesman*, op. cit., p. 40.

Jinnah exploited the communal flavour of certain public policies enacted by the Congress in the provinces where it had formed the government. He went on to criticise the Wardha scheme of education, named after the town where Gandhi's ashram was located, which antagonized the Muslims due

---

[66] A. Jalal, *The Sole Spokesman*, p. 39.

[67] See Lal Khan, *Pakistan's Other Story. The 1968–69 Revolution*, Lahore, The Struggle Publications, 2010, p. 96.

to the praise of Hindu heroes found in its textbooks, written moreover in Hindi.[68] The League drafted two reports, one in 1938, the other in 1939, on the way in which the Congress governments prevented Muslims from slaughtering cows, forced them to speak Hindi and interfered with their religious practices in general.[69] As Peter Hardy writes, these allegations may not have been justified, but "they were believed".[70]

As a result, Jinnah henceforth referred to the Congress routinely as a "Hindu body".[71] In his presidential address to the Muslim League at the party's annual session in December 1938, he even made the claim that a Congress-dominated parliamentary system would lead to a "totalitarian" regime.[72] He equated its pro-Hindu policies with a "kulturkampf".[73]

This is why Jinnah called on all his coreligionists to celebrate the resignation of the Congress governments when this party obliged its ministers to resign to protest the British decision to bring India into the war against the Axis Powers without consulting them. He did so in carefully chosen terms,

---

[68] Peter Hardy, *The Muslims of British India*, op. cit., p. 227.

[69] The first was prepared under the authority of the Raja of Pirpur and was titled Report of the Inquiry Committee appointed by the Council of the All India Muslim League to Inquire into Muslim Grievances in Congress Provinces, 1938. The second, drafted by S.M. Shareef, pertained only to Bihar but was distributed nationally: Report of the Enquiry Committee appointed by the Working Committee of the Bihar Provincial Muslim League to Inquire into some Grievances of Muslims in Bihar, 1939.

[70] Peter Hardy, *The Muslims of British India*, op. cit., p. 228.

[71] During the Muslim League session of December 1938, Jinnah delivered a virulent speech in which he declared "The Congress is nothing but a Hindu body (...) I ask does the Congress represent the Muslim? (Shouts of 'No, no'). I ask does the Congress represent the Christians? ('No.'). I ask does the Congress represent the Scheduled Castes ('No.') I ask does the Congress represent the non-Brahmans? ('No'.) I say the Congress does not even represent all the Hindus" ("Presidential address at the Muslim League's Session, Syed Sharifuddin Pirzada (ed.), *Foundations of Pakistan*, vol. 2, Karachi and Dhaka, National Publishing House, 1970, pp. 304–305.).

[72] Jamil-ud-din Ahmad (ed.), *Speeches and Writings of Mr. Jinnah, vol. 1*, Lahore, 1960, pp. 67–81.

[73] In an interview given to the British newspaper *Times and Tide*, he said in 1940: "In the six Hindu provinces a 'kulturkampf' was inaugurated. Attempts (sic!) were made to have Bande Mataram, the Congress party song recognised as the National Anthem; the party flag recognised as the National Flag, and the real national language, Urdu (sic!!) supplanted by Hindi". Faisal Devji, *Muslim Zion*, op. cit., p. 68.

as he invited "the Musalmans all over India to observe Friday the 22nd December as the 'Day of Deliverance' and thanksgiving as a mark of relief that the Congress regime has at least ceased to function".[74]

Then, the British considered that they needed at least the support of Congress opponents, including Jinnah, who claimed to represent a nation. It was in fact at this time that Jinnah declared that Indian Muslims were not a minority, but instead a nation. The nuance was not merely semantic, as it meant discarding a purely numerical logic: if a minority was defined by its demographic weight, a nation is equal to others, even if it is smaller. Reusing the terms he had begun to employ as soon as he returned to India in 1935, Jinnah pursued the quest for parity between Muslims and Hindus that Sir Syed had begun a half-century earlier and which constituted a major dimension of the Pakistani syndrome.

On 23 March 1940, this repudiation of the law of numbers—and hence democracy—became the matrix of a new turning point represented by the Muslim League's adoption in Lahore of a historical resolution moved by Fazlul Haq and backed by Jinnah. A few days prior to that, on 9 March 1940, Jinnah had published an article in *Time and Tide* that Sir Syed would have approved:

What is the political future of India? The declared aim of the British Government is that India should enjoy Dominion Status in accordance with the Statute of Westminster in the shortest practicable time. In order that this end should be brought about, the British Government very naturally would like to see in India the form of democratic constitutions it knows best and thinks best, under which the Government of the country is entrusted to one or other political party in accordance with the turn of the elections. Such, however, is the ignorance about Indian conditions among even the members of the British Parliament that, in spite of all the experience of the past, it is even yet not realized that this form of government is totally unsuited to India. Democratic systems based on the concept of a homogeneous nation such as England are very definitely not applicable to heterogeneous countries such as India, and this simple fact is the root cause of India's constitutional ills.[75]

The words Jinnah used here are those of Syed Ahmad Khan who also refuted the applicability of democracy to India. Like Sir Syed, Jinnah also

---

[74] "M.A. Jinnah's appeal for the observation of Deliverance Day, 2 December 1939", in B.N. Pandey (ed.), *The indian Nationalist Movement, 1885–1947. Select Documents*, London, Macmillan Press, 1979, p. 153.

[75] Cited in Vishwanath Prasad Varma, *Modern Indian Political Thought*, op. cit., p. 433.

rejected democracy because of its plebeian dimension. Jinnah did not have Sir Syed's aristocratic pedigree, but he shared his elitist mentality. Devji argues that Jinnah was very ambivalent vis-à-vis the Muslims for this reason and attributes this feeling to "his own dislike of Muslims in general, or perhaps his shame and pity at their 'backwardness'...".[76] This attitude may be explained by the fact that Jinnah came from a business community which knew how to prosper, as Devji suggests, but whatever the explanation, this dislike for the people Jinnah claimed to save reflects his elitist nature: he needed to mobilise large numbers of people not only or primarily to save them, but to obtain a separate state to rule, an objective for which Sir Syed had laid the groundwork.

But Jinnah went further than Sir Syed in that whereas the latter had called for the two communities to cohabit on an equal footing, Jinnah expounded what he called "the two-nation theory" (rather than two communities). He defended the idea that Hindus and Muslims formed two nations that could not cohabit because they "belong to two different civilizations [...] To yoke together two such nations under a single state, one as a numerical minority and the other as a majority, must lead to growing discontent...".[77] Jinnah used an ethnic conception of the nation against the Indian National Congress that claimed to represent all communities in an effort to establish a secular political regime. He presented Indian Islam as belonging to a separate culture and, by virtue of his "two-nation theory", thus demanded a separate state. Unlike Sir Syed, he now was asking for a form of political sovereignty for the Muslim nation. Indeed, the Lahore resolution

...resolved that it is the considered view of this session of the All-India Muslim League that no constitutional plan would be workable in this country or acceptable to the Muslims unless it is designed on the following basic principles, viz., that geographically contiguous units are demarcated into regions which should be so constituted, with such territorial readjustments as may be necessary, that the areas which the Muslims are numerically in a majority, as in the North-Western and eastern zones of India should be grouped to constitute Independent States in which the constituents units shall be autonomous and sovereign.[78]

[76] Faisal Devji, *Muslim Zion*, op. cit., p. 186.
[77] Excerpt from Jinnah's presidential address to the Muslim League, Lahore session, in March 1940 (Cited in Syed Sharifuddin Pirzada (ed.), *Foundations of Pakistan— All India Muslim League Documents: 1906–1947, vol. 2*, op. cit., pp. 337–338).
[78] "Text of the Lahore Resolution" in Ikram Ali Malik (ed.), *Muslim League Session 1940 and The Lahore Resolution*, Islamabad, National Institute of Historical and Cultural Research, 1990, pp. 298–299.

The idea that because of the inexorable democratisation of India, which amounted to making the Hindus masters of the country, the Muslims had to find another "homeland" was already publicised in the early 1930s. One of Jinnah's close associates, the poet-philosopher Muhammad Iqbal—who on occasion could also indulge in lyrical pan-Islamism[79]—also articulated a link between democratisation and ethnic-religious separatism for the first time in 1930 in his presidential address to the Muslim League session:

> To base a constitution on the conception of a homogeneous India, or to apply to India the principles dictated by British democratic sentiments is unwittingly to prepare her for a civil war (...) I would like to see the Punjab, the North-West Frontier Province, Sindh and Baluchistan, amalgamated into a single state. Self-government within the British Empire or without the British Empire, the formation of a consolidated North-West Indian Muslim State appears to me to be the final destiny of the Muslims, at least of North West India.[80]

Iqbal—who superbly ignored the Bengal Muslims as would so many other Punjabis after him—did not name the country.[81] In 1933, a student from Cambridge by the name of Rehmat Ali would make history by naming the country "Pakistan", an anagram meaning "the land of the pure" in which "P" stood for Punjab, "A" for the Afghans (actually the Pathans of the NWFP since "Afghan" means "Pathan" in Persian), the "K" for Kashmir, the

---

[79] In particular, he had written in 1908 about the Muslim nation that "the ideal territory for such a nation would be the whole earth". Cited in Peter Hardy, *The Muslims of British India*, op. cit., p. 179).

[80] Cited in Vishwanath Prasad Varma, *Modern Indian Political Thought*, op. cit., p. 456. Certainly, elsewhere, Iqbal claims that for Muslims, who belong to the universal *umma*, the quest for a home land was "idolatrous" and that the expression "Indian Muhammedan" was "a contradiction in terms". Faisal Devji, *Muslim Zion*, op. cit., p. 242 and pp. 110–111). But his 1930 speech shows that Devji is too radical when he says that Iqbal "dismissed geography as a basis for political life" (Ibid., p. 112). Iqbal simply stopped short of asking for a separate sovereign state. In a 1933 letter to the British historian Edward Thompson he said: "Pakistan is not my scheme. The one that I suggested in my address [of 1930] is the creation of a Muslim province—i.e. a province having an overwhelming population of Muslims—in the Northwest of India. This new province will be, according to my scheme, a part of the proposed Indian Federation". Cited in S. Hasan Ahmad, *Iqbal: His Political Ideas at Crossroads*, Aligarh, Printwell Publications, 1979, p. 80.

[81] In the year preceding his death in April 1938, Iqbal increasingly pressured Jinnah to step up the fight for a state that could accommodate the Muslims of colonial India. Hafeez Malik (ed.), *Iqbal: Poet-Philosopher of Pakistan*, New York, 1971, pp. 383–390.

"S" for Sindh and the "tan" for Balochistan—once again Bengal was conspicuously absent.

The Lahore resolution was less specific, even cultivating ambiguity. In its closing words it mentioned an entity that was at once "autonomous", as befits a component of a federation or confederation, and "sovereign", an epithet that applies only to states.[82] This is because Jinnah—who did not adopt the use of the word "Pakistan", absent from the Lahore Resolution, until 1941—not only did not know how far to carry the implications of his two-nation theory (do two nations require two states?),[83] but moreover he could not take the risk of clarification if he wanted to preserve the support of both "Minority Muslims" as well "Majority Muslims": neither wanted Punjab and Bengal to be truncated and Jinnah probably remained vague on the border issue because he knew that Punjab and Bengal had districts with a Hindu majority that were not meant to become part of Pakistan. The Punjabi and Bengali leaders wanted their provinces to remain whole, as to them it was inconceivable that the area over which they ruled should be curtailed in the slightest and leaders of "Minority Muslim" provinces thought alike. Indeed, Khaliquazzaman perceived the presence of Hindus in Pakistan as essential because "one of the basic principles lying behind the Pakistan idea [was] that of keeping hostages in Muslim Provinces as against the Muslims in the Hindu Provinces. If we allow millions of Hindus to go out of our orbit of influence, the security of the Muslims in the minority provinces will greatly be minimised"[84]—Khaliquazzaman assumed (rightly so) that not all the Muslims in those areas would migrate any time soon to

---

[82] These are the words of Ahmad Bashir, secretary of a Lahore-based movement, Majlis-i-Kabir Pakistan which, has R.J. Moore has shown, supplied Jinnah with the at once vague and sophisticated terminology that he began using in 1939. R.J. Moore, "Jinnah and the Pakistan Demand", op. cit., pp. 54–58. This point is worth underscoring, as it attests once again to the fact that Jinnah, while he may have been solitary in nature, was not isolated: his philosophy was the product of his personal thinking, but also of countless outside influences. Among them should be pointed out the role of many members of the Aligarh faculty.

[83] Jinnah moreover was unsure of the number of nations existing in India. In 1941, he discussed with the governor of the Madras Presidency the possibility of creating four nations within the British Raj: Pakistan, Hindustan, Dravidistan (within the South Dravidian borders) and Bengalistan, an indication that he did not view Islam as an identity marker that could transcend ethno-linguistic divides (Vappala Pangunni Menon, *The Transfer of Power in India*, London, Sangam Books Ltd. 1957, p. 105).

[84] Cited in Ayesha Jalal, *The Sole Spokesman*, op. cit., p. 59 (note 54).

the new state of Pakistan. This is why when in 1944, Jinnah—who had decidedly become a leading spokesman—was invited to negotiate with Gandhi in a round of discussions that would lead to naught, he reasserted his demand for a Muslim state that would include the aforementioned provinces within the borders at the time, a Pakistan that was destined to make treaties with what he called "Hindustan".[85]

Jinnah's assurances were not enough, however, to assuage the concerns of Muslim leaders in provinces where their community was a majority—and where they were accustomed to governing with minority representatives on a secular basis.

In Bengal, Haq resigned from the League in protest "against the manner in which the interests of the Muslims of Bengal and the Punjab are being imperilled by Muslim leaders of the Provinces where the Muslims are in a minority".[86] In May 1944, Abdul Mansur Ahmed, a journalist who had become the leader of the Bengal Provincial League—the regional variant of a League that had eventually shed its reference to Islam—delivered a presidential address before the Party's annual session in which he declared that the Muslims of Bengal were not only different from the Hindus but from Muslims of other provinces as well because "Religion and culture are not the same thing. Religion transgresses the geographical boundary but 'tamaddum' [meaning culture] can not go beyond [t]he geographical boundary".[87] In September 1944, the same regional "branch" of the League demanded "a sovereign state in N.E. India that will be independent of the rest of India".[88]

In Punjab, when Sikander Hayat Khan saw his Sikh and Hindu allies taking their distance after the Lahore resolution, he immediately denounced it and refrained from participating in the Pakistan Conference held by the League in March 1941.[89] Then he resigned from the League's executive committee in May 1942. Two years later, his successor at the helm of the Muslim League, Khizar Hayat Tiwana, decided to go back on the terms of the pact that Hayat Khan and Jinnah had agreed in 1937 stipulating that the unionists were affiliated with the Muslim League. Tiwana, by challenging

---

[85] Ibid., p. 122.

[86] Cited in ibid., p. 68.

[87] Cited in Harun-or Rashid, *The Foreshadowing of Bangladesh: Bengal Muslim League and Muslim League Politics, 1936–1947*, Dhaka, Asiatic Society of Bangladesh, 1987, p. 181.

[88] Cited in R.J. Moore, "Jinnah and the Pakistan Demand", op. cit., p. 65.

[89] A. Jalal, *The Sole Spokesman*, op. cit., p. 67.

this dual affiliation, left Jinnah with no alternative other than to expel him from the League.[90]

In Bengal, Jinnah managed to build a fragile Muslim League government by manipulating rivalries among factions. But its leader, Nazimuddin, only remained at its helm from May 1944 to March 1945. In the NWFP, the League took advantage of the resignation of Dr Khan Sahib's Congress government to take its place in 1939, but Mahatma Gandhi allowed Khan Sahib to return to power in March 1945. At that point, the League only held one provincial government, Sindh, a region in which the support of its members for the Pakistan idea competed with what must be called a form of Sindhi nationalism comparable to the Pashtun nationalism of the Pathans.

In Sindh, indeed, the Muslim League only belatedly gained a foothold— and a precarious one. Like in Bengal and in the NWFP, the League's emphasis on the Islamic identity of the Muslims of Sindh was in competition with ethno-nationalist sentiments rooted in a deep attachment to culture and language. While Sindhi had not been codified (by British grammarians) before the nineteenth century, there had been a rich literature before. Poets like Shah Abdul Latif (1689–1752)[91] have remained very popular for instance. Acknowledging the importance of language for the Sindhis, the British made their idiom the language of the courts in the second half of the nineteenth century. At the same time, the discovery of vestiges of the Indus civilisation gave historico-territorial roots to a new sense of collective pride. One of the founding fathers of Sindhi nationalism, Muhammad Ayub Khuro, wrote in his 1930 book, *A Story of the Sufferings of Sind*, that his province historically formed a separate entity by mentioning the newly exhumed site of Mohenjo-Daro.[92]

In the early decades of the 20th century, these feelings fostered a demand for the separation of Sindh from Bombay presidency, something the British agreed to in 1935. In fact, Sindh was the first province whose borders were redrawn according to linguistic criteria. The others would follow in India in the 1950s. The demand for a separate province was initiated by the Congress in 1913. The League supported it, considering it would give one more province to the Muslims and it was a popular demand anyway. But it could not fully capitalise on this movement in political terms.

---

[90] Ibid., p. 95.
[91] M.G. Chitkara, *Jiy-e-Sind. G.M. Syed*, Delhi, APH Publishing Corporation, 1996. See Chapter 3, "Shah Abdul Latif and Sindi Literature", pp. 41–64.
[92] Oskar Verkaaik, *Migrants and Militants. Fun and Urban Violence in Pakistan*, Princeton, Princeton University Press, 2004, pp. 30–31.

As in Punjab and Bengal, the League was in competition with two parties, the Congress, which was strong among the urban voters—mostly Hindu traders and professionals—and the Sind United Party of Shahnawaz Bhutto (Zulfiqar Ali Bhutto's father). Founded in 1936 at the same time as the new province, this party was designed along the same lines as the Punjabi National Unionist Party. Like the NUP, it tried to promote socio-economic interests beyond religious divisions. It was quite successful during the 1937 elections when it won 22 seats out of 33 in the provincial assembly. But in contrast with Punjab where the Muslim, Hindu and Sikh peasants shared some common interests, in Sindh, even more than in Punjab, Hindus were urban merchants and moneylenders whereas Muslims tilled (and owned) the land. And the latter depended upon the former to sell their produce and secure loans: so much so that in 1937 Muslim members of the assembly proposed a bill aiming to prevent the moneylenders from acquiring the land of defaulting peasants.[93] Hindu politicians resisted this move and rallied around the Congress, even when they were independent, for that purpose. The Sindhi chapter of the Muslim League took shape in this context in 1938. It was officially launched in the presence of Jinnah who paid particular attention to the development of his party in his native province (he was born in Karachi).[94] The League benefitted at the time from the communal atmosphere created by what became known as the Manzilgarh issue, named for a controversial place of worship in Sukkur that Muslims wanted to be officially recognised as a mosque.[95] This conflict resulted in a bloody Hindu-Muslim riot.

However, League leaders in Sindh, as in Bengal, were as much interested in defending their provincial identity and interests as they were in "Muslimhood" and the idea of Pakistan. The president of the Sindhi chapter of the League in 1943, G.M. Syed, probably the most influential political figure in the region, was a staunch Sindhi nationalist who admired all its historical heroes—including Shah Abdul Latif[96] and its last Hindu king, Raja Dahir (661–712).[97] While he supported the Lahore resolution and while the

---

[93] G.M. Syed, *Struggle for New Sind. A Brief Narrative of the Working of Provincial Autonomy in Sind during a Decade (1937–1947)*, Sehwan Sharif, Sain Publishers, 1949 (1996), p. 19.

[94] M.S. Korejo, *G.M. Syed. An Analysis of his Political Perspectives*, Karachi, Oxford University Press, 2000, p. 9.

[95] Ian Talbot, *Pakistan. A Modern History*, London, Hurst, 1999, p. 78.

[96] G.M. Syed, *The message of Shah Latif*, Sehwan Sharif, Sain Publishers, 1996.

[97] M.S. Korejo, *G.M. Syed*, op. cit., p. 77. See also G.M. Syed, *SinduDesh: A Study in*

League of Sindh was the first provincial chapter of the party to endorse it in 1943, he emphasized the provision of this text specifying that the entities comprising the new state would be "autonomous and sovereign".

Interestingly, G.M. Syed also took his distance from the League for class reasons. While he had been attracted to the party for religious beliefs,[98] he left the party in 1945 when Jinnah turned to Sindhi landlords to maximise its chances before the January 1946 elections.[99]

The 1946 Elections: What Turning Point?

In 1945, Jinnah appeared as politically isolated as he had been ten years earlier. But at this time, the British, worn down by five years of war, hastened the process of India's independence. Elections to renew the provincial Legislative councils, which were to designate a constituent assembly, were scheduled for February 1946. These elections, the last of the colonial period, were a turning point—but in what direction? No one really knew.

Jinnah's Muslim League, with its leadership dominated by "Minority Muslims",[100] stepped up the pressure on the "Majority Muslims". It especially exhorted the Punjabis and the Bengalis to realize what was at stake. India's independence was only months away. Given Congress' showing in 1937 and the popularity of its most recent movement called "Quit India" in 1942, post-colonial India would be governed by the party that Jinnah continued to define as "Hindu" and the Muslims would thus be trapped if they

---

    Its Separate Identity through the Ages, Karachi, Syed Academy, no date. The history of Sindh, for G.M. Syed, naturally begins with the Indus civilisation.

[98] Descending from a Sufi saint who was a Syed by caste, he had started his public career by creating a caste association to promote a pious lifestyle in tune with their traditional status among the Syeds. See ibid., p. 32.

[99] This class-based explanation of the severing of his links with the League is the one he gives in his autobiography where he writes: "While trying to get rid of the Hindu vested interests we are being dragged under the heels of the Muslims (sic) feudal-lords". (G.M. Syed, *Struggle for new Sind*, op. cit., p. 188). But Syed, after founding his own party, the Progressive League, would himself rely on feudal lords with whom he cultivated a kind of love-hate relationship. Factional fights should probably also be factored in to understand his decision to leave the League. M.S. Korejo, G.M. Syed, op. cit., p. 12, p. 24 and p. 53.

[100] For instance, the three members of the Central Parliamentary Board—Choudhry Khaliquzzaman, Liaquat Ali Khan and Nawab Ismail Khan—were from the United Provinces.

did not rally behind the League, the only political movement that was truly in a position to defend them and which was demanding a sovereign Pakistan in their name.

Such rhetoric drew on religious sentiments that were perfectly in tune with the slogan "Islam in danger", but it was at odds with the convictions of Muslim League leaders. Jinnah and most of his lieutenants were not religious. The party cadres used Islam as an instrument of ethno-nationalist mobilisation. One of them declared that a vote for the League was a vote for the Prophet and another that "the battle of the Karbala is going to be fought again in this land of the five rivers",[101] in other words Punjab. Many politicians used mosques to spread their propaganda, and the League relied on religious figures as well. In Punjab this strategy was reflected in their appeal to many *pirs* and *sajjada nashin* (lit. "one who sits on or occupies the prayer-rug").[102] These religious leaders were also men of power as they were usually descendants of "hereditary saints" who had been given land by emperors, sultans and nawabs over which they ruled like any other landowner—hence the notion of "pir-zamindar".[103]

Punjabi politics was already dominated by families of notables with vast patronage networks. Peasants voted for their masters from whom they expected protection, but *sajjada nashin* and *pirs* were even more power-ful[104] because they combined spiritual blessing (*baraka*) and the ability to perform miracles (*karamat*) as well as power over land. The *pir-zamindar* was therefore in a uniquely powerful position:

For the common villagers he is at the same time a source of spiritual solace and of fearful terror. He behaves regally. He expropriates their feelings and ther earnings.

---

[101] Cited in Anita Inder Singh, *The Origins of the Partition of India, 1936–1947*, Delhi, Oxford University Press, 1987, p. 133.

[102] David Gilmartin, *Empire and Islam: Punjab and the Making of Pakistan*, Berkeley, California University Press, 1988.

[103] K.K. Aziz makes the following difference: "The *zamindar* can sentence his ploughman to a lifetime poverty. The *pir-zamindar* can condemn his *murid* (disciple) to the eternity of hell" (K.K. Aziz, *Religion, Land and politics in Pakistan. A Study of Piri-Muridi*, Lahore, Vanguard, 2001, p. 2).

[104] On this sociological reality, with or without references to the 1946 elections, see Craig Baxter, "The People's Party vs. The Punjab 'Feudalists'", in Henry Korsen (ed.), *Contemporary Problems of Pakistan*, Leiden, 1974, Ian Talbot, "The 1946 Punjab Elections", *Modern Asian Studies*, 14 (1) (1980), pp. 66–69, Parvez A. Wakil, "Exploration into Kin-Networks of the Punjabi Society: a preliminary statement", *Journal of Marriage and the Family*, 32, Nov. 1970, pp. 700–707 and Hamza Alavi, "Kinship in West Punjab Villages" in *Contributions to Indian Sociology*, Dec. 1972.

He aggravates their poverty. He is demanding in every way: asking for their loyalty, devotion, money, support, votes, veneration, prostration. He prays for them, but only when they beg for it.[105]

In the Punjab, the *pir-zamindars* used to support the NUP. In 1923, when Fazl-i-Husain created the party, the five *pir-zamindars* of the Legislative Council joined it.[106] But in the 1940s, the *pirs* started to defect to the Muslim League. The Pir of Sial Sharif was the first one to do so,[107] but not the only one. Characteristic examples could be found in Jhelum district where Pir Fazl Shah had established a stronghold,[108] in Jhang district where Pir Shah Jiwana Bukhari Sayed had two relatives elected,[109] in the Rawalpindi Division where the support of the Pir of Golra contributed to the League's triumph.[110] The League also won in the districts of Multan and Karnal with the help of religious figures.[111] As Jalal writes,

there was an appeal to 'religion in danger'; it was an obvious cry. The League encouraged the prelates to give fatwas in its favour. Some propagandists threatened the voters that if they did not back the League they would cease to be Muslims; their marriages would be invalid and, if this did not frighten them, then they were told they would face 'ex-communication graveyards', and be debarred from 'joining in mass Muslim prayers'.[112]

Clearly, the *pir-zamindars* "had a large reservoir of votes in their *murid* population".[113]

In 1946, the Muslim League in Punjab scored a spectacular success at the polls. The leading party in terms of votes with 32.8 per cent of votes cast, it went from a single seat to 75 in less than ten years. The scale of its victory cannot be ascribed solely to the campaign conducted on the slogan "Islam

---

[105] K.K. Aziz, *Religion, Land and Politics in Pakistan*, op. cit., p. 88.

[106] Ibid., p. 38.

[107] Ibid. p. 46. In 1945, the Muslim League also benefited from the rallying around the party of Deobandi Ulema—including Maulana Shabbir Ahmzad Usmani—who, till then, where part of the Jamiat-i-Ulema-i-Hind. This group formed the Jamiat-i-Ulema-i-Islam.

[108] David Gilmartin, "Religious Leadership and the Pakistan Movement in the Punjab", *Modern Asian Studies*, 13 (3), 1979, pp. 497–98.

[109] Ayesha Jalal, *The Sole Spokesman*, op. cit., p. 148.

[110] Ian Talbot, "The 1946 Punjab Elections", *Modern Asian Studies*, 14 (1) (1980), pp. 68–69.

[111] Ibid.

[112] Ayesha Jalal, *The Sole Spokesman*, op. cit., p. 147.

[113] K.K. Aziz, *Religion, Land and politics in Pakistan*, op. cit., p. 51.

in danger". The desire for political change running through the province after more than twenty years of Unionist government also played a part.

Table 2.4: The 1946 election results in Punjab

Party	No. of votes	% of votes cast	No. of seats
Congress	477,765	23.1	51
Unionists	419,231	20.2	21
Panthic Sikhs	160,763	7.8	21
Muslim League	680,823	32.8	75
Communists	39,516	1.9	–
Other	295,238	14.2	7 (Independents)
Total	2,073,336	100	175

Source: Ayesha Jalal, *The Sole Spokesman*, op. cit., p. 150.

In Bengal, the League's triumph was equally resounding, at least in terms of seats, as its score in terms of votes was less striking. The party won 95 per cent of the urban Muslim vote and 84.6 per cent of the Muslim vote for the province on the whole, but only 37.2 per cent of the total, or 5 percentage points less than Congress. These votes were so concentrated, however, that the Bengal League won 115 seats out of 250, as opposed to 62 for Congress.

The Muslim League's growing popularity however meshed with a strong current of Bengali nationalism, and could even be explained by the strength of this sentiment. Ayesha Jalal points out this particular aspect in eloquent terms:

The Bengali Muslims' idea of 'Pakistan' was very different from that of Muslims in other parts of India, and certainly different from what Jinnah had in mind. It was not a question of how Muslims would get a share of power in the rest of India, but rather the ideal of an independent sovereign state consisting of the whole of Bengal and Assam (and free of the exploitative Permanent Settlement system), which was the real motivating force behind a movement which, for the lack of a better name, called itself the Bengal Muslim League.[114]

The Muslim Leaguers of Bengal, being Bengali nationalists as much as pro-Pakistan activists, were prepared to join hands with Hindus up until the last moment. The architect of the League's victory in Bengal himself, Abul Hashim (with the help of Suhrawardy and against K. Nazimuddin), tried to impose until the very last the idea of an independent Bengal along

---

[114] Ayesha Jalal, *The Sole Spokesman*, op. cit., p. 151.

with Sarat Chandra Bose, a Congress leader whose brother was none other than Subhas Chandra Bose.[115]

Table 2.5: 1946 election results in Bengal

Party	No. of votes	% of votes cast
Congress	2,337,053	42.2
Muslim League	2,057,830	37.2
Krishak Praja and Muslim Nationalists	172,880	3.1
Hindu Mahasabha	78,981	1.4
Communists	157,197	2.8
Other	736,882	13.3

Source: Ayesha Jalal, *The Sole Spokesman*, op. cit., p. 161.

The force of ethno-linguistic nationalism remained also strong in Sindh and the NWFP. In Sindh, the Muslim League won 46.3 per cent of the vote (79.3 per cent in urban Muslim constituencies but only 58.9 per cent in rural Muslim constituencies), compared to 29.6 per cent for the Congress, which enabled the League to win 28 seats out of 57, and therefore to form a minority government. In the NWFP, the party won only 17 of the 36 seats reserved for Muslims, as opposed to 23 seats (of which 19 were reserved for Muslims) for the Congress, which again won the majority. These figures reflect a certain erosion of the Red Shirts' popularity, which probably resulted from the propaganda of the Muslim League whose leaders accused Abdul Ghaffar Khan of betraying the Pashtun martial ethos by allying with Hindus in general and Gandhi in particular.[116] Moreover, the League came in ahead of the Congress in urban Muslim constituencies (45.6 per cent as against 22.2 per cent), but the opposite was true for the rural vote (41. per cent% as against 40.7 per cent).

Despite the League's relative setback in the NWFP, after the 1946 elections the party eventually managed to appear representative of Indian Muslims (see Table 2.6).

Jinnah then clarified somewhat his conception of what his future Pakistan should look like. It would be a political entity that would incorporate the Muslim-majority provinces in their existing borders and develop on equal

---

[115] Leonard Gordon, "Divided Bengal: Problems of Nationalism and Identity in the 1947 Partition", *The Journal of Commonwealth and Comparative Politics*, 16 (2), 1978, pp. 136–168.

[116] Sayed Wiqar Ali Shah, *Ethnicity, Islam and Nationalism*, op. cit., p. 107.

footing with Hindustan under the auspices of the British, who would continue to be responsible for India's defence and foreign affairs. The part played by the British in Jinnah's plans suggested that, in his view, neither Pakistan nor Hindustan were supposed to be full-fledged sovereign states, but he nevertheless argued in favour of the designation of a constituent assembly.

Table 2.6: Main party scores within the Muslim electorate in the 1946 elections

Party	Muslim League	Congress	Muslims nationalists	Unionists	Other
Total Muslims	74.7	4.6	6.4	4.6	9.7
Urban Muslims	78.7	2.3	5	–	14.0
Rural Muslims	74.3	4.8	6.6	6.1	9.2
Muslim women	51.7	–	27.9	–	20.4

Source: Table adapted from Ayesha Jalal, *The Sole Spokesman*, op. cit., p. 172.

The "Minority Muslims" in whose name Jinnah spoke were the only ones to push this agenda. The "Majority Muslims" were mainly concerned with preserving their regional boundaries, fearing that their province would be carved up along religious lines. They were also anxious to escape control of any sort of centre—as promised in the Lahore Resolution, one of the reasons why they supported it. The idea of winding up with their "Muslim brothers" of another culture did not particularly appeal to them. The Bengalis were not prepared to give up Calcutta,[117] a Hindu city that would probably not be part of Pakistan in the event of partition—but they were prepared to sacrifice the Muslim Assamese. In Punjab, Khizar Hayat, the Muslim League leader, "wanted no Pakistan centre or at most a weak centre over the Muslim provinces".[118] In Sindh, G. M. Syed, considering that "The problems of the Muslim majority and Muslim minority provinces were essentially different in character",[119] asked for the right of regional self-determination when he was interviewed by the Cabinet Mission.[120] Lastly, "The Pathans had no love for their Punjabi neighbours".[121] That they remained in a Congress-governed India and provoked no opposition to the idea of becoming independent in a Pashtunistan to be built together with

[117] Ayesha Jalal, *The Sole Spokesman*, op. cit., p. 180.
[118] Ibid., p. 181.
[119] G.M. Syed, *Struggle for New Sind*, op. cit., p. 170.
[120] M.S. Kujero, G.M. Syed, op. cit., p. xix.
[121] Ayesha Jalal, *The Sole Spokesman*, op. cit., p. 198.

the southern Afghans sparked a certain degree of enthusiasm among the staunchest Pashtun nationalists—who were in a minority.

The other obstacle Jinnah continually had to face was none other than the Congress, as had been evident from the 1945 Simla conference. In summer 1945, the Viceroy, Lord Wavell, had convened all the Indian leaders in this summer capital to prepare the Indian transition towards self-rule. The negotiations—rather promising until then—came to a standstill when Jinnah insisted not only that the Executive Council have the same number of Muslims members as Caste Hindus, but also that they would be appointed by the Muslim League alone, something the Congress, which claimed to represent Muslims as well, could not accept.

After the Muslim League's success in the 1945–6 elections that Wavell had decided to organise after the Simla conference, the League was more adamant than ever but the British once again tried to promote an agreement between the Congress and the League. Prime Minister Attlee having promised India speedy and full freedom on 15 March, the British government sent a Cabinet Mission on 24 March 1946, to prepare India's transition to independence. This meant designating an interim government and electing a Constituent Assembly. After consulting different parties, in May it submitted its report, which envisaged the formation of a loose confederal framework grouping of Muslim-majority provinces and the Hindu-majority provinces. Both groupings would observe parity. The central government, in charge of foreign affairs, defence and communications, would be composed of ministers appointed in equal numbers by the Congress and the League. The Congress and the Muslim League accepted this agreement in June. But it eventually failed, not only because the British gave one more portfolio to the Congress, but also because on 10 July Nehru declared that the government of India might not apply the plan after the departure of the British. He even declared, "The big probability is that... there will be no grouping".[122] Jinnah immediately withdrew his commitment at a time when he could claim more than ever before that the Muslim League indeed represented the Muslims of India since the party had won 73 of the 78 Muslim seats in the July–August elections to the Constituent Assembly.

The Muslim League then called on Muslims to demonstrate on 16 August to show their determination on the occasion of a "Direct Action Day". In Calcutta, this display of force turned to rioting, which claimed approxi-

---

[122] Cited in Sumit Sarkar, *Modern India, 1885–1947*, Madras, Macmillan, 1985, p. 430.

mately 5,000 to 10,000 victims, mostly among Hindus.[123] It seems that Jinnah, who had never handled such a massive show of strength, had lost control of the movement—whose real architect in Bengal was the Chief Minister, Shaheed Hussain Suhrawardy, who probably tried to assert his domination over the League and the province.[124] The Congress interpreted this event as a plot to make it virtually impossible to work with the Muslim League. After 16 August 1946, the cycle of riots that spread to Bihar and then Punjab and other places made Partition nearly inevitable.

Ayesha Jalal considers that this event "destroyed the India of Jinnah's dreams".[125] This statement, which rests on the assumption that Jinnah did not want Partition, is doubly problematic. It supposes that Jinnah had a well-defined political agenda[126] and that it could be made acceptable to all the parties, whereas his idea of a loose confederation wherein "Hindustan" and "Pakistan" would co-exist on the basis of some parity under the aegis of British referees was neither very clear nor very realistic. Second, Jalal's expression presents Jinnah as a victim. He was certainly under pressure from a party and a community that were both in a rush, given that the British were on the verge of leaving the country. But he was nevertheless responsible for two major contradictions that resulted in counterproductive decisions—if he wanted to avoid Partition. Jinnah was torn between the desire not to partition the provinces of Punjab and Bengal, and the two-nation theory that rests entirely on the idea that Hindus and Muslims cannot live together. Furthermore, Jinnah made a serious error in judgment in thinking that Congress could agree to a form of parity with the League—including in the interim government. This obsession with parity[127] had

---

[123] Claude Markovits, "The Calcutta Riots of 1946". Available at: http://www.massviolence.org/The-Calcutta-Riots-of-1946?decoupe_recherche=Markovits (Accessed on September 15, 2013).

[124] Suhrawardy, who had been one of the Bengali leaders of the Khilafat movement, "had left the Congress Swaraj Party in 1926 after the first Calcutta riots in 1926, because he was sickened by the miseries of the Muslims, and revolted by the cruelty of the Hindus" (Begum Shaista Suhrawardy Ikramullah, *Huseyn Shaheed Suhrawardy*, op. cit., p. 66).

[125] Ayesha Jalal, *The Sole Spokesman*, op. cit., p. 216.

[126] One may have doubts about the fact that Jinnah had a roadmap in 1946–47, given the League's strategic hesitations at that time. While it joined Nehru's government in October 1946, it decided to boycott the Constituent Assembly in January 1947.

[127] Farzana Shaikh has pertinently emphasised that this parity "implied not only the right of Indian Muslims to equality of representation as a 'nation', but also

been at the heart of Jinnah's actions for decades, in the wake of Sir Syed's own worldview. It is a major feature of the ethos of the "minority Muslims" who had both a sense of vulnerability and a superiority complex with regard to the Hindus. Jinnah may have put his quest for parity in his program as a basis for negotiation in the hopes simply of obtaining a greater share than what the Muslims actually represented. But this calculation turned out to be a poor one and ended up leading to the Partition of 1947.

* * *

The idea of Pakistan in the 1940s was thus a highly ambiguous and complex one. It first developed, in the wake of the Aligarh movement, in provinces with a Hindu majority among Muslim elite groups who, initially, did not aspire to create a separate sovereign state. Muslim League leaders were simply seeking to escape the Hindu domination inherent in the law of numbers with democratization underway so as to retain their traditional status. Hence their multifarious tactics and strategies: their rejection of democracy, their eagerness to form coalition governments with the Congress and finally their demand for parity. Hence, also, the two-nation theory that was intended, precisely, to substitute parity for the idiom of numbers and, last but not least, their initial approval of the Cabinet Mission. Until then, most of the Muslim League leaders and sympathisers were not diehard separatists. Some of them even claimed that the Congress had forced them to divide India. Chaudhry Khaliquzzaman, for instance, in his autobiography wrote paradoxically:

It is a great irony that the Muslims, who had endeavoured for centuries to unify India and made untold sacrifices for the cause, even to the last days of Emperor Aurangzeb's life in 1707, were themselves forced by circumstances so little of their own making, to seek the partition of the country. But it would be found on an impartial study of the deteriorating relations between the two communities from the early twentieth century that a major operation alone could have prevented the catastrophe of a civil war in the sub-continent.[128]

For Chaudhry Khaliquzzaman the Muslims of India were "forced" to partition British India, otherwise, there would have been a civil war. But "forced" by whom? And why? The Muslim League leaders argued that Islam was under the threat of the "Hindu Congress". But the religious fig-

---

the exclusive prerogative of a Muslim party to represent a Muslim electorate". See Farzana Shaikh, *Community and Consensus in Islam*, op. cit., p. 195.

[128] Chaudhry Khaliquzzaman, *Pathway to Pakistan*, pp. x-xi.

ures of their community, including the *ulema* of the JUH were, until 1946 at least, less interested in the League's political projects than in the defence of their creed as a *millat*.

Muslim League leaders felt that they had been "forced" to partition India because the Congress did not want to share power with them on their own terms. The Congress, indeed, did not want to apply the parity principle the way the League defined it and did not want to recognise this party as the only representative of the Muslims of India given the fact that it claimed to be a national and secular organisation—where, indeed, "Muslim Nationalists" were in large numbers. The Muslim League, therefore, was not "forced" to back the project of a separate state. Instead it initiated it because it represented elite groups anxious to retain their traditional status and power—and fearing Hindu domination—and which, as a result, wanted a state to govern. This is exactly what Iqbal himself told Jinnah in the 1937 letter cited in the epigraph of this chapter. And he adds that, if the Muslim League "remains a body representing the upper class", he does not see how it will attract the masses. In 1937, it was indeed difficult to imagine how the party could surmount this contradiction. But ten years later, it was partly resolved through the watchword "Islam in danger". This cry was used to mobilise Muslim voters in the 1946 elections. What was at stake was the socio-political condition of the elite represented by the Muslim League. The rationale of this party's separatism was therefore similar to that of Sir Syed, and its popularity relied largely on a calculated confusion since it did not fight primarily for Islam, but for certain vested interests.

The effectiveness of this tactic needs to be qualified, however. It enabled the leaders of the Muslim League to blur regional identities rather superficially. Indeed, the idea of Pakistan was also complicated in the 1940s because it originated among "minority Muslims" who could only create their new state in provinces where Muslims were in a majority. But their coreligionists of Punjab, Sindh and Bengal adhered to it belatedly without giving up their regional identity. Of all of them, the Northwest Frontier Province showed the greatest reluctance. This contrast between majority and minority provinces is easily explained in the virtually federal context of British India: the Muslim elite in the United Provinces and the Bombay Presidency pursued this agenda in order to have themselves a state to govern, whereas the elite in the Muslim majority areas were already in power and had little to fear from the Hindus. Pakistan could not, however, be achieved without securing the adhesion of all areas in which Muslims were settled and detaching them from India. This is why Jinnah sought to intensify the conflict between Hindus and Muslims via his campaigns against the "Hindu Congress" after its victory at the polls in 1937—and this is why the League adopted the slogan "Islam in danger". It thus managed to exacerbate "majority Muslims'" fears of the risk of Hindu domination with the approach of British withdrawal hastened by the Second World War: hence what Yunus Samad has called "a brief moment of political unity".[129]

The Muslim League also sought to woo the "majority Muslims" by presenting the future Pakistan as a loose structure in which each province would enjoy considerable autonomy. The famous Lahore resolution of 23 March 1940, during the session in which the party would officially demand the creation of an independent state for the first time, even stipulated that its "constituent units shall be autonomous and sovereign".[130] The style of government initiated by Jinnah after the proclamation of Pakistan's independence on 14 August 1947 was in fact to be far more centralising than this phrase suggested.

---

[129] Yunas Samad, *A Nation in Turmoil. Nationalism and Ethnicity in Pakistan, 1937–1958*, New Delhi, Sage, 1989, p. 90.

[130] Syed Sharifuddin Pirzada (ed.), *Foundations of Pakistan: All-India Muslim League Documents 1906–1947, vol. 2*, op. cit., p. 341. Regarding the debate over the Lahore resolution, see Ikram Ali Malik (ed.), *Muslim League Session 1940 and The Lahore Resolution*, op. cit..

3

ISLAMIC STATE OR A COLLECTION
OF ETHNIC GROUPS?

FROM ONE PARTITION TO THE NEXT

I want you to be on your guard against this poison of provincialism that our enemies wish to inject into our State. (excerpt from a speech made by Jinnah broadcast from Radio Pakistan, Dhaka, 28 March 1948).[1]

Up until at least the mid-1940s, Jinnah made it a point to present the plan for Pakistan as federal. In 1945 he committed himself to giving to the provinces of the future state as much autonomy as that enjoyed by states or provinces in the US, Canada and Australia.[2] After August 1947, when he had become Governor General and President of the Constituent Assembly of Pakistan, his approach would be different. He now denounced the "poison of provincialism" by arguing that it was one of the latent divisions of the nation that India sought to exacerbate, to its own benefit. In the meantime, the Muslim Legislators' Convention, which had met in Delhi in April 1946, had amended the Lahore Resolution in a centralising perspective. The provincial leaders of the League, including the Bengalis, had apparently not even "noticed"[3] this change. One provision of the Delhi Resolution read:

[1] M.A. Jinnah, "Farewell message to East Pakistan", in *Jinnah. Speeches and Statements, 1947–48*, Karachi, Oxford University Press, 2009, p. 174.

[2] Muntzra Nazir, *Federalism in Pakistan, 1947–58*, Lahore, University of Punjab, 2001, p. 91. Available at: http://prr.hec.gov.pk/Chapters/1601-3.pdf (Accessed on September 15, 2013).

[3] Philip Oldenburg, "'A Place Insufficiently Imagined': Language, Belief, and the

...the Muslims are convinced that with a view to save Muslim India from the domination of the Hindus and in order to afford them full scope to develop themselves according to their genius, it is necessary to constitute a sovereign independent state comprising Bengal and Assam in the North-East Zone and the Punjab, North-West Frontier Province, Sind and Baluchistan in the North-West zone.[4]

There was no longer any mention of the provincial autonomy and sovereignty emphasized in the Lahore Resolution. This new approach consequently revived tensions between national and regional leaders. The debate that crystallised in the late 1940s reflected two diverging conceptions of Pakistan. Provincial leaders were in favour of a federal structure guaranteeing, among other things, that the nation's ethnic groups would be able to use their own language. The Muslim League leaders on the contrary promoted not only Islam but also Urdu as factors of integration in the framework of a unitary state. They wanted to use their new power to contain the ethno-linguistic divisions that had made their life so complicated in the 1930s–40s. But if they were in favour of a unitary nation-state, it was not only to defuse centrifugal forces and build a new Homo Pakistanus, it was also to resist India more effectively since they saw this country as posing an existential threat after the first Kashmir war and New Delhi's rapprochement with Kabul.

This contradiction undermined the work of the Constituent Assembly for almost ten years during which this body tried in vain to invent an institutional framework that would satisfy all parties. Eventually, the dominant groups, the Muhajirs (that is, those newly arrived in Pakistan—especially West Pakistan—after Partition) and the Punjabis, unwilling to find a compromise, imposed a centralised state that further exacerbated ethnic tensions. One result of this process was the 1971 partition and the creation of Bangladesh.

Jinnah's Nation-State: Between "The Poison of Provincialism"
and the Indian Threat

Jinnah began his fight against "provincialism" in East Bengal where he made a 9-day visit in March 1948 (seven months after the creation of Pakistan), during which he gave a very telling speech:

Pakistan Crisis of 1971", *The Journal of Asian Studies*, vol. 44, no. 4, August 1985, p. 720.

[4] Ikram Ali Malik, *Muslim League Session 1940 and The Lahore Resolution*, op. cit., pp. 329–330.

Pakistan is the embodiment of the unity of the Muslim nation and so it must remain. That unity we, as true Muslims, must jealously guard and preserve. If we begin to think of ourselves as Bengalis, Punjabis, Sindhis, etc., first and Muslims only incidentally, then Pakistan is bound to disintegrate. Do not think that this is some abstruse proposition: our enemies are fully alive to its possibilities which I must warn you they are already exploiting. I would ask you plainly, when political agencies and organs of the Indian press, which fought tooth and nail to prevent the creation of Pakistan, are suddenly found with a tender conscience for what they call the 'just claims' of the Muslims of East Bengal, do you not consider this a most sinister phenomenon?[5]

Jinnah's stance was clearly overdetermined as much by domestic considerations (the need to contain ethnic divisions) as by the enormous external factor that is the fear of India—a country with which Jinnah had pursued his quest for parity;[6] indeed, in another speech made in Dhaka, he also warned the Eastern Bengalis against foreign agencies working with Pakistani communists against the new state.[7]

Even if Partition in 1947 had finally given the Muslim minority in the Raj its own state, the Pakistani elites continued to act under the sway of a strong sense of vulnerability toward India. Not only did Pakistan not carry the same weight as India in demographic, economic and military terms, but neither was the sharing of resources of the defunct Raj devoid of complications. Whereas the "migrant state"—to use Mohammed Waseem's apt expression—that is Pakistan was to be built virtually from the ground up, it did not manage to obtain its share of the inheritance. Nehru was reluctant to give Pakistan the share of the Raj's assets it was owed by right—which moreover prompted Mahatma Gandhi to go on a hunger strike to pressure him, convincing the latter's murderer to carry out the act.

In this context, Pakistani leaders were even more prepared to believe (or at least to argue in public) that India did not want their country to survive. This sentiment of vulnerability (which helped them to rally "their" people behind them and justified their rapprochement with the US in the 1950s),

---

[5] M.A. Jinnah, "Farewell message to East Pakistan", in *Jinnah. Speeches and Statements, 1947–48*, Karachi, Oxford University Press, 2009, pp. 173–174.

[6] Responding to the questions of a Swiss journalist in March 1948, Jinnah considered that Pakistan and India could have good relations "provided the Indian Government will shed its superiority complex and will deal with Pakistan on an equal footing..." M.A. Jinnah, "India should deal with Pakistan on equal footing", ibid., p. 131.

[7] Speech of M.A. Jinnah in Dhaka, 21 Mach 1948, "National Consolidation", in ibid., p. 146.

was fostered by statements by Hindu nationalists in favour of "Akhand Bharat" (undivided India) and the words of Congress leaders cited in the introduction of this book about India's potential reunification. Whether these Congressmen meant what they said (and whether they actually uttered these words) is uncertain, but apparently Jinnah himself took them at face value. In a handwritten note probably dating from late 1947–early 1948 he confided:

1. The Congress have accepted the present Settlements with mental reservations.
2. They now proclaim their determination to restore the unity of India as soon as possible.
3. With that determination they will naturally be regarded as avowed Enemies of Pakistan State working for its overthrow.[8]

This feeling of vulnerability was even more acute in the army ranks where the non-transfer by India of the military equipment that had been agreed upon before the British left was very much resented. Ayub Khan, who in 1948–9 was General Officer Commanding in charge of the Pakistani army in East Bengal, considered that "India's attitude to Pakistan continued to be one of unmitigated hostility. Her aim was to cripple us at birth. She denied us our share of financial resources and dishonoured solemn agreements for the supply of our share of stores and equipment".[9]

In 1948–9, in addition to the Kashmir war that was perceived as a defeat,[10] two smaller episodes would reinforce Pakistan in its inferiority complex vis-à-vis India.[11] First, on 1 April 1948, New Delhi decided to stop the water flowing in two canals irrigating West Punjab from tributaries of the Indus River. The matter was not fully settled until the Indus Treaty was signed in 1960.[12] Second, in December 1949, in reaction to the fact that Pakistan had not, like New Delhi, devalued its currency, India stopped exporting coal to its

---

[8] See Gohar Ayub Khan, *Testing Times as Foreign Minister*, Islamabad, Dost Publications, 2009, p. 309.

[9] Muhammad Ayub Khan, *Friends not Masters*, op. cit., p. 65.

[10] See the section "Why the War Failed" of Shuja Nawaz, *Crossed Swords. Pakistan, Its Army and the Wars Within*, New York, Oxford University Press, 208, pp. 70–73.

[11] On the relations between both countries at that time, see Chandulal Nagindas Vakil, G. Raghava Rao, *Economic Relations between India and Pakistan: need for international cooperation*, Bombay, Vora, 1968 and Golam Wahed Choudhury, *Pakistan's relations with India 1947–1966*, New York, Frederick A. Praeger, 1968.

[12] Aloys A. Michel, *The Indus Rivers: A Study of the Effects of Partition*, New Haven, Yale University Press, 1967.

neighbours. This issue was partly settled through trade agreements in 1951—which still did not lead these two countries to become trade partners.

Stillborn Federalism and the Unresolved Ethno-linguistic Issue

Certainly, the fear of India aggravated the Pakistani leaders' centralising attitude, but their political project was in any case one for a unitary nation-state. This is evident from Jinnah's approach to the language question. His dealing with the Bengalis' attachment to their language during his trip to Dhaka is a case in point. In March 1948, in his first speech during this official visit, he declared with sententious overtones:

...let me make very clear to you that the State Language of Pakistan is going to be Urdu and no other language. Any one who tries to mislead you is really the enemy of Pakistan. Without one State language, no nation can remain tied up solidly together and function. Look at the history of other countries.[13]

A zealous supporter of unitary state-formation, Jinnah believed in the "one country, one people, one religion, one language" equation in order to fight against "provincialism" and other divisive factors. Indeed, he seems to have been haunted by memories of tribal conflicts affecting Muslims in the past. In the speech cited above, he exhorted the Bengalis to come to their senses by asking them a question most of those present in the audience might have not understood: "Have you forgotten the lesson that that was taught to us thirteen hundred years ago?"[14] One month before, in a lecture on Australian radio, he had also invoked the legacy of the Mughal Empire, a glorious episode of Muslim unity he wanted to recapture: "We have had a place in India for many centuries. At one time, it was supreme place. This was when the edict of the Moghuls ran from shore to shore."[15]

Jinnah's advocacy of Urdu not only arose from the fact that it was the language Indian Muslims living in the cradle of the Mughal Empire had had to defend in the nineteenth century; it also stemmed from the idea that this language could not be identified with any province of Pakistan—which was good for national integration—and had clear affinities with the Middle East where Islam was born.[16]

---

[13] "Farewell message to East Pakistan", in *Jinnah. Speeches and Statements, 1947–48*, op. cit., p. 150.

[14] M.A. Jinnah, "National consolidation", in ibid., p. 148.

[15] M.A. Jinnah, 19 February 1948, "Pakistan and her people", in ibid., p. 119.

[16] Philip Oldenburg, "'A Place Insufficiently Imagined': Language, Belief, and the Pakistan Crisis of 1971", op. cit., p. 717.

Jinnah's rhetoric in 1947–8 relativises Faisal Devji's interpretation that the Quaid-e-Azam ("great leader") sought to invent, with Pakistan, a country based on an Islam free from its historical and geographical roots. In fact, Pakistan's identity has constantly been nurtured by references to the past (especially a Mughal golden age) and to places (especially the sacred Muslim geography of Islam—and Urdu in any case was territorialized). If the founding fathers of Pakistan intended to use this country as a "laboratory", as Liaquat Ali Khan said in 1945,[17] they showed little if any imagination and fell back on the old recipes of the unitary nation-state, at the expense of cultural diversity—and at their own expense, eventually, given the resistance put up by the ethnic groups comprising Pakistan.

While Bengalis were Jinnah's first target, he also focused on other communities during his tours of Pakistan. In June 1948, at Quetta (Balochistan) he made a forceful speech echoing those he had made in Dhaka: "We are now all Pakistanis—not Baluchis, Pathans, Sindhis, Bengalis, Punjabis and so on and as Pakistanis we must feel, behave and act, and we should be proud to be known as Pakistanis and nothing else."[18] Inviting the ethnic groups of Pakistan to merge in a new identity, he clearly aspired to create a new man, a Homo Pakistanus that would transcend the pre-existing regional cultures.

But his fear of fissiparous tendencies led him to adopt centralizing measures which were bound to be counterproductive. The interim Constitution of Pakistan allowed him to do so. After 1947, indeed, Pakistan was ruled by an amended version of the 1935 Government of India Act. This text was federalist-oriented as regards the autonomy it gave the provinces. While the Centre was in charge of 59 matters, the list of those pertaining to the provinces' domain was almost as long (54)—and the Concurrent list was 36 items long. But this Constitution endowed the governor general with some of the sovereign prerogatives that the viceroy had enjoyed up until 1947, including the power to appoint the governors of the provinces. Certainly, section 93 of the 1935 Act, which enabled governors to dismiss the governments of their provinces, was abrogated by the Constituent Assembly of Pakistan,[19] but Jinnah could use the article 51(5)—according to which the

---

[17] Cited in ibid., p. 249.

[18] Speech by Jinnah in Quetta on 15 June 1948, "Provincialism: a curse", in ibid., pp. 227–228.

[19] Muntzra Nazir, *Federalism in Pakistan, 1947–58*, Lahore, University of Punjab, 2001, p. 76. Available at: http://prr.hec.gov.pk/Chapters/1601-3.pdf (Accessed on September 15, 2013).

governors were supposed to execute orders issued by the governor general—to achieve the same results.

A few weeks after the creation of Pakistan, he had Dr. Khan Sahib, the Chief Minister of the NWFP, dismissed because he feared that this politician, brother of Abdul Ghaffar Khan, would promote a Pashtun nationalist agenda. In April 1948 he did the same in Sindh. He had the Chief Minister, M.A. Khuro, dismissed because the latter was opposed to the transformation of Karachi into the capital of Pakistan[20] and resisted interference from the Centre with the functioning of his government (the Quaid-e-Azam apparently had some of its ministers appointed without referring to the chief minister).[21] In August 1948, Jinnah declared a state of emergency in the NWFP and in Sindh (as permitted by section 102 of the amended Government of India Act) to twist the arms of their government and have 500,000 refugees settled in their provinces.

Liaquat Ali Khan pursued the same policy after Jinnah's demise. When in February 1948 a member of the Constituent Assembly tabled an amendment to allow the use of Bengali as a language of the Assembly along with English and Urdu he replied: "Pakistan is a Muslim state and it must have as its lingua franca, the language of the Muslim nation".[22] In December of the same year, his government "established adult language centers in East Pakistan to teach Bengali in Arabic script despite Bengali opposition".[23] In January 1949 Khan dismissed the Chief Minister of Punjab, Nawab Iftikhar Hussain Mamdot, because he was not docile enough. Indeed, beyond Jinnah's personality, these practices reflected the centralist philosophy of the ruling elite that was rooted in their more unitary than federal conception of the new nation-state. This view reflects the sociology of the new state. Indeed, Pakistan had been created by the "minority Muslims" who had strived for a state to rule. After 1947, this group would become known mostly as the Muhajirs.

---

[20] In February 1948 the Sindhi chapter of the Muslim League had already passed a resolution against this upgrading of Karachi which, as a result, was emancipated from the provincial government.

[21] Muntzra Nazir, *Federalism in Pakistan, 1947–58*, op. cit., p. 162.

[22] Cited in Aqil Shah, *The Army and Democracy. Military Politics in Pakistan*, op. cit., p. 56.

[23] Ibid., p. 57.

Muhajirs and Punjabis, Founding Fathers of a Unitary and Centralised State

The Muhajirs, Architects of a "Migrant State"[24]

From its inception, Pakistan was formed by the Muhajirs, literally "migrants". This word designates those coming from the provinces of the former Raj, but it does not only refer to a geographical move. Its previous use to describe those who had fled with Prophet Muhammad from Mecca to Medina during the *hijra* endowed it with a religious quality. In Pakistan, it was first used by the education minister of Sindh[25] and became the official name of the "persons who entered Pakistan on account of partition or for fear of disturbances connected therewith"[26] in the 1951 census. At that time, there were 7 million Muhajirs in the country, 700,000 of them in East Pakistan.[27] In West Pakistan, the community thus counted 6.3 million people, one-fifth of the total population of 33.7 million. Most Muhajirs merely crossed the border and settled in a similar cultural and especially linguistic environment: the East Punjabi Muslims moved to West Punjab and those from West Bengal migrated to East Bengal. But for the Muhajirs from Hindu majority provinces it was a different matter:[28] 100,000 Urdu-speaking Biharis migrated to East Bengal and 1.1 million Muslims from Uttar Pradesh, Bombay Presidency, Delhi, Rajasthan and Gujarat moved to West Pakistan—half of them in Karachi and the rest in the other cities of Sindh.[29] Soon the "Muhajir" label was restricted to this community whose influence would immediately outweigh its demographic size.

The Muhajirs came from the circles among which the Muslim League had initially enlisted support, and they continued to exercise control over the

---

[24] Mohammad Waseem, "Ethnic Conflict in Pakistan: Case of Mohajir Nationalism", in G. Peiris and SWR Samarasinghe (eds), *Millennial Perspectives: Essays in Honour of Kingsley de Silva*, Colombo, 1999.

[25] Oskar Verkaaik, *A People of Migrants. Ethnicity, State and Religion in Karachi*, Amsterdam, VU University Press, Comparative Asian Studies, no. 15, 1994, p. 11.

[26] Cited in Laurent Gayer, *Karachi. Ordered Disorder and the Struggle for the City*, London, Hurst, 2014, p. 2.

[27] Mohammad Waseem, *Politics and the State in Pakistan*, op. cit., pp. 104–107.

[28] This does not mean that their integration was necessarily more difficult than for the former as evident the problems the Eastern Punjabis encountered after settling in Multan or Jhang where they are still today viewed as outsiders to a certain extent.

[29] Ann Frotscher, *Claiming Pakistan: The MQM and the Fight for Belonging*, Baden-Baden, Nomos, 2008, p. 89.

party. As they came mainly from an intellectual and trading elite, they not only dominated the state that they had carved out for themselves, but also Pakistani society. They settled primarily in urban areas, particularly the large towns of Sindh where the Hindus made room for them, especially in the capital of the province—Karachi, Jinnah's birthplace. In August 1947, the Quaid-e-Azam not only shared memories of his childhood with the audience during a public dinner at the Karachi Club,[30] but he also thanked the city for welcoming the "Pakistan staff",[31] an interesting formula that designates a government and a bureaucracy which were totally exogenous indeed.

Karachi became the city of the Muhajirs par excellence, even if they settled in other places, including Hyderabad. In fact, Partition transformed it completely. Before this event, it counted only 360,000 inhabitants according to the 1941 census, only half the size of Lahore, and 51 per cent of its inhabitants were Hindus (against 42 per cent Muslims). In 1951, the population had reached 1.1 million. The Muhajirs, who accounted for one-fifth of the population of Sindh, made up 57 per cent of the city's population—where Hindus were only 2 per cent.[32] Urdu speakers made up 51.4 per cent of its inhabitants, Sindhi speakers 14.3 per cent and Gujarati speakers 11.6 per cent.[33] Those who could not settle there made their homes in Hyderabad and Sukkur, two other Sindh towns where they made up 65 per cent and 55 per cent of the population respectively.[34]

In 1947, the Muhajirs enjoyed real prestige in Sindh. They had been the driving force in the creation of Pakistan and had given up everything to go and live there. They dominated the state through the Muslim League, their party, and its two leaders, Jinnah as Governor General and Liaquat Ali Khan, the Prime Minister, whom the Quaid-e-Azam referred to as his "right hand man".[35] Muhajirs also took over the economy. Out of the 42 largest

---

[30] Speech by Jinnah in Karachi, 9 August 1947, M.A. Jinnah, "Reminiscence of early days", in *Jinnah. Speeches and Statements, 1947–48*, op. cit., p. 23.

[31] Speech by Jinnah in Karachi, 25 August 1947, "Karachi—City with a bright future", in ibid., p. 43.

[32] Feroz Ahmed, *Ethnicity and Politics in Pakistan*, Karachi, Oxford University Press, 1998, p. 95.

[33] Ann Frotscher, *Claiming Pakistan: The MQM and the Fight for Belonging*, op. cit., p. 60.

[34] In 1951, immigrants made up 46% of the population of the country's 12 largest cities: urban Pakistan was a world of migrants dominated without question by Muhajirs.

[35] Liaquat Ali Khan, after having asked Jinnah to return to India in 1933, became

private companies, 36 belonged to Muhajirs—mostly from Gujarat (be they Bohras, Khojas or Sunnis, like the Memons).[36] Last but not least, the Muhajirs also dominated the civil service (95 out of the 101 Muslims in the Indian Civil Service chose to leave India, among whom a third were Punjabis and many were Urdu-speakers)[37] and the professions. In Sindh prior to Partition, the occupations of lawyer, teacher and tradesman had generally been the preserve of Hindus who left in droves after 1947. The Muhajirs thus touted their expertise in these areas and filled the vacancies generated by the exodus. Still in the early 1960s, 34.5 per cent of the civil servants of Pakistan were not born in the areas which had formed the country in 1947—many of them came from the former United Provinces.[38]

Table 3.1: Karachi's demographic growth (1941—2011)

Year	Population	Variation over the previous survey	% increase
1941	435,887	135,108	45
1951	1,137,667	701,780	161
1961	2,044,044	906,377	80
1972	3,606,746	1,562,702	76
1981	5,437,984	1,831,238	51
1986	7,443,663	2,005,679	37
1998	9,802,134	2,358,471	32
2011*	21,200,000	11,343,470	115

* Pakistan has not taken a census since 1998. The 2011 figure is therefore based on a non-systematic enumeration of the population of Karachi.
Source: Adapted from Laurent Gayer, *Karachi*, op. cit., p. 26.

---

his closest associate. After Liaquat Ali Khan's election to the legislative assembly in Delhi in 1941, Jinnah appointed him Deputy Leader of his Muslim League parliamentary group. That same year he involved him in the founding of his newspaper, *Dawn*. Liaquat Ali Khan accompanied him to the Shimla Conference in 1946. He was also the only person, together with the Quaid-e-Azam's sister Fatima Jinnah, who was aware how serious the illness was that struck him and that would bring about his demise a few months after the creation of Pakistan.

36 Stanley Kochanek, *Interest Groups and Development. Business and Politics in Pakistan*, Karachi, Oxford University Press, 1983, p. 25.

37 K.B. Sayeed, *The Political System of Pakistan*, Boston, Houghton Mifflin, 1967, p. 132. Although they made up only 3.5 % of the population, the Muhajirs occupied 21 % of the posts in the Pakistan Civil Service. R. Braibanti, *Asian Bureaucratic Traditions Emergent from the British Imperial Tradition*, Durham, Duke University Press, 1966, p. 263.

38 Muhammad Wassem, *Politics and the State in Pakistan*, op. cit., p. 109.

While Sindhis appreciated that the Muhajirs took over jobs they needed (in the service sector especially),[39] their elite groups were frustrated not to obtain some of the positions the Hindus had abandoned.[40] In fact, the Sindhis were ambivalent toward the Muhajirs. They expressed some resentment (especially after they "lost" Karachi, the new federal capital) while at the same time they appreciated the fact that the Muhajirs had created Pakistan and had sometimes lost everything in Partition. Indeed, some of them, when they did not cram into the houses left behind by the Hindus,[41] lived in camps.[42] In 1953, 250,000 Muhajir were homeless—a situation responsible for recurring street demonstrations.[43]

But most of the Muhajirs—if not all of them—eventually did well. They were naturally helped by the fact that, as mentioned above, in keeping with Pakistani ideology, their leader promoted Urdu to the rank of official language, even if English remained the natural language of the elite and therefore the state.[44] While recognising that English was necessary for the smooth functioning of the administration in a multilingual country, the Pakistani government did its best to promote Urdu.[45] The budget allocated to the Anjuman-e-Taraqqi-e-Urdu, an organisation in charge of propagating the language, doubled between 1948–9 and 1950–51. The courts and regional assemblies were urged to use Urdu and in the early 1950s, the Committee for the Official Language set up by the government in Punjab, a trailblazer in the matter, invented thousands of Urdu words for English terms that as yet had no equivalent.[46] Indeed, the Punjabis abandoned the

---

[39] See the personal testimony of Afak Haydar, "The Mohajirs in Sind: a critical Essay", in J. Henry Korson (ed.), *Contemporary Problems of Pakistan*, Boulder, Westview, 1993, p. 117.

[40] Sarah Ansari, "Partition, migration and refugees: responses to the arrival of Muhajirs in Sind during 1947–48", in Donald Anthony Low and Howard Brasted (eds), *Freedom, Trauma, Continuities: Northern India and Independence*, Delhi, Sage, 1998, pp. 91–105.

[41] See the reminiscences of Akbar S. Ahmed cited in Steve Inskeep, *Instant City. Life and Death in Karachi*, New York, The Penguin Press, 2011, p. 76.

[42] Ibid., p. 75.

[43] Sara Ansari, *Life after Partition: Migration, Community and Strife in Sind, 1947–1962*, Oxford, Oxford University Press, 2005, pp. 126–127.

[44] Tariq Rahman, *Language and Politics in Pakistan*, Karachi, Oxford University Press, 1998, p. 232.

[45] Also in the 1973 Constitution, article 251 (2) indicated that "the English language may be used for official purposes until arrangements are made for its replacement by Urdu" (ibid., p. 239).

[46] Ibid., pp. 230–231.

use of their mother tongue (at least in public) more systematically than any other ethnic group. That was due to the fact that Punjabi, in its original form, written in the Gurumukhi script, was largely seen as the language of the Sikhs—and, when written in Shahmukhi characters, it had many affinities with Urdu. But it was also due to the fact that the Punjabis played the official national ideology game all the more assertively to occupy the vanguard of the new state.

The Roots of Punjabi Domination

The Punjabi Muslims, who for a long time had held reservations about the idea of Pakistan, wielded their demographic weight and political as well as economic strength to dominate the country from its very inception. Although according to the 1951 census they accounted for only a quarter of its population, they made up the principal community of West Pakistan. They had benefited from the modernisation of agriculture in their region during the colonial period and, even more importantly, were heavily overrepresented in the army, where they held about 80 per cent of the posts.[47]

The British had identified many Muslim "tribes" of Punjab as forming a "martial race" and had recruited them in large numbers as part of their "Afghan Policy" of establishing a line of defence against any future Russian incursion into Central Asia. Many Punjabis were later enrolled in the First World War.[48]

The Punjabis were also omnipresent in the administration. Certainly, in the first decades of the twentieth century, the Hindus of the province, being more urban dwellers than the Muslims, thus enjoyed a better education. But Mian Fazl-i-Husain, as soon as he was appointed Education Minister in 1921, had for this very reason set a 40 per cent quota for Muslims in institutions as important as the school of administration. As a result, after Partition, the Punjabis occupied 55 per cent of administrative posts, considerably more than the Muhajirs.[49]

---

[47] Stephen P. Cohen, "State Building in Pakistan" in Ali Bannazizi and Myron Weiner (eds), *The State, Religion and Ethnic Politics: Pakistan, Iran and Afghanistan*, Lahore, Vanguard, 1987, p. 318.

[48] Clive Dewey, "The Rural Roots of Pakistani Militarism", in Donald Anthony Low (ed.), *Political Inheritance of Pakistan*, Basingstoke, 1991, pp. 255–283.

[49] Charles H. Kennedy, *Bureaucracy in Pakistan*, Karachi, Oxford University Press, 1987, p. 194.

Furthermore, the major irrigation projects carried out by the British from the 1880s onwards in Punjab had turned it into a breadbasket, producing wheat especially, for the Raj and later for the whole of Pakistan. This relative prosperity laid the groundwork for the "green revolution" of the 1960s which had an especially spectacular impact in the districts of Lyallpur (renamed Faisalabad in 1977), Multan and Montgomery (Sahiwal after 1978), where agricultural production rose by nearly 9 per cent yearly between 1959–60 and 1964–1965 nearly doubling the national growth rate.[50] Fifteen years later, in the early 1980s, 80 per cent of the tractors and 88 per cent and of the tube wells were located in Punjab.

In 1951, Punjab (including Bahawalpur, which eventually would be incorporated into the province) already had a GDP that was three times larger than that of Sindh minus Karachi (see table 3.2.).

In its early years, Pakistan was thus dominated by two distinct groups: the Punjabis, dominant in the military and the bureaucracy, and the Muhajirs, overrepresented among the businessmen, in the administration and in the government. Liaquat Ali Khan's government was for instance formed mainly of members of his own community.[51] Yet the Muhajirs and the Punjabis did not share either the same political culture or the same interests. The Muhajirs had always regarded South Asian Muslims as an ethnic group on the basis of their culture and considered Islam as nothing more than an identity symbol as will be seen in the last part of this book. In contrast, Punjab finally rallied to the idea of Pakistan by heeding the cry of "Islam in danger", and that province, still very rural, continued to be guided by both a religious and conservative political ethos. Unsurprisingly, Punjab was one of the first provinces of Pakistan, if not the first, to reshape the colonial Muslim Personal Law (Sharia) Application Act of 1937. The 1948 West Punjab Muslim Personal Law (Sharia) Application Act was "a rather protracted effort to purge the terms of customary law from the courts of postcolonial Punjab. They did not, however, bring an end to the influence of kinship-based ('tribal') custom".[52] In particular, widows were deprived "of the ancestral property that they might have distributed, as

---

[50] Ian Talbot, "Le poids du Punjab", in Christophe Jaffrelot (ed.), *Le Pakistan, carrefour de tensions régionales*, op. cit., p. 92.

[51] Leonard Binder, *Religion and Politics in Pakistan*, Berkeley, University of California Press, 1961, p. 205.

[52] Matthew Nelson, *In the Shadow of Shari'ah. Islam, Islamic Law, and Democracy in Pakistan*, London, Hurst, 2011, pp. 161–62.

full-fledged 'owners', through inheritance", a clear reflection of the attachment of the Punjabi men to land.[53]

Table 3.2: Population and resources of Pakistan in 1951, by province

Provinces	Population (thousands)	% of the total	Annual revenue (x million rupees)	Revenue per capita
Punjab	18,815	24.9	246.2	12.0
Sindh	4,606	6.1	97.0	21.1
NWFP*	5,865	7.8	65.0	20.1
Bahawalpur	1,822	2.4	50.5	27.7
Khairpur	319	0.4	12.0	37.6
Balochistan	602	0.8	NA	NA
Karachi	1,123	1.5	NA	NA
Total West Pakistan	33,704	44.6	NA	NA
East Pakistan	41,932	55.4	234,5	5,6
Total	75,636	100.0	–	–

*Including the North West Frontier Agencies—which were to be renamed the Federally Administered Tribal Agencies (FATA).
Source: adapted from Keith Callard, *Pakistan, A Political Study*, London, George Allen and Unwin, 1957, p. 156.

Muhajirs and Punjabis also differed in socioeconomic terms. The Muhajirs were predominantly urban, active in the private sector, whether in the professions or in business, whereas the Punjabis mostly still farmed the land and owed their relative prosperity to state irrigation subsidies and policies regulating agricultural markets and land tenure.[54] The liberal Muhajir outlook thus contrasted with the Punjabi inclination toward state interventionism.[55]

The latent antagonism between Muhajirs and Punjabis finally turned to the latter's advantage in the mid-1950s. Jinnah died in 1948 and his party, the Muslim League, gradually slipped out of Muhajir control. Liaquat Ali Khan took over for Quaid-e-Azam as party leader with the faction he

[53] Ibid., p. 162. Matthew Nelson points out that in Punjab "most families sought to maintain a *de facto* attachment to the 'custom' of female disinheritance", even after the law was reformed in the 1980s (ibid., p. 169).

[54] By promulgating the Land Alienation Act in 1901, the British Raj protected indebted Punjabi peasants from the merchant-usurers who otherwise would have seized their land to recover their debts.

[55] Shahid Javed Burki, *Fifty Years of Nationhood*, Boulder, Westview Press, 1999, p. 29.

headed, the Muhajirs, solidly dominating the Bengali and Punjabi factions. But Liaquat Ali Khan was mysteriously assassinated in 1951. The post of prime minister first went to Bengalis before falling to Chaudhri Muhammad Ali, who hailed from East Punjab. The new president, Iskander Mirza, was from West Punjab. He presided over the creation of a new party in 1956, the Republican Party, made up essentially of Punjabis who had sometimes adhered to the movement for Pakistan only belatedly. In December 1957 the Republicans brought down Ali, who was replaced by a West Punjabi, Malik Feroz Khan Noon.[56]

The domination of the Muhajirs, and then the rise to power of the Punjabis largely explain why Pakistan failed to give itself a constitution for almost ten years. The ethnic groups forming the country could not agree about the form of the state (not to mention the regime): while the Muhajirs and the Punjabis wanted a unitary structure, the others, including the Bengalis, true to the initial Lahore Resolution, favoured federalism, but to no avail.

The Slaying of Federalism: the One-Unit Scheme and the 1956 Constitution

In the late 1940s, constitutional debates focussed to a large extent on the question of the state.[57] The Objectives Resolution that Prime Minister Liaquat Ali Khan submitted to the Constituent Assembly on 12 March 1949 stipulated in its article 6 that Pakistan would be a federation. However, in the first draft of the Constitution that the Basic Principles Committee of the Assembly prepared, the Central government was in charge of 67 subjects and the provinces of only 35 (the concurrent list was 37 items long). The state was plainly becoming centralised. The Bengalis objected that such an institutional framework would undermine the federal nature of the state.

Bengalis were bound to be the main opponents to the political views of the Muhajirs and Punjabis. While Pakistani territory was composed of two "wings" on either side of India, these two regions did not carry the same weight. East Pakistan—corresponding to East Bengal under the Raj—had a larger population than West Pakistan, 41.9 million compared to 33.7 million,

---

[56] Ibid., p. 30. The use of the word "indigenous" by Burki to refer to Pakistanis who were neither Muhajirs nor Bengalis is indicative of the scope of ethnic divisions. It was finally as "sons of the soil" that the Punjabis aspired to power.

[57] Rafi Raza, "Constitutional Developments and Political Consequences", *Pakistan in Perspective, 1947–1997*, Karachi, Oxford University Press, 1997, pp. 1–60.

in 1951. On these grounds, the people of East Pakistan demanded a federal system and democracy and at least equal representation in the institutions the Constituent Assembly was in charge of setting up. Moreover, a majority of the members of this body were from East Bengal (44 of them, compared to 22 from Punjab, 5 from Sindh, 3 from NWFP and 1 from Balochistan).[58]

The Basic Principles Committee (BPC—also known to stand for the Bengali Punjabi Controversy!) submitted its second report on 7 September 1950. It recommended the creation of a federal and parliamentary system, with two assemblies: one representing the provinces and the other elected by direct universal suffrage. The elected representatives from Punjab immediately demanded a parity system—again!—in which Pakistan's two wings would be allocated the same number of seats in the lower house and each province would have the same number of seats in the upper house (which would give more seats to the western wing than to East Bengal, which would get only one). The Bengalis rejected this counterproposal. The quarrel over representation thus became the main stumbling block that prevented the Constituent Assembly from making progress. To find a way out, the East Bengal representatives sought the support of their colleagues from Sindh, the NWFP and Balochistan within the BPC—which was then presided over by a Bengali, Khawaja Nazimuddin. In November 1952, the BPC proposed a compromise which, certainly, gave an equal number of seats to the western provinces and to the Bengalis in the lower house (200 seats out of a total of 400), but also in the upper house. This formula was devised by the Bengalis with the support of the small western provinces. The Punjabis and the Muhajirs rejected the compromise.

They instead continued to try to impose a centralised, unitary state that they would control. They hence attempted to push through legislation that would make not only Islam but also the Urdu language pillars of the Pakistani nation-state, although the Bengalis were particularly attached to their language and revered its literature, even when its authors were Hindus from West Bengal. In 1952, Urdu was elevated to the status of national language while it was "a largely alien language spoken by some among Bengal's exploitative Ashraf aristocracy but foreign to the masses".[59] Demonstrations were held in East Pakistan in protest over this decision. Some of them degenerated into riots, and police crackdowns resulted in three deaths, an event commemorated yearly by a day of remembrance.

[58] As mentioned above, the Constituent Assembly members were elected by the Legislative Assemblies of the Raj in 1946.

[59] S. Mahmud Ali, *Understanding Bangladesh*, London, Hurst, 2010, p. 17.

The political parties of Bengal also cashed in on the Urdu-only policy of Karachi in the early 1950s. After Partition, new parties capitalising on Bengali nationalism were created by leaders who sometimes had briefly joined hands with the Muslim League. Fazlul Haq and A.H. Khan Bhashani, a popular peasant leader from Assam, left the League to defend Bengali interests and Suhrawardy was expelled from it because he continued to advocate the unity of Bengal.[60] In June 1949 these men rallied around an Awami League (named after the party Suhrawardy had already created). The first meeting of the party was held in Lahore in 1950. But its stronghold was in Bengal where Bhashani was made president of the East Bengal branch. In 1954, this League was the core group of a larger United Front amalgamating smaller parties. It produced a charter in 21 points. In the first point the Front asked for recognition of Bengali as a national language whereas point 19 prefigured the program of the Bengali separatists in the 1960s:

East Bengal will get complete autonomy according to the Lahore Resolution. Our defence, currency and foreign policy will be joint subjects with the Centre. Army headquarters will be in West Pakistan and Naval headquarters are to be set up in East Pakistan, so that this wing can become strong enough to safeguard her freedom.[61]

The United Front won an overwhelming victory during the provincial elections of March 1954 at the expense of a decimated Muslim League, allowing Fazlul Haq to form the government.[62] Consequently, the Centre made some concessions and in May 1954 a constitutional amendment elevated Bengali to the status of "state language" on a par with Urdu.

The central government nevertheless continued to keep the Bengalis at bay. In order to counterbalance their main political resource—their numbers—it devised a plan for parity between the two wings of the country, the One-Unit Scheme. This plan consisted in merging all the provinces of west-

---

[60] Ibid., p. 15. Many years later he was to tell his biographer: "... in the Pakistan I had envisaged, Bengal would have remained an entity and the Muslims would have been in a majority there" (Begum Shaista Suhrawardy Ikramullah, *Huseyn Shaheed* Suhrawardy, op. cit., pp. 59–60). In May 1947 he had written a letter to Liaquat Ali Khan to get the permission to contact Congres leaders, Sarat Chandra Bose and Kiran Sanker Roy who were equally keen to preserve the unity of Bengal. The talks did not bear any fruits.

[61] Cited in Richard Sisson and Leo E. Rose, *War and Secession. Pakistan, India and the Creation of Bangladesh*, Berkeley and Los Angeles, University of California Press, 1990, p. 12.

[62] Haq would be dismissed soon afterward partly because of a speech he made in Calcutta in which he suggested that he was first a Bengali and then a Pakistani (Ibid., p. 13).

ern Pakistan into one unique province almost as big as eastern Pakistan. Khawaja Nazimuddin, the Bengali prime minister who had raised objections to this plan, had been dismissed on 17 April 1953 by Punjabi Governor General Ghulam Mohammad. The new Prime Minister, Mohammad Ali Bogra, although a Bengali, endorsed this new constitutional formula. The Constituent Assembly stuck to the BPC scheme mentioned above, however, not only because of its Bengali members but also due to the opposition of many other provinces to the One-Unit Scheme. Pirzada Abdul Sattar, Chief Minister of Sindh, wanted nothing to do with it.

The Constituent Assembly was about to ratify the BPC plan in October 1954 when Ghulam Mohammad exercised his right to dissolve the assembly and declare a state of emergency. In March 1955, he took it upon himself to formally create the province of West Pakistan, uniting Punjab with the regions of Sindh, Balochistan and the NWFP to offset the weight of East Bengal. The One-Unit Scheme then became an institutional reality. The slaying of federalism that it represented enabled the Punjabi (and Muhajir) elites to retain power and keep the Bengali majority in a marginal position.

A new Constituent Assembly, elected like the previous one by the provincial legislative councils, officially created the Province of West Pakistan on 30 September 1955, the decree formally giving birth to this new entity being promulgated on 14 October. East Bengal was renamed East Pakistan. Punjabi responsibility in this operation becomes clear in a document attributed to Mian Mumtaz Mohammad Khan Daultana in circulation at the height of the debate over the One-Unit Scheme. The author explains that the national identity issue poisoned life in Pakistan due to the mutual distrust of the two wings of the country. He claimed that the unification of West Pakistan would remedy the situation by placing the country's two constitutive units on an equal footing.[63]

This quest for parity certainly reflects the political will of the western Pakistani elites to dominate the Bengalis, but also their profound belief that in fact both wings were equally populated because the Hindus (about one-fifth[64] of the east Bengali population) should not be taken into account.[65] For them, they were second-class citizens as evident from the system of separate electorates that will be studied below.

[63] Cited in Rizwan Malik, *The Politics of the One Unit, 1955–58*, Lahore, Pakistan Study Centre, 1988.
[64] Hindus represented 22% of the population of East Bengal in 1951 and 18.5% in 1961.
[65] Philip Oldenburg, "'A Place Insufficiently Imagined'", op. cit., p. 726.

Why did some major Bengali leaders agree to political parity between East and West Pakistan? After several rounds of discussions in Murree (near Rawalpindi), a certain number of concessions were granted to them. These included respect for the provinces' autonomy, an effort to recruit Bengalis in the bureaucracy and the army until parity was achieved there as well, and, apparently, the fact that the Prime Minister of Pakistan would be a Bengali (while the Governor General would hail from West Pakistan).[66]

With the creation of West Pakistan, the Punjabis formed the core of a unit whose demographic and political weight counterbalanced that of the Bengalis. This manoeuvre was naturally accomplished with the support of a Punjabi-dominated army. Commander-in-Chief Ayub Khan, who would become the regime strongman in 1958, noted in his memoirs that unifying West Pakistan was an absolute priority.[67] He was familiar with Bengal since he had been in charge of the Pakistani army in this province for two years in 1948–50, and although he was not a Punjabi but a Pashtun,[68] he shared the prejudices of most Punjabis and army officers regarding the Bengalis.

Since the colonial period, Bengalis were stereotypically described as weak and effeminate.[69] The Punjabis and the Pathans, on the other hand, were "martial races" and considered their warrior ethic to be essential to the country's very survival. According to Ayub Khan, even if the Bengalis "belong to the very original Indian races", this autochthonous feature was not to their credit. First, it classified them as Ajlaf, who were subject to all sorts of dominant influences—including the Ashraf—without ever ruling themselves ("They have been in turn ruled either by the caste Hindus, Moghuls, Pathans or the British").[70] Second, it explains the fact "that they have been and still are under considerable Hindu cultural and linguistic influence".[71] Ayub Khan viewed these features as damning for Bengalis: "As such they have all the inhibitions of down-trodden races and have not yet found it possible to adjust psychologically to the requirements of the new-born freedom".[72] Thus Ayub Khan conceived the idea of merging together the Western provinces into a single unit that could stand up to the Bengali

---

[66] Ibid., p. 715.

[67] Ayub Khan, *Friends not Masters*, op. cit., p. 192

[68] But Hindi-speaking and Aligarh-educated (ibid., p. 20).

[69] John Rosselli, "The Self-Image of Effeteness: Physical Education and Nationalism in Nineteenth-Century Bengal", *Past and Present*, no. 86, 1980.

[70] Ayub Khan, *Friends not Masters*, op. cit., p. 210.

[71] Ibid.

[72] Ibid.

masses—a plan that took on the name "One-Unit Scheme", which he admittedly was not the only one to endorse. And this was only natural: the scheme catered to the interests of many West Pakistan leaders.

The One-Unit Scheme antagonised most of the Bengali leaders when they realised that the promises made in Murree would not be kept. The first commitment that was betrayed by the authorities regarded the post of prime minister. Indeed, a Punjabi, Chaudhri Muhammad Ali, not a Bengali, was named prime minister, which prompted the Awami League to withdraw its support for the One-Unit Scheme.[73] Then, while the Scheme was in the process of being tabled in one provincial assembly after another, the authorities continued to dismiss provincial governments, including that of Pirzada Abdul Sattar in Sindh in November 1954.[74] They also dissolved the assembly of the province of Bahawalpur and changed the government of another newly created province, Khairpur, which like Bahawalpur was a former princely state. Partly because of these methods, the governments of the NWFP and Punjab withdrew their support for the One-Unit Scheme although they had already pushed it through their provincial assemblies. The NWFP government of Sardar Adbur Rashid Khan was immediately dismissed on 18 July 1955. All the provinces, including Punjab, dreaded the formidable centralising effect induced by the One-Unit Scheme.

Yet, the One-Unit Scheme remained one of the mainstays of the Constitution that Pakistan finally adopted in 1956. Certainly, according to article 1, "Pakistan shall be a Federal Republic to be known as the Islamic Republic of Pakistan". Indeed, the number of "central" subjects was reduced to 30 whereas the two provinces, West and East Pakistan, were in charge of 94 (only 19 items figured on the Concurrent list). Besides, the provinces were entitled to amend or even reject laws passed by the central legislatures.[75] But federalism remained an illusion given the huge concentration of power in the hands of the President. Not only could the President decide to declare a state

---

[73] H.S. Suhrawardy, who probably expected to be selected for the post, would be appointed to this position in September 1956, but he occupied it for only one year, and that was not enough to dispel the Bengalis' sense of alienation.

[74] He was replaced by Ayub Khuro, who was not even a member of the provincial assembly but who pressured its elected members to vote for the One-Unit Scheme. This method of coercion was criticised by H.S. Suhrawardy, who nicknamed it "Khuhroism", a term the Bengalis would have many other occasions to use in the future.

[75] Murtaza Nazir, *Federalism in Pakistan*, op. cit., p. 144. Available at: http://prr.hec.gov.pk/Chapters/1601–4.pdf (Accessed on September 15, 2013).

of emergency, but he could also suspend the assemblies. In East Pakistan, recourse to this procedure was taken even to pass the budget.[76]

In West Pakistan, similar techniques were also used in order to save the government and have the budget passed in 1957. President Mirza was keen to help the Chief Minister of the province, Dr. Khan Sahib—a former Pashtun nationalist co-opted by the regime—in order to weaken the influence of his brother, Abdul Ghaffar Khan, who was combating the One-Unit Scheme. But in September 1957 the members of the West Pakistan assembly passed a resolution asking for the restoration of the former provinces and for greater decentralisation.[77] To no avail: the ideology of Pakistan was systematically invoked for justifying state centralisation, a process instrumentalised more by the bureaucrats and the soldiers than by the politicians.

Ayub Khan's Constitution: Authoritarianism and Centralisation

Ayub Khan's rise to power after the 1958 coup reaffirmed the domination of the Punjabis (who were still hugely overrepresented in the army), but also epitomized the crystallisation of some affinity with the Pashtuns, who were also overrepresented among military personnel although to a lesser extent. While 77 per cent of the recruits came from Punjab (mostly from Rawalpindi, Jhelum and Campbellpur—today Attock), 19.5 per cent of the troops hailed from the NWFP (mostly from Kohat and Mardan).[78] The relatively large number of East Punjabis in the entourage of Ayub Khan moreover tended to blur the division between the Punjabis of the East and those of the West. The influence of these groups gained momentum at the expense of the Muhajirs whose decline was symbolised, in 1960, by the transfer of the federal capital from Karachi to Rawalpindi, a Punjabi city close to the NWFP where the General Head Quarters (GHQ) of the army was already located.[79] In 1967, the capital was transferred once again to a nearby city, Islamabad, which had been built from the ground up.

However, the balance of power was changing mostly at the expense of groups that were attached to regional autonomy, the Bengalis in particular. The Martial Law regime established by Ayub Khan resulted in additional

---

[76] Ibid., p. 211.

[77] Murtaza Nazir, *Federalism in Pakistan*, op. cit., p. 221.

[78] Stephen Cohen, *The Pakistan Army*, Karachi, Oxford University Press, 1998, p. 44.

[79] The Muhajirs resented this transfer not only because it epitomized their marginalisation, but also because of the loss it implied in terms of job opportunities.

forms of centralisation simply because power was now concentrated in a few hands. But the 1962 Constitution scarcely made any difference. The federal character of the state was mentioned in the preamble, but in practice the provinces were given no autonomy. The Constitution maintained the One-Unit Scheme and parity between East Pakistan and West Pakistan. In these provinces, power remained concentrated in the hands of governors appointed by Ayub Khan who were empowered to dismiss regional governments by virtue of exceptional procedures designed to protect state security and which were quickly diverted from their original purpose to become almost routinised. When assemblies were established, they were elected indirectly by a small collegium and did not have the power to overthrow the government. Even the list of state subjects had disappeared.

The Bengalis were the first victims of the balance of power that emerged in the late 1950s, not only in political terms, but also economically. Mujibur Rahman protested actively against this twofold domination in the 1960s.

Bengali Separatism: Mujibur Rahman, the Two-Economy Theory and the Centre's Overreaction

Having begun his political career in the Muslim League as one of Suhrawardy's lieutenants, Mujibur Rahman followed his mentor to the Awami Muslim League, was elected under the United Front label in 1954 and then took part in several provincial governments. After Suhrawardy's death in 1963, he became the key leader of the Awami League and radicalised the party line.

While politicians of the previous generations had shown a strong attachment to the Bengali culture, sometimes without resisting the attraction of power, Mujibur Rahman highlighted socioeconomic issues and no Pakistani government could co-opt him. (Given the growing arrogance of the regime, it is quite possible that nobody tried.) For him, the One-Unit Scheme had adversely affected the Bengalis—who were already lagging behind in socioeconomic terms since Partition. Out of the 95 Muslims in the Indian Civil Service (ICS) who opted for Pakistan in 1947, only one or two were from Bengal. The administration of East Bengal was therefore in the hands of civil servants from West Pakistan. Certainly, the Bengalis had been granted quotas in the civil service: 20 per cent of the posts subject to competitive examination were allotted on merit alone, 40 per cent were allocated to East Pakistan and 40 per cent to West Pakistan, among which 23 per cent went to Punjab and Bahawalpur, 15 per cent to Sindh, the NWFP and

Balochistan taken together, and 2 per cent to Karachi. But these figures represented no sacrifice whatsoever for the Punjabis and did not truly enable the Bengalis to catch up.[80] Although Bengalis could be appointed district administrators and administrative heads answering to the government in Dhaka, they remained a minority in the central administrative bodies. In 1959, there were only 349 Bengali higher civil servants out of 3,532 (9.6 per cent). And at the same time, there was not even a single Bengali among the highest 47 Pakistan army officers.[81] In 1955, East Pakistani officers represented 1.5 per cent of the Army officers, 1.2 per cent of Navy officers and 8.6 per cent of Air Force officers.[82] In 1963, the proportions had hardly changed, with respectively 5, 5 and 11 per cent.[83]

Simultaneously, Bengalis also suffered from serious economic exploitation. The revenues reaped from their exports were used to finance the industrialisation of West Pakistan. Between 1947 and 1962, East Pakistan exported 13.08 billion rupees worth of goods (particularly jute) and West Pakistan, only 9.9 billion worth. Imports into East Pakistan amounted to only 7.9 billion, compared to 18.7 billion for West Pakistan, which was clearly able to purchase equipment abroad with the trade surplus produced by East Pakistan. The Bengalis complained all the more bitterly of this practice as their per capita income in the early 1960s was about 25 per cent below that of West Pakistan and the growth rate of their province amounted to half that of West Pakistan. Per capita income only rose by 17 per cent in East Pakistan from 1959–60 to 1969–70 whereas it grew by 42 per cent during the same period in West Pakistan.[84] In 1971, while East Pakistan has 75 million inhabitants and East Pakistan, 55, the former and the latter had respectively 6,000 and 26,000 hospital beds, 162 and 271 colleges, 16 and 84 per cent of the civil servants, 20,000 and 500,000 soldiers...[85]

The Bengali population, however, became more swiftly politicised, as education had made great strides. In 1961, 17.6 per cent of Bengalis could

---

[80] The 1961 census revealed that the population of East Pakistan was 50.8 million inhabitants, while there were 42.9 million in West Pakistan. The quotas were thus not proportional to the demographic weight of the two entities.

[81] Tariq Rahman, *Language and Politics in Pakistan*, op. cit., p. 121.

[82] Rounaq Jahan, *Pakistan: Failure of National Integration*, New York, Columbia University Press, 1972, p. 25.

[83] Aqil Shah, *The Army and Democracy. Military Politics in Pakistan*, op. cit., p. 102.

[84] M. Rashiduzzaman, "East-West Conflicts in Pakistan: Bengali Regionalism, 1947–1970", in A. Jeyaratnam Wilson and Dennis Dalton (eds), *The States of South Asia—Problems of National Integration*, London, Hurst, 1982, p. 117.

[85] S. Mahmud Ali, *Understanding Bangladesh*, op. cit., p. 31.

read compared to a literacy rate of 13.6 per cent in West Pakistan. The Bengali intelligentsia included a great number of influential economists who denounced the state of affairs that had taken hold in Pakistan, suggesting that a "two-economy theory" had replaced the "two-nation theory".

In 1966, the Awami League outlined a Six-Point Programme, which amounted to a challenge to the central government:

1. The constitution should provide for a federation in the true sense and a parliamentary democracy on the basis of direct universal suffrage.
2. The federal government should control only defence and foreign affairs; all other matters should be devolved to the state level.
3. Each wing of the country should have its own freely convertible currency; failing that, there will be a single currency but constitutional provisions will prevent the flight of capital from East Pakistan to West Pakistan. Furthermore, East Pakistan should have its own central bank and conduct a separate fiscal and monetary policy.
4. The power of taxation should be vested in states. A share of the revenue will be remitted to the federal government.
5. Each wing of Pakistan will manage its own currency reserves and trade with whatever country it chooses.
6. East Pakistan should have its own paramilitary force.

Ayub Khan responded to these demands by repression, arresting Mujibur Rahman along with many other members of his party on the ground that their actions threatened national cohesion. The government then sought to discredit Rahman, accusing him of having accepted arms from India. The Agartala trial, named for the Indian town where the alleged transaction had supposedly taken place, opened in 1968 in Dhaka where it provoked mass mobilisation of opponents to the regime. The judges dismissed the case for lack of evidence, and the entire episode merely bolstered Mujibur Rahman's popularity.

The attitude of the Pakistani government ended up fostering the radicalisation of the Bengali movement for self-determination, a pattern that was bound to repeat itself in other provinces. Ayub Khan realised this, but too late. In February 1969, he convened a Round Table Conference at which he proposed to the various parties to amend the Constitution toward greater federalism. The Conference, which Rahman agreed to attend in March 1969, produced no results, in particular due to the boycott by Zulfikar Ali Bhutto, who had founded the Pakistan People's Party (PPP) sixteen months before. An ageing Ayub Khan then decided to step down and hand over power to the army commander-in-chief, Yahya Khan.

Yayha Khan decided to repeal the 1962 Constitution and declared martial law, while announcing that elections would be held and a federal-style constitution drafted. In early 1970, he enacted a Legal Framework Order abolishing the One-Unit Scheme[86] and establishing a de facto federal regime which gave East Pakistan 169 seats in the 313-member assembly. For the first time this province had a political majority proportional to its demographics.

The elections held in December 1970 resulted in a triumph for Rahman's Awami League. His party won 160 seats compared to only 81 for Bhutto's PPP for which Sindh and Punjab voted in large numbers.[87] This election confirmed the parliamentary partition of Pakistan given that the Awami League contested almost no seats in the western wing and the PPP none in the eastern wing. The remarkable score made by the PPP in Punjab (where it won 62 of the 82 seats)—despite its being led by a Sindhi—attests to the determination of West Pakistan—still in search of parity—to unite forces against the Bengalis. Bhutto, who "demanded power without having won the election",[88] moreover sought to set himself up as the man who repre-sented the "real" Pakistan, claiming that Punjab and Sindh were the cradles of the country. Such rhetoric was reminiscent of Syed Ahmad Khan in his rejection of the democracy and Jinnah's quest for parity. Drawing inspira-tion from these illustrious predecessors, Bhutto maintained that the law of numbers wasn't everything. "Political importance", to use the expression introduced by the Aligarh school, also had to be taken into account, he suggested.[89] This idea however referred less back to the Muslims' glorious past when they ruled India, but to a de facto situation: the West Pakistanis held power and had no intention of giving it up. Bhutto's priority remained not to allow the Bengalis to govern. He, like the Punjabis, viewed the people of East Pakistan as being meant to remain second-class citizens.

---

[86] It should be noted, however, that not all the provinces prior to 1955 were rein-stated. The states of Khairpur and Bahawalpur, cradle of the Saraiki language whose speakers wanted their own province, were integrated into Punjab, which thus became the majority province within West Pakistan.

[87] Wolfgang-Peter Zingel, "Pakistan" in Dieter Nohlen, Florian Grotz and Christof Hartmann (eds), *Elections in Asia and the Pacific. A Data Handbook. Volume 1*, Oxford, Oxford University Press, 2011, pp. 661–695.

[88] Sarmila Bose, *Dead Reckoning. Memories of the 1971 Bangladesh War*, London, Hurst, 2011, p. 23.

[89] See Rafi Raza, "Constitutional Developments and Political Consequences", op. cit., p. 18.

Rahman, after winning the elections, demanded that the government implement his Six-Point Programme. Yahya Khan seemed prepared to call a constituent assembly in Dhaka to this end, but Zulfikar Ali Bhutto, the new strong man of West Pakistan, refused and declared that his party would boycott any such body.[90] On 1 March 1971, Yahya Khan announced that the appointment of the proposed constituent assembly would be postponed indefinitely. Rahman then launched a general strike throughout East Pakistan. He now demanded a Confederation in which the eastern and western regions would each have its own constitution.[91]

On 25 March 1971, Islamabad, where many leaders—military and civilian—were apparently convinced that India was behind this move,[92] reacted by sending troops to accomplish the infamous Operation Searchlight. The day before, General Tikka Khan had been appointed governor of East Bengal. During the night of the 25–26 March, Pakistani soldiers killed about 300 people on the campus of Dhaka University.[93] Bengalis responded by attacking Urdu-speakers known as Biharis because most of them had come from Bihar after Partition. The largest number of casualties probably occurred in the Crescent textile mill in Khulna.[94]

India apparently started to support the Bengali guerrilla force, the Mukti Bahini, in April 1971[95] and began to train its members in the course of that summer. But the nature of the conflict truly changed on 21 November when New Delhi, justifying its military intervention on humanitarian grounds, argued that it could not cope with the influx of refugees (10 million of them had already crossed the border).[96] The war was short, especially after a new front was opened on the West on 3 December, forcing Pakistan to concede defeat and surrender what would soon become Bangladesh.[97]

---

[90] Stanley Wolpert, *Zulfi Bhutto of Pakistan. His Life and Times*, New York, Oxford University Press, 1993, pp. 145–46.

[91] Philip Oldenburg points out that Rahman could have demanded the independence of Bengal at that time. In abstaining from doing it he showed his commitment to Pakistan, provided the state was democratised and decentralised. See Philip Oldenburg, "'A Place Insufficiently Imagined'", op. cit., p. 713.

[92] Ibid., pp. 728–730.

[93] Sarmila Bose, *Dead Reckoning*, op. cit., p. 65 and ff.

[94] Ibid., p. 81.

[95] Richard Sisson and Leo E. Rose, *War and Secession*, op. cit., p. 210.

[96] Gary J. Bass, *The Blood Telegram. Nixon, Kissinger and the Forgotten Genocide*, London, Hurst, 2014, p. 119.

[97] For a comprehensive study of the 1971 war, see the recent book by Srinath

The controversy over the human toll of this war continues, the figures mentioned by various sources ranging from 300,000 to 3 million dead.[98] But there is no doubt that this second Partition sealed the fate of the Pakistan project as it had been conceived in 1947. The failure was twofold. On the one hand, Pakistan was unable to retain in its midst an ethnic group that shared its Muslimhood but resented the over-centralisation and even the unitary form of the state. This structure, at odds with the Lahore Resolution, did not produce the kind of autonomy Bengalis expected from the new State and resulted in socioeconomic imbalances as well as exploitation. On the other hand, the creation of Bangladesh weakened Pakistan vis-à-vis India. Not only was defeat humiliating—even if the "official" figure of 93,000 war prisoners has been challenged recently[99]—but Pakistan could no longer claim that it encircled India.

* * *

Immediately after it came into being, Pakistan had to cope with the issue of national integration, a question some of the oldest nation-states in Europe have yet to resolve. This question pertained primarily to the form of the state—unitary or federal—that the new nation would choose. While they claimed to be faithful to the federal overtones of the Lahore Resolution, the founding fathers of Pakistan opted for a unitary arrange-ment that would comply with the old nationalist trinity, "One people, one religion, one language".

As Muhajirs, they had no regional identity to defend and on the contrary were anxious to subsume the ethnic groups that had so reluctantly rallied around the Pakistani project in the 1940s and could, according to Jinnah and his followers, still weaken it, if granted official recognition. Hence their emphasis not only on Muslimhood, but also on Urdu. This quest for unity—one of the three words of the official motto, "Faith, Unity, Discipline"[100]—was made even more imperative by a sense of vulnerability vis-à-vis India (and Afghanistan), which was presumably sincere, but also probably instru-mentalised by the rulers to rally "their" people around them.

This project would have not materialised if all the provinces had rejected it in the name of their specific identity and interests. But the Punjabis sup-

---

Raghavan, *1971, a Global History of the Creation of Bangladesh*, Cambridge (Mass.), Harvard University Press, 2013.

[98] Sarmila Bose, *Dead Reckoning*, op. cit., pp. 175–178.

[99] Ibid., p. 174.

[100] This motto, officially coined in 1954, was Jinnah's legacy.

ported it. In the army—where they were so omnipresent—they were used to transcending cultural differences in the name of collective security. And more importantly, because of their positions in the army and in the bureaucracy, the Punjabis were largely in command: it was in their interest to play the national game—and therefore to adopt Urdu, which was already a language with which they had affinities. This attitude allowed them not only to become identified with the national project but also to keep the Bengalis at bay.

All the other provinces demanded respect for their autonomy and specificity in keeping with the terms of the Lahore Resolution. All protested against the centralisation of the state and, in the 1950s, against the One-Unit Scheme. Bengalis rejected this framework all the more vehemently as it was intended to deprive them of their main asset—numbers—in the name of parity between East and West Pakistan. They were the new casualties of an ethos that had crystallised in the late nineteenth century when "minority Muslims" of the United Provinces began to fight to retain power by non-democratic means—in fact, against the democratization process.

From the mid-1950s onwards, the constitutional debates and texts resulting from them, the Constitutions of 1956 and 1962, reflected the determination of the elites of West Pakistan to marginalise the Bengalis. Gradually, this policy—and the correlative economic exploitation of the East by the West—completely alienated the political leaders of the latter. This process culminated in Mujibur Rahman's mobilisation, which Ayub Khan did not attempt to defuse. On the contrary, he responded to the Awami League's demands by repression, when a more conciliatory attitude might have made a great difference. In doing so, Ayub Khan followed in Jinnah's footsteps, but he went further—and set a pattern: in the future even civilian governments would tend to react to ethnic groups by repressive measures, which, in return, would further radicalise their movement along nationalist lines.

The official historiography of Pakistan presents the birth of Bangladesh as the result of an Indian operation to destabilise its neighbour—whose existence New Delhi allegedly had never accepted.[101] Certainly, New Delhi dealt the deathblow, but after months of popular mobilisation that Islamabad helped to radicalise by its repressive measures. It turned into a most traumatic defeat that would reinforce Pakistan's existential fear of India.

But the creation of Bangladesh had broader implications for the domestic scene since it called into question the country's very identity: Islam had not

<hr>

[101] Richard Sisson and Leo E. Rose, *War and Secession*, op. cit., p. 221.

enabled Pakistan to transcend ethno-linguistic divisions and to build a new man (in the spirit of Liaquat Ali Khan's metaphor of the country as a laboratory). This is not surprising given the fact that this laboratory, far from being creative, had fallen back on the old formula of the centralised, unitary state. Such was the perfect recipe for transforming a demand for more autonomy into a separatist movement, especially when the initial demands were met by repression.

After 1971, this trajectory was repeated in the NWFP and Balochistan—more than once. But most of the Sindhis, on the contrary, rallied around the idea of Pakistan just as the Punjabis had done 20–25 years before. This was largely due to the electoral success of the PPP which, however, further alienated the Muhajirs.

4

FIVE ETHNIC GROUPS FOR ONE NATION

BETWEEN SUPPORT AND ALIENATION

Post-1971 Pakistan, in theory, was likely to be more federal. Not only had the abolition of the One-Unit Scheme resulted in the creation of four provinces—Punjab, Sindh, the NWFP and Balochistan—but democratization under the aegis of Z.A. Bhutto's PPP was also more conducive to decentralisation than the previous concentration of power. On 21 April 1972 Bhutto promulgated an interim constitution that was the outcome of an agreement negotiated with the main political parties, including the regional forces of the four provinces. The Constitution proclaimed the following year, on 12 April 1973, was more favourable to a federalist system than its predecessors. It set up the Council of Common Interests in which representatives from the central government and the four provinces sat as equals to oversee a variety of matters such as the sharing of river waters among regions. It also granted small provinces the same number of seats as Punjab in the Senate. Although the Senate had almost no say in financial matters, the reform was intended to offset the influence of Punjab, which had become the majority province (see table 4.1.).

But the new government's practices contradicted the Constitution's stated ideal of decentralisation. Not only had Bhutto's PPP actually formed a tacit pact with the Punjabis, enabling Pakistan's two main communities (the Sindhis and the Punjabis) to dominate the state apparatus, but Bhutto's natural inclination towards authoritarian methods was at crosspurposes with the federal and parliamentarian spirit of the Constitution.

Table 4.1: Population of Pakistan,1972 (by province)

Population	in millions	in %
Punjab	37.5	58.0
Sindh	14.0	21.6
NWFP and FATA	10.8	16.7
Balochistan	2.4	3.7
Total	64.7	100.0

Source: Shahid Javed Burki, *Pakistan under Bhutto*, op. cit., p. 94.

While Sindhis rallied around the Pakistan project—like the Punjabis before—considering that they could govern the country through the PPP, the other groups did not follow a linear trajectory. Pashtun nationalism continued to ebb, but the rise of Islamism in the 1980s altered the rules of the political game in the NWFP. The Balochs, when their leaders were not co-opted by the Centre, were often at war with it because of forms of exploitation that called to mind the situation of East Bengal in the 1960s. Muhajirs oscillated between phases of violent opposition and episodes of collaboration with mainstream parties or military dictators, but their sense of alienation tended to prevail.

The Pakistanisation of Sindh

Sindhi nationalism traditionally relied on three pillars: language (and literature), "a strong historical-territorial element"[1] enshrined in the Golden Age that was the Indus civilisation, and a sense of victimisation due to the province's having had to wait until 1935 to be recognised officially and its socioeconomic deprivation. This last dimension needs to be elaborated upon. During the Raj, early Sindhi nationalists held up as symbols of their province's condition the exploitation of the local peasants, the (mostly Muslim) *haris*, by urban (mostly Hindu) moneylenders.[2] G.M. Syed created a Sindh Hari Committee as early as 1930. The social overtones of Sindhi nationalism exerted a certain attraction on the leftist intelligentsia after 1947.[3] All the more so as feelings of victimisation were, at that time, reinforced by the attitude of the Muhajirs who were settling in the cities of

[1] Oskar Verkaaik, *Migrants and Militants. Fun and Urban Violence in Pakistan*, Princeton, Princeton University Press, 2004, p. 31.
[2] Ibid.
[3] Ibid., p. 35.

Sindh. As Oskar Verkaaik points out, "To many Muhajirs hailing from the former heartland of the Moghul Empire, Sindh was a peripheral backwater of the subcontinent, a culturally barren outskirt, rural and tribal wilderness."[4] Sindhi leaders immediately resented this dismissive attitude. One of them remembers, "Muhajirs entertained notions of cultural superiority, and in over-enthusiasm, forgot that this can create a negative reaction among the local population. No local community can accept the superiority of an immigrant community, irrespective of its cultural level. As a reaction, this sentiment led to hatred".[5]

This superiority complex sparked Sindhi protest when it translated into adverse policies. In 1948 Sindhis contested in the courts the transformation of Karachi into the federal capital of Pakistan—in vain.[6] In the 1950s, the formulation of the One-Unit Scheme provoked strong reactions too in the province. G.M. Syed moved closer to Pashtun and Bengali nationalists to form a common front. Sindhis also resented their marginalisation in the army where they made up only 2.2 per cent of the troops in 1947.[7] In 1959, there was not a single Sindhi among the 47 senior most officers.[8] The situation was no better in the bureaucracy, as in 1959 Sindhis represented 2.5 per cent of Pakistan's 3,532 highest civil servants (against 48.9 per cent Punjabis and 30.3 per cent Muhajirs).[9] This marginalisation in the administration prevailed also in the Sindh regional bureaucracy. It was partly due to the fact that Urdu had become the official language of the province. The linguistic issue was a major bone of contention once Ayub Khan replaced Sindhi with Urdu after the sixth grade in schools.[10]

In this context, "the Sindhi movement became one of the most vocal components of the social uprising that bought down the military regime of Ayub Khan in 1968".[11] The man who channelled this energy was none other

---

[4] Ibid., p. 43.

[5] M.S. Korejo, *G.M. Syed*, op. cit., p. 35.

[6] Sarah Ansari, "The Movement of Indian Muslims to West Pakistan after 1947: Partition-related migration and its consequences for the Pakistani province of Sind", in Judith M. Brown, Rosemary Foot (eds), *Migration. The Asian Experience*, New York, St Martin's Press, 1994, pp. 149–168.

[7] Stephen P. Cohen, *The Pakistani Army*, op. cit., p. 44.

[8] Khalid B. Sayeed, "The Role of Military in Pakistan", in J. Van Doorn (ed.), *Armed Forces and Society*, The Hague/Paris, Mouton, 1968.

[9] Ann Frotscher, *Claiming Pakistan*, op. cit., p. 98.

[10] M.S. Korejo, *G.M. Syed*, op. cit., p. 63.

[11] Oskar Verkaaik, *Migrants and Militants*, op. cit., p. 36.

than Z.A. Bhutto who would gradually marginalise G.M. Syed's Jiye Sindh, a party founded after the creation of Bangladesh in order to obtain a "Sindhu Desh" along similar lines as Mujibur Rahman's achievement.

In the late 1960s, after leaving Ayub Khan's government in 1967, Bhutto fought against the former dictator in the name of socialism. This ideology held some appeal for Sindhi nationalists who had always defended the poor—at least in their rhetoric. Verkaaik argues that Bhutto would finally be identified with the cause of Sindh at the expense of G.M. Syed and his followers after he "appropriated their symbolism",[12] without being as radical as they were and thus not at all in favour of separatism. For instance he touted Shah Abdul Latif as "a Pakistani national poet rather than a Sindhi national one".[13] However, he had a real impact on the Sindhi nationalist movement in the 1970s when he rose to power in Islamabad. At that time he was in a position to persuade his compatriots from Sindh to think of themselves first as Pakistanis and then as Sindhis. One representative of the Sindhi intelligentsia, M.S. Korejo, interestingly confides, "For the first time in history, a Sindhi was the absolute ruler in Pakistan, and Sindhis had their presence felt in Islamabad".[14] This was bound to make a difference indeed.

From Anti-Muhajir Nationalism to Rallying Around the Pakistan Project

Once in office, Bhutto denounced G.M. Syed's separatism, eventually having him placed under house arrest in 1973, but at the same time he implemented pro-Sindhi policies that Syed could only support privately.[15] These policies were possible because the PPP had not only won power at the centre, but also in Sindh where one of Z.A. Bhutto's cousins, Mumtaz Bhutto, known for his pro-Sindhi leanings, became governor in 1971 and then formed the government in 1972. He immediately promoted a new piece of legislation, The Teaching, Promotion, and Use of Sindhi Language Bill, making Sindhi obligatory alongside Urdu from grade 4 to grade 12. Clause 6 of the bill provided for the gradual introduction of Sindhi in the administration, the courts and the provincial assembly. Within this body, where the bill was discussed during the summer of 1972, Urdu-speaking opponents suggested that a national tongue, their own as it happened, also

---

[12] Ibid.
[13] Ibid., p. 37.
[14] M.S. Korejo, *G.M. Syed*, op. cit., p. 82.
[15] Ibid., pp. 119–120.

be officially recognized as the language of the administration and the courts. But the final wording of the law passed in early July disregarded this demand.[16] This measure sparked a wave of Muhajir protest in Karachi, Hyderabad and Larkana, where a number of riots broke out. Bhutto nevertheless backed the decision made by the Sindh authorities—whom he himself had appointed—thus pandering to Sindhi nationalism. In defence of his stance, he declared before the National Assembly:

> We have given our lands; we have given our homes; we have given our lives [...] to people from all parts, to the Pathans, Punjabis, to the Muhajirs living in Sind [...]. What else can we do to show our loyalty, our love and our respect for Pakistan and our Muhajir brothers?[17]

However, the scale of the protest prompted Bhutto to curb the scope of the law in mid-July 1972. By an ordinance of his own devising, he specified that no discrimination against Urdu speakers would be tolerated in civil service recruitment and that the new provisions would not come into effect for 12 years to allow the Muhajirs time to learn Sindhi.[18]

Language was not the only focus of the Sindhis (or the only matter of concern to the Muhajirs). The issue of quotas was another. In September 1948, Liaquat Ali Khan's government had introduced a quota system regulating access to the civil service in order to promote parity between the eastern and western wings of Pakistan. In this framework, 2 per cent of federal civil service jobs were reserved for Muhajirs, although they made up only 1.5 per cent of the total population. Bhutto overhauled this system, which since the 1971 Partition was in any case based on skewed figures. Now 10 per cent of the vacant positions would be filled solely on the basis of merit, 50 per cent were reserved for Punjab, 11.5 per cent for the NWFP, 11.4 per cent for rural Sindh, 7.6 per cent for urban Sindh and 3.5 per cent for Balochistan. As native-born Sindhis came mainly from rural areas whereas the Muhajirs lived almost exclusively in cities, this measure aimed

---

[16] Farhan Hanif Siddiqi, "Intra-Ethnic Fissures in Ethnic Movements: The Rise of Mohajir Identity Politics in Post-1971 Pakistan", *Asian Ethnicity*, 11 (1), 31 March 2010, p. 31.

[17] Cited in Stanley Wolpert, *Zulfi Bhutto of Pakistan. His Life and Times*, New York, Oxford University Press, 1993, p. 199.

[18] They finally would never have to because General Zia, who was in power when the time limit expired in July 1984, repealed the law. See Feroz Ahmed, "Pakistan problems of national integration: the case of Sind", in S. Akbar Ali (ed.), *Regional Imbalances and the National Question in Pakistan*, Lahore, Vanguard Books, 1992, p. 168.

primarily to remedy Sindhi underrepresentation in the administration: in 1973 the Muhajirs still occupied 30.1 per cent of jobs in the central administration (and 33.5 per cent of the senior civil service posts), whereas they only made up 7 per cent of the total population; while Sindhis only held 3.1 per cent (and 2.7 per cent) of them—see Table 4.2.

Table 4.2: Breakdown of Pakistani communities in the administration and quotas set up in 1973 (%)

Province	Quota	General administration (1973)	Senior civil service (1973)	General administration (1983)	Senior civil service (1983)
Punjab	50.0	49.2	53.5	54.9	55.8
NWFP	11.5	10.5	7	13.4	11.6
Urban Sindh	7.6	30.1	33.5	17.4	20.2
Rural Sindh	11.4	3.1	2.7	5.4	5.1
Balochistan	3.5	2.5	1.5	3.4	3.1
Northern regions and FATA	4.0	2.6	1.3	3.6	3.4
Azad Kashmir	2.0	1.8	0.5	1.9	0.9
Total	90*	100.0	100.0	100.0	100.0
		N=84 749	N=6 011	N=134 310	N=11 816

* A total of 100 is arrived at by adding the 10% national recruitment on the basis of merit.
Source: after Charles H. Kennedy, *Bureaucracy in Pakistan*, Karachi, Oxford University Press, 1987, p. 194.

The new quotas did not radically alter the balance of power within the administration. But the trend at least moved in the right direction for the Sindhis, and countered certain Sindhi nationalist arguments, such as the one predicting for their "compatriots" an irreversible marginalisation within their own country. The spectre of decline actually loomed larger over the Muhajirs who lost posts in the nation's civil service.

The last of Bhutto's noteworthy measures, nationalisation of industries and businesses conducted in the framework of a leftwing policy that will be discussed in the second part of this book, particularly penalised the Karachi business community dominated by Muhajirs although the Sindhis did not necessarily reap the benefits of it.

During the PPP's first stint in power some of the grievances on which Sindhi nationalism prospered were thus defused. Not only did a minority that had never backed the "Pakistan project" en masse wound up being represented at the highest level of the state by one of its own, but this man, Z.A. Bhutto, and his party, the PPP, had managed to enact measures in favour of his community. It became all the easier to support a Pakistani nation as a Sindhi turned out to be in a position to govern it.

From Bhutto to Bhutto: The Conquest of Power as an Antidote to Sindhi Nationalism

This achievement was seriously called into question at the end of Bhutto's rule, a reconfirmation that the presence of one of their own at the head of the state was a decisive factor in the Sindhi's eyes. Toward the end of the 1970s, Sindhi nationalism was indeed rekindled when General Zia, a Punjabi, ousted Bhutto. His death sentence, handed down, in appeal, by a tribunal primarily composed of Punjabis[19] and his subsequent execution made him a Sindhi martyr, all the more so as his entire family was sent into exile or placed under house arrest.[20]

Furthermore, under Zia, Punjabis were once again favoured over Sindhis. By February 1978, 1,746 Sindhis had already been sacked from the provincial administration. As for the senior civil service, in 1983, 55.8 per cent of the staff were Punjabis, 11.6 per cent were from the NWFP, 20.2 per cent urban Sindhis (a large majority of them Muhajirs), 5.1 per cent Sindhis from rural areas in the province and 3.1 per cent Balochis. In state-owned enterprises, the proportion of Punjabis was estimated to be 41 per cent and urban Sindhis 47 per cent, compared to 6 per cent from the NWFP, 3.5 per cent from rural Sindh and 1 per cent from Balochistan.[21] Moreover, General Zia, anxious to stifle any dissidence from Sindhis who denounced his usurpation of power and the "murder" of Bhutto, tightened his grip on the regional administration.

These circumstances explain the success of the Movement for the Restoration of Democracy in Sindh. Although the movement was launched

---

[19] The four Punjabi judges upheld the death sentence against the three others hailing from "minority provinces" See Omar Noman, *Pakistan—Political and Economic History since 1947*, London, Kegan Paul International, 1992, p. 193.

[20] Michel Boivin and Rémy Delage, "Benazir en odeur de sainteté. Naissance d'un lieu de culte au Pakistan", *Archives de sciences sociales des religions*, no. 151, July–Sept. 2010, pp. 189–211.

[21] Charles H. Kennedy, *Bureaucracy in Pakistan*, Karachi, Oxford University Press, 1987, p. 194.

by a coalition of the main opposition parties nationwide, it met with particular resonance in Sindh due to the regional context and the PPP's pivotal role in this agitation.[22] 45,000 troops were deployed to quash it over a six-month period, resulting in about 300 deaths. Underground tracts circulating at the time called for a Sindhi Desh, a "Sindhi nation". One of the movement's leaders, Mumtaz Bhutto, outlined a programme reminiscent of Mujibur Rahman's Six-Point Programme in that its main demand was for the institution of a confederate structure in which Sindh would enjoy considerable autonomy.[23]

His cousin Benazir Bhutto, who had returned to Pakistan after years in exile, was however far more moderate.[24] The success of her father, Zulfikar Ali Bhutto, at the polls in 1970—particularly in Punjab—had proved to her that a Sindhi could govern Pakistan. This precedent probably induced her and many other Sindhis to shy away from a form of Sindhi nationalism that advocated a confederate or autonomist perspective. Benazir Bhutto instead chose the national political route, thereby following in her father's footsteps. She took over the PPP leadership and led the party to victory in the 1988 elections, which hailed a return to democracy after Zia's death that year. Although it won 52 out of the 113 seats reserved for Punjab in the general elections, the PPP still had the air of a Sindhi party in 1988, having won all the seats in the rural Sindh areas and a two-thirds majority in the provincial assembly, whereas it only managed to win 94 of the 240 seats in the Punjab assembly. The Sindhi nationalist parties, on the other hand, won no seats at all.[25] Benazir Bhutto—who, like her father in 1973, had arrested

---

[22] Omar Noman, *Pakistan*, op. cit., p. 196.

[23] For details on these eight demands, see ibid., pp. 196–197. The main ones were as follows:

1. The confederation would be made up of states (the word was preferred to 'province' at the time in the Pakistani institutional vocabulary).
2. These states would be autonomous and sovereign. They would each have their own flag.
3. The central authorities would only keep defence, foreign relations, currency, communications, coordination of the states' economy and national assembly elections.
4. The confederation would be a parliamentary democracy.
5. The Prime Ministership would rotate among the various states.

[24] Selig Harrison, "Ethnicity and the Political Stalemate in Pakistan", in Ali Bannazizi and Myron Weiner (eds), *The State, Religion and Ethnic Politics*, Syracuse, Syracuse University Press, 1986, pp. 281–82.

[25] Their fragmentation precipitated their decline. Jiye Sind, G.M. Syed's party, was

G.M. Syed in 1990 (he would die in 1995) without causing much emotion among the Sindhis—had emerged as representative of the Sindhis at the helm of a party that remained well entrenched in the province. The fact that a Sindhi became prime minister again argued in favour of renewed Sindhi allegiance to Pakistan, which did not mean that Sindhi nationalism was dead as evident from the creation of the Sindh Taraqqi Pasand Party in 1991.[26]

This oscillation between defiance towards and identification with the Pakistani project, depending on the ethnic identity of the country's leader, is however indicative of the weakness of state institutions. The state has not managed to free itself from regional particularisms. Instead of being above the fray, it has become the stakes in a contest among elites from different communities. In the case of the Sindhis, the fact that one of their own had become head of the government—and that there was a prospect of this accomplishment being repeated after he had been removed—helped to defuse the most virulent separatist tendencies. As of the 1970s, Sindh's political trajectory was largely in line with the rest of Pakistan. That was not so true of the other provinces.

The Baloch Self-Determination Movement

Balochistan came officially into existence in 1970 after the abolition of the One-Unit Scheme. But Baloch nationalism is much older. Its staunchest ideologues claim that it harks back to the twelfth century or at least to the creation, in 1666, of a Confederation comprising dozens of tribes and hav-

---

first affected by the defect of R.B. Palijo who created the Sind Awami Tehrik. In 1985 Mumtaz Bhutto had left the PPP to build an anti-Punjabi Sind-Baloch-Pashtun Front. See Ann Frotscher, *Claiming Pakistan*, op. cit., p. 206.

[26] In spite of its limited outreach, the STP "discreetly influences the politics of the PPP, because it has a tremendous barganing potential with that party. The latter is forced to take up the issues raised by the STP and other nationalist parties when it is in government. When the PPP is in opposition, it uses the nationakist groups to voice Sindhi nationalist issues" (Mohammad Waseem and Mariam Mufti, *Political Parties in Pakistan*, Organization & Power Structure, Lahore, Lahore University of Management Sciences, 2012, p. 69). However, in 2000, the STP was affected by the breakaway faction of Shafi Burfat who created the Jeay Sindh Muttahida Mahaz (JSMM), a movement that believed in armed struggle, whereas the STP Chairman, Dr Qadir Magsi, has opted for parliamentary politics (Sohail Sangi, "Sindhi nationalists stand divided", *Dawn*, 4 Dec. 2014 (http:// epaper.dawn.com/DetailImage.php?StoryImage=04_12_2014_001_005).

ing Kalat as its capital. Indeed, in the seventeenth century the Khan of Kalat was at the helm of a kingdom spreading from Kandahar (in today's Afghanistan) to the coast of Makran and Punjab. The British defeated the Khan in 1839 but gradually rebuilt an Agency of which the heir to the Khan of Kalat was the symbolic head in 1877, and whose capital was located in Quetta. Faithful to the indirect rule philosophy, the Raj abstained "from interfering with Baloch society but co-opted sardars (tribal chiefs), who retained considerable autonomy provided they had no objection to the (numerous) operations of the British army in Afghanistan".[27]

Although home to only 3 per cent of Pakistan's population—and nearly one-quarter of them live in Quetta—Balochistan makes up 42 per cent of the country's surface area and moreover occupies a strategic area on the border with Iran and Afghanistan. The Baloch population in fact is spread over several countries—Pakistan, Iran and Afghanistan—which explains the irredentist dimension of Baloch nationalism in Pakistan.[28]

The Making of Baloch Nationalism

After 1947, Baloch nationalism crystallised under the aegis of princely rulers opposed to the Pakistan project—and in reaction to Jinnah's policy.[29] In 1947, the Khan of Kalat opposed the new state but in March 1948 signed an instrument of accession with Jinnah, in spite of the opposition of tribal elders and his younger brother, Prince Adbul Karim—and after the Pakistani government sent in troops in March 1948.[30] This agreement "stipulated that all subjects except defence, external affairs and communication would be the domain of the state of Kalat".[31] It remained a dead letter, and Adbul Karim then tried to persuade the Baloch sardars to back the creation of an autonomous state in accordance with the Lahore Resolution of 1940. The

---

[27] Frédéric Grare, "Baloutchistan: fin de partie?" *Hérodote*, no. 139, 4th quarter, 2010, p. 105.

[28] During the period of British rule, in 1871 the Goldsmid Line gave one-quarter of the Baloch settlement area to the Persians, and later, in 1893, the Durand Line attributed a small portion of it to Afghanistan.

[29] Martin Axmann, *Back to the Future: the Khanate of Kalat and the Genesis of Baloch Nationalism, 1915–1955*, New York, Oxford University Press, 2008.

[30] On the origins of Baloch nationalism, see Taj Mohammed Breseeg, *Baloch Nationalism: Its Origins and Development*, Karachi, Royal Book Company, 2004.

[31] A report by Pak Institute for Peace Studies, *Conflict and Insecurity in Balochistan*, Islamabad, A Narratives Publication, 2012, p. 18.

Pakistani government managed to co-opt most of these leaders but Abdul Karim then founded a People's Party that continued to be the standard-bearer of Baloch nationalism.

This ideology was based less in a language than in an ethnic identity nurtured on invented traditions—including the "golden age" of the 12th Confederation of 48 tribes.[32] The Baloch actually come from two different linguistic groups, one that speaks Balochi, the other Brahui. Speakers of this latter language claim to be full-fledged Baloch, as the Kalat dynasty itself spoke Brahui. This linguistic fragmentation is coupled with another, tribal this time: the Baloch are divided into eighteen tribes. The largest of them, and the most inclined to resort to violent action against the central government, are traditionally the Marris, the Bugtis and the Mengals.[33] However divided, the Baloch had developed a certain solidarity over time, based on common resistance to outsiders attacks. But the Baloch nationalist movement developed mostly in reaction to the policies of the Pakistani state when they affected not only the interests of the Khan of Kalat but also of larger groups.

Several Baloch tribes shared common grievances against the government in the 1950s, ranging from Baloch underrepresentation in the local bureaucracy (which the People's Party had previously underlined) to the imposition of the One-Unit Scheme. It was in this context that the Baloch People Liberation Front took shape. While Marris had initiated the movement, it received the support of Bugtis and Mengals, especially after Ayub Khan's response to Baloch demands took a brutal turn. Indeed, in 1958–60, the Pakistani state arrested and executed many insurgents, including a 90-year-old chieftain, Sardar Nauroz Khan Zarakzai, who was hanged along with his son and five others after he had been invited to negotiate by the army.[34] Once again, the attitude of the Centre, instead of defusing an ethnic mobilisation, radicalized it.

---

[32] Paul Titus (ed.), *Marginality and Modernity: Ethnicity and Change in Post-Colonial Balochistan*, Karachi, Oxford University Press, 1996.

[33] Sylvia Matheson, *The Tigers of Baluchistan*, Karachi, Oxford University Press, 1967. On the Marris, see Robert N. Pehrson, *The Social Organisation of the Marri Baloch*, Chicago, Wenner-Gren Foundation, 1966.

[34] This episode was one of the reasons why Khair Bakhsh Marri turned to Baloch nationalism (Hasan Mansoor, "Khair Bakhsh Marri: a fighter all the way", *Dawn*, 11 June 2014, http://www.dawn.com/news/1111939/khair-bakhsh-marri-a-fighter-all-the-way/print).

This second Baloch uprising was still weakened by tribal divisions,[35] but a certain "detribalisation"[36] process had been initiated by a nascent middle class, and more especially by its youth, which drew part of its inspiration from Maoism and Marxism.[37] A third movement took place in the 1960s under the aegis of She Muhammad Marri. It was again crushed by the army.

The fourth "war of Balochistan", in 1973–7, was of a different magnitude— as its duration suggests. But it reconfirmed the key role of the state's policies. In 1972, a coalition formed by the National Awami Party (NAP—led by Wali Khan, son of Abdul Ghaffar Khan), which had its stronghold in the NWFP but into which the People's Party had merged, and the Jamiat-Ulema-i-Islam (an Islamic party also based in the NWFP—see infra—and backed by the sardars of Balochistan), won the elections in both provinces. The new Chief Minister, Attaullah Mengal, announced his determination to indigenize the administration of Balochistan by replacing civil servants from outside with "sons of the soil". The central government disapproved of this "spoils system" that would deprive much of the national elite—and primarily the Punjabis—of positions in the bureaucracy. Distribution of industrial investments was an additional bone of contention. Balochistan and the NWFP accused Islamabad of not doing enough to further development in their territory and thus wanted to take the reins of their own industrial policy.[38]

Z. A. Bhutto dismissed the Balochistan government in February 1973 on the grounds of its separatist activities, alleging that weapons—conveniently—discovered at the home of the Iraqi military attaché were intended for it. The NWFP government resigned in protest. With the Baloch national movement leaders in jail, its generally more radical second line of leadership then came to the fore. A guerrilla movement developed with many students in it ranks—whose nationalist rhetoric was again peppered with

---

[35] Malik Muhammed Saeed Dehwar, *Contemporary History of Balochistan*, Quetta, Third World Publications, 1994.

[36] Frédéric Grare, "Baloutchistan: fin de partie?" op. cit., p. 106.

[37] According to Selig Harrison, in 1963, there were 22 Baloch training camps stretching from Mengal tribal territory to the territory of the Marris, see Selig Harrison, *In Afghanistan's Shadow: Baluch Nationalism and Soviet Temptations*, New York/Washington DC, Carnegie Endowment for International Peace, 1981.

[38] For further detail, see Khalid B. Sayeed, *Politics in Pakistan—The Nature and Direction of Change*, New York, Praeger, 1980; in particular chapter 6 entitled "Pakistan's central government versus Baluchi and Pakhtun aspirations", pp. 113–138.

Marxist and Maoist references. For four years, the Baloch People's Liberation Front (BPLF)--created by Attaullah Mengal—and the Baloch Students' Organisation (BSO)—founded in 1967—were at the heart of an insurrection that involved over 10,000 combatants. But tribal divisions and the sardars' opportunism weakened the movement from the start. For instance, "Akbar Bugti, chief of the tribe that goes by the same name and one of the instigators behind the insurrection, refrained from taking part in armed struggle and was even considered a traitor by some of his peers".[39] In fact, after having suffered under the policies of Ayub Khan, Bugti allied with Z.A. Bhutto, backing the dismissal of the government in Quetta in 1973, for which he was rewarded with the post of provincial governor, a position he occupied for one year before falling out with Bhutto. More than any other, Akbar Bugti illustrates the facility with which sardars could switch from cause to enemy and vice versa according to what Anatol Lieven calls "the old tribal tradition of alternating between rebellion and participation".[40] This political culture has much to do with tribal rivalries. Some sardars aligned themselves even more strongly with the Centre when they needed allies to fight other local leaders. Bugti, for instance, was locked in a competition with the Marri elders. Each of these leaders had their semi-private army. The Balochistan Republican Army (BRA) therefore drew from "a personal tribal militia for Nawab Akbar Bugti amid his rivalries with Marri Tribes".[41] And the Balochistan Liberation Army (BLA) was created by the Marris in this manner emulating the guerrillas of the 1970s.

The Pakistan army sent in approximately 80,000 soldiers to crush the rebellion with logistical support from the Shah of Iran who was afraid that the disturbance would spill over into western Balochistan.[42] The war claimed about 5,300 lives among the Baloch and 3,300 among the army.[43] The insurrection, finally quashed in 1977, marked a turning point. While at first the Baloch "were not fighting for independence but rather for regional autonomy within a radically restructured, confederal Pakistani constitu-

---

[39] Frédéric Grare, "Balouchistan: fin de partie?" op. cit., p. 110.

[40] Anatol Lieven, *Pakistan. A Hard Country*, op. cit., p. 349.

[41] A report by Pak Institute for Peace Studies, *Conflict and Insecurity in Balochistan*, op. cit., p. 66.

[42] Tehran also tried to convince the Afghan authorities to recognize the Durand Line at the time when Prince Daud, who had just come to power in Kabul in 1973, was backing the Pakistani insurgents in the name of a "free Balochistan".

[43] Urmila Phadnis, *Ethnicity and Nation-Building in South Asia*, New Delhi, Sage, 1989 p. 183 and Selig Harrison, *In Afghanistan's Shadow*, op. cit., p. 274.

tional framework", by the time the hostilities were over in 1977, separatist sentiment had "greatly intensified".[44] Once again, state centralism had been a decisive factor in the emergence of self-determination movements.

General Zia wielded carrot and stick in dealing with the Baloch nationalists. He was intractable with the hardliners. But he promised economic development measures for the province. He also managed to appease a segment of the Baloch nationalists by releasing several thousand prisoners and granting amnesty to those who had fled to Afghanistan or Iran. Some chose to go into exile. One was Attaullah Khan Mengal, who went to London to found the Sindh Baloch Pashtun Front with the help of Mumtaz Bhutto. Mengal continued to advocate armed struggle to achieve a confederate regime. Another exile, Khair Bux Marri, instead chose Afghanistan, where he headed the Balochistan Liberation Army (BLA) formed in the early 1980s, and campaigned for the creation of a Great Balochistan that would include Baloch territories in Pakistan, Iran and Afghanistan.

Those who remained in Pakistan adopted a more moderate stance. Former governor Ghous Buksh Bizenjo for instance established the Pakistan National Party with the hope—or on the pretext—of putting pressure on Islamabad to enforce better administration of the federal arrangements enshrined in the Constitution of 1973. The PNP also campaigned in favour of redrawing the provincial borders, limiting them to areas where the Balochi language and/or culture were in use.[45] With Bizenjo's death in 1989, the PNP merged with other, smaller parties to form the Baloch National Party (BNP), which continued to play the political game.

Baloch nationalism in the 1980s was not toned down merely due to the departure of extremists and the collaboration of certain notables. It also resulted from the fact that the movement could hardly rely on support from the middle class and intelligentsia, both of which were fairly small in a province where the literacy rate is the lowest in the country, at 10.1 per cent in 1981.[46] The region's cultural homogeneity also continued to

---

[44] Ibid., pp. 274–75.

[45] Baloch speakers are now only a majority in four districts, Karan, Makran, Sibi and Shagai.

[46] In contrast, the literacy rate of Punjab, Sind and the NWFP were respectively 27.4%, 31.5% (thanks to Karachi) and 16.7%. See M.G. Ahmed, *Causes of Low Literacy Rate in Pakistan*, Faislabad, Institute of Engineering and Fertilizer Research, 2011, p. 13. Available at: http://www.academia.edu/944975/Causes_of_low_literacy_rate_in_Pakistan_by_Muhammad_Gulraiz_Ahmed (Accessed on September 15, 2013).

decline[47] as Balochistan attracted a large number of immigrants (in 1981, 57 per cent of the inhabitants spoke Balochi or Brahui, 28 per cent Pashto and 8 per cent Sindhi). More than that, the Baloch were migrating to other Pakistani provinces (one-third of the 4 million Baloch in Pakistan lived at the time in Sindh, the NWFP or Punjab) or were moving abroad at a steady rate, especially to countries in the Persian Gulf, depriving the province of its life-blood and a youth that otherwise might have been in the vanguard of nation-alist movement. Although this population drain defused certain centrifugal forces by enabling a whole generation of Baloch to "seek their fortune" elsewhere, the diaspora has maintained strong ties with the homeland and proved to be a useful resource in the nationalist revival of the 2000s.

The Collusive Transactions of the 1990s to the Current War

The return of democracy in 1988 hailed the return in force of Baloch nota-bles, who were prepared to make considerable compromises with the cen-tral government. Even if the traditional sardars who had been unable or unwilling to take part in the revolt in the early 1970s were losing ground,[48] they remained highly influential in Baloch areas, as was evident in the rise in power of the Baloch National Alliance (BNA), which had just emerged from the rapprochement of the BNM and the new party of Nawab Akbar Bugti, the Jamhoori Watan Party (JWP). The BNA won ten seats in the regional assembly in the 1988 elections. In Pashtun areas, the JUI strength-ened its positions and won four seats in the National Assembly, twice as many as the BNA. The Baloch party also had to reckon with national par-ties such as the PPP (one seat) and the other pan-Pakistani alliance, Islami Jamhoori Ittehad (IJI, the Islamic Democratic Alliance), at the time led by the chief minister of Punjab, Nawaz Sharif (two seats).[49]

Baloch politics remained prisoner of faction fights. While Nawab Bugti became Chief Minister in 1988, the alliance he relied on, the BNA, was

---

[47] The province's cultural unity had already been damaged by the redrawing of Pakistan's provinces decided in 1970 after the One-Unit Scheme was abolished. The Baloch-majority districts of Jacobadad and Dera Ghazi Khan were incorpo-rated into Sindh and Punjab respectively, whereas the Pashtun-majority districts of Pishin, Zhob and Loralai were included in Balochistan (International Crisis Group, *Pakistan: The Forgotten Conflict in Balochistan*, Asia Briefing no. 69 from Oct. 2007).

[48] Mohammad Waseem, *Politics and the State in Pakistan*, op. cit., p. 438.

[49] Akbar Zaidi (ed.), *Regional Imbalances and the National Question in Pakistan*, Lahore, Vanguard Books, 1992.

short-lived because the BNM splintered in 1990 in two groups, one directed by Dr. Hayee Baloch and the other by Akhtar Mengal. Soon after, leaders of the Mengal tribe formerly in favour of armed struggle entered electoral politics. Sardar Ataullah Khan Mengal himself, who had distanced himself from the Sindh Baloch Pashtun Front shortly after it was created, returned to Pakistan to preside over the merger of the BNM faction of his son and the Pakistan National Party (PNP) of Ghous Buksh Bizenjo. The party which emerged from this move in 1996, the Baloch National Party, was directed by Akhtar Mengal.[50]

Baloch politicians had already started to strike alliances with the parties in power in Islamabad. With the blessing of the then Prime Minister Benazir Bhutto, one of them, Zulfikar Ali Khan Magsi, led a coalition government formed on August 1996 with members from the PPP, the Pakistan Muslim League and the Jamiat-ul-Ulema Islam (JUI). In the February 1997 elections, no single regional party obtained the majority. Out of forty-three seats in the Balochistan assembly, the Balochistan National Party won only ten of them, placing it in the lead but still very much in a minority position. Akhtar Mengal, thus formed a government with the support of a four-party coalition including the PPP. At the same time, the BNP backed Prime Minister Nawaz Sharif in the National Assembly.[51] Mengal however resigned in 1998 on the pretext that Baloch honour had been tarnished by the central government's failing to inform the authorities in Quetta of nuclear testing in their region. In fact, the main bone of contention between Mengal and Sharif had to do with the central government's unlawful confiscation of revenues from the exploitation of natural gas in Balochistan. Once again, an identity discourse was overdetermined by conflicts of interests.[52] This issue and the general attitude of the Centre were to be the root causes for what is known as the fifth Baloch war.

The rekindling of Baloch agitation can in fact be explained here again as much by material as by cultural factors, and the radical turn it took by the government's centralising policies and the violent means used to achieve them.

The exploitation of natural gas resources in Balochistan is an old bone of contention. The deposits near Sui and Pirkoh (both in Dera Bugti dis-

---

[50] Mohammad Waseem and Mariam Mufti, *Political Parties in Pakistan*, p. 61.

[51] *The News*, 20 February 1997, p. 1.

[52] When he resigned, Mengal declared that he was acting in defence of Baloch identity. See *The Muslim*, 31 July 1998.

trict), discovered in 1953, have supplied Punjabi cities such as Multan and Rawalpindi since 1964. In the district of Dera Bugti only the main town itself is supplied with natural gas—and this only since the mid-1990s due to the establishment of a paramilitary camp by the federal state. In 2004, however, the dispute was revived on other grounds: the comparatively low pricing of the export gas, the percentage of royalties allocated by the central government to the province of Balochistan and the fact that the "centre owe(d) the province billions of rupees in gas revenue arrears".[53] The province was receiving far lower amounts than other natural gas producing areas, Punjab and Sindh[54] whereas, at that time, Balochistan supplied 70 per cent of Pakistan's total gas requirements (as against 45 per cent today).

This issue, which like the Bengal question of the past, can be analysed in terms of internal colonialism, is coupled with another issue pertaining to the development of a deepwater port in Gwadar, a place to which Baloch are emotionally attached—one of there heroes, Hammal Jeayand, apparently fought there a key battle against the Portuguese occupation. This construction project—developed with the help of China in a strategic location near the Persian Gulf through which so many supertankers pass—was not only undertaken without immediate economic benefits for the Baloch (out of 600 workers hired, only about thirty jobs were filled by local people), but further threatened the province's demographic balance. The government's proposed project foresaw a growth of the city's population from 60,000 to 2 million inhabitants, the newcomers originating mainly from neighbouring regions, particularly Punjab. This project became the focus of strong resentment.[55] All the more since the policy, which the Baloch labelled colonialist, went along with a plan to build three additional army garrisons in Balochistan, in Gwadar, in Kohlu (capital of the Marri tribe) and in Dera Bugti (capital of the Bugtis).[56]

Political considerations compounded these economic, demographic and military issues. In 2002, General Musharraf—who had seized power in 1999—prepared the ground for a Baloch insurgency in two different ways. First, "the military rigged the elections and reinvigorated its long-stand-

---

[53] A report by Pak Institute for Peace Studies, *Conflict and insecurity in Balochistan*, op. cit., p. 28.

[54] Frédéric Grare, "Baloutchistan: fin de partie?", op. cit., p. 113.

[55] From that time, many "outsiders"—particularly Punjabis—were able to buy land in Gwadar.

[56] Frédéric Grare, "Baloutchistan: fin de partie?" op. cit., p. 114.

ing alliance with the region's mullahs, helping the Muttahida Majlis-e-Mahal (MMA), a coalition of religious Islamic parties to gain power in Balochistan".[57] Secondly, Musharraf introduced a "decentralisation plan" that amounted to forming local governments that were directly linked to Islamabad. It was actually yet another political centralisation manoeuvre, which did not antagonise Baloch leaders alone, but the Baloch had other reasons than this for their discontent. Thus, the Baloch middle class—not as insignificant as in the 1970s and a factor of national unity through a "detribalization" process—mobilised through the Baloch Student Organisation (BSO) and the Baloch National Movement (BNM) led by Abdul Hayee Baloch to protest against its underrepresentation in the Pakistani state apparatus. In 2005, not only was there not a single Baloch at the helm of one one of the 200 corporations and not one Baloch among Pakistan's ambassadors but there were only 502 young Baloch recruited in the army.[58]

Those who had never compromised relaunched an agitation in this context. Khair Bux Marri, at the helm of the Baloch Liberation Army, came back from Afghanistan and attacked the gas pipelines.[59] Although all the Baloch nationalist forces had formed in 2003 a coalition, the Baloch Ittehad, which supported a guerrilla-based strategy,[60] the other leaders were usually more moderate. But they were further alienated by Musharraf's intransigence. In January 2005, the president-general warned the Baloch: "Don't push us. This is not the Seventies. They [the Baloch] will not even know what has hit them [when the army strikes]".[61]

Although the Marris—whose BLA has about 3,000 fighters[62]—were the first to get involved, shortly afterward the Bugtis stepped in behind Akbar Bugti. The radicalisation of the Bugtis had been precipitated by the rape of

---

[57] Frédéric Grare, *Balochistan. The State versus the Nation*, Washington DC, Carnegie Endowment for International Peace, 2013, p. 11.

[58] A report by Pak Institute for Peace Studies, *Conflict and Insecurity in Balochistan*, op. cit., p. 147.

[59] Farhan Hanif Siddiqui, "Security Dynamics in Pakistani Balochistan: religious activism and ethnic conflict in the war on terror", *Asian Affairs*, 39 (3), 2012, p. 165.

[60] Martin Axmann, "Phoenix from the Ashes? The Baloch National Movement and Its Recent Revival", in Carina Jahani, Agnes Korn and Paul Titus (eds), *The Baloch and Others. Linguistic, Historical and Socio-Political Perspectives on Pluralism in Balotchistan*, Wiesbaden, Reichert Verlag, 2008, p. 284.

[61] Cited in Farhan Hanif Siddiqui, "Security Dynamics in Pakistani Balochistan", op. cit., p. 165.

[62] Frédéric Grare, *Balochistan. The State versus the Nation*, p. 5.

a female doctor of their tribe by an army captain in Sui in January 2005.[63] Akbar Bugti might have been tempted by compromises again, since he was mostly interested in getting "for his tribe a greater share of the royalties" generated by gas exploitation,[64] but this criminal action complicated that option. Musharraf's policy in any event soon made any negotiations impossible: "Extrajudicial executions, torture, illegal arrests carried out by security forces and intelligence agencies were on the rise."[65] General Musharraf attributed the revival of the Baloch movement to aid that India was providing to the "insurgents" through its consulates in Afghanistan. In August 2006, Akbar Bugti was killed in an air raid he may not have been the target of. This action "virtually changed the entire landscape of the Baloch resistance against the center".[66] At Bugti's funeral in Quetta on 29 August 2006 young Balochs tore down portraits of Jinnah—whose residency in Ziarat (North Balochistan) was later torched in June 2013.[67] The Baloch war for national liberation had one more martyr around whom all the Baloch startyed to rally. On 21 September a Baloch National Jirga was convened in Quetta in order to reconsider "Balochistan's accession to Pakistan".[68] The Baloch Republican Army (BRA) immediately grew out of Bugti's JWP, at the instigation of his grandson, Baramdagh Bugti, now exiled in Switzerland. The following year, Balach Marri, the son of Khair Bux Marri, was killed in Afghanistan and Akhtar Mengal was put in jail. Between 2002 and 2007, fifty-four opponents disappeared according to the Human Rights Commission of Pakistan.[69] According to another NGO, Human Rights Watch, citing the Pakistan's Interior Ministry, "1,102 Baloch were forcibly disappeared during General Musharraf's rule".[70] In this con-

---

[63] Farhan Hanif Siddiqui, "Security Dynamics in Pakistani Balochistan: religious activism and ethnic conflict in the war on terror", p. 165.

[64] Frédéric Grare, *Balochistan. The State versus the Nation*, p. 3.

[65] Frédéric Grare, "Balouchistan: fin de partie?" op. cit.

[66] A report by Pak Institute for Peace Studies, *Conflict and Insecurity in Balochistan*, p. 113.

[67] It was restored in 2014 and reopened on August 14 in presence of Prime Minister Nawaz Sharif and COAS Raheel Sharif.

[68] Ibid.

[69] Human Rights Commission of Pakistan, "Balochistan, Blinkered Slide into Chaos: Report of an HRCP Fact-Finding Mission", Lahore, June 2011, pp. 31–34. Available at: http://hrcp-web.org/publication/book/blinkered-slide-into-chaos/ (Accessed on September 15, 2013).

[70] *"We can torture, kill, or keep you for years". Enforced Disappearances by Pakistan Security Forces in Balochistan*, New York, Human Rights Watch, 2011, p. 24.

text, a moderate like Akhtar Mengal preferred to leave for London immediately after he was freed. He returned soon afterwards but boycotted the 2008 elections which were rigged again (in September 2011 the Election Commission of Pakistan, after checking the electoral rolls, revealed that in 2008, 65 per cent of Baloch voters were fake).

In reaction to army abuse, involving in particular the disappearance of many Baloch activists and journalists, the head of the Supreme Court, Iftikhar Chaudhry, who had been the Chief Justice of the High Court of Balochistan, demanded explanations from Musharraf—to no avail. After he left office and the PPP won the 2008 elections, the new government pledged to change tack. In April it formed a Shaheed Benazir Bhutto Reconciliatory Committee on Balochistan which handed in its report in October 2008. It took another year, however, for the government to present thirty-nine concrete measures to parliament, including:

> the return of political exiles, the release of jailed Baloch political activists, the promise of an investigation into political murders (especially the death of Akbar Bugti), army withdrawal from certain key areas (particularly Sui), a moratorium on building new garrisons, a reform of the mechanisms by which federal resources are allocated to the provinces,[71] job creation and increased control over the resources in Balochistan, all new development projects requiring approval by the provincial government.[72]

The Baloch nationalists instantly rejected this roadmap and demanded greater autonomy as well as a halt to military operations. But Mengal came back from exile to propose a Six Points Plan. However, he was ignored and the Balochistan Package was not implemented.

The army's modus operandi has not changed since Musharraf. According to the Human Rights Commission of Pakistan, out of the 143 missing persons recorded in 2011, 89 of them disappeared between 2008 and 2010.[73] Between July 2010 and May 2011, 140 mutilated bodies of insurgents were recovered in Balochistan.[74] In 2014, the situation had not improved, as an article in *The Express Tribune* shows:

---

[71] The mechanism in effect considers population as the only relevant criterion, thereby favouring the most densely populated province, Punjab. In future, the socioeconomic lag (measured in particular by the share of the population living below poverty level) should be taken into account.

[72] Frédéric Grare, "Balouchistan: fin de partie?", op. cit., pp. 117–118.

[73] Farhan Hanif Siddiqui, "Security Dynamics in Pakistani Balochistan", op. cit., p. 174, note 45. In 2010, the government of Balochistan was approached by the families of 992 missing persons.

[74] Human Rights Commission of Pakistan, "Balochistan, Blinkered Slide into Chaos: Report of an HRCP Fact-Finding Mission", op. cit., pp. 31–34 and pp. 35–42.

According to a home department report, at least 164 bullet-riddled bodies have been found in Balochistan during the last 12 months. Of them, 80 were found in Quetta, 41 in Kalat division—comprising Khuzdar and Mastung districts—41 in Makran division—comprising Panjgur, Gwadar and Turbat districts—six in Nasirabad division, 13 in Zhob district and eight in Sibi Division, says the report, a copy of which is available with *The Express Tribune*. Of the victims, the report says 71 have been identified as ethnic Baloch, 35 Pashtun, 19 people of other ethnicities, while 41 victims could not be identified.[75]

The point of what was now known as "kill-and-dump operations" was probably not only to punish but also to intimidate the Baloch nationalists. On 3 April 2009, the president of the Baloch National Movement, who campaigned in favour of an independent Great Balochistan, was abducted from his lawyer's office and his body found in the mountains six days later.

In response, since the mid-2000s, Baloch nationalists have conducted targeted killings of "foreigners", whether Punjabi or of other origins, leading to the flight of those who had come from other provinces, particularly teachers, engineers and doctors. In 2006, Punjabis of Quetta created the Punjabi Ittehad Pakistan, whose president was attacked in 2007.[76] The situation has worsened since then. For instance on 14 August 2010, insurgents hijacked a Quetta-Lahore bus and killed ten Punjabi-speaking passengers. In 2010, 250 "outsiders", mostly Punjabis, were killed, which resulted in the departure of 100,000 people, mostly Punjabis. Those who stayed continued to suffer. Between January and May 2011, eighteen targeted killings (as they are now known) claimed twenty-eight lives.[77]

Lately, Balochistan has been one of the Pakistani provinces the most badly affected by political violence. In Quetta alone, terrorist attacks increased by 39 per cent compared to the previous year in 2012, according to the Pak Institute for Peace Studies.[78] The year 2013 was even more violent.

[75] Shezad Baloch, "164 bodies found in Balochistan this year: report", *The Express Tribune*, 31 December 2014 (http://tribune.com.pk/story/814993/164-bodies-found-in-balochistan-this-year-report/?print=true).

[76] Luc Bellon, "La ville de Quetta et la guerilla baloutche. Enjeux d'une violence politique urbaine", in Gilles Dorronsoro and Olivier Grosjean (eds), *Identités et politique. De la différenciation culturelle au conflit*, Paris, Presses de Sciences Po, 2014, p. 242.

[77] Human Rights Commission of Pakistan, "Balochistan, Blinkered Slide into Chaos: Report of an HRCP Fact-Finding Mission", op. cit., pp. 45–46.

[78] *Pakistan Security Report—2012*, Islamabad, Pak Institute for Peace Studies, 2012, p. 7.

Table 4.3: Terrorist attacks in Balochistan and resulting casualties

	No. of attacks	No. of killed	No. of wounded
2006	403	277	676
2007	536	224	564
2008	692	296	807
2009	792	386	1070
2010	737	600	1 117
2011	640	710	853
2012	474	631	1 032
2013	487	727	1 577

Sources: Pak Institute for Peace Studies, *Pakistan Security Report* for the years 2006, 2007, 2008, 2009, 2010, 2011, 2012 and 2013, Islamabad, PIPS (www.san-pips.com).

The data compiled by the Pak Institute for Peace Studies (PIPS) show that while the number of attacks has been diminishing since 2010, it remains high, and these attacks are, on average, more lethal. The figures are aggregates and it is not easy to identify the share of this violence that can be ascribed to the Baloch nationalists. But certain PIPS indications make it possible for certain years. For instance, in 2009, the Institute mentioned that Baloch nationalists were responsible for 92 per cent of the violent actions of the year.[79] In 2010, out of 737 terrorist attacks, 614 were perpetrated by "nationalist insurgents"—the others had a "religious" origin.[80] In 2012, out of 474 attacks, 373 were perpetrated by nationalists—121 by the Baloch Liberation Front and 131 by the Baloch Liberation Army—and 62 by sectarian groups (be they Sunni or Shia).[81] In its 2013 report, PIPS wrote that "Out of 487 reported terrorist attacks in Balochistan, 424 were perpetrated by nationalist insurgents".[82]

The 2013 elections did not defuse tensions in Balochistan. Mengal's BNP contested but lost and the party workers even asked their leaders to leave the assembly where they won two seats out of sixty-five.[83] They did not go

[79] *Pakistan Security Report—2009*, Islamabad, Pak Institute for Peace Studies, 2009, p. 12.
[80] *Pakistan Security Report—2010*, Islamabad, Pak Institute for Peace Studies, 2010, p. 9.
[81] *Pakistan Security Report—2012*, Islamabad, Pak Institute for Peace Studies, 2012, p. 10 and p. 17.
[82] *Pakistan Security Report—2013*, Islamabad, Pak Institute for Peace Studies, 2014, p. 18.
[83] Amanullah Kasi, "BNP-M workers want their leaders to quit assemblies", *Dawn*, 9 juin 2013 (http://www.dawn.com/news/1017000).

that far, but resorted to demonstrations when those who were already more radical continued to rely on violence. While attacks on gas pipelines had dropped from sixty-eight in 2009 to nine in 2010,[84] they are on the rise again. In 2014, gas pipelines were sabotaged eighty-four times.[85] In February 2014, militants attacked the installations of the Sui Northern Gas Pipelines Ltd and for the first time the three pipelines were blown up simultaneously near Rahim Yar Khan, depriving Punjab of gas for several days.[86] The Baloch Republican Army of Brahamdagh Bugti claimed responsibility for this action.

But why did the BNP (Mengal) fare so badly in the election? First of all, the demographic balance of power among ethnic groups in the province worked against it.[87] Pashtuns probably make up 40 per cent of the province's population and dominate twelve districts out of thirty, including Quetta.[88] They have sealed a sort of non-aggression pact with the army and play the electoral game that most Baloch nationalists have lately decided to boycott. Their main party is the Pakhtunkhwa Milli Awami Party (PkMAP) that has succeeded the Pakhtunkhwa National Party created by Abdul Samad Khan Achakzai, a follower of Abdul Ghaffar Khan, when he left the NAP in 1970.[89] His son, Mahmood Khan Achakzai, who took over from him after he was assassinated in 1973,[90] breathed new life into the party in 1986

---

[84] A report by Pak Institute for Peace Studies, *Conflict and insecurity in Balochistan*, p. 41.

[85] Shezad Baloch, "164 bodies found in Balochistan this year: report", *The Express Tribune*, 31 December 2014 (http://tribune.com.pk/story/814993/164-bodies-found-in-balochistan-this-year-report/?print=true).

[86] "Explosion near Rahim Yar Khan damages 3 gas pipelines", *The Express Tribune*, 11 Feb. 2014 (http://tribune.com.pk/story/669777/bra-insurgents-blow-up-three-gas-pipelines-near-rahim-yar-khan/?print=true).

[87] According to the 1998 census, the Baloch make up 54.7% of the province and the Pashtuns 29.6%. But this figure is underestimated due to the call to boycott the census issued by Pashtun parties who thus hoped not to appear to have too large a population in the eyes of native-born Balochs, so that Afghan Pashtun refugees could acquire Pakistani citizenship in greater numbers. Pashtuns claim to make up between 35 and 40% of the population in Balochistan.

[88] A report by Pak Institute for Peace Studies, *Conflict and insecurity in Balochistan*, p. 32.

[89] See: http://storyofpakistan.com/abdul-samad-khan-achakzai/ (Accessed on September 15, 2013).

[90] The Bugtis have been accused by some of his assassination. See: http://hatefsvoice.wordpress.com/tag/khan-samad-khan-achakzai/ (Accessed on September 15, 2013).

and changed its name three years later. The PkMAP, as it is now known, has gradually asserted itself, so much so that in 2013, it won fourteen seats (second only to the PML(N)'s twenty-two seats) in the provincial assembly and formed a ruling coalition with the PML(N) and the National Party (one of the few Baloch parties that contested the elections and won ten seats). Even more importantly, perhaps, the PkMAP was for the first time in a position to have one of its leaders appointed governor of Balochistan in the person of Muhammad Khan Achakzai, Mahmood's elder brother. As Luc Bellon points out, in Quetta, the question of the rivalry between Balochs and Pashtuns is usually not talked about. But it may become the elephant in the room if Balochs continue to lose ground vis-à-vis the Pashtuns who already dominate the local economy. Balochs may have to give up their claim on the political headquarters of the province.[91]

While the growing influence of the Pashtuns may be one of the handicaps facing the Baloch nationalists in their own province—which remains to be seen because the former may happily concentrate on the northern part of Balochistan and leave the rest to the ethnic Balochs who may concentrate on Southern Balochistan only[92]—there are possibly others. Aside from the Pashtuns, large numbers of Hazaras from Afghanistan migrated to Pakistani Balochistan, particularly to Quetta, where they are reportedly between 200,000 and 300,000[93] and thriving, particularly in the army, due to a decent level of education. Furthermore, ethnic boundaries have also been blurred by population shifts and interethnic mixing such that, for instance, "many 'Sindhis' are in fact from Baloch tribes".[94]

In addition to this ethnic dilution—which may explain why according to a 2012 survey only 37 per cent of the Balochistan people favoured inde-

---

[91] Luc Bellon, "La ville de Quetta et la guerilla baloutche", op. cit., 244–45.

[92] Jameel Bugti, the son of Nawab Akbar Bugti, argued that the Pashtuns may be entitled to ask for Northern Balochistan to merge with K-P, but that the redrawing of the provincial borders may result too in the inclusion of the Punjabi districts of Rajanpur, Jacobadad and Dera Ghazi Khan in Balochistan (A report by Pak Institute for Peace Studies, *Conflict and Insecurity in Balochistan*, p. 33).

[93] However, a report in *Dawn* stated that the Hazara population in Quetta had been up to 600,000 before 100,000 of them fled to Rawalpindi-Islamabad because of the anti-Shia persecutions that we'll study below (Irfan Haider, "A Tough Life for the Displaced Hazaras in Twin Cities," *Dawn*, 9 March 2014, http://http://www.dawn.com/news/1091921/a-tough-life-for-the-displaced-hazaras-in-twin-cities).

[94] Anatol Lieven, *Pakistan. A Hard Country*, op. cit., p. 342.

pendence[95]—Baloch nationalism may fail to achieve its goals mostly because of the inflexible attitude of the Centre. In addition to its usual rigidity, the Pakistani government may be all the more reluctant to adopt a conciliatory attitude because the Baloch movement has become an international issue with the awakening of Baloch separatism in Iran. In October 2009, the Jundallah movement fighting for the independence of Iranian Balochistan killed forty-two Iranian state officials in a suicide attack, including fifteen Revolutionary Guards[96]—prompting Tehran to accuse Islamabad of involvement.

In order to circumvent Baloch nationalists, the centre may make history repeat itself by co-opting Baloch leaders who have gained a solid reputation for opportunism based on a tradition of reversing alliances handed down through centuries of tribal politics. An old hand at Baloch politics moreover admitted to Anatol Lieven, "You always have to be prepared to negotiate with your enemies—who knows, they may change sides and become your allies tomorrow".[97] The new chief minister who was appointed with the blessing of Prime Minister Nawaz Sharif may illustrate this old modus operandi. Abdul Malik Baloch is the leader of the National Party which was formed in 2004[98] and came only third in 2013. But he was able to form the government with the support of the PML(N) and the PkMAP. He was certainly selected by his two partners because he is a moderate Baloch, but he does not seem to be in a position to defuse tensions. In Gwadar, for instance, the Pakistan Coast Guard and the Frontier Corps, according to press reports, continue to behave "like an occupation force"—which means that they are "rude and high handed".[99]

Even if the Baloch movement for self-determination does not achieve its ends and is crushed once again, it will probably re-emerge after some time, especially if other mineral resources of the province are exploited by the

[95] Ansar Abbassi, "37pc Baloch favor independence: UK survey", *News*, 13 August 2012.

[96] Farhan Hanif Siddiqui, "Security Dynamics in Pakistani Balochistan", op. cit., p. 163.

[97] Quoted in Anatol Lieven, *Pakistan. A Hard Country*, op. cit., p. 559.

[98] The National Party was formed out of a merger of the BNM and a faction of the Pakistan National Party (a founding constituent of the NAP), known as the Balochistan National Democratic Party (Mohammad Waseem and Mariam Mufti, *Political Parties in Pakistan*, p. 58).

[99] Salman Rashid, 'Unequal forces in Makran', *Dawn*, 21 Feb. 2014 (https://www.dawn.com/news/1088426/unequal-forces-in-makran).

central government[100] and Gwadar transformed into a non-Baloch area. Lately, Baloch have worried about the transfer of Gwadar Port to the China Overseas Port Holding Company.[101]

The cyclical trajectory of Balochistan shows that the national integration issue in Pakistan has yet to be settled and illustrates well-known facets of the Pakistani syndrome: especially the centralising reflex of a ruling elite keen to concentrate power, be it civilian or military. Indeed, the military establishment (and the Punjabi elite in general) has inflicted the same treatment upon the Baloch that Bhutto had meted out in the 1970s and that the Pakistani state in general, from Ayub Khan to Bhutto, had dealt out to the Bengalis even before. Each time, the group in power has refused to respect the spirit and/or the letter of a Constitution that was intended to be federalist (especially after 1973)—or to seek some sort of compromise likely to defuse tensions. They instead developed a centralist policy involving violent forms of oppression. This approach has resulted in the radicalisation of the Baloch nationalists, who have finally opted *for* an equally violent form of separatism. A similar scenario unfolded in the Pashtun belt.

The Pashtuns, from Pashtunistan to Pakhtunkwa

In 1947 Abdul Ghaffar Khan and his followers had rejected their incorporation in Pakistan on grounds of Pashtun nationalism and their loyalty to the Indian National Congress.[102] They were first betrayed by Congress leaders and more especially by Nehru whose visit to the tribal areas was

---

[100] Balochistan harbours large deposits of gold and copper. See Farhan Hanif Siddiqui, "Security Dynamics in Pakistani Balochistan", op. cit., p. 168.

[101] Sanaullah Baloch, "Gwadar, China and Baloch apprehensions", *The Express Tribune*, 8 Sept. 2013 (http://tribune.com.pk/story/601604/gwadar-china-and-baloch-apprehensions/?print=true) and Khaleeq Kiani, "China to finance, develop airport in Gwadar", *Dawn*, 13 June 2014 (http://www.dawn.com/news/1112334/china-to-finance-develop-airport-in-gwadar/print).

[102] All the Pathans were not Pashtun nationalists. In addition to those—mostly urban dwellers of the NWFP—who differed from Abdul Ghaffar Khan because they did not adhere to Gandhi's ideas and were not comfortable with the omnipresence of Hindus at the helm of Congress, there were two other groups of "dissenters": the rulers of the princely states of Chitral, Dir and Swat, who were bound to retain their autonomy after Partition, and the Pathans of Rohilkhand (a subregion of the United Provinces), who, like other "Minority Muslims" supported the Muslim League and migrated to Pakistan after 1947. Most of them went to the NWFP. Among them was Sahabzada Yaqub Khan who would become Minister of Foreign Affairs under Zia and then Benazir Bhutto.

a fiasco: while the Pashtun chiefs he met probably did not identify with this Hindu, Nehru similarly wondered to what extent the followers of the Pashtunwali were Indian.[103] One year later, Nehru not only accepted Partition (something Abdul Ghaffar Khan could not understand), but he also admitted the idea of organising a referendum in the NWFP (all the other provinces had to decide their fate through a vote of their legislative council). On the top of it, the question that was to be asked offered a simple alternative: the inhabitants of the NWFP had the choice only between Pakistan and India—an independent Pashtunistan was not an option. Ghaffar Khan's Red Shirts boycotted the referendum. As a result, the NWFP joined Pakistan after only 51 per cent of the 573,000 registered citizens cast their vote.[104] But an overwhelming majority of these voters were in favour of Pakistan. Ghaffar Khan resigned himself to their choice and took an oath of allegiance to the new country on 23 February 1948 during the first session of the Constituent Assembly. But he wanted to create a party in conjunction with other former opponents to the Pakistan project (including G.M. Syed) and that raised Jinnah's suspicion who had him arrested.[105] Up until 1954, he was repeatedly sent to jail. When he was freed in 1954, he protested against the One-Unit Scheme and was imprisoned again. In 1964, when he was liberated because of health problems he decided to go into exile to Afghanistan.[106]

By contrast, Ghaffar Khan's second son, Wali Khan, played by the rules of the political system. In 1957, he joined the National Awami Party, a leftist party. Among the founding members of the NAP in 1957 were, besides Wali Khan's father, Abdul Ghaffar Khan, the former Muslim League member and socialist Mian Ifikharuddin, the Sindhi nationalist, G. M. Syed, the Pashtun nationalist, Abdul Samad Achakzai, the Baloch nationalist Ghaus Baksh Bezinjo and the Bengali leftist and peasant leader, Maulana Bhashani. Tensions emerged in the mid-1960s between a pro-China faction led by

---

[103] See Mukulika Banerjee, *The Pathan Unarmed*, op. cit., p. 184.

[104] See Erland Jansson, *India, Pakistan or Pakhtunistan*, Uppsala, Acta Universitatis Upsaliensis, 1988 and S. Rittenberg, *Ethnicity, Nationalism and the Pukhtuns: The Independence Movement in NWFP*, North Carolina, Carolina University Press, 1992.

[105] Ajeet Jawed, "Pakistan failed Jinnah", *Mainstream Weekly*, vol. XLIX, no. 38, 10 Sept. 2011 Available at: http://www.mainstreamweekly.net/article2993.html (Accessed on September 15, 2013).

[106] Rajmohan Gandhi, *Ghaffar Khan: non-violent Badshah of the Pakhtuns*, Viking, New Delhi, 2004.

Bhashani and a pro-Soviet faction led by Wali Khan. The former became closer to Ayub Khan after the Pakistan-China rapprochement which followed the 1962 war, to such an extent that he supported him during the 1965 elections. Wali Khan, on the contrary, supported Fatima Jinnah (see below). The split took place in 1967 but the following year, a group defected from the NAP-Wali to form the Mazdoor Kisan Party (MKP) which started a kind of guerilla war under the aegis of former army officers who had been involved in the 1951 Rawalpindi conspiracy.[107]

Wali Khan was not as radical as the MKP or Bhashani. In contrast to the Bengalis, the Balochs and the Sindhis, who had been largely sidelined for one reason or another in the 1950s, the Pashtun elite—which was partly Aligarh-educated—was to a large extent part of the Pakistani establishment. That was primarily due to their strength in the army ranks.[108] In 1959 there were more Pashtuns than Punjabis among the top army officers—19 compared to 17 (there were 11 Muhajirs).[109] At the end of the 1960s, they made up 40 per cent of the 48 highest ranked officers (once again more than the Punjabis, 34 per cent) and by then three commanders-in-chief, including Ayub Khan and Yayha Khan, were proof of their presence at the highest levels of the state.

These factors of national integration largely explain Wali Khan's strategy of watering down his Pashtun nationalism to enhance the appeal of his party, which, until 1970 never garnered more than 20 per cent of the vote. In 1969 he recognized the borderline between the NWFP and Balochistan—a portion of which Wali Khan had hitherto claimed. The NAP government of 1972 even promoted Urdu to the rank of official language in the province. That move was probably a reflection of Wali Khan's ambition to be seen as a national leader, but it also reflected his admission of the linguistic diversity of the NWFP where, for instance, the Hazara region spoke Hindko.

The NAP's relative weakness had also to do with the competition it faced from the JUI. This party, founded in 1947, grew out of the Pashtun branch of the JUH, the party formed in 1919 by *ulema*, most of them linked to the Deoband seminary, who had promoted the Caliphate Movement and supported the Congress. When faced with the choice between India and

---

[107] Nadeem F. Paracha, 'When the mountains were red', *Dawn*, 1 August 2013 (http://dawn.com/news/1033407/when-the-mountains-were-red?view=print).

[108] As mentioned above, Pashtuns made up one-fifth of its numbers following independence. See Stephen P. Cohen, *The Pakistan Army*, op. cit., p. 44.

[109] Khalid Bin Sayeed, "The role of the military in Pakistan", op. cit., p. 278.

Pakistan, JUH leaders were divided. The pro-Partition faction had a Pashtun at its helm, Maulana Shabir Ahmed Usmani, who founded the JUI. While the NAP was dominated by agrarian notables, the JUI was dominated by religious leaders. En 1970, Maulana Mufti Mahmud—another Pashtun alim—took over from Usmani.

However, Pashtun nationalism was revived in the 1970s when it was again sustained by propaganda emanating from Kabul under the aegis of Muhammad Daoud. In 1947, the Afghan authorities had asked the British to allow the NWFP the opportunity to become part of Afghanistan or to set up an independent Pashtunistan. Daoud had promoted this political line while prime minister of Afghanistan between 1953 and 1963. It was put on the backburner when Daoud was marginalised by King Zaeer Shah. But in 1973 Daoud staged a comeback. He deposed the King and became president of Afghanistan. The new strong man in Kabul declared that he would work toward the establishment of an independent Pashtunistan on the model of the newly founded Bangladesh, in cooperation with Ajmal Khattak, the NAP secretary-general in exile in Kabul. This outside support would probably not have been enough to revive Pashtun nationalism in the NWFP if at the same time the Pakistani state had not hardened its centralist attitude.

Islamabad's centralising policies in fact reinforced Pashtun nationalism as it had done with the Baloch. As already mentioned, when Bhutto dismissed the JUI-NAP coalition government of Balochistan in 1973, the NWFP government also resigned.[110] The rivalry between Bhutto and Wali Khan, who had ambitions as a national leader, intensified and in 1975 Bhutto used the pretext of the murder of a PPP minister, H. M. Sherpao, in the NWFP to arrest Wali Khan—who was allegedly implicated in this crime—and dissolve the NAP. Wali Khan's trial dragged on until Bhutto's downfall in 1977, after which the accusations were dropped. These events did not, however, lead to any extensive violence, and Pashtun nationalism even ebbed to some extent. New socioeconomic developments probably contributed to this trend. On that front, the situation of the NWFP improved somewhat in 1970s because of the growing number of Pashtuns

[110] After the 1970 elections, the JUI had formed an alliance with the ANP that resulted in a coalition government in 1972. This two-party coalition was hence in a position to form a government whose Pashtun nationalist spirit was tempered from the start by the Islamic and national sentiment characteristic of the JUI. The JUI's Pashtunisation only gained momentum in the 1980s when it took the forefront of the jihad against the Soviets.

who migrated to the Gulf countries and Saudi Arabia after the oil boom. In the late 1970s–early 1980s, these migrants were probably half a million, one-third of the Pakistani expatriates in the region, and sent substantial remittances to their province of origin.[111]

The war in Afghanistan that started in late 1979 also diminished Pashtun irredentism. The influx of 3 million Afghan refugees of the same ethnic origin increased the NWFP population to 16 million, exceeding the Afghanistan population (about 15 million). This led some Pakistani Pashtun leaders to affirm that Pashtunistan existed de facto on their side since the administration of the province was already in the hands of Pashtuns.[112] But Pashtun nationalism has been more directly and negatively affected by the economic consequences of the Afghan war. The ANP began protesting against the cost of the war effort and the expense borne by the NWFP of the flow of Afghan immigrants.[113] Most of all, the war against the Soviets had no ethnic justification. It was not even a war of national liberation; it was a jihad in which all the communities that had fled to the NWFP— Pashtuns, as well as Tajiks, Hazaras and Uzbeks—were united in their rejection of the infidels. As will be seen in Part 3 of this book, the 1980s evinced a shift in the region from an ethnic discourse to an Islamist repertoire.

Last but not least, the watering-down of Wali Khan's Pashtun nationalist rhetoric in the 1980s had much to do with his personal tactics. He for instance backed the central government of Zia during the Movement for the Restoration of Democracy in 1983—not only because Zia had opportunistically freed some of the Pashtun leaders Bhutto had put behind bars, but also because the MRD was largely identified with both Zia's and Wali Khan's bête noire, Bhutto's PPP.

Wali Khan continued to pursue his national destiny by founding a new party in 1986, the Awami National Party (ANP), into which the NAP and smaller parties merged, including the Awami Tehrik (a Sindhi party), that did not have an NWFP base. Moreover, ANP Vice-President Rasul Bux Palejo, former leader of the Awami Tehrik, was a Sindhi. Wali Khan's efforts not to limit himself to Pashtun nationalism converged with those of the mainstream national parties to make inroads in the NWFP: the cumulative effect of both resulted in a dilution of this brand of ethnic nationalism.

---

[111] Robert Nichols, *A History of Pashtun Migration, 1775–2006*, Karachi, Oxford University Press, 2011, p. 143.

[112] Omar Noman, *Pakistan*, op. cit., p. 198.

[113] Mohammad Waseem, *Politics and the State in Pakistan*, op. cit., p. 437.

The 1988 elections demonstrated that the political scene in the NWFP was now open to national parties. While the ANP and the JUI each won three seats, the PPP came away with seven and the IJI with eight. The ANP at first joined hands with the PPP, at the Centre as well as in the province, but turned to the PML(N) in 1989. This shift was accompanied by a split, the left wing of the ANP fully disapproving of this new partnership.

However, this dilution of the party's Pashtun identity was challenged from the inside in the 1990s after Wali Khan retired. He was replaced in 1991 by a senior leader of the Red Shirts, Ajmal Khattak. In the 1997 elections, the ANP won twenty-eight seats (out of eighty-three) in the NWFP assembly and once again joined in an alliance with the PML(N), which had won thirty-one seats, to form the government.

The coalition broke apart, however, one year later when Nawaz Sharif opposed renaming the NWFP "Pakhtunkhwa", even though this ANP request reflected the growing moderation of Pashtun nationalists. After all, they had given up on the name "Pashtunistan", too loaded with separatist connotations. In fact, this issue probably served as a pretext. The real bone of contention lay elsewhere, in the Kalabagh Dam project. Construction was sited near the NWFP border, and the ANP criticised the project, arguing that it would only benefit Punjab. It maintained that the province would receive irrigation waters needed for its agriculture while the dam would increase the risk of flooding upstream. As in the case of Balochistan, economic interests were draped in ideological language. The acknowledged leader of the ANP, Wali Khan's wife Begum Nasim Wali, justified the break with the PLM(N) in emotional terms: "I want an identity [...] I want a name change so that the Pashtuns may be identified on the map of Pakistan".[114] But the ideological overtone of this discourse should be qualified. Paradoxically, this militant rhetoric shows that the Pashtuns were no longer motivated by nationalist ambitions, since they demanded territorial recognition within Pakistan's borders. For Mohammad Waseem, by that time the NWFP "had finally crossed the Rubicon" and "joined the mainstream politics of the country".[115]

Indeed, when Ajmal Khattak joined hands with a coalition of small regional parties, the Pakistan Oppressed Nations Movement, the cadres of the ANP criticised him for deserting the national scene. He eventually made an alliance with the PPP—whose founder had been Wali Khan's main

---

[114] Quoted in *The News*, 1 March 1998.
[115] Mohammad Waseem, *Politics and State in Pakistan*, op. cit., p. 437.

rival—in 1999. His successor, Asfandyar Wali Khan, Wali Khan's son, continued with this alliance during the 2002 elections which took place in a completely new context marked by the rise of the Islamic parties due to the United States intervention in Afghanistan in 2001.

This second Afghan war reinforced the socio-political impact that the first one had had and that was very costly to the ANP. Since Abdul Ghaffar Khan's time, Pashtun nationalism and particularly its principal mouthpiece, the NAP and then the ANP, have largely drawn on the network of *maliks* (or *khans*) at the head of more or less large tribes. Starting with the first war in Afghanistan, these figures of Pashtun society have been in competition with Mujahideens fighting infidels at the risk of their life. Unlike the hereditary hierarchies in Sindh and Punjab, in Pashtun areas a leader's authority derives to a great extent from his reputation which itself depends on physical courage. A *malik* that cannot demonstrate such courage thus loses all prestige, even his honour.[116]

Not only did the prestige of *khans* and *maliks* decline in comparison to the Islamists, but the latter took them as a target. The Afghan Taliban and then the Pakistani Taliban indeed have implemented a strategy to eliminate *khans* and *maliks* who could thwart their recruitment and mobilisation efforts. After an initial wave of targeted killings which claimed several hundred lives among *maliks* in the early 2000s, the survivors, stricken with fear, lost all prestige and hence all authority when they did not lose their life, all the more since the Islamists appeared as liberators to many of the Pashtuns. The *maliks*, even if they continued to propound a leftist discourse, justified primarily by their secularism, represented the feudal element of Pashtun society. The ANP had always been led by landowning *khans* in the Peshawar valley. The Islamists, on the contrary, were egalitarian and could play lawmen, even Robin Hood at least in the early 2000s. They were particularly appreciated for their ability to dispense justice more quickly and under less influence than government officials, known for their corrupt practices. This state of affairs, and even more so the visceral anti-Americanism among NWFP Islamists due to the United States bombing of the Pashtun area in Afghanistan in the autumn of 2001, explains their suc-

---

[116] Anatol Lieven reports that Asfandyar Wali Khan lost the respect of many Pashtuns when he fled by helicopter after having been targeted in an attack in Charsadda in 2008, an operation that killed his bodyguard and to whose funeral he did not have the guts to attend. See Anatol Lieven, *Pakistan. A Hard Country*, op. cit., p. 386.

cess at the polls in 2002, which will be discussed further in the last part of this book.[117]

In 2008, the ANP nevertheless returned to power on the back of a remarkable electoral triumph, as for the first time these Pashtun nationalists won thirty-eight seats, enabling the party to take the lead of a ruling coalition including the PPP (twenty seats).[118] This achievement was probably due more to a rejection of the Islamists, as their government did not keep any of its promises (as we shall see), than to popular support for Pashtun nationalism. Not only did the ANP continue to partner with a national party in the NWFP, but it also became part of the ruling coalition at the centre—where it had ministers. Instead of putting up resistance to the central authorities in the name of Pashtun nationalism, as was its custom, it allied with mainstream forces—and the army. Whereas the party had promised talks with the militants during the elections campaign, the rejection of their overtures by the Taliban persuaded the government of Peshawar to endorse and even support counterinsurgency operations the Pakistani army led under pressure from the US in the FATA.

The ANP government in Peshawar won a symbolic victory in 2009 when the Pakistani parliament amended article 1 of the Constitution, renaming the NWFP "Khyber–Pakhtunkhwa", a measure in favour of which the provincial assembly had voted in 1997. This measure nevertheless aroused protest from the Hindko-speaking minority concentrated in the Hazara region, bordering Punjab, and which did not identify with the ethnic repertoire henceforth contained in the new name.

Paradoxically, Pashtun nationalism found new areas into which to expand hundreds of miles from the NWFP, in Karachi, to which many citizens of this province had migrated in search of work starting in the 1960s. These Pashtun pockets enabled the ANP to win a modest but unprecedented electoral success in the 2008 elections, securing two seats out of 130 in the Sindh assembly and one seat in the national assembly. The Muhajir party, the MQM (see infra), accustomed to a monopoly position in Karachi,

---

[117] It should be noted that the JUI did not manage to ride this Islamist wave, the scope of which will also be put in perspective in the last part of this book, because this party threw its support behind General Musharraf, who was considered a lackey of the United States.

[118] Hassan Abbas, "Inside Pakistan's North-West Frontier Province". Available at: http://www.newamerica.net/publications/policy/inside_pakistan_s_north_west_frontier_province (Accessed on September 15, 2013).

was all the more upset by this breakthrough as at the same time the ANP had adopted a conciliatory tone with the Islamists. Moreover, the growing presence of Pashtuns in Karachi is a major factor of militant Muhajir mobilisation in Sindh.

During the 2013 elections, the ANP was the target of political violence. Out of 148 terrorist attacks which killed 298 people and injured 885 others between January and May, fifty took place in K-P, killing fifty-five and injuring 222. The ANP faced thirty-seven of these terrorist attacks, followed by the PPP and the MQM with twelve attacks each.[119] These attacks were mostly engineered by Pakistani Taliban (see part 3) but did not occur only in the Pashtun area. In fact, some of them took place in Karachi where the ANP eventually closed two-thirds of its offices.[120] This violence was one of the reasons for the electoral defeat of the ANP whose candidates could hardly canvass. The party won only one seat in the National Assembly.

Muhajir Militancy—and its Limitations

Spearheads of the Pakistan project, the Muhajirs first identified with the Muslim League and then, after the party's decline, with Islamic forces, the Jama'at-e-Islami (JI) and the Jamiat-e-Ulama-e-Pakistan (JUP) which promoted Islam as the cement of the Pakistani ideology.[121] In 1970, the JUP won seven seats (with 6 per cent of the valid votes) in the assembly of Sindh, mostly in Hyderabad, and the JI one (with 3 per cent) in Karachi. These parties received more than 17 per cent of the valid votes during the 1970 general elections in Sindh.[122]

But the 1970s were a turning point for the Muhajirs. By demanding a share of power in a province that the Muhajirs had become accustomed to governing from Karachi, Bhutto brutally reminded them of a demographic and territorial reality. As Feroz Ahmed writes:

---

[119] Pak Institute for Peace Studies, *Elections 2013: Violence against political parties, candidates and voters*, Islamabad, PIPS, 2013, p. 1, p. 2 and p. 5.

[120] Sohail Khattak, "Out of business? To keep threats out, ANP shuts its doors in Sindh", *The Express Tribune*, 9 July 2013.

[121] Muhajirs not only had affinities with the JI ideology, but also they appreciated the humanitarian aid they received from the party after Partition, as refugees. See Sayyed Vali Reza Nasr, *The Vanguard of Islamic Revolution. The Jama'at-i Islami of Pakistan*, Berkeley, University of California Press, 1994, pp. 88–89.

[122] The JI won 10% of the valid votes and 2 seats and the JUP, respectively 7% and 3 seats. See Ibid., pp. 166–167.

For 23 years the Mohajirs of Karachi had never even thought of being in Sindh; a majority of them had never seen Sindhi nor heard their language being spoken. Their youth had grown up, thinking that Karachi was a Mohajir enclave or a world unto itself. In everyday speech, as in the press, the expression 'Karachi and Sindh' was in vogue.[123]

An Ethnic Group Reinvented

In the 1970s, in reaction to Bhutto's pro-Sindhi policy, the Muhajirs increasingly tended to define themselves as a separate community and no longer as the spearheads of Pakistan. In theory, they had none of the characteristics of an ethnic group. As migrants, they had no ancestral territorial roots or any particular linguistic unity. Among them are found Urdu-speakers as well as Gujarati-speakers (as well as few others). But Muhajirs would invent for themselves a separate ethnic identity. Eventually they would claim that they were "sons of the soil" in the cities of Sindh. Gujaratis and Urdu-speakers would minimise their differences and "re-imagined themselves as Muhajirs",[124] the former to a certain extent adding Urdu to their linguistic repertoire. This process, which is revealing of the malleability of ethnic identities,[125] has developed at the interface of two dynamics: on one hand, the Muhajirs could capitalise on a stock of identity symbols; on the other, this stock is activated in reaction to the fear of Others.[126]

The list of more or less latent identity symbols that the Muhajir ideologues could use is long. The heroes of the past they worship comes first, ranging from Tipu Sultan (who fought the British until his "martyrdom" in

---

[123] Feroz Ahmed, "Ethnicity and Politics: The Rise of Muhajir Separatism", *South Asian Bulletin*, vol. 8 (1988), p. 37.

[124] Yunas Samad, "Le 'problème Mohajir'", in Christophe Jaffrelot (ed.), *Le Pakistan, carrefour de tensions régionales*, Bruxelles, Complexe, 1999, p. 77.

[125] Emphasizing the malleability of the notion of ethnicity in the case of the Muhajirs, Akbar S. Ahmed suggests that they invented the concept of "refugee ethnicity". Cited in Steve Inskeep, *Instant City*, op. cit., p. 175. Mohammad Waseem in the same vein shows that they have given substance to a form of "imagined autochthony" in "Mohajirs in Pakistan: A Case of Nativization of Migrants", in Crispin Bates (ed.), *Community, Empire and Migration. South Asians in Diaspora*, Delhi, Orient Longman, 2001, p. 250.

[126] One of the lessons that can be drawn from social science theory is precisely that ethnic groups can indeed display immense creativity to resist threatening others. See Christophe Jaffrelot, "For a Theory of Nationalism", in Alain Dieckhoff and Christophe Jaffrelot (eds), *Revisiting Nationalism*, London, Hurst, 2005, pp. 10–61.

1799) to brothers Muhammad and Shaukat Ali (most active during the Khilafat Movement), and, more importantly, Syed Ahmad Khan and Liaquat Ali Khan.[127] These prestigious ancestors allow them to establish some continuity with the aristocratic lineages of the Mughal Empire.[128] Indeed, the leaders of the MQM (which will be the focus in the following section) "see the Muhajirs as Ashraf, the direct descendents of the Arabs, Persians and Turks who once conquered the subcontinent".[129] This pedigree, which endows them with a form of Islam closer to the origins of the religion, supports their superiority complex that is mainly rooted in the fact that they created Pakistan to allow the Muslims of the former Raj to practice their religion freely.[130]

The very name "Muhajir" reflects this prestigious past, as evident from the use Liaquat Ali Khan made of it. He was probably the Muslim League politician who most assiduously compared the Muhajirs to those who had fled to Medina "at the time of departure of the Holy Prophet from Mecca".[131] While the older generation continued to pay tribute to Jinnah, Liaquat Ali Khan, whose family descended from an aristocratic North Indian lineage, is more often referred to by the MQM activists that Ann Frotsher has interviewed.[132] In his wake, Muhajir leaders make a point of emphasizing their education, their culture and even their purity.[133] This sense of superiority is fostered by reminiscences of the sacrifices made at the time of Partition,

---

[127] Ann Frotscher, *Claiming Pakistan: the MQM and the Fight for Belonging*, Baden-Baden, Nomos, 2008, p. 144.

[128] Ibid., p. 199.

[129] Ibid., p. 159.

[130] While Muhajirs claim to embody orthodox Islam, the less educated among them and Altaf Hussain himself fallen into the trap of popular Islam as shown by the title "Pir Sahib" given to Hussain. The label was given humorously, but ended up sticking due to the resonance it had with the masses. This is another indication of what probably remains the MQM's main characteristic: a cobbled-together ideology. See Oskar Verkaaik, "Ethnicizing Islam: 'Sindi Sufis', 'Muhajir Modernists' and 'Tribal Islamists' in Pakistan", in Saeed Shafqat (ed.), *New Perspectives on Pakistan. Visions for the Future*, Karachi, Oxford University Press, 2007.

[131] Cited in Ann Frotscher, *Claiming Pakistan*, op. cit., p. 90 (note 10).

[132] Farzana Shaikh points out that in 1917 the aristocratic leaders of the Muslim League had objections to the leadership of "men of low birth" such as Jinnah, who after all was a businessman. See Farzana Shaikh, *Community and consensus in Islam*, op. cit., p. 171.

[133] Ann Frotscher, *Claiming Pakistan*, op. cit, p. 161.

a recurring theme in the Muhajirs' identity repertoire. Their leaders continue to eulogise those who lost everything in 1947 and the 2 million people who died (an exaggerated figure).[134]

The crystallisation of Muhajir identity was overdetermined by the attitude of other communities—and the way the former related to the latter. As mentioned above, the Sindhis did not welcome them unreservedly: on the contrary. But similarly, the Muhajirs immediately despised these backward peasants while, according to the 1951 census, 40 per cent of their community was categorized as white collar and thus formed the bulk of the middle class in Sindh.[135] However, the Sindhis did not seem to pose any threat to them until the PPP rose to power in the 1970s. After that, they felt the need to organise against this group as well as the Pashtuns.

The Mohajirs, a Community of Interest Against the Sindhis—and the Pashtuns

In the early 1970s, having deemed detrimental to their interests the new policy of quotas set up in the educational system, Muhajir students took the lead in protest movements in the largest cities of Sindh.[136] Some of them joined existing student unions. In Karachi, Altaf Hussain, who was to become the main Muhajir leader in the 1980s, for instance, played an active role in the Islami Jamia'at Tulabah (IJT), the student union of the Jama'at-e-Islami (a party for which he was to canvass during the 1977 election). As Laurent Gayer has shown, in the 1970s, student unions were an important force to reckon with in Karachi. Their style made a major impact on the public sphere of the city. Now, most of them—including the IJT—resorted most systematically to violence on university campuses.[137] They terrorised students to assert their domination, using weapons which had become more easily available—especially after the US started sending arms to the mujahideen fighting the Soviets in Afghanistan. These weapons reached Karachi first, and some of them were immediately hijacked by other militant groups, including student unions.[138]

[134] Ibid., p. 164.
[135] Oskar Verkaaik, "A People of Migrants: Ethnicity, State and Religion in Karachi", *Comparative Asian Studies*, no. 15, 1994, p. 47.
[136] The first Mohajir student organization to come about was the Mohajir Medicos Association, founded by Salim Haider in May 1978.
[137] Laurent Gayer, *Karachi*, op. cit., p. 54.
[138] Ibid., p. 59.

In 1978, Muhajir students created their own union, the All-Pakistan Mohajir Students Organisation (APMSO) under the aegis of Altaf Hussain and others.[139] Hussain was representative of the lower middle class of Muhajirs who were the first to feel the brunt of Bhutto's reforms in the 1970s.[140] Born into a family of modest means, Hussain had trouble getting into medical school to study pharmacology. A clear indication of his social marginalisation is the scorn of the Muhajir business elite that he painfully experienced when he approached industrialists in Karachi to raise funds needed to operate APMSO.[141] The beginning of his career as a student leader was so difficult that in 1982 he left Karachi for Jeddah and then Chicago, where he became a taxi driver till 1985. As a result, the MQM was founded in his absence.

In the 1980s, the Muhajirs found Zia's policies just as detrimental to their community as Bhutto's: although they approved the establishment of courts in charge of enforcing sharia law, they protested against the quotas put in place in the administration after 10 per cent of civil service posts were reserved for retired military personnel, while Punjabis continued to dominate the army. The Muhajirs resented this move all the more since the other long term trends worked to their disadvantage in the 1980s.

The Green Revolution that benefited Punjab starting in the late 1960s strengthened Punjabi hegemony and enabled businessmen from this area

---

[139] Altaf Hussain had come to the conclusion that the IJT was a "Punjabi group" where Muhajir would never be able to play a significant role. Cited in Ann Frotscher, *Claiming Pakistan*, op. cit., p. 116.

[140] But Altaf Hussain's decision to embark on a Muhajir militant agenda was also probably due to an episode of personal humiliation that, rather than serving as a mere anecdote, demonstrates the extent of the ethnic divisions in Pakistan in the 1970s: "He underwent military training for a year in the National Cadet Corps, a college based training programme for civilian youths in Pakistan. It was here that Hussain experienced ethnic hatred against the Urdu speakers. Once he was ridiculed by his superior for belonging to Karachi where people drank a lot of tea, wore close-fitting trousers and were incapable and unfit for military service. This infuriated the young Hussain and led him to believe that other ethnic communities did not like his particular community, while he himself had joined the military training programme with the belief that Pakistan was one nation". Farhan Hanif Siddiqi, *The Politics of Ethnicity in Pakistan. The Baloch, Sindi and Mohajir Ethnic Movements*, London, Routledge, 2012, p. 103.

[141] Farhan Hanif Siddiqi, "Intra-ethnic Fissures in Ethnic Movements", op. cit., p. 34, note 41.

to invest in industry, even in Karachi.[142] Migrants poured into the city from all of Pakistan's provinces, seeking to take advantage of its dynamism; this was also true of refugees from the war in Afghanistan who had fled to Pakistan. According to the 1981 census, the city's population was 61 per cent Muhajir, 16 per cent Punjabi, 11 per cent Pashtun, 7 per cent "native-born" Sindhi and 5 per cent Baloch.[143] The growing Pathan influence in the upper ranks of the army after the Soviet invasion of Afghanistan further disadvantaged the Muhajirs just as they were losing government jobs as a result of the quotas set in 1973: ten years later, urban Sindhis only made up one-fifth of the senior civil service compared to one-third in 1973. In 1981 they represented only 22.3 per cent of the civil servants hired by the centre, against 30.3 in 1973.[144] Muhajir activists would use this as an argument to decry the pauperisation of their community. This was an excessive claim but a fairly common one among groups which, while continuing to form an elite, suffered from challenges to their former privileges—like the Sikhs in Indian Punjab at about the same time.

In 1978, the first APMSO manifesto, authored by Azim Ahmad Tariq, the organization's vice-president, had concluded with two demands that have constantly been repeated since then with more or less insistence: "Mohajirs should be provided with a province of their own where they can freely practice and exercise their culture", and "Draconian laws relating to the quota system and domicile should be abolished".[145] In 1984, Muhajir activists went one step further by creating the Mohajir Qaumi Mahaz (MQM) of which Altaf Hussain took the lead the following year after his return from the US. Its cadres continued to come from the youth of the Muhajir middle class whose expectations in terms of upward social mobility were frustrated—sometimes due to unemployment.[146] But their main enemies were no longer only (not even primarily) the Sindhis, but the Pashtuns.

---

[142] S. Akbar Zaidi, "Sindhi vs Mohajir in Pakistan—Contradiction, Conflict, Compromise", *Economic and Political Weekly*, May 18, 1991, p. 1296.

[143] The 1998 census was prevented from being carried out in Karachi, as the Muhajirs feared it would show a further decrease in their demographic weight. On the scale of the province, Urdu-speakers made up 21% of the population, as against 59% Sindhi-speakers, 7% Punjabi-speakers, 4% Pashto-speakers and 3% Gujarati-speakers considered as Muhajirs.

[144] Laurent Gayer, *Karachi*, op. cit, p. 298.

[145] Farhan Hanif Siddiqi, "Intra-ethnic Fissures in Ethnic Movements", op. cit., p. 34.

[146] In his autobiography, Altaf Hussain claims that some Muhajirs were not given

This antagonism was more or less latent since the 1960s, and even since the coup of Ayub Khan who did not like Karachi, "a centre of agitational politics".[147] This is one of the reasons why he transferred Pakistan's capital to Rawalpindi. Before that, as early as 1958, he had started building Korangi colony, a huge enterprise that Muhajirs interpreted as intended to give Pashtuns jobs and housing.[148] Similarly, they viewed his efforts to industrialise the city—whose share in Pakistan's industrial production jumped from 28 per cent in 1954 to 44 per cent ten years later[149]—as a device for promoting businessmen from Punjab and the NWFP. Indeed, the proportion of Pashto-speaking inhabitants of Karachi district increased from 5.2 per cent in 1961 to 11 per cent in 1981.[150] In this context, clashes with Muhajirs took place. In 1965 violence broke out for purely political reasons after Muhajirs supported Fatima Jinnah—Quaid-e-Azam's sister—against Ayub Khan during the presidential election, something the general-president clearly resented.[151]

But the Pashtun problem took on much larger dimensions for the Muhajirs in the 1980s because of the war in Afghanistan. This conflict led millions of refugees to migrate to Karachi where they indulged in all kinds of trafficking, including opium, leading to the development of a powerful Pashtun mafia.[152] The problem became even more acute when Pashtuns gained control over road transport, through not only their lorry companies running between Karachi and Peshawar, but also their bus companies.[153]

---

jobs because they were not considered as "sons of the soil". Altaf Hussain, *My Life's Journey, The Early Years (1966–1988)*, Karachi, Oxford University Press, 2011, p. 22.

[147] Muhammad Ayub Khan, *Friends not Masters*, op. cit., p. 115.

[148] Arif Hasan, "The Growth of a Metropolis", in Hamida Khuhro and Anwer Mooraj (eds), *Karachi. Megacity of Our Time*, Karachi, Oxford University Press, 1997, p. 182.

[149] Amtul Hassan, *Impact of Partition: Refugees in Pakistan. Struggle for Empowerment and State Response*, Delhi, Manohar, 2006, pp. 72–73.

[150] Ann Frotscher, *Claiming Pakistan*, op. cit., p. 44.

[151] The victory procession that Ayub Khan's son organised in Karachi purposely went through a Muhajir neighbourhood in provocation. The ensuing violence caused the death of several inhabitants. Amtul Hassan, *Impact of Partition*, op. cit., p. 73. In his autobiography, Altaf Hussain—who was 12 years old at the time—mentions this episode as one of the reasons why he joined student politics. Altaf Hussain, *My Life's Journey*, op. cit., p. 22.

[152] Ann Frotscher, *Claiming Pakistan*, op. cit., p. 79.

[153] Ann Frotsher considers that 50% of the 1500 minibuses of Karachi belonged to

On 15 April 1985 a minibus belonging to a Pashtun owner killed a Muhajir girl who was a student at the prestigious Sir Syed College in Karachi. There was a flare-up of violent protest on college campuses, repressed so harshly by the police that Muhajirs mobilised in larger numbers. Riots broke out between the two groups.[154] On the Muhajir side, this violence was not only the legacy of student politics in the 1970s, it was also encouraged by the expertise of veterans from the Bangladesh war, Biharis who had recently settled down in Karachi.[155]

In 1987, Pashtuns of Sindh joined hands with Punjabis to form the Punjabi-Pakhtoon-Ittehad (PPI). They claimed that they shared interests as well as an ethos as "the martial community in Pakistan".[156] The PPI contested elections in 1988 but received only 7.2 per cent of the votes and therefore invested more in street politics.[157] On the Muhajir side, another alliance took shape—with the Sindhis. In 1985, Altaf Hussain met G.M. Syed[158] whom he regarded as "the protector of the old Sindis", while he defined the Muhajirs as "the new Sindis".[159] Cadres from G.M. Syed's party, Jiye Sind, gave Muhajir sophisticated military training.[160]

But soon after this rapprochement, Muhajirs again fought the Sindhis. This U-turn was fostered by competition between two Muhajir organisations, the MQM and the Muhajir Ittehad Tehreek (MIT), an organisation formed in 1986[161] which criticised Altaf Hussain's flirtation with G.M. Syed's Sindhi nationalists, his enemies of yesterday. This rhetoric further damaged the MQM's image after clashes between Muhajirs and Sindhis multiplied in 1988. On 30 September 1988, in Hyderabad, Sindhi nationalists attacked Muhajirs during what is known as Black Friday. The Muhajir retaliated. 200 people died in the space of two days.[162] This episode made an impact on the

---

unlicensed Pashtun "companies" whose drivers, on the top of it, behaved very dangerously on the road. See ibid., p. 77.

[154] Akmal Hussain, "The Karachi Riots of December 1986: Crisis of State and Civil Society in Pakistan", in Veena Das (ed.), *Mirrors of Violence. Communities, Riots and Survivors in South Asia*, Delhi, Oxford University Press, 1990, pp. 194–214.

[155] Laurent Gayer, *Karachi*, op. cit.

[156] Cited in Ann Frotscher, *Claiming Pakistan*, op. cit., p. 195.

[157] Ibid., p. 197.

[158] See the fully empathetic chapter of Altaf Hussain's autobiography G.M. Syed. See Altaf Hussain, *My Life's Journey*, op. cit., p. 91 ff.

[159] Laurent Gayer, *Karachi*, op. cit., p. 161.

[160] Ibid.

[161] Oskar Verkaaik, *Migrants and Militants*, op. cit., p. 77.

[162] Ibid., p. 79.

discourse of Altaf Hussain who, after that, emphasised the physical suffering of his community as much as its socio-economic decline.[163] This was also the moment when he tried to broaden the scope of the MQM by presenting it not only as the party of the Muhajirs, but also as a party representing Pakistan's middle class in general. Hence the idea—first mentioned in 1991—of changing its name to the Muttehida Qaumi Movement (Movement of the United Nation).[164] The MQM would thus be renamed in 1997.

By the end of the 1980s, the Muhajirs had no friends left in the cities of Sindh. In addition to the Pashtuns and the Sindhis, the IJT had also become their enemy, as evident from clashes between this student union and the APMSO on university campuses in 1988.[165]

What Program?

The way Altaf Hussain and his followers shifted from one organisation to another and from one ally to another had a confusing effect in the 1980s. What did they really want? In 1986, Altaf Hussain demanded that the Muhajirs be recognized as the fifth nationality making up Pakistan and in 1987, he issued the MQM's "Charter of Resolutions" which, out of twenty-one points, included the following most important ones:

1) Sindh's domicile certificate should be given to such locals who could prove residency in the province for the last 20 years (the Bihari refugees from East Bengal excepted);
2) Only those who held such a certificate should be recruited into the police and related agencies;
3) Muhajirs and Sindhis should be allowed to purchase weapons as easily as a radio or television;
4) Afghan refugees should be confined to camps near the Afghan border;
5) To stop the unnatural growth in Sindh's population, people coming here from other provinces should be given jobs and business opportunities in their own provinces;
6) Only those illegal settlements that were built in Sindh before 1978 should be legalized;
7) In the cities of Sindh, government transport should be made the respon-

---

[163] Ibid., p. 82.
[164] Ibid., p. 83.
[165] Laurent Gayer, *Karachi*, op. cit., p. 119. In fact, the IJT constantly targeted Altaf Hussain after he had left the organisation. See ibid., pp. 186–187.

sibility of the municipal authority and education up to Matriculation level should be made a requirement for the issuing of a driver's licence;

8 and 12) Local persons from Sindh should be given preference for employment in all government and private oraganisations;

9 and 10) Nobody should be allowed to vote in Sindh except the local people and the minimum voting age should be fixed at 18 years;

11) The 10% quota for merit in employment on the federal level should be abolished and the share should be distributed among federal units on the basis of their population;

21) Shah Abdul Latif's death anniversary and Liaquat Ali Khan's day of martyrdom should be declared public holidays throughout the country.[166]

Altaf Hussain clearly intended to introduce two-stage citizenship, granting full civil rights only to families settled in Sindhi cities for a long period of time (the issue did not apply to rural dwellers) and making the others second-class citizens or forcing them to leave the province. Paradoxically, a migrant community claimed to be recognized as the natural ruler of a fraction of Sindh on behalf of an imagined autochthony.[167]

Along with the list of demands outlined by Altaf Hussain in 1987, an additional demand was implicit in them, that of setting up "Karachisuba", a Muhajir province corresponding to the country's largest city.[168] Muhajir ideologues have also called the land they wanted for themselves "Urdudesh" (in response to the Sindhi demand of a "Sindhudesh")[169] or "Jinnahpur", a comprise of Karachi and Hyderabad—two cities that would have been connected by a corridor[170] (This utopia is reminiscent of that of the Muslim League before 1947, when the party was trying to find ways and means to connect the two wings of Pakistan and/or the princely state of Hyderabad). But Altaf Hussain, who has declared on several occasions that Partition had been a mistake, has never truly been a separatist—although he has also said that the Muhajirs would follow the path of the Bengalis if they had no

---

[166] See the complete list in Altaf Hussain, *My Life's Journey*, op. cit., pp. 169–187.

[167] Mohammad Waseem, "Mohajirs in Pakistan", op. cit.

[168] J. Rehman, "Self-Determination, State-Building and the Muhajirs: An International Legal Perspective of the Role of the Indian Muslim Refugees in the Constitutional Development of Pakistan", *Contemporary South Asia* (1994), vol. 3, no. 2, pp. 122–23.

[169] This formula was used in the 1970s in reaction to the Sindhi demand of "Sindudesh". See Ann Frotscher, *Claiming Pakistan*, op. cit., p. 121.

[170] Oskar Verkaaik, *Migrants and Militants*, op. cit., p. 78.

other alternative.[171] More likely, what he wanted was to establish MQM control over the "Muhajir cities" of Sindh.

Hence the MQM's attempts to criss-cross this urban space with a dense network of well-trained activists. This organisation, emulating the pyramidal structure of the Jama'at-e-Islami,[172] was intended to establish a direct relationship between Altaf Hussain and the local cadres, including those in charge of fractions of the cities called "zones"—which were themselves subdivided into smaller units. As regards Karachi, Ann Frotscher points out that "The MQM has divided the city into zones, sectors, areas and sub-units. The 'zones' correspond to the municipal districts, 'sectors' to election constituencies, 'units' to a mohalla and 'sub-units' are made of just a few streets".[173] This dense presence of the MQM at the local level not only enables the organisation to exert social control over the inhabitants (and even to spy on them), but also to implement a strategy of social work, including the distribution of free food.[174]

Violence and Martyrdom

Immediately after its creation, the MQM cultivated techniques of violence which were part of the APMSO's legacy. In 1987 Altaf Hussain sent his bodyguards to Afghanistan for training in a mujahideen camp.[175] Another indication of the MQM's culture of violence pertained the use of torture, not only against enemies from other groups but also against "deviant" Muhajirs at a time when Altaf Hussain did not tolerate dissent in any form. The existence of torture chambers in almost a dozen Karachi neighbourhoods was revealed in 1992 after the army's intervention in the city.[176]

MQM cadres have routinely paraded with arms since the party's inception. In fact, it was the first political organisation to exhibit Kalashnikovs at public meetings in 1986.[177] Such practice fell in line with a policy of

---

[171] Ann Frotscher, *Claiming Pakistan*, op. cit., p. 121, note 24.

[172] Oskar Verkaaik, *Migrants and Militant*, op. cit., p. 74.

[173] Ann Frotscher, *Claiming Pakistan*, op. cit., p. 173.

[174] Ibid., p. 163.

[175] Laurent Gayer, *Karachi*, op. cit., p. 110.

[176] Ann Frotscher, *Claiming Pakistan*, op. cit., p. 135.

[177] Siddiqi believe that MQM was probably the first Pakistani party to authorise its members to exhibit firearms in its first major rally in Nishtar Park in December 1986. Farhan Hanif Siddiqi, "Intra-ethnic fissures in Ethnic Movements", op. cit., p. 36, note 51.

intimidation, as Altaf Hussain suggested in October of the same year when he said in the course of a press conference: "If our rights are not given to us, we will use every kind of force."[178]

Nichola Khan, in her study of the MQM cadres in one of Karachi's neighbourhoods, has shown that the cult of violence enabled them to display a form of "hypermasculinity".[179] Ann Frotscher has collected personal testimonies in the same vein. One of her interviewees thus confided, "Believe me, there is no greater feeling than having a well-oiled, loaded Kalashnikov in your hostel room cupboard, with the whole hostel knowing about it. You feel like a king".[180]

This discourse reflects the social profile of the MQM. The activists who thus improve their status are young Muhajirs from the lower middle class seeking to raise their self-esteem. They usually live in *katchi abadis*, the informal settlements of Karachi where 2.6 million people (about 43 per cent of the population) lived in 1985. (At the same time, one million people were living in slums.)[181] The MQM activists in charge of violent operations were usually "formerly petty criminals in the katchi abadis who were suddenly raised to the status of 'political' leaders".[182]

The sociological profile of the MQM was naturally not to the liking of the Muhajir elite who looked at this organisation as made up of a lumpen proletariat. They were all the more critical of the MQM as its actions were not good for their business when they disrupted law and order.[183] But their attitude changed at the turn of the 1990s when MQM activists and the Muhajirs generally speaking were victims of violence. In 1989, abuse committed by the Sindhi police started to make a difference. All Muhajirs, rich and poor, developed a new sense of solidarity when innocent women and children were killed. But the real turning point came with the state-sponsored army operation in 1992.

Operation Clean Up was decided just after the assassination of a senior army officer (who had been tortured) and two other soldiers—and just after

---

[178] Ann Frotscher, *Claiming Pakistan*, op. cit., p. 174.

[179] Nichola Khan, *Mohajir Militancy in Pakistan. Violence and Practices of Transformation in the Karachi Conflict*, London, Routledge, 2010.

[180] Ann Frotscher, *Claiming Pakistan*, op. cit., p. 144. Another activist told Ann Frotscher "The more you killed, the more praise you got from the party. This kicked off an unending competition amongst us". Cited in ibid., p. 175.

[181] Arif Hasan, *Participatory Development*, Karachi, Oxford University Press, 2010, p. 19.

[182] Ann Frotscher, *Claiming Pakistan*, op. cit., p. 147.

[183] Ibid., p. 138.

the demise of the governor of Sindh who up to then had been one of the patrons of the MQM. But these circumstances were probably not the only relevant factors. The operation was also decided at a time when Altaf Hussain, aiming to represent Pakistan's entire middle class, had started a campaign against the feudals and the capitalists of the country's establishment. He had gone to Lahore (to the very place where the Lahore Resolution had been passed in 1940) to make a speech with revolutionary overtones: "Rise, become aware of your rights and create leadership from among yourselves. How long will you keep voting for these plundering feudals?"[184] This discourse was probably also one of the reasons why the state decided to crush the MQM.

Approximately 20,000 Rangers—a paramilitary force—were deployed in Karachi to "clean up" the city. Certainly, it made a significant impact by shutting down the torture chambers. But they alienated the population by resorting to brutal house searches and arresting en masse people who sometimes had virtually nothing to do with the MQM. The army relied on the support of MQM dissenters. This group of opponents to Altaf Hussain was directed by Afaq Ahmed and Amir Khan, who resented the rise of the Biharis in the party and also criticised Altaf Hussain for his attempt to become a national leader, a move that diluted the MQM agenda.[185] Both leaders were expelled in 1991 and, fearing for their lives, fled to the United States. But their followers created the MQM (Haqiqi)—lit. "the true MQM". This faction indulged in criminal activities, including protection rackets. But the army used them nevertheless during Operation Clean Up.

The military finally withdrew in November 1994. The MQM (A)—"A" for Altaf—hailed its departure as a victory. In the course of this operation, 1,113 persons were killed by snipers in Karachi.[186] Some MQM(A) leaders went

---

[184] Ibid., p. 217.

[185] In fact, Altaf Hussain not only tried to mobilise the middle class throughout Pakistan, but also the poor. He declared for instance regarding the MQM, "No wadero, landowner, or wealthy capitalist leads, runs, or supports our organisation. It is the people of this very class, who are beset with problems, who lead and run this organisation (...) Because the MQM is a success story of the lower, middle, and poor classes, it is likely that, using it as an example, people belonging to the poor classes in NWFP, Punjab, and Balochistan might establish their own organisations and begin to demand their rights". See Altaf Hussain, *My Life's Journey*, op. cit., pp. 102–104.

[186] Farhan Hanif Siddiqi, "Intra-ethnic Fissures in Ethnic Movements", op. cit., p. 37.

underground or left the country—like Altaf Hussain, who settled down in London. But the worst was still to come. First, the army subcontracted part of the anti-MQM(A) fight to the Haqiqis, which further heightened violence due to vendettas and score-settling of all sorts. Second, Benazir Bhutto and her Minister of the Interior, General Babar, decided also to resort to torture on a larger scale[187] and to targeted killings—Altaf Hussain's elder brother was killed in December 1995.[188] In 1995 the official death toll reached 2,095, most of the deaths occurring in the course of police operations.[189]

By the middle of the 1990s, the Muhajirs not only formed a community of interest, but also a community of suffering where social differences were largely blurred by the sentiment of a common destiny. Once again, the intervention of the state had qualitatively transformed an ethnic move-ment, which was already well structured and actively violent. Indeed, the MQM(A) remained very influential and popular. In October and December 1995 it successfully called two general strikes in response to the murder of two of Altaf Hussain's close associates, crippling the city.

The MQM(A)'s Political Game

Violence is only one element of the MQM(A)'s repertoire among many others. Indeed, since it is keen to defend the Muhajirs by any possible means, party politics (including coalition-making and electoral competi-tion) is also an important part of its agenda. Altaf Hussain's party con-tested the municipal elections in Karachi and Hyderabad in 1987. It won in both places. In 1988 with thirteen seats, the party came away with a fine score in the general elections where the PPP came out in the lead, although without an absolute majority. Benazir Bhutto thus struck an agreement with the MQM, whose additional seats were enough to form a majority, taking up most of the demands in the Muhajir party charter. The new prime minister was nevertheless reluctant to honour her commitments. She in particular refused to admit the Biharis from Bangladesh who had long wanted to join the Muhajirs and who would have swelled the ranks of the latter. In reaction, the MQM organised large demonstrations that degener-ated into riots prior to breaking with the PPP. The violence reinforced

[187] See Ann Frotscher, *Claiming Pakistan*, op. cit., p. 229.
[188] Amtul Hassan, *Impact of Partition*, op. cit., p. 115.
[189] Adeel Khan, *Politics of Identity: Ethnic Nationalism and the State in Pakistan*, New Delhi, Sage, 2005, p. 180.

President Gulam Ishaq Khan's distrust of Benazir Bhutto, whom he later dismissed from office.

With the 1990 elections approaching, the MQM formed a new alliance, this time with the Islam-i Jamhoori Ittehad (IJI) led by Nawaz Sharif and which seemed more likely to win—and to help the Muhajirs. Sharif's party won and formed a coalition with the MQM but proved to be no better disposed toward the Muhajirs than the PPP. It is indeed under Sharif that Operation Clean Up took place. Even if, apparently, the army had not informed the prime minister of its decision,[190] the MQM could not continue in a coalition with his party.

In 1993, the MQM, in protest against Operation Clean Up, boycotted the next general elections, which saw Benazir Bhutto return to power. But it took part in the provincial elections in Sindh, which were also won by the PPP with fifty-six out of the 100 seats, compared to twenty-seven for the MQM(A)—which once again formed a coalition with the PPP.

The MQM(A) shifted alliances once again in 1997. While the February 1997 elections confirmed the PPP as the largest party represented in the Sindh assembly with thirty-six out of 100 seats, it was unable to lead a majority coalition. However, the PML(N) and the MQM(A) won fifteen and twenty-eight seats respectively. This success prompted Nawaz Sharif and Altaf Hussain to join forces and form a strong majority coalition of seventy-two seats, with the support of small parties and independents. The agreement between the MQM(A) and the PML(N) gave the MQM(A) three ministerial portfolios in the federal government, positions in the governorship of Sindh (in addition to Speaker of the Sindh assembly) and the same number of ministries as those held by the PML(N) in the government of Sindh. In addition, the "Biharis" of Bangladesh were to be repatriated, the quota of Muhajirs in the civil service raised to 11.5 per cent and the MQM(Haqiqi) disarmed.

As Nawaz Sharif failed to keep these last three promises—least of all the one concerning the disarmament of the MQM(Haqiqi), the MQM(A) walked out of the Sindh government. In autumn 1998, Prime Minister Sharif demanded that the MQM(A) hand over the murderer of Hakim Saeed, a former governor who had remained very popular. When the party refused, Sharif declared a state of emergency in the province after the MQM(A) withdrew its support.

In 2002, the MQM(A) suffered an electoral setback in terms of valid votes because of the appeal that Islamic parties held (at its expense) for voters who

---

[190] Laurent Gayer, *Karachi*, op. cit., p. 31.

had been very much upset by the American intervention in Afghanistan. But the party won a record number of seats (eighteen in the National Assembly and forty-one in the Sindh assembly). Once again, it entered into a coalition with the number one party—the PML(Q), the party of Musharraf. In exchange for its support in the National Assembly and in Sindh, it was granted the post of governor of Sindh and the promise of a more repressive policy vis-à-vis the Haqiqis—which was indeed carried out.[191] Between 1999 and 2008, the MQM(A) benefited from the benevolent attitude of General Musharraf (another Muhajir born in Delhi) who, for instance, supported Mustapha Kamal, Nazim (mayor) of Karachi for five years in 2005. This position was strategic since the nazim was in charge of the police, could hire municipal functionaries and distribute land as well as real estate.[192]

The close relationship the MQM(A) entertained with Musharraf largely explains why the party defended him against the Chief Justice of the Supreme Court, Iftikhar Chaudhry, in 2007. When Chaudhry came to Karachi during his tour of Pakistan that he undertook to protest against his dismissal by Musharraf, the MQM(A) demonstrations prevented him from leaving the airport. Officially, forty-two people died during the violence that ensued.[193]

Table 4.4: Vote share (%) of major political parties in Karachi (Sindh Provincial Assembly Elections), 1988–2008

	MQM	PPP	PML	ANP	MMA/JUI	PTI
1988	63	20	6	2	0	0
1990	71	16	7	2	0	0
1993	65	19	4	1	0	0
1997	56	10	22	1	0	0
2002	42	13	4	1	26	0
2008	68	22	4	2	1	0
2013	59	8	5	1	1 (JUI-F)	15
					3 (JI)	

Source: Laurent Gayer, *Karachi*, op. cit., p. 102.

In 2008, the PPP won the elections, but needed partners to form coalition governments at the Centre and in Sindh. The MQM(A), which had won twenty-five seats in the National Assembly and fifty-two in Sindh, joined

---

[191] Ann Frotscher, *Claiming Pakistan*, op. cit., p. 259.
[192] Laurent Gayer, *Karachi*, op. cit., p. 106.
[193] Ann Frotscher, *Claiming Pakistan*, op. cit., p. 262.

hands with the party of President Zardari once again. But at that time the positions of the MQM(A) and of the Muhajirs more generally speaking were not as secure as they had been under Musharraf, not only because they had lost their protector, but also because of the new demographic and political equations in Karachi.

Karachi, Crucible of Another Civil War?

For the Muhajirs of Karachi, growing Pashtun assertiveness has become a major challenge. According to the 1998 census, only 4 per cent of the city population were Urdu-speakers (to whom Gujaratis, with 8 per cent, must be added to obtain the proportion of Muhajirs), whereas Pashto-speakers made up 14 per cent, Punjabis 13 per cent, Sindhis 5 per cent, and Baloch 4 per cent.[194] But the war that started in 2001 in Afghanistan and growing instability in Pakistan's Pastun belt probably resulted in the migration of one million people to Karachi.[195] Today, Karachi is the lagest Pashtun city in the world with 4 to 6 million Pashtun people whereas the Urdu speakers, with 7 to 9 million, are probably in a minority.[196] Not only is the quantity of Pashtuns a problem for the Mohajirs, but their "quality" too. First, Pashtuns are not only drivers, watchmen, guards or cooks any more—but businessmen and entrepreneurs as well. This elite group feels discriminated against and resents its marginalisation in the city's power centres that the Mohajirs monopolise. They organised during the last decade, especially after Shahi Syed, the owner of petrol pumps who had migrated to Karachi in 1971, formed a Pashtun Loya Jirga which defends the interests of the Pashtuns of Karachi.[197] Secondly, among the Pashtun activists, ANP members have been gradually replaced by militants who appear much more dangerous to the Mohajirs. Indeed, "Karachi is increasingly becoming the most attractive hideout for Taliban, al-Qaida and other extremist elements, because of its massive make-up and all kinds of ethnic and linguistic societal fabric, where Pakistani and Afghan Taliban can melt in".[198] The Pakistani Taliban of the TTP are a case in point. In a few years, they have

---

[194] Laurent Gayer, *Karachi*, op. cit, p. 24–25.

[195] Robert Nichols considers that 500,000 Afghans lived in Karachi in 2004 (R. Nichols, *A History of Pashtun Migration, 1775–2006*, Karachi, Oxford University Press, 2004, p. 151).

[196] Zia Ur Rehman, *Karachi in turmoil*, Islamabad, Narratives, 2013, p. 29.

[197] Ibid., p. 31.

[198] Ibid., p. 43.

dislodged the ANP leaders who claimed that they represented the local Pashtuns, by resorting to intimidation or by assassinating them. The TTP has also sent some of its members to Karachi because of its economic and financial attractiveness. Not only, according to the police, did TTP members rob local banks of $18 million between 2009 and 2013, but "kidnapping high-profile figures and businessmen for ransom is a primary source of funding".[199]

In 2010, the MQM Nazim of Karachi, Mustapha Kamal, described the Pashtuns of his city not only as forming a mafia, but also as fundamentalists who sought to gain control over Karachi to impose sharia.[200] To resist them more effectively, the MQM has further improved paramilitary style and introduced sophisticated weaponry to allow the Muhajirs to defend their *lebensraum*. This has not deterred the Pashtuns, who stepped up their attacks in 2007 while they were mobilising in favour of Chief Justice Chaudhry.[201] But during this episode ANP activists who supported the Chief Justice were attacked by the MQM (which remained faithful to Musharraf and wanted to show the local Pashtuns that Karachi belonged to them). Fifty-eight Pashtuns died and according to Zia Ur Rehman that was "a watershed moment" because "on that day the Pashtuns of Karachi realized they were not welcome in the city".[202]

Pashtuns where not the only ones who were locked in an increasingly intense conflict with the Mohajirs. Sindhis were too, again. There were two reasons for that. First, in 2011 the MQM presented a bill in the National Assembly asking for the creation of new provinces and Sindhis "for the first time, have taken the threat seriously".[203] Second, Sindhis from the interior (not residents of the city) have been *de facto* excluded from Karachi educational institutions, including Karachi University and Dow Medical College.[204] In this context, Sindhi nationalist parties, which had become

---

[199] Ibid., p. 47.
[200] See interview by Steve Inskeep, available online at: http://www.npr.org/templates/ story/story.php?storyId=91071685, partly transcribed in his book *Instant City*, op. cit., pp. 176–177. See also http://sachaylog.blogspot.fr/2011/01/racist-abusive-mustafa-kamal-of-mqm.html (Accessed on September 15, 2013).
[201] They have, for instance "conquered" the predominantly Christian neighbourhood of De Silva Town (Taimur Khan, "Karachi in Fragments", *Critical Muslim*, no. 4, Oct.-Dec. 2012, p. 48).
[202] Zia Ur Rehman, *Karachi in turmoil*, op. cit., p. 32.
[203] Ibid., p. 37.
[204] Ibid., p. 36.

largely irrelevant since the 1970s, tried to stage a comeback. G. M. Syed's Jeay Sindh Tehrik, which had split into eleven groups, was relaunched by Safdar Sarki who in 2012 asked for the "independence" of Sindh, like the Jeay Sindh Qaumi Mahaz. Soon after, Bilawal Bhutto-Zardari, the Chairman of the PPP, launched the Sindh festival which was intended to make Sindhis "aware of [their] existence" and "civilisation".[205]

The escalation of violence in Karachi since 2011 is unprecedented. While the previous wave of killings had resulted in 1,742 deaths in 1995 before a quick return to normalcy, the number of casualties has kept rising since 2006, being multiplied by almost ten on a yearly basis between 2006 and 2012. In three years, 1,000 activists were killed.[206]

Table 4.5: Killings in Karachi, by year

Year	1999	2000	2001	2002	2003	2004	2005	2006	2007	2008	2009	2010	2011	2012
Number killed	85	84	107	87	76	163	130	278	344	777	801	1,339	1,724	2,174

Source: Citizens Police Liaison Committee, http://www.cplc.org.pk/content.php?page=26

But 2013 has been even worse and in fact the deadliest year so far—probably, in part, because of the general elections. According to the Human Rights Commisson of Pakistan, 3,251 people died.[207] The data released by the Sindh Police and the Rangers gave a lower figure (2,715), but also showed a steep rise of "incidents of heinous crimes"—which reached the unprecedented level of 40,848 in 2013.[208] The Pak Institute for Peace Studies, in its 2013 Pakistan Security Report, points out that during that year 356 terrorist attacks were carried out in Karachi, representing an increase of 90 per cent as compared to 2012.[209]

205 "Bilawal declares 'cultural coup'", *Dawn*, 22 Jan. 2014 (http://www.dawn.com/news/1081942/bilawal-declares-cultural-coup).

206 Laurent Gayer, *Karachi*, op. cit., p. 170.

207 Rabia Ali, "Death toll rises", *The Express Tribune*, 18 January 2014 (http://tribune.com.pk/story/660098/death-toll-rises-over-3200-killings-in-karachi-make-2013-deadliest-year-so-far/?print=true).

208 Faraz Khan and Gibran Ashraf, "Karachi 2013: the deadliest year of all", *The Express Tribune*, 6 January 2014 (http://tribune.com.pk/story/653889/karachi-2013-the-deadliest-year-of-all/).

209 *Pakistan Security Report—2013*, Islamabad, Pak Institute for Peace Studies, 2014, p. 19

In reaction to this wave of violence, the government of Nawaz Sharif—who had just visited the city—initiated a "targeted operation" in September 2013. In six months, according to the Rangers spokeperson, 1,839 "targeted raids" resulted in the arrest of 1,887 suspected criminals, including 126 suspected target killers, 181 suspected extortionists and 12 "high-profile terrorists". As many as 78 suspected criminals were killed in 52 encounters. Simultaneously, 3,236 weapons were confiscated, including rocket propelled grenades, hand grenades, rocket launchers, light and sub-machine guns, and explosives.[210] In July 2014, the authorities claimed that 31,336 criminals had been arrested.[211] In reaction, the TTP—one of the main targets of these raids—killed policemen (13 in a bus in January 2014) including the police chief Chaudhry Aslam who had already escaped 5 attacks since 2009.[212] During the first six months of 2014 alone, 91 policemen were killed in Karachi.[213]

Violence has sealed the fate of the remaining mixed neighbourhoods. The last inhabitants of localities dominated by "others" have left. This process, which Taimur Khan calls a form of self-cleansing, is in fact reminiscent of preventive, voluntary ethnic cleansing.[214] The homogenous nature of the areas resulting from this process is easily identifiable: Muhajir neighbourhoods bear MQM flags, whereas Pashtun localities display fewer and fewer ANP flags and more and more the colours of the Taliban who have "virtually wiped out [the ANP] of Karachi" within a year in 2012.[215] While Muhajirs and Pashtuns face each other in a kind of trench warfare, other groups are playing their own cards. The Baloch, for instance, are entrenched in Lyari, one of the oldest industrial neighbourhoods in

---

[210] "Operation cleanup", *The Express Tribune*, 6 March 2014 (http://tribune.com.pk/story/679571/operation-cleanup-rangers-arrest-80-suspected-criminals-in-karachi/).

[211] Asim Khan, "Karachi operation: Report says over 30,000 arrested so far", *Dawn* 10 July 2014 (http://www.dawn.com/news/1118314/karachi-operation-report-says-over-30000-arrested-so-far/).

[212] "Karachi car bomb kills 13 policemen; TTP claims attack", *Dawn*, 14 February 2014 (http://www.dawn.com/news/1086747) and Imran Ayub, "SP Chaudhry Aslam—a symbol of success for many, hatred for others", 10 January 2014 (http://www.dawn.com/news/1079525).

[213] "91 Karachi cops killed this year as police face backlash for targeted operation", *The Express Tribune*, 15 July 2014, (http://tribune.com.pk/story/735892/91-karachi-cops-killed-this-year-as-police-face-backlash-for-targeted-operation/).

[214] Taimur Khan, "Karachi in Fragments", op. cit.

[215] Laurent Gayer, *Karachi*, op. cit., p. 162.

Karachi, which used to be a stronghold of the leftwing unions and the PPP.[216]

Skirmishes take place at the "frontier" between ethnic localities, which are usually marked merely by wider streets. This war of position does not necessarily result in a large number of casualties if the frontlines are stabilised. But the growing assertiveness of the Pashtuns has apparently persuaded some Muhajir leaders that the best way to defend their positions is to be on the offensive. The new players, the Taliban, have also opened a new front by massively targeting Shias (mostly Muhajirs).[217]

The scale of violence in Karachi needs to be qualified. It is not on such a great magnitude if compared to the situation prevailing in other cities. Certainly, 15,000 to 20,000 were killed between 1985 and 2012, but in 2012, the homicide rate was "only" 12.3 for 100,000 inhabitants. Such figures rank Karachi in 13th place, behind many Latin American cities.[218] The chronic violence is a problem, however, because Karachi accounts for one-fourth of Pakistan's tax revenue and one-fifth of its GDP (almost one-third of the country's industrial production and half of its financial services).[219] This explains why more than one government has fallen because of troubles in Karachi.[220] Second, the situation in Karachi and other cities of Sindh shows that national integration has made no progress so far as the Muhajirs are concerned, on the contrary. Certainly, Altaf Hussain is probably bluffing when he says that he wants another Partition,[221] but he is sincere when he asks for the recognition of the Muhajirs as a "separate nationality"[222] and says that he is prepared to use all possible means—including violence—to exercise control over the cities of Sindh. Muhajirs consider that they are entitled to this territory—the only part of Pakistan that is left to them—the same way Sir Syed considered Muslims were entitled to special privileges. But at the same time, the MQM(A) continues to play a political game within the system in order to be represented in as many sites of power as possible. Consequently, on 22 April 2014 the party joined the PPP-led government in Sindh, where it obtained two ministers.

---

[216] Ibid. chapter 4.

[217] Ibid., p. 185.

[218] Ibid., p. 5.

[219] Ibid..

[220] More precisely, it explains why troubles in Karachi provided presidents with a good excuse to dismiss prime ministers they disliked in the 1990s.

[221] Interview in *India Today*, 15 July 1995, p. 42.

[222] Altaf Hussain, *My Life's Journey*, op. cit., p. 120.

FIVE ETHNIC GROUPS FOR ONE NATION

National Integration through Federalism and Regionalisation of Politics?

Although the issue of national integration is far from settled in Pakistan, largely because of virulent Baloch separatism and violent Muhajir politics, it should not be blown out of proportion as observers who periodically predict the break-up of the country tend to do. In addition to the gradual integration of Sindhis and Pashtuns into mainstream Pakistani politics, there are probably three other good reasons that this problem should be nuanced.

First, due to internal divisions, Punjab does not exercise absolute domination apt to foster more centrifugal forces. Second, the state, with the start of a new phase of democratisation in 2008, seems to be engaging in a decentralisation policy likely to restore some of the provinces' prerogatives. Third, provinces are becoming more multi-ethnic, particularly due to migratory flows, an evolution that has not, however, diluted the trend towards the regionalisation of politics, as evident from the results of the 2013 elections.

What Punjabi Hegemony?

Punjab seems destined to dominate the country, not only from an economic viewpoint (it represents 57 per cent of the GDP), but also politically. When the military holds the reins of power, the province takes advantage of its over-representation in army ranks. In phases of democratisation, the region continues to play a preponderant role on account of its demographics. Up until the 2008 elections, it held 55 per cent of seats in the National Assembly (115 out of 207, compared to 46 in Sindh, 26 in the NWFP and 11 in Balochistan). Its share diminished somewhat with the 2013 elections, as it now holds 54.4 per cent of the seats, 148 out of 272 (61 for Sindh, 35 for KP, 14 for Balochistan, 12 for the FATA and 2 for Islamabad).[223]

The political importance of numbers was one of the reasons why the 1991 census could not be organised on time. It turned out to be a highly sensitive issue partly because the minority provinces were afraid the population count would show a proportionally stronger population growth in Punjab, which would result in an increase in the number of its constituencies and its share of the federal budget. The census was also postponed because the Muhajirs and the Baloch feared that it would show an increase in the number of Pashtuns in Karachi and Balochistan respectively. It was finally held in 1998,

---

[223] Furthermore, when the PML(N), a party largely identified with Punjab, sweeps the polls, the government itself is dominated by Punjabis. In 2013, in the first government formed by Nawaz Sharif, 19 of the 25 ministers came from Punjab.

seven years late, under army supervision. Nationalist mobilisation in the smaller provinces in fact took on a new form in the 1990s with the creation of the Pakistan Oppressed National Minorities (PONM) movement, bringing together the minority provinces to counterbalance Punjabi domination.

Table 4.6: Pakistan in 2008, by province

Provinces	Surface (in sq. km)	%	Population (in million)	%	% of the GDP
Punjab	205,344	23.3	81,594	50.3	57.0
Sindh	140,914	16	35,471	21.9	27.5
Khyber–Pakhtukhwa	74,521	8.5	20,215	12.5	8.0
Balochistan	347,190	39.4	11,934	7.4	3.0
Gilgit-Baltistan	72,496	8.2	1,800	1.1	–
Azad Kashmir	13,297	1.5	4,568	2.8	–
Islamabad	906	0.1	0.956	0.6	1.0
FATA	27,220	3.1	5,600	3.4	1.5
Total	881,888	100.0	162,138	100.0	–

Source: Pakistan Bureau of Statistic, Government of Pakistan. Data available at http://www.pbs.gov.pk/content/pakistan-social-and-living-standards-measurement-survey-pslm-2008-09-provincial-district.

Punjab's influence, however, deserves to be qualified on a number of counts. First, as will be seen below, Punjabi-speakers are not in a majority if Saraiki-speakers are taken into account. Second, Punjab is also divided from a socioeconomic standpoint. The Lahore region is probably the most prosperous due to the influence of this city and Faisalabad, which has become the country's third largest metropolis on account of its booming textile industry. This area is where the "canal colonies" are located, which were developed by the British and were at the heart of the Green Revolution in the 1960s.[224] The Potohar plateau in northwest Punjab, with Rawalpindi for its capital, has a very different profile in particular due to the influence of the neighbouring region inhabited by Pathans, from whom much of the area's population in fact descends. It is more arid, and the low agricultural yields—in addition to Pathan influences—largely explain why many Potohar families send at least one of their sons into the army. Although the Punjabis have been said to dominate the Pakistan army since

---

[224] Ian Talbot, "The Punjabisation of Pakistan: Myth or Reality?" in Christophe Jaffrelot (ed.), *Pakistan, Nationalism without a Nation?* op. cit., p. 56.

the British designated them as a "martial race", this analysis in fact practically applies solely to the people of Potohar. Lastly, southern Punjab not only encompasses the Saraiki region, but also derives its specific identity in Punjabi-speaking districts such as Jhang from Baloch and Sindhi influences. This is evident in the system of farmland ownership, which is less egalitarian than in other subregions because it is dominated by large landholders. The cult of saints there is closer to the one practiced in the Sindhi culture, "feudals" sponsoring places of worship (particularly saints' tombs) linked with *pirs*—when they are not hereditary *pir-zamindars* themselves. These differences also reflect class conflicts or disputes between certain segments of the Punjabi elite. Whereas the most influential business communities—in particular large industrialists—live in the north of the province, the south is dominated by agrarian interests, which can be further subdivided between feudal landlords bordering Sindh and Balochistan and landowner-entrepreneurs in the centre.

Punjab is thus less unified than it first appears and therefore less capable of wielding the power of a hegemon. Otherwise, the Punjabis would have managed to push through the Kalabargh Dam for instance, planned since the 1950s but constantly postponed under pressure from the Sindhis and Pashtuns who are afraid of losing control over the waters from the rivers that run through their province. The fact remains that the sheer size of Punjab and the lust for power of a fraction of Punjabis sustains ethnic tensions in Pakistan by making the minority provinces insecure and resentful vis-à-vis the domination of the largest group.

As a result, even if Punjab is not in a position to exercise hegemony to the point that all the other provinces might be encouraged to stand together against it, the Punjabis are targets of widespread resentment among their neighbours. This relationship to their fellow citizens was underscored by the summer 2010 floods, when the province least affected by the disaster turned out to be Punjab. Differences in rainfall and better governance provide a rational explanation for this. But rumours circulating in Balochistan and Sindh claimed that the northern provinces simply allowed the water to gush toward the Indus, thus reflecting the extent of prejudice.

Toward a New Federalism? The Eighteenth Amendment

Ethnic centrifugal forces might also diminish in Pakistan because of new attempts to decentralise the political system since 2008. Just before, General Musharraf had gone in the opposite direction. Not only did he repress autonomist movements in Balochistan, but he also made an effort to weaken the provinces. In 2001, he introduced a reform strengthening the local political echelon at the expense of the provinces by turning many positions hitherto filled by civil servants into elective offices. Citizens now voted in the *nazims* (district council chiefs), *tehsildars* (subdistrict council chiefs) and municipal council officials who were formerly appointed by the administration. Musharraf intended this to be a means of renewing the political class by bringing out new leaders. The result was entirely different. Traditional notables were the first to occupy these new positions of power and join Musharraf's party, the PLM(Q), thus mirroring his influence at the local level. Afraid of being short-circuited by this new system, the provinces got it abolished at the end of the elected officials' term in 2009, and civil servants once again fill these offices that had been open to election.

But the new regime, well aware of the need for more decentralisation, went one step further. In August 2009 it attributed new responsibilities to the Northern Territories (NT), renamed Gilgit-Baltistan. Until then, this area lagged behind the other four, even behind neighbouring Azad Kashmir, which had an interim constitution and an assembly. Even if the NT had an elected legislative assembly, the federal government appointed its president. This is no longer the case. The Legislative Council elected in November 2009 under the new rules is now empowered to discuss the provincial budget. Although the chief minister of the province operates under the authority of a governor appointed by the federal government, which continues to appoint some of the ministers as well, a certain degree of decentralisation is underway in this strategic area due to its proximity to Indian Kashmir and the high Shia population living there.

More importantly, in April 2010, the Pakistani Parliament passed the 18th constitutional amendment, which not only re-established a parliamentary system, as will be seen in the next chapter, but also aimed to restore the prerogatives provinces enjoyed by virtue of the 1973 Constitution.

Indeed, this amendment substantively modified a number of internal balances as much to the detriment of the central authorities as to the country's main province, Punjab. First of all, the Concurrent List was abolished. The Constitution of 1973 originally had two lists of powers, the Federal Legislative List (FLL), which listed sixty-seven areas in which the centre could legislate, and the Concurrent List, which detailed forty-seven other subjects in which the centre could prevail over legislation enacted by a provincial assembly, any remaining areas falling within the competence of the provinces. The 18th Amendment abolished the Concurrent List and divided the FLL into two categories. The first category contains areas in which the federal government has sole power to legislate and the second, areas that would now be managed by the Council of Common Interests, the powers of the regional assemblies having been enlarged considerably, to the point where seventeen ministries were devolved from the centre. Furthermore, following discussions between the SPCCR and the 7th National Finance Commission (NFC), the 18th Amendment stipulated that the distribution of resources between the centre and the provinces could not be less than the share awarded by the NFC for the year 2011, in which 57.5 per cent of revenues—compared to 45 per cent under Musharraf—was allocated to the provinces. Moreover, the sharing of resources among the provinces would no longer be allocated on the basis of population, which placed Punjab at an advantage, but according to other criteria as well, such that even if 82 per cent of the total amounts allocated was awarded on the basis of population, 10.3 per cent would be awarded by level of development (a Baloch and Pashtun concern), 5 per cent on the basis of revenue generated by the provinces (in accordance with Karachi's wishes), and 2.7 per cent on the basis of inverse population density. As a result, Punjab saw its fund allocation decrease by 5.6 per cent, although its leaders had apparently received assurance that it would be compensated for its losses.[225]

Lastly, the 18th Amendment, in response to a long-standing demand from Balochistan, revised article 172 of the Constitution—which until then had vested the central authorities with exploitation of natural resources. Now "mineral oil and natural gas within the Province or the territorial waters adjacent thereto shall vest jointly and equally in that province and the Federal Government". Pashtun demands were also satisfied, as the NWFP was renamed Khyber–Pakhunkhwa. Contrary to the common belief that a majority of them—starting with the ANP leaders, who had featured the demand to change the province's name in the party manifesto—were disappointed by the more territorial than ethnic reference made by adding the name of the Khyber Pass to their preferred term, Pakhtunkhwa, they saw it as the first step in their crusade to join the FATA to their province.

In the same spirit, article 38 was augmented with a paragraph stipulating that provincial quotas for the national civil service should effectively be filled.

---

[225] Katharine Adeney, "A Step towards Inclusive Federalism in Pakistan? The Politics of the 18th Amendment", *The Journal of Federalism*, 2012, Vol. 42 No. 4, pp. 539–565.

Multi-ethnicity and the Regionalisation of Politics

In none of the four provinces of Pakistan does a dominant linguistic group represent more than 75–80 per cent of the population. The NWFP, now renamed Khyber–Pakhtunkhwa (KP), is a case in point. In 1984, a survey showed that only 68 per cent of its inhabitants spoke Pashto. The main linguistic minority was made up of Hindko-speakers. Hindko, an Indo-European language which may well be the sixth most widely-used language in Pakistan, is spoken in KP and Punjab respectively in the districts of Mansehra, Abbottabad, Haripur, Peshawar, Nowshera, Akora Khattak, Swabi and Kohat, and in Attock and Rawalpindi. While the urban Hindko-speakers also know Pashto and sometimes Urdu, they have staunchly defended their mother tongue in recent years. In 1993, they formed the Gandhara Hindko Board, the reference to Gandhara civilisation reflecting their attachment to a prestigious past. This Board produced the first dictionary of Hindko in 2003.

In Balochistan, Baloch-speakers, as mentioned above, are probably in a minority in their own province mostly because of the massive presence of Pashtuns whose ranks have increased with the inflows of refugees from Afghanistan. (In 1997, out of 1,350,000 Afghan refugees living in Pakistan, 352,700, mostly Pashtuns, were settled in Balochistan.)[226] Their party, the Pakhtunkhwa Milli Awami Party (PkMAP), asked for a separate province, "South Pakhtoonkhwa",[227] that the mainstream parties (including the PML(N)) are not likely to grant them simply because this party, for the moment, helps them to govern Balochistan. The separatist agenda of the Baloch nationalists is also somewhat weakened from the inside, to a much lesser extent, by the Hazaras[228]—but the relationship between Hazaras and Baloch nationalists are unclear as we'll see below, while studying sectarianism in Balochistan. This small community, which speaks a Persian dialect, Hazaragi, descends from the Mongols but converted to Shiism from the sixteenth century onwards when it was located in Afghanistan. Because of persecutions, many Hazaras left Afghanistan to settle in Quetta. The Hazaras have invested in education, so much so that they are over-represented among professionals and army officers. One of them, General

---

[226] *Economic Survey 1996–1997*, Islamabad, Government of Pakistan, 1997, p. 107.

[227] Amir Wasim, "Achakzai proposes 60 amendments, 6 provinces". See http://pkmap. 8k.com (Accessed on September 15, 2013).

[228] See http://www.joshuaproject.net/people-profile.php?peo3=12076&rog3=PK (Accessed on September 15, 2013).

Muhammad Musa, became commander-in-chief of the Pakistani army under Ayub Khan between 1958 and 1968. The Hazaras do not share the Baloch nationalist agenda, not only because the former disapprove—like the Pashtuns—of the positive discrimination measures that the government of Quetta has implemented in favour of the Balochs, but also because they are more and more identified as Shias. The last part of this book will focus on the sectarian conflict between Shias and Sunnis, a line of division that does not overlap with ethnic distinctions—and in fact weakens them.

Table 4.7.: Linguistic groups of Pakistan in 1984 (by region, in %)

Province/Language	Punjabi	Pashto	Sindhi	Saraiki	Urdu	Baloch	Other
Punjab	78.7	0.8	0.1	14.9	4.3	0.6	0.6
Sindh	7.7	3.1	52.4	2.3	22.6	4.5	7.4
NWFP	1.1	68.3	0.1	4	0.8	0.1	25.6
Balochistan	2.2	25.1	8.3	3.1	1.4	36.3	23.6
Pakistan	48.2	13.1	11.8	9.8	7.6	3	6.5

Source: *Government of Pakistan, Statistical Pocket Book of Pakistan, 1984*, Islamabad, Federal Bureau of Statistics, 1984, p. 61.

The last province in which unity is weakened by the presence of a linguistic minority is Punjab,[229] where Sraraiki-speakers, concentrated in the South, represented 17.5 per cent of the population in 1998. Their language, partly codified during the Raj, derived its emotional attraction from the poetry of a Sufi saint, Ghulam Farid, who has become an identity symbol.[230] The first Saraiki grammar saw the light of the day in 1953. The Saraiki movement subsequently became more political due to the forced integration of the former princely state of Bahawalpur into the province of West Pakistan in 1954. In 1970, when the One-Unit Scheme was abolished, the Saraiki-speaking zone was amalgamated with Punjab. Saraiki was then described as a dialect of Punjabi. Saraiki-speakers protested that they needed a separate province, also because they wanted to emancipate the local peasants from absentee landlords who had kept the area backward. In 1975 the Saraiki Literary Conference of Multan accelerated the politicisation of the Saraiki movement. The Saraiki Subha Mahaz (SSM—Movement for the creation of a Saraiki province) demanded a separate province com-

[229] Sindh is a special case that has already been analysed.
[230] Tariq Rahman, *Language and Politics in Pakistan*, op. cit., p. 180.

prising the divisions of Multan, Bahawalpur, Dera Ghazi Khan and Sargodha and the districts of Jhang and Dera Ismail Khan (located in the NWFP). Zia's regime did not allow this regional movement to air its grievances publicly, but in 1988 the SSM supported the PPP in exchange for the promise that it would consider its demands if voted in. This promise was not fulfilled and the SSM therefore transformed into the Pakistan Saraiki Party in 1989. The party was unable to make any inroads, but its very existence to some extent bears testimony to the resilience of a sub-regional ethno-linguistic movement in Punjab. During the term of Zardari, the upper house approved the creation of a Bahawalpur Janoobi Punjab province, but the government did not table the bill to the National Assembly.[231]

Despite the growing multi-ethnicity of the Pakistani provinces, the regionalisation of politics continued to develop during the 2013 elections. Almost all the provinces can be identified with one particular political force. The winner, the PML(N) obtained 118 of its 126 seats in the National Assembly from Punjab, in the assembly of which it won 214 out of 293 seats—including in South Punjab, among Saraiki voters. The PPP won 30 of its 31 seats in Sindh, a province where it also won 65 seats out of 125 in the regional assembly (naturally the MQM cornered most of the urban seats—it took 37 of them and did not win any outside of these ethnic strongholds).

The only political force that was not associated with a province was the Pakistan Tehrik-e-Insaf of Imran Khan, the former captain of the national cricket team who turned to politics in the 1990s. In fact, the PTI set out to transcend the regional logics of Pakistani politics by attracting middle class voters throughout the country. It tried to woo them (in particular the youth) by focusing on national issues such as anti-Americanism and corruption. But in the end, this party still won most of its seats (17 out of 29) from one province, KP, where it also won 35 of the 97 in the regional assembly. As a result, the PTI was unexpectedly in a position to lead the ruling coalition in Peshawar. This "Pashtunisation" was probably less due to the ethnic origin of Imran Khan,[232] who has written a book entitled

---

[231] Azam Khan, "National Assembly: a tenure of changes—bith good and bad", *The Express Tribune*, 17 March 2013 (http://tribune.com.pk/story/522062/national-assembly-a-tenure-of-changes-both-good-and-bad/).

[232] Imran Khan claims that he is a Pashtun. Imran Khan, *Pakistan, A Personal History*, London, Bantam Press, 2011, pp. 32–33 and 277, but he is probably not recognized as one of them by the KP voters, at least not by those who suspect that he does not speak Pashto fluently.

Warrior Race: A Journey through the Land of the Tribal Pathans,[233] than to the rejection of the ANP[234] by KP voters who were willing to try something else.

The 2013 elections showed that Balochistan and Karachi remained the main factors of national disintegration. In the former, most of the Baloch parties boycotted the elections and turnout was very low in many places.[235] In the latter, the MQM made a point to intimidate voters and violently resist the PTI's attempts to make inroads in "its" city. The PTI won 13 per cent of the votes, but there were many casualties.[236] Elsewhere, regionalisation of politics has remained the order of the day more than before (in the 1990s and in 2008 either the PPP won seats in Punjab or the PML(N) made inroads in Sindh), suggesting that even when they do not belong to the same community because of the growing multi-ethnicity mentioned above, the provinces of Pakistan tend to identify with one political party.

* * *

The trajectory of Pakistan, as an idea before 1947, and then as a country, offers a good illustration of a specific category of nationalism, that of "nationalisms without nations"[237] where the ideological construction of the national project precedes the formation (in sociological terms) of the nation. In this type of nationalism, elite groups play a major role since they shape the national project and then mobilise masses in support of it. Such a top-down modus operandi is not uncommon—on the contrary. In France, for instance, peasants have become Frenchmen (to paraphrase Eugen Weber) along these lines.[238] But in the case of Pakistan, in contrast to

---

[233] Advocating the case of the Pashtuns, Imran Khan claims that they are not in a better situation than the East Bengalis before 1971. See Madiha Tahir, "I'll be your mirror", *The Caravan*, 4(1), January 2012, p. 41.

[234] The Taliban's terrorist methods prevented ANP candidates from canvassing the way they did in 2008, as will be seen in the last part of the book.

[235] "Bizarre Numbers in Balochistan", *Dawn*, 18 May 2013. Available at: http://dawn.com/2013/05/18/bizarre-numbers-elections-in-Balochistan/ (Accessed on September 15, 2013).

[236] FAFEN, "Observation of General Election 2013. Key Findings and Recommendations", 22 May 2013. Available at: http://www.electionpakistan.org (Accessed on September 15, 2013).

[237] The title of a book I edited more than ten years ago, *Pakistan: Nationalism Without a Nation?* London/New York, Zed Books, 2002.

[238] Eugen Weben, *Peasants Into Frenchmen: The Modernization of Rural France, 1880–1914*, Stanford, Stanford University Press, 1976.

France, the national(ist) elite could not rely on a state apparatus and, more importantly, the ethnic identities it had to cope with were more numerous and vigorous—some of them irredentist. It had not only to build a nation, but a state as well, and, to further complicate matters, it came from outside the territory of the new country.

Indeed, the idea of Pakistan first took shape among Muslims in areas of British India such as the United Provinces where they were a minority, and in particular among an elite descended from the Mughal aristocracy whose status was threatened by a rapidly expanding Hindu majority in the 1860s. Pakistan's prehistory in fact dates back to the Aligarh movement whose leader, Sir Syed, strived not only to regain the trust of the British who accused the Muslims of having fomented the Revolt of 1857, but also to obtain from them a separate political status that would protect them from having to compete with the Hindus, and even put the Muslims on an equal footing with them. Sir Syed used the historical and social importance of the minority he represented to justify this ambition. Without granting them equal status, the British accorded a separate electorate to the delegation that eventually formed the Muslim League in 1906.

It was then up to Muhammad Ali Jinnah to pursue Sir Syed's work to campaign in favour of political sovereignty for Indian Muslims in colonial India, still in the name of an equal footing for the "two nations". In his mind, the entity to be built did not necessarily imply Partition of the British Raj, but the obstinacy (or tenacity, depending on one's point of view) he showed in his demand for parity was one of the explanatory factors of Partition. That this was not the goal of the Muslim League leaders, who experienced it as much as a failure as an achievement, attests to the blindness characteristic of the Pakistani syndrome. Its symptoms—combining a feeling of vulnerability toward the Hindus, heightened by the idea that the Muslims were those who suffered most from British rule, and a superiority complex inherited from past Mughal grandeur—are mainly manifested through a keen sense of entitlement: the conviction that Indian Muslims cannot be treated like everyone else in view of their past status and because they must be protected in light of their waning influence today. This perception of things clearly made "minority Muslims", for whom Jinnah was the principal spokesman, lose sight of reality and it cost them dearly in the final negotiations. A more moderate position than the headlong quest for equal status might have produced different results—provided that the Congress had proven accommodating, which it had begun to show signs of by accepting that the interim government counted as many Muslims as Hindus in 1946.

In the 1930s–40s, however, the main problem facing the Muslim League leaders came as much from the "majority Muslims" as from Congress. Although the sovereign Muslim political entity Jinnah dreamed of implied the rallying of Muslims in Punjab, Bengal, the NWFP and Sindh to his cause, their leaders were less attuned to the Islam-based identity arguments the League propounded than to their ethno-linguistic culture and their socio-economic agenda based on the convergence of the agrarian interests of Hindu and Muslim elites; all the more since, as they were a majority in provinces that moreover enjoyed increasing autonomy, they in no way perceived a Hindu threat the way the Muslims of the North—who had been discriminated against by the British and who suffered from the Hindus' competition—did.[239] The notion of a Hindu threat did not appear to them until after the 1937 election victory of Congress, which Jinnah made sure to portray as a Hindu party. Exploiting the impression of danger that this group represented for Indian Muslims in the 1946 elections, the Muslim League managed at the last minute to rally majority Muslims to his cause that year. This success, unhoped-for a year earlier, was incomplete—Jinnah still had not conquered the NWFP—and fragile—to the very end Muslim leaders would argue against the idea of Pakistan in the name of a particularly strong regional identity in Bengal and Sindh.

By all appearances, it would seem as though the "minority Muslims", descendents of an elite accustomed to ruling, had instrumentalised Islam to convince the "majority Muslims" to detach a piece of territory to give them a state to govern. Pakistan thus did not develop out of a long maturation process backed by the representatives of various provinces. It is the product of "a brief moment of political unity", in the words of Yunus Samad,[240] fostered and seized upon by an elite that thus achieved its ends: the Muhajirs indeed got their state in 1947, but the Pakistani nation still did not exist. As Salman Rushdie was to write about Pakistan, this country had probably not been "sufficiently imagined" before coming into being.[241]

---

[239] The Muslim elites of Punjab, Sindh, the NWFP and Bengal did not entertain the same nostalgia of the Mughal era either. Interestingly, among them, the Urdu speaking Ashraf who shared this ethos and sometimes descended from Mughal-related aristocrats joined the Muslim League first.

[240] Yunus Samad, *A Nation in Turmoil. Nationalism and Ethnicity in Pakistan, 1937–1958*, New Delhi, Sagen, 1995 p. 90.

[241] Salman Rushdie, *Shame*, New York, Alfred Knopf, 1983.

Indeed, as Benedict Anderson has shown,[242] nations are also (and perhaps primarily) the product of a collective imagination using means of mass communication. Without them—including what Anderson calls "print capitalism"—and a centralized state apparatus (including civil servants who play an important part in Anderson's model), ethnic identities make the shaping of a nation much more complicated. Pakistan had none of them in 1947, and that is why it epitomizes a kind of "nationalism without a nation" that was born against the Hindu other, but without much societal substance; all the more so as it was the product of a tiny elite.

This nationalist elite could have rallied most of the ethnic groups around the idea of Pakistan rather easily if it had opted for a federal state structure, as promised in the Lahore Resolution. But Jinnah and his successors promoted a unitary, centralised state—through their deeds, if not officially. This decision, which was partly overdetermined by the fear of India, reflected the political culture and the interests of the Urdu-speaking Muhajirs (whose language was elevated to the rank of national idiom).

Accounting for only 1–2 per cent of the new state, those who had done everything to win power were soon dislodged from the country's leadership by the Punjabis who adopted the new state's official line as their own, aware of the legitimacy it would lend their domination. Invoking Islam and adopting Urdu were the means they found to defuse criticism from minorities by posing as pure patriots. Not only were the other communities not fooled, but furthermore the Punjabi elites—especially those trained by the military establishment and the civil service—conducted centralist policies with just as much rigidity as the Muhajirs.

The Bengalis were the first to demand more autonomy, not only because of their attachment to their language, but also because of the economic exploitation they were subjected to. On top of it, they formed the country's majority and could rule it if power were not centralized undemocratically. The One-Unit Scheme, which the Muhajirs and the Punjabis had concocted to remain at the helm in defiance of democratic principles, could only alienate the Bengali majority and, after its abolition, the repressive measures of Ayub Khan against Mujibur Rahman further radicalized the Bengali nationalists. This process was bound to recur—and had already been seen in Balochistan: instead of seeking some sort of compromise, the state resorted to heavy-handed interventions that transformed autonomist

[242] Benedict Anderson, *Imagined Communities: Reflections on the Origin and Spread of Nationalism*, London, Verso, 1983.

movements into full-fledged separatisms. In Bengal, it ended up, with help from India, in a second Partition that was more traumatic that the first simply because it showed that Islam was not a sufficiently strong cement to keep the country together.

After 1971, Sindhis identified more with Pakistan when one of them— Z.A. Bhutto, and then his daughter—ruled the country and gave them greater recognition and a larger share of resources, including jobs. Similarly, Pashtuns—who had always been over-represented in the army— gradually turned their back on their old separatist agenda. Pashtun nationalists diluted their ideology in order to make more room for the non-Pashto speakers of the NWFP and form alliances with mainstream parties in Peshawar as well as at the Centre.

By contrast, Baloch nationalists and Muhajirs continue to support centrifugal trends fostered by the government's repressive attitude (be it in the hands of the army or civilians). The Baloch, like the Bengalis before them, continue to combat a classic case of domestic imperialism based on the exploitation of local resources by the state. The Muhajirs are prepared to resort to any means ranging from electoral coalitions to sheer violence to retain power in the cities of Sindh. As a result, Karachi has been the epicentre of a low intensity civil war because of competition between the MQM(A) and the Pashtuns, primarily.

This unresolved national question is part of the Pakistan syndrome. The architects and rulers of the country have always been anxious to concentrate power in their hands—Pakistan was essentially created for this reason. Hence the unitary form of the regime that was bound to alienate the provinces dominated until then by deeply entrenched ethnic groups.[243] This centralising attitude has been epitomized, in the course of history, by personal oppositions: Jinnah vs. Abdul Ghaffar Khan, Ayub Khan vs. Mujibur Rahman, Z.A. Bhutto vs. Wali Khan, Benazir Bhutto and Nawaz Sharif vs. Altaf Hussain, Musharraf vs. Akbar Bugti. But the national question is larger than that. It is, in a way, systemic.

However, it is not as acute as it was before the 1970s. First, ethno-linguistic violence is mostly circumscribed to two provinces. Second, the domination of Punjab is not as hegemonic as it once was. Third, federalism has

[243] See Samina Ahmed's analysis "Centralization, Authoritarianism and the Mismanagement of Ethnic Relations in Pakistan", in Michael Edward Brown and Sumit Ganguly (eds), *Government Politics and Ethnic Relations in Asia and the Pacific*, Cambridge (Mass.), MIT Press, 1997, p. 88.

staged a comeback, at least on paper, since the 2008 transition to democracy. Certainly, the grammar of politics continues to be regionalised, so much so that even mainstream parties could not claim that they covered the entire nation after the 2013 elections, but this regionalisation shows that ethnic identities can be transcended since most provinces are now multi-ethnic—and ethnic groups, when they are out of their province, adjust to the political culture of their new region.[244] Whether regional tensions are easier to defuse than ethnic tensions remains to be seen.

---

[244] A recent survey illustrates this capacity of regional identities to prevail over ethnicity. While 49% of the Punjabis in Punjab think that the sharia should play a much larger role in the state, only 15% of the Punjabis interviewed out of Punjab think the same—and 50% of the non-Punjabis in Punjab concur (C. Fair, *Fighting to the End*, New York, Oxford University Press, 2014, p. 272).

PART TWO

NEITHER DEMOCRACY NOR AUTOCRACY?

Since independence in 1947, Pakistan has had three constitutions and three military coups d'état, democratic-leaning regimes alternating with dictatorships at almost regular ten-year intervals. In 1958 the coup led by General Ayub Khan brutally put an end to eleven years of constitutional debates. His successor, General Yahya Khan, resigned himself to organising elections that finally brought Zulfikar Ali Bhutto to power after the "Partition" of Bangladesh. But Bhutto was overthrown in 1977 by another military coup orchestrated by General Zia ul-Haq, who remained in power for eleven years, until his death in an airplane accident. The democratisation process was then marked by the return of another Bhutto, Benazir, to the post of prime minister. For eleven years, she would alternate with Nawaz Sharif at the head of governments which, despite being chosen at the polls, were allowed little room to manoeuvre by the military and successive presidents. Neither of them in fact reached the end of her or his mandate. In October 1999, the civilian government, led by Nawaz Sharif, was overthrown by General Musharraf, who brought the military back to key positions of power. But nine years later, in 2008, shortly after shedding his soldier's uniform and rising to the presidency through a questionable electoral procedure, Pervez Musharraf was compelled to resign by a democratisation process that landed Asif Zardari, whose wife Benazir Bhutto had been assassinated in December 2007, in his post. It was not until the year 2013 that an elected parliament completed its full term and, moreover, another democratically chosen government took over from its predecessor. Significantly, this new government was of a different political colour.

This succession of civil and military regimes contrasts with the stability of institutions in neighbouring India, which placed democracy on hold only for a period of eighteen months in 1975–7. Why have two countries born of the same colonial womb and consequently heir to the same political experience diverged to this extent?[1] Yielding to the simplifying charms of culturalism, many commentators have argued that Islam and democracy are incompatible.[2] In fact, the ups and downs of democracy in Pakistan flow largely from the legacy of the British Raj, and even more so from post-Partition power struggles. For one, Pakistan suffers from such a feeling of vulnerability vis-à-vis India that in its process of state-building it gave priority to national security to the detriment of civil liberties. In addition, due to the arithmetic of ethnic groups, the democratic rule of "one man, one vote" would have undermined the power of the communities that dominate the state in government, and even more in the army and the civil service.

But beyond the colonial legacy and power struggles, factors entering into a more nuanced political sociological analysis should be taken into account as well. In keeping with the elitist authoritarianism of the founders of the Muslim League, the architects of Pakistan did not develop a democratic culture or political parties, so much so that the opposition between "democratic civilians" and "the autocratic military" is debatable. These categories tend to be oversimplifying in the case of Pakistan, where the dividing lines are unclear. Departing from a chronological perspective, the second part of this book is divided into three chapters that analyse first the civilian and then the military polities, politics and policies that have alternated at the highest level of the state, before turning to the role of alternative actors and power centers, particularly the judiciary.

---

[1] I suggested an interpretation for the divergence of the Indian and Pakistani trajectories in Christophe Jaffrelot "India and Pakistan: interpreting the divergence of two political trajectories", *Cambridge Review of International Affairs*, 15 (2), July 2002, pp. 251–268.

[2] Lawrence Ziring, *Pakistan: The Enigma of Political Development*, Boulder, Westview Press, 1980, p. 97.

5

IMPOSSIBLE DEMOCRACY
OR IMPOSSIBLE DEMOCRATS?

The failure of democracy in Pakistan in the 1950s has given rise to a number of interpretations.[3] Explanations abound and need to be compared and ranked. Two of them should remain present in the background. First, the legacy of the British Raj: as previously discussed, during the colonial era the areas that formed West Pakistan in 1947 experienced a more authoritarian form of administration than the rest of the Empire, starting with Punjab, which has been called a "garrison state".[4] Second, since 1947, Pakistan has lived in fear of India. This sense of vulnerability—whether sincere or instrumentalised by political entrepreneurs exploiting the fear of the Other—remains a constant that is hardly conducive to political liberalism.

The first factor explaining the failure of democracy in Pakistan to be examined here is situated precisely at the intersection of the colonial legacy and the relationship to India: this is what Khalid bin Sayeed has called the viceregal model of government.[5] This model has permeated the political

[3] An excellent survey of these can be found in Philip Oldenburg's book, *India, Pakistan and Democracy. Solving the Puzzle of Divergent Paths*, London and New York, Routledge, 2010.

[4] Tan Tai Yong, *The Garrison State. The Military Government and Society in Colonial Punjab, 1849–1947*, Lahore, Vanguard, 2005.

[5] Khalid bin Sayeed, *Pakistan: The Formative Phase*, London, Oxford University Press, 1968. See the second part of his book, "Continuation of the Viceregal System in Pakistan", pp. 221–300.

culture, starting with the father of the nation, Jinnah, under whose rule, however brief, a pattern was set up that concentrated power in the hands of a single man. Far from a mere holdover from British rule, this political culture was overdetermined by considerations of a realpolitik nature. A democrat deep down, Jinnah justified his approach by the need to build a strong state practically from scratch to cope with the threat posed by India. Whatever its justification, the priority given to state-building with a security-based orientation worked to the detriment of political parties perceived as adverse to national unity, whether they were in the opposition or in power. Pakistan's early rulers even weakened their own already fragile movement, the Muslim League. The dysfunctional nature of the party system is the second variable that will be considered.

The third factor is a combination of tensions among ethnic communities, social classes and interest groups, the three lines of division overlapping to hamper the implementation of a democratic regime. Not only were the numbers on the Bengali side while power was in the hands of the Muhajirs (who controlled the administration) and then the Punjabis (predominant in the army), but the "Punjabi faction" that rose to power in 1953–4 in defiance of the rules of democracy represented much more than an ethnic group. First of all, Pashtuns were also included in this group, and second, they also shared a socio-economic bond: being made up of "bureaucrats"— to use the standard expression in Pakistan—and members of the military, it represented the agrarian interests of the rural elite, whereas the Muhajirs embodied the modern sector of the urban economy. Lastly, the dividing lines between the "Punjabis" and the "Bengalis" had an international angle: whereas the latter were inclined toward a form of third-worldism, the former chose to align itself with the United States from which they started receiving subsidies in the early 1950s and from which they expected financial as well as military support.

The fourth parameter to be examined in this chapter will focus on political figures. Although the military and the "bureaucrats" seized power in the 1950s, civilians share a large part of the responsibility in the failure of democracy for still other reasons than those mentioned up to now. They in fact cultivated a factionalism (that is at the root of considerable instability) and a system of political patronage that could only perpetuate the most extreme social hierarchies. The two phenomena are moreover closely linked: to remain in power, the agrarian elites—the "feudal lords"—owing their position to clientelistic relationships devoid of any ideology, formed factions, thereby fuelling political instability and opportunism that the military turned to its advantage. Most of the usurpers (including the generals who led coups) actually found support among Pakistani politicians to consolidate their power. This was the case for Mirza and later Ayub Khan in the 1950s, and Zia and then Musharraf even more so.

In fact, if the years 1947–58 require such detailed study, it is because it was during this period that a political class was formed, the functioning, culture and sociology of which would evolve very little thereafter. After that time, not a single political leader—not even Z. A. Bhutto, who was the most effective against the military—would manage to break the pattern set in the 1950s to break away from the authoritarian, factionalist and clientelistic models. The main political parties remained influenced by the traditional elites accustomed to nepotism (when they were not simply owned by a given family). Once in power, their mode of government would reflect this democratic deficit—and even a marked propensity for corruption. In addition to the centralising tendency studied in Part One, these authoritarian leanings (which have clearly never been the monopoly of the military rulers) form the second pillar of the Pakistani syndrome. It is another of the root causes of the country's instability, as democratic forces never remain dormant for long. Pakistan, therefore, keeps oscillating between the suppression and (re)conquest of public liberties.

An Initial Democratic Design Aborted (1947–1958)

Priority to Building—and Defending—the State

In 1947, the British raised India and Pakistan to the status of Dominions. The Indian Independence Act of July 1947 simply did away with every reference to control by the British crown given by the Government of India Act (1935), which thus became the basic law for both countries. But while India drew up its own Constitution as early as 1950, Pakistan maintained this framework in a scarcely amended form until 1956. And while New Delhi, in keeping with the practice of every other Dominion in the Commonwealth, appointed as governor general a figure that commanded respect but had no great political authority, C. Rajagopalachari, in Pakistan, Mohammad Ali Jinnah himself decided to assume this function, despite Mountbatten's reticence.[6] Jinnah viewed this office as similar to the British governors general who bore the title of viceroy after 1858. He thereby

[6] Ayesha Jalal, "Inheriting the Raj: Jinnah and the Governor-Generalship Issue", *Modern Asian Studies*, 19 (1), February 1985, pp. 29–53.

promoted the authoritarian and centralising dimension of the British legacy, while India drew inspiration more from its parliamentary and federal features.

That did not mean that Jinnah was not in favour of democracy. On 9 June 1947, a few weeks prior to Independence, he stated at a meeting of the Muslim League that Pakistan's Constitution would be "a democratic type, embodying the essential principles of Islam".[7] He believed these two aspects were inseparable. He elaborated on these plans in a broadcast speech in February 1948:

The constitution of Pakistan has yet to be framed by the Pakistan Constituent Assembly. I do not know what the ultimate shape of this constitution is going to be, but I am sure that it will be of the democratic type, embodying the essential principles of Islam. Today they are as applicable in actual life as they were 1,300 years ago. Islam and its idealism have taught us democracy; It has taught equality of men, justice and fairplay to everybody.[8]

Although Jinnah considered himself a democrat, he did not hold the parliamentary system of government in high esteem. In July 1947 he had remarked that a "presidential form of government [was] more suited to Pakistan".[9] From the outset, he introduced a strong personalisation of power that Pakistan has never managed to shed. Jinnah not only held the position of governor general, but was also president of the Constituent Assembly,[10] an unprecedented concentration of power in the history of the British dominions. As minister in the cabinet of his Prime Minister, Liaquat Ali Khan, he also held two portfolios, one named Evacuation and Refugees

---

[7] Cited in Allen McGrath, *The Destruction of Pakistan's Democracy*, Karachi, Oxford University Press, 1998, p. 42.

[8] M.A. Jinnah, "Pakistan and her People", in *Speeches and Statements*, op. cit., p. 123.

[9] Cited in McGrath, *The Destruction of Pakistan's Democracy*, op. cit. p. 35. See the handwritten, undated note penned by Jinnah who shortly after "The Land of the Pure" was created, presented the presidential system as the "most suited to Pakistan". This note is reproduced in Gohar Ayub Khan, *Testing Times as Foreign Minister*, Islamabad, Dost Publications, 2009, p. 309.

[10] This assembly was made up of officials elected to the Constituent Assembly of 1946, (at the time appointed by the provincial assemblies) who came from the constitutive regions of Pakistan in 1947 and/or who had chosen this country at the time of Partition. This assembly acted as a house of parliament. The Muslim League had a majority but this did not reduce the length of constitutional debates, in particular due to conflicting interests among the various ethnic communities (cf. infra).

Rehabilitation, the other State and Frontier Regions. In keeping with his title, Quaid-e-Azam ("great leader"), he directed debates among ministers that he himself had chosen. As Ian Talbot writes, "The central cabinet was even more docile than the Working Committee of the AIML (All India Muslim League) had formerly been. Its members were not only hand-picked by the Quaid, but he chaired their meetings and was authorised to overrule their decisions".[11]

The concentration of power Jinnah orchestrated went hand in hand with a strong centralisation of the state, as shown in chapter 3. Both aspects—authoritarianism and centralism—could no doubt be partly explained by the situation prevailing in the country at the time: the state remained to be built on the basis of provincial administrations that had suddenly been deprived of a decision-making center.[12] But Jinnah's viceregal style put a lasting strain on the democracy to which he claimed to aspire.

In Search of a Party System: the Decline of the Muslim League

Jinnah's death on 11 September 1948 might have provided an opportunity to alter Pakistan's political course since the country's leading figure was now its prime minister, Liaquat Ali Khan, and its new governor general, Khawaja Nazimuddin, readily acknowledged his authority. But Khan pursued Jinnah's policies. In July 1948, he had introduced a bill to amend section 92A of the Government of India Act authorizing the federal government to dismiss a provincial government on the model of the prerogative given to the Viceroy of India by virtue of section 93. Liaquat Ali Khan used it as early as 24 January 1949 to dismiss the government of Punjab on the pretext of mismanagement, even though it enjoyed a solid majority in the provincial assembly; for two years this key province was placed under direct administration of the central authorities. Like Jinnah, Liaquat Ali Khan held different posts of responsibility simultaneously, taking over the leadership of the Muslim League in 1950—not to strengthen it, paradoxically, but to weaken it.

The weakness of the Muslim League and the party system in general already stood as a tremendous obstacle for the future of parliamentary

---

[11] Ian Talbot, *Pakistan. A Modern History*, op. cit., p. 135.
[12] Regarding the difficulty Jinnah encountered of building a state while promoting citizen's political participation in the Pakistan of the 1940s and 50s, see Ayesha Jalal, *The State of Martial Rule.*

democracy. Pakistan had no doubt inherited a rich form of multipartism that could have served as a basis for political pluralism—a condition for democracy. But the party system suffered from three handicaps.

First, a large number of parties were identified with provinces and served as mouthpieces for ethnic movements. Not only did the country's rulers perceive these forces as centrifugal (and even separatist), often disqualifying them as "anti-Pakistani", but such groups also fostered the dissipation of the party system. The Jinnah Awami Muslim League is a case in point. It was founded in 1952 by former Muslim League leaders from Punjab (such as the Nawab of Mamdot), Bengal (Suhrawardy) and the NWFP (including the Pir of Manki Sharif). But gradually the party was divided "along regional lines".[13] Suhrawardy allied with Fazlul Haq's Krishak Sramik Party to form the United Front, which was confined to Bengal, where it won the elections in 1954. Certainly, another national political force took shape under the aegis of leftists disillusioned by leaders they regarded as opportunists (like Suhrawardy). From 1957 onwards, this National Awami Party gathered together regional figures including G. M. Syed, the followers of Abdul Ghaffar Khan in the NWFP and Maulana Bhashani, the Bengali socialist. However, the NAP could not resist the regionalisation of politics and the rise of Bengali nationalism in particular. The only organisations that boasted a "pan-Pakistani" coverage were naturally those based on Islam, mainly the Jama'at-e-Islami.

Second, Liaquat Ali Khan conducted a policy that was hostile to political parties even when they were not based in ethnicity, in the name of sacrosanct national unity, in a context still dominated by the fear of India and divisions that might weaken the country facing it. Pakistan was "the child of the Muslim League" and those who joined other political movements in his eyes were "enemies of Pakistan who aim[ed] to destroy the unity of the people",[14] which explains, for instance, Khan's attacks against the remnants of the Unionist Party in Punjab. Liaquat Ali Khan's distrust of other political figures was evident in the passage of the Public and Representatives Officers (Disqualification) Act (PRODA) on 26 January 1950—the date on which, in an irony of history, the Constitution of India was proclaimed in New Delhi. This law enabled the governor general, provincial governors and even ordinary citizens to lodge a complaint against a minister or elected official suspected of corruption, nepotism, favouritism or misman-

---

[13] Mohammad Waseem, *Politics and the State in Pakistan*, op. cit., p. 117.
[14] Quoted in A. McGrath, *The Destruction of Pakistan's Democracy*, op. cit., p. 67.

agement. The charges were then investigated by a tribunal made up of two judges appointed by the governor general. The maximum penalty was exclusion from public office for a period of ten years. Instead of resorting to the verdict of the ballot box to punish its politicians, Pakistan thus resorted to a new type of legal action that turned out to be highly pernicious. Politicians prepared to wager 5,000 rupees—the fee required to start proceedings—used PRODA to attack their rivals, giving rise to partisan vendettas that tarnished the reputation of the entire political class. The Assembly repealed this law in 1954.

Third, the Muslim League itself demonstrated considerable weakness. For a long time, the League had been nothing more than a small elite group representing a landowning milieu and an educated middle class. This microcosm had scarcely been able to mobilise the Muslim masses until the mid-1940s, and even then only for a short while. After independence, Jinnah and Liaquat Ali Khan cut it off from the seat of power in a very counterproductive fashion. Whereas all the regional Congress "bosses" (who in fact also held key posts in the Congress Working Committee) sat on Nehru's cabinet, in February 1948, Jinnah had decided that no party cadre could be minister out of fear that the (divisive) party spirit would contaminate the state apparatus. This divorce took a heavy toll, as the government thus lost important anchorage points throughout the country that could have relayed its policies and been in tune with shifts in public opinion. Liaquat Ali Khan tried to remedy this by taking over leadership of the party in October 1950, but he was assassinated shortly thereafter and in any event, his highly centralising exercise of power was incompatible with setting up local political leaders the way Congress had done with its regional cadres who enjoyed considerable freedom in adapting to public opinion, even if that meant contradicting Nehru.[15] In the League, neither its national nor local leaders ever tried to oppose the executive, even when the party fell into the hands of Ghulam Mohammad.[16] On the contrary, League activists were called on to rally behind leaders sent in by the executive from on high, which cast doubt on the party's credibility. The centralisation of decision-making power in the hands of the government and the

---

[15] In the "Congress system" as theorised by Rajni Kothari, the Congress was thus, in many ways, its own opposition.

[16] They for instance "were not courageous enough to take a stand against the bureaucracy or the government of the days when some of their leaders were removed from office arbitrarily by the government". Khalid B. Sayeed, *The Political System of Pakistan*, Boston, Houghton Mifflin Company, 1967, p. 83.

bureaucracy and the infrequency of elections moreover did not encourage party cadres to devote themselves to grassroots activism.

The country's rulers in fact focused all their energies on setting up a centralised administration that escaped electoral sanction all the way down to the local level. In Punjab, for instance, the few existing municipal and district councils were presided over by a bureaucrat appointed by the central government, as was the case under colonial rule. At the end of the 1950s, over half of these councils were for one reason or another directly administered by the state, which was reluctant to organise elections that might give political parties a stronger local foothold.[17] The Pakistani leaders thereby deprived themselves of the representatives and channels of communication that were indispensable to complete the plan for democracy they professed to pursue, because they gave priority to state-building.

Rather than building a party apparatus from the ground up, the power structure encouraged the League's leaders to indulge in court politics and factional battles.[18] The movement was in fact wracked by countless factions at both the regional and national level. In Punjab, where the League had won, the struggle between Finance Minister Mian Mumtaz Dautlana and Chief Minister Nawab Iftikhar Husain of Mamdot took on such proportions that the central authorities had to step in to dissolve its government in 1949. In 1951, the Muslim League won the provincial elections in Punjab, the NWFP (where the Pashtun nationalists of the Khudai Khidmatgaar had been banned for being "anti-Pakistan") and Sindh, but it had split into many different parties according to factional lines. In Punjab the Jinnah Awami Muslim League won thirty-two seats, against 140 to the Muslim League.[19]

The Ethno-Political Obstacle: Bengali "Democrats" vs. Punjabi Bureaucrats (and Military)

Beyond the categorical imperative of defending the state and the correlative decline of the Muslim League, the arithmetic of ethnic groups posed a

[17] Ayesha Jalal, *The State of Martial Rule.* op. cit., p. 300.

[18] S. Mahmood, "Decline of the Pakistan Muslim League and Its Implications (1947–54)", *Pakistan Journal of History and Culture*, 15 (2), July–December 1994, pp. 63–84.

[19] Nadeem F. Paracha, "Various shades of green: an ideological history of the Muslim League", *Dawn*, 1 August 2014 (http://www.dawn.com/news/1122395/various-shades-of-green-an-ideological-history-of-the-muslim-league).

number of obstacles to the constitutional debate, for—as mentioned above—while the Bengalis were the majority community, the Punjabis (and to a lesser extent the Pashtuns) dominated the army and the bureaucracy. This superposition of lines of division proved to be crippling, all the more since it tied in with class factors and a different assessment of the international alliances the new state should form.

Liaquat Ali Khan's proposed constitution, in line with the perspectives opened by Jinnah, was intended to be of a democratic type. In March 1949, his government submitted an "Objectives Resolution" to the Constituent Assembly stipulating that in the future political system, "the principles of democracy, freedom, equality, tolerance and social justice as enunciated in Islam [shall] be fully observed."

The Constituent Assembly, which was composed of Muslims elected in 1946 by the provincial assemblies and who had chosen Pakistan after Partition, organised several committees. The committee in charge of outlining the "fundamental principles" was subdivided into several subcommittees, whose reports formed the basis of a draft constitution known as the "Interim Report". Liaquat Ali Khan submitted it to the Assembly in September 1950. It immediately sparked protest among Bengali representatives, who were worried both by the elevation of Urdu to the rank of national language as well as by their underrepresentation in the proposed institutions. Although the Bengalis were a majority in the country, in the draft constitution they were represented on an equal basis with the other administrative entities of West Pakistan (Punjab, NWFP, Balochistan, Sindh and Karachi) in the upper house of parliament. This parity was even more prejudicial to their interests in that the two parliamentary assemblies were to have the same legislative competence. Faced with opposition from the Bengalis as well as from religious groups who felt that the Interim Report did not place enough emphasis on Islam, Liaquat Ali Khan ended up withdrawing it in November 1950.

The next twelve months would be a wasted year from an institutional standpoint, seriously damaging politicians' credibility, as they were incapable of reaching an agreement over a constitution—while India already had its own. The military and the bureaucrats were irritated not only at the politicians' immobilism, but also at their weakness regarding India. General Akbar Khan, who had played a key role in the first Kashmir war, "felt that the civilians had let the country down"[20] by doing nothing to recover the

---

[20] Shuja Nawaz, *Crossed Swords. Pakistan, Its Army and the War Within*, New York, Oxford University Press, 2008, p. 83.

province lost in Partition. He considered that "the civilian leadership's ultimate decision to accept a cease-fire that left the Kashmir vale under Indian control as a national surrender that deprived the army of a potential victory".[21] Khan fomented a plot in 1949, known as the "Rawalpindi conspiracy," along with twelve other soldiers and a few communists (whose pro-Soviet ideas Akbar Khan did not share but whose organization he hoped to make use of). This conspiracy, which aimed to overthrow Liaquat Ali Khan, was found out in time, in February–March 1951, but it reflected an uneasiness in army ranks that was only exacerbated by the ensuing trial. The defence lawyer, former chief minister of Bengal, H.S. Suhrawardy, used the opportunity to put the army in the hot seat when cross-examining witnesses who were theoretically officers above suspicion. This made the new army chief, Ayub Khan, extremely bitter. In his memoirs he recalls that Suhrawardy "took great delight in attacking the army officers who appeared as witnesses and I felt he far overstepped the mark in his cross-examination".[22]

Ayub Khan already felt a certain contempt for politicians—particularly the Bengalis—whom he'd seen at work in his previous position as general officer commanding (GOC) East Pakistan. At the time he had frequented the chief minister of the province, Khawaja Nazimuddin—who became governor general of Pakistan upon Jinnah's death—remembering that "it was a torture for him to give a decision".[23] But Liaquat Ali Khan had little choice but to rely on the Pakistani military after the last British army chief of staff left in January 1951—whom Ayub Khan thus replaced, stating that "After nearly two hundred years a Muslim army in the sub-continent would have a Muslim Commander-in-Chief".[24] Liaquat Ali Khan paradoxically gave Ayub Khan more freedom than he wanted to because he had "considered it prudent to hold the dual offices of prime minister and defense minister, ostensibly to exercise direct control over the national defense effort. But his full-time prime ministerial and party responsibilities meant that he could not devote his undivided attention to the Ministry of Defense".[25] The prime minister also left the bureaucracy considerable leeway, all the more since, caught up by Muslim League infighting, he had

[21] Aqil Shah, *The Army and Democracy. Military Politics in Pakistan*, op. cit., p. 42.

[22] Muhammad Ayub Khan, *Friends Not Masters*, op. cit., p. 53.

[23] Ibid., p. 40.

[24] Ibid., p. 51.

[25] Aqil Shah, *The Army and Democracy. Military Politics in Pakistan*, op. cit., p. 61.

"ceded the work on the constitution to the bureaucrats who gained an ascendant position in the hierarchy."[26]

On 16 October 1951 Liaquat Ali Khan was assassinated during a political meeting in Rawalpindi. Khawaja Nazimuddin took over as prime minister, leaving his post of governor general to Ghulam Mohammad, who was officially appointed by Queen Elizabeth II on 18 October. This arrangement paved the way for the rise of the "bureaucrats"[27] at the expense of politicians, and the Punjabis at the expense of the Bengalis. This distinction does not refer only to two ethnic groups, but to two opposing social, cultural and professional circles as well. Former Finance Minister under Liaquat Ali Khan, Ghulam Mohammad had begun his career as a member of the Indian Civil Service. From his years as a senior civil servant of the Raj he had retained his nostalgia for the efficiency of the British "steel frame"—a term used to refer to the colonial administration. This sentiment was far more developed in Punjab—his home province—than in others, particularly Bengal.

Bengal was the first region to be conquered by the British East India Company and by the end of the eighteenth century, political institutions and procedures were set up there. The governor general governed in concert with his council, in which Indians had gradually made their place over the years. The notion of collective deliberation became ingrained as the regime grew more democratic. Punjab, by contrast, conquered last, in 1849, established the rule of the bureaucracy, and more particularly of bureaucrats: individuals whom the colonial imagery portrayed as strong personalities in daily contact with their citizens. District magistrates thus travelled the countryside not only to levy taxes but also to mete out justice. They were the pillars of the state, accountable to no assembly but deriving their prestige from their supposed devotion to the public good. The Lawrence brothers who governed the region after it was annexed embodied better than anyone this blend of paternalism and authoritarianism.[28]

The arrival of Ghulam Mohammad marked the triumph of this typically Punjabi bureaucratic-authoritarian ethos. He trusted politicians even less

---

[26] Shuja Nawaz, *Crossed Swords. Pakistan, Its Army and the War Within*, op. cit., p. 84

[27] On the role of the civil service in Pakistan prior to 1970 see Shahid Javed Burki, "Twenty Years of the Civil Service of Pakistan: A Reevaluation", *Asian Survey*, IX, April 1969, pp. 239–254.

[28] See Charles Aitchison, Lord Lawrence and the Reconstruction of India under the Crown, Oxford, Clarendon Press, 1916 and R. Bosworth Smith, *Life of Lord Lawrence*, New York, Charles Scribner, 1883.

than Jinnah and Liaquat Ali Khan[29] and distrusted the parliamentary system, with its divisive debates and delays, even more. This political culture alone does not explain Ghulam Mohammad's reservations toward a democratic regime. He also knew where his interests lay: the Punjabis he represented at the pinnacle of the state stood to lose everything from the development of institutions based on the law of numbers given their lack of demographic strength, however relative it may have been. The Bengalis, on the other hand, were in favour of democracy not merely because of their constitutionalist tradition but again and above all because they made up the majority of the population.

Another important factor in the growing opposition between the so-called Punjabi and Bengali factions had to do with their perception of international affairs. The former—and particularly the military among them—wanted to cultivate a closer relationship with the United States, which saw Pakistan as an important element in its containment of communism in Asia. The Pakistani army could hope for considerable financial and military aid from such a rapprochement. The "Bengalis", on the other hand—and especially Nazimuddin—viewed this evolution with circumspection in accordance with a certain third-worldism and in particular a great sense of solidarity among Muslim countries.[30]

In November 1952, Prime Minister Nazimuddi submitted a new report to the Constituent Assembly's Committee of Fundamental Principles. He had contributed to removing the advantages in the upper house the previous report had given to the provinces of West Pakistan: that area no longer carried more influence than East Bengal.[31] The Muslim League in Punjab rejected the proposals contained in the report, and Ghulam Mohammad also came out against it. Nazimuddin thus withdrew the report on 21 January 1953 and then adjourned the Constitutent Assembly sine die. On

---

[29] It seems that Ghulam Mohammad had been disturbed by the way Liaquat Ali Khan promoted himself at the expense of Jinnah before his death in 1948, while the Quaid-e-Azam was seriously affected by cancer (See the pages of Fatima Jinnah's book which had been censured till 1988 as reproduced in Akhtar Baloch, "The deleted bits from Fatima Jinnah's 'My Brother'", *Dawn*, 27 December 2014, http://www.dawn.com/news/1153284/the-deleted-bits-from-fatima-jinnahs-my-brother).

[30] Ian Talbot, *Pakistan. A Modern History*, op. cit., p. 141.

[31] This assembly no longer had the same prerogatives as the lower house in approving the budget, the most sensitive legislative issues and confidence motions—in all these areas it could do little more than make recommendations.

17 April he was dismissed by the governor general who—having privileged relations with the army—also disapproved the reduction of military expenditure by a third contained in the finance bill. Nazimuddin's attempts to point out the unconstitutional nature of his dismissal—in particular to Queen Elizabeth II, but also to the judicial apparatus—were quickly discouraged by the physical pressures he underwent.

Nazimuddin's dismissal was a turning point: first in terms of the methods behind it, as when he decided to call on London to suggest that the Queen discharge Ghulam Mohammad, he realized his telephone line had been cut and that police had surrounded his residence;[32] then in terms of substance, as it confirmed the rise of a community that was hostile to democracy at the expense of another that was more favourable to it. Up until then, Jinnah's Muslim League, dominated by Muhajirs and Bengalis, led the debates in the name of a parliamentary system. As of 1953, the Punjabi bureaucrats, wary not only of East Pakistanis (as an ethnic majority) but also the Muhajirs, were gaining the upper hand. This evolution fit in with a process of indigenisation—to use Shahid Javed Burki's term[33]—that should be analyzed in terms of social class and not solely of ethnic groups. After 1947, West Pakistan was dominated by the Muhajirs, due to their political influence and educational level, which gave them an edge in the intellectual professions, and due to their economic and financial capital: twenty years later, out of the twelve major Pakistani companies, ten of them were controlled by Muhajirs.[34] These urban, modern milieus were vulnerable, not only because they depended on the protection of their political patrons (who were disappearing one after the other), but also because they were outsiders whose integration depended on the whims of the autochthonous population. With Liaquat Ali Khan's death, the powerful landed aristocracy, particularly in Punjab, organised and identified with Ghulam Mohammad's leadership.

The already very weakened Muslim League was the first victim of the polarisation between Punjabis and Bengalis. In April 1954, it lost the East Bengal elections by a wide margin. These were won by a coalition, the United Front led by Fazlul Haq. The League won only ten seats compared to 223 for a front that united three groups: the Awami Muslim League, the

---

[32] Mc Grath, *The Destruction of Pakistan's Democracy*, op. cit., p. 95.

[33] Shahid Javed Burki, *Pakistan under Bhutto*, op. cit., p. 21.

[34] Hanna Papanek, "Pakistan's Big Businessmen: Muslim separatism, entrepreneurship and partial modernization", *Economic Development and Cultural Change*, vol. 21, Oct. 1972, p. 27.

Krishak Sramik Party and Nezam-e-Islam.[35] The new government immediately organised an "anti-US-Pakistan Military Pact day" to protest against Pakistan's joining the Baghdad Pact. This prompted Ghulam Mohammad to appoint a firm-handed bureaucrat, Mirza, as governor of East Bengal. Ghulam Mohammad reacted to the Bengali call to arms by dismissing Haq by virtue of section 92A. He accused the chief minister of Dhaka of speaking out in favour of a reunification with India's West Bengal.

On 21 September 1954, the Constituent Assembly approved the report of the Committee of Fundamental Rights, which continued to acknowledge the considerable political weight of East Pakistan—and this against the opinion of all the Punjabi members. One month later, Ghulam Mohammad blocked the final adoption of a constitution that would have set up a genuine parliamentary regime in Pakistan by declaring a state of emergency on the pretext that "the constitutional machine [had] broken down". He imposed press censorship and prevented the elected members from commencing their Assembly session on 28 October 1954. No street protests followed this show of force, even in Bengal, as the governor general had co-opted the province's two leaders, Haq and Suhrawardy, by naming them ministers in the new government.[36] Politicians had been either sidelined or won over in exchange for a position in the administration—or the promise that the post of prime minister would go to a Bengali as mentioned in chapter 3. Prime Minister Chaudhri Muhammad Ali himself came from the ranks of the bureaucracy in October 1955. The only person to take a stand against the regime's drift toward authoritarianism was the President of the Assembly, Tamizuddin Khan—another Bengali—who lodged a complaint in vain. (see infra)

The Supreme Court, presided by a Punjabi by the name of Munir, ratified the dissolution of the Constituent Assembly. Ghulam Mohammad had another one elected in 1955. Before that, he asked Mirza to create a new party, the Republican Party. It gathered together factions of the Muslim League, including, in Punjab, the one led by Firoz Khan Noon and Nawab Iftikhar Husain of Mamdot. Sponsored by Pakistan's leading figures, the party attracted many political notables, to such an extent that it became the number one party in the Constituent Assembly, with twenty-one seats compared to fifteen for the Muslim League.[37]

[35] Kamran Tahir, "Early phase of electoral politics in Pakistan: the 1950s", *South Asian Studies* vol. 24, no. 2, July–December 2009; pp. 257–282.

[36] Begum Shaista Suhrawardy Ikramullah, *Huseyn Shaheed Suhrawardy*, op. cit. p. 81.

[37] Mohammad Waseem, *Politics and the State in Pakistan*, op. cit., p. 118. These fig-

Ghulam Mohammad hastened the decline of the Muslim League, and more generally speaking of civilian politicians, by replacing Nazimuddin with Mohammad Ali Bogra—a more obscure figure than Nizamuddin—but even more importantly by appointing Ayub Khan, the army chief, Defence Minister and Mirza Interior Minister. Last but not least, he imposed the One-Unit Scheme that enabled the Punjabis to resist Bengali pressure.

If the Constitution that the new Constituent Assembly produced in record time appeared to have all the attributes of parliamentarianism, it nevertheless endowed the governor general—renamed president—with prerogatives that were incompatible with such a regime. The president could thus dismiss the central government as well as those of the provinces. Once the Constitution of 1956 was promulgated, Ghulam Mohammad resigned in favour of Iskander Mirza, who thus became the first President of Pakistan. Mirza, a senior civil servant like his predecessor, although he was born in Bengal, "had formed alliances with the Punjabi bureaucrats throughout his career".[38]

By the mid-1950s parliamentary democracy in Pakistan had thus foundered on the demographic power struggle between Bengalis and Punjabis who refused to bow to the law of numbers. The principal leaders of these two communities, Ghulam Mohammad and Iskander Mirza, were moreover both senior civil servants moulded by the values of the British "steel frame" and thus hostile to political parties, the failings of which admittedly tarnished their credibility. This political evolution paved the way for a takeover by the military, a "corporation" also dominated by the Punjabis, after the failure of the 1956 Constitution.

Factionalism and Feudalism: The Failure of the Constitution of 1956

In 1956 the country finally had its Constitution, but was lacking the political parties that could have brought it to life. A form of multipartism did emerge with the decline of the Muslim League,[39] but it remained very unstable because of forms of factionalism that were rooted in the social structures of the country.

---

ures well reflect the appeal of the Republican Party since just prior to its creation the Muslim League had 20 seats, the United Front, 16 and the Awami Party, 12.

[38] Allen McGrath, *The Destruction of Pakistan's Democracy*, op. cit., p. 120.

[39] According to Mohammad Waseem, as early as 1949, out of the 13 existing Pakistani parties, 9 derived from breakaway factions of the Muslim League. Mohammad Waseem, *Politics and the State in Pakistan*, op. cit., p. 114.

While a distinction must be made between the tribal world west of the Indus River and the world of caste east of the Indus, in politics, the two realms converge toward the same two-sided phenomenon: the clientelism of the "feudal lords" and factionalism. Castes and tribes in this case share common features that is aptly rendered by the word *biradari* ("phratry" in Persian), applied indifferently to both. As Pierre Lafrance explains in a remarkable overview of the question, "in broad terms, the *biradari* is the community of descendants from an ancestor who is still present in the elders' memory".[40] These endogamous groups by birth and by status fit into hierarchies still dominated by those who own the most land. In Punjab and in Sindh, they are the Rajputs and Jats; among the Baloch, they are the most prestigious tribal chiefs, the *sardars*; and among the Pashtuns, those who are recognised by the prestigious titles of Khan or Malik.[41]

Under the Raj, the ascendancy of the rural grandees was strengthened by the British recognition of property deeds held by those whom the colonial power considered to be "natural" leaders. In 1955, 6,061 large landowners possessed holdings greater than 500 acres. They represented 0.1 per cent of the total number of farms, but the surface area of the land they owned amounted to 15.4 per cent of the total.[42] These notables went into politics—sometimes even before Pakistan was founded—to perpetuate their domination. They generally won a seat in their regional assembly by activating the standard mechanisms of clientelism in rural areas whereby a patron receives the votes of "his" peasants in exchange for his protection and the distribution of largesse.[43]

This class of large landowners are known as "feudal lords" in Pakistan. S. Akbar Zaidi points out that the term is inaccurate as they are actually capitalists, but he aptly describes how their mindset and attitudes are akin to feudalism:

---

[40] Pierre Lafrance, "Between Caste and Tribe", in Christophe Jaffrelot, *A History of Pakistan and its Origins*, op. cit., p. 192.

[41] However, one must bear in mind that acknowledgement of superiority is never guaranteed once and for all, whether among tribes or castes, or even within one or the other: the *biradari* from these various backgrounds are in fact always in competition and only stifle their divisions when they must face a common opponent. See Alain Lefebvre, *Kinship, Honour and Money in Rural Pakistan*, London, Curzon Press, 1999.

[42] Mahmood Hasan Khan, *Underdevelopment and Agrarian Structure in Pakistan*, Boulder, Westview, 1981, p. 68.

[43] Stephen Lyon, *Anthropological Analysis of Local Politico and Patronage in a Pakistani Village*, New York, Edwin Mellen Press, 2004.

Pakistan society has a darbar culture, where ostentatiousness is the norm and privilege is misused and flaunted; patronage from those in power is the norm; corruption, from the thana [police station] and kutchery (judicial court) level to the highest public office in the country, is a standard and even accepted practice; there is a serious law and order problem at the local level caused by propertied and influential people who have their own private jails; there are large landholders and 'traditional' land owning families; nepotism (or bribes), rather than merit, determine access to the public sector employment market.[44]

The domination of these "feudals"—an expression that gained currency in the 1950s to refer to those who won the first elections—is especially clear in Punjab and in Sindh where the large landlords went into politics.[45] In Punjab, 1,936 landowners (0.1 per cent of all of them) holding farms greater than 500 acres possessed 9.9 per cent of the arable land in the province. In Sindh, these figures were 3,045 (or 0.9 per cent) and 29.1 per cent respectively—a sign of even greater inequality (at the other end of the Sindhi pyramid, 29.8 per cent farmers responsible for farms smaller than five acres, only cultivated 3.6 per cent of the total arable land in the province).[46] The grip of this social elite on political power explains why agrarian reform got bogged down. The Agrarian Reform Committee of the Muslim League had made proposals to improve the situation in July 1949, but they resulted in a wave of evictions of tenants and remained largely theoretical.[47] The Committee's recommendations were shelved partly because twenty-eight out of the forty West Pakistan members elected to the National Assembly were big landowners.[48]

The feudal nature of Pakistani politics explains to a large extent the intensity of factional strife. The choice of leader or party was mainly dictated by quarrels between *biradaris* sometimes dating back several generations. In Punjab, for instance, the Republican Party was backed by the Qizilbashs, the Noons, the Tiwanas, the Gardezis, the Legharis and the Gilanis because

---

[44] S. Akbar Zaidi, *Issues in Pakistan's Economy*, op. cit., p. 20.

[45] In Sindh, the rural grandees took full advantage of the Hindu exodus in 1947. Although the latter were primarily urban dwellers, they owned vast amounts of land. Those remaining behind helped themselves to 800,000 of the 1,345,000 acres abandoned by the deserters.

[46] Mahmood Hasan Khan, *Underdevelopment and Agrarian Structure in Pakistan*, op. cit., p. 68.

[47] Matthew Nelson, *In the Shadow of Shari'ah. Islam*, op. cit., pp. 147–8.

[48] Whereas 20 of the 40 elected members from the eastern wing were "lawyers"—an additional indication of the East-West divide. Mushtaq Ahmad, *Government and Politics in Pakistan*, Karachi, 1963, p. 115.

these *biradaris* (or some of their factions) were in conflict with others who backed the regional Muslim League figure, Mian Mumtaz Daultana. Factional strife led to government instability because of the volatility of their support in the Assembly, a tendency further reinforced by the central government's "divide-and-rule" strategy. Iskander Mirza was particularly versed in such practices, as his capacity to play Haq off against Suhrawardy in East Pakistan attests.[49] The Bengalis were not above factional battles motivated by personal interest. Suhrawardy thus backed the One-Unit Scheme to win the favour of Ghulam Mohammad and become prime minister at the expense of his province's interests. As his biographer attests, Suharawardy had accepted the One-Unit Scheme and parity bertween East and West Pakistan because he "had been promised the Prime Ministership".[50]

From 1956 to 1958, three prime ministers, Suhrawardy, I.I. Chundrigar and Firoz Khan Noon, belonging to three different political parties (Awami League, Muslim League and Republican Party), followed in rapid succession. No wonder Ayub Khan remarked in his memoirs, "No one knew any longer who belonged to which political party; it was all a question of swapping labels: a Muslim Leaguer today; a Republican tomorrow; and yesterday's 'traitors' were tomorrow's Chief Ministers, indistinguishable as tweedledum and tweedledee!"[51]

But this instability did not only reflect the opportunism of elected officials who were always ready to switch alliances, all the more because the dividing lines between parties were artificial. It also mirrored the structural conflict between the prime minister and the president. H.S. Suhrawardy thus tried to break free from Mirza's control by seeking a vote of confidence from the Assembly. Mirza, unwilling to acknowledge the Assembly's power to approve and dismiss governments, refused to convoke it and forced Suhrawardy to resign on 11 October 1957—he officially resigned on the joint electorate issue. Mirza replaced him with Firoz Khan Noon, who was no more docile and even made contact with Suhrawardy. In fact,

---

[49] Allies in the United Front, their two parties won the regional elections of 1954. The coalition, deprived of victory by central government intervention, was asked once more to form a government in September 1956, but its members were soon at each other's throats and the Awami League was reduced to governing during brief periods of time when its two leaders, Haq and Suhrawardy, managed to reach an understanding.

[50] Begum Shaista Suhrawardy Ikramullah, *Huseyn Shaheed Suhrawardy*, op. cit., p. 82.

[51] Ayub Khan, *Friends Not Masters*, op. cit., p. 72.

Pakistan was faced with a difficulty it would have to confront repeatedly until the 1990s. The Constitution had the trappings of parliamentarianism but allowed the president such prerogatives that he could not bring himself to leave the business of governing up to "his" prime minister. In the event of a conflict, the only solution was to dissolve the government and/or the Assembly, or even suspend both institutions. Mirza chose the latter option by proclaiming martial law on 7 October 1958.

*

It is not easy to rank by order of importance the reasons for the failure of democracy in Pakistan in the 1950s, given the extent to which political and social factors are intertwined. If eleven years after Partition, the country's efforts to establish a democratic regime failed, it is probably because the democratic ideal of Jinnah and his followers was subordinated to the security imperative spawned by the fear of India. This reality was bound to be the parameter serving as a backdrop for the entire period, as indicates the astounding amount of military expenditure in Pakistan when civilians were in power: defence spending accounted for over half the national budget, peaking at 71–73 per cent per year between 1948 and 1950 after the first war in Kashmir.[52] With such a financial outlay—which went along with an increase in the number of men doing their military service—the army gained in strength.

But if the bureaucrats seized power in the mid-1950s, it was less in the name of national defence in face of the threat of India than due to two other factors. First, the West Pakistani elites (starting with those in Punjab) who controlled the army and the bureaucracy could not resign themselves to losing power to the Bengalis by accepting the law of numbers. Second, the political class was not equal to the task. Regardless of the role played by the Bengalis—bound to awaken the suspicion of those in power in West Pakistan—it lacked political parties that might have brought parliamentarianism to life and was discredited by a factionalism stamped with feudalism and opportunism. It was easy for the bureaucrats and the military to criticize politicians for negligence while the "Indian threat" required the Pakistani elites to develop a keen sense of responsibility. But as will be seen in the following chapter, the army that finally came to power in 1958 with General Ayub Khan was not in a position to remain at the helm any longer

[52] Hasan-Askar Rizvi, *Military, State and Society in Pakistan*, Lahore, Sang-e-Meel Publications, 2003, p. 63.

than the civilians and after twelve years of military regime, politicians were back in control and once again tried to establish a democracy.

Democratisation, Separatism and Authoritarianism (1969–1977)

The post-Ayub Khan phase of democratisation is mainly the result of Khan's power-weariness in the wake of the failed military operation against India in 1965 and the ensuing demonstrations—particularly among students—in the late 1960s, as well as the rise of Bengali nationalism. Yahya Khan—to whom Ayub handed over power in 1969—made attempts at compromise to defuse these tensions. But it was too late, and especially, as the arithmetic of ethnic groups was freely expressed in the first free general elections, it dealt national unity a final blow. The creation of Bangladesh as the outcome of a war lost to India no doubt had the advantage of bringing to power a man, Zulfikar Ali Bhutto, who could stand up to the military. But Bhutto made the usual mistakes of the political class and turned out to be a dubious democrat.

Yahya Khan, Gravedigger of the Military Regime...and National Unity

Yahya Khan came to power with no preconceived plan.[53] Inheriting a delicate situation in which presidential power was increasingly challenged, he was convinced of the need to make concessions to his opponents, as much in terms of political liberalisation as of recognition of ethnic particularisms.

The first thing Yahya Khan did after his instalment was to announce free elections, before calling into question the One-Unit Scheme. On 30 March 1970 he also proclaimed a Legal Framework Order stipulating that the future National Assembly would have 313 seats, 169 of which would go to East Pakistan, thereby giving it a majority, and that the provinces would enjoy greater autonomy. Yahya Khan believed he was taking a calculated risk after intelligence agencies had assured him that Mujibur Rahman's Awami League would not win any more than eighty seats.[54]

From the start of the election campaign, the government, true to a custom that dated back to Ghulam Mohammad's Republican Party, formed its own "khaki party"—to use the standard expression to refer to groups "spon-

[53] Regarding his two-year reign, see H. Feldman, *The End and the Beginning: Pakistan, 1969–1971*, Karachi, Oxford University Press, 1976.

[54] Ian Talbot, *Pakistan. A Modern History*, op. cit., p. 195.

sored" by the military. This was a heavily subsidised Muslim League whose leadership was entrusted to Abdul Qayyum Khan, former chief minister of the NWFP. Yahya Khan also more or less directly supported the Islamic parties: the Jama'at-e-Islami, the JUI and the JUP. None of these organisations won more than nine out of the 300 seats to be filled, not only because they couldn't manage to gain a foothold in East Pakistan (where they did not win a single seat) but especially because they had to contend with a new rival in West Pakistan, the Pakistan People's Party.

The PPP newly formed by Z. A. Bhutto focused its efforts on West Pakistan alone, to the extent of not fielding a single candidate in the country's eastern wing. Bhutto held meeting after meeting for months all over West Pakistan in a typically populist style embodied in India at the same time by Indira Gandhi. He "reached out to the people", promising them "*Roti, Kapra aur Makan*" ("bread, clothing and a house"). The religious parties answered this slogan with a purely negative cry of "*Socialism kufir hai. Muslim millat ek ho*" ("Socialism is a heresy. Let's unify the Muslim people"). Bhutto graciously donned the epithet of socialism while fending off the criticism of the clerics and the fundamentalists by labelling his doctrine "Islamic socialism",[55] a notion he associated with *musawat*, the equality of all Muslims as defined by their religion. What was more, the extreme anti-Indian line he had taken since his stint as Foreign Minister gave him the image of a hardcore nationalist. Bhutto thus overcame the potential handicap of his Sindhi origins.

In the 1970 elections—which saw a comparatively high voter turnout of 63 per cent,[56] the PPP won 81 seats, including 62 in Punjab (out of a total of 82 to fill) and 18 (out of 27) in Sindh. It won hands down in West Pakistan despite its patent defeat in Balochistan and the NWFP, two provinces where Islamic and ethnic parties triumphed, a sign of the growing regionalisation of Pakistani politics.[57]

Though considerably mitigated by Bhutto-the-Sindhi's success in Punjab, this trend was illustrated most clearly by the Awami League landslide in East Pakistan. Confounding military intelligence forecasts, Mujibur Rahman's

---

[55] His slogan was "Islam is our faith, democracy is our polity; socialism is our economy". See Z.A. Bhutto, *Pakistan and the Alliances*, Lahore, Pakistan's People Party, 1969.

[56] This national average needs to be disaggregated. As mentioned above, the turnout was surprisingly lower in East Bengal (56%) and significantly higher in Punjab (67%). It was 58% in Sindh, 47% in the NWFP and only 39% in Balochistan.

[57] Craig Baxter, "Pakistan Votes—1970", *Asian Survey*, 11 (3), March 1971.

party carried 160 of the 162 seats up for grabs in the province—with 75 per cent of the valid votes. Such a victory was unlikely to tone down his demands for autonomy.

The 1970 elections confirmed West Pakistani fears that implementing democratic procedures would automatically transfer power to the Bengalis by the mere application of demographics to the balance of power. Bhutto couldn't resign himself to it. As soon as the results were announced, he declared that majority rule was not the only consideration in national politics[58] and that the PPP's historic role in the fight against Ayub Khan gave it the right to a share of power. Mujibur Rahman replied on 3 January 1971 that the Awami League was a majority party on a nationwide scale and that he intended to give Pakistan a new constitution based on his Six-Point Programme. The ensuing negotiations between Rahman, Yahya Khan and Bhutto yielded nothing, these last two refusing to concede the power Rahman claimed. When Yahya Khan announced that convocation of the National Assembly was postponed *sine die*, the Awami League organised demonstrations for 3 March, the day the Assembly should have convened. Yahya Khan immediately announced that elected Assembly members would meet on 25 March. Rahman then placed several conditions on his party's participation in this session, including the lifting of martial law and the immediate transfer of power to the Assembly. Discussions resumed, but on 23 March, the anniversary of the Lahore Resolution, Rahman declared that he would agree to nothing less than a Pakistani confederation in which the central government retained only certain sovereign powers. Yahya Khan's military advisors encouraged him immediately to use force to eradicate the Awami League.

Mujibur Rahman was arrested, but some of his lieutenants managed to flee to India where they formed a government in exile on 17 April. In all, 10 million refugees from the East found asylum in India. The Indian army lent its support to the Mukti Vahini liberation forces, commandos that were recruited largely among the youth to carry out guerrilla warfare in the name of Bangladesh. India launched an attack on November 1971 that it had been preparing for some time. The war lasted only two weeks, in the course of which Pakistan lost half its navy, a third of its army and a quarter of its air force.[59] On 16 December Islamabad was forced to sign a humiliat-

---

[58] On Bhutto's role in this crisis, see Golam Wahed Choudhury, *The Last Days of United Pakistan*, Bloomington, Indiana University Press, 1974.

[59] Robert Victor Jackson, *South Asia Crisis: India, Pakistan and Bangladesh: A political and historical analysis of the 1971 war*, New York, Praeger, 1975.

ing ceasefire under which terms India held prisoner the 93,000 soldiers captured in the net around Dhaka. The rout was such that the army had to persuade Yahya Khan to resign and agree to entrust power to a civilian, Bhutto. On 20 December he assumed the posts of president and chief administrator of martial law.[60]

This episode, although it showed the Pakistani military in its worst light, was not particularly flattering for Bhutto, either, as he rejected the law of numbers and preferred repression at the risk of civil war and ultimately secession to respect for the verdict of the polls. In fact, Bhutto soon turned out to be a rather mediocre democrat, the zealous incarnation of the vice-regal political culture that Jinnah had initiated.

The Bhutto Era or the Failure of Democratic Reform

Z. A. Bhutto's rise to the head of Pakistan could have been the opportunity for a new departure for the country. The army, discredited by its defeat at the hands of India and the loss of East Pakistan, was on the defensive and for the first time, a political figure at the head of a structured party (and one that claimed an ideology) enjoyed a legitimacy that only universal suffrage can accord. This window of opportunity closed in 1977, not so much—or not only—due to the coup led by General Zia, as to the various failings of the Bhutto government. In many regards, it had fallen into the same ruts as the political class of the past, even if it created a new repertoire, destined to remain the main alternative to the army.

The PPP: a Revolutionary Party?

In the early 1970s, Bhutto's PPP seemed to offer a last hope for the heirs of the leftist parties and movements that Ayub Khan had systematically crushed. Eager to do away with the members of the Communist Party that had been banned in 1954 after the Rawalpindi Conspiracy, he had brought the left to heel, for instance placing the press group that published the *Pakistan Times* under state control—as members of its staff, such as the poet Faiz Ahmad Faiz, were affiliated with this organisation. He also persecuted trade unionists,[61] as the following chapter will show.

[60] Regarding internal army tensions, particularly officer resentment toward the high command, see Herbert Feldman, *The End and the Beginning: Pakistan 1969–1971*, London, Oxford University Press, 1976.

[61] Gerald A. Heeger, "Socialism in Pakistan", in Helen Desfossés and Jacques Levesque (eds), *Socialism in the Third World*, New York, Praeger, 1975, p. 291 ff.

Despite the crackdown, four leftwing currents—to borrow Shahid Javed Burki's typology[62]—had survived: the "traditional left," a remnant of the Communist Party represented by men of letters such as Faiz Ahmad Faiz, the publisher (and poet) Mohammad Hanif Ramay and the lawyer (and poet as well) Kurshid Hasan Meer; the "rural left" which, behind Sheikh Mohammad Rashid, called for collectivisation of the countryside;[63] "socialist industrial labour", represented by Mirza Ibrahim and Miraj Mohammad Khan, which aspired to bring industry under control of the working class; and the "urban ultra left", a sort of intelligentsia which, under Mubashir Hasan's leadership, aimed to restructure both the political system and the economy.

These leftist figures turned to Bhutto as soon as he resigned from Ayub Khan's cabinet in 1967, at a time when he sensed that the president-general had been worn out by the exercise of power and his popularity was diminished by the defeat of 1965. Bhutto's resignation was above all a tactical move, as was the socialist agenda he set for himself.

Until then, Bhutto had not demonstrated any democratic commitment. Son of a large landholder-turned-politician who had sent him to study in the United States and Great Britain, he first began practicing as a lawyer in Karachi, his native city. As a youth, he wanted to join G. M. Syed's Awami Party, but his father forbade him to. Iskander Mirza—whose wife knew Bhutto's wife (both were Iranian)—offered him a government post.[64] Bhutto apparently had no qualms about joining Mirza's government following the latter's anti-constitutional offensive in 1954. Nor did he feel the need to quit the government when Ayub Khan ousted Mirza. For nine years, he would be in charge of prestigious portfolios, including the Ministry of Foreign Affairs. When Bhutto jumped ship in 1967, it was because he knew Ayub Khan's rule was on the wane. He went with him to Tashkent to sign the peace treaty with India, and then accused him of having lost the war before leaving the government. He thus sought first to rise in the ranks of the Muslim League where he hoped to become spokesman for the large land-owners, whose social background he shared. But he was countered by the party's secretary-general, Malik Khuda Bux Bucha, who fully intended to

---

[62] Shahid Javed Burki, *Pakistan under Bhutto*, op. cit., p. 50.

[63] Bhashani's group, a faction of which would join the PPP, also belongs to this category.

[64] See the interview with Sobho Gianchandani, Newsline, Oct. 2008. Available at: http://www.newslinemagazine.com/2008/10/interview-comrade-sobho-gianchandani/ (Accessed on September 15, 2013).

continue playing this role: "Having been abandoned by the landlords, Bhutto turned towards the left".[65]

The survivors of the Pakistani left, lacking a leader, had appreciated his work as Minister of Oil, Electricity and Natural Resources and later as Foreign Minister. He had demonstrated firmness toward the United States and openness toward the USSR and China in both positions. These early followers remember having taken to Bhutto very quickly due to his charisma (including his oratorical gifts) as much as the socialist rhetoric he had opportunely opted for.[66]

The PPP from its inception seemed strongly anchored to the left. The founding meeting of the party was held from 30 November to 1 December 1967 at the home of Mubashar Hasan in Lahore with veteran socialists in attendance, including Jalaluddin Akbar Rahim,[67] who had drafted the documents submitted for discussion with Bhutto in Paris in 1966. This initial charter was extremely radical. It stated that "The ultimate objective of the party's policy is the attainment of a classless society which is only possible through socialism in our times".[68]

Bhutto used the same language during the tour he began immediately afterward, seeking to erase any doubts his social origins might arouse. In a speech he made in 1968 he for instance declared,

My dear friends, it is said that I am a wealthy man and a feudal lord. It is said that I have no right to struggle for socialism without distributing my wealth among the people. (...) But you cannot fool the people by such useless arguments. I believe in socialism: that is why I have left my class and joined the labourers, peasants and poor students. I love them. And what can I get from them except affection and respect? No power [what the masses had best to offer Bhutto!] on earth can stop socialism, the symbol of justice, equality, and the supremacy of man from being introduced in Pakistan. It is the demand of time and history. And you can see me raising this revolutionary banner among the masses. I am a socialist, and an honest socialist, who will continue to fight for the poor till the last moment of his life.[69]

In fact, Bhutto was more a rebel than a revolutionary, and without a doubt a talented populist, with all the opportunism that implied. In 1967, Bhutto accented the rebellious side of his temperament once again—in a very timely

---

[65] Shahid Javed Burki, *Pakistan under Bhutto*, op. cit., p. 50.

[66] Cited in Lal Khan, *Pakistan's Other Story. The 1968–69 Revolution*, op. cit., p. 192.

[67] Mubshar Hasan gave Lal Khan an account of the event, op. cit., pp. 171–2.

[68] Cited in ibid., p. 261.

[69] Quoted in Stanley Wolpert, *Zulfi Bhutto of Pakistan*, op. cit., p. 124.

fashion, as he had gauged the level of exasperation that ten years of military rule had aroused. Shortly thereafter, student protests would mark the beginning of a movement (its rise throughout all sectors of society will be retraced below). Bhutto consulted in particular with the student leaders during the unrest in Rawalpindi in November 1968. He led a PPP delegation at the funeral of Abdul Hamid, the student whose death had served as a spark for the agitation. He later went to Lahore to hold rallies that were instantly popular, including one on 11 November before the District Bar Association at which he urged the members to disobey Ayub Khan's injunction asking the lawyers to appeal to the students for calm. On 13 November, he was arrested as he was leaving for Multan. On 10 February, he was released from prison to be placed under house arrest in Larkana. On 14 February he began a fast unto death to protest against the Emergency Rule Laws that Ayub Khan had just introduced. He was released on 17 February, on which day these laws were suspended. He then made a triumphant entry into Karachi. The following day, he decided not to take part in the Round Table Conference (RTC) Ayub Khan had summoned to defuse tensions: he did not want to discuss concessions but a regime change. Seeking allies, on 23 February he went to Dhaka to consult with Mujibur Rahman—although he disapproved of certain aspects of the Six-Point Programme. He in particular demanded that the proceedings against Rahman in the Agartala Conspiracy Case be dropped immediately.[70] It should be remembered, however, that the PPP, after its East Pakistan wing was disbanded on 4 March 1969, no longer had any official presence to compete with the Awami League in what was to become Bangladesh.[71]

Rahman's view that his Six-Point Programme was non-negotiable constituted a stumbling block for the RTC. Ayub Khan thus handed power over to Yahya Khan, who immediately asked Bhutto on what conditions he would support the new regime. Bhutto listed three: an independent foreign policy (a most ambiguous expression); the dissolution of the One-Unit Scheme; and general elections within the year—which the PPP was determined to win. Yahya agreed to all of them and Bhutto put an end to the agitation.

[70] Lal Khan, *Pakistan's Other Story. The 1968–69 Revolution*, op. cit., p. 273.
[71] Occupying the media spotlight, Bhutto, while Mujibur Rahman was attending the RTC, declared in a press conference late February that he would only go if all the opposition parties agreed to demand the election of a new Constituent Assembly—which was highly unlikely given that Jama'at-e-Islami wanted to reinstate the Constitution of 1956. On 2 March he made a different declaration: he would take part if Ayub Khan resigned.

From that point on, Bhutto shifted the PPP from revolutionary into electoral mode. He gradually allowed or directly solicited membership among conservative notables who could help him cull votes from their dependents (tenant farmers, workers, debtors, etc.). In the summer of 1969, Muslim League leaders who had felt the wind turn thus threw their support behind Bhutto—who was very glad of this additional backing. This alarmed the left wing of the PPP[72] and on 29 March 1970, the Punjab-Bahawalpur Council, an organization of district and city party officials, passed a resolution of which the first three clauses read:

- Individuals with class interests contradictory to the party manifesto should not normally be given party membership.
- In no case should party membership, office or ticket be given without the agreement of the relevant local party committee.
- Opportunists, i.e. professional politicians, landlords and capitalists with 'family boroughs' should be kept out of the party.[73]

This resolution displeased Bhutto. He had Amanullah Khan suspended (although he was reinstated a few months later). This leader of the PPP's left wing in Punjab exercised greater caution in the future and no longer opposed Bhutto's cooptation of influential conservatives.[74] Among them finally were Makhdum Talib ul Maula (Pir Jhandewaro of Hala Sharif), who became party vice-chairman, Mian Mahmud Ali Kasuri (who also became vice-chairman) and Maulana Kausar Niazi, who was appointed Propaganda Secretary (see below).

Even if Bhutto maintained a radical line toward the working class, he considerably tempered his remarks concerning rural reforms for fear of losing the support of feudal lords who continued to make the election. He moreover did not hesitate to endorse landowners as PPP candidates—for instance in Sargodha to defeat the Noon-Tiwana clan and in Multan—one more indication that he was less a socialist than a populist.

---

[72] The party's left wing was not always consistent. It brought together the Mazdur Majlis-i-Amal (Workers Action Committee) of Multan, the Taraqqipasand Mazdur Mahaz (Progressive Workers' Front) of Lyallpur, Rifat Hussain's People's Labour Front of Rawalpindi and the Muttahida Mazdur Mahaz (United Workers' Front) of Lahore. Added to that were Thal Mehnat Kash Mahaz (The Labourers' Front), a worker and peasant alliance formed by the fraction of the National Awami Party (Bhashani) present mainly in the districts of Mianwalli and Muzzafargarh.

[73] Cited in Lal Khan, *Pakistan's Other Story. The 1968–69 Revolution*, op. cit., p. 279.

[74] Ibid.

Bhutto, Socialist or Populist?

Populism is an "elusive and protean" notion[75] that requires some definition. First, as Edward Shils has shown, populism "proclaims that the will of the people as such is supreme over every standard, over the standards of traditional institutions, over the autonomy of institutions and over the will of other strata. Populism identifies the will of the people with justice and morality".[76] Second, populism is the discourse of those politicians who claim that they are above parties and that they stand on the side of the workers against their exploiters,[77] hence a personalisation of their direct relation with the people. Third, populism is a political device in the sense that the politicians articulating this discourse are less interested in social reforms than in the vote of the masses and aim more to defuse tensions than to transform society.

Bhutto's populist style was clear from his first speech as head of state, broadcast over the radio and television on 20 December 1971, the day after Yahya Khan resigned:

My dear countrymen, my dear friends, my dear students, labourers, peasants... Those who fought for Pakistan, I have come in at a very late hour, at a decisive moment in the history of Pakistan. We are facing the worst crisis in our country's life, a deadly crisis. We have to pick up the pieces, very small pieces, but we will make a new Pakistan, a prosperous and progressive Pakistan, a Pakistan free of exploitation, a Pakistan envisaged by the Quaid-e-Azam. With your co-operation... I'm taller than the Himalayas.[78]

Bhutto here was seeking to establish a direct relationship between himself and his people from whom he claimed to draw his strength, using the hyperbolic style he was fond of. Other images show him haranguing the crowd, on the verge of knocking down a forest of microphones[79] to pro-

---

[75] To use the words of Ionescu and Gellner in their introduction to G. Ionescu and E. Gellner (eds), *Populism—Its Meanings and National Characteristics*, London, Weindenfield and Nicholson, 1969, p. 1.

[76] Edward Shils, *The Torment of Secrecy*, Melbourne, Heinemann, 1956, p. 98.

[77] Margaret Canovan, *Populism*, New York, Harcourt Brace Jovanovich, 1981, p. 260.

[78] "Z. A. Bhutto, Addresses to a Nation—20 December 1971", in Z. A. *Bhutto, Speeches and Statements. Vol. 1*—December 20, 1971–March 31, 1972, Karachi, Government of Pakistan, 1972, p. 1.

[79] In one of his speeches, he ended up knocking down the microphones. See: http://tune.pk/video/57240/Zulfiqar-Ali-Bhutto-Great-Speech (Accessed on September 15, 2013).

claim "There are two Zulfikar Ali Bhuttos, the one standing in front of you and the one who is within each of you".[80] The populist leader he truly was—at once like Mrs Bandaranaike in Sri Lanka and Mrs Gandhi in India—claimed to be a socialist, but his only real aim was power, which he exercised in a conservative vein once he attained his goal.

Here an anecdote may be more meaningful than a long-winded speech—this was at least the conviction that emerges from a personal account narrated to Lal Khan by Munnoo Bhai, one of Bhutto's lieutenants from the start. He relates in detail an episode of his tour by car with Bhutto from Lahore to Jhelum during the 1970 election campaign:

When we reached the town of Gujarat there was a procession of shirtless workers from the local factories that stopped Bhutto's motorcade and asked him to give a speech. Some were lying down on the hot tarmac and blocked further movement. Bhutto was reluctant as they were already late for the public meeting in Jhelum. Sensing the delicate situation [Mustafa] Khar [one of his followers and later governor of Punjab] persuaded Bhutto to come out and say a few words. Bhutto gave a fiery revolutionary speech and thrilled the procession. When he came back into the car and motorcade speed off towards Jhelum, the naked chest workers were shouting slogans of 'Socialism! Socialism!' and were beating their wrists on the bonnet of the car. When they passed them, after a few minutes Bhutto turned back from the front seat and addressing [Hanif] Ramay [another of his lieutenants who became chief minister of Punjab] and Munnoo Bhai said, 'We may not mean it but they really mean it!'[81]

The limits of Bhutto-style socialism soon appeared in certain aspects of his politics after he took over power, as much in terms of his party strategy as the policies (both public and secret) that he implemented once in power.

The Progressive Phase

Zulfikar Ali Bhutto's main achievement as a democrat has to do with the way he asserted the primacy of elected officials over the military and the civil service. In this endeavour he benefited from a popularity not seen since Jinnah—including in the army ranks—and from the discredit affecting the generals in place—including among the officers.

---

[80] See the film by Arnaud Mandagaran, "La saga des Bhutto ou la politique dans le sang" Information available at: http://www.film-documentaire.fr/La_Saga-Bhutto_ou-politique_dans-sang.html,film,34002. (Accessed on September 15, 2013) See also: http://archive.org/details/JareseGulKeySadaSpeechesOfZulfikar AliBhutto (Accessed on September 15, 2013).

[81] Lal Khan, *Pakistan's Other Story. The 1968–69 Revolution*, op. cit., p. 178.

Bhutto began by showing the military that he was indeed master of the ship. In fact, Bhutto alone appointed "his" commander-in-chief on two occasions. On 20 December 1970, just after having replaced Yahya Khan as president and chief martial law administrator, Bhutto summoned Lieutenant General Gul Hassan Khan to ask him to take the post. If his memoirs are to be believed, Gul Hassan Khan at first refused to take on such heavy responsibility after the very recent and stinging defeat. He finally accepted on several conditions, including that there would be "no interference from anyone, himself or any of his ministers included".[82] Bhutto agreed, but four months after taking office, twenty-nine senior officers were suspended, including commander-in-chief Gul Hassan Khan, who was replaced by General Tikka Khan.[83]

This decision was justified by Gul Hassan Khan's behaviour during the Bangladesh war as described in the Hamoodur Rahman Commission report. The commission, named after its chairperson, the chief justice of the Supreme Court, was appointed by Bhutto to investigate the causes of the war, the reasons for the break-up of Pakistan and the role of the Pakistan Armed forces in these events. Officially named the War Enquiry Commission, it submitted its report on 23 October 1974. It recommended that several top generals should be put on trial before martial courts. Even before the report was submitted, Bhutto used it against Gul Hassan Khan. But it was not used against many other senior generals. In fact, it was not even made public because the commission also highlighted Bhutto's own responsibility in the war.[84]

Bhutto sought to build a more professional army in the service of the civilian authorities.[85] Some of the functions that had devolved to the army chief of staff were transferred to the prime minister. All promotions and transfers of officers above the rank of brigadier-general were henceforth decided by Bhutto and Tikka Khan, who was staunchly loyal to the prime minister. Bhutto took advantage of the situation to rebalance the ethnic makeup of the army, where Pashtuns (the community from which hailed the country's first four commanders-in-chief from Ayub Khan to Yahya Khan

---

[82] Lt. Gen. Gul Hassan, *Memoirs of Lt. Gen. Gul Hasan Khan*, Oxford, p. 351.

[83] Hasan-Askari Rizvi, *The Military and Politics in Pakistan, 1947–1986*, Delhi, 1988, pp. 198–199.

[84] The report was unearthed by the Times of India in 2000. It is now available at the following address: http://www.bangla2000.com/Bangladesh/Independence-War/Report-Hamoodur-Rahman/default.shtm (Accessed on September 15, 2013).

[85] He explained this in *If I Am Assassinated...*, New Delhi, Vikas, 1979.

and Gul Hassan Khan, with the exception of Mohammad Musa) and natives of Potwar (a region of Punjab that includes the districts of Campbellpur (Attock since 1978), Rawalpindi and Jhelum) had become dominant.

He gradually redesigned the architecture of the political-military apparatus. He took away the title of commander-in-chief, making it "chief of service" (COS)—renamed Chief of Army Staff (COAS) in 1972—and separating the functions previously concentrated in the post. Although the COS continued to oversee strategy and coordination of the three military branches (the army, the navy and the air force), the prime minister's defence advisor was now in charge of domestic security and the defence secretary administered the ministry of the same name. In addition, a Defence Committee of the Cabinet (DCC) henceforth assisted the prime minister in defining defence policy while another committee assisted the defence secretary in carrying out this policy. Bhutto also gave the prime minister final decision-making power in defence matters—including the nuclear dimension.[86] Bhutto's actions show that the democratic transition had led to the total subordination of the military.[87]

The military staff at first approved of these reforms, which opportunely replaced officers who had been discredited by the defeat,[88] all the more since defence expenditure remained very high, even if it showed a considerable linear erosion—59.3 per cent of the budget in 1972–3 and 44.7 per cent in 1976–7.[89] Compared to GDP, this expenditure, which had hovered between 4.8 and 5.7 per cent between 1966 and 1970, increased to between 5.6 and 6.7 per cent during the period 1971–5. The size of the armed forces also increased considerably, going from 350,000 troops to 502,000 between 1972 and 1975.[90]

But to offset the military's influence, in October 1972 Bhutto created a Federal Security Force (FSF) that answered to the central government and which was assigned the task of aiding the police with its law enforcement

---

[86] On 24 January 1972, one month after assuming power, Bhutto called together the country's fifty most eminent scientists to announce he would launch a nuclear programme under his personal authority. See S. Nawaz, *Crossed Swords*, op. cit., p. 339.

[87] A. Heeger, "Politics in the post-military state: some reflections on the Pakistani experience", *World Politics*, XXIX, January 1977, pp. 242–262.

[88] Stephen P. Cohen, *The Pakistan Army*, op. cit., p. 73.

[89] I. Cordonnier, *The Military and Political Order in Pakistan, The Military and Political Order in Pakistan*, Geneva, Programme for Strategic and International Security Studies, 1999, p. 32.

[90] Shahid Javed Burki, *Pakistan under Bhutto*, op. cit., p. 105.

operations.[91] The army never accepted this new institution (which was soon 18,500 men strong), seeing it as a rival force.[92] In the same spirit, he created an intelligence agency, the Federal Investigating Agency, in order to counterbalance the growing influence of the Inter-Services Intelligence. The ISI, which had become the main agency for intelligence,[93] had been created in 1948 in order to coordinate the army, the air force and the navy, something Military Intelligence had not done very well during the first Kashmir war.[94] At first, therefore, the ISI was not supposed to play any role on the political scene, except in the Pashtun belt and in Azad Kashmir, two sensitive areas. But Ayub Khan assigned the ISI with the surveillance of Pakistani politicians and gave it additional resources after the 1965 war, a conflict that had been "a real fiasco"[95] for the intelligence services of Pakistan which had failed to assess the atmosphere in Indian Kashmir. It also failed to anticipate the reslts of the 1970 elections,[96] but played a major role in East Bengal in 1970–71. The turning point came later anyway, with Bhutto and Zia. First, "it was Zulfikar Ali Bhutto, after the disaster in East Pakistan, who helped the downbeat military leadership gain a new self-confidence. This meant that in the '70s for the first time the ISI was headed by a three-star general".[97] While "a political cell for the observation and manipulation of the internal political scene had already existed under Ayub and Yayha", the Internal Security Wing was officially created by Bhutto.[98] To control the ISI more effectively, Bhutto appointed General Ghulam Jilani at its head.[99] But Jilani was to play truant after the 1977 coup.

---

[91] On the attitude of Bhutto vis-à-vis the army, see Aqil Shah, *The Army and Democracy. Military Politics in Pakistan*, op. cit., pp. 122–131.

[92] Hassan-Askari Rizvi, Military, State and Society in Pakistan, London, Macmillan, 2000, p. 146. The Constitution Bhutto had passed in 1973 also contained a number of clauses designed to avert the risk of military coups. It required the military staff to swear not to engage in political activity and defined as treason any act aiming to subvert the Constitution by force.

[93] There were two others: Intelligence Bureau and Military Intelligence.

[94] Hein Kiessling, *Faith, Unity, Discipline: the ISI of Pakistan*, London, Hurst, forthcoming.

[95] Ibid., p. 8.

[96] Ibid., p. 10.

[97] Ibid., p. 11.

[98] Ibid., p. 19.

[99] Frédéric Grare, *Reforming the Intelligence Agencies in Pakistan's Transitional Democracy*, Washington DC, Carnegie Endowment for International Peace, 2009, p. 18.

Still, by placing the army under the control of elected civilians, Bhutto democratised the regime. He also worked toward this aim when he brought an end to martial law on 21 April 1972, four months after taking office, by promulgating an interim constitution. It was replaced on 14 August 1973 by the country's third constitution, which is still in effect today. It changed Pakistan's political system over to parliamentarianism, placing power in the hands of the prime minister, elected by the Assembly, rather than vesting it in the president. Article 48, for instance, stipulated that presidential decrees had to be countersigned by the prime minister. Bhutto occupied the post of prime minister as soon as the Constitution was promulgated, in August 1973, and the post of president went to a secondary figure, Fazlal Elahi Chaudhry.

In addition to the suspension of military officers and the adoption of a parliamentary constitution, Bhutto's efforts at democratisation were reflected in rather accommodating socio-economic reformism initially engineered by Minister of Finance Mubashir Hasan, one of the four social-ist-affiliated members of government.[100]

In accordance with his election platform, in January 1972 Bhutto nation-alised thirty-one major enterprises in a dozen industrial sectors ranging from the iron and steel industry to petrochemicals and including electrical equipment. His real aim was to bring to heel the twenty-two families who still controlled the Pakistani economy in an oligopolistic structure.[101] Nationalisation was extended to the financial sector, affecting insurance companies and later banks by early 1974. No compensation was paid during this process given that the families who had founded the companies affected remained their owners. They simply could no longer sell them or sell off their shares, and the management were appointed by the government—and assisted by worker committees.[102] On 10 February 1972, Bhutto announced a significant set of worker-oriented measures: trade unions gained in influ-ence through the introduction of labour courts before which they could bring conflicts that pit them against the management. Employee representa-tives also henceforth had to be elected, and companies were obliged to dis-tribute between two and four percent of their profits to their employees.

In the business community, even if owners did not systematically opt for exile, they invested a considerable amount of their capital abroad and espe-

---

[100] The others were J.A. Rashim, Sheikh Rashid and Kurshid Hasan Meer.

[101] In 1968, it was estimated that two-thirds of industry, 80 % of the banks and 70 % of insurance companies were held by these 22 families. Shahid Javed Burki, *Pakistan under Bhutto*, op. cit., p. 64.

[102] Ibid., p. 114.

cially, curbed their investment in Pakistan. Whereas under Ayub Khan's rule, private investment oscillated between 930 and 990 million rupees per year on average, it tapered off to between 648 and 767 million rupees during the Bhutto years.[103]

The (Narrow) Limits of Progressivism

Bhutto came from a family of *waderos*, a term that denotes large landowners in Sindh. His estate in the district of Larkana stretched as far as the eye could see—and was probably smaller only than that of the Jatois. All of his biographers have pointed out the ambivalence of a man who at once shared modern values and those of a feudal landlord.[104] Even if Bhutto showed a certain leftist voluntarism with regard to the urban capitalists, he was in fact far more cautious in rural areas, as the limited nature of his land reform indicates. On 11 March 1972, the ceiling on land holdings was lowered from 500 to 150 acres of irrigated land and from 1,000 to 300 acres of non-irrigated land. This measure did not, however, lead to a very substantial redistribution of land to poorer tenants, as the land they acquired was often of poor quality. Moreover, property deeds could be transferred within a family and those who owned tractors or tube wells were entitled to additional land over and above these ceilings. Land reform was only substantial in three districts of the NWFP—Charsadda, Mardan and Swabi—where Bhutto thus tried to weaken the position of his archenemy, Wali Khan.[105]

Bhutto's land reform was in fact not as ambitious as Ayub Khan's (see infra). Only 0.6 million acres were redistributed, which is far less than in the 1958–69 period.[106] In all, "only 50,548 persons benefited from the redistribution of 308,390 acres during 1972–8. Only 1 per cent of the landless tenants and small owners benefited by these measures".[107] Furthermore, the prime minister satisfied agrarian interests by putting an end to a practice of his

[103] Ibid., p. 119.

[104] Stanley Wolpert, *Zulfi Bhutto of Pakistan. His Life and Times*, New York, Oxford University Press, 1993 and S. Taseer, *Bhutto: A Political Biography*, London, Ithaca Press, 1979.

[105] As a result, one-third of the landless peasants of the NWFP received some land. Omar Noman, *The Political Economy of Pakistan, 1947–85*, London, KPI, 1988, p. 94.

[106] Akmal Hussain, "Land reform in Pakistan", in Akmal Hussain (ed.), *Strategic Issues in Pakistan: Economic Policy*, Lahore, Progressive Publishers, 1988, p. 182.

[107] S. Akbar Zaidi, *Issues in Pakistan's Economy*, op. cit., p. 36.

predecessors which involved rewarding their supporters (particularly retired officers) by granting them plots of land out of state property. This practice, which resulted in the arrival of new agricultural producers on an already heavily competitive market, immediately aroused hostility among traditional landowners. Eager to satisfy them, "Bhutto, despite his rhetoric demanding change in the countryside, continued to receive the support of the more important landed groups".[108]

By the end of 1974, all sorts of feudal families were found in the PPP: the Legharis,[109] the Khosas of Dera Ghazi Khan, the Pirachas, Tiwanas, Bandials and Qureshis of Sargodha, the Daultanas, Khakwanis and Gilanis of Multan, the Kharrals of the Ravi in Faislabad, the Pirs of Makhad, Manki Sharif and Taunsa Sharif, the Khorejas of Rahim Yar Khan, the Tammans and Jodhras of Attock, various descendants of the Bukhari Sayyid lineages: Pir Mahal, Kuranga and Shah Jiwana. In addition to these big landowning families, Lal Khan adds those he calls "civil service moguls" such as Aziz Ahmed and Malik Khuda Baksh Bucha,[110] before concluding:

The entry of the elitist class representatives, upper middle class, traders and even leaders of criminal gangs and *rassagir* (police pimps) elements, was undoubtedly a protective reaction, for access to the power system has always been crucial to the gaining and holding of land and wealth. For the most part, in return for lip service to the PPP Manifesto and an expression of loyalty to Bhutto, they found easy entry into the PPP.[111]

Further along, Lal Khan gives a striking summary of the drift taken by the party:

By 1974, the names of the old local feudalists had begun to emerge in the lists of district PPP officeholders, as well as on the District Councils of the People's Work Programme (PWP), the successor of the Rural Works Programme and the major

---

[108] Shahid Javed Burki, *Pakistan under Bhutto*, op. cit., p. 139.

[109] Lal Khan gives details concerning Farooq Ahmed Leghari that informed observers prefer to treat as rumour: "He was a vicious feudal lord and had his private prisons where the poor peasants and youth who dared to question the tyranny in his estates in South Punjab were incarcerated and tortured. Several were killed...". See Lal Khan, *Pakistan's Other Story. The 1968–69 Revolution*, op. cit., pp. 315–316. The same man was appointed minister without portfolio in the Bhutto government and the country's president by his daughter a few years later. Meanwhile, after Zia's removal of Z. A. Bhutto, Leghari was the first landowner to dispute the land reform he suffered from in court.

[110] Lal Khan, *Pakistan's Other Story. The 1968–69 Revolution*, op. cit., p. 281.

[111] Ibid.

channel of development funds to the local level. By mid-1975, members of aristo-cratic families held the Secretary-Generalship of the Punjab PPP (Syed Nasir Ali Shah), the Punjab Chief Ministership (Nawab Sadiq Hussain Qureshi) and the Punjab governorship (Sadiq Muhammad Khan, Amir of Bahawalpur).[112]

This scenario is comparable to the trajectory followed by the Congress(R) in the 1970s. Indira Gandhi also fairly quickly gave up the idea of making Congress a party of cadres touting a socialist ideology. She instead used it as the instrument of a populist approach based on a network of local notables.[113]

Trade unionists such as Miraj Muhammad Khan—elected in 1970 under the PPP label to Lalu Khait, then government minister without portfolio—broke with Bhutto by 1973 due to the rather "unsocialist" nature of his poli-cies. This was also the case of another trade union leader in Karachi, Usman Baloch, whom Bhutto sacrificed on the altar of his good relations with the leaders of the Pakistan National Federation of Trade Unions.[114] The NSF and the Thal Mehnat Kash Mahaz—among others—did the same for similar reasons.

In fact, once the euphoria of nationalisation was over, Bhutto's industrial policy was a bitter deception for the union leaders and more generally the workers who had backed him. The New Labour Policy he announced in February 1972 created the conditions for greater control over the labour world, repressive practices being evident as early as 7 June 1972. On that day, the police fired on employees at Feroz Sultan (a textile mill in Karachi) who were demanding payment of their wages. One of the workers was killed. The victim's funeral the following day gave rise to demonstrations that were even more brutally crushed. Ten people were killed, including a woman and a child.[115] In October 1974, a presidential order again reformed industrial relations, this time explicitly in favour of the business commu-nity. In February 1975, the labour minister moreover indicated his goal was to reduce the number of trade unions, supposedly to give more power to the workers.[116] In fact, in October 1974, Bhutto had gotten rid of three of

---

[112] Ibid., p. 282.

[113] See Christophe Jaffrelot, *Inde: La démocratie par la caste*, Paris, Fayard, 2006.

[114] Lal Khan, *Pakistan's Other Story. The 1968–69 Revolution*, op. cit., p. 170. Right after the 1970 elections, the West Pakistan Federation of Trade Unions that had just backed the JUI gradually threw its weight behind the PPP. Its ally, the Pakistan Labour Party, merged with it in March 1971.

[115] Lal Khan, *Pakistan's Other Story. The 1968–69 Revolution*, op. cit., p. 236.

[116] Ibid., p. 237

his four socialist ministers—including Mubashir Hasan, replaced by Rana Mohammad Hanif, a PPP member of a more centrist vein. This decision was naturally greeted with favour by the business community.

Certainly, the business world was taken by surprise by the belated nationalisation, in July 1976, of 4,000 small family agrifood concerns: flour mills and vegetable oil factories thus came under state control. But this was in no respect the tail of the socialist comet, but instead yet another demonstration of good will toward the traditional large landlords a few months before the elections. These notables had always been excluded from the high added-value activities of marketing and processing handled during the Raj by Hindu and Sikh merchants which after Partition had been taken over by immigrants with greater entrepreneurial sense. By nationalising these activities, the PPP-state was able to hand their management to the large landowners in an effort to win their support and thus accomplish unprecedented vertical integration. In fact, nearly three-quarters of the 4,000 new managers "had close links with the large landlords who had now become prominent in the PPP".[117]

This move was carried out at the same time as a similar reorganisation of the PPP structure. Like Indira Gandhi, Bhutto sought to use his party as an instrument to establish a lasting foothold in rural areas and like her, he relied on rural notables. Out of the fifty-two district-level party committees, thirty-two were dominated by "large landlords, prosperous lawyers and large industrialists".[118]

In addition to his social conservatism, Bhutto also showed a tendency toward authoritarianism—which moreover was not new. This inclination was already apparent in 1962 in a long memorandum addressed to Ayub Khan and other government ministers when the new Constitution was being drafted. In it he advocated a "one-party system in which the roles of the legislative and judicial branches of the government were to be completely subservient to the all-powerful central authority".[119] This single party was to cover all of society down to the village level and urban communities—where it was destined to assume control of schools and dispensaries. Eventually, civil servants, judges and possibly even soldiers should belong to it. Bhutto ascribed Ayub Khan's rejection of his plan to excessive timidity and later saw it as a political mistake that eventually drove the president-general to resign.

---

[117] Shahid Javed Burki, *Pakistan under Bhutto*, op. cit., p. 160.

[118] Ibid., p. 162.

[119] Ibid., p. 80.

In 1973, Bhutto would have preferred to give Pakistan a presidential constitution, but opposition from the PPP's left wing forced him to give up the idea.[120] He did, however, manage to have a clause inserted in the Constitution that was hardly in line with the spirit of parliamentarianism: if the prime minister could be dismissed following a no-confidence motion voted by Members of Parliament, it had to mention the name of his successor.[121] A number of his speeches following the adoption of the Constitution show that he did not resign himself to seeing the head of government's power overseen to a large extent by Parliament. For instance, he did not hide his fascination for "the tremendous advance made in the countries in the Middle East and in the countries in the Pacific because the administrations there were free to act without being inhibited by a handful of people of the type who have used the excuse of parliamentary democracy to stop me, my administration and my people from making similar progress in Pakistan".[122] It would appear that Bhutto, who admired Singapore and Dubai, would probably have used a new victory at the polls to revise the Constitution and take greater distance from the Westminster model. As it was, the shift from libertarian rhetoric to freedom-crushing practices was already evident in Bhutto's treatment of the media. He used the Press and Publications Ordinance introduced by Ayub Khan with the same harshness as Ayub Khan, including with regard to the English language press. The left-leaning weekly *Outlook* (Karachi) was thus obliged to fold.

Similarly, Bhutto had resigned himself to federalism when actually he had a preference for a centralised political system—his Justice Minister, Mahmud Ali Kasuri, moreover resigned as soon as he realised this. Whereas the letter of the Constitution was federal, the use Bhutto made of it was considerably different. His aim in abolishing the Civil Service of Pakistan was not to get rid of a centralised bureaucracy, but instead to concentrate more power in his hands once he had disposed of an administration that had controlled the state for years. He moreover prosecuted the senior officials who had implemented Ayub Khan's policies and might thus act as an opposition force.[123] As we saw in chapter 4, Bhutto had not hesitated to

---

[120] Craig Baxter, "Constitution Making: the development of federalism in Pakistan", *Asian Survey*, XIV, December 1974, p. 1075.

[121] Such a motion could not be put to the vote during the budget session, and if it did not go through, no other such motion could be made for another six months.

[122] Cited in Shahid Javed Burki, *Pakistan under Bhutto*, op. cit., p. 183.

[123] The President-General's right-hand man, Altaf Gauhar, was jailed and others (S.M. Yusuf, Ghiassudin Ahmad and Afzal Agha) dismissed.

dismiss the government of Balochistan in 1973—provoking the resignation of the NWFP government—to maintain control over provinces that wanted to regain their autonomy in a truly federal framework.

Bhutto's authoritarian and conservative tendencies came into full light with the 1977 elections. Whereas in 1970, he had mainly attempted to appeal to the urban middle class (including its worker segment—factory workers, who should be distinguished from informal labourers), in 1977, after having lost the backing of his socialist allies and abandoning reforms, Bhutto counted more on a coalition of extremes bringing together land-owners and the rural poor who often depended on the patronage of these same landowners. Even if on 5 January 1977 Bhutto announced another reform lowering land holding ceilings to 100 acres of irrigated land and 200 acres of non-irrigated land, he backed the PPP candidacies of a record number of large Punjabi landowners: the Noons and Tiwanas in Sargodha district, the Maliks in Mianwali, the Qureshis in Multan, the Hayats of Rawalpindi and Campbellpur, the Legharis and Mazaris of Dera Ghazi Khan, and so on.[124] The list of PPP candidate reads like a "'who's who' of the families that dominated electoral politics in Punjab from 1920 to 1958".[125] In a sign of his reorientation toward other social milieus, out of 100 PPP members in the incumbent Assembly, the party slate for re-election excluded forty of them (including two ministers).[126]

Not only did the campaign confirm the remarkable personalisation of power that prevailed within the PPP, an organization that was undergoing the same deinstitutionalisation process that Indira Gandhi's Congress Party was experiencing at the same time, but Bhutto also circumvented the constitution to counter opponents that put up more of a fight than expected. He had, for instance, waited until 7 January to announce an election set for the month of March in order to catch his opponents off guard. But already on 11 January, nine opposition parties had united under the Pakistan National Alliance (PNA). This coalition grouped parties ranging from traditional Islamic organisations to leftist groups and included various factions of the Muslim League as well a new party, Asghar Khan's Tehrik-e-Istiklal (Independence party).[127]

---

[124] Shahid Javed Burki, *Pakistan under Bhutto*, op. cit., p. 192.

[125] Lal Khan, *Pakistan's Other Story. The 1968–69 Revolution*, op. cit., p. 282.

[126] Shahid Javed Burki, *Pakistan under Bhutto*, op. cit., p. 193.

[127] Asghar Khan was the first Pakistani air force chief, from 1957 to 1965. He resigned from the army when he discovered that Ayub Khan had not informed

Most observers believed that the PPP would certainly suffer in the face of a unified opposition.[128] The results were therefore regarded with suspicion abroad and denounced by the opposition as the product of widespread fraud. 155 of the 200 candidates fielded by the PPP were elected, whereas the opposition won only thirty-six seats out of the 169 it contested.[129] Bhutto himself was taken aback by the scope of his victory—and the manipulation he concealed. As he watched the results for one constituency after another come in on television in the company of US ambassador Henry Byroade (a privilege indicating the close relations between the two countries), he was particularly disturbed by his party's performance in Punjab, where the PPP won 93 per cent of seats. Byroade recounts that "Then he became absolutely quiet and started to drink heavily, calling Lahore he said: 'What are you guys doing?'".[130] The results were truly amazing indeed: the PPP had won 155 seats out of 200, including 107 seats in Punjab.[131]

The PPP repeated a similar performance in the regional elections, all the provinces except one falling into its pocket on 10 March. The opposition parties, which had boycotted this round of elections, reacted on 11 March with a general strike that paralysed a number of cities in Pakistan. Some observers feared that Bhutto was keen to achieve a two thirds majority "to amend the constitution to create a strong presidential system".[132] The Jama'at-e-Islami mobilised its activists in the street. In response, Bhutto announced on 17 April that he would make sharia the law of the country, which implied that alcohol would be banned and that Friday would replace

---

him of Operation Gibraltar, which was to lead to the second Pakistan-India war. In 1968–1969, he entered politics to fight against nepotism and the incompetence of the political class (See his public speeches appended to his book, *Pakistan at the Cross-Roads*, Karachi, Ferozsons Ltd, 1969, p. 88–117). He had created his own party in 1970 and emerged as the other rising star of Pakistani politics—along with Bhutto, and against him. In 1977, he was elected at Karachi and Abbottabad, in the two constituencies where he contested—against all odds.

[128] M.G. Weinbaum, "The March 1977 Elections in Pakistan", *Asian Survey*, 17 (7), July 1977, pp. 599–618.

[129] Ibid.

[130] Quoted in Stanley Wolpert, *Zulfi Bhutto of Pakistan. His Life and Times*, New York, Oxford University Press, p. 279.

[131] According to Frédéric Grare, Bhutto had asked the political cell of the ISI to rig the elections. (Frédéric Grare, *Reforming the Intelligence Agencies*, op. cit., p. 18).

[132] Aqil Shah, *The Army and Democracy. Military Politics in Pakistan*, op. cit., p. 141.

Sunday as the day when people would not work. Since this made hardly any difference, Bhutto resorted to strongarm tactics. He enforced section 144 of the Criminal Procedure Code prohibiting any gathering of more than five persons. He had opposition leaders arrested. And then he imposed martial law. The Chief Election Commissioner, who had pledged to investigate electoral malpractices on 6 April, left the country on 8 May for medical reasons.

On 2 June, the judiciary declared that martial law was illegal. Talks between Bhutto and the opposition parties resumed. But in the night of 4–5 July, while it seemed that they were about to reach some compromise,[133] the army took power.[134]

Not only had Bhutto called the military in for reinforcement to repress street demonstrations, but it had already returned to a centre-stage role when it had been asked to fight the Baloch guerrillas in 1973. The initiative came from General Zia ul Haq, whom Bhutto had appointed not long before as COAS, believing he had engaged the services of a docile man. The military took over on 4 July 1977 without bloodshed while, according to some observers the PNA and Bhutto had "agreed to hold fresh elections at the centre and in the provinces".[135] But Lieutenant General Faiz Ali Chisti, the then Comander of the X Corps, told Aqil Shah that the "PPP and the PNA were like two children".[136] Zia first announced that new elections would be held within 90 days. The leaders of the PPP—including Bhutto—and the PNA were arrested, but released three weeks later. Zia nevertheless assumed the title of Chief Administrator of Martial Law and, reneging on his promises, subjected the country to eleven years of an extremely repressive military regime, though not without periodically announcing that elections would soon be held.

*

The Bhutto years were both a missed opportunity and a founding moment in the history of Pakistan. For the first time a democratically elected civil-

---

[133] This compromise would have led to the dissolution of the assemblies and the organization of new elections under the supervision of a council in which the PPP and the PNA would have been equally represented.

[134] Mohammad Waseem, *Politics and the State in Pakistan*, op. cit., pp. 335–339.

[135] Syed Sami Ahmad, *The Judiciary of Pakistan and its role in Political Crises*, Karachi, Royal Book Company, 2012, p. 89.

[136] Cited in Aqil Shah, *The Army and Democracy. Military Politics in Pakistan*, op. cit., p. 141.

ian authority backed by a lasting majority political party restricted the army and the bureaucracy to their primary role (defence of the nation and administration of the country under the authority of elected representatives of the people) and gave the country a parliamentary and federal constitution that respected civil liberties. Moreover, the PPP had won the elections on a socialist-inspired programme and the making of this party was another major legacy.[137]

Z. A. Bhutto's term in power left a mixed record, however. Although he established a lasting democratic repertoire that serves as a reference for opponents to the army, his use of institutions often contravened the democratic ideal. In addition to his highly populist penchant for personal power that inhibited democracy within the PPP, Bhutto quickly turned his back on his progressive friends to renew ties with his original background of very conservative landowners. Most of all, his sense of democracy was not developed enough to allow voters to freely decide their fate, as the fraud that marred the 1977 election attests. In fact, the sincerity of Bhutto's democratic commitment is itself doubtful. The authoritarian nature of his political agenda (one-party system, personalisation of power) are reminiscent of the viceregal model advocated by Jinnah, who had also wished to set up a presidential system. Bhutto added to this legacy a dimension that the Quaid-e-Azam could not have by collaborating with military rulers: after being part of Mirza's anti-democratic cabinet, Bhutto participated in Ayub Khan's government and in this way foreshadowed a grey area between civilians and the military, two categories that tend too often to be contrasted outright.

In terms of institutions, while the PPP is Bhutto's major legacy, far from remaining a revolutionary party, the PPP under Bhutto (and finally the Bhutto family) became a populist party whose apparatus fairly quickly hewed to Pakistan's social structure after most of the leftists were eased out.

If the army and the bureaucracy were so easily able to return to power in 1977, it was also because Bhutto contributed—partly in spite of himself—to putting these two institutions back in the saddle during his term in office. His partial reliance on the army began in 1973 when the dismissal of the government of Balochistan led to a war involving up to 80,000 troops

---

[137] Philip Jones, *The Pakistan People's Party: Rise to Power*, Karachi, Oxford University Press, 2003. See also Anwar H. Syed, "The Pakistan's People Party: Phases One and Two", in Lawrence Ziring, Ralph Braibanti and Howard Wriggings (eds), *Pakistan: The Long View*, Durham, Duke University Press, 1977.

through 1977. This show of force replaced the military at the heart of government action and illustrated the civilian authority's dependence on it. Bhutto did not truly manage to free himself from the influence of the bureaucracy either, for two reasons. For one, like his predecessors, he resorted to the spoils system in handing out civil service posts to his supporters. He even abolished the Police Service of Pakistan and the Civil Service of Pakistan, the state nobility that still served as the country's "steel frame", merging them into a new "All-Pakistan Unified Grade".[138] Second, Bhutto gave bureaucrats new responsibilities through the nationalisations he undertook in the early 1970s, which required the skills of a larger number of administrators.

After 1977, the military and bureaucrats ruled supreme for eleven years, but once again had to step aside and yield power to a civilian government in 1988 for yet another democratic transition—which turned out to be no more lasting or complete.

Civilians under Influence—and Prone to Lawlessness (1988–1999)

The democratisation of Pakistan in the late 1980s and 90s has often been analysed as being part of "the third wave"[139] that had begun in Europe in the 1970s and was destined to spread to Latin America and Asia.[140] The democratic transition approach has proven to be limited in the case of Pakistan, however, as power has largely remained in the hands of unelected institutions: the military and the president. This is not only because these two institutions have sought to govern in the wings, but also because politicians and political parties have proved to be incapable of administering the country, whether because they were prone to corruption or authoritarianism, or both. The way in which some politicians have colluded with the army against their counterparts further confirms the existence of a grey area between two categories, civilians and the military, that are too often described as antagonistic.

---

[138] Charles H. Kennedy, *Bureaucracy in Pakistan*, Karachi, Oxford University Press, 1987, p. 89.

[139] Samuel Huntington, *The Third Wave: Democratization in the Twentieth Century*, Norman, University of Oklahoma Press, 1991.

[140] Christophe Jaffrelot, "Comment expliquer la démocratie hors d'Occident", in Christophe Jaffrelot (ed.), *Démocraties d'ailleurs. Démocratie et démocratisations hors d'Occident*, Paris, Karthala, 2000.

The Return of the Bhutto Family, or of "Diarchy"?

The PPP, in 1988, was the only organization having a popular leader, Benazir Bhutto.[141] She rode high on her family's legacy, a mostly emotive capital drawing on the "martyrdom" of her father. In 1988, she was 35 years old. Trained at Radcliff and Oxford, she had also been initiated into politics by her father who had taken her with him during some of his official visits abroad. More importantly, she had learned from her personal experience and more especially from the tragic end of her father and the periods during which she had been under arrest alone or with her mother.

After three years in more or less self-imposed exile abroad, she was back on 11 April 1986 to lead the Movement for the Restoration of Democracy. When Zia died two years later, she was in a position to contest elections. Her party, the PPP, was better organised than the others (the JI excepted) and she could rely on dedicated activists who sometimes worshipped the Bhutto family. The two main themes of her campaign were the return to democracy and the cause of the poor, both of which had been the centrepiece of Z. A. Bhutto's programme in the early 1970s.

In reaction to the PPP's return to the front of the political stage, an opposition coalition was formed, the Islami Jomhuri Ittihad (IJI—Islamic Democratic Alliance),[142] which was backed by and even issued from the military establishment. The leading figure in this group, Nawaz Sharif, had collaborated with General Zia for nearly ten years, largely as a reaction to the effect Bhutto's policies had had on his family. Nawaz was from a family of Punjabi businessmen. His father, Muhammad Sharif, a Kashmiri from Amritsar who had moved to Lahore in 1947, had slowly built up a smelting works when he was stripped of his property in 1972 by the wave of nationalisation ordered by Z. A. Bhutto. The episode left the entire family—including the youngest brother, Shahbaz—with a hatred for the Bhuttos that first encouraged Nawaz to join the Pakistan Muslim League in 1976, a party firmly grounded in the Punjabi business community and that had set as its goal the restitution of property to despoiled entrepreneurs. Nawaz, a dynamic young politician, attracted the attention of the new governor of Punjab, Ghulam Jilani, in the late 1970s.

---

[141] On Benazir Bhutto, instead of her autobiography, one may read Katherine M. Doherty and Craig A. Doherty, *Benazir Bhutto*, London, Franklin Watts, 1990. Available online at: http://www.bhutto.org/Acrobat/Benazir%20Bhutto. pdf. (Accessed on September 15, 2013).

[142] Sayyed Vali Reza Nasr, "Democracy and the Crisis of Governability in Pakistan", *Asian Survey* 32 (6), 6 June 1992, p. 523.

A seasoned officer, Jilani had been director of the ISI from 1971 to 1977 before becoming a close advisor to Zia as secretary-general of the Defence Ministry and then being named by him governor of Punjab, a post he would hold until December 1985. Looking for new leaders who could act as a counterweight to the feudal lords in the province, Jilani appointed Sharif finance minister of Punjab.[143] This post would help him secure Zia's authorisation to privatise the companies Bhutto had nationalised, including his own.[144] Once this Zia regime boss had thus taken him under his wing, Sharif played fully along with the dictator's game. In 1981, he joined the Punjab Advisory Board chaired by Zia himself. In 1985, Sharif contested a very closely supervised election that the PPP had boycotted to protest against Zia's authoritarianism. Jilani, who continued to chaperon him, then appointed him chief minister of the province, while Zia relied on him to help develop the Muslim League in Punjab.

In 1988, the military continued to count on Nawaz Sharif to contain the PPP. It had essentially two things to fear from this party: that it would impede the nuclear programme and that it would call into question the jihad operations conducted jointly by the Islamists and the Pakistani army in Kashmir and Afghanistan.[145] The ISI, which had become more powerful under Zia (see below), played a key role in promoting the opposition to the PPP. Its chief, Hamid Gul, not only persuaded a dozen other parties to join him under the IJI banner, but also influenced its rhetoric—which explains the emphatic references to Zia's Islamisation policy, with which Nawaz, a devout Muslim, had affinities.[146] The ISI thus backed the IJI while trying to set Zia up as a martyr, with some success in fact, as the commemoration of the first anniversary of Zia's death at the Faizal mosque in Islamabad drew a crowd of 1 million. The IJI moreover included Islamic parties such as the Jama'at-e-Islami among its affiliates.

---

[143] According to Hein Kiessling, Jilani, "together with Maulana Fazlur Rehman groomed Sharif as the new political candidate" (Kiessling, *Faith, Unity, Discipline,* op. cit.).

[144] See the well-informed work of a Pakistani senior civil servant, Aminullah Chaudhry, *Hijacking from the Ground,* Central Milton Keynes, AuthorHouse, 2010, p. 14. The entire chapter entitled "Politicians and the Army" (pp. 13–29) makes for instructive reading.

[145] Shuja Nawaz, *Crossed Swords. Pakistan, Its Army and the War Within,* op. cit., p. 412.

[146] Hussain Haqqani, an advisor to Nawaz Sharif who later moved toward the PPP under Zardari (to whom he owed his post of ambassador for Pakistan to the United States in 2008)—played a major role in formulating the IJI's programme.

The coalition also enjoyed the support of many other politicians who were theoretically hostile to the military establishment. Ghulam Mustafa Jatoi can be considered typical in this regard. This Sindhi aristocrat—the Jatois are reputed to be the largest landowners in the province—had joined Z. A. Bhutto as soon as the PPP was created and had headed the provincial government from 1973 to 1977. He had also taken part in the Movement for the Restoration of Democracy (MRD) until personal rivalry led to a break with Benazir Bhutto. He then founded his own party in 1986, the National People's Party. In 1988, the NPP came under the umbrella of the IJI, of which Jatoi was formally president—even if Sharif was its leading figure (especially after Jatoi lost his seat during the 1988 elections). Factionalism within the PPP thus produced yet another reversal of alliances that further blurred the decidedly hazy dividing line between civilians and the military.

The military establishment's co-opting of PPP cadres via the IJI does not explain all the defections. Benazir Bhutto's behaviour was also a factor. In 1988, she sought to run the PPP as she saw fit, without necessarily relying on the cadres who had built up the party alongside her father, nor on those who had campaigned with her mother and herself in the MRD. She was even prepared to turn brutally away from this base if it served her. She thus alienated such founding members of the PPP as Mumtaz Bhutto, Z. A. Bhutto's cousin, Hafeez Pirzada, the author of the 1973 Constitution and one of its advocates in 1978–9, and Dr Ghulam Hussain, PPP secretary-general under Z. A. Bhutto. The latter describes in very revealing terms how Benazir ignored him when it came time to name a party candidate in his constituency:

Benazir, who couldn't read Urdu[147]—she had to write her speeches in English—bypassed me and gave the PPP ticket in Jhelum to Chaudry Aftaf, who was from the Pakistan Muslim League—Zia's party!—because he was a jagirdar, a man so powerful as a feudal master that he owned serfs. This same man, who violated all the party's principles ideologically, had also sat in Zia's Majlis e Shoora [parliament]! I didn't even learn about my demotion from Benazir. I read about it in the press the next day.[148]

Z. A. Bhutto's rivals were promoted within the party in a similar fashion. Nisar Khuro thus became party boss in Sindh province.

---

[147] Fatima Bhutto has pointed out in her memoir that Z. A. Bhutto family worshiped English to an extent that could only have a negative effect on its use of vernacular languages.

[148] Cited in Fatima Bhutto, *Songs of Blood and Sword. A Daughter's Memoir*, New York, Nation Books, 2010, p. 290.

Although the 1988 elections were supposed to hail the return to democracy, only a minority fraction of registered voters—43 per cent—went to the polls. And the PPP, far from repeating its performance of 1970, only won ninety-two seats out of the 207 with 38.5 per cent of the votes cast—against fifty-five seats and 30 per cent of the vote for the IJI.[149] It lost in the country's main province, Punjab, where the IJI tallied its highest scores. This coalition also carried a majority in the regional elections of this province, enabling Nawaz to remain head of government there. The PPP was thus obliged to enter into an alliance with the MQM, which had taken thirteen seats in Sindhi cities, whereas Benazir had mainly been backed in the rural areas of the province where "native" Sindhis hostile to the Muhajirs lived. The mismatched nature of this coalition was not, however, the only factor of dysfunction in the government she formed in December 1988.

Immediately after the election, the army sought to curb Benazir Bhutto's power. COAS Aslam Beg, after having tried in vain to draw PPP leaders away from the party to form a coalition with the IJI,[150] brokered a five-point compromise in which Bhutto promised not to bother Zia's family and not to alter the Afghan policy, the nuclear programme or defence strategy, and that she would not interfere with the country's administrative architecture[151]—in other words, promotions within the army.

To ensure that Benazir would honour this division of responsibilities, the army benefited from a very influential backer, the president. This man, Ishaq Khan, a career senior civil servant, had been Z. A. Bhutto's Defence Secretary and in this capacity had played a key role in launching Pakistan's nuclear programme. A close associate of the "father of the Pakistani bomb", Abdul Qadeer Khan, he had chaired the committee that had led to establishing his laboratory in Kahuta. But Ishaq Khan had accepted Zia's coup and he became minister of finance before running for election in 1985. Upon his election as senator, he was appointed to preside over the Upper House of Parliament and it was in this capacity that he became acting

---

[149] http://www.elections.com.pk/contents.php?i=7. 217 seats (207 Muslim, 10 non-Muslim) were filled by direct election, with 20 reserved for women chosen by the elected members.

[150] The ISI in particular allegedly approached Makhdoom Amin Fahim to offer him the post of prime minister if he defected. Fahim refused, a sign that certain PPP remained faithful to their party. See Shuja Nawaz, *Crossed Swords. Pakistan, Its Army and the War Within*, op. cit., p. 414.

[151] Ibid., p. 415.

president in 1988 on Zia's death, in accordance with the Constitution. He was officially elected to this post in December of the same year.

The president had acquired a predominant role with the passage of the Eighth Amendment to the Constitution under Zia. When General Zia had begun to liberalise the regime (see infra), he had made sure to reorganise state institutions so as to strengthen the power of the president and, through him, the military. In November 1985, the National Assembly had modified the 1973 Constitution in this direction with the Eighth Amendment, which had transformed the office of the president from a mere honorary figure to chief of the executive. Benazir Bhutto had always criticized this provision, but to annul the amendment she would have needed a two-thirds majority that she could not put together. She thus remained subordinate to President Ishaq Khan through whom the army continued to exercise considerable influence, particularly in the conduct of foreign affairs. She was moreover obliged to keep Zia's Foreign Affairs Minister, Yakub Ali Khan, in her cabinet. The ISI largely retained control over the Afghan and Kashmir policies. The only domain in which Benazir Bhutto managed to change things somewhat was in the nuclear agenda, which the Americans pressured her over, concerned as they were about Pakistani proliferation.[152] She cut down on the president's monopoly over the matter, apparently with the COAS' approval.[153] After a few months in the post of prime minister, she however admitted to her friend Tariq Ali: "I can't do anything. The army on one side and the president on the other".[154]

Having basically given up on wielding any influence in strategic and geopolitical affairs, Benazir focused her energies on domestic issues. She challenged Ishaq Khan's right to appoint provincial High Court justices, even seeking to appeal the decision to the Supreme Court before changing her mind. Benazir Bhutto also tried to regain control over the ISI—which she suspected of fomenting a coup.[155] She dismissed the director of this powerful institution, Hamid Gul, replacing him with Lieutenant General Rahman Kallu, who was not on good terms with COAS Beg. As a result, the

---

[152] Ibid., p. 416.

[153] Ibid., 422.

[154] Quoted in Tariq Ali, *The Duel. Pakistan and the Flight Path of American Power*, London, Pocket Books, 2008, p. 135.

[155] On 6 October 1989, during the "night of the jackals", two senior ISI officers, IJI representatives and PPP dissidents allegedly hatched a plot to bring down the prime minister.

ISI "was suddenly cut off from the Pakistan Army".[156] Hein Kiessling points out that in the security establishment, "there was a feeling that Kallu was more loyal to politics than to the military; some even saw him as a turn-coat. Kallu was not invited to meetings of the corps commanders and there-fore not informed about important decisions".[157]

The first free elections since the 1970s thus produced a new version of the colonial "diarchy", to borrow Mohammad Waseem's term.[158] Under British rule, this term referred to the system set up by the reform of 1919: although a protoparliamentary system had been introduced in the provinces, the governors, as the viceroy's local representatives, controlled the activity of the ministers, thereby giving rise to the notion that the executive was at once double-headed and hierarchical. Pakistan remained prisoner of this authoritarian aspect of the British legacy: the prime minister was named by a democratically elected assembly but remained under the thumb of a president who was not elected by the people and owed his authority to military support.

In such a context, a united front of political figures against the old alli-ance of bureaucrats and the military could have made all the difference. But the civilians instead supplied arguments for those who doubted the benefits of democratisation. Indeed, the long-distance duel between Benazir Bhutto and Nawaz Sharif tended to discredit the entire political class. Just after her election, Benazir had tried to oust Sharif from his post of chief minister of Punjab,[159] in vain. And Nawaz used this regional stronghold to do battle with Bhutto on a nearly daily basis. For the first time in Pakistan history, its most heavily populated province, which generally crystallised resent-ment from minority regions, led the opposition against "the Centre". Benazir was obliged to devote much of her energy to responding to Sharif's criticism, thereby hampering the government's action when it was not totally paralysed by obstructionism.

If the politician's lack of discipline exasperated the military and the presi-dent, the degradation of relations between Benazir and the security estab-

---

[156] Shuja Nawaz, *Crossed Swords. Pakistan, Its Army and the War Within*, op. cit., p. 425.

[157] Hein Kiessling, *Faith, Unity, Discipline*, op. cit.

[158] Mohammad Waseem, "Pakistan's lingering crisis of diarchy", *Asian Survey*, 32(7), July 1992, pp. 612–634.

[159] The PPP had opened hostilities on 7 December 1988 by pulling all its elected members from the Punjab Assembly in response to Sharif's amended finance bill.

lishment was mostly due to another factor. COAS Beg realised quickly that "the new Prime Minister attached little importance to his advice and was seeking purposefully to bring the Army to heel—without consulting him. She even "demanded from her Army Chief a list of military personnel who had been closely linked to the Zia regime"[160]—obviously not with a view to promoting them. Beg asked her not to interfere in the internal affairs of the army and suggested the creation of a National Security Council. This Council—which was to be introduced years later by General Musharraf—was intended, in his view, to ensure better coordination between the civilians and the military. According to Beg, the past coups had resulted from a lack of such coordination. Benazir rejected the idea of such a Council and the fate of her government was sealed soon after when the security establishment could use the situation of Karachi to remove her.

On 2 December 1988, the PPP and the MQM had ratified a "Charter of Peace, Love and Rights" aiming to "reunite the urban and rural populations of Sindh".[161] This 59-point document aimed in particular to raise the job quotas for Muhajirs, help them integrate the educational system and "repatriate" the some 250,000 Biharis still living in camps in Bangladesh. In exchange, the MQM would renounce its separatist demands. The Bihari question quickly became a bone of contention between the MQM and the government. Such an influx of immigrants was unacceptable for most native Sindhis who were already so jealous of the Muhajirs. The PPP did not honour its promise, and so the MQM reversed its alliance and joined forces with the IJI. The two parties drafted a 17-point protocol agreement that placed particular emphasis on the return of the Biharis. This strengthened opposition filed a motion of censure on 1 November 1989 that nearly succeeded. On the ground, these political realignments were followed by an unleashing of violence in Karachi as well as in Hyderabad, site of the infamous police massacre in Pucca Qila on 27 May 1990.[162]

---

[160] Hein Kiessling, *Faith, Unity, Discipline*, op. cit.

[161] Quoted in Ian Talbot, *Pakistan*, op. cit., p. 304.

[162] On that day, Sindhi police officers conducting searches for a weapons cache opened fire on civilians, killing some 40 Muhajirs, including women and children. They justified their action by alleging "snipers", an allegation that could not be substantiated for lack of an independent investigation. The army on several occasions requested full powers to restore order in Sindh (which would have enabled it to bypass the power of the judges). Benazir Bhutto turned them down, thus avoiding the establishment of a sort of parallel government.

According to Shuja Nawaz, it was during a meeting between Beg and the Corps Commanders held on 21 July 1990 that "the army high command decided that the Bhutto government was no longer acceptable".[163] This message was communicated to President Ghulam Ishaq who was of the same opinion and dismissed Benazir Bhutto from her post of prime minister on 6 August. He cited the Pucca Qila "incident" to explain his decision. In his view, the government had proven incapable of maintaining "law and order".

Nawaz Sharif in Power: a Façade of Democratisation

Unlike in 1988, the PPP went into the 24 October 1990 elections in a position of weakness, even if it had put together a coalition, the People's Democratic Alliance, which included three other small parties.[164] Benazir Bhutto had been a disappointment and was unable to hold on to all her allies (including the MQM). The IJI seemed to provide an alternative. In Nawaz Sharif it had an enterprising leader who enjoyed the support of the military.

General Beg wanted to prevent Benazir Bhutto's re-election at all costs. One of the first things he did after her removal was to replace the ISI director she had appointed with the director-general of Military Intelligence, Lieutenant General Asad Durrani, who immediately promoted Benazir's opponents. In 1990, the army and the ISI:

had realised that a PPP election victory could not be prevented; internal ISI reports make that abundantly clear. Their intention was to avoid a one-sided distribution of power. As in 1971, they sought a balanced parliament that would secure the military's future influence. The ISI screened the available politicians: Ghulam Mustafa Jatoi, hailing from a Sindhi family of old politicians and great landowners, was selected as the top candidate for the IJI. In the election campaign two well-known personalities from the same province would compete against each other, thereby splitting their constituency.[165]

In 1990, the situation was different. The ISI was in charge of "fund-raising" for the campaigns of Benazir's opponents. Two banks (Habib Bank and Mehran Bank) granted a total of 140 million rupees that the ISI's political wing distributed to dozens of politicians and political parties. Among the beneficiaries, in addition to Ghulam Mustafa Jatoi were Nawaz Sharif,

---

[163] Shuja Nawaz, *Crossed Swords. Pakistan, Its Army and the War Within*, op. cit., p. 430.

[164] The Tekrit-i-Istiqlal, the Pakistan Muslim League (Chatta Group) and the Nifaz Firqah Jafariya.

[165] Hein Kiessling, *Faith, Unity, Discipline*, op. cit.

Mohammad Khan Junejo and Altaf Hussain, the MQM leader. This case yet again confirms the need to put the common sense opposition between military and civilians in perspective.[166]

In the 1990 elections, the IJI won ninety-two of the 105 parliamentary seats in Punjab while the PDA, whose driving force was still the PPP, relied on its Sindhi stronghold: twenty-four of its forty-five seats came from there. The scope of its defeat in terms of seats—the PDA carried only half as many seats as the IJI—should nevertheless be viewed in light of the small difference in percentage of votes: 36.65 per cent compared to 37.27 per cent, a distortion linked to the single-ballot system. With ninety-two seats out of the 198 at stake, the IJI had an absolute majority but not the two-thirds necessary to amend the Constitution.

(Like in 1988, 217 seats (207 Muslim, 10 non-Muslim) were filled by direct election, with 20 reserved for women chosen by elected members).

Appointed prime minister in December 1990, Nawaz Sharif made gestures of goodwill toward the military, particularly by appointing Zia ul Haq's son, Ijazul Haq, to his cabinet and leaving responsibility to his government as well as the president for nuclear affairs and the Afghanistan and Kashmir policies. He shared their view of these issues anyway and was just as determined to help the jihadists as Ishaq Khan himself.[167] Nawaz focused his energies more on economic questions and engaged the country on a path of economic liberalism as demanded by the business community he originated from. In February 1991, he announced the relaxing of exchange restrictions, and eight months later no fewer than eighty-nine state-owned companies were in the process of privatisation. But he also paid attention to small-scale industries. He allowed 40,000 households to secure subsidized loans to purchase taxis, buses or trucks under a self-employment scheme that was soon renamed the Yellow Taxi Scheme. He also introduced a minimum wage of 1,500 rupees in July 1992, a largely populist measure publicised with great media fanfare.

---

[166] The scandal, revealed by General Naseerullah Babar, Interior Minister under Benazir Bhutto in 1994, was brought before the courts following a complaint filed by Air Marshal (Rtd) Asghar Khan that enabled the police to extract confessions (and details) in 1996. Sharif's return to power in 1997 caused the case to be shelved—until the current Chief Justice of the Supreme Court reopened it (see chapter 7). Khaled Ahmed, "Soldier of misfortune", *The Friday Times*, 16–22 March 2012, 25 (2) http://www.thefridaytimes.com/beta2/tft/article.php?issue=20120316&page=2 (Accessed on September 15, 2013).

[167] Shuja Nawaz, *Crossed Swords. Pakistan, Its Army and the War Within*, op. cit., p. 437.

Sharif's other pet theme, the revival of the Islamisation policy, resulted in the introduction of a Sharia Bill that was finally passed in May 1991. This law did not, however, satisfy all the Islamic parties in the coalition as it hardly extended the powers of the sharia courts and allowed non-Sunnis the right to apply their version of Muslim Personal Law. This measure, intended to placate the Shias, angered the Jama'at-e-Islam, which withdrew from the coalition on 5 May 1992 after Nawaz Sharif had offered his support for a United Nations proposal to set up an interim consensus government in Afghanistan—whereas the JI supported the Islamist groups, including Hekmatyar's Hezb-e-Islami.[168]

Nawaz Sharif nevertheless sought to assert himself vis-à-vis the president and the COAS more than anything else. Although he finally agreed to let the president handpick Beg's successor when he reached retirement age, replacing him with General Asif Nawaz, he took it upon himself to replace the ISI chief with Javed Nasir, a general known for his Islamic activism (see below), to the great displeasure of Asif Nawaz, who was presented with a fait accompli.[169] And when Asif Nawaz suddenly—and mysteriously—died a few months later, Nawaz Sharif wanted a say in choosing the next COAS. He nominated someone different from the person chosen by the president who, after a heated exchange, finally settled on another officer, General Abdul Waheed Kakar.[170]

The main bone of contention, however, was over the dissolution of provincial assemblies.[171] Sharif was trying to free himself from presidential supervision, though without calling into question the Eighth Amendment. In July 1991, he thus introduced a 12th amendment that would authorise the prime minister to take over the administration of a province. The IJI did not go along with him on this for fear of displeasing President Ishaq Khan. From then on, the president distrusted his prime minister, and his wariness only increased when Nawaz Sharif dodged the question of whether or not he would support Ishaq Khan's re-election when his term was up.

As it did with Benazir Bhutto, the Muhajir question brought about Nawaz Sharif's downfall. The disturbances in Karachi once again gave the presi-

---

[168] The JI's unease was also caused by its rivalry with another member of the coalition, the MQM, which also held Islam to be the symbol of the nation and found support among the Muhajir middle class which previously provided the JI with solid backing.

[169] Shuja Nawaz, *Crossed Swords. Pakistan, Its Army and the War Within*, op. cit., p. 454.

[170] Ibid., p. 459.

[171] I. H. Malik, *State and Civil Society in Pakistan*, London, Macmillan, 1997, p. 36.

dent and the army an excuse to put the blame on civilian rule. Partly due to the split of the MQM into an MQM (Haqiqi) and an MQM (Altaf), the outbreak of violence in Karachi and other cities in Sindh prompted the army to launch Operation Clean Up in May 1992. The MQM pulled out of the IJI, reducing its parliamentary majority proportionally.

On 18 April 1993, the president dismissed the prime minister and dissolved the Assembly but Nawaz Sharif, who the day before had had the gall to denounce a "plot" of Ishaq Khan on television, appealed this decision to the Supreme Court. The judges ruled in his favour on 26 May, declaring his dismissal unconstitutional. Nawaz Sharif recovered his post and then fought to get the High Court of Lahore to reinstate the government of Punjab, which had been dismissed as well. The justices of this tribunal followed the Supreme Court's example, thus confirming the new dynamism of the courts (see chapter 7). The triumph of the rule of law was short-lived. The Corps Commanders called an emergency meeting on 1 July to resolve the political crisis, showing that they still had the upper hand in the democratisation process. On 18 July, the Chief of Army Staff devised a compromise whereby Ghulam Ishaq Khan and Nawaz Sharif were both required to resign.

Benazir II: Impotence, Corruption and Lawlessness

The October 1993 elections brought the PPP back to power despite a lower number of votes than the Pakistan Muslim League (Nawaz), competing on its own this time—37.9 per cent as against 39.9 per cent—due to distortions inherent to the voting system. With eighty-six seats out of 202—compared to seventy-three for the PML (N)[172]—Benazir Bhutto's party was nevertheless far from having a majority. It once again had to find allies among the independents, certain factions that had grown out of the Muslim League (such as the group led by Junejo) and once more the MQM. This was a persistent weakness. The prime minister's position looked more secure, however, when the PPP managed to get one of its senior members, Farooq Leghari, elected president in November 1993. This achievement would remove the threat of the Eighth Amendment and strengthen the regime's parliamentary position. Unlike his predecessors, Leghari was more receptive to the prime minister's will. In accordance with her wishes, he for instance suspended the government of the NWFP and installing a PPP government.

---

[172] http://www.elections.com.pk/contents.php?i=7 (verified on February 5, 2015).

However, far from accelerating, the "democratic transition" suffered from another type of setback,[173] as the government resisted the temptations of corruption even less than in the past.[174] The prime minister's husband himself, Asif Ali Zardari, embodied this trend; as head of the Investment Ministry, he was better known as "Mr Ten Percent" due to the commissions this position enabled him to pocket.

Asif Zardari was viewed as an outsider in the PPP, never having been accepted by veteran party members.[175] It is true that his father, Hakim Zardari, had been a member of the party of Wali Khan (a rival of Z. A. Bhutto).[176] His influence was particularly resented by Murtaza Bhutto, Benazir's brother who in the 1993 elections competed for the Larkana seat from Syria and won. Upon his return to Pakistan, Murtaza was arrested on six different charges, including the hijacking of a plane in 1981. Before he was even released on parole in 1994, it was clear that he enjoyed widespread popularity, even more so as he had his mother's backing. Benazir thus removed her from the position of chair of the PPP and got herself appointed Chairperson-for-Life in her place. At the same time, a number of PPP activists who were dedicated to Murtaza's cause were arrested and

---

[173] The transition also suffered incidentally from the continuing marginalisation of Parliament: rather than seeking to get legislation passed by its elected members, the prime minister preferred to resort to presidential orders, which rose from an already high number of 93 in 1994 to 133 in 1995. See M. Waseem, "Dix ans de démocratie au Pakistan?" in Christophe Jaffrelot (ed.), *Démocraties d'ailleurs*, op. cit., p. 477.

[174] In 1991, the IJI government had already been accused of approving loans for an amount of 1.2 billion rupees illegally granted by state cooperatives to the Ittifaq Industrial Group owned by the Sharif family. This group, as well as one owned by the Minister of the Interior, had borrowed millions of rupees from the National Industrial Credit Financial Corporation (NICFC) even though the Cooperative Societies Act of 1925 forbade such loans to limited companies. This misuse of funds led to a succession of bankruptcies of several cooperatives and losses of up to 17 billion rupees suffered by 2 million shareholders.

[175] There were not many veteran Bhutto followers left in the party, most of them having been sidelined or dismissed. In the mid-1990s, it came turn for Aftab Sherpao to leave the party. Z. A. Ali Bhutto had convinced him to resign from the army to join him and in 1988 Benazir had appointed him chief minister of the NWFP.

[176] "Who is Hakim Asif Zardari?" 2 June 2011, available at: http://alaiwah.wordpress.com/2011/06/02/who-was-hakim-ali-zardari/ (Accessed on September 15, 2013).

tortured so they would desert him or even turn against him.[177] One of them, Ali Hingoro, died in prison.[178] After making a major tour of the country, Murtaza Bhutto accused Asif Zardari of corruption head on,[179] demanded internal PPP elections and declared himself in favour of a return to the ideological bases of 1970. Having made no headway, he drew up a policy document in 1994 entitled "New Direction: Reforms in the PPP and Pakistani Society" and then on 15 March 1995 founded a new party, the Pakistan People's Party (Shaheed Bhutto). He was assassinated on 20 September 1996 not far from the Bhutto family home on 70 Clifton in Karachi. The finger was immediately pointed at Asif Ali Zardari. Former President Leghari, about whom Zardari allegedly said in 1996 "it's him or me", stated in January 2010 on television with regard to Zardari: "He has Murtaza's blood on his hands, and Allah knows how many others."[180] In December 2009, one year after Zardari became the nation's president, a court in Karachi acquitted the police officers accused of this crime. For Hein Kiessling, the guilty men came from the ISI who wanted "to eliminate the Bhutto factor entirely from Pakistani politics".[181]

Benazir fell from power a few weeks after her brother's assassination, for other reasons. Her personalisation of power and her growing authoritarianism had gradually alienated Leghari, a president who had at first been on her side. In 1994, Benazir made it a point of honour to nominate eleven judges to the High Courts, including three women who did not have the required seniority and who according to the Constitution should have been appointed by the Chief Justice of the High Court in Lahore. The matter was taken before the Supreme Court, which declared the appointments illegal on 20 March 1996. Benazir disregarded the decision, prompting lawyers in Karachi and Lahore to boycott these "political judges". This episode is revealing of the propensity Benazir Bhutto had to abuse power, which she

---

177 See the interviews conducted by Murtaza's daughter, Fatima Bhutto, *Songs of Blood*, op. cit., pp. 328–331.

178 See Mir Murtaza Bhutto's address on 1st anniversary of Ali Muhammad Hingoro's death, available at: http://www.youtube.com/watch?v=7dW6WklWJ hU (Accessed on September 15, 2013).

179 Murtaza Bhutto coined an expression that met with great success: "Asif Baba and the Chalees Chor" (Asif Baba and the Forty Thieves).

180 Cited in Fatima Bhutto, *Songs of Blood*, op. cit., p. 423. See also "President Zardari accomplice in murder of Murtaza Bhutto: Farooq Leghari" http://www.thefreelibrary.com/resident+Zardari+accomplice+in+murder+of+Murtaza+Bhu tto%3A+Farooq...-a0217554764 (Accessed on September 15, 2013).

181 Hein Kiessling, *Faith, Unity, Discipline*, op. cit.

demonstrated when she asked the president to dismiss the chief justice of the Supreme Court.[182] Leghari resisted the pressure all the more easily as he realised the string of corruption scandals was dilapidating the government's credibility. On 21 September, Leghari came out of his reserve and backed the Supreme Court. Benazir finally gave in and suspended the 11 nominations, but the incident had further strained her relations with Leghari.

Two other events tarnished the prime minister's image, finally giving the president the arguments he needed to dismiss her. First, the revelation by *The Independent* in London that she had just purchased a luxurious estate in Surrey, and second, her attempt to purchase enough Punjabi elected officials to ensure that the Assembly would side with her. On 5 November 1996, Leghari decided to dismiss the prime minister and dissolve the National Assembly. This time the Supreme Court upheld Benazir Bhutto's removal.

Nawaz Sharif II: Parliamentarianism and Autocracy

The February 1997 elections took place in a climate made ponderous by President Leghari's attitude. Whereas he had appointed a senior PPP official, Malik Mairaj Khalid, as acting prime minister, surrounded by liberals (Shahid Javed Burki, Najam Sethi, Maleeha Lodhi, etc.), Leghari set up a Committee for Defence and National Security (CDNS) which he chaired and which included the four chiefs of staff. This committee officially had only a consultative role but it was immediately perceived as an attempt on the part of the military and the president to supervise elected government officials.

The low voter turnout, 35.2%, reflected less the impact of the Jama'at-e-Islami and JUP's call for a boycott (probably preferring to avoid another defeat at the polls)[183] than the disillusionment of the PPP electorate and the people's weariness toward corrupt politicians and parliamentary instability.[184] Partly because of the absention of traditional PPP supporters, the elections handed a crushing victory to Nawaz Sharif's Pakistan Muslim League (N), 137 seats (with 45.8 per cent of the vote) out of 204 (including 107 won in Punjab), compared to 18 (with 21.8 per cent of the vote) for the PPP—which even lost Sindh to an alliance between the PML(N) and the

---

[182] Shuja Nawaz, *Crossed Swords. Pakistan, Its Army and the War Within*, op. cit., p. 485.

[183] The sole Islamic party to face the voters, the JUI only won seats in the National Assembly.

[184] Voter turnout had continued to drop, falling from 54% in 1970 (for West Pakistan) to 43.07% in 1988, 45.46% in 1990, 40.92% in 1993 and 35.92% in 1997.

MQM: the prime minister was finally in a position to make significant changes to the Constitution since he benefited from a two-thirds majority.

On 1 April 1997, the two houses passed the Thirteenth Amendment which called into question four articles of the Eighth Amendment: article 58 (2) allowing the president to dissolve the National Assembly was repealed; article 101 now obliged the president to consult with the prime minister before naming provincial governors; article 112 (2)(b) allowing the governors to dissolve the provincial assemblies was abolished; article 243 (9)(2) was altered in such a way that the president could no longer appoint military chiefs at his discretion. A number of observers believed these reforms should have established true democracy in Pakistan. Nawaz Sharif soon dispelled this illusion by setting up a true parliamentary dictatorship instead.[185] With the PPP decimated and its leaders snagged in legal entanglements,[186] Sharif mainly used his authority to undermine any opposition,[187] in total contempt for the separation of powers.[188]

The judiciary was the first victim of his methods, as Nawaz Sharif did his best to diminish the Supreme Court's influence by reducing the number of justices from 17 to 12. On 30 September 1997, Chief Justice Sajjad Ali Shah appealed to President Leghari, asking him to confirm the pending nomination of five justices in accordance with paragraph 190 of the Constitution. Nawaz Sharif then had a motion passed by the National Assembly requesting that the president dismiss the Chief Justice—who had been appointed under Benazir Bhutto, superseding three senior colleagues. Leghari refused to comply and on 31 October the prime minister accepted Sajjad Ali Shah's recommendation concerning the five justices. But on 2 December Shah

---

[185] Conscious of the fact that all his power emanated from his parliamentary majority, in the spring Sharif did his best to have a law voted to prevent Assembly members from changing parties in the course of a legislative term, a common practice that had the potential of significantly altering the balance of power. The Chief Justice ruled the law anti-constitutional and Leghari refused to sign it—but Sharif achieved his ends through the 14th Amendment.

[186] Asif Ali Zardari, Benazir Bhutto's husband, was arrested as soon as she was removed in November 1996. His trial, in which he faced the charge, among others, of murdering Murtaza Bhutto, began while he was in jail.

[187] In Parliament, the Senate alone resisted Nawaz Sharif when he tried to have the famous Sharia Bill passed as the 15th Amendment. This reform would have enabled the prime minister to interpret and apply sharia. Nawaz Sharif could not get the two-thirds majority he needed because of the opposition Senators.

[188] Sharif had the police harass PPP leaders, especially in Sindh. Human Rights Commission of Pakistan, *State of Human Rights in 1997*, Lahore, 1998, p. 174.

resigned, along with the president. Responsibility for these developments lay primarily with the COAS, Jahangir Karamat, in office since January 1995, who considered that the prime minister, as an elected official, had greater legitimacy and that he should thus be given a clear playing field.

Nawaz Sharif used the incident to secure his authority by having a friend of his father's and a Tablighi Jamaat sympathiser, Rafiq Tarar, elected president. The growing influence of the Sharif family moreover tended to lend the regime a neo-patrimonial aspect. All the more so as the prime minister's brother Shahbaz headed the province of Punjab.

The media—the last remaining opposition power—did not refrain from criticising the dereliction of a government in which the public had placed high hopes for a complete restoration of the democratic process. The Jhang group, which published the English-language daily *The News*, was especially critical. The tax administration punished it for its audacity, harassing the management with searches designed to intimidate it. Sharif further hardened his tactics in the spring of 1999 following a BBC documentary on corruption among Pakistani politicians. The ISI placed *Friday Times* editorialist Najam Sethi in custody for twenty days for an interview he had granted the BBC for this documentary. During that summer, the government set up the Press Council, which was vested with the same powers as the civil courts to punish reputedly deviant press organs. Only the army, the most powerful of all opposition forces, would be able to bring an end to this parliamentary dictatorship.

Musharraf's "Countercoup"

In 1977, concerned by Z.A. Bhutto's authority, if not authoritarianism, the army had seized the opportunity of rigged elections to oust him from power. Twenty-two years later, a similar scenario would be played out. The military establishment resented the treatment they received at the hands of Nawaz Sharif—who in their view exploited the relative weakness of Jahangir Karamat, the first COAS to resign under pressure from a civilian since Gul Hassan Khan in 1972.

On the top of it, before resigning, Karamat had placed the army in the service of the government, thereby seeking to palliate the deficiencies of a fairly inefficient administration. The census for instance was organised in March 1998, seven years late, under close military watch. Management of the Water and Power Development Authority (WAPDA), which oversaw distribution of water and electricity, was also placed under army control—30,000 soldiers were detailed to ensure that recalcitrant Pakistanis paid their bills. Last but not least, in spring 1998, 1,400 military crews were also deployed to uncover the "ghost schools" that were collecting state subsidies without ever operating—4,000 of the 56,000 public schools were thus found out.[189]

The army was of course rewarded for its efforts—and for strengthening national defence. Military spending remained very high—almost two-thirds of the budget every year on average under Nawaz Sharif—despite a dire economic crisis. The army was authorised to set up court martial tribunals to try certain crimes and carry out sentences. It particularly appreciated this measure in Sindh where it continued the fight against Muhajir militants. The military approved even more of Sharif's support, however halfhearted it may have been, for nuclear activism reflected in the June 1998 nuclear tests in answer to India's "provocation".[190]

But it was reluctant to become further involved in the maintenance of services and law and order for fear of appearing to support Nawaz Sharif's misdeeds. This is one explanation for Karamat's decision to resign in October 1998 out of disagreement with the prime minister's policies. Sharif then rounded out his neo-patrimonial arrangements by naming another family friend, Lieutenant-General Ziaduddin, to replace him, but the army's reservations vis-à-vis this man were such that he finally backed down. He instead came out in favour of General Musharraf[191] whom Sharif believed, due to his Muhajir origins, did not have the same network of support as the Punjabi or even Pashtun officers.

Like Zia, Musharraf had been promoted to the rank of COAS after the prime minister personally examined the other potential candidates and rejected better-placed generals. Sharif finally appointed Musharraf on 7 October 1998 while at least two other generals ranked above him in terms of seniority—and both of them immediately resigned.

The first signs of a rift between Sharif and the army appeared in the wake of the Kargil conflict, named after the Indian Kashmir city that hundreds of Pakistani soldiers and mujahideen secretly infiltrated in spring 1999. Combat

---

[189] Ian Talbot, *Pakistan*, op. cit., p. 364.

[190] See the account that Nawaz Sharif's Minister for Foreign Affairs (and Ayub Khan's son) gave of the Prime Minister's discussion with the emissaries of Bill Clinton (Gohar Ayub Khan, *Testing Times as a Foreign Minister*, Islamabad, Dost Publications, 2009, p. 15 ff).

[191] He settled on this choice in two stages, as he did not appoint Musharraf as head of the Joint Chiefs of Staff Committee until April 1999.

broke out between the Indian troops in charge of dislodging the "infiltrators" and the Pakistani fighters who had built solid bunkers in the mountains. Indian forces had carried off their first success when Sharif went to Washington on 4 July 1999 to request aid—claiming to be unaware of an operation for which, he claimed, the army was apparently entirely responsible. He was urged to withdraw the Pakistani troops and their support for the mujahideen. The prime minister complied, much to the displeasure of the military chiefs who felt betrayed by a civilian authority that, it seems, had not even bothered to consult them before giving in to American demands.[192] In his autobiography, Musharraf highlighted the importance of this factor in explaining the deterioration of his relations with the prime minister.[193]

Nawaz Sharif again antagonised the military establishment in September 1999 by reminding it that he had pledged before the UN General Assembly to sign the Nuclear Test Ban Treaty. He would not go through with his promise unless India pledged to do the same, but the reminder reinforced the military's impression that Sharif was likely to yield to American pressure in exchange for the lifting of sanctions enforced since the 1998 nuclear tests—that, indeed, weighed heavily on an economy in recession.

United States pressure regarding relations between the Pakistani army and Islamists was a third bone of contention. Even though the United States had backed Islamist groups waging war in Afghanistan when they served American interests in the region, they gradually considered these groups highly dangerous. In 1997, Washington placed one of them, Harkhat-ul-Ansar—since renamed Harkat-ul-Mujahideen—on its list of terrorist groups. American vigilance was further heightened after the bomb attacks against the American embassies in Kenya and Tanzania in the spring of 1998. The alleged instigator of these terrorist attacks, Osama bin Laden, was a Taliban protégé. Washington demanded that Islamabad obtain his extradition from the government in Kabul and at the very least that Pakistan stop supporting the Taliban. Sharif seemed to take his distance from these Islamist groups in October 1999 when he accused the Afghan fundamentalists of being behind the rise in sectarian conflict in Punjab and announced that the *dini madaris* would be searched for arms caches he suspected were stored there. The Pakistan military feared that as a result they would lose their special relationship with Kabul that they believed crucial to the "strategic depth" of Pakistan.

---

[192] Isabelle Cordonnier, *The Military and Political Order in Pakistan*, op. cit., p. 50.

[193] Pervez Musharraf, *In the Line of Fire. A Memoir*, London, Simon and Schuster, 2006, pp. 136–137.

Musharraf carried out his coup on 12 October 1999 in response to Nawaz Sharif's decision to replace him as COAS with Kwaja Ziauddin, whom he had finally managed to put at the head of the ISI. Sharif announced this decision at 5 p.m. Three hours later power had changed hands, and Sharif was under arrest. The sequence of events points up the loyalty certain officers displayed for their leader, particularly the Director General of Military Operation (DGMO), Shahid Aziz, without whose consent the order could never have been carried out, the Head of the General Staff, Mohammed Aziz Khan, and the Commander X Corps stationed in Rawalpindi, Mahmood Ahmed. Instead of swearing allegiance to Ziauddin, Shahid Aziz, who was related to Musharraf, ordered the corps headquarters in all regions except Balochistan to arrest key members of the Sharif clan, including the governor of Punjab. In a panic, the prime minister ordered Musharraf's plane to be denied permission to land and diverted to another country, at the risk of running out of fuel. The order was not carried out, and instead, officers loyal to Musharraf arrested Sharif, his brother—chief minister of Punjab at the time—and ritually took control of the national television network. This lent credence to Musharraf's claim that he never planned to take over and that in this case it was more a "countercoup" than a coup d'état.[194]

Once again, the episode took place without any bloodshed, the army met with no resistance of any kind, either physical or apparently psychological, due to increasing general hostility toward Sharif. The announcement of the coup did not provoke a single demonstration. The pervading sentiment seemed to be relief, a sign that the Pakistani citizens no longer placed any hope in the civilian government.

In contrast to the way Zia dealt with Bhutto, Musharraf did not try to execute Sharif, but the latter was tried anyway (even after his defence lawyer Iqbal Raad was shot in Karachi and some of his documents stolen). Nawaz Sharif was eventually convicted of "tax evasion, corruption, hijacking and terrorism". He was sentenced to a 20-million-rupee fine for tax evasion and a life sentence for preventing Musharraf's return flight from Colombo from landing till the last minute. The court also banned him from taking office for 21 years. He was in detention for 14 months and allowed to go to Saudi Arabia in exile in December 2000.[195]

*

[194] This is the title of the chapter Musharraf devoted to the event in his autobiography.

[195] Hein Kiessling, *Faith, Unity, Discipline*, op. cit.

The democratisation phase extending from Zia's accidental death to Musharraf's "countercoup" seems to bear little resemblance with the previous phase in which, from 1970 to 1977, civilian authority was in the hands of a charismatic figure, Z. A. Bhutto, who served until the end of his term and brought the military to heel. From 1988 to 1999, on the other hand, the army maintained considerable influence particularly through the Eighth Amendment, giving predominance to the president—an ally of the military until 1993.

The cause of democracy was no better served by Benazir Bhutto's and Nawaz Sharif's assertion of their power. The PPP had become trapped in a rut of corruption—even lawlessness—and Nawaz Sharif exhibited an authoritarianism that placed him in line with the viceregal tradition inaugurated by Jinnah and perpetuated by Z. A. Bhutto—whose daughter, Benazir, could also be criticised for a disrespectful attitude vis-à-vis her party colleagues as well as the judiciary. If civilians then had trouble regaining ground lost to the military with respect to the Z. A. Bhutto years, when they manage to reconquer it, it was only to repeat the same failings and thereby facilitate the return of a military government: the people of Pakistan actually greeted Musharraf's coup d'état in 1999 with relief.

The opposition between civilians and the military must also once again be qualified. The 1990s evidenced collusion between politicians and the military on a growing scale. If Bhutto had shown the way by serving Ayub Khan as minister, Nawaz Sharif took this collaboration a step further, even crossing the Rubicon. From the start of his career in Punjab under Zia's patronage until the election campaign of 1990, Sharif owed his political success wholly to military support. But even if he was the most famous client of the security establishment, he was not the only one to enjoy its protection. The dividing line between civilians and the military was thus highly relative.

A Democratic "Transition" without Transfer of Power? (2007–2013)

The fourth and latest phase of democratisation, that started in 2007, was atypical in many respects—and does not fully comply with the criteria of democratic transition. Certainly, for the first time, Pakistan was presided over for a full five-year term by the leader (Asif Zardari) of the largest party in Parliament (the PPP) and the parliamentary system that had been battered as much under Musharraf as under Zia has been restored. But the country has not for all that reverted to an era where the strong man was a civilian, for unlike Z. A. Bhutto, Zardari, his son-in-law, was unable to recover a number of powers that the army has assumed. This relative powerlessness was partly due to the divisions among civilians which for once Benazir Bhutto and Nawaz Sharif had successfully contained in 2006.

"Democrats" United against Musharraf, but Divided vis-à-vis the Judiciary

On 14 May 2006, considering, finally, that they needed to put up a united front against Musharraf and the army, Benazir Bhutto and Nawaz Sharif signed a "Charter of Democracy". The 36 points of this document formed a detailed and refreshing programme. Not only did it aim to fully restore the 1973 Constitution, but it also outlined the procedure by which judges should be appointed in order to remain independent. It contained most of the pro-federal recommendations that would be the mainstays of the 18th Amendment. It prescribed that the ISI should be accountable to the prime minister and that defence budget should be placed before Parliament "for debate and approval".[196] Last but not least, Benazir and Nawaz committed themselves "not [to] join a military regime or any military sponsored government". It also said that, contrary to what Nawaz Sharif had done in the 1990s, "No party shall solicit the support of military to come into power or to dislodge a democratic government". (In fact, in 2005, Benazir Bhutto had started to negotiate with Musharraf under the auspices of Washington—but the talks failed. They were to bear fruit in 2007[197]—see below).

Despite their new and unprecedented unity, the PPP and the PML(N) were not responsible for the fall of Musharraf, which was mostly due to the judiciary. Indeed, Musharraf precipitated his own downfall by entering into conflict with the Supreme Court and particularly Chief Justice Iftikhar Chaudhry, who denounced disappearances—especially of Baloch nationalists and Islamists—in the context of army repression (see chapter 7). In response to criticism, Musharraf attempted to dismiss the chief justice who resisted and mobilised support throughout the country. Musharraf declared a state of emergency on 3 November 2007 and enacted a provisional constitutional order. The hardening of the regime gave rise to protest at home and pressure from abroad that forced Musharraf to allow Benazir Bhutto

[196] "Charter of Democracy: Full Text", available at: http://www.stateofpakistan. org/time-to-implement-the-charter-of-democracy-and-bury-the-legacies-of-army-rule (Accessed on September 15, 2013).

[197] Aqil Shah, *The Army and Democracy. Military Politics in Pakistan*, op. cit., p. 218.

and Nawaz Sharif to return from exile, shed his military uniform and organise general elections. These were postponed due to the assassination of
Benazir Bhutto on 27 December 2007 (which will be discussed further on),
but they were eventually held on 18 February 2008. The army, now led by
General Kayani, having decided to stay out of politics, the country experienced "probably its best election—in terms of being free and fair—since
1970".[198] The PPP, headed by Benazir's widower (Asif Zardari) and son
(Bilawal Zardari-Bhutto) in accordance with her last testament, won the
most votes in the election though not enough to be in a position to form a
government on its own.

With over 30 per cent of the votes cast, the PPP carried only 91 seats out
of 258, while Musharraf's party, the PML(Q), which came in second in terms
of votes, showed considerable resilience with 41 seats—but the PML(N) was
number two in terms of seats, 67. Even if the PML(Q) politicians' show of
loyalty to Musharraf confirmed that the military (or rather their former
leader) could still co-opt civilians, those who had suffered most from the
regime, Zardari (heading the PPP) and Nawaz Sharif (heading the PML(N))
managed to set aside their differencess and stand together to implement the
Charter of Democracy. They formed a "large coalition" with the ANP before
being joined by the MQM(A)—which could not remain in the opposition—
and the JUI (F). This group backed the government of Prime Minister Yousaf
Raza Gilani, a senior PPP official from Multan in Punjab.

Zardari's prevarication, however, eroded this unity. He could not make
up his mind to reinstate Chief Justice Iftikhar Chaudhry—probably for fear
that the judge would cancel the amnesty he had won from Musharraf
before the general left office.[199] Zardari's reluctance to honour a commitment he had made—especially to Nawaz Sharif—prompted the former
prime minister to pull his PML(N) out of the government, without for all
that joining the opposition. In August 2008, the coalition parties voted in
favour of "impeaching" Musharraf, who finally resigned, nine years less
one month after having taken over—after losing the army's support.[200]

---

[198] Philip Oldenburg, *India, Pakistan, and Democracy*, op. cit., p. 204.

[199] Zardari had spent eight years in jail from 1996 (after the fall of Benazir Bhutto's
government) till 2004.

[200] According to Aqil Shah, "Kayani and his army corps commanders decided in
meetings on August 7 and 8 that they would not support the presidential decree
to oust the government, in light of its negative consequences for political stability and public opinion" (Aqil Shah, *The Army and Democracy. Military Politics in
Pakistan*, op. cit., p. 220).

Parliament elected Zardari President of Pakistan on 9 September 2008. He still did not reverse Chaudhry's suspension until the judge Musharraf had appointed to replace him reached retirement age, at which time he was obliged to reconsider his position. On 22 March 2009, Zardari finally agreed to reinstate the Chief Justice, as well as about one hundred judges who had been unfairly punished. The Court immediately examined complaints regarding Musharraf's declaration of a state of emergency, a decision it declared "void, illegal and unconstitutional".

Table 5.1: The 2008 National Assembly Elections

Party	Total General Seats	Total Ind. Joined	Total Non-Muslims	Total women
	272		10	60
Pakistan People's Party Parliamentarians (PPPP)	91 (30.6)	8	4	23
Pakistan Muslim League (PML-N)	67 (19.9)	4	3	17
Pakistan Muslim League (PML-Q)	41 (22.9)	0	2	10
Muttahida Qaumi Movement (MQM)	19 (7.2)	0	1	5
Awami National Party (ANP)	10 (2)	0	0	3
Muttahida Majlis-e-Amal (MMA)	6 (2.3)	0	0	1
Others & Ind	24 (15.1)	0	0	1
Total	258 (100.0)	12	10	60

Source: Adapted from Election Commission of Pakistan, *General Elections 2008. Report, vol. II*, Islamabad, 2008, p. VII (http://www.ecp.gov.pk/Misc/ReportGeneral Election2008Vol-II.pdf).

The Return of Parliamentarianism? Shadow Play Democratisation

Even if Zardari's PPP was at first ambivalent toward the independence of the judiciary, he strove like his predecessors to restore parliamentarianism and federalism. The most important measure of all was the passage of the 18th Constitutional Amendment that restored the parliamentary system of the initial 1973 regime and accorded greater autonomy to the provinces. The way in which Pakistan's political personnel proceeded with this modi-fication indicates a new mindset. In 2009, Zardari appointed a Special Parliamentary Commission on Constitutional Reforms (SPCCR) made up of twenty-seven representatives from the various parties to lay the groundwork for restoring the 1973 Constitution to its original form. In December of that same year, the SPCCR reached a compromise with the 7th National Finance Commission (NFC) regarding the distribution of resources among the provinces of Pakistan. It handed in its 133-page report in April 2010, and the 18th Amendment that grew out of it was passed unanimously by the two houses of Parliament. The president was able to sign the new law into force on 19 April 2010. The speed with which this process was accomplished is directly related to the consensus underlying it and for which Katharine Adeney, on completion of a meticulous study, gives a compelling explanation. While the military did not believe the Commission would manage to reach an agreement—which explains the leeway the army left it—the political parties on the other hand were aware "of the dangers of returning to the politics of the 1990s, where politicians co-opted the army [and vice versa] to undermine their political opponents. Politicians appreciated that the short-term political gains of army intervention against opponents was outweighed by the weakening of the democratic process".[201]

The united front symbolised by the co-signing of the Charter of Democracy by Benazir Bhutto and Nawaz Sharif in 2006 and then the coalition formed after the 2008 elections thus was restored in 2009 after the tensions between the PPP and the PML(N) due to Zardari's reservations. regarding I. Chaudhary.[202] Civil leaders had every interest in banding together in the name of a democratic process they had more or less faith in to reduce the ascendancy of the military. In this case, the politicians of Punjab—the dominant province—had made the greatest sacrifices (unless they never really believed that the law would be implemented).

The promotion of federalism emphasized in the previous chapter was only one of the purposes of the 18th Amendment. Its primary vocation was to restore the parliamentarianism outlined in the 1973 Constitution. This amendment, 102 articles long,[203] did not set out merely to reverse the constitutional changes crafted by Musharraf (starting with the Legal Framework

---

[201] Katharine Adeney, "A Step towards Inclusive Federalism in Pakistan? The Politics of the 18th Amendment", *The Journal of Federalism*, Oct. 2012, Vol. 42 Issue 4, pp. 539–565.

[202] Unless Benazir Bhutto had attempted to make a deal with Musharraf in 2007 under pressure from the United States, which is highly possible, but no one today has the proof to back up such a hypothesis.

[203] http://www.scribd.com/doc/30269950/18th-Amendment-in-the-Constitution-of-Pakistan-Complete-Text (Accessed on September 15, 2013).

Order of 2002 and the 17th amendment). It gave the Pakistani people new rights—or strengthened existing ones, such as those pertaining to freedom of association and expression, access to education etc. Above all, the 18th Amendment was intended as a guide to good governance, as is evident in a number of fairly new clauses: the size of the central and provincial governments should not exceed 11 per cent of the members of the assemblies that it answered to (whereas appointing ministers was one of the most prized clientelistic techniques of chief ministers); the National Assembly could only be dissolved if following a motion of no confidence in the prime minister, no one was in a position to replace him; to be admissible, such a motion could no longer stipulate the name of a successor; the head of the Election Commission had to be appointed by a parliamentary committee out of three candidates suggested by the prime minister after consultation with the opposition leader; Supreme Court judges were to be appointed by a commission named for two years, presided over by the Chief Justice and including the two other senior-most Supreme Court judges, a former Chief Justice or a retired Supreme Court judge, the Minister for Law and Justice, the Attorney General and a senior advocate of the Supreme Court nominated by the Bar Council.[204] This mechanism drew its inspiration from the Charter of Democracy.

The provisions concerning civil-military relations followed the same rationale. The prime minister was thus called upon to appoint the chiefs of staff of the three branches of the military after consultation with the president. Certainly, the new executive has tended to recover a certain authority over the army. On 28 November 2008, Gilani announced the dissolution of National Security Council that Musharraf had created to enable the military to exert legitimate influence over public affairs once they were no longer in power. The gesture proved to be mainly symbolic, the body never having really used its power. But the lack of reaction on the part of the military, however, did not mean that it had renounced control.

The Army and the Civilian Government: Barbed Exchanges or Daggers Drawn?

The new COAS, Ashfaq Kayani wanted to bring the military back to its primary vocation. He considered that the army had drawn considerable dis-

---

[204] Created in 1973, the Bar Council is in charge of supervising the provincial Bar Councils and regulating the admission of lawyers into the legal profession.

credit upon itself and become dispersed under Musharraf. The president-general had in fact appointed military figures to all sorts of positions designed for civilians (see infra), and this at a time when the army's professionalism was put to the test by the war in Afghanistan and Islamic terrorism. Kayani thus called some 300 three-star generals back into army ranks.[205]

But that did not mean that the army had become weak. In July 2010, it fell to Gilani, after consultation with Zardari, to grant Kayani—who was approaching retirement age—a three-year "extension". As Saeed Shafqat writes, in a country where the right to appoint generals (and judges, as a matter of fact) had often given rise to violent disputes, "In theory and constitutionally this establishes the norm of the supremacy of civilian leadership".[206] Except that such an extension, unprecedented in Pakistan's history, above all reflected Kayani's influence over the civilian government—for he was indeed the one who was seeking the deferral. This ascendancy had become apparent three months earlier when Kayani called a meeting of the federal secretaries at army general headquarters (GHQ) just before an official visit to the United States: "This earned him the distinction of being the first and the only COAS who summoned a meeting of the country's top civil servants in the presence of a civilian democratic government".[207]

Among these senior civil servant positions, one of them gave rise to particularly stiff competition between civil and military, the "defence secretary" who since Bhutto had been in charge of administering the ministry of the same name. In December 2008, the civilian who occupied the post retired and was replaced by a former Lieutenant General, which "revived the practice of appointing retired senior army officers to this position".[208] But Gilani removed him in January 2012 in the context of "Memogate" (see below) because in his testimony before the Supreme Court, he had declared that the government did not exercise "operational control" over the army. The PPP considered these remarks a provocation.[209] That the prime minister could react in this way was an illustration of the evolution in the balance of power between the civil authorities and the army.

---

[205] Mohammad Waseem, "Civil-Military Relations in Pakistan", in Rajshree Jetly (ed.), *Pakistan in Regional and Global Politics*, New Delhi, Routledge, 2009, p. 205.

[206] Saeed Shafqat, "Praetorians and the people", in Maleeha Lodhi (ed.), *Pakistan. Beyond the "Crisis State"*, London, Hurst, 2011, p. 110.

[207] Ibid., p. 111.

[208] Hasan-Askari Rizvi, "Protecting democracy", *Daily Times*, 20 March 2009.

[209] "Gilani removes Lodhi from Defence Secretary post", *The Express Tribune*, 11 January 2012. See: http://tribune.com.pk/story/319790/gilani-removes-lodhi-from-defence-secretary-post/ (Accessed on September 15, 2013).

The resilience of the Pakistani executive in the face of the military was confirmed by the Memogate scandal in a most instructive fashion. The case takes its name from a memo the Pakistani ambassador to Washington, Hussain Haqqani, a former advisor to Nawaz Sharif who had gone over to Benazir in the 1990s, allegedly sent the then US Chairman of the Joint Chiefs of Staff Admiral Mullen, following the killing of Bin Laden in May 2011. At the behest of Zardari, whom he was very close to, Haqqani reportedly had a memo delivered to Mullen in which the Pakistani president expressed his fear of a military coup, the Pakistani army being unable to bear the humiliation of the Bin Laden raid carried out by American forces. Zardari thus called on the Obama administration for help—at a time when the Americans harboured increasing doubts about the Pakistani army's sincerity in the fight against the Islamists anyway. The memo should have remained secret, but Haqqani's intermediary, Mansoor Ijaz, a Pakistani businessman living in the United States, mentioned it in an editorial in the *Financial Times* in October 2011. The memo was published in November on the website of *Foreign Policy*. It stated that:

Civilians cannot withstand much more of the hard pressure being delivered from the Army to succumb to wholesale changes. If civilians are forced from power, Pakistan becomes a sanctuary for UBL's [Osama bin Laden's] legacy and potentially the platform for far more rapid spread of al Qaeda's brand of fanaticism and terror. A unique window of opportunity exists for the civilians to gain the upper hand over army and intelligence directorates due to their complicity in the UBL matter.[210]

The memo asked the American authorities to talk sense into Kayani and Ahmad Shuja Pasha, director of the ISI, before adding,

Should you be willing to do so, Washington's political/military backing would result in a revamp of the civilian government that, while weak at the top echelon in terms of strategic direction and implementation (even though mandated by domestic political forces), in a wholesale manner replaces the national security adviser and other national security officials with trusted advisers that include ex-military and civilian leaders favourably viewed by Washington, each of whom have long and historical ties to the US military, political and intelligence communities.

[210] "Exclusive: secret Pakistani-U.S. offering overthrow of military leadership revealed", 17 Nov. 2011, (memo: http://thecable.foreignpolicy.com/posts/2011/11/17/exclusive_secret_pakistan_us_memo_revealed_ijaz_calls_amb_haqqani_architect_of_sche). See the full text at the following URL: http://www.foreign-policy.com/files/fp_uploaded_documents/111117_Ijaz%20memo%20Foreign%20Policy.PDF (Accessed on September 15, 2013).

The plan outlined by the author of the memo first provided for Zardari's nomination of a commission of inquiry—which the United States would take part in appointing—to identify those who had protected Bin Laden in Pakistan. The memo also assured that if the United States made the chiefs of Pakistan's security apparatus toe the line, Pakistan would hand over Al Zawahiri, Mullah Omar and Sirajuddin Haqqani (probably the three most wanted Islamists in the world). "This commitment has the backing of the top echelon on the civilian side of our house", concluded the author of the memo.

The document caused a considerable stir in Pakistan. The military viewed it as an act of high treason. Zardari was obliged to recall Ambassador Haqqani, who denied having authored the memo. Zardari dismissed him and the Pakistani judiciary opened an investigation—while authorising Haqqani to leave the country, to the dismay of the Pakistani generals. In June 2012, the commission of inquiry appointed by the Supreme Court submitted its report, concluding that Haqqani had indeed authored the memo.[211]

This case is revealing of the state of civil-military relations in Pakistan at the time, no matter which interpretation of the Memogate prevails—or almost.[212] If Zardari penned the memo, it attests to a strong sense of vulnerability on his part—and of course a highly clumsy effort to exploit one of the Americans' priorities. If it is a fake concocted by the ISI, it is evidence of a very sophisticated strategy by the Pakistani military to destabilize the civil authorities.[213] Whether the idea of such a memo germinated in one camp or the other, it attests to the vigour of mutual distrust.

---

[211] Sidra Moiz Khan, "Memogate: Commission's report says Haqqani authored memo", 12 June 2012. Available at: http://tribune.com.pk/story/392485/memogate-commissions-report-claims-haqqani-authored-memo/ (Accessed on September 15, 2013).

[212] If Haqqani wrote the memo on his own initiative or if it is a farce invented by Mansoor Ijaz, it is naturally of little interest.

[213] This hypothesis is accredited by two elements that the ongoing inquiry will either disqualify or substantiate. First, James Logan Jones, Obama's National Security Advisor at the time of the incident, claimed in a written statement to the Supreme Court of Pakistan on 17 December 2011 that Mansoor Ijaz had asked him to deliver the memo in question without ever mentioning Haqqani. As the memo used the same language Ijaz had already used in a prior conversation, Jones believed that the text was written by Ijaz (See Jones' deposition in Faisal Shakeel, "Memogate: James Jones submits statement in Supreme Court" http://tribune.com.pk/story/307993/memogate-general-jones-submits-statement-in-supreme-court/). Second, Ijaz indicated in December 2011 that the

Clearly, the army had not resigned itself to come under civil supervision in Pakistan. Although it no longer managed the country as it did under Musharraf—a task that moreover made it unpopular and diverted it from its priorities—it has retained most of its prerogatives. Since the Zia years, the Pakistani army has designed the country's foreign policy most definitely in the region, with a near monopoly over the Afghan and Kashmir issues, but also beyond, as can be seen in the intensity of its exchanges with the United States and Chinese authorities. As regards the country's nuclear programme, it was still the preserve of the military. As Saeed Shafqat very justly points out, "a system of power sharing seems to be evolving rather than military subordination to civilian supremacy."[214]

In fact, Zardari and Gilani did not manage to impose their will on the military the way Bhutto had. In July, the government announced that the ISI would have to be brought back into the fold of the Interior Ministry. But "one day later, another government statement was issued stating that the ISI would continue to be directly subordinate to the PM". As Hein Kiessling points out: "COAS Kayani had prevailed and shown who held the power in Pakistan".[215] The attempt was fully aborted in September 2008 when Kayani took it upon himself to replace the ISI director general with one of his trusted associates, Lieutenant-General Ahmad Shuja Pasha, although he was near retirement.[216] Zardari was also unable to convince Pasha to go to India and work with New Delhi to investigate the Mumbai attacks in November 2008, when a dozen Islamists affiliated with Lashkar-e-Taiba stormed the Mumbai train station and luxury hotels, killing 173. A diplomatic cable sent to the State Department from the United States embassy dated 1 December 2008 and revealed by Wikileaks shows that Zardari agreed with this suggestion that came from London but that the army had

---

Director of the ISI, Pasha,—who paid him a long visit in London after the scandal broke out—had made a tour of Arab countries to ensure their neutrality in the event Zardari was deposed by the Pakistani army. See Omar Waraich, "Pakistan's 'Memogate': Was there ever going to be a coup?" *The Independent*, 13 December 2011. Available online at: http://blogs.independent.co.uk/2011/12/13/pakistans-memogate-scandal-was-the-isi-planning-a-coup/ (Accessed on September 15, 2013).

[214] Saeed Shafqat, "Praetorians and the people", op. cit., p. 112.

[215] Hein Kiessling, *Faith, Unity, Discipline*, op. cit.

[216] Editorial in the *Daily Times*, 1 October 2008 http://www.webcitation.org/60fc6n4 FA (Accessed on September 15, 2013).

vetoed it.[217] Zardari and Gilani, despite these rebuffs, had no choice but to grant Pasha two one-year extensions, in 2010 and 2011.

Partisan Microcosm and Citizen Disillusionment

The fact that the military has been able to stand up to the civil authorities—even engaging in a tug of war with them—can be explained partly by the attitude of politicians who have not been able to preserve their initial unity and popularity.

Considerable political haggling took place in the parliamentary coalition backing Gilani which weakened it. The JUI walked out by 2010 and the MQM(A) continually raised the ante throughout the entire period. Altaf Hussain's party threatened desertion to obtain lower petrol prices, the repression of Pashtuns accused of Islamic extremism in Karachi and greater involvement in controlling law and order in the city—which the local chapter of the PPP did not want to hear of.[218] The MQM(A) thus made Gilani's government face the prospect of being reduced to minority status. The prime minister brought the party back into his parliamentary coalition in January 2011—in exchange for lower petrol prices—but the MQM(A) continued to boycott the government.

Second, "Memogate" reawakened the old demons of the PML(N). Nawaz Sharif saw it as an opportunity to put his rival, Zardari, in a difficult position, even if that meant playing into the military's hands. While the government had put the case in the hands of the Parliamentary Committee on National Security with the unanimous support of both houses—including PML(N) representatives—Nawaz Sharif took the matter before the court, going so far as to present his case himself. Without naming Zardari, he accused Haqqani of high treason and violating state sovereignty—as did the military.[219]

---

[217] "Zardari agreed to send ISI chief to India after 26/11", 2 December 2010, available at: http://www.ndtv.com/article/wikileaks-revelations/zardari-agreed-to-send-isi-chief-to-india-after-26–11–70035 (Accessed on September 15, 2013).

[218] Abrar Saeed, "Another battle between PPP, MQM brewing up", *The Nation*, 27 May 2012, http://www.nation.com.pk/pakistan-news-newspaper-daily-english-online/Islamabad/27-May–2012/another-battle-between-ppp-mqm-brewing-up/ (Accessed on September 15, 2013).

[219] "Zardari snubs Kayani's call, ready to fight till the last bullet", www.rediff.com, 19 December 2011. See: http://www.rediff.com/news/slide-show/slide-show-1-zardari-snubs-kayani-s-call-ready-to-fight-till-the-last-bullet/20111219.htm (Accessed on September 15, 2013).

Third, in the face of PML(N) attacks and (partial) JUI and MQM defections, the PPP sought out other sources of support, particularly, against all expectation, in its opponent from 2008, Musharraf's PML(Q). The PML(Q) had been founded prior to the 2002 election in order to give President Musharraf a party, like Mirza's Republican Party or Ayub Khan's Muslim League before. Four years after Musharraf's resignation, the PML(Q) remained a force to be reckoned with. The PML(Q) was the second largest party in the senate until March 2012, when twenty-one senators retired.[220] In the 2008 elections, the party had won the second largest number of seats in the National Assembly, eighty in the assembly of Punjab, nineteen in that of Balochistan and six in what was still the NWFP. After months of negotiation, in April 2011 the PML(Q) joined the PPP coalition, in exchange for five federal ministerial positions and eight junior ministerial appointments.[221] One year later, on 24 June 2012, Chaudhry Pervez Elahi, one of the party leaders, became deputy prime minister of Pakistan.[222] The deal reached between the PPP and the PML(Q) also provided for splitting Punjab and the new province of Khyber–Pakhtkhunwa each into two parts to create a region for Saraiki speakers in southern Punjab and give the Hazaras an administrative unit in KP. This would enable both parties to weaken Nawaz Sharif in his Punjabi stronghold while presenting the manoeuvre as an element of public policy.

By allying with PML(Q), Musharraf's party, the PPP disowned the principles that had guided its combat for democracy against the general turned president all the more openly as he continued to influence Pakistani politics from exile in London. In January 2012, Chaudry Shujaat Hussain, the PML(Q) president, said that his party's decision to support the PPP in Balochistan—and thus make it possible to form a government in the province—had come at the orders of Musharraf.[223] This prompted one leftwing observer to write:

---

[220] See: http://www.nation.com.pk/pakistan-news-newspaper-daily-english-online/ Islamabad/03-Mar-2012/pml-q-shrinks-in-upper-house (Accessed on September 15, 2013).

[221] On this occasion, the MQM also joined the government in Islamabad.

[222] The Chaudhrys have held out for the Rs17 billion in party development funds promised them when they entered the ruling coalition.

[223] See: http://www.nation.com.pk/pakistan-news-newspaper-daily-english-online/ national/29-Jan-2012/pml-q-voted-ppp-govt-in-balochistan-at-musharraf-s-order-shujaat (Accessed on September 15, 2013).

The PPP's alliance with the military-sponsored PML (Q) is a further demonstration of its utter political putrefaction. The PPP, a party that one postured as "socialist" and which traditionally has appealed for support by pointing to the abuse and machinations it has suffered at the hands of the military-bureaucratic establishment, now courts the military's political satraps in a desperate bid to cling to power. Top leaders of the PPP, it need be recalled, were not long ago publicly accusing several senior PML (Q) leaders of having been co-conspirators in the December 2007 assassination of PPP Chairperson-for-life Benazir Bhutto.[224]

Indeed, by entering into an alliance with the party of the former dictator, Zardari's PPP lapsed into unparalleled opportunism which fuelled the already exacerbated disillusionment of Pakistan's citizens with their politicians.

Beyond the PPP, all political parties arouse suspicion in particular due to two practices that have become routine: party nomadism and dynastic patrimonialism. Party nomadism, which denotes politicians' propensity to change parties, switching to whichever one offers the best deal, is not specific to Pakistan. In India, the scope of the phenomenon even prompted Rajiv Gandhi to have a law passed to regulate the practice in the 1980s. In Pakistan, elected officials have managed to retain full latitude—all the more since they lay down the laws—so as to preserve the advantages of a free market in the political sphere. A local notable can thus often be bought. He will change parties naturally if the one whose banner he was elected under no longer selects him as a candidate, but he might also migrate during a legislative term if the party in power or in a better position to take it needs additional votes—and is prepared to give something in return. Thus after the 2002 elections, the PML(Q) managed to "persuade" seven elected PPP members to join its ranks and support the Jamali government. They were rewarded with ministerial portfolios. This defection in favour of the dictator's party foreshadowed Zardari's practices.

Most elected members, however, remain in the same constituency. This is because their electoral base is their main capital, which they cultivate by constantly touring their area. Some politicians have won their base after the vigorous struggle of a grassroots campaign. Such is the case of Sheikh Rashid Ahmed, a newspaper vendor in his youth who managed to get elected to the Islamabad municipal council, then as mayor and later Assembly representative—as an independent in all three cases—before

[224] Ali Ismail, "Pakistan: Military sponsored-PML (Q) joins PPP-led coalition government", *World Socialist Web Site*, 27 May 2011. See: http://www.wsws.org/articles/2011/may2011/paki-m20.shtml (Accessed on September 15, 2013).

becoming minister.[225] In fact Sheikh Rashid has become a typical politician, in the sense that he has shifted from one regime to another, including the one established by Musharraf whom he has served as Minister of information. His is a rare case, however. Most politicians are recruited from among landowners who continue to dominate the electoral scene. In 1990, 15,400 landowners with farms of at least 150 acres (or 0.9 per cent of all the farmers), owned 10 per cent of the arable land—whereas at the bottom of the pyramid, 35 per cent of the farmers work 11 per cent of the land.[226] It is true that the large majority of farmers now own their properties—except in Sindh where 49 per cent were still tenant farmers in 1980.[227] It is also true that most large landowners do not derive most of their revenue from their land—they in fact often live in the city. But first, a number of feudal lords still remain attached to their lands, where things have changed little in fifty years,[228] and second, even for those who have migrated to the city, the old relation of patronage remains, and it still takes shape around the land—which prompts most feudals to tour "their" villages at regular intervals.

---

[225] Interview with Sheikh Rashid Ahmed in Islamabad on 17 April 2012. See also his autobiography, *Farzand-e-Pakistan. An Autobiography*, Islamabad, Midas advertising, no date.

[226] Government of Pakistan, *Agricultural Statistics of Pakistan—2001–2002*, Islamabad, 2003

[227] The last reliable agricultural census is the one taken in 1980. S. Akbar Zaidi provides some very useful figures from it. See S. Akbar Zaidi, *Issues in Pakistan's Economy*, op. cit., p. 42.

[228] See the short stories by Daniyal Mueenuddin, who himself lives in a southern Punjab village and the quality of whose ethnographic observation is worth many lessons in political anthropology. He describes thus the role of a landlord turned member of Parliament: "Jaglani could order men arrested released, could appoint them to government posts, could have government officers removed. He decided whose villages the new roads passed through the canal. He could settle cases, even cases of murder, by imposing a reconciliation upon the two parties and ordering the police not to interfere". See Daniyal Mueenuddin, *In Other Rooms, Other Wonders*, New York/London, W.W. Norton and Co., 2009, p. 80. The short story that lends its name to the book's title is indicative of the persistence of a feudal mentality over and above a relationship to land: "At that time, in the 1980s, the old barons still dominated the government, the prime minister a huge feudal landowner. Their sons, at least the quick ones, the adapted ones, became ministers at thirty, immaculate, blowing through dull parties, making an appearance, familiar with their elders, on their way to somewhere else, cool rooms where ice and alcohol glowed on the table, those rooms where deals were made". Ibid., p. 120.

Abida Husain, an elected representative from Jhang district, admitted to Anatol Lieven, "Very little of our income actually comes from land any more, but land is our essential link to the people and our voters".[229] As a result, in the 1990s, a majority of National Assembly members were still recorded in the "Landlords and Tribal Leaders" category according to the figures Saeed Shafqat has compiled (see table 5.2).

Table 5.2: Sociological profiles of parliamentarians in the Pakistani National Assembly (and, in parenthesis, of the governments resulting from these elections).

Category	1985	1988	1990	1993	1997
Landlords and tribal leaders	157 (12)	156 (15)	106 (12)	129 (17)	126 (8)
Businessmen/industrialists	54 (3)	20 (1)	38 (9)	37 (3)	39 (6)
Urban Professionals	18 (8)	9 (14)	46 (12)	26 (13)	32 (8)
Religious leaders	6 (1)	15 (0)	11 (1)	8 (0)	3 (0)
Retired Military Officers	– (2)	7 (3)	3 (1)	5 (2)	2 (1)
Others	3 (1)	– (1)	3 (2)	3 (2)	2 (0)
Politicians					
Non identified		(5)	(2)	(2)	(1)
Total	(27)	207 (44)	207 (39)	207 (39)	207 (39)

Adapted from Saeed Shafqat, "Democracy and Political Transformation of Pakistan", in S. Mumtaz, J.-L. Racine and I.A. Ali (eds), *Pakistan. The Contours of State and Society*, Karachi, Oxford University Press, 2002, pp. 225–6.

Table 5.2. also shows that although the Benazir Bhutto governments included a relative majority of feudals, Nawaz Sharif's cabinets also counted a great many of them.

Many "feudal" families have undeniably lost their status as local grandees over the years. This is true of the Khuhros of Larkana, the Tiwanas of Sargodha, the Dautlanas of Vehari, the Qazi Fazlullahs of Sindh, the Gardezis of Multan, the Nawabs of Qasur and the Mamdots in Ferozpur and Lahore.[230] But many other families have endured or taken the place of the losers, having the same profile, like the Gilanis, the Makhdums of Hala, the Qureshis, the Tamans, Mehars, Birjanis, Rinds, Raisanis, Jhararanis, Shahs of Nawabpur and Nawabs of Kalabagh.

The situation described by Saeed Shafqat in the 1990s continued to prevail during the following decade. A survey of the Members of the National

---

[229] Cited in Anatol Lieven, *Pakistan, a hard country*, op. cit., p. 219.
[230] This list was drawn up by Raza Ahmad Rumi, "Dynasties and Clientelism in Pakistan", *Seminar*, no. 622, June 2011, p. 37.

Assembly elected in 2002 showed, for instance, that these parliamentarians where "immensely rich"[231]—but it unfortunately does not mention their occupation.

The resilience of agrarian interests fosters such opportunistic practices as described above: irrespective of any ideology, a rural notable will seek the highest yield for his capital (the influence he exercises over "his" voters) by shifting his allegiance from one party or even one regime to another as the need arises.[232] Moreover, politics in this case is regarded more as an enterprise, the basic unit of which is the constituency, but of which the political party can also be more than a metaphor. In fact, patrimonial practices explain the dynastic inclinations of all families at the head not only of constituencies, but also of political organisations.

Lineage practices—which are generally described as dynastic—are on the rise throughout Asia,[233] but in Pakistan they have taken on exceptional proportions. Most parties are in fact associated with a family. This is of course the case of the PML-F whose head has to be the chief of "the Pagaro clan that represents the hereditary leadership of the Hurs in Sindh": "Following Pir Pagaro's death in January 2012, the party nominated his son Sibgatullah Rashdi as the new Pir Pagaro of the Hurs and President of the PML-F".[234] His brother became president of the PML-F's Sindh chapter.

---

[231] S. Akbar Zaidi, "Elected Representatives in Pakistan. Socio-economic Background and Awareness of Issues", *Economic and Political Weekly*, 6 November 2004, p. 4941.

[232] The chronic renegades are many. Besides Jamali, who has returned to the PML(N) after its victory in 2013, one may mention the extreme case of Manzoor Wattoo. Elected to the Punjab Assembly as an independent in 1988, he first joined the IJI, and then the PML(Junejo) in order to dislodge—with the support of the PPP—the PML(N) from power and to become Chief Minister in 1993. After severing his ties with the PPP, he created his own PML(Jinnah) in 1995 and finally joined the PML(Q). But he went full circle when he shifted to the PPP in 2008. He was even appointed president of the Central Punjab's chapter of the party by Zardari to the dismay of the local party cadres, "Manzoor Wattoo", *Dawn*, 23 April 2013. See http://dawn.com/2013/04/23/mian-manzoor-ahmed-wattoo/ (Accessed on September 15, 2013).

[233] See the October–December 2006 issue of *Critique internationale* that I coordinated entitled "Asie: la démocratie à l'épreuve du phénomène dynastique?" and in particular my article: "Inde: démocratie dynastique ou démocratie lignagère?" in *Critique internationale*, no. 33, Oct.-Dec. 2006, pp. 135–152. See also Mariam Mufti, "Dynastic Politics in South Asia", *South Asian Journal*, no. 20, April–June 2008, pp. 9–19.

[234] Mohammad Waseem and Mariam Mufti, *Political Parties in Pakistan. Organization*

Baloch parties associated with a tribe, and its leaders have cultivated the same modus operandi. In 2006 the eldest grandson of Nawab Bugti (whose son had died young), Aali Bugti "was named the tribal chief on the basis of being Bugti's eldest grandson"—and he took over as leader of the Jamhoori Watan Party too. However, another grandson of Nawab Bugti, Brahamdagh, has declared him as his heir, hence a faction fight.[235] But non ethnic parties have also become family affairs. The PPP is a case in point since its leaders have come from the same family for three generations. Its official head, Bilawal Zardari-Bhutto, was designated along with its "regent", Asif Zardari, by his mother Benazir's handwritten testament, in a practice that harks back to that of material inheritances. The Bhutto-Zardari line (to which Zardari's sister, Faryal Talpur—elected in Larkana in 2008—also belongs) is opposed by the one founded by Benazir's brother Murtaza Bhutto, whose widow, Ghinwa, established a party and whose daughter, Fatima, has become a public figure. The other major party, the PML(N) is only in its first genera-tion but managed to maintain *biradari* unity because although Nawaz is the party "Quaid", his brother Shahbaz is the official chairman. He has also been chief minister of Punjab since 2008. After becoming prime minister in 2013, Nawaz has appointed his daughter in charge of the youth program with a huge budget at her disposal.[236] The ANP on the other hand has in some regard entered its third generation, because even if Abdul Ghaffar Khan did not form a party, he started a movement—"The Red Shirts"—which spawned the ANP created by his son, Wali Khan, and whose own son, Asfandyar Wali Khan, leads the ANP today. The PML(Q) also belongs to the club of the "three generation plus" parties since the son of Chaudhry Pervez Elahi (for-mer Chief Minister of Punjab, son of Chaudhry Zahoor Elahi, a lieutenant of Ayub Khan after 1962), Chaudhry Moonis Elahi, was elected to the Punjab assembly in 2008. These lineage practices are just as customary among the Islamic parties, as Maulana Fazlur Rehman succeeded his father, Mufti Mahmud, as head of the JUI—or at least the main fraction that bears his

---

& *Power Structure*, Lahore, Lahore University of Management Sciences, 2012, p. 52.

235 Ibid., p. 56.

236 Not only has Nawaz established a lineage at the helm of the PML(N) but "he continues to run his own party and government like a small-time shop-keeper, who trusts no-one with the accounts, except a family member or two" (Arifa Noor, "Analysis: PM Sharif, one year on", *Dawn*, 5 June 2014 (http://www.dawn.com/news/1110699).

name, the JUI(F). Anas Noorani also replaced his father, Shah Ahmad Noorani, as head of the JUP and even the Jama'at-e-Islami, despite its being known for the key role played by ideology, is affected by this syndrome—to a lesser extent—as the daughter of the former leader, Qazi Hussain Ahmad, was elected to Parliament.[237]

The percentage of Members of the National Assembly and Members of Provincial Assemblies who belong to a political family increased from 37 per cent in 1970 to 50 per cent in 1993, before falling to 44 per cent in 2008, according to *The Herald*. In Punjab, 50 per cent of the seats were held by such politicians (in South Punjab, the proportion rises to 64 per cent), followed by Balochistan 44 per cent, Sindh 41 per cent, and KP 18 per cent.[238] Since 1970, 597 families have controlled 3,300 seats out of the 7,600 one generation after another. Among the most pervasive lineages, the Legharis have had fourteen elected representatives in the family since 1970 and the Jatois, 11.[239] Punjab—partly because it has the largrst number of seats— accouns for 379 dynastic families, Sindh 110, KP 56, and Balochistan 45.[240]

If political parties have become family enterprises, it is also because politics pays. Pakistani leaders amass large fortunes which encourages lineage practices because beyond the name, a party leader has a legacy to hand down: symbolic capital and financial capital are bound up into one. In 2007, the list of the richest personalities in Pakistan thus cited Asif Zardari—who was not yet even president of the country—in second place with an estimated fortune of $1.8 billion[241] and the Sharif brothers in fourth place with a fortune evaluated at $1.4 billion. Six years later, Nawaz—who had become prime minister for the third time—turned out to be the richest parliamentarian with declared assets of Rs. 1,824 billion. One of his ministers, Shahid Khaqan Abbassi, was also a billionaire.[242]

---

[237] Aluzeh Kohari, "Political Dynasties in Pakistan", *The Herald*, 14 May 2013. See http://dawn.com/2013/05/09/herald-exclusive-political-dynasties-in-pakistan/ (Accessed on September 15, 2013).

[238] Alizeh Kohari, "The cost of kin(g)ship", *Herald. Special issue Election 2013: Political dynasties*, May 2013, pp. 28–30.

[239] Ibid., and Ali Cheema, Hassan Javid and Muhammad Farooq Naseer, "The paradox of dynastic politics", op. cit., pp. 11–15.

[240] Shahid Zahid, "The family connection", op. cit., p. 18.

[241] Among his properties abroad are eight estates in Great Britain and 13 in the United States (where Zardari is also said to own the Holiday Inn in Houston). "Pakistan Rich list 2008, see: http://teeth.com.pk/blog/2007/12/08/pakistans-rich-list-of-2008 (Accessed on September 15, 2013).

[242] Meena Menon, "Nawaz, the richest of them all", *The Hindu*, 27 Dec. 2013, p. 22.

Such personal enrichment is related to the scale of corruption that affects Pakistani politics. Zardari in this regard can be held up as a symbol. In a highly detailed investigative report, John Burns showed not only that Zardari had spent $4 million to purchase the Surrey Palace and $660,000 in less than a month in shops such as Cartier and Bulgari, but also and above all that this money indeed came from ill-gotten gains: the Swiss judiciary has determined that Benazir and Asif Zardari had received $15 million in kickbacks in an arms contract with a Swiss manufacturer. They were obliged to reimburse $11.5 million to the Pakistani state. A gold bullion dealer also reportedly paid $10 million into the Bhutto-Zardari account after the Benazir government had granted him a monopoly on gold imports in Pakistan.[243]

Alongside these extreme forms of corruption, there are others on a smaller scale involving mere National Assembly members. A report drawn up by PILDAT (Pakistan Institute of Legislative Development and Transparency) based on the declarations of assets by elected members of the Assembly showed that in 2010 the average value of Assembly member assets was three times higher than the average value of assets of members of the previous National Assembly—many of them being the same.[244]

Opportunism, patrimonialism and corruption of the Pakistani political class not only explained the spectacular unpopularity of those in power in the Zardari era, but also a certain indifference among the citizenry toward the so-called democratic process. Even before entering into his unnatural alliance with the PML(Q), Zardari's popularity had faded as his exercise of power lent credence to charges of corruption[245] and nepotism.[246] According

---

[243] John Burns, "House of Graft: Tracing the Bhutto Millions—a special report; Bhutto clan leaves trail of corruption", *The New York Times*, 9 January 1998. See http://www.nytimes.com/1998/01/09/world/house-graft-tracing-bhutto-millions-special-report-bhutto-clan-leaves-trail.html?pagewanted=all&src=pm (Accessed on September 15, 2013).

[244] This report is available on a website close to the security establishment: http://www.defence.pk/forums/national-political-issues/72754-how-rich-pakistani-mnas-pppp-mna-tops-list-rs3-288bn.html (Accessed on September 15, 2013).

[245] From the start, Zardari drew well-founded suspicion by refusing to reinstate Supreme Court Chief Justice Iftikhar Chaudhry for six months, out of fear that the judge would reactivate proceedings against him.

[246] He has been all the more incapable of cultivating a relationship with the people since, for fear of becoming an Islamist target, he has given up the idea of holding such public rallies as his wife (and the Bhuttos in general) were accustomed to.

to a Pew Center survey, only 11 per cent of Pakistanis interviewed by the Pew Centre in 2011 had a favourable opinion of him, compared to 20 per cent in 2010, 32 per cent in 2009 and 64 per cent in 2008.[247] In 2010, this loss of popularity was hastened by the mismanagement of rescue operations after the unprecedented floods that hit the country. At the time, Zardari had the tastelessness to maintain his tour of Europe—which in particular took him to his castle in Normandy—while his country was under water.

Notwithstanding the Pakistani president's record unpopularity, voters have tended to stay away from the polls in considerable proportions for decades.

Table 5.3: Turnout rate in Pakistan since 1971 (% of registered voters)

1977	1985	1988	1990	1993	1997	2002	2008
55	52.9	43.1	45.5	40.3	35.2	41.8	44.6

Source: Philip Oldenburg, *India, Pakistan and Democracy*, op. cit., p. 79.

Such abstention rates—the accuracy of which may be questionable[248]—reflect the scepticism of many citizens toward democracy. This fact appeared clearly in the 2008 survey of Lokniti.[249] But things seem to have improved somewhat in the 2013 elections.

The 2013 Elections: What "New Pakistan"?

The 2013 elections have been hailed in the media as marking the advent of a "New Pakistan" (*naya Pakistan*). This enthusiasm was inspired by the comparatively high turnout rate (53 per cent), which was indeed remarkable given the intimidation and violence that the Taliban and others had unleashed either to secure success for their candidate or to derail the con-

---

[247] "Pakistani Public Opinion Ever More Critical of U.S.", 27 June 2012, http://www.pewglobal.org/2012/06/27/pakistani-public-opinion-ever-more-critical-of-u-s/. (Accessed 3 August 2012). In 2012 the percentage of respondents holding a positive opinion of Zardari rose to 14%.

[248] The participation rate in elections organised by Zia in 1985 and Musharraf in 2002 should be viewed with particular caution, but ballot stuffing cannot be ruled out on other occasions either (especially in 1990, a year marred by many irregularities, as we have seen).

[249] Lokniti (CSDS), *State of Democracy in South Asia: A Report*, Delhi, Oxford University Press, 2008, pp. 226–227.

stitutional process.[250] The parties the most directly targeted were the ANP, the PPP and the MQM (which resorted to violence as well). Their candidates were physically assaulted or kidnapped (like the son of the former Prime Minister, Ali Haider Gilani, who contested in his father's constituency). The candidates of these three parties had to replace their usual style of campaigning based on mass meetings with door-to-door canvassing. Contesting and voting in such a context was an achievement in itself.

The other reason why the media saw the making of a new Pakistan was the rise of Imran Khan's party, the Pakistan Tehreek-e-Insaf (PTI—Pakistan Movement for Justice). While the party had been founded in 1996 and benefited from the popularity of its leader, it managed to bag only one seat in 2002, Imran's. (In 2008, the PTI had boycotted the elections.) The PTI began its rise in 2011 by capitalising on two themes: the defence of national sovereignty vis-à-vis the US (especially the drone strikes they carried out in Pakistan) and the fight against corruption, the scourge of Pakistan that had reached new heights under Zardari. In 2011, Imran Khan held a meeting in Lahore that is generally considered as a turning point since it attracted about 100,000 people. Imran Khan's popularity was largely due to the fact that he was in tune with the expectations of many Pakistanis, including the urban middle class, and among them, the youth. The formula "Naya Pakistan", interestingly, was originally the PTI's campaign slogan.[251] And the party indeed made inroads in the big cities. It came second in Faisalabad and Karachi, for instance. It also came second at the national level with 16.7 per cent of the valid votes against 15.1 per cent for the PPP which, for the fist time, was relegated to third position.

However, the PTI did not provoke the "tsunami" Imran Khan envisaged. In fact, KP was the only province that massively supported the PTI, as mentioned in chapter 4. Second, Imran Khan was not such a novelty because of his rather conservative election campaign, as evident from his defence of the Anti-Blasphemy Law and his discourse on sharia. Third, while the PTI has primarily attracted new blood, the politicians who had joined the party lately had a long career behind them—and sometimes

---

[250] In Peshawar, the TTP distributed pamphlets presenting democracy as un-Islamic. See Zahir Shah, "TTP distributes pamphlets against elections", *Dawn*, 26 April 2013.

[251] Sher Khan, "The coining of the 'Naya Pakistan' slogan", *The Express Tribune*, 15 May 2013. See http://tribune.com.pk/story/549650/the-coining-of-the-naya-pakistan-slogan/ (Accessed on September 15, 2013).

dubious records.[252] Fourth and last, among the party leaders, one found personalities who had worked closely with Musharraf (including the party spokesperson, Shirin Mazari).

More generally speaking, the 2013 elections did not change the political landscape a great deal. First, the traditional hierarchy has remained the same. While the PPP came in third in terms of valid votes (largely due to power-weariness and unpopularity of its corrupt leaders), it remained number two in terms of seats. It garnered forty seats out of 342, including seven seats reserved for women and one seat reserved for minorities,[253] whereas the PTI won thirty-five seats. The PPP's stronghold of Sindh remained intact, so much so that the party could form a government on its own.[254]

With twenty-three seats (including four reserved for women and one reserved for minorities), the MQM(A) was no longer on the podium but now number four (which was probably the main reason why Altaf Hussain revamped the party apparatus immediately after the elections).[255] But it continued to dominate Karachi where it won fifteen of the nineteen seats that it contested during the general elections. Another thing has not changed: the MQM(A) offered its unconditional support to Nawaz Sharif after the victory of the PML(N).[256]

Second, the winner, Nawaz Sharif, who was appointed prime minister on 5 June 2013, was not new to politics and in fact his triumph was not unprecedented. In fact, the PML(N) did not win as many seats as in 1997—"only" 185, including thirty-five reserved for women and two reserved for minorities.

---

[252] Among the most prominent ones are Javed Hashmi (former leader of the PML(N), who had been a protégé of Zia and, even before that, a IJT activist), Shah Mahmood Qureshi (former leader of the PML(N) and the PPP—and long-time rival of Hashmi in Multan) and Kurshid Kasuri (former leader of the PML(Q) and Minister of Foreign Affairs of Musharraf).

[253] According to the new distribution of seats introduced by Musharraf, 60 seats reserved for women and 10 seats reserved for minorities were attributed to the parties according to their share of valid votes.

[254] The PPP sustained its most substantial losses in South Punjab where it did not win a single seat, even in its former strongholds of Layyah, Muzaffargah and Rahimyar. It is perhaps in rural areas—the cities never having been the PPP's strong point—that a new Pakistan is on the verge of emerging, if these setbacks reflect a loss of influence for the old feudals, which remains to be seen.

[255] "Altaf revamps MQM's organisational setup", *Dawn*, 26 May 2013.

[256] "MQM extends unconditional support to Nawaz for PM's office", *Dawn*. See http://beta.dawn.com/news/1015822/mqm-extends-unconditional-support-to-nawaz-for-pms-office (Accessed on September 15, 2013).

If Nawaz Sharif was not a new man, he claimed that he had changed. Just before the 2013 elections, in a long interview given to Najam Sethi's daughter, he said that he meditated on his past mistakes during his six-year exile in Saudi Arabia and learnt from them. He now wanted to solidly establish democracy in Pakistan and keep the army at bay.[257] But the government he had formed was made of personalities who were not newcomers either and who may not have changed as much as he claimed. Sartaj Aziz, a former minister under Zia, has become the prime minister's foreign affairs advisor. The Minister of the Interior, Chaudhry Nisar Ali Khan, belonged to Nawaz Sharif's previous governments—and Zia's before that. Other ministers had worked with Musharraf, including Abdul Qadir Baloch, former Corps Commander of Balochistan who had been appointed governor of that province by Musharraf in 2003 and Zahid Hamid, Musharraf's former Law Minister who had first been given this portfolio before being shifted to the Ministry of Science and Technology.[258]

While the 2013 elections have not given birth to a "New Pakistan", they seemed to represent an important step in the democratisation process because for the first time a democratically elected parliament that completed its five-year term was replaced by another one which, on top of it, permitted a changeover in power between two forces locked in an age-old rivalry. This achievement needs to be qualified on one front: the electoral process. In addition to the multiple forms of violence and intimidation mentioned above, many irregularities were observed by NGOs such as the Free and Fair Election Network.[259] The weakenesses of the Electoral Commission were also noticeable vis-à-vis the Supreme Court during the presidential election of July 2013. Indeed, the Court disregarded the schedule the Commission had prepared for this election, which prompted the PPP and the ANP to boycott the election. Certainly, the PML(N) candidate, Mamnoon Hussain, was not elected unopposed, but the fact that the second largest party in Parliament abstained from taking part in this competition was not good for democracy.

---

[257] Mira Sethi, "Watch the throne", op. cit., p. 28.

[258] Irfan Ghauri, "Federal cabinet unveiled: enter the ministers", *The Express Tribune*, 8 June 2008. See http://tribune.com.pk/story/560553/federal-cabinet-unveiled-enter-the-ministers/ (Accessed on September 15, 2013).

[259] The FAFEN issued a report on the 2013 elections which, however imperfect is enlightening: Observation of General Election 2013. Key Findings and Recommendations-22 May 2013, which can be consulted on www.fagen.org (Accessed on September 15, 2013).

The 2014 Crisis: Imran Khan, Qadri, Nawaz Sharif and the Army

The euphoria of the 2013 election was shortlived—not only because of the malpractices mentioned above, but also because of the manner in which the army continued to prevail. It had already shown its "tutelary mentality", to use Aqil Shah's formula, when Kayani was the referee between Zardari and Nawaz Sharif in 2009. The COAS informed Zardari at the time that if he did not reinstate Iftikhar Chaudhry as Chief Justice, he would "implement the minus-one formula, that is, the ouster of President Zardari while keeping the rest of the government intact".[260] Four or five years later, Kayani and his successor, Raheel Sharif, played an even more active role vis-à-vis Nawaz Sharif.

The fact that the army wanted to assert itself in the power structure was evident from its will to create a "National Security Council that institutionalised the role of the armed forces in civil decision-making, a demand he [Nawaz Sharif] had been resisting since the Jahangir Karamat days".[261] This NSC, created by Musharraf but which had remained dormant under the Zardari-Gilani government, was reconstituted in August 2013 during the first meeting of the Defence Committee of the Cabinet. It was then announced that it would be chaired by the prime minister and would comprise the ministers for foreign affairs, defence, interior and finance as well as three corps chiefs (Army, Navy and Air Force) and the chairman of the Joint Chiefs of Staff Committee.[262]

During the fall of 2013, the Military Intelligence made the Supreme Court understand that "the military personnel involved in any offence should be tried under the Pakistan Army Act 1952", and therefore by military courts, not by any other court, including the Supreme Court. The police could not investigate army personnel either.[263] This point was hammered in regarding the case of missing persons, an issue that will be discussed further below.

---

[260] Aqil Shah, *The Army and Democracy. Military Politics in Pakistan*, op. cit., p. 223.

[261] Nazish Brohi, "Civil-military ties, not back to square one", *Dawn*, 30 August 2014 (http://www.dawn.com/news/1128558/civil-military-ties-not-back-to-square-one).

[262] Sumeira Khan, "Battling militancy: Govt revives National Security Council", *The Express Tribune*, 23 August 2013 (http://tribune.com.pk/story/594103/battling-militancy-govt-revives-national-security-council/).

[263] Nasir Iqbal, "Military officials fall under Army Act, MI tells SC", *Dawn*, 27 November 2013 (/news/1058805/military-officials-fall-under-ary-act-mi-tells-sc) and Nasir Iqbal, "SC, police cannot investigate army personnel, says MI", *Dawn* (http://www.dawn.com/news/1017672).

Certainly, Nawaz Sharif himself chose Kayani's successor in November 2013 when he retired after his three-year extension.[264] Sharif then promoted the third-most senior man "to make a statement about the civilian government's primary role in formulating foreign and security policy".[265] But the new COAS, Raheel Sharif, appeared to be very independent-minded.

Under Raheel Sharif, the growing influence of the army found expression in Nawaz Sharif's withdrawal from the front of his Indian policy: he resigned himself not to accept New Delhi's proposal regarding the mutual granting of the Most Favored Nation status. More generally spreaking, he could not explore the possibility of developing Indo-Pakistani trade. His attendance at the swearing-in ceremony of Narendra Modi in June 2014 was not well received among the security apparatus.

One month later, Nawaz Sharif ensured the passage of the Pakistan Protection Act that the PPP had resisted during the Zardari years. This new piece of legislation has given large powers to the law enforcment authorities, including the right to "enter and search, without warrant any premises to make any arrest or to take possession of any firearm, explosive weapon, vehicle, instrument or article used, or likely to be used and capable of being used, in the commission of any scheduled offence".[266]

While the army grew more and more assertive, Nawaz Sharif alienated the military by claiming that his government wanted to negotiate with the Pakistani Taliban when the COAS had decided to deploy troops in North Waziristan (see below) and, more importantly, in making the Musharraf trial possible.

After leaving Pakistan for a self-imposed exile in London, Musharraf was indicted in five cases: the detention of judges (including Iftikhar Chaudhry) in 2007; the 2007 Red Mosque operation (see below);[267] the death of Benazir

---

[264] Nawaz Sharif thus did not follow Kayani's recommendation of Gen. Mahmood (who was appointed Chairman of the Joint Chiefs of Staff Committee—a mostly ceremonial post), nor the principle of seniority (Kamran Yousaf, "New GHQ boss: four stars and top slot for Raheel", *The Exprress Tribune*, 28 Nov. 2013 (http://tribune.com.pk/story/638181/new-ghq-boss-four-stars-and-top-slot-for-raheel/).

[265] "Pakistan's delicate civil-military balance", *Strategic Comments*, Volume 20 Comment 5, February 2024.

[266] Irfan Haider, "Protection of Pakistan Bill 2014 approved in NA", *Dawn*, 2 July 2014 (http://www.dawn.com/news/1116529).

[267] In September 2013, the police registered a case against Musharraf over the alleged murder of cleric Ghazi Abdul Rasheed and his wife. "Lal Masjid cleric's

Bhutto; the death of Akbar Bugti; and the imposition of the state of emergency declared illegal by the Supreme Court on 31 July 2009. In spite of these substantial charges against him, he came back to Pakistan in March 2013 to contest elections. However, the returning officers of the Election Commission rejected his nomination papers in four constituencies. He was arrested on 21 April 2013, put under house arrest and judicial procedures were started. In August 2013 Musharraf was indicted in the Benazir Bhutto case by an Anti-Terrorism Court in Rawalpindi. The ATC had named him in the case and declared him offender in 2011.[268] Still more importantly, in January 2014, the Supreme Court disposed of the review petition filed by Musharraf against the 31 July 2009 verdict denouncing the 3 November 2007 proclamation of a state of emergency. As a result, he was to be tried for treason. Soon after, in February 2014, the special court constituted to try him ruled that his treason trial would not take place in a military court. Musharraf immediately criticised the way the tribunal had been formed: it "involved the prime minister and the ex-chief justice, this itself smacks a little bit of a vendetta". He added: "the whole army is upset".[269] (Ex-)Army men were indeed alarmed by the fact that the prosecutor assumed that Musharraf should identify his accomplices.[270] Chaudhry Shujaat Hussain declared in that respect: "If you want a fair trial then you should initiate cases against Kayani and Elahi too"—as well as against himself, he admitted—since the imposition of the emergency was a collective decision.[271]

Musharraf was probably right: "the whole army" might have been upset by the idea of a former COAS going through a treason trial—especially if his "accomplices" (who were sometimes still in office) were affected. Back

murder case registered against Musharraf", *Dawn*, 2 Sept. 2013 (http://www.dawn.com/news/1040040).

[268] "Benazir murder case: Musharraf to be indicted on Aug 6", *Dawn*, 20 August 2008 (http://www.dawn.com/news/1032961).

[269] "Musharraf says army backs him over treason 'vendetta'", *The Express Tribune*, 29December2013(http://tribune.com.pk/story/652196/musharraf-says-army-backs-him-over-treason-vendetta/?print=true).

[270] Azam Khan, "Treason case hearing: Court says abettors' names can be added to accused list", *The Express Tribune*, 26 January 2014 (http://tribune.com.pk/story/661753/treason-case-hearing-court-says-abettors-names-can-be-added-to-accused-list/).

[271] "Musharraf treason trial: Shujaat offers himself for trial", *The Express Tribune*, 7 January 2014 (http://tribune.com.pk/story/655821/musharraf-treason-trial-shujaat-offers-himself-for-trial/).

door channels of communication were opened by the new COAS with the Home Minister, Chaudhry Nisar Khan, a former minister of Zia-ul-Haq whose brother had been a senior general in the army and who appeared as the contact person for the military in the government. In early 2014, "Khan assured Chief of Army Staff (COAS) General Raheel Sharif that General (retd) Pervez Musharraf would be allowed to go abroad after he had been indicted for imposing emergency in November 2007".[272] This promise did not materialise because other ministers, including Defence Minister Khawaja Asif, argued that "allowing Musharraf to go abroad would seriously damage the credibility of the government"[273] and because Nawaz Sharif himself wanted the Musharraf trial to take place (his determination might have eroded in the fall of 2014 as will be seen below).

When it appeared in late 2013-early 2014 that the prime minister was adamant, the security establishment decided to make his life difficult by using other politicians. That was not something new. Beg and Durrani had used Junejo and Nawaz Sharif himself against Benazir in the past. Musharraf had used the Jama'at-e-Islami and the Jamiat-ul-Ulema (and their coalition the MMA at large) in 2002 in order to weaken the PPP and the PML(N). This time, the military gave the green light to two a-typical politicians, Tahir-ul-Qadri and Imran Khan.[274]

The former was primarily a Barelwi preacher who hailed from Jhang (Punjab) where he had received his early education in a madrassa, before getting a law degree from Lahore.[275] His activity was at the interface of party politics and the socio-religious domain. He had started a political party in 1989, the Pakistan Awami Tehreek (PAT), which contested the elections in 2002—when Qadri was elected MNA from Lahore. In 1981, Qadri had also created Minhajul Quran, an NGO which runs a large number of *dini madaris* in Pakistan and abroad. The headquarters of the organisation

---

[272] Umer Farooq, "Interior differences", *The Herald*, August 2014, p. 33.

[273] Ibid., p. 34.

[274] A third actor, the PML(Q) cintinued to play a more ambiguous role. In July 2014, leaders of the PTI and the PML(Q) had reached an agreement on three points: "May 2013 elections were rigged, the election commission did not play its due role and that protests should be held constitutionally and legally for securing rights". The PML(Q) leaders mediated also between the PTI and PTA ("Alliance in the making: PTI,PML-Q agree on three points", *The Express Tribune*, 10 July 2014 (http://tribune.com.pk/story/733025/alliance-in-the-making-pti-pml-q-agree-on-three-points/?print=true).

[275] Ayesha Siddiqa, "Revolutionary or stooge?", *Newsline*, July 2014, p. 44.

in Lahore were inaugurated in 1987 by a renowned Sufi, Tahir Allauddin. After 9/11, Qadri received considerable support from the West, and especially from the US, where his 600-page fatwa against Islamic terrorism in 2010 and his promotion of a moderate islam were most appreciated.

For some time Qadri left the Pakistani scene. He resigned his seat in 2004 (he was to boycott the subsequent elections) and settled down in Toronto in 2005. He eventually became a Canadian citizen, but came back to Pakistan in 2012 to launch a protest movement against government corruption in Islamabad. Although Qadri called for a "million-men" march, the sit-in before the parliament in Islamabad mobilised only 50,000 people, mostly followers who literally worshipped him. After four days, he signed an agreement with the government which committed itself to electoral reforms and more political transparency. Since these promises had remained dead letters, he returned in 2014 and started a new agitation. On 17 June violent clashes between PAT activists and the Punjab police in Model Town (Lahore) resulted in several deaths among the former. Soon after, Qadri announced a new protest movement.

This march from Lahore to Islamabad was to start at the same time—and to follow the same route—as the one organised by another Pakistani politician, Imran Khan, who claimed, similarly, that the government of Nawaz Sharif was corrupt and anti-democratic.[276] His main complaint was that the 2013 elections had been rigged and that his party had been deprived of victory by Nawaz Sharif.

He now demanded the resignation of the government and new elections. This is why he launched an "Azadi march" from Lahore to Islamabad on Independence Day, 14 August. Launching the march, Imran Khan said about Nawaz Sharif: "He became the prime minister in a fixed match with the help of the Election Commission, caretaker government and other major players. Nawaz's victory was unconstitutional as he snatched the public mandate in a massive rigging".[277] Besides, Imran Khan accused the ex-Chief Justice, Iftikhar Chaudhry, and the judges who had served as returning officers during the 2013 election.[278]

---

[276] Ironically, the PTI topped the list of the 19 lawmakers who have been suspended in 2014 "for failing to submit their own statements of assets and of their spouses and dependants, more than five weeks after the deadline" (Iftikhar A. Khan, "PTI tops list of lawmakers yet to file statements of assets", *Dawn*, 10 November 2014 (http://www.dawn.com/news/1143273).

[277] Anwer Sumra, "Azadi march takes off", *The Express Tribune*, 15 August 2014, p. 1.

[278] Waseem Ahmed Shah, "Rigging charges against judiciary causing anxiety

The reasons for the Azadi march and its timing need to be scrutinized. While the elections had not been transparent and fair enough, out of the 410 election petitions that had been filed by losing candidates before the fourteen election tribunals across the country, 292 (73 per cent) had been decided. But, unfortunately for Imran Khan, none of the thirty-nine petitions filed by PTI candidates—and decided upon (nineteen others were still pending)—had resulted in a favourable verdict, whereas ten elected parliamentarians of the PML(N) had been unseated. This unprecedently high number for a ruling party suggested that the independence of the election tribunals was more respected than before.[279]

There were probably other reasons for Imran Khan's decision to embark on the Azadi March. First, Mohammad Waseem convincingly pointed out in July that the "spectre of Qadri stealing the show ha[d] now led Imran Khan back to the issue of election rigging".[280] Second, Nawaz Sharif, after one year, not only had not significantly improved the economic situation (in particular on the energy front), but he had also been very much absent from parliament—and from the country!—as well as surprisingly "indecisive".[281] In this context, as Talat Masood pointed out, Imran Khan was "clearly working towards destabilising the government with a view to capturing power".[282] Indeed, after starting his "Azadi march", Imran Khan demanded the same thing as Qadri: Nawaz Sharif's resignation.

Their processions were distinct. I saw them arrive in Islamabad one after another on 15 August, in the afternoon for the PAT and in the night for the PTI. They were not massive—not more than 50,000 for sure.[283] On the PAT

among officers", *Dawn*, 11 August 2014 (http://www.dawn.com/news/1124575/rigging-charges-against-judiciary-causing-anxiety-among-officers/print).

[279] Zahid F. Ebrahim, "Ten truths about electoral rigging", *The Express Tribune*, 5 August 2014 (http://tribune.com.pk/story/743813/ten-truths-about-electoral-rigging/?print=true).

[280] Mohammed Waseem, "Go Nawaz Sharif, go", *The Express Tribune*, 26 July 2014 (http://tribune.com.pk/story/740934/go-nawaz-sharif-go/?print=true).

[281] Zahid Hussain, "A part-time leader", *Dawn*, 23 July 2014 (http://www.dawn.com/news/1120931/a-part-time-leader/print). See also Shamshad Ahmad, "A leaderless nation", *The Express Tribune*, 2 August 2014 (http://tribune.com.pk/story/743165/a-leaderless-nation/).

[282] Talat Masood, "Leadership on the wrong course", *The Expres Tribune*, 5 August 2014 (http://tribune.com.pk/story/744642/leadership-on-the-wrong-course/?print=true).

[283] Few figures were suggested in the media—interestingly. *The Express Tribune*

side, "most of the participating families, including women and children, (we)re either students, employees or ther beneficiaries of the schools and charity institutions of Minhajul Quran".[284] The federal capital had been cordoned with containers in such a way that access to the city centre could have been made impossible. But the government let the demonstrators enter Islamabad, possibly because the June violence in Lahore against PAT activists had already given a bad name to the Sharif family. The PAT accused Shahbaz Sharif, the Chief Minister of Punjab, of having blood on his hands and his brother was precisely not willing to spill blood again. The PTI and the PAT therefore organized meetings right in the city centre, in which Imran Khan in a strident populist style exhorted the crowd to fight to the finish to remove the government,[285] while Qadri said that he believed only in one thing: a revolution. They both issued one ultimatum after another and forced their way to the Red zone even though they had previously pledged not to. On 20 August, Imran Khan declared: "We will march towards the PM House if Nawaz Sharif does not resign till tomorrow [sic]".[286] He subsequently besieged it with his supporters.

In this context, the government tried to negotiate with the demonstrators and establish the right balance of power to do so. Nawaz Sharif received Asif Zardari (who came back from Dubai to meet him).[287] Zardari met with the leader of the Jama'at-e-Islami, Sirajul Haq, who, despite the fact that his party was in a coalition with the PTI in the KP government disapproved of Imran Khan's attitude. Zardari and Haq agreed to recommend the holding of "an inquiry into alleged polls rigging through a judicial commission which should submit its report within a month or so".[288] Imran Khan

estimated that the PAT group was not larger than 16,000 (Hassan Naqvi, "Inqilab fervour peaks at PAT camp", *The Express Tribune*, 15 August 2014, p. 5.).

[284] Muhammad Amir Rana, "Dilemma of Barelvi politics", *Dawn*, 24 August 2014 (http://www.dawn.com/news/1127288/dilemma-of-barelvi-politics/print).

[285] "I have burnt all bridges and will not turn back, says Imran", *The Express Tribune*, 19 August 2014 (http://tribune.com.pk/story/750750/i-have-burnt-all-bridges-and-will-not-turn-back-says-imran/?print=true).

[286] Qamar Zaman, "Islamabad sit-in updates: Wait till evening for Nawaz to resign, then march to PM House, Imran", *The Express Tribune*, 20 August 2014 (http://tribune.com.pk/story/751019/islamabad-sit-in-updates-patpti-set-up-protest-camps-in-front-of-parliament-house/?print=true).

[287] "Deadlock persists as third round of talks yields no result", *Dawn*, 24 August 2014 (http://www.dawn.com/news/1127260/deadlock-persists-as-third-round-of-talks-yields-no-result/print).

[288] "Siraj warns of 'third force' intervention", *Dawn*, 24 August 2014 (http://www.

objected that such a commission would not be in a position to tell the truth if Nawaz Sharif had not stepped down. On 1 September, Nawaz Sharif convened a joint session of parliament during which all the parties—except PTI—supported the Constitution and claimed that they stood behind the democratic institutions. Javed Hashmi, the president of PTI—who was the only member of his party to take part in this meeting—made an emotional speech in this vein.[289] He was immediately expelled by Imran Khan who had asked the elected representatives of the PTI to resign their seats—they had almost all obeyed his order.[290]

After seven or eight rounds of talks over a few days between teams—ministers on one side and the PTI and the PAT on the other—the stalemate was obvious since Khan and Qadri wanted nothing less than the resignation of Nawaz Sharif who was not prepared to step down. On 27 August, Khan and Qadri declared that they would not continue to negotiate. Two days later, for the first time, they addressed their supporters together and joined hands.[291] On 31 August, Qadri's supporters stormed the headquarters of PTV and randsacked the place. The day after, protesters broke the gate of Pakistan Secretariat, the head office of the administration.[292] Clashes with the police resulted in three deaths.

Then, the army stepped in. That was expected since on 27 August, during his joint meeting with Qadri, Imran Khan had said that he "was waiting to hear from the army, which was acting as a go-between, mediating between

---

dawn.com/news/1127351/siraj-warns-of-third-force-intervention/print).   See also Sirajul Haq statement of the 20th of August: "Dire straits: 'Democratic institutions in the country must be protected", *The Express Tribune*, 20 August 2014(http://tribune.com.pk/story/750827/dire-straits-democratic-institutions-in-the-country-must-be-protected/?print=true).

[289] "In the midst of crisis, Parliament speaks with one voice", *Dawn*, 2 Sept. 2014 (http://www.dawn.com/news/1129413/in-the-midst-of-crisis-parliament-speaks-with-one-voice/print).

[290] Aamir Yasmin, "PTI lawmakers want Sheikh Rashid, Dasti to resign from NA", *Dawn*, 30 August 2014 (http://www.dawn.com/news/1128674/pti-lawmakers-want-sheikh-rashid-dasti-to-resign-from-na/print).

[291] Baqir Sajjad Syed and Irfan Haider, "PTI,PTA leaders on same platform", *Dawn*, 30 August 2014 (http://www.dawn.com/news/1128723/pti-pat-leaders-on-same-platform).

[292] "Islamabad stand-off: Protesters outside PM House", *Dawn*, 1 Sept. 2014 (http://www.dawn.com/news/1129011/islamabad-stand-off-protesters-outside-pm-house).

the two parties and the government".[293] In the night of 28 August, Imran Khan met the COAS[294] who allegedly "assured him that the army would ensure a transparent and fair investigation of the election rigging".[295] On 31 August, Raheel Sharif held a Corps Commanders conference after which the army issued the following communiqué:

While reaffirming support to democracy, the conference reviewed with serious concern the existing political crisis and the violent turn it has taken, resulting in large scale injuries and loss of lives. Further use of force will only aggravate the problem.

It was once again reiterated that the situation should be resolved politically without wasting any time and without recourse to violent means.

Army remains committed to playing its part in ensuring security of the state and will never fall short of meeting national aspirations.[296]

Once again, the army appeared as the ultimate referee, faithful to national interest, in contrast to power-hungry politicians. But as *Dawn* emphasized, the army had "constructed [its] veneer of neutrality". The fact that it did not intervene—only the police did—to stop the PTI and PAT supporters when they physically attacked official buildings including Parliament House was a manner of taking sides,[297] and not the side which "clearly had the law and Constitution in its favour".[298] In fact, it had taken probably that side at a very early stage with one clear objective in mind: to weaken Nawaz Sharif, if not to dislodge him.

Observers have noted several indications of the army's involvement in favour of Qadri and Imran Khan.

---

[293] Cited in Baqir Sajjad Syed and Irfan Haider, "PTI, PAT leaders on same platform", *Dawn*, 30 August 2014 (http://www.dawn.com/news/1128723/pti-pat-leaders-on-same-platform).

[294] Qadri also met the COAS separately (Khawar Ghumman, "Politicians decry army's role in politics", *Dawn* (30 August 2014, http://www.dawn.com/news/1128517/politicians-decry-armys-role-in-politics/print).

[295] Baqir Sajjad Syed and Irfan Haider, "Enter the chief", *Dawn*, 29 August 2014 (http://www.dawn.com/news/1128518/enter-the-chief).

[296] "Islamabad protests", *The Express Tribune*, 1 September 2014 (http://tribune.com.pk/story/756071/islamabad-sit-in-updates-imran-...spare-sharif-brothers-for-attacking-unarmed-protesters/?print=true).

[297] "Army's questionable decisions", *Dawn*, 2 Sept. 2014 (http://www.dawn.com/news/1129263/armys-questionable-decisions/print).

[298] "Blow to democracy", *Dawn*, 30 August 2008 (http://www.dawn.com/news/1128637/blow-to-democracy/print).

First, according to Federal Information Minister Pervaiz Rashid, before starting his Azadi march, Imran Khan met the ex-DG ISI, Ahmed Shuja Pasha, who had already helped the PTI in 2011, before he retired and who remained very influential.[299]

Second, the Pakistan Ex-Servicemen Association, headed by Rtd Vice Admiral Ahmed Tasnim, called for dissolution of assemblies and fresh elections in a meeting held on August 20 in Rawalpindi.[300]

Third, the supporters of Imran Khan and Qadri could reach the centre of Islamabad, in spite of the relatively small number of participants, because the army did not intervene and even let them enter the Red Zone. The military remained passive observers while the government had asked them to guarantee the security of Islamabad by virtue of Article 245 of the Constitution (that is, if there is a situation pertaining to internal security)—the same way Z.A. Bhutto had operated when he was facing demonstrations from the PNA in 1977. On 14 June 2014, 352 troops were deployed in the federal capital.[301] Six weeks later, five companies of the army were deployed to secure the main offices of the judiciary, Parliament House, Presidency, Prime Minister Houses, embassies etc.[302] Interstingly, the Red Zone's security had been handed over to the army by the Interior Minister, Chaudhury Nisar Khan, who insisted that the agitation had nothing to do with the army when other members of the government, including Ahsan Iqbal, the Minister for Planning, Development and Reforms, pointed out that the PTI, the PAT and the PML(Q) were trying hard to create a "situation wherein the army will have no choice but to take over".[303]

---

[299] "'Imran being advised by ex-spymaster Pasha'", *Dawn*, 14 August 2014 (http://www.dawn.com/news/1124864/imran-being-advised-by-ex-spymaster-pasha/print).

[300] Amin Ahmed, "Ex-military men back call for dissolution of assemblies", *Dawn*, 20 August 2014 (http://www.dawn.com/news/1126538/ex-military-men-back-call-for-dissolution-of-assemblies/print).

[301] Azam Khan, "No active deployment: Defence aide says troops only in forward position", *The Express Tribune*, 3 August 2014 (http://tribune.com.pk/story/743632/no-active-deployment-defence-aide-says-troops-only-in-forward-position/?print=true).

[302] Mateen Haider, "Army deployed in capital today", *Dawn*, 1 August 2014 (http://www.dawn.com/news/1122611/army-deployed-in-capital-from-today/print).

[303] "Red Zone's security handed over to Pakistan Army: Nisar", *Dawn* 19 August 2014 (http://www.dawn.com/news/1126356/red-zones-security-handed-over-to-pakistan-army-nisar) and "August 14 protests", *The Express Tribune*, 14 August 2014 (http://tribune.com.pk/story/746421/azadi-march-updates-if-anything-happens-to-me-hold-the-pm-responsible-says-imran/).

Fourth, Imran Khan and Qadri were in relation with the army, to such an extent that on 29 August, they themselves "announced that Chief of Army Staff General Raheel Sharif ha[d] been appointed by Prime Minister Nawaz Sharif as a 'mediator' and 'guarantor' for bringing the current crisis between the government and protesters to an end".[304]

Fifth, PTI president Javed Hashmi revealed on 1 September 2014 that Imran Khan had told "the core committee" of the party that in this movement it "can't move forward without the army" and that "all the matters had been decided and there will be elections in September".[305]

Immediately Imran Khan claimed—like Qadri—that he had nothing to do with the army.[306] The military, symmetrically, declared that it was a-political but Ayesha Siddiqa pointed out: "One wonders what to make of the statement when we see the army chief meeting Imran and Qadri and the army not intervening in pushing back the protesters who would certainly show deference to the armed forces and not use the sticks to beat soldiers as they did with the police".[307] The question was even more germane in early September as there were days then "when Imran Khan would address less than a couple of thousand people from among his supporters".[308] But other non-military power centres had become even weaker. The Supreme Court's advice and ruling, for instance, had made no difference.[309]

---

[304] "COAS Raheel Sharif made 'mediator' to end political crisis", *Dawn*, 29 August 2014 (http://www.dawn.com/news/1128362/coas-raheel-sharif-made-mediator-to-end-political-crisis).

[305] "'Imran Khan said can't move forward without army': Javed Hashmi", *The News*, 1 September 2014 (http://www.thenews.com.pk/article-158478-Imran-Khan-said-cant-move-forward-without-army:-Javed-Hashmi).

[306] This claim was somehow contradicted (1) by Imran Khan in November when he declared that members of the ISI and MI (Military Intelligence) should take part in a commission headed by the Supreme Court to investigate rigging in the 2013 elections ("ISI and MI should sit on commission to investigate vote rigging: Imran", *Dawn*, 9 November 2014 (http://www.dawn.com/news/1143355) and (2) by Tahirul Qadri five days later when he said: "Army chief should also launch Zarb-e-Adal (the name of the North Waziristan military Operation) in Lahore and Islamabad or God forbid the country could descend into anarchy" (Ali Usman, "Model Town case: Qadri asks army chief to intervene", *The Express Tribune*, 14 November 2014 (http://tribune.com.pk/story/791220/model-town-case-qadri-asks-army-chief-to-intervene/).

[307] Ayesha Siddiqa, "Politics and the military", *The Express Tribune*, 4 Sept. 2014 (http://tribune.com.pk/story/757411/politics-and-the-military-2/?print=true).

[308] Ibid.

[309] Hasnaat Malik, "Govt hopes for SC intervention to resolve impasse with PAT,

Certainly, the parliament could assert itself after Nawaz Sharif convened a joint session that lasted four days. During these four days, most of the parties, including the PPP, the JI, the JUI and the MQM, stood by the government, not because they supported its policies, but on behalf of democracy.[310] But the prime minister had lost most of his prestige and authority. By asking the army not only to protect Islamabad but also to mediate in the political crisis, Nawaz Sharif had acknowledged that the military was the key institution of the country. As Babar Sattar pointed out: "khakis now have Nawaz Sharif on a tight leash".[311] This new balance of power was almost made publicly explicit by the media. According to media reports, Nawaz had been told on 20 August that "there would be no coup but if he wants his government to survive, from now on it will have to share space with the army".[312] The decision to let Nawaz Sharif continue was made during the late August meeting of the Corps Commanders mentioned above. Five of the eleven participants in the meeting—including the DG ISI, Zaheer-ul-Islam—wanted to dislodge the government, but according to a senior security source cited by Reuters, "Raheel Sharif (wa)s not interested in direct intervention".[313] This sense of restraint was probably due to the

---

PTI", *The Expres Tribune*, 20 August 2014 (http://tribune.com.pk/story/751003/govt-hopes-for-sc-intervention-to-resolve-impasse-with-pat-pti/?print=true).

[310] This demonstration of parliamentarian unity was breached when Chaudhury Nisar Khan accused the PPP leader Aitzaz Ahsan of being part of the "land mafia". The PPP leader of the opposition in the national assembly then told Nawaz Sharif: "That man has breathed life into the dying forces which were trying to oust you", that is the army (Qamar Zaman, "Nisar, Aitzaz spat shatters veneer of Parliament's unity", *The Express Tribune*, 5 September 2014, http://tribune.com.pk/story/758211/nisar-aitzaz-spat-shatters-veneer-of-parliaments-unity/). It seemed indeed, that it was Nisar "who persuaded the prime minister to involve the military leadership" in the exercise of crisis resolution that started in late August. (Khanwar Ghumman, "Army as 'facilitator' was Nisar's brainwave", *Dawn*, 30 August 2014, http://epaper.dawn.com/DetailImage.php?StoryImage=30_08_2014_001_005).

[311] Babar Sattar, "Return of the game-keeper", *Dawn*, 5 August 2014 (http://www.dawn.com/news/1123086/return-of-the-gamekeeper/print).

[312] "'From czar-like prime minister to deputy commissioner type character'", *Dawn*, 20 August 2014 (http://www.dawn.com/news/1126545/from-czar-like-prime-minister-to-deputy-commissioner-type-character/print).

[313] Mehreen Zahra-Malik, "Army chief holds off generals seeking Pakistan PM's ouster", Reuters, 5 Sept. 2014 (http://in.reuters.com/article/2014/09/05/pakistan-crisis-army-idINKBN0H015K20140905).

fact that there was no need to replace the prime minister and deal with a difficult economic situation when Nawaz Sharif was no longer in a position to resist the army as much as before. It can also be explained by the fact that Raheel Sharif did not necessarily trust the DG ISI and the Corps Commanders whom he had not appointed himself—most of them were Kayani's appointees.

* * *

The opposition between the forces of freedom and those of oppression in Pakistan cannot be grasped by resorting to a simple equation. These two camps do indeed exist, but to present the former as relying on the body of civilians hostile to the military would be an oversimplification. The limits on Pakistan's democratisation are explained by a web of complex factors, not the least of which is the weak sense of democracy among the politicians: democracy may be possible, but the so-called democrats often behave impossibly.

Since the country's inception, Jinnah, a product of the viceregal system, favoured the construction of a centralized state over a parliamentary system, toward which in any event he was less inclined than toward presidentialism. His successor, Liaquat Ali Khan, continued in the same vein, reining in political parties which he saw as a divisive force for the nation and even neglecting his own Muslim League, which would thus never become a cornerstone similar to the Congress Party in India, partly for this reason. The disappearance of these two Muhajir leaders left the democratically inclined Bengalis in a face-off with the Punjabis who were averse to such a regime, due to demographic reasons as well as their political culture bequeathed by the Raj. The Punjabi bureaucrats and the military were not, however, the only ones to reject the democracy ideal backed mainly by the Bengalis: politicians in Punjab—and in West Pakistan in general—displayed the same attitude. Z. A. Bhutto even rejected the rise of Mujibur Rahman and the deepening of democracy. Not only did they not wish to fall under Bengali rule, but they also embodied a political culture stamped with "feudalism", made up more of clientelism and factionalism than democratic ideology. This ethos sealed the fate of Pakistan's political class by denying the country the stability that the bureaucrats and the army easily presented as a categorical imperative in the face of India to justify the 1954 offensive, the 1958 coup d'état and the return of martial law in 1969.

The second attempt to democratise Pakistan was without a doubt the most convincing of all in that, thanks to Bhutto's PPP and owing to its defeat in 1971, the military was brought back under the authority of a civilian government, which gave the country a parliamentary constitution and undertook large-scale social reforms. But the momentum did not last long, primarily because of Bhutto's own contradictions. Less a democrat than a populist, more an authoritarian than a parliamentarian, more a centraliser than a federalist and as much a product of his landlord background as a socialist, he turned his back on part of his platform—and thus on the middle and working classes which supplied much of the PPP leadership—to co-opt the landowning elite. Most of all, having little respect for basic freedoms—including of the press—he denied Pakistan free elections in 1977, giving the army, already reinvigorated after the war in Balochistan, the arguments it was waiting for.

The period from 1988 to 1999 contrasts with the Bhutto era due to the control the military continued to exercise over civilians who were supposedly back in command—at least till 1997. Neither Benazir Bhutto nor Nawaz Sharif would even manage to complete their terms. But if the army has become so powerful, it is also because of the weakness of the political class, some elements of which prefer to collaborate with the military rather than join forces with their democratic adversaries against the military. This was mainly true of Nawaz Sharif, who in a sense was the army's creature and who would play into its hands against Benazir Bhutto. But Benazir herself accepted the little bit of power the military allowed her instead of playing the regime opposition card, as her brother Murtaza had advised. There is another point in common between the Zulfikar Ali Bhutto years and the 1990s: when Prime Minister Nawaz Sharif was finally at the helm, he abused his power just like his rival's father had, an additional sign of the weakness of democratic culture among civilians.

The phase known as the "Zardari years" was probably at the midpoint on a scale of civil-military relations. The government had greater power than in the 1988–99 period, but less than during the Bhutto era, as the army, even if it could no longer dismiss the people's elected representatives, retained supreme control over key issues (nuclear power, Afghanistan, Kashmir, etc.). Once again, civilians had somewhat suffered from their divisions which were not as profound, however, as in the 1990s when Nawaz Sharif had collaborated with the army to destabilise Benazir Bhutto. Nawaz Sharif, after being forced into exile by his former COAS in 1999, had struck an unprecedented alliance with Benazir Bhutto to oust the military from power. But once that was achieved, he was once again tempted to play into the military's hands during "Memogate". At the same time, the PPP sealed an alliance with Musharraf's party, the PML(Q).

It is more difficult to place the current regime on a democracy/authoritarianism scale. Certainly, political parties have greater influence on the course of public affairs than in the 1988–99 period, and the 2013 elections have made history with a democratically elected parliament not only completing its term but also being replaced by another one. But this new democracy lacks democrats to function effectively. Aside from ongoing practices of patronage among the "feudals"—who are also urban, businessmen such as the Sharif family having copied their clientelistic and factional ways—almost all the political parties have become family enterprises over time—in financial terms as well—and most of the senior politicians have indulged in forms of corruption which contradict the spirit of democracy. As Maleeha Lodhi writes:

> The personalized nature of politics is closely related to the dominant position enjoyed throughout Pakistan's history by a narrowly-based political elite that was feudal and tribal in origin and has remained so in outlook even as it gradually came to share power with well-to-do urban groups (...) The urban rich functions much like their rural counterparts with their efforts at political mobilisation resting more on working lineage and biradari connections and alliances than representing wider urban interests.[314]

The disconnect of this political milieu from the public good is patent in its refusal to levy taxes—so as not to pay any themselves—while there can be no public good without tax revenue (not to mention tax fairness—see the conclusion to the next chapter). But the disconnect is aggravated by the transformation of political parties into (unofficially) lucrative family enterprises, as is evident in the personal enrichment of the political elite. The regime's corruption—in all senses of the term—during the democratisation period alienated many citizens who instead took refuge in abstention.

More importantly, the 2014 crisis that followed the "Azadi march" has shown that the army continued to play a "tutelary" role—to use Aqil Shah's words. The way Raheel Sharif "solved" the Imran Khan problem was well in tune with the manner in which his predecessor, Kayani, had already acted as a referee between Nawaz Sharif and Asif Zardari in 2009. Similarly, the COAS intervened in August/September 2014 and found a way out of the rivalry in which Imran Khan and Nawaz Sharif were locked. This tutelary mindset was different from previous interventions of the same kind. In 1977, when Bhutto and the PNA were at loggerheads because of similar

---

[314] Maleeha Lodhi, "Beyond the Crisis State", in Maleeha Lodhi (ed.), *Pakistan, Beyond the Crisis State*, London, Hurst, 2011, pp. 54–55.

problems (the rigging of elections), Zia seized this opportunity to take power. In 2014, the army was not interested in a military coup—primarily because the military does not want to manage the country (to do it under Musharraf was painful) but to be in a position to fight Islamist militants (as well as India if need be). But the army wants to prevail and dictate its terms to the civilians who—additional bonus—give Pakistan a façade of democracy. That means that the army will "intervene in governmental affairs whenever the high command determines that the civilian government is not acting properly, and that its actions or performance are undermining political stability, military institutional autonomy, and national security".[315] This "tutelary mentality" means that not only has the army resisted Nawaz Sharif's attempts at eroding its authority (as evident from the composition of the CCNS), but it has also been able to weaken the prime minister by supporting the month-long agitation of Imran Khan and Qadri—and finding a way out.

---

[315] Aqil Shah, *The Army and Democracy. Military Politics in Pakistan*, op. cit., p. 221.

6

VARIABLE-GEOMETRY MILITARY DICTATORSHIP

From the very start, beginning with the 1947–48 war in Kashmir, the army officers have shown deep contempt for civilians, with whom they never had close contact in the time of the Raj. Besides, the Pakistani army always aspired to play an active role because of what it perceived as the Indian threat as well as because of its "strategic culture" that Christine Fair defines as "a stable ensemble of preferences that has endured for much of the country's existence: resist India's rise; restrict its presence and ability to harm Pakistan; and overturn the territorial status quo at all costs".[1] The army's lack of consideration for civilians and this "strategic culture" have been the touchstones of its political assertiveness. As Fair points out, this army "has long justified its dominant role in running the state by arguing that it is uniquely positioned to protect not just Pakistan's territorial integrity but also the very ideology of Pakistan, which centers on protecting Pakistan's Muslim identity from India's supposed Hindu identity".[2]

The army's contempt for civilians, its sheer hunger for power and the Indian imperative have been recurring explanations for the three military coups. The authoritarian dimension of the regimes instituted by the generals in 1958, 1977 and 1999 is undeniable, given the extent of curbs on freedoms and the severity of the repression each time—the recurrent subjection

---

[1] C. Christine Fair, *Fighting to the End. The Pakistan Army's Way of War*, New York, Oxford University Press, 2014, p. 6.

[2] Ibid., p. 21.

of political prisoners to torture (especially under Zia) attesting to this. Moreover, once the army takes over, it militarises the administration—with the complicity of the bureaucracy—and seizes part of the state budget, even the economy, making it truly predacious.

But military regimes have never survived more than a decade in Pakistan and have always needed to reform (even sometimes constitutionalise) their rule. In fact, the successive military regimes that have followed the virtually immutable pace of every other decade have also been characterised by references to democracy which at first are purely rhetorical but as time goes by translate into concessions in favour of this form of government—an evolution that should be ascribed less to international pressure than to the army's search for legitimacy[3] and the mobilisation of a highly resilient opposition. Furthermore, not all army chiefs display the same distrust of civilian rule and democracy.

Ayub Khan, an "Enlightened Dictator"?

The threat of India partly explained Jinnah's viceregal style. But this threat had even more immediate implications for the military: the country needed a powerful army,[4] all the more since the troops Pakistan had inherited at the moment of Partition in 1947 represented only 36 per cent of the British Indian Army (140,000 men out of 410,000), giving New Delhi a considerable advantage,[5] as the Land of the Pure soon realized with the first war in Kashmir in 1947–8. The government therefore made an exceptional financial effort to strengthen the army and modernise its equipment. Defence spending between 1947 and 1959 on average accounted for more than half of the annual budget, peaking at 73 per cent for the 1950–51 fiscal year

[3] Amélie Blom convincingly points out that the Pakistani army in fact suffers from a historic legitimacy deficit: "It was not a national liberation army, it was not a key player in the fight for independence, nor was it a decisive actor in the creation of Pakistan...". Amélie Blom, "'Qui a le bâton, a le buffle'. Le corporatisme économique de l'armée pakistanaise", *Questions de recherche*, no. 16, December 2005, 56 pages), p. 6. Available online at: http://www.ceri-sciencespo.com/publica/question/qdr16.pdf (Accessed on September 15, 2013).

[4] Isabelle Cordonnier, *The Military and Political Order in Pakistan*, Geneva, Programme for Strategic and International Security Studies, 1999, p. 16.

[5] Ayesha Jalal, *The State of Martial Rule. The Origins of Pakistan's Political Economy of Defence*, Cambridge, Cambridge University Press, 1990, p. 42. In fact, Pakistan received only 30 % of the army, 20 % of the air force and 40% of the navy (Aqil Shah, *The Army and Democracy. Military Politics in Pakistan*, op. cit., p. 39).

(from July to June)[6] and 64 per cent in 1955–6.[7] The country's political economy was clearly dominated by security considerations.

This army thus bolstered by the authorities had complex relations with the civilian rulers. Here the colonial legacy previously discussed merits another look, but this time from the military's standpoint. The Raj had shaped a deeply peculiar, virtually topographical estrangement by separating "cantonments" (garrisons) from "civil lines" (administrative quarters) in each of the large cities of colonial India, especially in the most militarised areas of Punjab and the NWFP located on the western front facing Russia and the buffer state of Afghanistan. As Shuja Nawaz, himself from a family of officers in Punjab, writes:

The gap between the cantonment and the city, where the civilians lived, was huge and almost insurmountable. This divide continued well into the first couple of decades of independent Pakistan, leading not only to separate economic and social systems for these entities, but also to a different worldview and indeed to a different view on national issues.[8]

In 1947, this gap was symbolised—and materialised—by the distance between the new capital, Karachi, and the military headquarters based in Rawalpindi in a former regional British Army HQ.

From Mirza to Ayub Khan: a Double-barrelled Coup

Civil-military relations deteriorated in the late 1940s. While Prime Minister Liaquat Ali Khan had taken care to keep hold of the defence portfolio, he and his government proved incapable of assuming responsibility for conducting the war of 1947–8 in Kashmir. Obsessed with the fear of being found out, they claimed to the end, even within power circles, that it was an operation led by mujahideens in which the regular army had no role. The most heavily involved officers were therefore not given the support they felt they had a right to expect. According to Shuja Nawaz, "the political leadership [was] unable to come to terms with the fact that they were in fact fighting a war", which "strengthened the view [among a coterie of officers] that Pakistan needed a stronger central leadership".[9] The war in question, which the senior

---

[6] That year, the defence budget absorbed virtually all of the state revenue (Ibid., p. 99).

[7] H.A. Rizvi, *The Military and Politics in Pakistan (1947–1986)*, New Delhi, Foundation Books, 1988, pp. 44–45.

[8] Shuja Nawaz, *Crossed Swords. Pakistan, Its Army and the War Within*, op. cit., p. 16.

[9] Ibid. pp. 70–71.

officers experienced as a defeat or at best an incomplete victory, not only created a context that was conducive to coup attempts (such as the Rawalpindi Conspiracy—see supra), but also sowed doubt in the minds of generals who prior to that were resigned to civil control.

This feeling was heightened, as we have seen, by prevarication among the civilian authorities, unable to overcome their factional divisions and give the country a constitution. Government instability was reflected in the succession of eight prime ministers in ten years over the course of the 1947–57 period, while it had only taken India three years to draft and approve a Constitution and the country remained governed by the same prime minister and the same dominant party. The contempt in which certain officers held the political class spread to the senior civil service, starting with Ghulam Mohammad, the governor general who invited commander-in-chief Ayub Khan to take over. The general turned down the offer[10] but finally accepted the post of defence minister in Malik Firoz Khan Noon's cabinet. With regard to his prime minister, Ayub Khan made the following eloquent journal entry: "Noon is a nice man, means the country well, but he is very impetuous, lacking in ability and has no guts. He has a very bad memory, can't read anything. So it is very difficult to do any serious business of life with him. But I am used to dealing with a galaxy of morons starting with Khwaja Nazimuddin downwards".[11]

Why did Ayub Khan go into politics in 1954? From his studies at the Sandhurst Military Academy in England and his years under the command of British officers, he had adhered to the notion that soldiers should stay away from politics.[12] The shortcomings of the civilian government, however, had convinced him that Pakistan's survival depended on the army. But the desire to wield greater influence over the course of public affairs alone does not explain his cabinet entrance. Ayub Khan would later say that in 1954 he had "two clear objectives: to save the armed forces from the interferences of the politicians, and to unify the provinces of West Pakistan into one unit".[13] His desire to counterbalance the weight of the Bengalis explains the second objective.

---

[10] Muhammad Ayub Khan, *Friends Not Masters*, op. cit., p. 70.

[11] Cited in Altaf Gauhar, *Ayub Khan: Pakistan's First Military Ruler*, Lahore, Sang-e-Meel Publications, 1993, p. 128.

[12] He had drafted a memo along these lines upon being appointed COAS in 1951. H. Feldman, *Revolution in Pakistan. A Study of the Martial Law Administration*, London, Oxford University Press, 1967, p. 35.

[13] Muhammad Ayub Khan, *Friends Not Masters*, op. cit., p. 216.

In the early 1950s, not only did the increasing power of senior civil servants in key state posts pave the way for a military takeover, but political leaders set the fox to mind the geese, so to speak, by calling in the military to put down the anti-Ahmadi agitation in 1953 (see infra)—which should have been handled by the police. The army asserted its authority by temporarily declaring martial law. Bhutto later would also place the army centre stage by relying on the military after the outbreak of war in Balochistan in 1973.

It was finally a bureaucrat, Mirza, who sealed the fate of civilian politicians. His affinities with the army were strong, however. Iskander Mirza was in fact a career military officer. He was Pakistan's first defence secretary before being appointed governor of East Pakistan, then interior minister and finally governor general to replace Ghulam Mohammad in 1955. Like Ayub Khan, Mirza did not hide his profound contempt for politicians. He moreover wrote to his son, "The country, to put it bluntly, is being ruined by the politicians".[14]

The senior civil service and the army, represented respectively by Mirza and Ayub Khan at the head of the state, worked together to dislodge civilians from power. Appointed president once the Constitution of 1956 had been promulgated, Mirza declared martial law and promoted Ayub Khan to the rank of chief administrator of this exceptional law. Mirza quickly realized, but still too late, that he was no longer the country's strong man:[15] after swearing to secrecy the Corps Commanders (regional military officials) who formed the collective framework of the Pakistani army, Ayub Khan forced Mirza to resign and then forced him into exile—in London, a city that would become the primary destination in such circumstances before competing with Dubai and Riyadh—and launched a campaign to discredit him for corruption. The press thus accused him of personal enrichment.[16]

Aqil Shah points out that three major factors precipitated this double-barrelled coup d'état. First, the army had developed an anti-civilian mindset that was bound to remain a structural feature of Pakistani politics: in contrast to the divisive and somewhat childish attitude of the politicians,

[14] Cited in Humayun Mirza, *From Plassey to Pakistan: The Family History of Iskander Mirza, the First President of Pakistan*, Lanham, MD, University Press of America, 1999, p. 212.

[15] The senior military officers Mirza ordered to arrest Ayub Khan informed their commander about the plan and persuaded him instead to have Mirza arrested.

[16] Mirza would be buried in Iran (his wife's country of origin) because the Pakistani authorities refused to have him buried in Pakistan.

the military started to look at themselves as "the center of gravity that ensures the survival and stability of Pakistan".[17] Second, in 1958, the bureaucracy and the military feared that "a Bengali or Bengali-led coalition in the forthcoming elections might have put the military's resources and even its vision of internal stability and foreign policy in danger".[18] Third, beyond the Bengalis, "even the Muslim League and others West Pakistani leaders had started to question the utility of the Cold War alliance with the United States because of the country's lack of commitment to resolving the Kashmir and other disputes with India".[19] For the army, the American partnership was seen as guaranteeing access to sophisticated weapons and first clas training.

The 1958 coup took place without any bloodshed or even a single shot being fired. Ayub Khan's narrative of the event in his memoirs—however embellished—indicates the chain of command followed by the military and the relative acceptability of them by the rest of the Pakistani population:

On the night of the Revolution [the word will be discussed further on] we informed the Commanders-in-Chief and all local Commanders of what had happened and required them to ensure that law and order was maintained. That was all (...) I did not think that there would be any occasion for the use of force at all. The people were completely fed up with the state of affairs and desperately wanted a change. And they had great respect for the army.[20]

The 1958 coup d'état drew on a military hierarchy clearly hinging on the Corps Commanders and their unfailing discipline: their obedience to their chief was such that Ayub Khan apparently informed some of them of the secret only after the coup d'état had taken place. But in fact, the army had a rather collegial decision-making process and the Corps Commanders were probably implicated in the coup right from the beginning. The coup in fact was surrounded with a sort of consensus among the military and the bureaucrats, and even found a certain echo among the citizens: many of them felt that the political class, having lost its historic leaders, Jinnah and Liquat Ali Khan, who both died prematurely, was not in a position to govern the country. This scenario would repeat itself in the future, with a significant nuance, as the senior civil service would not necessarily play the same role, and for good reason: the army had gained considerable influence

---

[17] Aqil Shah, *The Army and Democracy. Military Politics in Pakistan*, op. cit., p. 23.
[18] Ibid., p. 84.
[19] Ibid.
[20] Muhammad Ayub Khan, *Friends Not Masters*, op. cit., p. 90.

and would no longer need allies. From that standpoint, the coup of 1958 marked a turning point.

Signs of continuity in the transition from Mirza to Ayub Khan were evident, however, in the fact that martial law remained in force, as well as that Khan retained his predecessor's cabinet in which there were already eight ministers, four general and four civilians (including the young Ali Bhutto) with no party affiliation.

While the bureaucracy would play a lesser role in future military take-overs, the 1958 coup introduced the prototypical coup by consensus that was destined to repeat itself. This "model" is defined by five complementary features: (a) the army behind its leader (and never behind some colonel); (b) takes over peacefully; (c) to replace politicians or bureaucrats made out to be dangerous for the nation—and corrupt; (d) with the blessing, as the next chapter will show, of the judicial apparatus; (e) the general leading the coup having been placed at the head of the army by the very figure he removed from power. This model would repeat itself with variants in 1977 and 1999.

The Bell Curve of a Praetorian Regime

Ayub Khan's trajectory, as well as the characteristics of his coup d'état, established a model that his successors would more or less follow, too. After an authoritarian takeover that politicians are the first to suffer from, the regime initiates a form of relative liberalisation via a constitutional arrangement that is supposed to give the general-become-president in civilian life a degree of legitimacy.

From Martial Law to "Controlled Democracy"

Ayub Khan's political agenda was known since 1954—at least in some circles of the Pakistani establishment. In October of that year, on a stopover in London on his way to the United States, he had drafted a constitutional framework that he later shared with members of the Bogra administration when the governor general appointed him defence minister. In it he advocated "a controlled form of democracy"[21] with a chain of command somewhat reminiscent of the army's: the president was responsible for appointing the provincial governors who supervised the provincial govern-

---

[21] Muhammad Ayub Khan, *Friends Not Masters*, op. cit., p. 212.

ments. The president could also dismiss ministers. Ayub Khan implemented this plan soon after assuming power.

In a sign that he wanted to make a clean sweep of politicians and their misrule, he abrogated the Constitution of 1956, dismissed both the central and provincial cabinets, dissolved the assemblies—the National Assembly and the two provincial assemblies alike—and outlawed political parties. Over 150 former cabinet members and 600 former assembly members were indicted for corruption, including Suhrawardy and Firoz Khan Noon. The civil service did not escape the purge; the commissions of inquiry set up by the new authorities led to the dismissal or early retirement of 1,662 public officials.[22]

In March 1959, Ayub Khan issued a decree confirming his desire to oust politicians from the public sphere: the Elective Bodies (Disqualification) Order (EBDO) stipulated that those suspected of improper behaviour or corruption had the choice of either going on trial or retiring from politics. Those found guilty were banned from elective office until 31 December 1966. Such important political figures as Mian Mumtaz Daultana, Firoz Khan Noon and M.A. Khuro were ensnared by the EBDO. In this way Ayub Khan managed to behead the main political parties in one fell swoop and for a long time to come.[23]

He then promulgated the Basic Democracies Order on 26 October 1959 to mark the first anniversary of his rise to power. The new regime established a sort of indirect democracy. At the local level, 80,000 "basic democrats" were elected by universal suffrage—to which Ayub Khan had resigned himself[24]—each of these people's representatives being elected by approximately 1,000 voters. These elected officials then met in "Town Committees" and at the rural level, in "Union Councils" of which there were about 4,000 in each wing of the country. These bodies also included a high proportion—as much as 50 per cent—of members appointed by the central government or bureaucrats acting in its name.

The "basic democrats" elected in January 1960 formed an electoral college 80,000 persons strong, half chosen by West Pakistan and half by East Pakistan, who were responsible for electing the president. Revisiting this period, Ayub Khan writes in his autobiography, "At this stage, I felt that I

---

[22] Ibid., p. 74.

[23] M. Waseem, *Politics and the State in Pakistan*, op. cit., p. 149.

[24] He nevertheless wrote in his 1954 draft: "It is too late now to resile [sic] from universal suffrage however great its shortcomings may be". See Muhammad Ayub Khan, *Friends Not Masters*, op. cit., p. 212.

should have a mandate from the people to continue in my task".[25] Being the only candidate in the running, he was elected president of Pakistan for five years on 15 February 1960 with 75,084 votes out of 80,000.[26] The question put to the "basic democrats" in what strongly resembled a mini-referendum, was, "Have you confidence in the President Field Marshal Muhammad Ayub Khan, Hilal-i-Pakistan [Crescent of Pakistan], Hilal-i-Jurat [Crescent of courage]?" The wording of the question itself is noteworthy: while Crescent of Pakistan is a civil award, Crescent of Courage is a military one. The fact that they were both mentioned on a ballot paper was a clear indication of the Janus-like figure of Ayub Khan.

Ayub Khan had thus become president of a country without a constitution. However, he was determined to stamp his authority with constitutional legitimacy. To achieve this, he appointed a Constitution Commission chaired by a Supreme Court justice, Muhammad Shahbuddin, and five representatives per province. The commission's first mission was to examine the "progressive failure of parliamentary government in Pakistan leading to the abrogation of the Constitution of 1956" and make proposals for the introduction of a new constitution. To Ayub Khan's great satisfaction, the Commission recommended adopting a presidential regime, which had long been his preference. The most interesting aspect here has to do with the way in which Ayub Khan linked this presidential orientation to the father of the nation himself, Jinnah:

During the brief period that the Quaid-e-Azam was Governor-general of Pakistan we had, in effect, a Presidential form of government in the country. The Quaid-e-Azam was Governor-general and he was also President of the Constituent Assembly. The Governor-general, and not the Prime Minister, presided at Cabinet meetings and this was done at the instance of the Cabinet itself.[27]

Ayub Khan claimed to follow in Jinnah's footsteps even if he came from the army and was highly critical of the Muslim League, the Quaid-e-Azam's party. This is because the founding father's political culture fitted Ayub Khan like a glove. This interchange further blurs the distinction between civilians and the military.

Ayub Khan's draft Constitution was examined in October 1961 during a meeting of provincial governors (who clearly played the role for Ayub

---

[25] Ibid., p. 235.

[26] In his autobiography, Ayub Khan gives an even higher figure: 75,283, or 96.6% of the vote.

[27] Muhammad Ayub Khan, *Friends Not Masters*, op. cit., p. 217.

Khan as president that the Corps Commanders played for him as com-mander-in-chief). He presented the Constitution to the nation on 1 March 1962 as "a blending of democracy with discipline". It made considerable reuse of the previous system, with the exception that the "basic democrats" first had to elect a National Assembly (in addition to the provincial assem-blies)—the Parliament being unicameral, contrary to Constitution Commi-ssion recommendations, of which Ayub Khan also rejected the idea of a vice-president. Furthermore, the president had an absolute right of veto over all decisions of parliament except for those concerning finances.[28] In financial matters, in the event of a two-thirds majority vote, he could then submit the decision to a referendum. In any event, the president had no trouble controlling the National Assembly, especially since it was elected by the electoral college formed by the 80,000 "basic democrats" whose votes were easy to buy or coerce. Even if opponents managed to get elected, as was the case in 1962 when Ayub Khan failed to obtain a two-thirds major-ity (required for passing constitutional amendments), he had no lack of means to achieve his ends. Rural elected officials for instance were threat-ened to have the water supply for their irrigation canals cut off if they voted the wrong way.[29]

In April 1962, the "basic democrats" elected the members to the National Assembly and in May those of the provincial assemblies. Finally, on 8 June, the martial law was lifted. The elections were thus held at a time when the judiciary's margin for manoeuvre was curbed, the press was subjected to censorship[30] and political parties were still outlawed.

---

[28] The Assembly, however, could only vote on new expenditures, previous appro-priations being automatically renewed.

[29] Khalid B. Sayeed, *The Political System of Pakistan*, op. cit., p. 106.

[30] In 1963, Ayub Khan had a constitutional amendment passed, the first one, that reduced judicial control over conformity of the laws with the fundamental prin-ciples of the Constitution. The courts nevertheless tried to resist pressure. In October 1964, the High Court of West Pakistan ordered the immediate release of Maududi, leader of the Jama'at-e-Islami who had been arrested ten months earlier along with 43 other party cadres, and the party was outlawed. The press was subjected to the iron law of two presidential orders in 1963 authorising the executive to take control of newspapers and printing presses that were guilty of issuing publications that tended "to incite hatred or contempt of the govern-ment" or that could fan rivalry between the two wings of the country.

Discipline—and the Army—Rule

Ayub Khan clamped down on liberties from the very start, considering that his country was not ripe for democracy and that its priorities should lie elsewhere, particularly the pursuit of national security.

Propaganda and disinformation became the regime's trademarks.[31] In 1947 the Pakistani press, like its Indian counterpart, was one of the mainsprings of pluralism. In 1949, the journalists' ability to mobilise became apparent in the forty-nine-day strike for better wages that affected the daily *Sindh Observer*, called by the Sindh Union of Journalists. The following year, this trade union was the kingpin for a new organisation, the Pakistan Federal Union of Journalists (PFUJ), which organised another memorable strike in 1954 at the *Times of Karachi*.

Ayub Khan changed the rules of the game. Press organs known for their independence (and their leftist inclinations) such as the *Pakistan Times* and *Imroze*, both belonging to a socialist-leaning press group, Progressive Papers Limited, were brought to heel in 1959 when Ayub Khan took control of PPL in the name of the Pakistan Security Act.[32] In 1960, the government passed a Press and Publications Ordinance that subjected press organs to stringent controls. Any criticism of the authorities was liable to heavy sanctions.[33] The government soon set up the Bureau of National Research and Reconstruction (BNR&R) having as one of its primary missions to promote journalists likely to publish pro-government articles. A National Press Trust was also formed—in particular to take control of the fourteen press organs, which thus lost their independence. One of the aims of the propaganda was to make Ayub Khan out to be an irreproachable leader, even the protective father of the nation.

Despite his election to the civilian post of president, Ayub Khan gave the army a preponderant role, even after he had shed his uniform. So it was that a provision was laid down in the Constitution, neglected by many analysts, stipulating that the defence minister should be a military officer for the twenty coming years. In the same spirit, Ayub appointed a growing number of military officials to administrative positions—despite his stated

---

[31] On the Pakistani press, see Zamir Niazi, *The Press in Chains*, Karachi, Karachi Press Club, 1986.

[32] See the account by Tariq Ali, son of the editor-in-chief of *Pakistan Times* in Tariq Ali, *Military Rule or People's Power*, London, Jonathan Cape, 1972.

[33] Shuja Nawaz, "The Mass Media and Development in Pakistan", *Asian Survey*, 23 (8), 1983.

fears of seeing the army contaminated by the bureaucrats' less disciplined ethic.[34] In addition to the bureaucracy, the army acquired positions in the economy via the creation of institutions destined to play a major role, such as the Fauji Foundation and the Army Welfare Trust, which overstepped their original mission of taking care of the needs of the military personnel. Ayub Khan also implemented a policy emulating those of the Mughal Emperors and the British during the Raj by distributing land to officers in the newly irrigated areas of Punjab and Sindh and authorised the Corps Commanders to grant plots to their men in the cantonments.[35]

Beyond that, Ayub Khan's rule marked the development of the military institution as such. In the early 1960s, the Pakistani army exceeded 250,000 troops. It passed the mark of 278,000 troops in 1965–6, and then reached 351,000 in 1967–8, culminating at 390,000 in 1969–70. According to the figures compiled by Jasjit Singh, its budget also grew apace, especially after the war of 1965. Military spending as a percentage of GDP, already very high—they were in the range of 4.66 to 5.79 per cent of the GDP in the first half of the 1960s—, doubled (from 4.66 per cent in 1962–3 to 9.86 per cent in 1965–6) before finally stabilising at 6 per cent in the late 1960s.[36]

Shahid Javed Burki gleaned from American sources slightly more modest figures marked by a downward turn in the late 1960s—from 5.7 per cent of GDP in 1966 to 4.8 per cent in 1970[37]—which remains considerable. Hasan-Askari Rizvi has suggested another indicator, the share of military spending in the state budget on the basis of the annual *Economic Survey*. Even if these figures are again lower than those found by Jasjit Singh, it is only marginally. Rizvi shows that over the 1958–69 period, the percentage of military spending in the state budget wavered between 46.13 per cent and 63.47 per cent, the 50 per cent mark having been surpassed in eight out of ten budgetary years.[38] Shuja Nawaz offers an edifying comparison of funds allocated to the country's defence and those devoted to its development. The defence expenditure/GDP ratio increased by 125 per cent between the

---

[34] He also admitted in his autobiography that he believed "the army would be destroyed if it go too mixed up in running the civil administration". Muhammad Ayub Khan, *Friends Not Masters*, op. cit., p. 95.

[35] S. Nawaz, *Crossed Swords*, op. cit., pp. 252–254.

[36] Jasjit Singh, "Trends in Defence Spending", in J. Singh (ed.), *Asian Defence Review 2006*, New Delhi, Knowledge World, 2006, pp. 87–88.

[37] Shahid Javed Burki, *Pakistan under Bhutto*, op. cit., p. 105.

[38] Hasan-Askar Rizvi, *Military, State and Society in Pakistan*, Lahore, Sang-e-Meel Publications, 2003, p. 107.

1960–65 period and the 1965–70 period, whereas the development expenditure/GDP ratio grew only by 56 per cent.[39]

The army's rise in power at the expense of civil authority—and at the same time the Punjabis at the expense of Mohajirs, was of course symbolised by the transfer of the nation's capital from Karachi to Islamabad, and even before that, in 1961, to Rawalpindi.

Ayub Khan, a Revolutionary?

In his memoirs, Ayub Khan referred to his coup d'état as a "revolution" (this is even the title of chapter 6). For him, it was one in the sense that he brought down a regime, but also in that the country's new leader saw himself as an enlightened dictator tackling conservative interests—those of the landowners—in the name of the people. Ayub Khan's sensitivity to public opinion is all the more noteworthy as his backers in the army simply did not understand it: "What they did not understand," he recounts in his autobiography, "was that civil action was subject to the limitations of the law and had to take into account currents and cross-currents of public opinion".[40] Ayub Khan's political sense nevertheless made plain to him the need for certain populist measures: once he had dislodged the politicians who represented the interests of the traditional property-owning class—or those from their ranks—he had to weaken them by all possible means and rely on other sectors of society. This explains the priority he gave to land reform, which was supposed to spawn a new category of farmers.

No sooner had he come to power in October 1958 than Ayub Khan asked his lieutenants which reform listed on his agenda appeared the most difficult to them. Land reform, they all replied. That is where Ayub Khan thus wanted to begin, if his autobiography is to be believed.[41] On 31 October 1958, he appointed a Land Reforms Commission which determined that in West Pakistan, 15 per cent of the land was in the hands of 0.1 per cent of the landowners (all with landholdings of at least 500 acres).[42] The Commission submitted its report on 7 February 1959 and on the basis of its recommendations, Ayub Khan set a ceiling on individual landholding: 500 acres of irrigated land and 1,000 acres of non-irrigated land, a measure

---

[39] S. Nawaz, *Crossed Swords*, op. cit., p. xxxviii
[40] Muhammad Ayub Khan, *Friends Not Masters*, op. cit., p. 96.
[41] Ibid., p. 105.
[42] Ibid., p. 106.

allowing millions of acres to be distributed to thousands of tenant farmers who thus became independent farmers. Shahid Javed Burki estimates that one-fifth of the land owned by the landed aristocracy in 1959 slipped through their hands ten years later: "Of the 10 million acres of land that the landed aristocracy gave up, mostly through sale, the bulk went to middle-sized farmers".[43] The figures supplied by Mahmood Hasan Khan are more modest: out of 5,064 landowners whose acreage was above the ceiling, land reform affected only 763 of them. The others subdivided their estates among members of their family in order to remain under the ceilings. As a result, only 1.9 million acres were recovered—against payment of an indemnity—and of this total only approximately 500,000 were distributed to new owners, the remainder comprising non-arable land (due to semi-desert conditions or the relief). Finally, only 67,000 landless peasants ben-efited from land reform.[44] A third source considers that in 1959 over one million acres (1,022,927) were recovered and that 955,656 acres were distrib-uted to 186,555 beneficiaries (compared to 481,244, 295,937 and 71,501 respectively in 1972).[45] These figures are closer to the dominant analysis among economists—including S. Akbar Zaidi, who holds that the land reform of 1959 went further than that of 1972.[46]

The effect of the land reform was amplified by the Green Revolution in the mid-1960s involving the introduction of high-yield seed and fertilizer which, in areas that were well-enough irrigated to profit from them, would significantly increase yields as well. The Green Revolution would foster the rise of a new category of owner-farmers who can be described as capitalists in that they would put money into their farms and reinvest their profits to further modernise them. According to Shahid Javed Burki, these new farm-ers who benefitted from land reform came from the middle class. According to Hazma Alavi and Akmal Hussain, they were mostly feudals who had discovered the charms of capitalism.[47] Indeed, as Akbar Zaidi explains, "While the three systems of agriculture—peasant [the term Zaidi uses to

[43] Shahid Javed Burki, *Pakistan under Bhutto*, op. cit., p. 42.
[44] Mahmood Hasan Khan, *Underdevelopment and Agrarian Structure in Pakistan*, op. cit., p. 166.
[45] Government of Pakistan, *Agricultural Statistics, 1993–94*, Islamabad, 1995, p. 129.
[46] S. Akbar Zaidi, *Issues in Pakistan's Economy*, op. cit., p. 35.
[47] Hamza Alavi, "The rural elite and agricultural development in Pakistan", in Kramat Ali (ed.), *Pakistan: the Political Economy of Rural Development*, Lahore, Vanguard, 1986 and Akmal Hussain, "Technical change and social polarization in rural Punjab", in Ibid.

refer to small individual properties], capitalist and feudal—can and do coexist, the trend has been for feudalism to give way to capitalism."[48]

Whatever the case, these "rural progressives", to borrow Burki's expression, became Ayub Khan's effective political backers when they were elected to the posts of "basic democrats"—which Khan seems to have personally made sure of.[49] He hence had at his disposal a force to counter the traditional feudals—and party members—who resented him terribly for ousting them from power, and even excluding them from politics using the EBDO. (Incidentally, 80 per cent of the charges on which these notables were indicted under the EBDO had to do with the illegal diversion of irrigation waters to farmers whose landlord-politicians could then solicit votes at election time).[50] In the 1962 elections, the landed aristocracy thus tried—to little avail—to maintain its local power in face of the new wealthy, whom Ayub Khan liked to describe as born of the common people to hone his image as a revolutionary.[51]

In addition to this rural support base, Ayub Khan added urban backers, again by enacting reforms. He emphasised industrial development and expressed this priority by making himself chair of the Planning Commission, a position he decided to take over in 1961. This effort, which was partly[52] responsible for a rise in the average growth rate for manufacturing of 11.5 per cent in the second five-year plan (1960–65), was conducted jointly with the business community. Only a minority, however, profited from this boom, in particular the twenty-two families said to "own Pakistan". Although this is an exaggeration, a study conducted in 1962 showed that the four largest merchant communities—the Memons, the Chiniotis, the Bohras and the Khojas—controlled two-thirds of the country's industrial assets even though they only made up 0.5 per cent of the population.[53] A study in 1968 confirmed this trend, finding that two-thirds

[48] S. Akbar Zaidi, *Issues in Pakistan's Economy*, op. cit., p. 49.

[49] Shahid Javed Burki, *Pakistan under Bhutto*, op. cit., p. 33.

[50] Ibid., p. 29.

[51] In 1962, in the elections to the provincial assemblies and the National Assembly, notables from the landed aristocracy who sought (re)election had to solicit votes from the "basic democrats" of a much lower rank, which Ayub Khan caricatured thus: "The masters were going to household servants and the elite to 'turbaned natives' for votes. It was a fitting nemesis!" Muhammad Ayub Khan, *Friends Not Masters*, op. cit., p. 255.

[52] Foreign aid (the US contribution in particular) played a role as well.

[53] Anita Weiss, *Culture, Class and Development in Pakistan: The Emergence of an Industrial Bourgeoisie in Punjab*, Boulder, Westview Press, 1991, p. 34.

of industry and 87 per cent of the banking and insurance sector were in the hands of a couple dozen families: "These industrial families, together with an estimated 15,000 senior civil servants belonging to approximately 10,000 families, and about 500 generals and senior military officials, formed the core of the regime's bases of support in urban areas".[54]

Although the traditional political parties and their aristocratic backers had been destabilized by Ayub Khan's strategy, they put up a fine show of resistance. Above all, they were not the regime's sole opponents starting in the mid-1960s, nor were they the most effective.

A Remarkably Vigorous Opposition

If Ayub Khan introduced in Pakistani politics a model of a bloodless coup d'état followed by a phase of constitutional liberalisation, his opponents on the other hand paved the way for a method of resisting autocracy, forcing the dictator to make concessions, even to leave.

The Resilience of Politicians

As soon as the new National Assembly was elected in 1962, Bengali leaders in the Awami League and the Krishak Sramik Party (KSP) rebelled against the ban on political parties in a joint communiqué on 24 June 1962. Their campaign forced Ayub Khan to legalise them in July by signing the Political Parties Act. Suhrawardy then formed the National Democratic Front bringing together the Awami League, the KSP and the Jama'at-e-Islami, the latter being the quickest to reorganise. Ayub Khan was forced to concede that political parties were back. He accepted the consequences and formed his own political organization, the Convention Muslim League, in September 1962 on the remnants of a fraction of the Muslim League. Although he was loathe to become a party man, Ayub Khan became its chairman in December 1963. Like Ghulam Mohammad's and Mirza's Republican Party, this was however merely a collection of courtiers, a coterie having no local base. Most of the veteran Muslim League members did not join him but instead founded the Council Muslim League which under Khawaja Nazimuddin's chairmanship joined the National Democratic Front.

This return to party politics remained highly inadequate, however, due to the disqualification of many politicians by virtue of the EBDO. This decree

---

[54] Ayesha Jalal, *The State of Martial Rule*, op. cit., p. 306.

prevented the heavyweights of Pakistani politics from running in the 1965 presidential election. Fatima Jinnah, the Quaid-e-Azam's sister, thus was approached by opposition parties to run against Ayub Khan with the support of most of the parties, including the Jama'at-e-Islami.[55] Her election campaign, with the slogan of "Democracy against dictatorship" met with a huge echo in the population, as attested the dense crowds that attended her rallies in all parts of the country. 65 per cent of the "basic democrats" voted for Ayub Khan, but he came out of this election weakened, especially in cities. Not only Dhaka and Chittagong, but also Karachi—partly because of the Jama'at-e-Islami local sympathisers—supported Fatima Jinnah.

The Impact of the 1965 Defeat

The September 1965 defeat shortly thereafter marked a far more decisive turning point. Whereas India's defeat against China in 1962 had given Pakistan confidence, prompting it to take initiative for the conflict, Ayub Khan and his army had underestimated the Indian army's capability to react—and overestimated the determination of the Indian Kashmiris to conduct a real uprising against New Delhi.[56] After the initial altercations concentrated in Rann of Kutch (Gujarat) during the first half of 1965, the Pakistanis launched Operation Gibraltar in July—the name referring to the Arab conquest of Spain. This operation—as in 1947–8—involved infiltrating (para-) militaries in Indian Kashmir to provoke an uprising among the population.[57] According to General Musa, "7,000 Mujahidin from Azad Kashmir" took part in Operation Gibraltar. Most of the members of this force had been "given some guerilla training within the short time available before it was launched. It was armed with light machine guns and mortars, besides personal weapons, and was equipped with wireless sets".[58]

---

[55] On the available sources regarding Fatima Jinnah, see Riaz Ahmad, "The works on Madar-i-Milat Fatima Jinnah: an evaluation", *Pakistan Journal of History and Culture*, vol. XXVII, n° 2, July–Dec. 2006, pp. 155–158.

[56] Which is not surprising when one reads Ayub Khan's account of the Indian debacle in 1962 which ends on a condescending note: "But let me not denigrate the Indian soldier, for some of them are as good as any in the world. They were badly served". Muhammad Ayub Khan, *Friends Not Masters*, op. cit., p. 169).

[57] On the war of 1965, see P.V.S. Jagan Mohan, *The India-Pakistan Air War*, New Delhi, Manohar, 2005.

[58] Gen. Retd. Mohammad Musa, *My Version: India-Pakistan War 1965*, Lahore, Wajida lis Ltd., 1983, p. 36.

The operation failed for two reasons: not only did the Indian troops expose the infiltrators, but the Indian Kashmiris did not revolt. In August the Indian army carried out reprisals, but it was Pakistan that started the air war on 1 September by launching Operation Grand Slam on the poorly protected border zone of Chamb. India's air force attacked Lahore, Sialkot and especially Sargodha, 150 km from the border, where half of the Pakistani air force was stationed. The following week, Indian aircraft attacked Peshawar and Kohat, 600 km from the border. At the same time, the largest tank battle since the Second World War, involving 1,000 vehicles, took place in Pakistani Punjab. On 22 September, the UN Security Council passed a ceasefire resolution, which was signed the following day.

The responsibility of Ayub Khan, "who had thought India would crumble under a couple of quick blows",[59] in what Pakistani history textbooks continue to present as a victory, is undeniable. But his foreign minister, Z.A. Bhutto, also shared some of the blame. On 19 September, Ayub Khan made it clear to the United States ambassador that he was "disenchanted with Bhutto's reckless adventurism".[60] But Bhutto was smart enough to criticise the Tashkent Declaration of January 1966 (which prepared the ground for a proper treaty) and to resign in June of that same year before Ayub Khan had a chance to dismiss him. In any event, Ayub was head of state and he could not obviate his responsibility for what was at the very least a diplomatic defeat.

Ayub Khan never recovered from the defeat of 1965 which all the opposition parties were quick to capitalise on. On 13 January 1966, the leaders of organizations as diverse as the Awami League and the Jama'at-e-Islami held a joint press conference in Lahore condemning the Tashkent Declaration. This opposition was considerably strengthened by the creation of the Pakistan People's Party in November 1967 on Z.A. Bhutto's initiative. His blend of nationalism and socialism managed to channel student unrest against the humiliation of Tashkent and the anger of the working class, which economic growth had left by the wayside.[61]

[59] Shuja Nawaz, *Crossed Swords. Pakistan, Its Army and the War Within*, op. cit., p. 235.

[60] Cited in ibid.

[61] Z.A. Bhutto, *The Myth of Independence*, Karachi, Oxford University Press, 1969.

Revolutionary Inspiration in the Streets: A Pakistani Student Revolt

The Pakistani left had undergone ordeals and defections that had drained it of its lifeblood. The Communist Party, which had once been very strong, had been banned in 1954. Some communists, such as Danial Latifi, who drafted the Muslim League's manifesto in the 1940s, joined Jinnah's party.[62] But others were against it as much before as after Partition[63] and were repeatedly arrested.[64] Trade unionists were also subject to severe repression under Ayub Khan—strikes having been declared illegal.[65]

The so-called forces of revolution were thus concentrated in more or less unofficial trade unions and student movements. The main student union, the National Students Federation (NSF), had been formed in 1953 but was banned a number of times, particularly after Ayub Khan's coup d'état.[66] Worker unions were very fragmented[67] and generally restricted to a single industry, even sometimes to one enterprise, except those that were affiliated with the Pakistan Trade Union Federation founded in 1947 and close to the communists. But workers and students readily joined forces. In 1963, the NSF backed striking union workers in the railroads, at KESC (Karachi Electric Supply Corp.) and among the dockers.[68] In 1964–5, the NSF also

[62] Muhammad Amir Hamzah, "Role of the Communist Party of India in Pakistan Movement with Reference to the Right to Self-determination", 4 February 2006. See: http://groups.yahoo.com/group/cmkp_pk/message/4157 (Accessed on September 15, 2013).

[63] Interestingly, the Pakistani branch of the Communist Party had remained under the moral authority of the Communist Party of India. See Kamran Asdar Ali, "Communists in a Muslim Land: Cultural Debates in Pakistan's Early Years", *Modern Asian Studies*, vol. 45, no. 3, 2011, p. 515.

[64] A veteran such as Sobho Gianchandani spent five years under house arrest for instance, from 1959 to 1964. See Salam Dharejo, "Interview: Comrade Sobho Gianchandani", 13 October 2008, op. cit.

[65] Many trade union members had also been co-opted and even paid by the regime, according to one veteran of the worker movement. See Lal Khan, *Pakistan's Other Story. The 1968–69 Revolution*, op. cit., p. 125.

[66] Matthew J. Nelson, "Embracing the Ummah: Student Politics beyond State Power in Pakistan", *Modern Asian Studies*, vol. 45, no. 3, 2011, pp. 565–596.

[67] While the number of unions had almost doubled between 1951 and 1964, union membership increased to a much lesser extent, some of them having fewer than 300 members. See Mohammad Waseem, *Politics and the State in Pakistan*, op. cit., p. 201.

[68] This strike provided incentive for other labour leaders such as Usman Baloch who founded the first labour union at the Karachi Atomic Nuclear Power Plant in 1967.

threw itself behind Fatima Jinnah before experiencing a classic split in the region between pro-Beijing and pro-Moscow members.

Students and workers nevertheless seized the occasion of a sick and age-ing Ayub Khan[69] weakened by the war of 1965, to foment unprecedented agitation in the context of a latent socio-economic crisis. The poor were indeed at the receiving end in the 1960s. Not only was agriculture being mechanised in the wake of the Green Revolution, depriving some landless workers of their job, but this modernisation process benefited those who could invest in the new machines (including tractors). Those who were impoverished and/or had lost their jobs were forced to look for work in the city. As a result, the "income of the poorest 10% of households declined from 2.6% of West Pakistan GDP in 1963 to 1.8% in 1968–69".[70]

Demonstrations and strikes multiplied in this context. In 1967, a thirteen-day railroad strike served as a prelude to a widespread student movement. Student demonstrations that at first had local causes grew in scale after police repression claimed one life in November. On the 10th, a student took a shot at Ayub Khan—without hitting him—while he was making a speech in Peshawar.[71] On the 13th, Wali Khan and Z.A. Bhutto—who had been touring the country campaigning against Ayub Khan since September—were arrested under section 38 of the Defence of Pakistan Rules. On the 15th, lawyers joined in the fray, their demonstrations spreading from Lahore to Karachi. On 7 December, a general strike was observed in Dhaka. The repression was such that Maulana Bhashani's National Awami Party called for an extension of the movement to all of East Pakistan. On 8 December, while Ayub Khan was in Dhaka, the police killed two more students. On 10 December, it was the journalists' turn to call a general strike organised by the PFUJ. This movement was a reaction to tightened censorship—in 1966, the government had shut down two major newspa-pers, *Purbani* in Dhaka and *Ittefaq* in Lahore—but it produced a further intensification of the phenomenon: the government had journalists arrested, pulled its ads from *Nawa-i-Waqt* (Lahore), *Ibrat* (Hyderabad) and three publications out of Dhaka: *Pakistan Observer*, *Azad* and *Sangbad*.[72]

---

[69] Ayub Khan reportedly suffered a heart attack in January 1968.

[70] Mohammad Waseem, *Politics and the State in Pakistan*, op. cit., p. 219.

[71] Lal Khan, *Pakistan's Other Story. The 1968–69 Revolution*, Lahore, The Struggle Publications, 2008, p. 129.

[72] See the PFUJ website for more detail: http://pfuj.pk (Accessed on September 15, 2013).

On 20 January, a communist activist was killed in Dhaka. The following day, doctors marched on Lahore where a general strike on the 24th prompted the government to declare curfew. Curfew was later extended to Karachi, Gujranwala, Dhaka and so on. On 14 February, railway workers, WAPDA (Water and Power Development Authority) employees and rickshaw drivers demonstrated in Lahore. On the 17th, employees of the Pakistan Industrial Development Corporation in Multan went on strike. On the 19th, 30 trade unions in Lahore marched side by side. On the 21st, it was the state civil servants and on the 23rd health care personnel. On the 24th transport workers and teachers were in the street in Bahawalpur. On 4 March postal workers joined the movement and on the 5th those of the Karachi Port Trust. On 18 March, 2.5 million stopped work in answer to a call from the Joint Labour Committee. A total of 239 people died during this movement, 196 in East Pakistan, the other 43 in the west.[73]

At the beginning of that same month, Ayub Khan made notes in his diary suggesting that the climate was resolutely revolutionary in much of the country: "gangs of communists and terrorists on the prompting of Bashani are raiding police stations, the houses and properties of Muslim Leaguers, and asking the chairmen and members of Basic Democrats to resign (...) in consequence, most of the civil officers have left their posts and so have the local rent collectors, and their records have been burnt".[74]

Bhashani, a peasant leader, repeated his slogans: "He who tills the land, shall reap the harvest" and "The tenants have rights, landlords should abdicate" ("*Hari Haqdar, Jagirdar Dastbardar*"). His Bengali base was all ready to go, but he also managed to mobilise farmers in the Chambar district of Sindh and Hasht Nagar in the NWFP. On 22 and 23 March 1970, a half-million tenant farmers took part in the huge Kisan Conference (peasant convention) in Toba Tek Singh (Faislabad district), where one had already taken place in 1948. Veterans of the communist movement spoke there, including Abdul Hammid Bhashani and Faiz Ahmed Faiz as well as Ahmad Rahi and Mairaj Muhammad Khan.[75] Another group, the Mazdoor Kisan Party (born from a breakaway faction of the NAP as mentioned above),

---

[73] Lal Khan, *Pakistan's Other Story. The 1968–69 Revolution*, op. cit., p. 130.

[74] Ayub Khan, *Ayub Khan Diaries*, Oxford, Oxford University Press, p. 305 (entry on 9 March 1969).

[75] Another movement, the Mazdoor Kisan Party that brought together small Bengali and Punjabi groups (such as the one led by Major Ishaque Mohammad) worked out a Maoist strategy of rural insurgency.

which had members in Punjab and Bengal, developed a Maoist guerrilla strategy.

The army itself was affected by the movement. Even if the soldiers did not express themselves, the high command could not be unaware of the mood prevailing among them. The soldiers had already expressed their disagreement with the official line on occasion by refusing to fire on demonstrators, such as in Lahore in February 1969.[76] This frame of mind became apparent soon afterward in the soldiers' voting behaviour. Philip Jones' analysis of postal ballots—most of which were sent by soldiers who could not cast their vote—shows that in 1970, the PPP attracted strong support among the residents of several garrison towns (see table 6.1).

Table 6.1: Vote in selected cantonments (soldier ballots sent by post)

Cantonment	Muslim League	PPP	JI	Other Islamic parties	Ind.	Others
Wah	3.2	67.2	16.7	5.2	1.9	5.8
Jhelum	21.2	61.2	7.1	5.6	1.4	3.6
PAF Bases Areas	11.6	37.8	11.9	13.1	25.5	–
Sargodha Cant.	8.0	58.3	8.8	8.1	16.9	–
Shorkot Rd	–	67.6	–	22.8	9.6	–
Lahore Garrison	29.2	58.2	–	–	0.7	11.9
Lahore Cant.	25.7	64.7	–	–	0.7	8.0
Sialkot lines	7.2	72.3	8.4	8.8	3.1	0.2
Sialkot Cant.	20.8	55.7	8	14.6	0.7	0.2
Gujranwala	23.4	67.4	7.5	1.7	–	–
Multan	–	55.9	–	44.1	–	–

Source: Philip E. Jones, *PPP: Rise to Power*, op. cit., p. 324.

Ayub Khan held two Round Table Conferences, the first on 26 February, the second from 10–13 March. In them he acceded to demands of the opposition led by Bhutto and Wali Khan: constitutional reform introducing elections by universal suffrage and the establishment of a parliamentary system. But these concessions came too late. The opposition wanted the dictator's head. Ayub Khan finally resigned on 25 March 1969 after a highly revealing speech broadcast over the radio:

[76] Lal Khan, *Pakistan's Other Story. The 1968–69 Revolution*, op. cit., p. 157.

"This is the last time I am addressing you as President of Pakistan (...) The administrative institutions are being paralysed. The mobs are resorting to gheraos at will and get their demands accepted under duress. The persons who had come forward to serve the country have been intimidated into following these mobs. (...) Every problem of the country is being decided in the streets".[77]

The demonstrators had managed to unseat the dictator. But Ayub Khan had decided to turn his rule over to the Commander-in-Chief of the Army, Yayha Khan (who had taken over from General Musa after the 1965 war). Yayha Khan started by declaring martial law and carrying out even more severe repression than his predecessor. In the city of Karachi alone, 45,000 workers were dismissed. On 4 November, the government passed a new Industrial Relations Ordinance that legalised lockouts. Targeted killings of revolutionary leaders also increased in the countryside. Thus Haq Nawaz, the sworn enemy of local landowners, was killed on 25 August 1970 in D.I. Khan. At the same time, the authorities stepped up pressure on the press. The Pakistani army set offices of *Ittefaq* on fire on 25 March—which did not prevent it from being back in print by the month of May. On 10 December 1971 in Dhaka, Serajuddin, Vice President of the Pakistan Federal Union of Journalists, was kidnapped and killed. But the mobilisation did not die down for months. The peasant movement, for instance, kept going, especially in the NWFP. In July 1971 the Mazdoor Kisan Party, a Maoist organization as mentioned above, stood up to 1,500 troops. The clash left some twenty dead.[78] Malakand Agency was the theatre of a massive crackdown on the MKP which would be the matrix of future tensions in the Swat valley.

Last but least, the regime's new strongman, disregarding the cultural modernisation promoted by Ayub Khan, drew support from the Jama'at-e-Islami which went after the PPP.[79]

But the students in particular resisted this policy. At the Punjab University of Lahore, the regime tried to prevent leftist student unions from winning elections that they had finally managed to have organised. Shaheed Mahmood Nadeem, a leader of the local National Students Federation who later became a theatre and television director, thus recalls,

---

[77] Ayub Khan, *Ayub Khan Diaries 1966–72*, op. cit., pp. 547–8.

[78] Lal Khan, *Pakistan's Other Story. The 1968–69 Revolution*, op. cit., p. 147. In Malakand Agency the MKD experienced more massive repression at the end of the ANP-JUI government period. At that time the party's vice-president, Maulvi Mohammad Sadiq, was killed.

[79] Lal Khan, *Pakistan's Other Story. The 1968–69 Revolution*, ibid., pp. 218–9

The Punjab University Union was restored and the elections called. But very soon it became apparent that the Yahya regime wanted to hoist Islami Jamiat-i-Talba [the student wing of Jama'at-e-Islami] on the University. When we protested at the rigged, manipulated elections, we were arrested again. This time we were tried by a summary military court. We challenged the court and bravely faced the trial. This time I spent a couple of months in prison. We were now a part of the left-wing popular movement for a democratic change. The time I spent in prison gave me a rare chance to meet political activists, hardened criminals and the poor hapless prisoners. It was like an internship after my University degree in political activism. Some of my prison mates became characters in my plays and the prison governance system gave me invaluable insights into the political and social system in the country. When I was released, I was even more determined to work for the revolutionary cause. I almost went straight to the legendary Toba Tek Singh conference of peasants and workers, a convention of red-capped workers, passionate students, fiery trade unionists, and socialist intellectuals, all committed to the cause of revolutionary change".[80]

Already months before in West Pakistan, the opposition had found a leader in the person of Z.A. Bhutto, as discussed in the previous chapter. No one can say if the mobilisation of the West Pakistanis would have been enough to bring down the military regime because the Bengalis finally dealt the deathblow. It is even reasonable to believe that the last straw had been Mujibur Rahman's campaign for greater autonomy in East Pakistan, which had led Ayub Khan to declare martial law on 17 March 1969, and then resign on the 25th. Yahya Khan, who succeeded him in defiance of constitutional procedures stipulating that in the event of a president's resignation power would be handed over to the Speaker of the Assembly, applied strongarm tactics from the very start. He abrogated the Constitution, dissolved both the national and provincial assemblies and banned political parties, just as Ayub Khan had done eleven years earlier. But pressure from the street soon prompted him to organise elections that would seal the fate of national unity and consequently of the regime.

*

The Ayub Khan years defined a typical trajectory of Pakistani-style military regime. All the ensuing coups d'état would, like his, be initiated by the army chief, certain of his Corps Commanders' backing. They would not be greeted with violent opposition, but instead almost with relief. Ayub Khan also—unsurprisingly—paved the way for a model for militarising the

---

[80] Cited in ibid., pp. 196–197.

administration and the economy that his successors would pursue. Furthermore, in the wake of Ayub Khan, all Pakistani military rulers would show strong pro-American leanings.

If the Pakistani generals, starting with Ayub Khan, always rise to power in more or less the same way, they also lose it in a very similar fashion after about ten years. Each time, they come up against a political opposition that in Ayub's case combined the resurgence of the old parties and the emergence of new forces—particularly among students. Each time the resilience of opposition forces the dictator to make concessions so as to offer their regime a semblance of respectability. Ayub Khan thus gave the country a Constitution—and legalised political parties. But to oust the military regime, the Pakistanis had to await an external clash—the war of 1965—and another one that was virtually externally as well, the secession of East Bengal.

Although very largely due to Ayub Khan's adventurism, the defeat of 1965 in fact did not lead to challenging the army's political control, quite the contrary. At the end of a perfectly anti-constitutional transition, Ayub Khan—who could no longer survive the discredit and physical wear and tear of power—handed over the reins of power in 1969, not to the Speaker of the National Assembly, but to army commander-in-chief Yahya Khan. He imposed martial law, claiming to do so in order to protect the people's freedom.[81] The defeat of 1971 against India would finally brought down the military and enabled civilians to return to power.

The bell-curve trajectory that the first military regime in Pakistan described in the 1958–70 period was largely reproduced in the Zia years— but this episode was qualitatively different and even, probably, that of the worst tyranny that Pakistan has yet to see.

Zia: A Modern Tyrant

General Zia had been appointed head of the army by Bhutto—who had thus passed over a dozen more officers with greater seniority—in the spring of 1976, due to "his piety, patriotism and professionalism".[82] But this positive assessment was not enough to defuse the hostility Bhutto and politicians in general aroused among the military institution and some sectors of public opinion in general. This time it was not the incompetence and divisions

---

[81] See the speech he gave when coming to power. Abdurrahman R. Siddiqi, *The Military in Pakistan: Image and Reality*, Lahore, Vanguard, 1996, p. 15.

[82] Ian Talbot, *Pakistan*, op. cit., p. 255.

of the civil government that irritated the generals, if their words are to be believed, but its authoritarianism—in particular Bhutto's, whose biggest mistake was of course the rigging of the 1977 elections, which the opposition parties disputed in the streets. The army once again had an opportunity to perpetrate a more or less consensual coup d'état by presenting itself as the politicians' mediator.

The sequence of events moreover suggests that Bhutto placed the army in a position to step in as arbitrator. In reaction to the demonstrations organised by the opposition, he left the matter in army hands, even declaring martial law in five cities on 22 April. He then sought out a negotiated settlement by initiating talks with the opposition. But on 4 July Zia decided to intervene after sounding out the military institution and spreading the message among the Corps Commanders. A brigade was positioned at all strategic points in Islamabad. Eleven PPP leaders were arrested (including the prime minister) along with nine of the most influential opponents, a way of showing that the army was not taking sides but instead neutralising politicians who were harmful for the national interest as a whole.[83] On 1 September, in a speech that came shortly after Bhutto's final imprisonment, Zia declared, "This country can be kept together by the armed forces and not by politicians".[84] Zia suspended the Constitution of 1973 and proclaimed himself Chief Martial Law Administrator (CMLA)—without defining a clear line, even announcing that elections would be held in 90 days.

Compromising Politicians and Militarization of the State

Unlike Ayub Khan—who had already devised plans for a constitution in 1954—Zia's coup in 1977 did not reflect the army's desire to run the country. It above all wanted to preserve its interests, which Bhutto more than any other politician had threatened. Zia moreover conceived his action in collaboration with other politicians, which introduced an entirely new arrangement of civil-military collusion that was bound to last. As Hasan-Askari Rizvi writes, "The military did not visualize any problem in organizing new elections within 90 days and transferring power to the PNA which, was, in their estimation, bound to win the forthcoming polls".[85] Zia thus

---

[83] Shuja Nawaz, *Crossed Swords. Pakistan, Its Army and the War Within*, op. cit., p. 352.

[84] Cited in Lt. Gen. Faiz Ali Chisti, *Betrayals of Another Kind: Islam, Democracy and the Army in Pakistan*, Rawalpindi, PCL Publishing House, p. 135.

[85] Hasan-Askari Rizvi, *Military, State and Society in Pakistan*, op. cit., p. 167.

released Bhutto, who instantly went on a triumphant tour of Lahore, Multan and Karachi, threatening that Zia would be punished for his misdeeds and accusing the PNA of scheming. Zia thus postponed the elections *sine die* and "discovered" that Bhutto had blood on his hands: he was accused of having ordered the murder of a former associate, Ahmed Raza Kasuri (whose father was killed in the attack supposedly targeting his son) and sent back to prison. Furthermore, an investigation into the 1977 elections determined that they had been rigged. The judicial proceedings undertaken against Z.A. Bhutto that will be analysed in the next chapter lasted from October 1977 to March 1979. He was hanged on 4 April 1979, after General Zia had come to consider the "Bhutto problem" in terms of "him or me", understandably so. Zia, in this regard, had the support of the PNA parties which did not feel quite up to rivalling with this man.

Zia went further than Ayub Khan in militarising the state but did not operate in a linear fashion. Due to improvisation and displays of resistance, militarisation was accomplished in fits and starts.

When he suspended the Constitution and proclaimed himself Chief Martial Law Administrator, Zia created five areas—Punjab, NWFP, Sindh, Balochistan and the Northern Provinces—and placed at their head five administrators of martial law who answered only to him. Zia was seconded by a five-member Military Council including the president of the Joint Chiefs of Staff Committee (JCSC),[86] General Sharif,[87] himself as COAS, the air force chief, the navy chief and one civilian—which was reminiscent of the Ayub Khan era—and a senior bureaucrat, Ghulam Ishaq Khan who went from being COAS Zia's secretary-general to becoming secretary-general of the Military Council.

This body was however gradually supplanted by another institution, the Conference of Martial Law Administrators, which in addition to Zia included the five provincial martial law administrators, the chairman of the JCSC, the Vice-COAS, the director-general of the ISI and "senior military officers holding political or bureaucratic posts".[88] The DG ISI was probably the most powerful person in this list. The ISI had indeed become even more important

---

[86] In theory, the JCSC is the summit of the military institution since it supervises the army, the air force and the navy. In practice, it has solely an advisory role.

[87] An indication of Zia's respect for the military hierarchy, he asked Sharif, theoretically his superior, to chair the meetings of this body.

[88] Shuja Nawaz, *Crossed Swords. Pakistan, Its Army and the War Within*, op. cit., p. 362.

under Zia than under Bhutto. First, "Zia had no political power base, apart from the army, and therefore he utilized the intelligence service to observe and control his oponents and the political scene". Second, the Soviet invasion of Afghanistan was "a stroke of good luck for the ISI" which became the main actor of the Pakistani strategy during the Jihad.[89] The Afghanistan Bureau of the ISI, with its headquarters in Ojhri, became a key body.

Besides the Conference of Martial Law Administrators, Zia also regularly convened a Council of Federal Secretaries. The direct relationship he maintained in this way with the bureaucrats in charge of the country's major administrations was also reminiscent of Ayub Khan's approach. However, in January 1978, this council was replaced by another, the Council of Advisers, composed of military officials and civilians not associated with political parties, such as Agha Shahi, the foreign minister who like Ghulam Ishaq Khan had been one of Bhutto's "secretaries" (in this case Foreign Secretary). Going from a democracy to a military dictatorship apparently did not particularly bother these bureaucrats.

The Council of Advisers in turn was replaced in July 1978 by a cabinet made up this time solely of civilians. Aside from a bureaucrat such as Shahi, its members were also from one of the PNA parties, the PML-Pagaro, as Zia was seeking to legitimate his power by associating with political party representatives. The PML-Pagaro—also known as the PML (Functional), had come about after the 1965 elections when Fatima Jinnah had declared the Muslim League "functional" and assigned its chairmanship to the Pir Pagaro (Sindh), a locally popular politico-religious leader. This fraction of the PNA was joined by others in August 1978, pointing up the weakness of democratic convictions in this segment of the political system. But "the cabinet was nothing more than a public relations exercise and it had very little role in decision-making on key domestic and foreign policy issues".[90] Some PNA leaders had sensed this or instantly learned a lesson from it: the NDP, the Tehrik-e-Istikal and the JUP quickly deserted the alliance, while the rest of the PNA did not withdraw from the government until April 1979, after having lending a veneer of respectability to a dictator at the time when he was busy ousting Bhutto. The PNA did not join the opposition for all that; on the contrary it announced that it would continue to back the ruling general.[91]

---

[89] Hein Kiessling, *Faith, Unity, Discipline*, op. cit.
[90] Hasan-Askari Rizvi, *Military, State and Society in Pakistan*, op. cit., p. 166.
[91] Ibid., p. 175.

Since Zia sought to legitimate his power by obtaining the backing of certain parties, he had not outlawed them but settled for exercising drastic supervision over them. All of them had to register with the administration in a terribly cumbersome procedure spelled out in an amendment to the Political Parties Act of 1962. Only parties that yearly submitted their accounts and their roster to the Election Commission, published an electoral platform and elected their leaders each year were recognised by the state. Most parties having refused to register, Zia used it as an argument to hold local elections on a non-partisan basis. But to his dismay, candidates from the PPP made a fine showing as independents.

After Bhutto's execution, Zia further toughened his regime and sought more to cement his authority by invoking Islam rather than seeking endorsement from politicians.[92] He once again postponed the elections in October 1979, a date that marks a turning point in his dictatorship. Two Martial Law Regulations, numbers 13 and 33, were enforced with increasing rigor. The first give an idea of the extent of the army's new impunity:

No person shall, by word, either spoken or written, or by signs or by visible representation or otherwise, bring or attempt to bring into hatred or contempt or excite or attempt to excite disaffection towards the Armed Forces or any member thereof.

The second was more laconic but just as portentous: "No person shall in any manner whatsoever directly or indirectly indulge or participate in political activity".[93]

All party leaders likely to thwart Zia had been rendered harmless after his coup d'état, the Bhuttos first of all. Bhutto's wife, Begum Nusrat had been placed under house arrest, like her daughter Benazir, from December 1977 to January 1978. Afterward she was arrested on three occasions for criticising the conditions of her husband's trial as unfair.[94] Upon her husband's execution she was detained with her daughter in the Sihala camp

---

[92] He completed his scheme toward the end of 1981 by appointing 350 members of a purely consultative assembly, the Majlis-i-Shura, the main purpose of which was to guide the regime's Islamisation policy, Zia's master plan, as will be seen in chapter 8.

[93] Amnesty international, Pakistan, *Human Rights Violations and the Decline of the Rule of law. An Amnesty Internatonal Report*, pp. 28–29. Available at: http://www. amnesty.org/en/library/asset/ASA33/024/1981/en/d95b691b-0920–4420-b814– 7c45a23d6365/asa330241981en.pdf (Accessed on September 15, 2013).

[94] On the Begum Nusrat Bhutto Case, see Syed Sami Ahmad, *The Judiciary of Pakistan and its role in Political Crises*, op. cit., pp. 75–98.

from 1 April to 28 May 1979. Both of them were arrested on 16 October 1979, after the turning point of that date and held until 8 April 1980. They nevertheless were heavily involved in the organisation of the Movement for the Restoration of Democracy (MRD). In retaliation, they were held in the Sullur prison from 8 March 1981 to the end of the year.

Z.A. Bhutto's eldest son, Murtaza, as his father requested in his last letter to him, left for Kabul—a traditional place of exile in the region where he was welcomed by the president recently installed by the communist coup d'état. He was joined there by his brother Shahnawaz, and the two of them founded a movement that advocated violent action, the Al Zulfikar Organisation (AZO). They were accused of an airplane hijacking on 2 March 1981 (see below)—in which Murtaza denied any involvement.[95] The movement did, however, claim the missile attack on Zia's plane—but the assailants missed their target.

Zia, who had the MRD to deal with, used these terrorist methods as an argument for harsher crackdowns. In March 1981, 6,000 political prisoners were put behind bars. Many of them were released shortly thereafter, but in July between 1,500 and 2,000 were still behind bars.[96] Torture was resorted to. A human rights organisation, the Political Prisoners Release and Relief Committee, which defended over 150 political prisoners, stated in its report that "the tortures range from solitary confinement to sustained beatings, water ducking, introducing chillies in the rectum, electric shocks, deprivation of sleep for long periods, burning the body with cigarettes, beating the genitals and threats to relatives and so on".[97] The Lahore Fort was a place of choice for these treatments.[98] Under Ayub Khan, only one political prisoner died in custody; under Zia, dozens of them died—including the student leader Nazir Abbasi, trade unionist Inayat Masih and political activists Mehr Chandio, Kalu Brahmin and Qamar Abbas.[99]

Not only politicians, but also labour and leftwing activists in general were preferred targets, even when they were not affiliated with the PPP. In late December 1977–early January 1978, workers at the Colony Textile Mills

---

[95] The courts cleared him posthumously in 2003.

[96] Amnesty International, *Pakistan. Human Rights Violations*, op. cit., p. 17.

[97] Cited in Anthony Hyman, Muhammed Ghayur and Naresh Kaushik, *Pakistan Zia and After*, Shakti Malik for Abhinav Publications, New Delhi, 1989, p. 44.

[98] See the novel by Mohammed Hanif who describes the fort during that time with a realism that only fiction allows. Mohammed Hanif, *A Case of Exploding Mangoes*, New York, Vintage Books, 2009.

[99] Amnesty International, *Pakistan. Human Rights Violations*, op. cit., pp. 35 ff.

went on strike for an unpaid bonus. Zia, a friend of the mill owner, Mughees Sheikh, was invited to the wedding of his daughter, whose dowry was ten times higher than the bonus owed. Zia got wind of a rumour (apparently unfounded) that the strikers were going to attack the wedding reception. He ordered the movement crushed.

The paramilitaries started firing directly at the workers who were gathering for a peaceful gate meeting. In a scene of indescribable horror workers screamed and stampeded over the bloodstained corpses of their workmates, crushing many others as they desperately tried to evade the carnage. Blood was everywhere, streaming from the bodies of the workers whose only crime was to ask for their basic rights.

The fire continued uninterrupted for three hours. By six o'clock in the evening, when darkness had set in, the state forces had 'conquered' the textile mill workers.

In the factory compound and lawns the state forces had prevented the bodies of the injured from being taken to hospital. Those who tried to pick them up were hampered by the police. Dozens had died on the spot. Several injured had died due to excessive loss of blood because they were prevented from being rushed for medical treatment.

In the darkness of the night the state forces, without differentiating between the dead and the injured, brought up trucks and threw the bodies into them. Some were thrown in the huge factory gutter, while others were buried without coffins in the nearby village of BagaSher (...) In its callousness the state arrested and charged with murder the members of the Worker Action Committee, some of whom had been killed in the massacre. Those who escaped it were prosecuted by the state.[100]

Press censorship also became more severe.[101] A correspondent for the *Far Eastern Economic Review*, Salamat Ali, was even arrested and tried by a military court for an article on Balochistan in November 1979. Academics critical of the regime were also punished. For instance, three University of Punjab professors in Lahore were transferred. Three others, from Quaid-e-Azam University in Islamabad, were tried by a military court in 1981 for distributing anti-martial law posters.[102]

Zia did not settle for relying more heavily on the military courts; he also brought the civil courts to heel. At the beginning of 1980, a former officer turned party leader, Asghar Khan, arraigned the Zia regime in the High Court of Lahore on charges that it had not organised the elections on which the Supreme Court had conditioned the legality of his regime.

[100] Lal Khan, *Pakistan's Other Story. The 1968–69 Revolution*, op. cit., pp. 299–300.

[101] See Zamir Niazi, *The Press in Chains*, Karachi, Royal Book Company, 1986.

[102] Hasan-Askari Rizvi, *Military, State and Society in Pakistan*, op. cit., p. 275 (notes 42 and 43).

Fearing an unfavourable decision, Zia promoted its chief justice to the Supreme Court. At the same time, he developed a system of exceptional courts that answered to the martial law administrators, in addition to sharia courts tied in with his Islamisation policy (see chapter 8). Zia introduced two types of courts. The "Summary Military Courts" (SMC) had only one judge (who was not necessarily a member of the bar). As their name indicated, full records were not made of the trials held in these courts, only summaries. The accused were not entitled to be represented by a lawyer. Sentences could be up to one year in prison and 15 strokes of the cane. Decisions could not be appealed. The "Special Military Courts" were made up of three people, a magistrate and two army officers having the rank of at least Major or Lieutenant Colonel. Again, only a synopsis of the hearing was expected. But in this case, sentences could be as severe as the death penalty. Several trials were held in secret.

Having established his domination over the public sphere, Zia undertook a gradual but unprecedented authoritarian militarisation of the state. Unlike Ayub Khan, Zia retained his position as Chief of Army Staff (COAS) and the uniform that went with it. He also filled the administration with active or retired military officials—whether it was in the Central Superior Service (the elite civil service corps), the Foreign Service (which provided Pakistan's diplomats) or the Police Service (which produced officer cadres in charge of national security). Between 1980 and 1985, 96 army officers entered the CSS while 115 were recruited on contract and in 1985, a military official was appointed head of the civil intelligence bureau for the first time. In 1982, eighteen of forty-two Pakistani ambassadors posted abroad came from the military.[103] In the end, 10 per cent of the posts in the civil administration were reserved for active or retired military personnel.[104]

Zia also catered to the army through many other "well-mannered" measures not devoid of ulterior motives counterbalanced by a certain degree of paranoia. He preserved the collegial tradition introduced by Ayub Khan— the Corps Commanders were always consulted in important matters—but took additional precautions. As Shuja Nawaz explains, "The dynamics of governance under a dictatorship led Zia to rely on a cohort of like-minded and pliable officers whom he would rotate out of office periodically before they struck roots or gained too much influence".[105] Like Ayub, Zia rewarded

[103] Ibid., p. 182.
[104] Regarding these issues, see K.L. Kamal, *Pakistan: The Garrison State*, New Delhi, Intellectual Publishing House, 1982.
[105] Shuja Nawaz, *Crossed Swords*, op. cit., p. 360.

his loyal supporters in coin, but in much higher amounts. Shuja Nawaz adds, "He plied these officers with gifts and favours, producing a new crop of millionaire generals who became part of the vested interest group that ran the country for over a decade".

Lastly, Zia took pains to promote mid-ranking officers by retiring more senior officials, who enjoyed golden retirements, particularly due to facilitated access to land. One will remember that Ayub Khan had granted his officers land, in particular to counter the domination of rural Punjab landowners. Zia perpetuated this tradition, such that between 1977 and 1985, the government of Punjab granted 450,000 acres to 5,538 military personnel.[106]

The Movement for the Restoration of Democracy (MRD)

Despite the severity of the repression Zia subjected them to, PPP activists organised their resistance. The Bhutto family was naturally the vanguard for it given the aura surrounding the founder of the line and the sympathy—even devotion—that his martyrdom aroused. Although Zulfikar Ali Bhutto's two sons, Murtaza and Shanawaz, went into exile in Afghanistan to better pursue the fight from abroad, Benazir and her mother remained in Pakistan and received the unwavering support of party cadres and activists who were entirely devoted to the PPP cause.

The party took the initiative of federating the opposition. In February 1981, leaders of eight parties met in Karachi to form the Movement for the Restoration of Democracy. Z.A.Bhutto's widow, Begum Nusrat, represented the PPP of which she was the chairperson. The Qasim group of the Muslim League was also represented, along with Mufti Mahmood's JUI, Sirdar Sherbaz Mazari's National Democratic Party,[107] Nawabzada Nasrullah Khan's Pakistan Democratic Party, the Pakistan National Party led by Mir Ghous Buksh Bizenjo (who had just left the NDP to form his own party), the leftwing party, Kisan Mazdoor Party led by Fatehyab Ali Khan and the Qoumi Mahaz Azadi led by Meraj Mohammad Khan, a Bhutto lieutenant who had left the PPP following a dispute with its founding father. Only the Muslim League and the Jama'at-e-Islami—except the Sindhi branch which went with the MRD[108]—always prepared to collaborate with the authori-

---

[106] Hasan-Askari Rizvi, Military, *State and Society in Pakistan*, op. cit., p. 182.

[107] The NAP had taken this name in 1975 after it had been banned by Bhutto. It was to merge into the ANP in 1986.

[108] Shuja Nawaz, *Crossed Swords*, op. cit., p. 382.

ties, did not join the alliance, as well as the Pashtun and Baloch national-ists.[109] The coalition consequently lacked ideological unity, with Islamists rubbing shoulders with militant socialists. But all were united by the same desire to bring back democracy—a regime they believed in and/or without which, as professional politicians, they lost their raison d'être.

The MRD was hampered practically upon its inception by the hijacking of a PIA plane on 2 March 1981 mentioned above. The episode, which forced the aircraft to land in Kabul—was attributed to Al Zulfikar Organization (AZO). While Murtaza Bhutto always denied responsibility for the hijacking, it was well in tune with his modus operandi. The hijacker, Salamullah Tipu, demanded the release of fifty-five political prisoners, some of whom belonged to the PPP. He upped the ante by executing a hostage. The government of Zia caved in and the hijackers disappeared.[110]

Zia used this episode to quash the MRD, which as a result never really took off until 1983. Then, the most massive mobilisation was in Sindh, the PPP's stronghold. Peasants in the Sukkur, Larkana, Jacobadad and Khairpur districts demonstrated as much for a return to democracy as in the name of Sindhi nationalism, as is apparent in the secret literature that circulated clandestinely. The opposition also drew its strength from the rigour of martial law and the harshness of the new Islamic law (see infra).[111] It took three divisions and military helicopters to quell the agitation. In those three weeks of repression alone, the governor of Sindh recorded 189 deaths and 1,999 prisoners. In all, it left 1,200 dead and 20,000 were taken pris-oner.[112] Zia finally resigned himself to a few concessions.

The Time of Concessions

Like Ayub Khan and later Yayha Khan when confronted with protest movements, Zia had to compromise. Stephen Zunes describes the actual

---

[109] The Baloch were grateful to Zia for having released 9,000 prisoners captured under Bhutto. As for the Pashtuns, Zia continued to co-opt them into the army and they approved of his involvement in Afghanistan against the Soviet invasion.

[110] Raja Anwar, *The Terrorist Prince. The Life and Death of Murtaza Bhutto*, London, Verso, 1997.

[111] Lal Khan, *Pakistan's Other Story. The 1968–69 Revolution*, op. cit., p. 379.

[112] Ibid., p. 302. See also Bin Sayeed, Khalid, "Pakistan in 1983: Internal stresses more serious than external problems", *Asian Survey*, vol. 24, no. 2, A Survey of Asia in 1983: Part II, 1984, pp. 219—228.

dialectic that took shape between the MRD and Zia: in 1983, "Zia sensed the MRD would likely choose Independence Day, August 14, to renew its offensive. To cut them off he announced a plan for the restoration of democracy on August 12, 1983".[113] He assured the country that elections would be held before March 1985. While pursuing the repression—45,000 troops were sent into Sindh province, 15,000 were arrested and between and 60 and 200 others killed[114]—Zia undertook a form of authoritarian decompression[115] to defuse mobilisation that was taking on national proportions, even if its base was Sindhi. In December 1984, Zia held a referendum in order to give his regime constitutional approval and improve its legitimacy. The question was:

Do you endorse the process initiated by the President of Pakistan, General Muhammad Zia-ul Haq, for bringing the laws of Pakistan in conformity with the injunctions of Islam as laid down in the Holy Quran and Sunnah of the Holy Prophet (peace be upon him), for the preservation of and further consolidation of that process, and for the smooth and orderly transfer of power to the elected representative of the people?

The MRD called for a boycott of the polls. The dismal turnout at the ballot boxes on 19 December 1984 made a number of observers doubt the accuracy of the official tally, putting voter turnout at 62.15 per cent and the "yes" vote at 97.71 per cent. Zia nevertheless deemed he was in office for another five years. He did not give up his uniform, but wore it less and less often and took his distance from his former brothers in arms better to appear as president of the entire nation. He organised general elections just afterward, but candidates could not display any party affiliation. The MRD once again called a boycott, but it was not widely followed given the voters' relative enthusiasm for the election.[116] The National Assembly and the

---

[113] Stephen Zunes, "Pakistan's Movement for the Restoration of Democracy (1981–1984)" http://www.nonviolent-conflict.org/index.php/movements-and-campaigns/movements-and-campaigns-summaries?sobi2Task=sobi2Details&sobi2Id=24 (Accessed on September 15, 2013).

[114] Ibid.

[115] This concept was first used in the context of Latin America. See James M. Malloy and Eduardo Gamarra, "The Transition to Democracy in Bolivia", in James M. Malloy and Mitchell A. Seligson (eds), *Authoritarians and Democrats: Regime Transition in Latin America*, Pittsburgh, The University of Pittsburgh Press, 1987, p. 108).

[116] William L. Richter, "Domestic politics in the 1980s", in Craig Baxter and Syed Razi Wasti (eds), *Pakistan Authoritarianism in the 1980s*, Lahore, Vanguard, 1991, p. 79.

provincial assemblies produced by the ballot box in February 1985 thus consisted largely of landowners and representatives of the business community—people who could afford to run for election without the backing of a political machine.

These elections marked a turning point in the recovery by civilians of a fraction of power, what Hasan-Askari Rizvi calls the "civilianization of military rule". Zia's aim was not to put the army back in the barracks, but he was resigned to a partial and organised "civilianization". To do so, he made sure to reform the Constitution of 1973, brought back in force by the Revival of Constitution 1973 Order (RCO) of 2 March 1985 which radically altered the original text to the point of completely distorting it. The president of the Islamic Republic of Pakistan could now appoint governors, heads of federal administrations, regional court justices and those sitting on the Supreme Court. By virtue of the Eighth Amendment,[117] he could also dismiss the prime minister and dissolve the National Assembly, either at the prime minister's request or when the prime minister had been rejected by an Assembly that was not in a position to replace him, or when the president did not believe the Assembly was in a position to make the Constitution work. The parliamentary debates preceding the vote on the Eighth Amendment induced Zia to accept to include in the text a provision that the National Assembly could name the prime minister as of 1990 and that the provincial assemblies could do likewise as of 1988. With that laid down, Zia finally lifted martial law on 30 December 1985.

Even if the prime minister did not have much influence in the political system in the process of "civilianization", his role was not negligible. Zia—to whom it fell to appoint one during the first session of Parliament—named Muhammad Khan Junejo to the post. He chose a man from Sindh in the hope of preventing the province from mobilising behind the MRD. But Junejo would not be his puppet. The new prime minister handpicked his cabinet, rejecting names Zia suggested to him, except Lieutenant General Yaqub Ali Khan, who had replaced Agha Shahi as head of Foreign Affairs in 1982. The Assembly even chose Syed Fakhar Imam for its Speaker, a man who was not Zia's candidate, and passed resolutions requesting that martial law be lifted—which it finally was at the end of 1985, as noted above.

Politics was back, and with it political parties, which recovered their legal right to exist in February 1986. The PML(F) reformed itself under the aus-

---

[117] On the Eighth Amendment see Mohammad Waseem, *Pakistan under Martial Law*, Lahore, Vanguard, 1987, pp. 50–52.

pices of Junejo who convinced Pir Pagaro to let him chair it. Even if it was still impossible officially to put together parliamentary groups in the Assembly, Junejo circumvented the problem by naming his party the Official Parliamentary Group and his opponents the Independent Parliamentary Group. In May 1986, Junejo convinced Zia to allow members of the assembly to state their party affiliation. In the exchange, the Speaker—a man clearly hostile to Zia—was replaced and parties had to comply with the registration procedure described above. The PML, the Tehrik-e-Istiqal and the JUP were the first to register, but the PPP refused.

The PPP was in fact on the rise again with the return of Benazir Bhutto. After years in self-imposed exile, Benazir received an enthusiastic welcome when she returned to the country for her brother Shahnawaz's funeral in August 1985. She was immediately placed under house arrest, then left the country again in November. On 10 April 1986, she returned for good. She resuscitated the MRD, demanded general elections on a party basis and reinstatement of the 1973 Constitution. This agitation also spread to Punjab where on 14 August 1986 the government sought in vain to prevent the PPP from demonstrating—killing four activists in the process.

The atmosphere had changed to the point where, when they met in session again in May 1987, Assembly members had the courage to ask Zia to choose between the role of president and that of COAS and even criticised the army budget, which was constantly on the rise. In early 1988, Junejo appears to have mentioned reducing this very large budget line. Added to that was Yakub Ali Khan's resignation in November 1987—whom Junejo did not bother to replace, the fact that the prime minister did not look kindly on the creation of new barracks, and lastly, his efforts to extract a consensus among all the parties regarding Pakistan's strategy in Afghanistan. Whereas this issue was part of the president's and the army's preserve, Junejo held a round table meeting on the subject in March 1988, inviting all the political parties, including the PPP. The army also drew sharp criticism for the explosion of a huge ammunition depot on 10 April 1988, which reflected serious professional negligence, causing a heavy loss of human life and property.[118]

The return of politicians and political parties to the fore antagonised Zia to the point that he decided to dismiss his prime minister on 29 May 1988, as well as the federal and provincial governments. He also dissolved the National Assembly and provincial assemblies. The army took control of the

---

[118] Hasan-Askari Rizvi, *Military, State and Society in Pakistan*, op. cit., pp. 201–202.

prime minister's residence as well as the national radio and television networks. Zia justified his decision by citing the need to bring the situation in Karachi under control, as it was threatened by Mohajir unrest. This pretext would be used time and again in the years to come. But Zia also announced elections for 16 November.

While Junejo was sliding into the opposition, another leader of his party, the Pakistan Muslim League, Nawaz Sharif, accepted the post of chief minister of Punjab on 31 May 1985—hence the split resulting in two PMLs. On 9 June, a new government was formed.[119] Eight of Junejo's formers ministers were retained—including Chaudhry Shujaat Hussain—while new figures appeared, such as Zaffarullah Khan Jamali (future prime minister under another dictator, Musharraf), Chaudhry Nisar Ali Khan and Ellahi Baksh Soomro, who would both remain associated with Nawaz Sharif (the former was appointed home minister in 2013). Last but not least, Ahmad Nawaz Bugti, the brother of Nawab Akbar Bugti, was also co-opted and became part of the government.

By mid-July, Zia announced elections that would be organised on a non-partisan basis on 16 November 1988. But he died in an airplane accident on 17 August 1988.[120] Mobilisation of the opposition can thus not be claimed to account for the end of another dictator, as was largely the case with Ayub Khan's resignation. But Zia had been forced by political pressures in the street to initiate a process of "civilianisation" of the government which had began the democratic transition.[121]

The new COAS, General Mirza Aslam Beg, immediately declared that the military was withdrawing from politics and decided to follow the procedure outlined in the Constitution, letting the chairman of the Senate, Ghulam Ishaq Khan, take over as acting president. He announced that the

---

[119] "New Cabinet Sworn In", *The Pakistan Times* (overseas weekly), 12 June 1988, p. 1.

[120] The causes of this disaster gave rise to much speculation. The Pakistani commission of inquiry concluded it was sabotage—without ever managing to identify the perpetrators—while the Americans stuck to the hypothesis of a mechanical failure. Khaled Ahmed has interestingly connected this event to the nuclear-related negotiations that were being held at that time between Aslam Beg (the army second in command), Abdul Qadir Khan (the father of the Pakistani bomb) and Iran. See Khaled Ahmed, *Sectarian War. Pakistan's Sunni-Shia Violence and Its Links to the Middle East*, New York, Oxford University Press, 2011.

[121] Hasan-Askari Rizvi (*Military, State and Society in Pakistan*, op. cit.) does not perceive a break in 1988 between the Junejo government and Benazir Bhutto's.

elections called by Zia on 16 November would indeed be held on that date. That ballot marked the return to a multiparty system, the Supreme Court having ruled that holding elections on a non-party basis was against the Constitution.

*

The Zia years were marked by the worst tyranny Pakistan has seen to date. Never had liberties been crushed to that extent and political prisoners tortured in that way. A major difference between Ayub and Zia has to do with their relationship to the clerics and religion in general. As much as Ayub saw himself as progressive and was distrustful of heralds of Islam, as much Zia, a religious man who described himself as a "soldier of Islam",[122] tried to legitimate his power by drawing on religion and its most zealous champions. Islamisation, as we will see in chapter 8, would finally exceed the limits of being a mere strategy of political legitimation to become a lasting influence in Pakistani society.

Zia's dictatorial government was not contested as much from the US[123] as in the streets of Pakistan. The resilience of the opposition is suggestive of a pattern already noted under Ayub Khan, with an important qualification: in the years 1958–69, those who put up resistance to the president-general prior to Pakistan's student revolt were recruited mainly among politicians (often large property owners); in the years 1977–88, these notables partly rejoined the dictator's camp according to a rationale of collusion that would later be exemplified by Nawaz Sharif as we have seen and that the PML(F) took to great heights in 1978–9. The true opponents come from different circles, the Bhutto partisans who had already joined them in the student movement of the late 1960s and who returned to the streets together with a new generation of PPP activists and a new political culture, even a mystique—that of Bhuttoism, buoyed by a sharp sense of sacrifice and martyrdom. In Sindh, this ethic underlay the Movement for the Restoration of Democracy that forced Zia to make concessions.

---

[122] In his first speech after taking power, he thus declared, "I want to make it absolutely clear that neither I have any political ambitions nor does the army want
to be taken away from its professional soldiering. I was obliged to step in to
fill the vacuum created by the political leaders. I have accepted this charge as
a true soldier of Islam. My sole aim is to organize free and fair elections which
would be held in October of this year [1977]". See Shuja Nawaz, *Crossed Swords.
Pakistan, Its Army and the War Within*, op. cit., p. 362.

[123] Like Ayub Khan, Zia enjoyed the Americans' unwavering support after the
Soviet invasion of Afghanistan in 1979.

Zia did not make concessions like Ayub Khan did: he kept the title of COAS and dismissed his prime minister in order to fully retain power. But his career is reminiscent of his predecessor's. In response to mobilisation from the opposition, he resigned himself to "civilianizing" his regime. And once again it was an external event that sent the military back to their barracks: the death of the dictator—an unforeseeable shock that in this case had a similar function to the defeat of 1965 in the case of Ayub Khan and that of 1971 under Yayha Khan.

But in 1988 the military did not allow civilian rule as much leeway as it did in the 1970s, and the generals even reconquered power eleven years later with Musharraf's "countercoup".

Musharraf, a New Ayub Khan?

Immediately upon seizing power, Musharraf opted for the most novel and neutral title possible—Chief Executive. He also sought to reassure his countrymen by presenting his takeover as a step toward democracy. Addressing the nation on 17 October 1999, he thus declared,

The Constitution has only been temporarily held in abeyance. This is not martial law, only another path towards democracy. The armed forces have no intention to stay in charge any longer than absolutely necessary to pave the way for true democracy to flourish in Pakistan.[124]

In fact, Musharraf had persuaded his Corps Commanders—with difficulty according to his autobiography[125]—not to declare martial law. He also allowed the president chosen by Sharif, Rafiq Tarar, to remain in office. But he reorganised the executive, which was dominated by the army, and included technocrats and bureaucrats like the cabinets that Ayub Khan and Zia had put together before him.

On 17 October he also announced the formation of a National Security Council (NSC), chaired by the Chief Executive and made up of only six members, the chief of navy staff, the chief of air staff and four advisors competent in financial, legal, foreign policy and national security matters—a framework similar to Ayub Khan's government. This NSC supervised a council of ministers made up of businessmen such as Razzaq Dawood[126]

---

[124] Cited in Shuja Nawaz, *Crossed Swords. Pakistan, Its Army and the War Within*, op. cit., p. 528.

[125] Pervez Musharraf, *In the Line of Fire*, op. cit., p. 144.

[126] Razzaq Dawood is 17th on the list of the 40 richest Pakistanis mentioned in the previous chapter. The biographical note presenting him connects him with

and advisors such as the former manager of City Bank, Shaukat Aziz and the legal expert, Sharifuddin Pirzada—men who had no ties with political parties. The decision-making process in fact increasingly escaped the political-administrative sphere for other reasons: "Often, meetings of corps commanders preceded cabinet meetings and the latter only rubber–stamped the decisions that had been discussed and approved by the corps commanders under Musharraf's guidance and control".[127]

Even if censorship was not instituted,[128] the president-general only tolerated free expression from a segment of the English-language press involving a tiny elite who argued for the benefit of his Western partners that his regime was not anti-liberal. Actually, Musharraf established a Pakistan Electronic Media Regulatory Agency (PEMRA), which granted licences in a very selective fashion and closed down the most recalcitrant press organs. Beyond that, his regime was "known for expressing displeasure about news reports that create[d] a negative image for it, and journalists [we]re targeted selectively, resulting in the harassment and disappearance of approximately 48 journalists to fate (2007) under his rule".[129]

In Musharraf's autobiography the classic terms describing the opposition between an army acting as the nation's saviour and corrupt politicians can once again be found:

---

the club of 22 families who dominated the Pakistani economy in the 1950s-60s: Razzaq Dawood Pakistan/UAE Ranking: 14 (tied at 14) Worth: £250m ($500) Industry: Businessman Razzaq presently heads one of Pakistan's biggest construction and engineering conglomerate known as Dawood group/Descen group. With a roster of impressive clients. His group has won many contracts in Dubai, Saudi Arabia and Iraq and employs over 1,000 people directly. His name was more prominent among the top 22 richest families in 1970 until the Bhutto nationalizations, which then made him set up abroad. He returned to Pakistan in the early 90s and started from scratch and today makes it in the top 22 easily. The group also has investments of $300m in Bangladesh in the fertiliser, energy and infrastructure and development sectors. See http://teeth.com.pk/blog/2007/12/08/pakistans-rich-list-of-2008 (Accessed on September 15, 2013). His interesting biography is also available on the following website: http://jamilgoheer.wordpress.com/2010/07/30/ard/ (Accessed on September 15, 2013).

[127] Shuja Nawaz, *Crossed Swords. Pakistan, Its Army and the War Within,* op. cit., p. 557.

[128] Jean-Luc Racine, "Le Pakistan après le coup d'état militaire", *Critique internationale,* no. 7, April 2000, p. 25.

[129] Ayesha Siddiqa, *Military Inc. Inside Pakistan's Military Economy,* London, Pluto Press, 2007, p. 98.

It is not unusual in Pakistan for the general public and the intelligentsia to approach the army chief and ask him to save the nation. In all crises, everyone sees Pakistan's army as the country's savior. Whenever governments have malfunctioned (as has frequently occurred), whenever there has been a tussle between the president and the prime minister (especially during the 1990s), all roads led to the general headquarters of the army. The army chief was regularly expected to put pressure on the prime minister to perform—to avoid corruption, nepotism, and sometimes, downright criminality.[130]

Militarising the State… and the Economy

Although Musharraf may resemble Ayub Khan in many regards, he follows in Zia's footsteps in one essential aspect: the militarisation of the state apparatus and the economy. Like Zia, moreover, he sought to carry for as long as he could the titles of both president and COAS.

The defence budget, contrary to the impression purposely created by official figures, did not diminish under Musharraf. In fact, in 2001, military pensions were removed from the defence budget to trim it down. Yet they represented huge sums. In 2001–2, they reached 26.4 billion rupees, 33.5 in 2002–3, 30.8 in 2003–04 and 30.1 in 2004–5, compared to 5.3, 6.1, 6.3 and 6.1 respectively for civilians.[131] This means that the military budget actually continued to account for 4 per cent of GDP,[132] in other words double that for education (1.6 to 2.1 per cent a year in the first half of the 2000s), and represented more than six times health expenditure (0.6–07 per cent).[133]

The militarization of the administration was once again reflected in a record number of active or retired servicemen in civilian posts. In 2003, a journalist for *Dawn* calculated that there were 1,087 of these servicemen, including 104 active or retired Lieutenant Generals, active or retired Major Generals and other active or retired officers of similar rank.[134] Many of them ended up in the Defence and Interior Ministries, but in embassies as well—fourteen of the ambassadors appointed between 1999 and 2003 were active or retired military officers.

---

[130] Pervez Musharraf, *In the Line of Fire*, op. cit., p. 137.

[131] Ayesha Siddiqa, *Military Inc. Inside Pakistan's Military Economy*, op. cit., p. 207.

[132] Shahid Javed Burki, "An expansionary budget", *Dawn*, 21 June 2005.

[133] A. Siddiqa, *Military Inc.*, op. cit. 163.

[134] Nasir Iqbal, "1,027 civilian posts occupied by servicemen", *Dawn*, 30 October 2003. See http://archives.dawn.com/2003/10/03/nat12.htm (Accessed on September 15, 2013).

Beyond filling the administration with servicemen, Musharraf wanted to institutionalise the army's role in the state so that civilians would not be left to rule on their own. This was not a new idea. The first to outline it with precision had been General Karamat, Musharraf's predecessor, who on 6 October 1998 gave a speech before the Naval Staff College of Lahore calling for the formation of a National Security Council. Musharraf took up the idea, and the name.

To gain greater acceptance for his plan, Musharraf explained that this council would be placed under the president's authority and be made up of the prime minister, the chief ministers of the four provinces, the Speakers of the Senate and the National Assembly, the opposition leader in the National Assembly, the Joint Chiefs of Staff Committee and the chiefs of staff of the three military branches (army, air force and navy). Even so, this boiled down to giving the military considerable weight. But Musharraf explained that the council would make coups unnecessary: "The army chief can never take over, because he has an institution available to voice his concerns (and the concerns of a worried public) to the prime minister and can then allow the constitution and the political process to take their course".[135] The NSC was one of the goals that Musharraf pursued with the greatest determination until a law was passed institutionalising it in 2004.

At the same time, Musharraf reinforced military presence in the Pakistani economy like never before, even if the previous dictators had laid the groundwork.[136] This process, the outcome of which Ayesha Siddiqa has termed "Military Inc." or "Milbus" (for "military business"),[137] was a particularly old practice in the domain of property ownership. It will be remembered that Ayub Khan had allocated land to active and retired officers to reward them for their services, as the Great Mughals gave *jagirs* (land grants) or even more like the British (especially in the Canal Colonies) who handed out property deeds,[138] also to counter the feudal lords' influ-

---

[135] Pervez Musharraf, *In the Line of Fire*, op. cit., p. 171.

[136] The Zia years spectacularly accelerated the personal enrichment of Pakistani military personnel and the decade of civil power that followed did not bring a stop to this. In 1997, out of the 17 wealthiest Pakistanis, 8 of them were retired generals or their sons (7 of them, including General Fazle Haq, had made their fortunes under Zia). See S. Akbar Zaidi, *Issues in Pakistan's Economy*, op. cit., p. 518 (note 5).

[137] Ayesha Siddiqa, *Military Inc. Inside Pakistan's Military Economy*, op. cit., p. 292. On this topic, see also Amélie Blom, "'Qui a le bâton, a le buffle'. Le corporatisme économique de l'armée pakistanaise", *Questions de recherche*, op. cit.

[138] This is not merely a random comparison. A. Siddiqa points out that "The mili-

ence at the head of opposition parties. This policy, according to Ilhan Niaz, gave birth to a "neo-mansabdari" system since it echoed the political build-up of the Mughal Empire where *mansabdars* were the representatives of the emperor. While, being state functionaries, they were supposed to rotate, they gradually developed hereditary fiefdoms. Similarly, the officers who had been given land by Ayub Khan and his successors became feudals themselves as much because of the acreage they controlled as their mentality. According to Ayesha Siddiqa, the army controls about 11.58 million acres, or about 12 per cent of the arable land owned by the state.[139] In 2007, the value of land owned by the army was estimated at $11,653.79 million.[140] 59 per cent of the total land was in rural areas, 6.8 million acres having been allotted to army personnel.[141] On average, starting with the rank of Major General, the size of the allotment was a minimum of 240 acres, for Brigadiers and Colonels, 150 acres, and for Lieutenant Colonels, 124 acres.[142] These allocations have thus made it possible to establish large estates. Not only do these new agriculturalists use their influence to gain better access to water and fertilizer, but they also behave like feudal lords. In 2001, the conflict that erupted in Okara gave a caricatural illustration of this. In this area of central Punjab where there were seven military farms in operation, the landlords decided to change the terms of their arrangement with the peasants working the land by arbitrarily replacing share-cropping with rent paid in cash. Fearing that if they failed to pay rent, the military would evict them from their homes, the peasants protested. The military reacted by indulging in forms of torture that alerted human rights organizations. Human Rights Watch published a report on the incident in which the account of one of the demonstrators provides a graphic description of the atmosphere:

We were produced before Major Tahir Malik. He asked why we had not made the contract payments. We answered that we had no money. They took us to the torture cell and Jallad ["tormentor"] Munir started thrashing us with a leather whip. He made us all strip naked and whipped us till we bled. Major Tahir Malik would

---

tary justifies its acquisitions of agricultural land as part of the inherited colonial tradition of granting land to military personnel". Ayesha Siddiqa, *Military Inc. Inside Pakistan's Military Economy*, op. cit., p. 174.

[139] Ibid.

[140] Ibid., p. 182.

[141] Ibid., p. 175.

[142] Ibid., p. 183.

personally supervise the whippings, abuse us, laugh at us, and punch us... We were produced before officers again in the morning. They would insist that we pay the contract money. Upon our refusal, it would begin again.[143]

The crackdown left eight people dead, most of them victims of torture. The treatment of these peasants is reminiscent of the brutality used by the *waderos* in Sindh against their peasants and their use of private prisons. A sign of this convergence lies in the fact that many retired officers who had acquired or been allotted farmland were given the title of *numberdars* (a position that involves collecting taxes on irrigation water), generally reserved for a local notable. Musharraf himself, a Delhi-born Mohajir who never tilled the land, thus became the *numberdar* of a village in Punjab. As Ayesha Siddiqa explains, this evolution is rooted in the prestige that land has in the Pakistani imaginary, yet another sign of the persistence of the feudal mentality.[144]

In addition to its rural properties, the army also acquired considerable urban real estate, the value of which is proportionally even higher. As Ilhan Niaz points out, under Ayub Khan, to "begin with the rule was one plot per officer but as senior commanders secured the authority through the defense housing societies to 'autonomously allocate plots in the cantonments' multiple plots in different schemes enabled officers to build considerable urban landholdings at throwaway prices in Pakistan's urban centres".[145] The most common technique involved converting training grounds in the major cantonments into residential areas where large plots of land were allotted for a paltry sum to active or retired officers. In all, in 1947, forty-six housing schemes had been built in the main cantonments (Lahore, Karachi, Rawalpindi, Kamra, Taxila, Peshawar and Quetta).[146]

Land, however, is only one aspect of the economic empire the Pakistan army has built up, especially under Musharraf. In addition to the department labelled "Military Land and Cantonment", the defence minister also

---

[143] Human Rights Watch, "Soiled Hands: Pakistan Army's repression of the Punjab's farmers' movement", *Human Rights Watch Report*, vol. 16, no. 10, July 2004, p. 4. See http://www.hrw.org/sites/default/files/reports/pakistan0704.pdf (Accessed on September 15, 2013).

[144] Ayesha Siddiqa, *Military Inc. Inside Pakistan's Military Economy*, op. cit., pp. 200–201.

[145] Ilhan Niaz, *The Culture of Power and Governance of Pakistan, 1947–2008*, Karachi, Oxford University Press, 2011, p. 155.

[146] Ayesha Siddiqa, *Military Inc. Inside Pakistan's Military Economy*, op. cit., pp. 188–189.

controls a number of foundations, the oldest and largest of which is the Fauji Foundation (FF). Established by the army in 1954 in the framework of the Charitable Endowments Act (1890), the FF's initial mission was to ensure the welfare of soldiers and their families through supplementary retirement packages, health care, education, and so on. But aside from hospitals and schools (the FF has about ninety of them), it began developing its own business enterprises, from sugar mills to cement factories and including fertilizer production. The FF was capitalised at $750 million in 2007.[147] The air force followed its example and established the Shaheen Foundation in 1977 (which manufacturers a wide variety of products from pharmaceuticals and shoes). Not to be left out, the navy established the Bahria Foundation in 1982 (which aside from manufacturing paint is also involved in industrial bread-making). In addition to these three foundations is the Army Welfare Trust, set up in 1971, which operates as an investment fund, hence in the financial sector, but also has a stake in cement manufacturing and pharmaceuticals. For all these reasons, "the assets of a Pakistani general are at present estimated in the range of two to five million US dollars".[148]

The sheer scale of economic interests the military has acquired and developed partly explains why Musharraf did not only concern himself with keeping the army in power, but also pursued the colonisation of the state by the military. He thus appointed military officers in key civilian posts and institutionalised the army's presence at the heart of the state by setting up the National Security Council (NSC). Musharraf also wanted to renew the political class.

How to Replace the Political Class... with Another One?

Musharraf's desire to renew the political class reflected two considerations. One of them was structural, and was inferred from recent history: the military had never managed to administer the country without the help of politicians. Therefore, it made sense to change the politicians that had handled the nation's affairs so badly, in the army's view, up to then. The other was related to the legal constraints: in a decision handed down in May 2000, the Supreme Court ratified Musharraf's coup d'état by virtue of the "law of necessity" that will be analysed in the following chapter, but required him to hold elections

---

[147] Ibid., p. 228
[148] Ilhan Niaz, *The Culture of Power and Governance of Pakistan,* op. cit., p. 158.

within three years following the coup and forbid him to distort the framework provided by the Constitution of 1973.[149] It was on such terms that Musharraf would operate in order to replace the political class not only with military personnel but also by a new political class.

The first thing to do was to banish the existing political class—something the previous dictators had tried to do as well. Musharraf did not outlaw political parties, but their leaders were prosecuted for corruption, the fight against this scourge being a centrepiece of Musharraf's rhetoric.[150] He associated the corruption eating away at the state with incompetence, following a mindset that the Pakistani army has cultivated since Ayub Khan.[151] Musharraf thus worked to rid the country of its corrupt politicians. He established the National Accountability Bureau (NAB) reminiscent of Ayub Khan's EBDO—he moreover appointed a military officer to lead it: "a general who was scrupulously honest, clearheaded, and bold enough to move against the rich and powerful without being swayed by their influence".[152] The NAB launched an anti-corruption campaign that claimed its first victims among politicians—including Benazir Bhutto and her husband, Asif Zardari.

Benazir went into exile—dividing her time between Dubai and England—while her husband, whom Sharif had already sent to prison, stayed there. In all, dozens of politicians were fined or put out of action, bearing in mind that Musharraf's primary target was of course Nawaz Sharif. For a while, it looked like Pakistan's new leader was going to duplicate the treatment Zia had inflicted on Bhutto. Indeed, the main charge against him—for barring the pilot of the plane carrying Musharraf back from Colombo from landing on Pakistani soil—was liable for the death penalty. Sharif escaped Bhutto's fate, perhaps due to pressure from abroad (Bill Clinton had men-

---

[149] The decision stipulated "That no amendment shall be made in the salient features of the Constitution i.e. independence of the judiciary, federalism, parliamentary form of government blended with Islamic provisions".

[150] He thus explains in his autobiography that upon coming to power he suddenly realised the scale of the problem and that he should make it a priority: "Corruption and nepotism were all too common. All government institutions and organizations and public-sector corporations had fallen prey to the most blatant corruption, facilitated at the highest levels of government, through the appointment of inept managers and directors. Corruption permeated effectively down from the top". Pervez Musharraf, *In the Line of Fire*, op. cit., p. 146.

[151] Musharraf moreover hammered out, "Financial corruption aside, the government was rife with nepotism and incompetence". Ibid., p. 148.

[152] Ibid., p. 150.

tioned this eventuality in a disapproving tone in March 2000 during a five-hour stopover in Pakistan), but he was sentenced to life imprisonment, then exiled to Saudi Arabia (whose rulers had probably interceded in his favour) for ten years before being allowed to move to Great Britain in 2005.[153]

The Nazims: New "Basic Democrats"?

Beyond historic party leaders such as Benazir Bhutto and Nawaz Sharif, Musharraf like Ayub Khan before him also wanted to rid Pakistan of a political class dominated by feudals: "This small elite comprises feudal barons, tribal warlords, and politicians of all hues".[154] To do so, using the Local Government Ordinance of 2000 he devised a scheme that recalled Ayub Khan's "basic democrats". The idea was to elect local officials, called *nazims*, through whom he hoped to build a support network. In any case, he expected the scheme to renew the political class, all the more since he introduced a clause intended to disqualify a whole swath of the old political class: only individuals who had attended university could be candidates. The aim was to disqualify certain rural notables. If party cadres could have run for election as independents, they were unable to dodge this provision.

Musharraf introduced a Local Government Plan in 2000 and enacted Provincial Government Ordinances in 2001. The new arrangement replaced the system of local administration. In accordance with the new District Government System, officials were instituted to manage four urban districts (the major cities), ninety-two rural districts, 307 sub-districts (*tehsils*) and 6,022 villages (joined under the leadership of union councils).

From December 2000 to July 2001, Musharraf thus organised these various local "councils". The most hotly contested ones were those at the district level. There, the *nazims* were to have funds earmarked for local development. The elections—which were non-partisan—were intended to enable new politicians to occupy part of the public space. The same exercise was repeated in 2005.

---

[153] Musharraf thus explains the strategy he pursued with Nawaz Sharif: "We struck a deal. I would give Nawaz Sharif a conditional pardon, and he and certain members of his family would go to Saudi Arabia for ten years and remain out of politics. They would also give up some of their properties as reparation for their misdeeds. This deal was signed by all the elders of the Sharif family, including Nawaz Sharif, his brother Shahbaz Sharif and their father". Ibid., p. 166.

[154] Ibid., p. 154.

Musharraf clearly intended for the *nazims* to represent his authority at the local level. They met at a large convention in December 2003 at which they all complained of the same problem: politicians—and of course the bureaucrats, whom they more or less replaced—were very hostile toward them in most of the provinces where they attempted to extend their power down to the local level, that of the electorate[155] (in Pakistan the first step in a political career is to be elected to a local body: in 1985, out of 240 provincial assembly members, 124 were municipal elected officials and in 1993, an estimated 70 per cent of the Punjabi representatives in the assemblies in Lahore and Islamabad had begun their career at the local level).[156] The provincial politicians knew that if Musharraf could establish a direct link between his person and the *nazims*, he could bypass the provincial government and the politicians.

On 30 April 2002, Musharraf sought to assure his authority—like Zia in the past—in a referendum. Unsurprisingly, the new local government system was among the first question in a long series:

For the survival of the local government system, establishment of democracy, continuity of reforms, end to sectarianism and extremism, and to fulfil the vision of Quaid-e-Azam, would you like to elect President General Pervez Musharraf as president of Pakistan for five years?

According to the Election Commission, 71 per cent of Pakistani citizens went to the polls and 97.5 per cent of the cast a "yes" vote. Fraud occurred on such a broad scale that Musharraf had to make a public apology,[157] without for all that drawing the appropriate conclusions as he immediately become the president of Pakistan for five years and would remain in office. Musharraf's plan to set himself up as national leader in close collaboration with a host of new local leaders was unable, however, to withstand the force of politics, even politicking.

---

[155] "The problem with local government", *The Daily Times*, 15 December 2003. Available online at: http://www.dailytimes.com.pk/default.asp?page=story_15–12–2003_pg3_1 (Accessed on September 15, 2013).

[156] *The News*, 30 September 1994, cited in S. Akbar Zaidi, *Issues in Pakistan's Economy*, op. cit., p. 518 (note 5).

[157] In his autobiography, he admitted to "irregularities". See Pervez Musharraf, *In the Line of Fire*, op. cit., p. 168.

Musharraf Caught up in the Game of Politics: the PML(Q)
and the 2002 Elections

Although the local elections in 2001, like those in 1962 and 1985, were organised on a non-party basis, Musharraf was obliged to bring parties into the organisation of the 2002 elections. As Ayub Khan had done, he thus founded his own political party. Like him, for the umpteenth time he resuscitated the old Muslim League. He justified this decision in highly instructive terms in his memoirs when he writes, "I needed a national political party to support my agenda. I had the option of forming a new party, but I decided—and the emotion of a soldier had a lot to do with this—to revive the Pakistan Muslim League (PML), the party of Quaid-e-Azam Muhammad Ali Jinnah that had led us to freedom to our own country".[158] Every word matters in those backward-looking sentences that manifest the grip of a history and a political system that are not rooted in military references, however authoritarian they may be. First, the name chosen for the party harks back to Jinnah, thereby attempting ground Musharraf in a political culture that draws its legitimacy from much different sources than the army. Second, he admits that even if he is all-powerful, he cannot disregard the political arena in which parties confront "agendas": competition for power entails a minimum of pluralism.

Musharraf became all the more bogged down in Pakistani-style politics as he preferred to rely on existing forces. Instead of carrying his plan for renovation to completion by starting his own party, he counted on notables known as "politicos".[159] The contradiction is obvious: while he was trying to combat the politicians, Musharraf, like Zia before him, turned to them because he needed the backing of political figures with connections at the grassroots level.[160] Once again the key region in this case was Punjab. Zia had sought Nawaz Sharif's support, but this possibility was naturally out of the question for Musharraf. He thus struck a deal with a leader of a rival faction to Sharif—Chaudhry Shujaat Hussain—to build his own "khaki party", to use the common expression in Pakistan, the PML(Q)—the "Q" standing for Quaid-e-Azam.

[158] Ibid., p. 166.
[159] Tariq Aziz, his principal secretary, suggested this shortcut to him. See ibid., p. 166.
[160] This paradox was already at the center of Indira Gandhi's strategy when she founded Congress (R) in 1970.

The PML (Q) was founded before the 2002 election to provide President Musharraf with party backing, the same way Ayub had started his Convention Muslim League from a breakaway faction of Jinnah's Muslim League when he had to contest elections for the first time in 1962. The key leader of Ayub's party at the time was Chaudhry Zahoor Elahi, a nouveau riche from rural Punjab who had risen from a police constable during the Raj to become a powerful industrialist after Partition.[161] At the helm of a powerful, clientelistic network, Zahoor Elahi opposed Ayub Khan's Elected Bodies Disqualification Ordinance 1959, an act of resistance for which he was sentenced to six months' imprisonment by the martial law courts. But then, realising who was the real master, he joined Ayub's party and became its General Secretary in 1962. Elahi represented all Ayub was looking for to fight the conservative landlords: a non-upper caste (he was Jat) "rural progressive" who had invested in industry.

The Convention Muslim League did not survive Ayub's regime, and the Bhutto years (1971–1977) were a period that Chaudhry Elahi spent in the cold. The new prime minister, who was hostile to these "rurban" capitalists "made it clear that he regarded the Chauhrys of Gujrat [their home town] as thieves and pimps who should be treated as such".[162] Elahi was imprisoned for five years by a special tribunal. He naturally welcomed Zia's coup, and even became a friend of the Chief Justice of Punjab who sentenced Bhutto to the death penalty. They were travelling in the same car when the AZO, Bhutto's sons' militia, killed Zahoor Elahi—who was probably not the main target.

His son, Chaudhry Shujaat Hussain, succeeded him as a powerful power broker under Zia. He took part in his prime minister's government as minister of industry and held several other ministerial portfolios till 1988.

Again, the democratisation phase, from 1988 to 1999, was not a good time for the Chaudhry. Benazir had not forgotten the way he had behaved with his father and Nawaz Sharif was his main rival in Punjab, even if Hussain became a member of the PML(Nawaz) and took part in its government once, briefly. Hussain's relationship with Nawaz had become frayed when Sharif froze foreign currency accounts and took control of the Karachi Stock Exchange (to minimise the effect of anticipated sanctions after the 1998 nuclear tests).

---

161 See: http://www.gujratpakistan.com/2010/07/chaudhary-zahoor-elahi.html (Accessed on September 15, 2013).

162 Tariq Ali, *The Duel*, op. cit., p. 128.

But Musharraf took over soon after. Then Shujaat Hussain Chaudhry seceded from the PML(N) and contributed to the creation of the PML(Q) to provide Musharraf with a party machine in 2002—when the split was formalised.

The 2002 elections were held in accordance with a Legal Framework Order,[163] which in particular stipulated that only those who held a university degree or equivalent—could contest the general elections.

The PML(Q) won 118 seats with 26.3% of the valid votes. It also won the state elections in Punjab where Shujaat Hussain's first cousin, Chaudhry Pervez Elahi, became Chief Minister. But this was not enough to form a government, as 171 seats were required for a majority. If the PML(N) had hit the low-water mark (18 seats with 12.71 per cent of the votes), the PPP, which had to change names to the Pakistan People's Party Parliamentary, with 80 seats (and more votes than the PML(Q), 28.4%), showed remarkable resilience, a sign that it was probably the only party capable of surviving the physical absence of its leader. The PML(Q) then engaged in endless negotiations to form a parliamentary majority. Even if the MQM quickly threw its weight behind Musharraf, its contribution of 13 seats was not enough. Several independents and members elected from micro-parties willingly "sold" themselves, but that was still not enough. The regime finally purchased the defections of 7 elected PPPP members who gave themselves the paradoxical name of "Patriots"—and who were immediately rewarded with ministerial portfolios. The group leader, Makhdoom Faisal Saleh Hayat, from Jhang district (Punjab), was even appointed Interior Minister.

Shujaat Hussain Chaudhry was of course in the front line throughout these negotiations. But they inevitably tarnished Musharraf's image, as he was clearly no longer above the fray. All the less so since the prime minister he had chosen, Zafarullah Khan Jamali, did not withstand the accelerated wear and tear of power that the struggle among factions produced. He was replaced by Shujaat Hussain Chaudhry in June 2004. However, Chaudry, who preferred to keep only the party chairmanship, merely prepared the transition with Shaukat Aziz, who was appointed prime minister in August 2004.

Political stability was not guaranteed for all that. Musharraf had to enter a new round of negotiations to ensure passage of the constitutional amend-

---

[163] This was already the name of the constitutional framework that Yayha Khan had enacted before the 1970 elections. History repeats itself so often in Pakistan that its leaders sometimes lack imagination in naming temporary measures.

ments he felt most strongly about. But this required a two-thirds majority in the Assembly. To achieve this proportion, Musharraf appealed to the coalition of Islamic parties, the MMA, which had 59 seats. After a year of haggling, the MMA agreed to add its votes to the other support Musharraf had secured to pass the 17th Amendment, which largely amounted to unravelling the Nawaz Sharif's 13th Amendment and reverting to Zia's Eighth Amendment. The text stipulated that the president—who would now be elected by the parliament—could dissolve the Assembly and thus dismiss the prime minister, as long as the decision was ratified by the Supreme Court. The governors could do the same with the provincial assemblies under the same condition. In exchange, the MMA convinced Musharraf to renounce holding the office of president and COAS simultaneously as of 31 December 2004, date on which an article of the Constitution would come into effect, forbidding a person to hold "political office" and "office of profit" simultaneously. It was understood that Musharraf, who was confirmed as president in November 2002 by 658 votes out of 1,170 in the electoral college (made up of the Senate and the National Assembly) would give up his uniform on 31 December 2004.

But relations between Musharraf and the MMA deteriorated soon after the 17th Amendment was passed when this group refused to vote in favour of the law instituting the National Security Council. As already noted, Musharraf placed great store in the NSC, viewing it as the guarantee that the military would have a structuring influence over the public arena even when he would no longer be in charge. The opposition leader from the MMA, Fazlur Rehman (chairman of the JUI) persistently refrained from taking part in NSC meeting so as not to compromise himself by participating in a predominantly military body and refused to vote in Parliament in favour of establishing it—which did not rule out its passage since a simple majority was sufficient. Musharraf used the excuse[164] that the MMA did not keep its word on this issue not to keep his word either: he did not give up his post as COAS on 31 December 2004, to the great dismay of the political class.

Yet, politicians were not responsible for his fall. He retained a comfortable majority in Parliament and bargained effectively with the elected representatives in 2005–2006. He obtained from them a modification of the article of the Constitution regarding the incompatibility between political office and office of profit. He mollified the MMA, of which opposition

---

[164] In fact, the MMA joined forces with the au NSC. See Ayesha Siddiqa, *Military Inc. Inside Pakistan's Military Economy* op. cit., p. 107.

leader Fazlur Rehman seemed close to the government. He managed to defuse MQM anger at the treatment of A.Q. Khan, the father of Pakistan's atom bomb whom the United States held responsible for acute nuclear proliferation. Even though he let Prime Minister Shaukat Aziz handle the most delicate matters to regain a certain nobility, he had become a politician to some extent, and dealt with his peers rather effectively. Yet like some of his predecessors, Musharraf was forced to step down against his will. Simply, unlike them, he was not pushed out by politicians—with whom he had finally achieved a modus vivendi—or by street demonstrators, but by lawyers—who mobilised not only in the court but were the architects of a full-fledged protest movement.

The Lawyers' Movement

As the next chapter will discuss in detail and as already alluded to, the Pakistani judges have not always been up to their task, an admittedly delicate one. In 2007, the Chief Justice, Iftikhar Chaudhry, seemed determined to enforce the rule of law in at least one case, that of the "missing persons" of Balochistan, whereas nothing indicated he would have the courage to stand up to the government. In fact, he had sworn allegiance to Musharraf in a rather dishonourable fashion in 2000: after the Provisional Constitution Order (PCO) suspending the Constitution of 1973 was issued on 26 January 2000, the justices were required to swear allegiance to it; four Supreme Court justices refused and it was to replace one of them that Justice Chaudhury, who had pledged to uphold the PCO as Chief Justice of the High Court of Balochistan, was appointed to the Supreme Court. In 2002, he had ratified the LCO as Supreme Court member and in 2005 Musharraf had promoted him to Chief Justice.

If he then made an unexpected show of independence, it is perhaps because he was familiar with Balochistan where a growing number of activists involved to various degrees in the nationalist movement had been reported missing: born in Quetta, where his father had migrated from Punjab, he was appointed justice to the Balochistan High Court in 1990 before becoming its Chief Justice in 1999. He engaged increasingly forceful proceedings against the mistreatment of the Baloch, particularly at the hands of the army and paramilitary forces responsible for the disappearance of over one thousand individuals.[165] In December 2006, the relatives

---

[165] Tariq Ali, *The Duel*, op. cit., p. 156.

of some 105 persons reported missing for five or six years (among which some Islamists were included)[166] were prevented by police, using brutal methods, from presenting a memorandum to army General Headquarters in Rawalpindi.[167]

In 2007, Musharraf, already displeased at the Supreme Court decision regarding the sale of the Pakistan Steel Mills,[168] was disturbed by its involvement in the case of the "disappeared" and was also concerned about the trouble Chief Justice Chaudhry might cause when his presidential term came to an end that fall. He summoned him on 9 March 2007 and, in the presence of five other generals and the director of the ISI, asked him to resign for serious misconduct. Chaudhry refused. Musharraf dismissed him and submitted his case to the Supreme Judicial Council, the body in charge of dismissing the justices of Pakistan—see chapter 7. Iftikhar Chaudhry appealed the decision before the Supreme Court. Five lawyers pleaded his case: Aitzaz Ahsan, Hamid Khan, Munir A. Malik, Ali Ahmad Kurd and Tariq Mehmood. These seasoned magistrates not only pleaded Iftikhar Chaudhry's cause in court, but they also started a vast protest movement.[169]

All of these men enjoyed considerable prestige and had more or less extensive experience in politics. Aitzaz Ahsan, President of the Bar Association of the Supreme Court at the time,[170] had been elected to the Punjab assembly under the PPP label in 1988 before becoming Interior Minister under Benazir Bhutto—he had been Minister of Law and Justice

---

[166] Musharraf retorted to his critics that the people who had supposedly disappeared had joined the jihadists. M. Ziauddin, "Amnesty: Reveal details of missing persons in Pakistan", *One World South Asia*, 27 July 2008. See: http://southasia.oneworld.net/todaysheadlines/amnesty-reveal-details-of-missing-persons-in-pakistan/ (Accessed on September 15, 2013).

[167] Adil Najam, "Brutally Shameful", *All Things Pakistan*. See: http://pakistaniat.com/2006/12/28/police-shame-pakistan/

[168] In June 2006 the Supreme Court refused to approve the sale of 75% of the shares of this state-owned enterprise to a Saudi-Russian-Pakistani consortium for $362 million, which the unions considered undervalued. See Adil Najam, "President removes Chief Justice. Why?" *All Things Pakistan*, 9 March 2007. See http://pakistaniat.com/2007/03/09/pakistan-president-chief-justice-removes-dismiss-judiciary-freedom-judge-letter-naeem-bokhari-supreme-court/ (Accessed on September 15, 2013).

[169] For a chronology of this movement, see the *Daily Times*: http://www.daily-times.com.pk/default.asp?page=2008\11\03\$story_3-11-2008_pg7_40 (Accessed on September 15, 2013).

[170] See: http://www.scbap.com/Presidents.html (Accessed on September 15, 2013).

from 1993 to 1996 in the second Bhutto cabinet. A leftwing activist in his youth, Ahsan had joined the PPP in 1975. He had been elected to the provincial assembly of Punjab and had held the Information Planning & Development portfolio, but had resigned from the government following the crackdown on demonstrators protesting against the rigging of the 1977 elections. He was expelled from the PPP shortly thereafter but joined again in the framework of the Movement for the Restoration of Democracy in which he took an active part—which landed him in prison.[171]

In 2007, lawyers such as Ahsan replicated a protest movement against the dictatorship of a military leader reminiscent of the MRD. They organised a tour for Chaudhry that turned out to be a huge success. The dismissed Chief Justice gave well-attended lectures before bar associations throughout the country in spring 2007. In them he defended the rule of law and the independence of the judiciary. Lawyers were the vanguard of the movement, but they drew support from a much larger swath of the population. On the road that took him from Islamabad to Lahore on 4 May 2007, for instance, the crowd was so dense that a normally five-hour journey took the whole day. The next day he gave a speech railing the dictatorship.[172]

On 20 July, the 11 Supreme Court justices ruled unanimously that the chief justice should be reinstated. Musharraf, however, continued to take him as his favourite target as high-risk presidential elections approached. In September, the Supreme Court cleared the way, with six votes to three, for Musharraf's candidacy.[173] He was re-elected president on 6 October 2007, but one of his rivals—a retired judge, Wajihuddin Ahmed, who represented his peers in the battle—challenged Musharraf before the Supreme Court, considering that he could not hold the posts of both president and COAS at the same time. The Court announced that it would hand down its verdict on 12 November—then moved the date up to the 5th, given that Musharraf's term expired on the 15th. Fearing the Supreme Court judgment, Musharraf declared a state of emergency on 3 November 2007, ahead of the verdict.

The page-long text proclaiming the state of emergency contained a record number of preambles—six out of thirteen—against the judicial apparatus.[174]

---

[171] See: http://www.elections.com.pk/candidatedetails.php?id=1242 (Accessed on September 15, 2013).

[172] "States cannot survive under dictatorship: CJ", *Dawn*, 7 May 2007. See http://www.dawn.com/2007/05/07/top1.htm (Accessed on September 15, 2013).

[173] See: http://www.guardian.co.uk/world/2007/sep/29/pakistan.international (Accessed on September 15, 2013).

[174] See the text of the 'Proclamation of emergency' on the Associated Press of

Musharraf denounced a government of judges that prevented the executive from combating terrorism and stimulating the economy. The first thing he did, moreover, was to produce a new Provisional Constitutional Order (PCO) that suspended the Constitution and to which the judges were required to swear allegiance. Out of eighteen judges, only five of them submitted to the president, which nevertheless enabled Musharraf to appoint other judges and have his offensive validated by the Supreme Court on November 24.

The lawyers' movement was relaunched. As soon as the state of emergency was proclaimed, Chief Justice Chaudhry put together a bench of seven judges who issued an interim order against this decision.[175] The Chief Justice then appealed to the troops Musharraf had deployed not to obey illegal orders. Under house arrest—his home surrounded by armed men—Iftikhar Chaudhry continued to organise the resistance over his mobile phone. In a tone befitting a political leader, he called on the lawyers to mobilise: "The constitution has been ripped to shreds. The lawyers should convey my message to the people to rise up and restore the constitution. This is a time for sacrifices. I am under arrest now, but soon I will also join you in your struggle."[176]

In all, 80,000 lawyers took to the streets,[177] and were met with severe repression by the regime. Accounts of lawyers mistreated by the police abound,[178] confirmed by photographs that made international headlines. Not only was there a media blackout for several days, but all the leaders were imprisoned or placed under house arrest. In all, some 3,500 persons were taken out of action.[179]

But Musharraf seems to have hesitated to use strongarm tactics for an extended period.[180] On 4 November, Information Minister Tariq Azim Khan

---

Pakistan website: http://web.archive.org/web/20071105231711/http://www.app.com.pk/en/index.php?option=com_content&task=view&id=20109&Itemid=1 (Accessed on September 15, 2013).

[175] See: http://www.dailytimes.com.pk/default.asp?page=2007%5C11%5C04%5Cstory_4-11-2007_pg7_3 (Accessed on September 15, 2013).

[176] See: http://news.bbc.co.uk/2/hi/south_asia/7080433.stm (Accessed on September 15, 2013).

[177] Cited in Ali Khan, *The Lawyers' Movement in Pakistan. Law Beyond Politics*, 26/12/2007, Washburn University. See http://papers.ssrn.com/sol3/papers.cfm?abstract_id=1078727 (Accessed on September 15, 2013).

[178] See the one recounted by Tariq Ali, *The Duel*, op. cit., p. 164.

[179] "As many as 3,500 detained in Pakistan", *Daily News*, May 11, 2007.

[180] He moreover gave a speech in which he justified the state of emergency in a

announced that the elections scheduled for the year's end, might be delayed for up to a year.[181] But on 29 November, as soon as the new Supreme Court validated his re-election, President Musharraf set the date for lifting the state of emergency in mid-December and announced elections for January 2008. The day before, he had already made a significant concession: he had given up his post as COAS, handing it over to the head of the ISI, General Kayani.

This decision can only be explained by the mounting pressure on the president-general. Campaigns by the lawyers and the intelligentsia—particularly in the media—had probably convinced the United States and perhaps even the army that it was risky to continue to support Musharraf. That he gave up his uniform was also one of the conditions Benazir Bhutto had set to come to the President-General's aid.

Musharraf and Benazir Bhutto: Collusive Transactions

Subject to increasing pressure from the streets, Musharraf was in need of new sources of support. They could only come from the political sphere. He had already used the services of a party, the PML(Q), but it was worn down by the test of power like the president was. Musharraf thus resigned himself to opening up a channel of communication with Benazir Bhutto.[182] The decision was made very much under the benevolent pressure of George W. Bush (through the intercession of John Negroponte) who had certainly always shown great confidence in Pakistan's head of state in whom he had already invested heavily, but who had to draw the consequences of his declining popularity and who could not remain impervious to Benazir Bhutto's promises. Indeed, currying favour with the United States authorities in hopes that Washington would help her return to power, Benazir had apparently promised to help the Americans in their fight against Al Qaeda and nuclear proliferation from Pakistan. Benazir, who for the Americans represented a more progressive polity, could not help them any less than Musharraf, whom the Bush administration was suspecting of doubletalk regarding his fight against the Islamists. For the Americans, a Musharraf/ Benazir Bhutto ticket with one in the role of president and the other as

state of terrible mental confusion. See Mohammad Hanif's comments in Tariq Ali, *The Duel*, op. cit., p. 166.

[181] See: http://web.archive.org/web/20071106094745/http://www.cnn.com/2007/WORLD/asiapcf/11/04/pakistan/index.html (Accessed on September 15, 2013).

[182] Regarding these negotiations, see Tariq Ali, *The Duel*, op. cit., p. 159 ff.

356

prime minister had a number of advantages—which was also true for those concerned: Musharraf would slip out of the stranglehold that the citizenry and the judiciary held him in; Bhutto would come to power once again.

Benazir Bhutto and Musharraf had their first meeting on 27 July 2007 in the United Arab Emirates, along with leading Arab figures, foreign diplomats and the chief of the ISI, General Kayani.[183] Discussions then stretched out over several months. The first deal Benazir and Musharraf made involved a dual concession. On one hand, Musharraf gave up his uniform, because Benazir could not agree to serve as prime minister under a general. On the other hand, Musharraf revoked the cases that had forced Benazir into exile and landed her husband in prison. This was accomplished via a National Reconciliation Ordinance, which amounted to eluding justice[184] for "any person including an absconding accused who is found to be falsely involved for political reasons or through political victimization in any case initiated between 1st day of January, 1986 to 12th day of October, 1999", in other words between the two phases of purely military regime in Pakistan. The text of this ordinance owed its name to its stated objective of "promoting national reconciliation, fostering mutual trust and confidence amongst holders of public office and removing the vestiges of political vendetta and victimisation, and to make the election process more transparent". Prime Minister Shaukat Aziz even tried to explain that this would help reduce corruption![185]

Musharraf proclaimed this ordinance on 5 October so that Benazir could return as soon as he was re-elected the next day. He was re-elected as planned, but the Supreme Court suspended the NRO on 12 October. This is another reason why Musharraf declared a state of emergency, for it enabled a new Supreme Court, "rid" of Chief Justice Chaudhry, to ratify the NRO (albeit not until 27 February 2008). Benazir nevertheless started on her journey home. She wanted to return before Nawaz Sharif, who also benefitted from the NRO. In September, the Sharif brothers were not allowed to leave their plane on arriving in Pakistan. But on their return to Saudi Arabia, they convinced the royal family to plead their case with Musharraf. Not to be outdone, Benazir landed in Karachi on 27 October, but the parade

[183] Adil Najam, "ATP Poll Redeaux: Benazir-Musharraf deal", *All Things Pakistan*, 27 July 2007, http://pakistaniat.com/2007/07/27/pakistan-musharraf-ppp-benazir-meeting-abu-dhabi-dubai-deal/ (Accessed on September 15, 2013).

[184] "NRO to end politics of revenge: PM", *Dawn*, 10 Oct. See: http://archives.dawn.com/2007/10/10/nat3.htm (Accessed on September 15, 2013).

[185] See their website: http://www.movementforruleoflaw.com/ (Accessed on September 15, 2013).

that was supposed to lead her to Jinnah's tomb for her homecoming speech was attacked, killing 130. She nevertheless pursued her campaign for the upcoming elections, all the more since Nawaz Sharif had been authorised to return to Pakistan and had started his own campaign on arrival on 25 November.

Even if the assassination of Benazir Bhutto one month later on 27 December derailed Musharraf's plans, it would appear that he was seeking a compromise with the PPP that would have enabled him to continue his presidential career. But after Benazir Bhutto's death, the PPP clinched a deal, not with Musharraf, but with the PML(N), which the party now led by Zardari—who did not have the same quarrel with Nawaz Sharif as Benazir did—chose as partner to form a majority. Although Musharraf, after congratulating himself on bringing Pakistan into "an era of democracy" attempted to work with the new cabinet led by Yousaf Raza Gilani (PPP), the parliamentary coalition refused to compromise itself with him, despite obvious divergences between the PPP (which feared Iftikhar Chaudhry more than Musharraf, as noted) and Nawaz Sharif's PML(N) that wanted to make the president pay for the coup in 1999. On 8 August, after months of negotiations, the PPP and the PML(N) reached an agreement to undertake impeachment proceedings against Musharraf. He resigned ten days later and fled to London. He thus did the same as many others, from Mirza to Nawaz Sharif and Benazir Bhutto; but it was the first time that a former army chief had taken such a route.

* * *

Throughout Pakistan's political history, civil and military regimes have alternated with almost metronomic precision. The same model is reproduced with each phase, as can be seen in the choreography of coups d'état since Ayub Khan and of which five features have been identified above: (1) each time, the army takes control peacefully, hands power over to its chief—wherefore the notion of consensual coup d'état—and replaces the "politicians" presented as harmful to the nation; (2) with the more or less clear approval (cf. next chapter) of the judicial apparatus—thereby reinforcing the impression of a consensus, a notion that does not exclude authoritarianism, even if variants appear here and there. The Zia years thus contrasted with the Ayub Khan/Yayha Khan era in their harshness and the Islamisation policy for which they were the framework. But Musharraf revamped the initial "model". Furthermore, the abiding features of these variants carry greater importance than differences in degree; (3) each episode of dictatorship results in the violent crushing of political, union and ethno-nationalist leaders (cf. the Baloch who "disappeared" under Musharraf), more or less strict control of the media; (4) greater rapprochement with the United States; (5) militarization of the state apparatus ("former" officers appointed to posts usually reserved for civilians) and the development of what Ayesha Siddiqa calls Milbus, an ongoing process that reached its height under Musharraf, placing the army at the head of an empire.

Not only do the phases of state militarization always begin (and more or less unfold) the same way, but they also generally end in the same fashion. After a number of years, civilians mobilise and manifest their desire for regime change. At the vanguard of such protest movements are students and trade union activists (as in the late 1960s, with Z. A. Bhutto's rise to power and his political appropriation of the unrest), bona fide political parties (such as the MRD of 1981–3) or legal professionals (as in the anti-Musharraf movement of 2007). But agitation itself never explains the fall of dictators. Each time external events also play a role, such as the war of 1965 in the case of Ayub Khan, the loss of East Bengal under Yayha Khan, the plane crash in the case of Zia and the intensity of anti-American sentiment following the second war in Afghanistan which contributed to bringing an end to Musharraf's rule, as will be seen further on—not to mention the direct impact of American policy after 2007. when Washington became suspicious of Musharraf.

But even if public opinion and street protest alone cannot bring down dictatorships, they largely explain their trajectory and especially the way in which all the military autocrats have been induced to make concessions each time. All have had to seek new sources of legitimacy in constitutive elements of the democratic process: the people, a façade of constitutional legality and political parties. None have been able to dispense with a referendum—however rigged. Beyond that, all have given the country a constitutional framework, leading them if not systematically to give up their uniform, at least to don the title and sometimes the attire of president. All have carried the process of "civilianization" to the point of appointing a prime minister and legalising political parties.

The trajectory of Pakistani military regimes is without a doubt the sign of the resilience of a democratic culture based as much on its attachment to the law (the liberal/legal aspect of democracy) as on the strong foothold of political parties—especially the PPP (the pluralist aspect of democracy). Consequently, politics in Pakistan moves within much better defined limits than what its chronic instability might suggest: the ground could not be better mapped out—and even its tempo seems regulated: just about every ten years, power changes hands between politicians and the military and vice-versa.

That said, the opposition between democratic politicians and dictatorial military officers should be placed in perspective.

Not all military chiefs have been inclined to exercise absolute power; to wit, not all COAS have systematically tried their hand at a coup d'état. In 1991, Asif Nawaz for instance brought in a brief but interesting series of COAS who had little inclination to conquer power. When he became COAS, Nawaz made his troops read a communiqué written in both English and Urdu which in particular stated:

as the democratic process has now taken hold, I would like it to be clearly under-stood that the Army must have nothing to do with politics. Let the elected repre-sentatives do their job, while we concentrate on acquiring ever greater professional excellence.[186]

According to his brother, Shuja Nawaz, Asif, in the name of the separa-tion of powers, even ignored a chief justice who had asked for his opinion before handing down a judgment.[187] Shortly thereafter, he punished sol-diers responsible for blunders in Karachi. Their actions were usually cov-ered by their hierarchy, giving them a sense of impunity. The sanctions forced the respect of the left-leaning weekly *Friday Times*, which wrote:

Gen. Asif Nawaz, Chief of Army Staff, has been better than his word. For the first time in living memory, army heads have rolled for an anti-public act—a Major General, two Brigadiers and one Colonel were sent packing and a major will most certainly face a court martial for the Tando Bahawal tragedy. The COAS has now moved into second gear and demonstrated his resolve to be ruthlessly fair.[188]

Asif Nawaz died of a heart attack that his brother, in light of post mortem tests, attributed to poisoning.[189] But his successor, Gen. Abdul Waheed, again selected by President Ghulam Ishaq Khan, also turned out to honour state institutions, so much so that when he reached retirement age, Benazir Bhutto—prime minister at the time—although she hadn't chosen him, would have liked him to stay. She told Shuja Nawaz:

I wanted Waheed to continue. (...) I found him to be a very shrewd person and a brilliant strategician or tactician (...) And he was (a) totally non-interfering Army

[186] Cited in Suja Nawaz, *Crossed Swords*, op. cit., p. 444.

[187] Ibid., p. 451

[188] "Put Pakistan first", *The Friday Times*, 25 June–1 July 1992, p. 1.

[189] See the post mortem in Suja Nawaz, *Crossed Swords*, op. cit., p. 607.

Chief. Many attempts were made to politicize him. All sorts of malicious, poisonous letters were circulated to provoke him into acting against the political government. But he did not do so. He was an honourable man. He spoke bluntly (...) So I wanted him to stay on for a year. Unfortunately, he did not want to continue".[190]

Clearly, not all COAS are power-hungry. This remark is illustrated in a very similar fashion by Waseed's successor, Jahangir Karamat. With Karamat as head of the army and Sharif as head of government, Pakistan underwent a real swap of roles traditionally played by the COAS and the prime minister. After having asserted his power by pushing through the Thirteenth Amendment, which cancelled the Eighth and deprived the president of the power of dismissing the government and dissolving Parliament, Sharif tackled the last remaining civilian opposition force that he had any reason to fear, the judiciary. He managed to force Chief Justice Sajjad Ali Shah to resign for appointing figures to the Supreme Court who were not to the prime minister's taste. At the time, a civilian member of the PPP, President Leghari, and a military official, Karamat, joined forces to resist the country's new strong man. In vain. The president resigned himself to relinquishing his post, not without having asked the military chief not to do the same, as he had intended to, because it would have left Sharif alone on the dance floor, which he said was akin to giving "a razor to a monkey".[191]

Aware of this risk, Karamat eventually envisaged a constitutional role for the army that would serve as a safeguard. Before the Naval Staff College in Lahore on 6 October 1998, he gave a speech calling for the formation of a National Security Council—which Musharraf took up later—to stabilise the Pakistani political system—a plan that held a number of dangers for democracy but which, given Sharif's lack of popularity, received the assent of several opposition parties and much of the media. Sharif took offense and forced Karamat to resign. The general retired two months early.

The careers of COAS Nawaz, Waseed and Karamat blur the image of more or less enlightened despotism that is traditionally associated with the person at the helm of the Pakistani army: those three men honoured state institutions—even while power was in civilian hands. Not only are military officers not all potential despots, but civilians are far from all being democrats.

As it has become clear, Jinnah from the start codified a political culture that has been described as viceregal because it gave priority to security—and hence to state authority—over political participation (which in par-

---

[190] Cited in ibid., p. 481.
[191] Cited in ibid., p. 489.

ticular would have implied greater decentralisation). Z.A. Bhutto, who like the founding father favoured a presidential system, showed little concern for the freedoms of his fellow citizens and did not hesitate to rig the 1977 elections. As for Nawaz Sharif, the inventor of another form of parliamentary dictatorship, he did not even hesitate to get mixed up with the military—as will be seen further on. The political culture of Benazir Bhutto, presented as the most liberal of all, especially in the United States, has just as many flaws as her predecessors. One of her close associates, Tariq Ali, summed up the situation that prevailed with the formation of her second cabinet in 1993:

> The high command of the Pakistan Peoples Party now became a machine for making money, but without any trickle-down mechanism. This period marked the complete degeneration of the party. The single tradition that had been passed down since the foundation of the party was autocratic centralism. The leader's word was final. Like her father in this respect, Benazir never understood that debate is not only the best medium of confutation, of turning the ideological tables. It is also the most effective form of persuasion.[192]

Beyond the personalisation of power common to all political parties in Pakistan (including the MQM(A))[193]—which has eventually led to the dynastic syndrome pointed out above—many parties have ended up making compromises with the military. The PML(Q) is the very prototype of these "khaki parties" which cropped up as soon as Ayub Khan founded his party—which the father of the current PML(Q) president moreover already led. But as of the 1980s, Nawaz Sharif placed his sense of political manoeuvring in the service of Zia, and then played into the hands of the ISI to undermine Benazir Bhutto. She returned the compliment to the very end, as attests the "deal" made in 2007 at the expense of the PML(N). As Ayesha Siddiqa writes, "The very fact that the prominent politicians continue to use the military as a political balancer of power, and refuse to negotiate their power or power interests through democratic means, allows the armed forces to play a dominant role".[194] The strategy employed by Nawaz Sharif and Benazir Bhutto during the 1990s shows that civilians gradually ceased to be a rampart against the military, and collusive transactions became the unwritten rule of politics.

---

[192] Tariq Ali, *The Duel*, op. cit., p. 173.

[193] Despite the fact that Altaf Hussain remains in England, he is fully in command of the MQM(A).

[194] Ayesha Siddiqa, *Military Inc. Inside Pakistan's Military Economy*, op. cit., p. 103.

This convergence is also due to the military's decision to "civilianize". Ayub Khan was the first to feel the need for party backing, and Musharraf later sought the same, both of them because of pressure from the streets and the resilience of the constitutional imperative. As soon as they were at the head of a political movement, these military chiefs felt that they had no other choice than to take part in the haggling involved in everyday Pakistani politics. Musharraf agreed to play the game—as much as he was drawn into it, as shown by his decision to make a comeback, having decided to try his chances in the 2013 general elections. As Ilhan Niaz points out:

Some of Pakistan's military officers can be legitimately described as politicians manqué who prefer the 'cut-and-thrust of political manoeuvring to that of the battlefield' and rise by practising the art of the courtier'[195] (...) What is fascinating about Pakistan's praetorians is their timidity. All of them came to power through bloodless coups. All of them sought an accommodation with political elements soon after coming to power, though in Yayha's case the attemps failed miserably. Except for Zia, who perished in an air crash in suspicious circumstances at a time when he was transparently fumbling and losing ground, all have been bloodlessly forced from power by a combination of civil disobedience and loss of support within the military. No military ruler has carried out purges of officer corps to eliminate perceived political rivals and install political allies. All have worked through the regular system of promotions, transfers, and postings, and sought to influence appointments through the existing procedures, rules and mechanisms for inputs though quite naturally such evaluations are partially subjective. While politics is a privilege reserved for a minuscule praetorian elite, the power exercised has secured for a large number of officers and men economic wealth and social mobility and consolidated a neo-*mansabdari* system in Pakistan.[196]

In the end, is there really such structural antagonism between civilians and the military?

A structural tension, latent or explicit, stems from the competition between these two poles of power. When the army is in office, it subjects the state to its domination and when the civilians are in power, the army insists on retaining prerogatives incompatible with a democratic regime. This balance of power has been reconfirmed by recent developments. Zardari was not able to tame Kayani—in fact he was obliged to grant him an extraordinary extension.

---

[195] Brian Coughley, *A History of the Pakistani Army: Wars and Insurrections*, Karachi, Oxford University Press, 2006, p. 138.

[196] Ilhan Niaz, *The Culture of Power and Governance of Pakistan*, op. cit., pp. 151–153.

However, this structural tension has been mitigated by an equally structural convergence. So much so that many observers have come to consider
political and army leaders as belonging to the same world. Ayesha Siddiqa
thus speaks of an "elite partnership".[197] Steven Cohen, like Mushahid
Hussain, refers to the domination of an "establishment".[198] Hussain, himself
a member of it—he was information minister under Nawaz Sharif before
joining the PML(Q) and becoming its secretary general—describes this
establishment as made up of only some 500 people belonging to various
circles, as much civilian and military.[199]

The border between these two worlds has been particularly porous on the
right side of the political chessboard, Muslim League leaders having gone
over to Zia (cf. Nawaz Sharif) and later Musharraf (cf. the PML(Q)).[200] But
this process ended up affecting PPP leaders as well. Aftab Ahmed Sherpao,
an officer whom Z.A. Bhutto had persuaded to leave the army to join him
and who became chief minister of the NWFP in 1988, after Benazir Bhutto
rebuffed him, created his own party faction and then joined Musharraf's
cabinet as Minister of the Interior from 2004 to 2007. Similarly, General
Naseerullah Babar, who had trained the first Afghan Islamist leaders as
Commandant of the Frontier Corps in the early 1970s, resigned from the
army in 1975 to join the PPP. He immediately became governor of the
NWFP and then Minister of Interior in Benazir Bhutto's second government. Another General, Air Marshal Mohammad Asghar Khan, resigned
from the army to create his own party. His son, Omar Asghar Khan, was
appointed minister in Musharraf's government in 1999.

Some generals' sons have also gone into politics after the death of their
fathers. The son of Ayub Khan, Gohar Ayub Khan, joined the PNA in 1977
and then the PML(N)—he was Minister of Foreign Affairs in Nawaz Sharif's
second government. Ijaz ul Haq, the son of Zia ul Haq, and Humayun
Akhtar Khan, the son of General Akhtar Abdur Rahman, joined the

---

[197] Ayesha Siddiqa, *Military Inc. Inside Pakistan's Military Economy*, op. cit., p. 103.
[198] Stephen P. Cohen, *The Idea of Pakistan*, op. cit., p. 69. This notion of "establishment" fits well in the political economy of Hamza Alavi who argued that the
military-bureaucratic "oligarchy" was connected to the landlord and the industrialists of Pakistan (Hamza Alavi, "The State in Post-Colonial Society: Pakistan
and Bangladesh", *New Left Review*, no. 74 (1972), pp. 59–81).
[199] See his articles in *The Nation*, 3 November 1996 and 18 June 2002.
[200] Even a former DG ISI, Javed Ashraf Qazi, who was the head of the intelligence
agency in 1993–5, became a civilian senator of the PML (Q)—as well as Minister
of Education under Musharraf...

PML(Q). These three persons show that the dynastic syndrome has not affected civilians alone. Some families are also part of both worlds, civilian and military, in the same generation. For instance, Chaudhry Nisar Ali Khan (who was a minister under Zia and under Nawaz Sharif) had a brother in the upper ranks of the army, Maj. Gen. Iftikhar Ali Khan. He was Chief of General Staff in 1996–7.

Other figures epitomize the convergence of civilian and military circles. The most significant is probably Syed Sharifuddin Pirzada, a lawyer who was Jinnah's personal secretary before going on to work with all the perpetrators of coups d'état from Ayub Khan to Zia and Musharraf, in particular to counsel them in legal (sic!) matters. But S.S. Pirzada also performed services for Z.A. Bhutto and Nawaz Sharif. Commenting upon the help Pirzada gave to Zia to draft the Laws (Continuance in Force) Order of 1977, Syed Sami Ahmad writes:

Mr. Sharifuddin Pirzada had strongly assailed Kelsen's doctrine in the case of Asma Jilani [see below]. At that time when he did it, usurpers were not in the field. They were no longer monarchs [...] When he came under the umbrella of Martial Law and became one of the beneficiaries [of the new regime], he was a different person as a lawyer.[201]

In 2013, Pirzada became part of the team of advocates defending Musharraf before the court. One of the arguments he made to counter the accusation of treason due to the 2007 declaration of emergency was that the 1973 Constitution was "a mere act of parliament" and that, therefore, "its violation technicaly does not amount to high treason".[202]

Pirzada is the quintessential establishment man, with his share of corruption—moreover admitted, as he confesses his wrongs to journalist Ardeshir Cowasjee in these words: "Accept me as I am with warts, blemishes, briefcases and all. If it were not for all the weak and corrupt governments of Pakistan, I would not be where I am today."[203] Pirzada examplifies a type of personality that became pervasive in the course of Pakistan's history, that

[201] Syed Sami Ahmad, *The Judiciary of Pakistan and Its Role in Political Crises*, op. cit., p. 85

[202] Azam Khan, "Analysis: for Musharraf, 1973 document wasn't the Constitution", *The Express Tribune*, 12 January 2014 (http://tribune.com.pk/story/658067/analysis-for-musharraf-1973-document-wasnt-the-constitution/).

[203] Jane Perlez, "On Retainer in Pakistan, to Ease Military Rulers' Path", *The New York Times*, 7 December 2007, (http://www.nytimes.com/2007/12/15/world/asia/15pirzada.html?pagewanted=all).

of technicians (in this case, of law) prepared to serve any regime—civilian or military—provided the job gives access to the top echelons of the state. Sartaj Aziz is another case in point. A professor of economics, he had joined the Planning Commission under Z.A. Bhutto before becoming one of Zia's ministers in 1984. He then joined Nawaz Sharif's second government in 1997 where he held the portfolio of foreign affairs. In 2013 he became his advisor on foreign affairs.

A few establishment figures are even at the intersection of the military, the PPP and rightist parties (including the PML (N) and the PML (Q)). Zahid Hamid, a lawyer by training, is a case in point. The son of Retd. Brigadier Hamid Khan who had been elected a PPP MNA in 1977 (and again—on a non-party basis—in 1985) and the son-in-law of Nawab Sadiq Hussain Qureshi (a close associate of Z.A. Bhutto who had been governor of Punjab and then Chief Minister of Punjab between 1973 and 1977), he unsuccessfully contested the 1997 general elections on a PPPP ticket in 1997 from Narowal district (Punjab). The same year, his brother, who was one of the PML(N) leaders, became governor of Punjab. In 2002, Zahid Hamid joined the PML(Q) and became a key minister in the Musharraf regime—he was holding the portfolio of Law in 2007 when the state of emergency was declared. In 2008 he shifted to the PML(N) and was elected again and appointed Law minister again in the first government of Nawaz Sharif. He changed his portfolio when the Prime Minister decided to press on with Musharraf's trial for treason because of the 2007 declaration of emergency—and eventually offered to resign when the judges made him a co-accused in this case in November 2014.[204]

At the lower level, the convergence of civilian and military circles in politics is evident in the profiles of the provincial governors, a very powerful category. Although under Musharraf they were logically all recruited among active or retired officers, this was already the case for a number of them under Benazir Bhutto and Nawaz Sharif in the 1988 to 1999 period. Then, it was the case of all those who followed in succession at the head of the NWFP, of three of them appointed in Punjab, three of them appointed in Balochistan and one of them appointed in Sindh. When Z.A. Bhutto was prime minister, only one governor came from the army.[205]

---

[204] Khawar Ghumman, "Zahid Hamid the indispensable?", *Dawn*, 22 November 2014 (http://www.dawn.com/news/1146103).

[205] Amélie Blom, "'Qui tient le bâton, a le buffle'", op. cit., p. 16.

What binds together the Pakistani establishment is a sense of class[206]—of caste even. In this highly inegalitarian society, social hierarchy has become less and less a matter of differences in status and increasingly one of differences in financial means. For a long time, this characteristic was only true of the political personnel dominated by rural "feudals" (such as the Bhutto family), and later urbans (such as the Sharif family). But since the 1980s, the quest for personal enrichment has spread to the army, which as we have seen has become a lucrative enterprise that is not exempt from corruption.[207] Even if Pakistan has no real "democrats" or real "autocrats" that have survived over time like the Burmese junta, it has a wealth of authoritarian "plutocrats" that can be labelled an establishment. This is an old component of the Pakistani syndrome with its elitist character that Iqbal had already mentioned to Jinnah in one of his letters, as mentioned above.

This class element of the Pakistani syndrome finds it clearest expression in the absence of social reform. After more or less timid attempts by Ayub Khan and Bhutto to implement land reform, no ruler has shown any real interest in tackling social inequalities—and they have increased steadily. The Gini coefficient rose from 0.345 in 1971–2 to 0.407 in 1990–1.[208] The most flagrant indication of the class element is the lack of fair taxation—and redistribution. Pakistan is one of the countries with the lowest tax burden in the world. The tax-to-GDP ratio rose from 9 per cent in 1964–5 to 14 per cent in 1990. This low figure is due to fraud (one specialist estimates that less than 1 per cent of the people who are supposed to pay income tax do so),[209] as well as the rise in tax exemptions on profits, particularly on agricultural products. Pakistan had to wait for the non-elected interim government of Moeen Qureshi, in 1993, to see the introduction of

---

[206] Probably marriage ties as well. Beyond the dynastic dimension mentioned earlier, it would also be worth studying the inter-marriages that in their own way structure the political class—likely including the military.

[207] Amélie Blom thus indicates that bribes associated with arms contracts were an estimated $164 million dollars in 2000, that in 2001 the Public Accounts Committee published the amount of funds misappropriated from the defence budget in the previous fiscal year: 1.3 billion rupees and that the National Accountability Bureau (NAB) stated in 2004 that it had recovered more money from corrupt military officials than from politicians (A. Blom, "'Qui tient le bâton tient le buffle'", op. cit., p. 48).

[208] Ishrat Husain, *Pakistan: the Economy of an Elitist State*, Karachi, Oxford University Press, 2000, p. 233.

[209] Hafiz Pasha, "Political economy of tax reforms: the Pakistan experience", *Pakistan Journal of Applied Economics*, 10 (1–2), 1994, p. 50.

some agricultural income tax and wealth tax. Then, Musharraf vaguely tackled the problem, but he only managed to raise the income tax-to-GDP ratio to 3.6 per cent in 2002/03, while it is over 5 per cent on average in other developing countries.[210] The Musharraf years were not very conclusive on that front: the percentage of income tax payers rose from 0.7 per cent in 2000 to 0.9 per cent in 2006. Only one million people paid income tax, out of which 475,000 were salaried employees (mostly civil servants) who could not escape this tax.[211] His successors did not achieve anything more substantial. In 2013, the income tax-to-GDP ratio had fallen to 3.5 per cent with taxpayers numbering about 1.5 million people.[212]

Elected representatives were among those who did not pay taxes. In 2014, one day after the deadline for submitting statements of their assets, about 400 legislators (from the parliament and from provincial assemblies) had not done so[213]—most probably in order to avoid paying taxes.

In 2013, the Nawaz Sharif government passed a budget that was supposed to tax the rich more, even though wage-earners remained the easier target and "the tax liabilities of the lowest income group having annual income of Rs 400,000 to Rs 500,000 [was] increased by 22%".[214] But the rich continued not to pay taxes (in a country of almost 200 million people, there were only 711,940 income tax filers in 2013 and about 770,000 in 2014).[215] The 700,000 households that the National Database and Registration Authority (NADRA) had identified as rich (and which are not made up of wage-earners) have continued to escape tax hikes (among other reasons because land revenue is not taxed).[216]

---

[210] Hafiz Pasha and M. Asif Iqbal, "Taxation reforms in Pakistan", *Pakistan Journal of Applied Economics*, 11 (1–2), 1995, p. 129.

[211] Ilhan Niaz, *The Culture of Power and Governance of Pakistan*, op. cit., pp. 219.

[212] Sakib Sherani, "Fixing the Tax System", *Dawn*, 14 June 2013. See http://beta. dawn.com/news/1018130/fixing-the-tax-system (Accessed on September 15, 2013).

[213] Iftikhar A. Khan, "ECP wants power to suspend legislators over assets", *Dawn*, 2 Oct. 2014 (http://www.dawn.com/news/1135625/ecp-wants-power-to-suspend-legislators-over-assets).

[214] Shahbaz Rana, "New Tax Measures", *The Express Tribune*, 13 June 2013 (http://tribune.com.pk/story/563251/new-tax).

[215] Shahbaz Rana, "Hunt for rich tax evaders", *The Express Tribune*, 29 August 2013 (http://tribune.com.pk/story/596813/hunt-for-rich-tax-evaders-fbr-to-zero-in-on-residents-of-upscale-areas/) and "Unsatisfactory: Despite extensions, tax collection remains dismal", *The Express Tribune*, 9 December 2014 (http://tribune.com.pk/story/803809/unsatisfactory-despite-extensions-tax-collection-remains-dismal/?print=true).

[216] "Government Misses Chance to Slap Wealth Tax", *The Express Tribune*, 15 June

In addition, the government gave tax exemptions—one-third of them in income tax—which represented almost Rs 240 billion. As a result, the tax-to-GDP ratio has declined to 8.9 per cent in 2013.[217] It further diminished to 7 per cent in 2014[218] partly due to the doubling of tax exemptions—Rs 477.1 bn (including Rs 96.2 bn on income tax)—which shows that the government continued with its pro-rich policy.[219] Finance Minister Ishaq Dar declared during the budget session: "We believe that the engine of growth has to be the private entrepreneurship and all mesures are taken to promote it across the board".[220] In this vein, the corporate tax rate was reduced from 33 to 20 per cent.[221] Tax revenue therefore does not enable the government to offer basic public services. The education budget decreased by 11 per cent in 2014, in real terms at Rs 86.4 billion,[222] while military expenditure—including military pensions—reached Rs 863 billion (ten times more).[223] Nor does the fiscal structure allow the kind of redistribution that might foster a sense of social justice. In 2013, 80 per cent of the state's revenues were generated through indirect taxation and the richest 10 per cent of the Pakistanis ended up paying only 5.9 per cent in indirect taxes according to Dr Kaiser Bengali, the former Managing Director of the Social Policy and Development Centre.[224] And this at a time when, according to the Oxford Poverty and Human Development Initiative, 64 per cent of the Pakistani rural population are landless and 48 per cent of the urban popula-

2013. See http://tribune.com.pk/story/563266/government-misses-chance-to-slap-wealth-tax/ (Accessed on September 15, 2013).

[217] Shahbaz Rana, "Breaks for the elite: Tax exemptions cost exchequer Rs 239.5 bn in FY13", *The Express Tribune*, 12 June 2013.

[218] Zeenia Shaukat, "What's in it for the poor?", *Newsline*, July 2014, p. 63. Another source gives a higher tax-to-GDP ratio at 10.5% (Khaleeq Kiani, "Tax-to-GDP ratio down", *Dawn*, 17 May 2005 (http://www.dawn.com/news/1106847).

[219] Mubarak Zeb Khan, "Economic survey 2013–14: tax exemptions double to Rs 477 bn", *Dawn*, 3 June 2014 (http://www.dawn.com/news/1110220).

[220] Cited in Zeenia Shaukat, "What's in it for the poor?", op. cit., p. 61.

[221] Khaleeq Kiani, "Relief for the rich, peanuts for the poor", *Dawn*, 4 June 2014 (http://www.dawn.com/news/1110429).

[222] Ikram Junaidi, "Education budget decreased despite promises", *Dawn*, 5 June 2014 (http://www.dawn.com/news/1110706).

[223] Khaleeq Kiani, "Relief for the rich, peanuts for the poor", op. cit..

[224] Kaiser Bengali, "Descent into chaos; evolution from an economic state to a security state", *The Express Tribune*, 15 Sept. 2013 (http://tribune.com.pk/story/604634/descent-into-chaos-evolution-from-an-economic-state-to-a-security-state/).

tion live in slums. Applying a Multidimensional Poverty Index, the Oxford Department of International Development showed that in 2012–13, 44.2 per cent of the Pakistanis were poor and 20 per cent could even be considered as "destitute".[225] In contrast, the "string of wedding halls in Lahore Cantonment's Garrison Club are lit up even when the city's lights are down and are often referred to as the Punjab's Las Vegas strip".[226]

The explanation for social inequalities that Ishrat Husain provided more than ten years ago remains, valid: "Given the political clout of both the urban industrialists and the feudal landlords, there is little possibility of targeting and taxing their income directly".[227] Politicians themselves were guilty. Some of the tax evaders were politicians who had sent their money abroad. In June 2014, the Minister for Planning and Development, Ahsan Iqbal declared that he had started negotiations with Switzerland "to bring back around $200 billion stashed by Pakistani politicians in Swiss bank accounts".[228] Around the same time, the Lahore High Court issued a notice to 64 politicians— including the Sharif brothers, Imran Khan, Chaudhry Shujaat Husain and Asif Ali Zardari—"on a petition seeking directions for the politicians to bring their foreign assets back to Pakistan".[229] Ironically, in late 2014 the Sharif government prepared bills which were intended to make tax evasion more difficult—in order to meet IMF conditions and continue to receive the $6.6. bn loan that Pakistan has been granted in 2013.[230]

The pervasiveness of social inequalities is partly due to the decline of the left. After it was repressed by Ayub Khan, it was betrayed by Z.A. Bhutto

---

[225] "OPHI Country Briefing January 2015: Pakistan", http://www.google.com/url?sa=t&rct=j&q=&esrc=s&source=web&cd=5&ved=0CEQQFjAE&url=http%3A%2F%2Fwww.dataforall.org%2Fdashboard%2Fophi%2Findex.php%2Fmpi%2Fdownload_brief_files%2FPAK&ei=LIWiVKChA-Pd7ga63oHwDg&usg=AFQjCNEIiAgbolFw1ilu81xL0NLVVPBu9A&bvm=bv.82001339,d.ZGU

[226] Shahid Javed Burki, "Inequality and extremism", *The Express Tribune*, 23 February 2014 (http://tribune.com.pk/story/675215/inequality-and-extremism/).

[227] Ishrat Husain, *Pakistan: the Economy of an Elitist State*, op. cit., p. 380. Husain also emphasizes the role of corruption of tax collectors in this state of affairs (ibid., p. 381).

[228] Shahbaz Rana, "$200 b stashed abroad", *The Express Tribune*, 10 June 2014 (http://tribune.com.pk/story/719722/200b-stashed-abroad-talks-with-swiss-authorities-will-begin-in-august-says-ahsan/).

[229] "64 politicians issued notices over foreign assets", *Dawn*, 11 May 2014 (http://www.dawn.com/news/1105340).

[230] Shahbaz Rana, "Tax evasion: Govt moves to make laws stricter", *The Express Tribune*, 26 December 2014 (http://tribune.com.pk/story/812332/tax-evasion-govt-moves-to-make-laws-stricter/?print=true).

and the triumph of populism sealed the fate of socialist ideas. Populists, indeed, claim to work for the people in order to better help the elite (their group) to retain power.

The convergence of political and military elites to form the Pakistani establishment partly explains the rise in power of the judiciary as the only alternative. In fact, in the movement against Musharraf in 2007, lawyers protested as much against the army's authoritarianism as its growing taste for bourgeois comforts. In 2007, the president of the Supreme Court Bar Association, Muneer Malik, thus wrote:

The Pakistan Army was once renowned for its discipline, its fighting skills and its unflinching fortitude in the face of adversity. It is now notorious for its commercial avarice and its skill in making political deals. When its generals spend their time establishing real estate projects, farming, constructing roads, managing utilities, manufacturing cornflakes, running aviation companies, operating banks, administrating educational institutes and playing politics, it is unsurprising that both national and international observers question their ability and willingness to fight and win the war against militants in Waziristan.[231]

In 2007, lawyers assumed the role of the quintessential opposition force, coming out against both civilians and the military in the name of the rule of law. But the extent to which this new actor can alter Pakistan's political and social situation remains to be seen.

---

[231] Muneer A. Malik, "The Rocky Road Ahead", *Dawn*, 7 August 2007, reprinted in Muneer A. Malik, *The Pakistan's Lawyers' Movement. An Unfinished Agenda*, Karachi/Lahore/Islamabad, Pakistan Law House, 2008, p. 312.

7

THE JUDICIARY, THE MEDIA AND NGOs

IN SEARCH OF OPPOSITION FORCES

The convergence of political and military circles, to the point of forming an establishment sharing numerous legal and illegal interests, makes the need for assertive opposition forces outside these spheres all the more pressing. Civil society, taken in the Tocquevillian sense to mean intermediary organizations through which individuals can resist the state, in Pakistan has had to overcome onslaughts of repression. Trade unions and leftist organizations were for instance very quickly dismantled. As for student movements, they have been more sporadic, as is often the case. But the press has fulfilled an important function despite recurrent episodes of censorship. Of all the institutions that contribute to a sort of balance of power, it is the judicial apparatus, however, that, when it has shown some independence, has acted the most effectively. This apparatus is primarily epitomized by the Supreme Court, but the High Courts play a major role as well. The Election Commission has also begun to assert itself and NGOs have made a big impact in some domains. In both such organisations, retired judges and lawyers are generally well represented.

The Judges: From Submission to Control?

The history of Pakistan has been punctuated not only by three Constitutions but also by a series of constitutional amendments that have altered the nature of the regime (such as the infamous Eighth Amendment), Provisional Constitutional Orders (PCOs) and Legal Framework Orders (such as in 1970 and 2002). This intense production of legal norms—which persisted even when the army ruled the country—reflects a sustained interest in the form that politics should take from a legal perspective. This is partly the result of a colonial heritage that India also shares: not only did the British institute all manner of courts in the Raj as well as a wide variety of legal codes, but moreover, the intelligentsia involved in founding both the Congress Party and the Muslim League practically all took their bachelor of law degree in the United Kingdom or in India. Jinnah, who for a long time was a member of both parties, thus became a barrister, the curriculum that Z.A. Bhutto also followed in the same institution, Lincoln's Inn, at a later date.[1]

But while in India the preponderance of "lawyers" in the public sphere facilitated the drafting of the Constitution of 1950, in Pakistan, constitutional debates would be hostage to and later victims of security considerations, as we have seen, and the judges would end up being courted by both civilians and the military, sometimes even arbitrating uneasily between the two camps, but lately acquiring more room for manoeuvre.

The Judiciary's Fluctuating Docility

The constitutional backbone the British bequeathed to its former colony first of all followed from the Government of India Act of 1935, which gave the Governor General (GG) considerable powers. Jinnah and his successors used these liberally and repeatedly. This law was supplemented by the "1947 Act" right after Partition, designed to set up an Assembly in charge of drafting the Constitution and enacting laws. The GG was however more active than the Constituent Assembly (which did not meet for either very long or very frequently): from 1947 to 1956, the Assembly passed 160 laws while the GG promulgated 376 ordinances.[2] The Government of India Act of 1935 granted the courts a degree of autonomy, especially the Federal Court, which acted as Supreme Court. It was further reinforced by section 223-A, an amendment the Assembly passed in 1954, giving individuals the power to petition the High Courts (provincial-level courts) when they believed they were victims of an abuse of power by the state.

---

[1] Bhutto took his first Law degree at Oxford University.
[2] Paula Newberg, *Judging the State. Courts and Constitutional Politics in Pakistan*, Cambridge, Cambridge University Press, 1995, p. 37.

The Assembly then strove to broaden the scope of its action. On 21 September 1954 it amended the Government of India Act to oblige the GG to choose the prime minister—and then the ministers—from among its ranks. The head of government thus had to remain in office as long as he had a majority among the members of the Assembly. The GG had to heed the government's opinion and act only upon its initiative. In reaction to this erosion of his prerogatives, Ghulam Mohammad went on the offensive on 24 October 1954, dismissing the Assembly and declaring a state of emergency.

On 8 November 1954, Speaker of the National Assembly Maulvi Tamizuddin Khan lodged a petition by virtue of section 223-A with the Sindh High Court disputing the validity of the measures taken by Ghulam Mohammad. The Court broke the issue down into three questions: was the GG's assent needed to validate Assembly decisions? Did it have the right to dissolve the Assembly? And did the petition filed by Tamizuddin Khan fall within the High Court's jurisdiction? The judges answered the last question in the affirmative and ruled in favour of the Assembly for the other two: the Assembly was sovereign and the GG's power to dissolve it was thus limited.[3]

The "Law of Necessity" Debated: Justice Munir vs. Justice Cornelius

Ghulam Mohammad appealed the decision before the Federal Court (which was to be renamed the Supreme Court). Before that, he promoted Justice Muhammad Munir, a Punjabi who was then Chief Justice of the Lahore High Court to the post of Chief Justice of the Federal Court on 30 June 1954. Munir was close to Ghulam Mohammad with whom he communicated secretely during the procedure.[4] Eventually, the Court ruled in the GG's favour, considering in its majority opinion that Assembly decisions had to be validated by the GG. Since the amendment to section 223-A of the Government of India Act hadn't received the GG's assent, the Sindh High Court did not have the necessary jurisdiction to rule on the case. The majority of judges behind Munir who handed down this verdict deduced it from relations between the British Crown—which the GG answered to— and its dominions: a dominion could not have a sovereign assembly. One

---

[3] Ibid., p. 43.

[4] Syed Sami Ahmad, *The Judiciary of Pakistan and Its Role in Political Crises*, op. cit., p. 13. He had also an "intimate" relation with Mirza (ibid., p. 59).

judge, Justice Cornelius, dissented from the majority opinion, arguing that Pakistan was to a certain extent an independent dominion, and therefore its Assembly was sovereign. It could only self-dissolve (or be brought down by revolution).

As regards the power to dismiss the Assembly that the GG claimed, Justice Munir justified it on the basis of the Assembly's lack of sovereignty and in the name of the principle of authority, while politicians had manifested their divisions for the previous seven years and one more conflict pitting them against the GG carried ominous consequences: "If the result is disaster, it will merely be another instance of how thoughtlessly the Constituent Assembly proceeded with the business and by assuming for itself the position of an irremovable legislature to what straits it has brought the country".[5]

The GG then petitioned the Federal Court for an opinion defining the scope of his powers. While stipulating that the GG should work constructively and peacefully with the Assembly, the Court considered that the dissolution he had ordered fell within his prerogatives. It added that proclamation of emergency was also within his powers and that he had done so "with a view to preventing the State from dissolution".[6] Justice Munir was referring here to a doctrine that he had already invoked as Chief Justice of the Lahore High Court during the anti-Ahmadi riots in Punjab in 1953: the "doctrine of necessity". Justice Munir, who had legally approved the way in which the governor of Punjab had assumed full powers to put an end to the violence in 1953, validated Ghulam Mohammad's offensive almost in the same terms:

"Subject to the condition of absoluteness, extremeness, and imminence, an act which would otherwise be illegal becomes legal if it is done *bona fide* under stress of necessity being referable to an intention to preserve the Constitution, the state, or the society, and to prevent it from dissolution, and affirms (...) that necessity knows no law (...) necessity makes lawful what otherwise is not lawful".[7]

The Court thus approved the Governor General's action in a decision handed down on 21 March 1955, with Justice Cornelius once again giving the only dissenting opinion.

---

[5] Cited in Paula Newberg, *Judging the State.* op. cit., pp. 47–48.

[6] Cited in ibid., p. 58.

[7] Cited in "Why did they have to kill the judges?" available at: http://www.sea-monitors.org/id37.html (Accessed on September 15, 2013).

Returning to this episode in his retirement speech in 1960, Munir stated, "If the court had upheld the enforceable writs, I am sure that there would have been chaos in the country and a revolution would have been formally enacted, possibly by bloodshed, a far more serious situation than that created by the invalidation of a whole legal system which the new Assembly promised by the Governor-General in his Proclamation could have easily validated".[8] These words prove if need be that Munir had given precedence to political considerations over the law he was in charge of administering.

History was to repeat itself nearly to the letter three years later after Iskander Mirza declared martial law on 8 October 1958. Muhammad Asghar Khan, the then Air Force Commander-in-Chief of Pakistan Air Force remembered about this episode:

"The following day or the day after, I attended a meeting presided over by Iskander Mirza at which Ayub Khan, the Chief Justice of Pakistan and the newly appointed members of Ayub Khan's cabinet were present. At this meeting, the Chief Justice, Muhammad Munir was asked by Ayub Khan as to how he should go about getting a new constitution approved by the people. Justice Munir's reply was both original and astonishing. In olden times in the Greek States, he said, constitutions were approved by 'public acclaim' and this could be done in Pakistan as well.[9]

Ayub Khan, as Martial Law Administrator, promulgated the Laws (Continuance in Force) Order which excluded the government from the courts' jurisdiction. Interestingly, "Justice Munir was the main player behind this piece of legislation".[10] As Paula Newberg points out, the judiciary "chose to keep its doors open and to live within its new limits".[11] Drawing on Hans Kelsen's theory of revolutionary legality, Munir established an unusual equation for a chief justice among "force, efficacy and legality"[12] and considered that "a successful coup d'état is an internally recognized legal method of changing a constitution. (...) If what I have already stated is correct, then the revolution having been successful, it satisfies the test of efficacy and becomes a basic law-creating factor".[13]

---

[8] Cited in Paula Newberg, *Judging the State. Courts and Constitutional Politics in Pakistan*, op. cit., p. 67.

[9] Muhammad Asghar Khan, *Generals in Politics*, cited in Syed Sami Ahmad, *The Judiciary of Pakistan and its role in Political Crises*, op. cit., p. 55.

[10] Ibid., p. 57.

[11] Paula Newberg, *Judging the State*, op. cit., p. 74.

[12] Ibid. p. 75.

[13] Cited in "Why did they have to kill the judges?" op. cit.

In the same vein, the judges validated the executive's actions against freedom of the press. In April 1959, the authorities took control of Progressive Papers Ltd. Its owner, Mian Iftikhar-ud-din, lodged a complaint with the Lahore High Court which, drawing on the Federal Court decision legalizing the forceful measure taken in 1958, declared that the President of Pakistan was exercising one of his legal prerogatives. The Supreme Court appeal judgment confirmed the ruling in terms amounting to than abdication of the rule of law: "even if the Central Government did contravene a principle of natural justice, its order would not be liable to challenge in a Court of law".[14]

Paula Newberg notes that "Bar Councils agitated for an end to martial law",[15] but there were not large-scale demonstrations. Nor were they responsible for bringing about the lifting of martial law in 1962 after the president's party carried the elections: the political process was much more directly responsible for this liberalisation than pressure from lawyers who, under the aegis of a highly conservative and docile chief justice till 1960, hardly put up a fight.

The early 1960s marked a dual change. First, Justice Cornelius replaced Justice Munir as Chief Justice in 1960, a post he would hold until 1968. Second, as of 1962, Pakistan had a Constitution to which judges could refer. The Supreme Court did just that in a ruling against Ayub Khan in 1963. He had wanted to amend the Constitution by ordinance to enable members of his cabinet to speak before the National Assembly even if they were not members. Justice Cornelius seized the opportunity of a court decision rejecting two of the President's plans to underscore that the Constitution was "the master-law"[16] that could only be amended according to a very strict procedure.

The judges acquired additional leverage after the fundamental rights were enshrined in the Constitution in 1963–4. On this basis, in 1964 the Supreme Court invalidated the executive's decision to dissolve the Jama'at-e-Islami, a party that the government accused of disturbing law and order. Interestingly enough, the High Court of West Pakistan had first rejected JI leader Maududi's petition, while the East Pakistan High Court had ruled in his favour.

---

[14] Cited in Paula Newberg, *Judging the State. Courts and Constitutional Politics in Pakistan*, op. cit., p. 91.

[15] Ibid., p. 83.

[16] Cited in ibid., p. 95.

The Supreme Court exercised caution, however, and did not confront Ayub Khan directly. In 1965, for instance, in an appeal ruling it invalidated a decision by the High Court of Dhaka condemning the Basic Democrats system, which in the eyes of the East Bengal judges confused executive, legislative and administrative powers. Likewise, in 1968, the Court, still presided by Cornelius, upheld Ayub Khan's use of preventive detention, however abusive it may have been, once again going against a ruling by the Dhaka High Court.

Judging Z.A. Bhutto's Democracy

After Ayub Khan stepped down in 1969 and Yayha Khan instituted an even harsher martial law regime than the previous one, the judges lost all their influence. Their authority wasn't restored until the democratisation of 1970–71. In 1972, the Supreme Court took the opportunity of a particular judgment—Asma Jilani v. Government of the Punjab with respect to the arrest of a human rights activist, Malik Ghulam Jilani[17]—to revisit certain basic principles. The notion of "revolutionary legality" was invalidated and Yayah Khan's regime—including its imposition of martial law—was declared illegal retrospectively. The Supreme Court did not hesitate to condemn what is described as Chief Justice Munir's errors.[18] Justice Hamoodur observed in his regard: "A person who destroys the national legal order in an illegitimate manner cannot be regarded as a valid source of law-making".[19]

Justice Yaqub Khan inferred from the rulings handed down in the Tamizuddin Khan (1955) and Dosso (1958) cases that they had transformed "a perfectly good country... into a laughing stock, and converted the country into autocracy and eventually... into military dictatorship". He sharply criticized the abrogation of the Constitution of 1956, noting that "Iskandar Mirza and Ayub Khan committed treason, and destroyed the basis of representation between East and West Pakistan".[20]

Ayub Khan's subsequent regime was shielded from such opprobrium by the 1962 Constitution, which conferred upon it a certain form of

---

[17] Jilani, the father of Asma Jilani (who was to become Asma Jehangir after her marriage), was a civil servant who entered politics after retirement in order to defend the cause of the Bengalis in 1970–71.

[18] Cited in "Why did they have to kill the judges?", op. cit.

[19] Syed Sami Ahmad, *The Judiciary of Pakistan and Its Role in Political Crises*, op. cit., p. 68.

[20] "Why did they have to kill the judges?" op. cit..

legality.[21] Furthermore, the Court followed the advice of two *amicus curiae*, A.K. Brohi and Syed Sharifuddin Pirzada (respectively a former and a future law minister) for asserting the power of the judges to identify what are bad laws and good laws.[22]

The judges applauded the promulgation of a new Constitution in 1973 and the creation, through the Legal Practitioners and Bar Councils Act, of a Bar Council endowed with the mission of "regulat[ing] the entry of lawyers into the legal profession".[23] In fact, the "main functions of the Bar Council [were] to admit persons, fulfilling the requirements of law, as Advocates entitled to practice before the Supreme Court of Pakistan and to maintain Roll of such Advocates and to remove advocates from the said Roll". In each province, regional Bar Councils were now doing the same vis-à-vis the High Courts.

But the judges proved to be powerless, or in any event passive, in the face of the authoritarian drift taken by Bhutto. This trend was reflected in a long series of constitutional amendments that (1) framed the freedom of association as defined by article 17, (2) limited the rights of the Ahmadis (cf. next chapter), (3) broadened the state's margin for manoeuvre in matters of preventive detention and (4) abrogated the requirement to submit any extension of emergency rule to the National Assembly. Other amendments whittled away the prerogatives of the judiciary. Bhutto thus "amended Article 199 by seriously restricting the High Courts from granting interim relief to detainees; and prohibited the courts from ordering the release of prisoners awaiting trial or already convicted by tribunals".[24]

Although article 8 of the Constitution invalidated any law entering into contradiction with the fundamental rights, the Fifth Amendment declared laws passed in the framework of a state of emergency "to have been validly made and shall not be called into question in any court" by virtue of a possible conflict with the fundamental rights.

The regime's freedom-curtailing evolution partly flowed from the fight against the Baloch and Pashtun nationalists that Bhutto's government was waging. In 1975, the government chose to seek out the Supreme Court's opinion regarding the dissolution of the NAP, the party then led by Wali

[21] Paula Newberg, *Judging the State. Courts and Constitutional Politics in Pakistan*, op. cit., p. 120 ff.

[22] Ibid., p. 125.

[23] http://pakistanbarcouncil.org

[24] Paula Newberg, *Judging the State. Courts and Constitutional Politics in Pakistan*, op. cit., p. 139.

Khan, Z.A. Bhutto's nemesis (or, at least, perceived rival). Endorsing the official line that held the NAP to be a separatist party, the Court declared that this organization had sought "to destroy the concept which formed the very basis for the creation of this country". In fact, the judges subscribed to the Attorney General's description of the NAP's strategy as "the sowing of the seed of secession as we have had the misfortune of experiencing from the course of events that took place in East Pakistan in the recent past".[25] The NAP decided to cease defending itself in the case, which only ended with Zia's coup d'état, resulting in the release of NAP prisoners.

Along with the trial of Pashtun nationalists, the judges also yielded ground in the wake of the previously mentioned constitutional amendments. In April and May 1976, the National Assembly amended the Defence of Pakistan Rules (DFR), making it possible to create special courts in charge of crimes and misdemeanours outlined by these DFR—members of the Assembly moreover authorised the transfer of certain cases from civilian courts to these special courts. The Chief Justice of the Punjab High Court, Sardar Muhammad Iqbal, resigned in protest. But most of the other judges tended to adapt to the regime's freedom-slaying policies. Chief Justice Muhammad Yaqub Ali could only deplore "the complete negation of the right of appeal and revision in majority of the cases arising under the Defence of Pakistan Rules"[26]—all the more since many cases falling under the DPR were transferred from the regular courts to military courts. Furthermore, court injunctions—particularly those forbidding torture in prisons—were not acted upon.[27]

On 5 September 1976, the Fifth Amendment set a five-year limit on the chief justice's term of office. Prior to that, a chief justice was appointed for the entire time remaining before his retirement at 65.[28] But Bhutto once again changed the rules of the game with the Sixth Amendment, stipulating that a chief justice who had reached retirement age could remain in office until completion of his five-year term.[29] This reform was to enable Chief Justice

---

[25] Cited in Paula Newberg, *Judging the State. Courts and Constitutional Politics in Pakistan*, op. cit., p. 148.

[26] Cited in ibid., p. 158.

[27] Ibid.

[28] Ibid.

[29] "Chief Justice of the Supreme Court who attains the age of sixty-five years before he has held that office for a term of five years may continue to hold that office until he has completed that term. Chief justice of the High Court who attains the age of sixty-two years before he has held that office for a term of five years may continue to hold that office until he has completed that term."

Muhammad Yaqub Ali to remain in office beyond retirement age since his protests against the regime remained rather soft. It antagonized judges whose promotion was thus delayed—they were the only ones who protested.

Zia and the Judges

Following Zia's coup d'état, the new military regime developed two judicial systems that competed with the one already in existence. One was a fairly classic system of military courts, including courts martial (as mentioned above). The other was made up of courts administering the sharia (see next chapter). The Supreme Court and High Court justices once again adjusted to this evolution and to the militarization of the political system generally speaking.

Following her husband's arrest, Begum Nusrat Bhutto disputed the legality of Zia's coup in the Supreme Court. But the Court, in a ruling that bears Mrs Bhutto's name, upheld it and by the same token brought the doctrine of necessity up to date. According to the judges, the army had saved the country from disaster, whereas the civilian government had led it into an impasse. They moreover decided not to take seriously the politicians' attempt to seek a compromise until 4 July 1977:

It can only be a matter of conjecture at this stage, whether an accord between the Government and the Pakistan National Alliance would have finally emerged if the Army had not intervened (...) it has become abundantly clear that the situation was surcharged with possibilities of further violence, confusion and chaos.[30]

The Court did not invoke the principle of revolutionary legality—particularly because the Constitution was not abrogated but merely held in abeyance. Instead, it broadened the perimeter of the law of necessity. It validated the suspension of the Constitution, the introduction of new oaths that the justices were expected to take under the Provisional Constitution Order, the decrees passed under martial law and "all acts which tend[ed] to advance or promote the good of the people (...), [which were] required to be done for the ordinary orderly running of the State [and] which have been consistently recognized by judicial authorities as falling within the scope of the law of necessity".[31]

[30] Cited in Paula Newberg, *Judging the State. Courts and Constitutional Politics in Pakistan*, p. 163.

[31] Ibid., p. 165.

Another example of the manner in which Zia limited the independence of the judiciary pertains to the way judges were appointed. On realizing that Chief Justice Yakub Ali Khan had passed retirement age, Zia immediately decided to replace him, thereby assuming the power to appoint judges. On 22 September 1977 he thus appointed Anwarul Haq as chief justice, who omitted the line about defending the Constitution when he took oath—an omission that the other justices of "his" court also made. Not only was the legality of these procedures not challenged, but the justices also willingly lent themselves to the exercise.

The Bhutto trial confirmed shortly thereafter that the judges submitted to Zia as much as he subjected them to his power. Z.A. Bhutto was officially accused of murdering the father of Raza Kasuri, a legislator who was initially a Bhutto supporter before becoming a virulent critique of his policies in the Assembly. His vehicle was attacked by gunfire on 11 November 1974 (Kasuri survived the attack, but his father did not). Bhutto was accused of this murder after two members of the Federal Security Force were arrested on 24 July 1977, 20 days after Zia's coup, following an attack on the Lahore train station in which they were allegedly involved. They accused the former prime minister of having ordered the killing. Their court-appointed lawyer, Irshad Qureshi, admitted during a press conference on 3 April 1996 that their testimony was concocted after General Faiz Ali Chisti assured them that the regime would give them favourable treatment if they stuck to their story before the court.[32]

An even more important witness, Masood Mamood, found himself in a similar situation. Director General of the Federal Security Force, he was arrested at the time of the coup d'état as an accomplice in the crime and held in solitary confinement for two months—after which time he implicated Bhutto in the murder of Raza Kasuri's father. T.W. Rajaratnam, a former justice of the Supreme Court of Sri Lanka who analysed the Bhutto trial many years later, expressed surprise that his Pakistani counterparts could accept Mahmood's testimony given that he was clearly released in exchange for testifying against Bhutto: "He obtained his pardon on condition that he will abide by his confessional statement and implicate Bhutto".[33]

---

[32] A. Basit, *Bhutto's Murder Case Revisited.* See http://bhutto.org/Acrobat/Bhuttos_Murder_Case_Revisited.pdf, p. 16. (Accessed on September 15, 2013).

[33] T.W. Rajaratnam, *A Judiciary in Crisis. The Trial of Zulfikar Ali Bhutto,* Madras, 1988, p. 16. See: http://www.archive.org/stream/AJudiciaryInCrisisTrialOfZulfikar AliBhutto/AJudiciaryInCrisis_djvu.txt (Accessed on September 15, 2013).

The Bhutto trial began on 11 October 1977 before the Lahore High Court. All of the accused were found guilty and sentenced to death on 18 March 1978 in a ruling that was remarkably partial. The Chief Justice, who treated Bhutto and his lawyers harshly hearing after hearing,[34] had considered the above-mentioned prosecution witnesses perfectly admissible. Symptomatically, the judgment condemning Bhutto to death ended by criticising Bhutto's practice of Islam, describing him as a Muslim "only in name."

Z.A. Bhutto appealed his case before the Supreme Court on 25 March. Shortly afterward, on 7 May, he wrote to the chief justice asking him not to preside over the trial for a number of reasons: his close relationship to the Chief Justice of the Punjab High Court that had just condemned him; the very direct criticism he had made of Bhutto after Zia's coup; and more importantly, the fact that he had been first deprived of the post of chief justice due to the Sixth Amendment promoted by Bhutto—and that he had finally been appointed to that post once Zia repealed the amendment.[35] Bhutto's letter was in vain. The hearings were held from 20 May to 23 December 1978. The judgment was handed down on 6 February 1979. Bhutto's appeal was dismissed by 4 votes (the Punjabi justices) to 3. The reasons cited by the minority justices to justify their vote were all different: Safder Shah doubted Bhutto's guilt because Kasuri had never suspected him; Dorab Patel and Mohammad Haleem did not consider Masood Mahood's testimony to be reliable.

Although, under Zia, the Supreme Court justices were generally docile, some of the High Courts demonstrated greater courage. Thus was the case of the Sindh High Court. Petitioned by Mumtaz Bhutto and Abdul Hafeez Pirzada, it disputed the legality of detentions without trial that were becoming increasingly frequent.[36] As for the High Court of Balochistan, it objected to the transfer of cases from civil courts to courts martial. The High Court of Sindh followed suit. The High Court of the NWFP disputed both the law of necessity and the power of the courts martial.

---

[34] This is one of the reasons that Bhutto requested in vain that his trial be transferred out of the country. See: http://panhwar.com/Books_By_Sani/CHAIRMAN-BHUTTOS-APPLICATION-IN-THE-LAHORE-HIGH-COURT-FOR-THE-TRANSFER-OF-THE-CASE.pdf (Accessed on September 15, 2013).

[35] http://www.bhutto.org/Acrobat/Bhuttos%20letter%20to%20Anwarul%20Haq.pdf (Accessed on September 15, 2013).

[36] Paula Newberg, *Judging the State. Courts and Constitutional Politics in Pakistan*, op. cit., p. 175.

Lawyers mobilised beyond the framework of the courts, particularly in the context of the Movement to Restore Democracy. Thus 200 of them were imprisoned in March 1981. Amnesty International adopted 37 of them, including Aitzaz Ahsan who would again be in the vanguard of the "lawyers' movement" of 2007.[37]

Zia reacted in 1981 to such forms of resistance by promulgating a Provisional Constitution Order that deprived the courts of a number of their prerogatives: military personnel were no longer subject to civil law and the civil courts no longer had any say in matters of preventive detention. Furthermore, the judges had to take an oath under this PCO in the following terms: "...I will discharge my duties and perform my functions honestly, to the best of my ability and faithfully in accordance with Provisional Constitutional Order, 1981, and the law". Chief Justice Anwarul Haq preferred to resign, as did two other members of the Supreme Court, Dorab Patel and Fakhruddin Ibrahim (who was to become Chief Election Commissioner in 2012), along with sixteen High Court justices. The government did not even ask the five other justices to take this new oath. They were instead excluded from office, thus flouting the official procedure according to which only the Supreme Judicial Council could dismiss justices.[38] According to article 209 of the 1973 Constitution, the SJC, composed of the Chief Justice, two most senior members of the Supreme Court, and the two most senior chiefs of the High Courts, was the only competent institution for dismissing a judge.

The judiciary did not benefit from the liberalisation of the regime that began in 1985. In fact, the Legal Practitioners and Bar Councils Act of 1973 was amended in such a way as to give the regime greater leeway to appoint to these bodies friends of the government deserving of reward. Magistrates were thus transferred arbitrarily for political reasons. A 1985 Presidential Order even stipulated that anyone who refused transfer would be forced to retire.[39] Furthermore, even though the PCO had lapsed and the 1973 Constitution brought back into force, the judges could not prosecute him for his misdeeds.

In 1985, magistrates taking part in the All-Pakistan Lawyers Convention unanimously condemned a policy that validated "all sentences passed by

---

[37] Amnesty International, *Pakistan. Human Rights Violations*, op. cit., p. 21.

[38] Ibid., p. 15.

[39] Paula Newberg, *Zia's law: Human Rights under Military Rule in Pakistan*, New York, Lawyers Committee for Human Rights, 1985.

Military Courts and reject[ed] the blanket indemnity of all excesses, torture, and violence perpetrated by the regime and its Civil and Military functionaries during the past eight years".[40] Once again it was the provincial High Courts that took the boldest initiatives. In March 1987 The Karachi High Court ruled in favour of extending its jurisdiction to actions undertaken by virtue of Martial Law Orders and Regulations. The Lahore High Court followed suit three weeks later in the Mustafa Khar case (named after a former Punjab PPP chief minister in exile in the United Kingdom).

On her return to Pakistan, Benazir Bhutto petitioned the Supreme Court in late 1987 to have it restore political parties' full freedom of action. The Chief Justice, Mohammad Haleem, answered with caution but positively that the 1973 Constitution—which had been partly revived—should "receive inspiration from the triad of provisions which saturate and invigorate the entire Constitution, namely the Objectives Resolution (Article 2-A), the Fundamental Rights and the directive principles of State policy so as to achieve democracy, tolerance, equality and social justice according to Islam".[41]

Zia's death instantly changed the situation, not only because of the army's decision to go back to their barracks, but also because of the Supreme Court decision to hold elections on a party basis. Mohammad Waseem has emphasized the fact that the Court "demonstrated the keen interest of the judiciary in facilitating the election process with a view to restore the constitutional rule in the country".[42]

Judges, the More or Less Passive Object of Power Politics (1989–1999)

After 1988, Benazir Bhutto, somewhat like her father in the 1970s, did little to honour the principle of an independent judiciary. In March 1989, she declared unconstitutional the nomination of judges made by the interim government that preceded her. The Supreme Court—with some of the justices appointed in these conditions on the bench—rejected this decision. But Benazir refused to back down, demanding that at least three of the Supreme Court justices step down. The Court joined forces against what it considered a frontal attack.

---

[40] Cited in Paula Newberg, *Judging the State. Courts and Constitutional Politics in Pakistan*, op. cit., p. 190.

[41] Cited in ibid., p. 203.

[42] Mohammad Waseem, *Politics and the State in Pakistan*, op. cit., p. 423.

Yet, some judges defended the PPP when it was under attack and attempted to resist what they considered President Ishaq's abuse of power. In 1990, the judiciary did not budge when he dismissed Benazir Bhutto's government, but some of them reacted when he also dissolved both the national and regional assemblies. In the NWFP, incumbent Chief Minister Aftab Sherpao took the matter before the High Court of Peshawar, which declared the decision illegal. As a result, the President did not confirm the permanent appointment of the acting chief justice of the High Court, who then appealed his case before the Supreme Court. The Supreme Court validated the dissolution and the organisation of new elections. Consequently, the Punjab High Court did the same. Paula Newberg concluded that this "court took its direction from political winds and refused to examine the soundness of the President's arguments or the sufficiency of his claims".[43]

History only partly repeated itself in 1993, given that President Ghulam Ishaq Khan indeed dismissed Nawaz Sharif, just as he had Benazir Bhutto, but this time the Supreme Court annulled the decision. The terms of the judgment in the *Mian Muhammad Nawaz Sharif v. President of Pakistan and others* case were unusually clear, as they stated that Ghulam Ishaq had demonstrated an "incorrect appreciation of the role assigned to him".[44] But the court's arbitration was quickly replaced by another. The army stepped in and dismissed both the prime minister and the President without pronouncing in favour of either, forcing both of them to resign.

The following episode, which saw Benazir Bhutto return to power from 1993 to 1996, was marked by the same violations of the law as in the years 1989–90. In 1994, Benazir made it a point of honour to appoint eleven justices of the High Courts herself, including three women who did not have the required seniority and who, in keeping with the Constitution, should have been appointed by the Chief Justice of the Lahore High Court. The case was taken before the Supreme Court, which on 20 March 1996 declared her action illegal. Benazir disregarded the ruling, which prompted lawyers in Karachi and Lahore to boycott these "political judges". On 21 September, Leghari came out of his reserve and backed the Supreme Court's action. Benazir gave in and suspended nomination of the 11 judges. More than ever, the judges were trophies to be won and served as symbols of power.

---

[43] Paula Newberg, *Judging the State. Courts and Constitutional Politics in Pakistan,* op. cit., p. 216

[44] Cited in ibid., p. 219.

In April 1996, the Supreme Court had issued a well-known writ in the Al-Jihad Trust Case stipulating that henceforth judges could only be appointed by the executive from a list of names recommended by the Chief Justice. But Nawaz Sharif's return to power in 1997 further confirmed the value of judges as political trophies. The new prime minister had retained a bitter memory of Sajjad Ali Shah, the chief justice. He had been the only one of eleven Supreme Court justices to vote against reinstating the Nawaz Sharif government in 1993. That is probably why Benazir Bhutto had appointed him chief justice in 1994, although two other judges were in line for the post due to their seniority. But that did not stop Sajjad Ali Shah from validating Benazir Bhutto's dismissal in 1996.

The first bone of contention between Nawaz Sharif and Sajjad Ali Shah in 1997[45] typically had to do with the nomination of new justices. The chief justice intended to fill five vacant posts. The prime minister vetoed this move, claiming that there were no vacant posts to be filled. He had to renege on this decision, but still did not appoint or allow the appointment of any new justices.

The conflict between the prime minister and the chief justice had consequences on the Supreme Court justices. Some of them refused to acknowledge the chief justice's authority, arguing that he had been appointed by Benazir Bhutto and that his promotion, being political, was not valid. Sajjad Ali Shah then proclaimed the Thirteenth Amendment—granting the prime minister greater powers than the president—illegal which another Supreme Court bench disputed. The chief justice finally undertook to charge the prime minister with "contempt of court" because he did not implement the decisions of the Supreme Court. In retaliation, on 30 November 1997, supporters of Nawaz Sharif (including members of his Cabinet) stormed the Supreme Court, devastating the premises.[46]

President Leghari, asked by Nawaz Sharif to replace the Chief Justice with another justice, Ajmal Mian—who had been eclipsed by Sajjad Ali Shah in 1994 despite the former's seniority—preferred to resign, as did the

---

[45] In the background of this conflict was the Supreme Court judgment of January 1997 in the Mahmood Khan Achakzai Case in which the justices declared the Eighth Amendment to be a permanent feature of the Constitution given that the legislators elected in 1988, 1990 and 1993 had not sought to do away with it. See http://www.seamonitors.org (Accessed on September 15, 2013).

[46] Amir Mir, "Bitter Memories of 1997 Contempt Case against Sharif", *The Tribune*, 19 January 2012. Available online at: http://www.thenews.com.pk/Todays-News-13-11847-Bittermemories-of-1997-contempt-case-against-Sharif.

COAS, General Karamat. The chairman of the Senate who replaced him in the interim dismissed Sajjad Ali Shah and appointed Ajmal Mian in his stead.[47] In 2006, Shahaz Sharif apologised to the nation for the behaviour of his brother and his party nearly ten years earlier.[48]

Musharraf's countercoup gave rise to a repetition of prior judicial decisions. In January 2000, when the Supreme Court was on the verge of ruling on the legality of the coup, Musharraf asked the judges in all jurisdictions to take an oath under the latest Provisional Constitutional Order (PCO) which had placed the 1973 Constitution in abeyance and banned the courts from ruling against the Chief Executive or anyone under his authority. Six justices, including the Chief Justice, and nine High Court justices preferred to resign, while three-fourths of the judges concerned took the oath.[49] The Supreme Court once again validated the coup d'état by virtue of the "law of necessity" but asked Musharraf to organise elections within three years.

*

From 1947 to 2007, the oscillation of Pakistan's judges to a certain extent replicated the monotonous cycle of Pakistani politics, alternating between military regimes and phases of democratisation. They usually validated coups d'état by virtue of the famous "law of necessity" reflecting a foundational priority with state security and have only rarely had the gumption to resign. While they have tried to maintain certain aspects of the rule of law, in general they have chosen to support acts of force in order to protect their interests.

The fact that the judges submitted to authorities that came to power by force as much as they were brought under submission by them is all the more significant as, in Pakistan, generals involved in a coup have always placed great store in the façade of legality that only the judicial apparatus could give them. Lacking historic legitimacy, military overthrows, once justified by a more or less credible existential threat, have tended first to seek the benediction of the judiciary and then a constitutional framework. Judges have rarely tried to exercise their bargaining power with the military.

---

[47] See Sajjad Ali Shah, *Law Courts in a Glass House: An Autobiography*, Karachi, Oxford University Press, 2001.

[48] "PML-N apologizes the nation on attack at the SCP", 29 November 2006. See http://paktribune.com/news/PML-N-apologizes-the-nation-on-attack-at-the-SCP-161516.html (Accessed on September 15, 2013).

[49] Available online at http://jurist.law.pitt.edu/world/pak.htm (Accessed on September 15, 2013).

They have been more concerned with expanding their dominion with regard to civil governments, giving rise to conflicts that have finally been more intense than with the military. For one thing, judges assessed the balance of power as being in their favour in a context of democratisation in which the rule of law was one of the pillars. Second, the successive PPP and PML(N) prime ministers have proven quick to intrude on the judges' preserve, either because they had no other ground to occupy given the military's ascendancy over the political checkerboard, or because they were eager to keep a tight rein on courts that were likely to pick a quarrel with them (especially in light of the many corruption scandals).

As of the 2000s, the convergence between the military and civilian power circles has made such distinction largely obsolete. Magistrates thus found themselves in a position to become an alternative to the establishment. They would seize this opportunity after 2007 under the aegis of Chief Justice Iftikhar Chaudhry.

The Iftikhar Chaudhry Phenomenon

There were no signs foretelling the rise of Justice Chaudhry, who in the space of a few years became one of the most powerful men in Pakistan. After practicing law in Quetta—his native city—he was appointed additional judge there and then chief justice in 1999.[50] Shortly thereafter he took oath under Musharraf's constitutional inventions that aimed to lend his regime a façade of respectability—including the PCO of 2002, promulgated two years after Chaudhry joined the Supreme Court. It was probably for this reason that Musharraf promoted him chief justice in 2005, counting on his docility. But just as Nawaz Sharif was betrayed by Musharraf, Musharraf was to a certain extent betrayed by Iftikhar Chaudhry, who demonstrated increasing independence once he became chief justice.

Judicial Activism Pakistani style: Chaudhry v. Musharraf

Iftikhar Chaudhry ushered the Supreme Court of Pakistan into the era of what in India had been labelled judicial activism ten years previously. It first became evident in the increase of proceedings initiated by the courts

---

[50] See the biographical note about Iftikhar Chaudhry in *Profile of the Chief Justice and the Judges*, pp. 14–15. See: http://www.supremecourt.gov.pk/Annual_Rpt/ Profile%20of%20the%20Chief%20Justice.pdf (Accessed on September 15, 2013).

themselves (*suo moto* actions): nearly 21,000 *suo moto* proceedings in the space of about two years.[51] Judges began calling governments to account on any number of issues. Chief Justice Chaudhry first established his reputation in a financial matter, the plan to privatise the Pakistan Steel Mill that the state was preparing to sell to a close associate of Prime Minister Shaukat Aziz for next to nothing. But his celebrity came with the case of the "missing persons". The Supreme Court first began looking into the fate of Baloch victims and then turned its attention to Islamists who had similarly "disappeared".[52]

Supreme Court activism, which Musharraf correctly attributed to Iftikhar Chaudhry, antagonized the General to the point of calling on him to resign on 9 March. The chief justice refused to step down, so Musharraf dismissed him from his office, referred his case to the Supreme Judicial Council and appointed a new chief justice. His chosen replacement, Javed Iqbal, immediately took oath and summoned his predecessor before the SJC that he presided on 13 March. Chaudhry then had to answer accusations made by Naeem Bokhari, an attorney with the Punjabi bar council, regarding favours he secured for his son, reportedly obtained from him to exercise a medical profession and then enter the police force.[53]

Musharraf should have come out unscathed from this incident due to the opportunism—even careerism—typical of unscrupulous lawyers. All the more since the man who replaced Javed Iqbal as chief justice on 22 March by virtue of the principle of seniority, Bhagwandas, seemed prepared to play his game. But it was the lawyers, on the contrary, who in a burst of activism on an unprecedented scale mobilized behind the deposed chief justice against Musharraf.

The Bar Associations network played a major role in this regard. The Punjab council revoked Naeem Bokhari's license on 10 March. The Lahore Bar Association moreover was "one of the main centers of protest",[54] local lawyers taking to the streets, braving the risk of being roughed up by the police. Similar demonstrations spread throughout the country, to Karachi, Quetta, Peshawar, Muzzafarabad and so on. Beyond that, one after the other regional Bar Associations invited Iftikhar Chaudhry to come speak to them. The Rawalpindi Bar Association was the first to do so, and on 13 March the

---

[51] Laurent Gayer, "Le général face à ses juges: la fronde de la magistrature pakistanaise", *Critique internationale*, no. 42, January–March 2009, p. 99.

[52] Ibid.

[53] Ibid., pp. 105–106.

[54] Ibid., p. 106.

chief justice thus gave an address on the importance of the separation of powers.[55] On 5 May, at the invitation of the local Bar Association, he left for Lahore from Islamabad. The procession, 2,000 vehicles long, took 24 hours to make the trip (six times longer than usual). He was greeted by a crowd of 50,000 people. On 12 May in Karachi, violence in the wake of an MQM rally associated with his visit claimed some forty lives. Each time, the lawyers played a key role in organising the demonstrations.

Among them, four nationally renowned personalities deserve particular mention: Aitzaz Ahsan, Hamid Khan, Munir Malik and Ali Ahmed Kurd, all four of whom acted as Iftikhar Chaudhry's counsel before the SJC.[56] The first of them was introduced in the previous chapter. Like him, Munir Malik, who was president of the Supreme Court Bar Association, had taken part in the lawyers' struggle against Zia. But he was not a member of any political party (Ahsan was a PPP member and had been a minister under Benazir Bhutto). Malik was profoundly a revolutionary and worked to establish the lasting "civilian supremacy over the military".[57] Ali Ahmad Kurd symbolised Iftikhar Chaudhry's "Baloch connection". They had known each other for twenty-five years: he too hailed from Balochistan and had benefited from the Chief Justice's support when he was abducted by an organised criminal gang. A militant lawyer like Malik, he on the other hand had joined a party, like Ahsan, but not the PPP, the NAP, when he was a student. He had spent "six or seven years" of his life in prison[58] before rising to the prestigious post of Vice-Chairman of the Pakistan Bar Council. On 26 May 2007, before the Supreme Court Bar Association (which would make him its president in 2008) he gave a speech—in Urdu as was his custom—directly attacking Musharraf:

Long ago, we said ... we said to that man (Pervez Musharraf) beware. The battle that you started by manhandling the Chief Justice of Pakistan, by assaulting the constitution... this battle is not any ordinary battle. It is a battle between two uniforms. And we also said that be careful, 150 million people of Pakistan are neither anyone's fiefdom, nor anyone's slaves.

[Crowd (all lawyers) jumps to their feet in applause and start chanting, "Go Musharraf Go!"]

---

55 Ibid., p. 107.
56 Ibid., p. 103.
57 Cited in ibid.
58 http://www.pakistanherald.com/newprofile.aspx?hofid=189(Accessed on September 15, 2013).

The people of Pakistan are no one's property nor are they slaves! (In Urdu, "*Pakistan kay awam na kisi kay baap ki jaagir hein na ghulaam hein*") This is the voice! This is that nation! These are the sons and citizens of this land! Today their valor and their courage! You and your disciple generals, do you have this courage, this power? You and those generals who were not ashamed to imprison a man (in the army headquarters) for 5 hours!

This is our declaration, we declare, we don't recognize this man, we don't recognize his throne (referring to Pervez Musharraf).

While talking to you in the life, living, breathing, independent, my head is held high; by God, even if I am beheaded you'd still hear my voice from my grave that I don't recognize this man, I don't recognize this throne (referring to Pervez Musharraf).

Don't dare to come in front of us. For you, we got fire in our eyes, and hatred in our hearts! By God if anyone goes against us, this is a war, beware, it will be our hand and your neck!

What does a man want? All he wants is to make his bread and butter with dignity; he wants the right to say proudly this land is his land; a right to say he is not a slave in his own country.[59]

Kurd's talents as an orator—his tone contrasting with the ever-moderate tone of the chief justice—is evident here.

Hamid Khan was president of the Bar Association of the Lahore High Court (1992–3), Vice-Chairman of the Pakistan Bar Council (1996–7) and president of the Supreme Court Bar Association (2001–3). Like some of his colleagues, he had invested himself in party politics, himself being a founding member and a vice-president of Imran Khan's party, Pakistan Tehrik-e Insaf (Pakistan Justice Party).

These four lawyers as well as a fifth man, Tariq Mehmood, former president of the Supreme Court Bar Association who was one of the three Supreme Court justices who refused to take oath after Musharraf's coup, defended the chief justice before the Supreme Court after he referred the matter to this court so as not to appear before the SJC as Musharraf wished. On 20 July, the Supreme Court repealed the decision Musharraf had taken against Iftikhar Chaudhry. The bench responsible for this verdict was not only presided by a man who came from a long line of Pakistani lawyers, Khalil-ur-Rehman Ramday, but it moreover was quite sizeable, being made up of thirteen justices, and was nearly unanimous (only three of them did not vote in favour of the chief justice). Never before in the history of

---

[59] See video at: http://www.youtube.com/watch?v=BdS9Ru450Lc (Accessed on September 15, 2013).

Pakistan had legal professionals demonstrated such independence in the face of military authorities.

This mobilisation did not weaken when Musharraf declared a state of emergency on 3 November 2007, fearing that the Supreme Court might not endorse his re-election as president of Pakistan. Though the offensive was validated by justices under the government's thumb who had agreed to take oath under the new PCO, they were few in number. Anil Khan calculated that "over sixty High Court and Supreme Court justices, including the Chief Justice of Pakistan, refused or were not asked to take oaths of office under the PCO, a number unprecedented in Pakistan's history".[60] Out of the eighteen Supreme Court justices, only five of them took the new oath. While all the members of the High Court of Balochistan took oath, twenty-four justices of other High Courts refused (twelve in Sindh, ten in Punjab and two in the NWFP).[61]

The new Supreme Court led by Chief Justice Abdul Hameed Dogor validated Musharraf's re-election once he renounced his post of COAS. It also validated the declaration of emergency rule and the new PCO. But the 2008 elections reshuffled the cards by bringing back a civilian government.

Civilian Figures, New Supreme Court Targets

Once the February 2008 elections set the democratic transition in motion, the judges pursued their movement, as the new government did not resolve to reinstate Iftikhar Chaudhry in office. As already discussed in chapter 6, the PPP leadership with Zardari at its head was obviously afraid of a backlash of judicial activism. Prime Minister Yousaf Raza Gilani settled for lifting the order of house arrest on 24 March 2008 Chaudhry had been under. The government then indicated that the chief justice would be reinstated on 12 May, but nothing of the sort occurred on that date. The new government in fact strove to divide the lawyers' movement, with a degree of success:

The PPP broke the solidarity of the sixty-four Supreme Court and high court judges who had stood by Chaudhry and who had refused to take the oath under the PCO;

---

[60] Anil Kalhan, "Constitution and 'Extraconstitution': Colonial Emergency Regimes in Postcolonial India and Pakistan", in Victor V. Ramraj and Arjun K. Thiruvengadam (eds), *Emergency Powers in Asia: Exploring the Limits of Legality*, Cambridge, Cambridge University Press, 2010, pp. 89–120.

[61] "324 judges of high courts 'cease to hold office'", *Dawn*, 5 December 2007. See http://archives.dawn.com/2007/12/05/top4.htm (Accessed on September 15, 2013).

fifty-eight judges accepted reappointment without insisting on Chaudhry's rein-statement. In the end, the issue of the restoration of the judges was reduced to Chaudhry and a few other judges.[62]

Nevertheless, agitation resumed. On 17 May, the Pakistan Bar Council announced a grand protest march from which the Peoples Lawyers Forum (the organisation of PPP lawyers) dissociated itself, however, so as not to put the government in an awkward position. The march took place on 14 June, mobilising thousands.

On 8 August, Nawaz Sharif and Zardari agreed to reinstate the chief justice, but after Musharraf resigned on the 18th, Zardari backed down and on the 25th the PML(N) walked out of the government coalition, although he did not join the opposition. Zardari was elected president on 6 September. The Supreme Court then reverted to its bad habits of submitting to the authorities. On 25 February 2009 it went as far as denying Nawaz Sharif and his brother the right to hold or apply for a government job (by contesting elections, for instance).

Ali Ahmad Kurd, who became president of the Supreme Court Bar Association on 28 October, helped to rekindle the lawyers' movement. On 21 January 2009, its leaders announced through the Lahore High Court Bar Association that they were initiating a campaign to collect 10 million signatures requesting the repeal of measures Musharraf had taken against the judiciary. In early March they called for a "long march"—the goal of which was to present the petition with its 10 million signatures to the parliament. On 11 March, the police made hundreds of preventive arrests among lawyers and opposition parties.[63] On 15 March, Nawaz Sharif launched the march. In the night of 15–16 March, the chief justice was reinstated, apparently after an intervention by the COAS that reinforced the pressure Sharif had mounted.[64]

Back at the head of the Supreme Court, Iftikhar Chaudhry first set about getting rid of the "PCO judges" (those who had taken oath under Musharraf, about 104 of them in all, including 45 in Punjab)[65] and second, strengthen-

---

[62] Ghias. Shoaib A., "Miscarriage of Chief Justice: Judicial Power and the Legal Complex in Pakistan under Musharraf," *Law and Social Inquiry*, vol. 35, no. 4 (Fall 2010), p. 1021.

[63] Muhammad Anis, Shakeel Anjum et Khalid Iqbal, "Govt panics ahead of lawyers march", *The News*, 12 March 2009. See: http://www.thenews.com.pk/TodaysPrint Detail.aspx?ID=20868&Cat=13&dt=3/12/2009 (Accessed on September 15, 2013).

[64] Amir, Ayaz, "The Hangover Recedeth", *The News International*, 29 October 2010.

[65] Following the decision of 31 July 2009, several "PCO judges" moreover were

ing the Pakistani judicial system. Appointment of judges was once again at stake in the first battles with Zardari. Without consulting the chief justice, he had appointed both the Lahore High Court Chief Justice to the Supreme Court and an acting chief justice. The Supreme Court suspended this decision which contravened articles 177 and 260 of the Constitution. The second sparring match had to do with a related subject, the extension of the terms of six additional judges in the High Courts of Sindh and Punjab. The Supreme Court annulled the decision in light of the judgment in the Al-Jihad Trust case of 1996 that had put an end to additional judges.

The drafting and the revision of the 18th Amendment that marked the restoration of the 1973 Constitution gave the Supreme Court the opportunity to push its advantage further. It stipulated that the President of the Pakistani Republic would henceforth appoint the judge with the greatest seniority to the post of chief justice when it became vacant. When a vacancy of a judge would occur, an ad hoc Judicial Commission would nominate one person for each vacancy to the Parliamentary Committee. This Committee, made up of four members of the Assembly and four Senators, would confirm the appointment within fourteen days. If the Committee could not confirm the nominated person or persons by a three-fourths majority, the Commission would send another nomination. This procedure, which gave a key role to the lawyers in the designation of the judges, was made official. The main indication of the power the judges thus acquired lies in the makeup of the Judicial Commission. According to the 18th Amendment, only two judges were to sit on it. But the Supreme Court objected to this small number and forced the parliament to pass a 19th Amendment, thereby doubling the number of judges on the Commission, so that the number of legal professionals exceeded the number of politicians, resulting in a Commission composed as follows:

(i) Chief Justice of Pakistan; Chairman
(ii) four most senior Judges of the Supreme Court; Member
(iii) a former Chief Justice or a former Judge of the Supreme Court of Pakistan to be nominated by the Chief Justice of Pakistan, in consultation with the [four] member Judges, for a term of two years; Member
(iv) Federal Minister for Law and Justice; Member

---

offered government jobs by the Gilani administration. Azam Khan, "Contentious decision: PCO-era judges appointed to key ministry slots", *The Express Tribune*, 29 July 2012 http://tribune.com.pk/story/414528/contentious-decision-pco-era-judges-appointed-to-key-ministry-slots/ (Accessed on September 15, 2013).

(v) Attorney-General for Pakistan; Member
(vi) a Senior Advocate of the Supreme Court of Pakistan nominated by the Pakistan Bar Council for a term of two years. Member.[66]

To affirm the parliamentary nature of the regime, the 19th Amendment introduced the prime minister in the process of appointing judges, as the Parliamentary Committee must now send him the name or names of the confirmed nominee(s), who then forwards the same to the President.[67]

Having thus strengthened the Supreme Court's independence, the Chief Justice made the fight against corruption his top priority. Mohammad Waseem listed the main decisions, which, although non-exhaustive, is already eloquent: the Supreme Court

blocked a controversial sale of 240 acres of land in Karachi. It asked the Haris Steel to repay a loan worth Rs. 9 billion to the Bank of Punjab. It took suo motu notices of the increase in the price of sugar; mega corruption in the Pakistan Steel Mills worth Rs. 22 billion; the cutting down of trees because of the extension of a canal road in Lahore; the alleged links of the Chief Justice of Islamabad High Court Bila Khan with an underworld don Nannu Goraya; the illegal allotment of land by the federal Government Housing Foundation; embezzlement of Rs. 0.07 million by the Pakistan Cricket Board; and electricity theft by Musharraf and other residents of a wealthy area, Chak Shehzad, near Islamabad.[68]

Beyond criminals and mobsters, the Chief Justice also wanted to tackle politicians involved in a number of the above scandals. Interior Minister Rehman Malik thus faced court charges for changing the investigation team responsible for probing the Pakistan Steel Mill scandal.[69] But to better fulfil its task, the Supreme Court had to remove two obstacles. The first was the National Reconciliation Ordinance that Musharraf had passed, which enabled those having committed acts of corruption from 1986 to 1999 to escape prosecution. The Supreme Court had at first asked the government to submit the 2006 NRO to parliament to make it law. But the PPP did not manage to muster the required majority due to the MQM's prevarication. As a result, on 16 December 2009, the Court declared the ordinance null and void, thereby

---

[66] "Article 175 (A), Appointment of judges." See http://www.supremecourt.gov.pk/web/page.asp?id=432 (Accessed on September 15, 2013).

[67] Irfan Bukhari, "19th Amendment draft tabled in National Assembly", *The News*, 22 December 2010. See http://www.pakistantoday.com.pk/2010/12/22/news/national/19th-amendment-draft-tabled-in-national-assembly/ (Accessed on September 15, 2013).

[68] Mohammed Waseem, "Judging Democracy in Pakistan: Conflict between the Executive and Judiciary", *Contemporary South Asia*, 20 (1), March 2012, p. 26.

reactivating the some 8,000 legal proceedings it had quashed—including one against political leaders such as Zardari and Nawaz Sharif.

Second, the chief justice had to ensure that the National Accountability Bureau (NAB) was functioning as it was designed to. Established by Musharraf in 1999, the NAB was "charged with the responsibility of elimination of corruption through a holistic approach of awareness, prevention and enforcement".[70] Up until September 2010, the NAB was all powerful in such matters, but at that time, Zardari, fearing investigation by the NAB, transferred most of its prerogatives to the Ministry of Law, headed by a loyal supporter. In the following months, he took further measures to protect himself by appointing Deedar Hussain Shah as its head. This former judge, after retirement, had joined the PPP (under which label he had been elected twice in Larkana).[71] According to the 18th Amendment, this nomination had to receive the assent of the opposition leader. His party, the PML(N), objected strongly to this highly political choice and the Supreme Court blocked his nomination. Seven months later, Zardari submitted a new name, former chief of naval staff, a four-star admiral, Fasih Bokhari, who finally assumed the post.[72]

The Supreme Court then focused its efforts on acts of corruption blamed on President Zardari. In 2012 it asked Prime Minister Gilani to write to the Swiss authorities to reopen their investigation into the Zardari-Bhutto family bank accounts. Gilani replied that he would do no such thing, as Zardari benefited from presidential immunity. The Supreme Court disputed this,[73] and finally Gilani was found in contempt of court on 26 April 2012 for having disobeyed the SC order. These developments have been analysed

[69] Sohail Khan, "Rs 22 billion PSM corruption big dacoity: SC", *The News*, 9 March 2010. See http://www.thenews.com.pk/TodaysPrintDetail.aspx?ID=27692&Cat=13&dt=3/9/2010

[70] http://www.nab.gov.pk/home/introduction.asp (Accessed on September 15, 2013).

[71] Zahid Gishkori and Zia Khan, "Deedar named new NAB chairman", *The Express Tribune*, 9 October 2010. See http://tribune.com.pk/story/60007/deedar-hussain-appointed-as-nab-chairman/ (Accessed on September 15, 2013).

[72] Zahid Gishkhori, "Controversial appointment: Zardari picks retired admiral as NAB chief", *The Express Tribune*, 9 October 2011. See http://tribune.com.pk/story/270282/nab-chairman-appointment-president-zardari-nominates-fasih-bokhari/ (Accessed on September 15, 2013).

[73] The Chief Justice observed that immunity protected the actions the president and other office-holders performed in official capacity, not in personal functions. See http://www.dailytimes.com.pk/default.asp?page=2012%5C07%5C26%5Cstory_26–7–2012_pg1_2

by a number of observers as reflecting a "judicial coup" that undermined the process of democratisation underway. Paula Newberg points out that while "The tough standards imposed by the court may be welcomed by some, [...] by its judgement the court has also weakened the parliamentary sovereignty that was the aim of these reforms".[74] Mohammad Waseem likewise concluded that the incidents of summer 2012 could be "interpreted as a clash of institutions between the judiciary and parliament".[75]

Under pressure from the Supreme Court, Gilani resigned on 19 June 2012. But his successor (one of his former PPP ministers), Raja Pervaiz Ashraf, was subjected to the same Supreme Court pressures. On 12 July the National Assembly passed a Contempt of Court Act "exempting all government office holders, including the prime minister and all other ministers, from court proceedings under contempt charges".[76] The Court declared this law illegal on 4 August and asked Prime Minister Raja Pervaiz Ashraf to approach the Swiss authorities. He refused, but the Supreme Court then started to investigate bribes he allegedly received when he was minister for water and power in 2008–11.

In the face of the PPP's obstinacy, which finally considered that it stood to gain in the process of victimisation to which the judges were subjecting it,[77] on 27 August 2012 the Supreme Court granted Prime Minister Raja Pervaiz Ashraf an extension until 18 September to write his letter to the Swiss authorities. In January 2013, the Supreme Court ordered his arrest. The authorities did not implement this order and the court did not press the case, probably because elections were approaching.

But the PPP and politicians in general were not the only ones targeted by the Supreme Court. (Ex-)army officials were not spared either as the Chief Justice's action against Musharraf had already shown. After the reinstatement of Chief Justice Chaudhry the Court also reopened a case thirteen years old involving the former COAS, Aslam Beg and former ISI Director General

---

[74] Paula Newberg, "The Court Rules in Pakistan", 21 June 2012, *The Yale Global Online. See* http://yaleglobal.yale.edu/content/court-rules-pakistan (Accessed on September 15, 2013).

[75] M. Waseem, "Clash of institutions in Pakistan", *Economic and Political Weekly*, 14 July 2012, vol. XLVII, no. 28, p. 16.

[76] Sohail Khan, "SC declares Contempt of Court Act 2012 illegal", The News, 4 August 2012 Available online at: http://www.thenews.com.pk/Todays-News-13–16535-SC-declares-Contempt-of-Court-Act-2012-illegal (Accessed on September 15, 2013).

[77] Ayesha Siddiqa, "The case of exploding lawsuits", *Tehelka*, 24 August 2012.

Asad Durrani, in a case of covert financing of Benazir Bhutto's opponents in 1990. In 1996, in a preliminary hearing following a petition filed by Asghar Khan, Beg and Durrani had admitted taking some 140 million rupees out of Mehran Bank and Habib Bank, which they subsequently distributed to Benazir's opponents: Nawaz Sharif had received 3.5 million, Mir Afzal Khan, 10 million, Abida Hussain, 1 million, Altaf Hussain Qureshi, 0.5 million, Ghulam Mustafa Jatoi, 5 million, Jam Sadiq, 5 million, Muhammad Khan Junejo, 250,000 Rs., Pir Pagaro, 2 million, Maulana Salahuddin, 300,000 Rs., Humayun Marri, 1.5 million—to which should be added 5 million for the Jama'at-e-Islami and 5.6 million in handouts to journalists.[78]

In 1992, as a sign of its gratitude, the ISI deposited its secret funds in Mehran Bank. But shortly thereafter, its new chairman returned them to the state and the bank went into bankruptcy. Its chief executive, Yunus Habib, was arrested on 7 April 1994 (he would be sentenced to ten years in prison). On the 20th, Benazir Bhutto's Interior Minister, General Babar, with the COAS's assent, informed the National Assembly that the main beneficiary of these deals was General Beg—who had distributed some of the money to political opponents. It was on these grounds that Asghar Khan petitioned the Supreme Court in June 1996. Beg and Durrani were convicted during the first hearings, but Chief Justice Sajjad Ali Shah was unable to go through with proceedings in the case, as he was forced to resign in the wake of Nawaz Sharif's return to power.[79]

In March 2012, the Supreme Court reopened the investigation and summoned the main protagonists to appear in court. While Gilani felt humiliated to be called before the bench twice, Aslam Beg was exasperated to have to perform what he called a "hat trick" (after which the chief justice firmly requested him to change his tone). He denied everything, whereas Durrani provided new details in his affidavit:

Durrani told the Supreme Court on Friday that he was told by Beg that a business community in Karachi had raised some funds to support the election campaign of Islami Jamhoori Ittehad (IJI)—an alliance of nine political parties formed against the Pakistan People's Party (PPP) during 1990 elections. He said Beg had asked him if he could distribute those funds among certain politicians according to a

---

[78] Terence J. Sigamony, "SC issues notice to ISI-ex-chief Durrani", *The Nation*, 1 March 2012.

[79] "Asghar Khan's petition finally finds its way to SC", 25 February 2012 http://www.brecorder.com/top-news/1-front-top-news/47172-asghar-khans-petition-finally-finds-its-way-to-sc-.html (Accessed on September 15, 2013).

formula which would be conveyed to him through the Election Cell at the president's office.[80]

During his hearing, Yunus Habib declared that "due to pressure from the 'higher-ups', he had arranged for Rs 1.48 billion out of which Rs 140 million were distributed among political parties while the rest were invested in army welfare schemes and transferred to account numbers provided by ISI officials on the directives of Baig".[81]

Never before had the courts made the army's fraudulent practices so plain to see. When the decision of the Supreme Court was made public, the style it adopted to deal with former army top-officers sounded radically new—from the Court:

The general election held in the year 1990 was subjected to corruption and corrupt practices as in view of the overwhelming material produced by the parties; during hearing it has been established that an "Election Cell" had been created in the Presidency, which was functioning to provide financial assistance to the favoured candidates, or a group of political parties to achieve desired result by polluting election process and to deprive the people of Pakistan from being represented by their chosen representatives.

[...] Late Ghulam Ishaq Khan, the then President of Pakistan, General (R) Aslam Baig and General (R) Asad Durrani acted in violation of the Constitution by facilitating a group of politicians and political parties, etc., to ensure their success against the rival candidates in the general election of 1990, for which they secured funds from Mr. Younas Habib. Their acts have brought a bad name to Pakistan and its Armed Forces as well as secret agencies in the eyes of the nation, therefore, notwithstanding that they may have retired from service, the Federal Government shall take necessary steps under the Constitution and Law against them.

[...] Similarly, legal proceedings shall be initiated against the politicians, who allegedly have received donations to spend on election campaigns in the general election of 1990.[82]

---

[80] "Durrani admits doling out money on Baig's order", *Pakistan Today*, 9 March 2012. See http://www.pakistantoday.com.pk/2012/03/09/uncategorized/mehran-gate-scandal-money-distributed-on-orders-of-aslam-baig/ (Accessed on September 15, 2013).

[81] "Mehrangate case: SC tells AG to overview investigative reports from Mehran, Habib banks", *Tribune*, 9 March 2012. See http://tribune.com.pk/story/347651/asghar-khan-petition-aslam-beg-submits-reply-to-sc/ (Accessed on September 15, 2013).

[82] "Asghar Khan Case Short Order: Full Text", *The Express Tribune*, 19 October 2012. See http://tribune.com.pk/story/453773/asghar-khan-case-short-order-full-text/ (Accessed on September 15, 2013).

The Supreme Court requested the government to have the Federal Investigation Agency (FIA) enquire.

The Politics of the Judiciary and the Pakistanis' Thirst for Justice

In 2007, after Musharraf dismissed him from office, Iftikhar Chaudhry had a single goal: to restore the Judiciary's independence, while some of the lawyers' movement leaders had more political ambitions. One year later, the suspended chief justice began to demonstrate a similar inclination. In 2008, he was invited to the United States to receive the "Medal of Freedom" from Harvard Law School (Nelson Mandela had been the first recipient). The New York Bar Association also named him an Honorary Member on 17 November 2008. He gave there one of his rare speeches indicating his view of the judiciary:

...it is not the province of the courts to step into areas that are exclusively within the domain of the Executive or the Parliament. But, if these two institutions remain indifferent to the duties entrusted to them under the Constitution; or if they have acted contrary to the principles enshrined therein; or if their acts discriminate between the rich and the poor, or on religious, class, regional, or ethnic grounds; then judges are called upon by the Constitution, their oath and their office to act.

We do not seek to deprive any other constitutional pillar of its authority or strength. In fact we seek to bolster and strengthen that authority. And above all, we owe it to the citizens of Pakistan to do our duty according to our original oath, the Constitution, the law and our conscience.

Parliament is no doubt supreme but the judiciary must be equally independent and authoritative. That is how the state and its institutions retain the confidence of the people. This is how nations develop and people prosper. People must not only have rights but must also have the means to enforce those rights.[83]

Iftikhar Chaudhry presents the judiciary here not only as the guardian of the Law as defined in the Constitution, but also as protector of the Pakistani people. And in both cases, he posits the judiciary as an active safeguard with respect to the other centres of power: the parliament and the Executive (namely the prime minister and the president). The key word here is "active", since Chief Justice Chaudhry set for the judiciary an extremely broad field of action: entitled to act not only if the Constitution

---

[83] Chaudhry, Iftikhar Muhammad, "Pakistan: Judicial Independence Vital for Democracy," *Address to the New York City Bar Association*, November 17, 2008. Online at http://www.hrsolidarity.net/mainfile.php/2008vol18no04/2664/ (Accessed on September 15, 2013).

is violated but also if the state discriminates between groups or classes of people. Some, as we will soon see, have called this a populist agenda. But it met the expectations of many Pakistanis. Basically, Chief Justice Chaudhry sets the judiciary up as a political actor called upon to make sure that those in charge of public action—legislators, the prime minister and the president—not only respect the Constitution, but also that they implement the public policies they are responsible for.

The Supreme Court's actions once its chief was reinstated gradually antagonised a number of former lawyers' movement leaders. The first fault line was political: lawyers close to the PPP were the first to take their distances as soon as their party came under fire. Aitzaz Ahsan is a case in point. He was not one of the first to change course. He on the contrary backed the movement until the PML(N) finally took lead of it against Zardari, whose hostility toward Iftikhar Chaudhry was untenable. But the showdown between the Supreme Court and Gilani—who Ahsan represented before the judges, which ended with the prime minister's resignation, convinced him that Iftikhar Chaudhry was overstepping his bounds. He reacted as a party member on 15 August 2012 in stating "The judiciary is crossing the limits. If the apex court's orders to write the letter to Swiss authorities are a siege around the ruling party's fort, the latter has announced, indirectly, that it is prepared to brave this out".[84]

On the other hand, supporters of Pakistan Tehrik-e Insaf (PTI), of which Hamid Khan was still a vice-president, continued to back the Supreme Court in its crusade against corruption. This theme, along with anti-Americanism, was one of Imran Khan's favourite hobbyhorses. But eventually the Supreme Court also initiated contempt of court proceedings against the PTI leader, Imran Khan.

Lawyers' movement leaders disapproved of the way the Supreme Court treated a government chosen by a democratically elected parliament. Muneer Malik for instance considered that "In the long run this is a very dangerous trend. The judges are not elected representatives of the people and they are arrogating power to themselves as if they are the only sanctimonious institution in the country. All dictators fall prey to this psyche—that only we are clean, and capable of doing the right thing."[85]

[84] Faisal Farooq, "Aitzaz Ahsan voices concerns against exceeding boundaries of judiciary", *News Pakistan*, 15 August 2012. Available at: http://www.newspakistan.pk/2012/08/15/aitzaz-ahsan-voices-concerns-exceeding-boundaries-judiciary/ (Accessed on September 15, 2013).

[85] Cited in a fine article by Abbas Nasir, former editor-in-chief of *Dawn*: "Sancti-

Asma Jahangir, who was to be elected president of the Supreme Court Bar Association in October 2010, also expressed concern about the way the Supreme Court was undermining the parliament's authority. She described 8 August, the day on which Gilani's fate was sealed, as a "black day" for the Pakistani judiciary before adding, "We want a strong judiciary, not a powerful one."[86] It is precisely in this regard that she diverged from the Chief Justice.

In August 2013, the Pakistan Bar Council "passed four resolutions against the role of the superior judiciary, condemning the overuse of contempt of court power by the Supreme Court against the politicians".[87]

The notion that Iftikhar Chaudhry was a populist soon replaced his image of victim and then saviour in a number of Pakistani editorials. For instance, on 13 August 2012 the new leading newspaper, *The Express Tribune* wrote:

Iftikhar Chaudhry's populism has been his greatest strength in empowering the Supreme Court but it has also been his biggest failing, causing him to cast himself as a saviour who can and will fix every problem in the country.[88]

One of the reasons why the intelligentsia expresses such reservations toward Iftikhar Chaudhry had to do with his relations with certain figures from Islamist circles, relations that were formed around the issue of the disappeared. Under Musharraf, along with Baloch activists, Islamists were among the main victims of security forces—which were responsible for a number of disappearances. Family members and sympathisers of these disappeared organised. Former ISI officer Khalid Khawaja formed an NGO called the Human Rights Defence Council, which would denounce the disappearance "of hundreds of presumed jihadists in the framework of

---

monious slide into chaos?" *Dawn*, 28 January 2012. See http://dawn.com/2012/ 01/28/sanctimonious-slide-into-chaos/ (Accessed on September 15, 2013). The quote comes from an interview published in the *New York Times* on 22 January 2012.

86 Qaiser Zulfiqar, "PM contempt: Asma Jahangir terms August 8 as 'black day in judicial history'", *The Express Tribune*, 8 August 2012. See http://tribune.com.pk/ story/419356/pm-contempt-asma-jahangir-terms-august-8-as-black-day-in-judi- cial-history/ (Accessed on September 15, 2013).

87 Hasnaat Malik, "'Cold war' between bar and bench intensifying", *Daily Times*, 17 August 2013 (http://archives.dailytimes.com.pk/main/07-Aug-2013/cold-war- with-bar-costs-bench-its-popularity).

88 Nadir Hasan, "The Gate keepers", *Tribune*, 13 August 2012. See http://tribune. com.pk/story/421555/the-gatekeepers/ (Accessed on September 15, 2013).

Pakistan's contribution to the war on terror".[89] In November 2006, this NGO organised demonstrations in front of the Supreme Court, in response to which the chief justice, shortly before his dismissal by Musharraf, ordered an inquiry. The probe led to "releases of prisoners held illegally by the army intelligence services"[90] in August 2007.

At that time Islamic parties had already joined forces with the movement in favour of reinstating the Chief Justice. On 12 March, the Muttahida Majlis-e Amal (MMA), a coalition of six religious parties, had taken the initiative of forming a national consultative assembly (Qaumi Majlis-e Mushawirat) that also included the PML(N), Pakistan Tehrik-e Insaf, Islami Tehrik and figures such as Hamid Gul, former Director General of the ISI who made no secret of his Islamist sympathies.[91] The support that such a group extended to the lawyers' movement could only irritate the more progressive elements of the PPP.

After Musharraf stepped down and Gilani formed his government, the progressive intelligentsia, particularly those who displayed traditional affinities with the PPP, showed greater reservations toward the lawyers' movement, not only because it had Zardari in its sights and even more because it was undermining the foundations of the parliamentary system, but also because of their affinities with such conservative, even Islamist circles. This affinity came to light in the wake of the assassination of Salman Taseer. This PPP veteran whom the new government had appointed governor of Punjab in 2008 had taken up the defence of Asia Bibi in 2010. This Christian woman had been sentenced to death under the so-called anti-blasphemy law (see infra). The Islamists harshly criticised the governor for his stance. On 4 January 2011, Taseer was shot twenty-seven times by one of his bodyguards, Malik Mumtaz Qadri, who had ties with an Islamist organisation. The progressive intelligentsia was all the more stunned as many lawyers called Qadri a hero, and it was very difficult to find a lawyer who would bring the case before the courts, even though the murderer surrendered on the spot. As he came out of the courthouse after his first hearing, lawyers showered him with rose petals, proclaiming that they were prepared to defend him for no fee.[92]

[89] Laurent Gayer, "Le Général face à ses juges", op. cit., p. 111.
[90] Ibid., p. 111.
[91] Ibid., p. 107.
[92] Bashir Ahmad Gwakh, "The Deep Roots Of Pakistan's Extremism", Radio Free Europe Radio Liberty, 8 January 2011. See: http://www.rferl.org/content/the_

This attitude does not seem to be compatible with the democratic objectives of the lawyers' movement. One may argue that the pro-Qadri lawyers did not take part in the movement. But it can also be argued that they shared some common ground with certain Islamist organisations. Many lawyers fought against Musharraf primarily because of his pro-American game and some of the verdicts frequently handed down by judges in local courts in favour of Islamists (or the causes they defend) may not only be due to intimidation:[93] many magistrates also shared the anti-American leanings of the Islamist organisations.

The strength of this sentiment was again on display a few months after Taseer's assassination in the case of Raymond Davis, an American secret agent who slayed two Pakistani pursuers (probably from the ISI) and whom the United States refused to allow to be tried in Pakistan, against the request of a number of lawyers as well as Pakistani citizens. The courtroom where Davis's extradition was finally pronounced was stormed by lawyers in robes who wrote "American Court of Injustice" on the entrance.[94]

The problem persisted after Nawaz Sharif became prime minister. In September 2013, Maulana Abdul Aziz, the chief cleric of the Red Mosque (see below) against whom 27 different cases had been registered because his inflammatory speeches, was acquitted by a judicial magistrate of Islamabad.[95] One month after, the government revealed that between 2007 and 2013, the courts had "released 1,964 alleged terrorists" and out of them, "722 have rejoined terrorist groups while 1,197 are still actively involved in anti-state activities".[96]

---

deep_roots_of_pakistans_extremism/2270457.html (Accessed on September 15, 2013).

[93] An editorialist for the *Daily Times* thus noted, "Judges are also scared of the religious warriors who constantly threaten and punish them with impunity from law—warriors, it may be added, who have been trained by the state to fight its covert wars. Indeed, that is why the world no longer believes that a case against a terrorist can be fairly heard in Pakistan because the 'fair' judges can be killed" ("Did judiciary fail democracy?" *Daily Times*, 22 July 2009 http://www.dailytimes.com.pk/default.asp?page=2009\07\22\story_22-7-2009_pg3_1 (Accessed on September 15, 2013).

[94] *Express Tribune*, 3 April 2011.

[95] Malik Asad, "Lal Masjid cleric aquitted in all cases", *Dawn*, 24 Sept. 2013 (http://www.dawn.com/news/1045051).

[96] Malik Asad, "722 suspects rejoined terrorist groups after acquittal", *Dawn*, 21 Oct. 2013 (http://www.dawn.com/news/1050293).

The holier-than-thou image that the lawyers have acquired thanks to their action under the aegis of Iftikhar Chaudhry needs to be qualified also because provincial lawyers are often known for their corruption. Judges in civil and criminal courts at the local level are poorly remunerated and suffer from a lack of consideration. These realities are no excuse but may explain the propensity of some judges for corrupt practices, giving them their nickname, the *kane*, in other words, "one-eyed".[97] In a collection of short stories by Daniyal Mueenuddin, in which fiction competes with reality, one of his characters, a judge in a regional court, describe himself as follows:[98]

I am a sessions judge in the Lahore High Court. (...) despite my profession I don't believe in justice, am no longer consumed by a desire to be what in law school we call 'a sword of the lord'; nor do I pretend to have perfectly clean hands, so am not in a position to view the judicial system with anything except a degree of tolerance. I render decisions based on the relative pressures brought to bear on me.[99]

This explains the concern with which the progressive intelligentsia greeted the rise of the lawyers in the wake of their 2007–09 movement. Khaled Ahmed writes:

The lawyers were already criminalised to some extent through 'qazba groups'[100] and touting; but now their ability to cow the judges into submission threatens to make them a threat to society.[101]

It would be a serious mistake to place lower-ranking judges on a par with Iftikhar Chaudhry's Supreme Court. Paradoxically, the dilapidated state of the Pakistani justice system, particularly due to corruption, explains Iftikhar Chaudhry's popularity. The thirst for justice is indeed fostered by

---

[97] Laurent Gayer, "Le Général face à ses juges", op. cit., p. 98.

[98] For an ethnographic presentation of the judicial system at the local level, see Muhammad Azam Chaudhary, *Justice in Practice: Legal Ethnography of a Pakistani Punjabi Village*, Karachi, Oxford University Press, 1999.

[99] Daniyal Mueenuddin, *In Other Rooms, Other Wonders*, New York/London, W.W. Norton & Company, 2009, p. 97.

[100] According to the Pakistan Law Commission in 1993, "a 'qabza group' means a person or group of persons committing an act of illegal possession of or illegal dispossession from property by means of fraud, intimidation, duress, assault or in any manner otherwise than in due course of law". See http://www.ljcp.gov.pk/Menu%20Items/Publications/Reports%20of%20the%20LJCP/reports/report19.htm (Accessed on September 15, 2013).

[101] Ahmed, Khaled, "Legal Anarchy: A 'decline and fall' in the offing?" *The Friday Times* 22, p. 35 (October 15–2010).

the loopholes of the judicial process, including the slowness of legal proceedings which is the result of a multitude of factors ranging from mere
incompetence to sheer corruption—for the longer a case is protracted, the
more profitable it is to dishonest lawyers and judges—and including the
flagrant problem of staffing. In May 2009, the courts in Karachi had over
100,000 cases pending.[102] Today, it still takes years to obtain a judgment and
it requires a considerable outlay of money. A thirst for justice was therefore
probably a major explanation for Iftikhar Chaudhry's popularity. As
Laurent Gayer writes,

Chaudhry meets a demand for social justice (*adl-e ijemai*) that transcends class,
caste and ethnic identity. The suo moto procedures engaged by the Supreme Court
have restored hope in a population that had given up on turning to the judicial
system to claim its rights. These procedures seem to offer a perspective of popular
justice that is accessible to all.[103]

That is probably why Iftikhar Chaudhry was not only a populist, but
popular as well. When he retired in December 2013, the comments were
ambivalent. Ayesha Siddiqa acknowledged that "the ordinary Pakistani (...)
had begun to view the highest court as a place where he could find an
alternative when there was none to be found elsewhere", but regretted that
"the Court did not create institutions within its own jurisdiction".[104]
Similarly, Arifa Noor considered that the chief justice "became the medieval king whose *darbar* (court room) was open to all those who could send
a petition or get a journalist to report their story", while admitting that
during his years, "cartel owners, investors and prime ministers were
dragged to the courts".[105] Lastly, Sarrop Ijaz highlighted that, while the
disqualification of PM Gilani was "problematic at muyltiple levels", under
Iftikhar Chaudhry, Pakistan saw in respect to the missing persons case, "the
first serious attempt by the judiciary to hold the military establishment
accountable for impunity and violation of fundamental rights".[106]

---

[102] Anatol Lieven, *Pakistan. A Hard Country*, op. cit., p. 108.

[103] Laurent Gayer, "Le Général face à ses juges", op. cit., p. 112.

[104] Ayesha Siddiqa, "Tomorrow is another day?" *The Expres Tribune*, 11 Dec. 2013
(http://tribune.com.pk/story/644119/tomorrow-is-another-day/).

[105] Arifa Noor, "Man without a legal legacy", *Dawn*, 11 Dec. 2013 (http://www.
dawn.com/news/1061767).

[106] Saroop Ijaz, "5-and-5: The highs and lows of the outgoing CJ of Pakistan", *The
Express Tribune*, 10 Dec. 2013 (http://tribune.com.pk/story/643710/5-and-5-the-
highs-and-lows-of-the-outgoing-cj-of-pakistan/).

Interestingly, this legacy has prospered since Nawaz Sharif took power—and after Iftikhar Chaudhry's retirement. In June 2013, in a 400-page report, the Commission of Inquiry on Enforced Disappearances, which had been created under Zardari, directed the interior and defence ministries to lodge criminal cases against 117 officials of secret agencies, police and the Frontiers Corps involved in enforced disappearances—including a dozen of serving military officials. And the Commission had come to this conclusion after disposing of only 415 of the 1,172 cases it had been asked to investigate.[107] In July 2013, a federal task force for missing persons was formed in Islamabad, which worked in relation with the judiciary. The Peshawar High Court, after hearing 425 petitions of enforced disappearances, announced in December that after working in collaboration with this task force it had enumerated 643 missing persons in K-P and 64 in the tribal areas—all in internment centres.[108] On the basis of this investigation, Iftikhar Chaudhry, a few days before retiring, ordered the federal government to produce 35 missing persons who had been in the detention centre of Malakand (KP). The order stated that the "intelligence agencies or the police have no power to carry out enforced disappearances or unlawful custody".[109] The Sharif government continued with this policy after the chief justice's retirement. In March 2014, the government told the Supreme Court that it wanted two military officers to be tried for their alleged involvement in enforced disappearances of Baloch people. According to one investigation, the Frontier Corps were responsible for the disappearance of 19 of 33 persons.[110]

The Musharraf trials are bound to be another test for the judiciary. In early November 2014, the Anti-Terrorism Court rejected the former President's medical reports and ordered him to appear before the court in the Nawab Bugti murder case and the judges did the same in the Lal Masjid case (while, in that case, they also ordered police to provide additional security to Musharraf who had narrowly escaped an apparent assassination attempt in

---

107 Zahid Gishkori, "Missing persons cases: Inquiry commission calls for arrest of military officers", *The Express Tribune*, 19 June 2013 (http://tribune.com.pk/story/565196/missing-persons-cases-inquiry-commission-calls-for-arrest-of-military-officers/).

108 Noorwali Shah, "K-P's 643 'missing' persons detained at internment centres PHC told", *The Express Tribune*, 11 Dec. 2013 (http://tribune.com.pk/story/643774/k-ps-643-missing-persons-detained-at-internment-centres-phc-told/).

109 "SC orders govt to produce 35 'missing persions' in one week", *Dawn*, 10 Dec. 2013 (http://www.dawn.com/news/1061702).

110 Nasir Iqbal, "Govt wants 2 military officers tried under army act, SC told", *Dawn*, 26 March 2014 (http://www.dawn.com/news/1095593).

April on his way to the court).[111] However, ten days later the "special court" in charge of the "treason case" (relating to the imposing of the emergency in 2007) accepted Musharraf plea to include co-conspirators. The judges by including the then prime minister, Shaukat Aziz, the then law minister, Zahid Hamid and the then chief justice, Adbul Hammed Dogar reset the case back to the investigation stage.[112] Doubting of the independence of the judiciary, some PML(N) dissidents have accused the Sharif brothers of "making an agreement with retired Gen. Pervez Musharraf...".[113]

*

All in all, the chief justice has restored the institution's dignity using a method reminiscent in its excesses of that employed by T.N. Seshan, head of the Indian Election Commission in the 1990s. Before him, most observers agred that in Pakistan's history the judges had contributed more to weakening democracy than to strengthening it by usually siding with the military. As Phil Oldenburg writes, "On balance, the judiciary has played the role of a rubber–stamp institution legitimizing military-bureaucratic rule".[114]

While the lawyers' movement brought together figures whose only point in common was their enemy—Musharraf—wherefore the fleeting nature of their unity, and while the judicial apparatus is still marred by corrupt practices, the fact nevertheless remains that Iftikhar Chaudhry stood up to a military dictator as no other of his predecessors had dared to before him. Although his intransigence toward democratically elected politicians is apt to undermine the foundations of restored parliamentarianism,[115] it is clear

---

[111] Shezad Baloch, "Musharraf ordered to appear in court or else face cancellation of bail orders"? *The Express Tribune*, 10 November 2014 (http://tribune.com.pk/story/788664/musharraf-ordered-to-appear-in-court-or-else-face-cancellation-of-bail-orders/) and "Musharraf summoned over Lal Masjud cleric's murder", *Dawn*, 8 November 2014 (http://www.dawn.com/news/1143142).

[112] Malik Asad, "What's next in the Musharraf treason saga...", *Dawn*, 22 November 2014 (http://epaper.dawn.com/DetailImage.php?StoryImage=22_11_2014_151_004).

[113] "PML-N stalwarts make no secret of indignation", *Dawn*, 2 November 2014 (http://www.dawn.com/news/1141941).

[114] Philip Oldenburg, "The Judiciary as a Political Actor" in Christophe Jaffrelot (ed.), *Pakistan at the Crossroads. Domestic Dynamics and External Pressures*, New York, Columbia University Press, (forthcoming).

[115] It is to be noted in this regard that Iftikhar Chaudhry's Supreme Court, in its judgment regarding the Seventeenth Amendment, recognized the parliament's power to profoundly reform the Constitution as long as it respected its basic

that democracy will not rise from its ashes for any length of time unless it is supported by political parties and politicians that enjoy a minimum of legitimacy.[116] Otherwise, there is a considerable risk that the military will use their corruption as an argument to oust them from power. In the years 2007–9 it was as if the convergence between civil rulers and the military in an establishment out of touch with the masses had left the judiciary as the only opposition force. This largely explained Iftikhar Chaudhry's popularity in a country where the craze for justice was already exacerbated by a dysfunctioning judicial process at the local level. His discourse was all the more intelligible as it was stated in terms of a quest for justice. As Imran Aslam, President of Geo TV, told Anatol Lieven, "Ask ordinary people here about democracy, and they can't really explain it; but ask them about justice, and they understand it well, because unlike democracy, issues of justice are part of their daily lives".[117]

The media made no mistake about this, having thrown their support behind the lawyers' movement in a rare show of virtual unanimity.

The Press: A Fifth Estate?[118]

The press played a role of sounding board in the lawyers' movement, a development that was all the more remarkable as in Pakistan the media has

---

structure. A judgment handed down in 2010 by five justices, including the Chief Justice, thus reads "The superior courts of this country have consistently acknowledged that while there may be a basic structure to the Constitution, and while there may be no limitations on the power of Parliament to make amendments to such basic structure, such limitations are to be exercised and enforced not by the judiciary (...) but by the body politic, i.e., the people of Pakistan". Cited in Philip Oldenburg, "The Judiciary as a Political Actor", op. cit.

[116] A sign of the times, since the prime minister also had to give up his seat in the Assembly after having been condemned by the Supreme Court, portraits of Justice Chaudhry appeared on campaign posters for his age-old rival in his constituency in the by-election that followed: the Chief Justice had become a symbol of political morality, which party politicians so desperately lacked in the Pakistani imaginary. It did not suffice, however: Gilani's son won the election by a slim margin. See Umair Javed, "Of patrons and elections", *Economic and Political Weekly*, 11 August 2012, vol. XLVII, no. 32, pp. 27–30.

[117] Cited in Anatol Lieven, *Pakistan. A Hard Country*, op. cit., p. 85.

[118] In traditional democracies, the press is known as the fourth estate, after (or in opposition to) the executive, the legislative and the judiciary. In Pakistan, due to the army's role, it can only be referred to as the fifth estate.

long suffered from censorship and self-censorship. But despite an even more sinusoidal trajectory than that described by the alternation of military and civil regimes, the Pakistani press should at least partly be categorized as an opposition force as well.

Pakistan inherited from the Raj a press just as rich as India's. Jinnah himself had founded a newspaper in 1941, *Dawn*, which became a daily the following year and moved from Delhi to Karachi in 1947. Owned by Jinnah until his death, it acted as the government's official mouthpiece until then, after which it was more critical of those in power. The other major newspaper, with a circulation that for a long time was well ahead of the other Pakistani dailies, was *Nawa-e-Waqt*, a paper founded in 1940 that was also transferred from Delhi to Karachi after Partition.[119]

Journalists, already organised before Partition, formed new unions such as the Sindh Union of Journalists, which led a strike for better wages that lasted almost 50 days at the *Sindh Observer* in 1949 and was the crucible of the Pakistan Federal Union of Journalists (PUFJ) in 1950.[120] This union, true to article 12 of its constitution which stated as one of the organization's goals "To defend, maintain and struggle for freedom of the Press",[121] campaigned against the Security Act of Pakistan which in 1953 granted the authorities the means to keep the press under its thumb in the name of higher national interests and reasons of state. In a resolution adopted in one of its meetings, taking the Constituent Assembly to task, the PFUJ declared that this law:

...confers on the executive power to detain without trial or otherwise victimise any person on a vague charge of prejudicing the external affairs of Pakistan, an undefined offence which even an alien government did not penalise under their most arbitrary laws...The special provisions in the Act to control the national press from [sic] the most objectionable part of the Act. It gives the government power to stifle free expression of opinion on external affairs and suppress the dissemination of correct information by forcing newspapers to disclose the source of their information on pain of being thrown into jail. The PFUJ is of the considered view that in a country where the executive is armed with such arbitrary powers there can be no free press and without a free press there can be no true democracy. This meeting therefore demands the repeal of this reprehensible law.[122]

---

[119] This paper belonged to the leader of the PML(N), Aleem Khan, until 2008–2009, when it was bought by the Jang Group (see infra).

[120] See the union website: http://pfuj.org/history/ (Accessed on September 15, 2013).

[121] http://pfuj.org/archive/constitution/ (Accessed on September 15, 2013).

[122] http://pfuj.org/history/3/ (Accessed on September 15, 2013).

The PUJF then organised another memorable strike in 1954 at the *Times of Karachi*, in the city where the union had its base. However, the main press group voicing opposition, Progressive Papers Ltd. (PPL), was based in Lahore, the stronghold of the Punjabi revolutionary tradition. It belonged to Mian Iftikharuddin. This man had quit the Congress Party for the Muslim League in 1946, and Jinnah appointed him Minister for Rehabilitation of Refugees after Partition. In 1949, true to his leftist ideas, he proposed a land reform that the right wing of the party opposed, which led him to resign from his government post. He was expelled from the League in 1951. His press group included several influential titles, starting with the *Pakistan Times* whose successive editors-in-chief in the 1940s–50s were none other than the great communist poet Faiz Ahmed Faiz (as of 1947), and then Mazhar Ali Khan (who took over from Faiz in 1951, when he was arrested in the Rawalpindi Conspiracy Case).

The first episode of censorship occurred in 1954 under Ghulam Mohammad. But it was the military overthrow led by Ayub Khan that sealed—temporarily—the fate of the Pakistani press in general and—definitely—that of PPL in particular. Propaganda and misinformation became hallmarks of the regime. A form of "pre-censorship" was imposed, stipulating that journalists for the *Pakistan Times*, for instance, had to submit their articles to the relevant authority prior to publication. In April 1959, the regime went a step further and brought Progressive Papers Ltd group under state control. It was Zulfikar Ali Bhutto, Minister of Commerce under Ayub Khan, who came to announce the news to the *Pakistan Times* editor-in-chief, Mazhar Ali Khan.[123] Zamir Niazi notes, "The only organisation to condemn this deadly attack on the Press came from the working journalists through their organisation, the PFUJ and its affiliated unions".[124]

In 1960, the government issued the Press and Publications Ordinance submitting press organs to very strict control. The third paragraph was particularly severe, as it threatened any press organ that took the risk of bringing "into hatred or contempt the government established by law in Pakistan or any class or section of the citizens of Pakistan" with heavy financial sanctions and even cessation of publication.[125]

---

[123] See the account by Tariq Ali, son of the *Pakistan Times*' editor-in-chief at the time, Mazhar Ali Khan, in Tariq Ali, *Military Rule or People's Power*, London, Jonathan Cape, 1972.

[124] Zamir Niazi, *The Press in Chains*, Karachi, Karachi Press Club, 1986, p. 84.

[125] Ibid., p. 97. See as well the account of former journalist, Suja Nawaz, "The mass media and development in Pakistan", *Asian Survey*, 23 (8), 1983.

As mentioned above, Ayub Khan quickly set up the Bureau of National Research and Reconstruction (BNR&R) of which one of the main missions was to promote journalists apt to publish articles favourable to the government. The National Press Trust was also established, in particular to take control of fourteen press organs.[126] In 1961, the government took over the Associated Press of Pakistan (APP), making newspapers that did not have a large stable of correspondents dependent on an official source of information. One of the goals of the propaganda was to set Ayub Khan up as faultless leader, even the protective father of the nation.

In 1963, after martial law was lifted, the regime protected itself by further hardening its attitude through the Press And Publications (West Pakistan) (Amendment) Ordinance—and its counterpart in East Pakistan. These amendments allowed the press to report proceedings of the courts (other than the Supreme Court)[127] and assemblies elected in 1962 only on the basis of official accounts.[128]

Once again the PFUJ protested vehemently and even organised a 24-hour strike on 9 September. The following day, Ayub Khan agreed to receive a group of press people.[129] But on 10 October, he promulgated an ordinance that scarcely differed from the previous version.[130] The journalists had by then begun to suffer from divisions created by a regime that, as previously noted, had an aptitude for co-opting "liberals", starting with Z.A. Bhutto, and make them endorse liberticide measures. Specifically, the union of newspaper publishers, the All Pakistan Newspapers Society (APNS), which had taken an active part in the September strike, backed down and chose to seek common ground with the regime. The government promised to observe a moratorium on use of the press ordinance as long as the journalists subscribed to a "Code of Ethics". The PFUJ refused, the APNS signed, and the government shortly afterward reneged on its commitment, invoking the reprobate ordinance to ban the Bengali opposition newspaper *Ittefaq* in 1966.

---

[126] Zamir Niazi gives the list of them in *The Press in Chains*, op. cit., p. 88.

[127] A sign that the government was certain of the apex court's docility.

[128] Zamir Niazi, *The Press in Chains*, op. cit., p. 98.

[129] Ibid., p. 101.

[130] The only nuance pertained to accounts of Assembly proceedings: "Printers/publishers/editors were barred from publishing an account of Assembly proceedings containing anything that was not part of the proceedings or had been ordered expunged, or against the publication of which the Speaker had issued a direction or which did not give a reasonably fair and correct version of the proceedings." Cited in Zamir Niazi, *The Press in Chains*, op. cit., p. 103.

The receptiveness of certain journalists to the appeal of sirens of power— and the security discourse the authorities formulated as of the 1950s—is quite apparent in the career of Altaf Husain. Jinnah had appointed him editor-in-chief of *Dawn* before independence. He transferred the newspaper from Delhi to Karachi in 1947 and retained his post there until he was picked by Ayub Khan as Minister for Industries and Natural Resources in 1965—a post he remained in until 1968. Shamsul Islam Naz, a veteran of the Pakistani press and secretary-general of the PFUJ, recalls some interesting details about him:

It may be added here that Mr. Altaf Husain was the person known to have submitted a list of what he considered as "subversive" journalists to the Intelligence Department through the then Information Minister for" necessary action". This was the time when liberal and progressive political workers, writers, journalists, student leaders and trade unionists were being arrested and detained under the Security Act of Pakistan following the signing of economic and military pacts with the United States in 1954. The result was that senior journalists like Messer M.A. Shakoor, Eric Rahim, Ahmed Hasan—all from "Dawn"—and several others were arrested and detained under the Security Act (including the author of this article).[131]

Ayub Khan's ability to co-opt journalist was matched only by the faculty that some journalists had for renouncing their freedom of speech for a government post and/or out of ideological conviction. But these black sheep were a minority.

Journalists took an active part in the early stages of the great 1968–69 protest movement. On 10 December 1967, the PFUJ called a general strike. This movement resulted in a tightening of censorship—in 1966 the government had shut down another major Bengali paper, *Purbani*, in Dhaka—but it only intensified the phenomenon: the government had journalists arrested and withdrew its advertisements from *Nawa-i-Waqt* (Lahore), *Ibrat* (Hyderabad) as well as from three publications in Dhaka: *Pakistan Observer*, *Azad* and *Sangbad*.[132]

The martial law declared by Yayha Khan, however, subjected the press to even worse treatment than Ayub Khan. "Enemies of Islam" and communists in editorial offices were hunted down on a sweeping scale, and in reaction to a 10-day wage strike in 1970, press barons and the regime (prodded by Information Minister General Sher Ali) colluded to dismiss 250 journalists.[133]

---

[131] See http://pfuj.pk/history, in particular page 8. (Accessed on September 15, 2013).
[132] See the PFUJ website for more detail (http://pfuj.pk) (Accessed on September 15, 2013).
[133] http://pfuj.pk/history In particular page 9. (Accessed on September 15, 2013).

In East Pakistan, when repression by the regime took a violent turn, *Ittefaq*'s offices were burned down by the army on 25 March 1971—which didn't prevent it from coming back out again in May. On 10 December 1971, Serajuddin, the vice president of the Pakistan Federal Union of Journalists, was kidnapped and killed in Dhaka.[134]

The Bhutto years reversed the trend, at least in the early 1970s. The prime minister honoured his campaign promises: the 250 journalists dismissed in 1970 were reinstated after Information Minister Abdul Hafeez Pirzada negotiated with the APNS for their return. On the other hand, Ayub Khan's ordinances remained in effect and the National Press Trust was not dismantled. Furthermore, the Bhutto government threatened one newspaper to withdraw some of its advertising—even to suspend some titles—to ensure its docility. In 1973, this fate struck three dailies, *Hurriyat*, *Jasarat* and *Mehran*. The PFUJ organised a general strike to bring them back to the newsstands and obtain the release of their editors-in-chief.

Unsurprisingly, Zia's methods regarding the Pakistani media were different from all the others.[135] He did not settle for imposing censorship—through the notorious Martial Law Regulation no. 49[136]—and having a record number of journalists and editors-in-chief arrested. He also had them brought before special courts dominated by the military and they were subjected to abuse ranging from torture to public floggings.[137] As a result, "Self-censorship replaced pre-censorship..."[138] and the Pakistanis began listening to the BBC and even All India Radio. As of 1982, systematic "pre-censorship" (submission of articles to the relevant authorities for publication approval) was suspended, but the government made use of it on a case-by-case basis (along with other methods such as withdrawing its advertising).

In response to the regime's exceptional harshness, journalists organised unprecedented forms of resistance. As of November 1977, in reaction to the banning of the Karachi edition of a major daily paper, *Musawaat*, the PFUJ and the All Pakistan Newspapers Employees Confederation launched a

---

[134] Lal Khan, *Pakistan's Other Story. The 1968–69 Revolution*, op. cit., p. 147.

[135] Iqbal, Zafar and Shabir, Ghulam, "Press-Government Relations in Structural-Functionalist Perspective: A Case of Pakistan under General Zia (from 1977 to 1988)", *Pakistan Journal of Social Sciences*, vol. 30, no. 1, September 2010, pp. 167–179.

[136] The full text of this directive is reproduced in Zamir Niazi, *The Press in Chains*, op. cit., p. 181.

[137] Ibid., p. 178.

[138] Ibid., p. 187.

widespread hunger strike that forced the government to lift the ban eight days later.[139] A similar movement took place the following year when the Lahore edition of *Musawat* and weeklies such as *Al-Fatah* and *Meyar* were banned and their editors-in-chief arrested. The movement, orchestrated by the PFUJ and the APNEC, was launched on 30 April 1978 in Lahore where it lasted until 30 May, after which it was revived on 18 July in Karachi—and lasted there until 10 October.

Like Ayub Khan, Zia managed to sow divisions among journalists, not so much through co-optation of individuals as by creating rival factions.[140] This is how the All Pakistan Newspapers Employees Confederation, formed back in the early 1970s, was eventually split under the aegis of Zia's Information Minister Farooqi, leader of the Jama'at-e-Islami—and with the help of a large faction of the PFUJ that was more accommodating. Once again, the opportunism of some offered the dictator a certain margin for manoeuvre—while at the same time reinforcing the fighting spirit of others.[141]

The journalists who took part in the MRD in the early 1980s were some of the regime's preferred targets. Ten journalists and management staff of the Pakistan Times, Imroze and Mashriq were thus dismissed for signing an appeal for "Peace in Sindh", the heart of the movement.

The democratisation process undertaken in 1988, like the one in the 1970s, resulted in a return to greater freedom of expression. Benazir Bhutto did away with the system of allocating newsprint to press organs—a means of pressure that all of her predecessors had made use of. Press organs now pay market prices for their paper supply. Nevertheless, media workers continued to be subject to forms of intimidation that were incompatible with the rule of law. During her second term, Benazir Bhutto cancelled publication of six Karachi newspapers by virtue of the Maintenance of Public Order Ordinance, which had clearly replaced the Press and Publication Ordinance, fallen into abeyance.

---

[139] See http://pfuj.org/history/ In particular page 11. (Accessed on September 15, 2013).

[140] Shamsul Islam Naz, "July 5; A black day in the history of Pakistan", 4 July 2008. See http://ja-jp.facebook.com/notes/pfuj-pakistan-federal-union-of-journalists/july-5-a-black-day-in-the-history-of-pakistan-pfuj/281850289956?comment_id=12109517&offset=0&total_comments=1 (Accessed on September 15, 2013).

[141] See the account by Afzal Khan, Secretary General of PFUJ from 1980 to 1985. Available online at: https://groups.google.com/forum/#!msg/PressPakistan/5o0tUndFLtg/bpvBIpoo7_MJ (Accessed on September 15, 2013).

The press was subjected to much more severe control under the Nawaz Sharif government. During his first term, in 1991, he reactivated the government newsprint allocation system that Benazir had abolished. But it was especially during his second term that he used strongarm methods against the press, the last active opposition force after the Supreme Court was brought to heel, which did not hesitate to criticise the government's authoritarian drift. The Jang Group was particularly vocal in its criticism. It was punished for its boldness by the tax administration, which harassed the management with intimidating searches. Sharif further toughened his methods in the spring of 1999 following a BBC documentary on corruption among Pakistani politicians. The editor-in-chief of the *Friday Times*, Najam Sethi, was placed in preventive detention for twenty days for an interview he gave the BBC journalists. During the summer the government set up the Press Council having the same power as civil courts to sanction reputedly dissenting press organs.

The Musharraf regime seemed liberal in comparison.[142] It is true that censorship was not imposed[143] and that in 2002 the airwaves were privatised, bringing an end to the state monopoly over the media and leading to the creation of dozens of television stations (see infra). But Musharraf also took this opportunity to establish the Pakistan Electronic Media Regulatory Authority (PEMRA), which granted licenses in a highly selective fashion. Beyond that, his regime was "known for expressing displeasure about news reports that create[d] a negative image for it, and journalists [were] targeted selectively, resulting in the harassment and disappearance of approximately 48 journalists under his rule [between 1999 and 2007]".[144]

Musharraf amended the PEMRA rules first in June 2007 to limit coverage of the "lawyers' movement" by the private media.[145] It was intended to make it easier to suspend the broadcast licences of private television and radio stations and confiscate their equipment. In the face of protest, the government was forced to withdraw the amendments a few days later and shortly thereafter, media coverage of the army's assault on the Red Mosque

---

[142] Tariq Ali thus writes, "In fact there was more interference in the media during Nawaz Sharif's tenure than under Musharraf prior to the desperate state of emergency imposed in the fall of 2007". See Tariq Ali, *The Duel*, op. cit., p. 156.

[143] Jean-Luc Racine, "Le Pakistan après le coup d'Etat militaire", *Critique internationale*, no. 7, April 2000, p. 25.

[144] Ayesha Siddiqa, *Military Inc. Inside Pakistan's Military Economy*, London, Pluto Press, 2007, p. 98.

[145] Geo TV, which broadcast from Dubai, was ordered by the local authorities to cease its live programming.

(see infra) cast Musharraf in an unfavourable light. He thus took advantage of his declaration of emergency rule in November to tighten his control on the press.

The state of emergency was moreover decided explicitly to combat the courts and the media on the grounds of "glorification of violence",[146] according to the President. Two decrees amended the PEMRA rules, turning them into a weapon for censoring the broadcast media. The first prohibited printing or broadcasting "anything which defames or brings into ridicule the head of state, or members of the armed forces, or executive, legislative or judicial organs of the state". The second threatened non-compliant media outlets[147] with 30-day suspension and with up to three years' imprisonment and/or a fine of 10 million rupees. "Men in black"—the famous "uniform" ISI—raided station offices, and editorial boards generally submitted to their orders. Aaj TV and ARY TV even dismissed some of their journalists whose programmes had been cancelled at the authorities' request. Only Geo TV resisted this pressure.

But the Musharraf regime had other means of coercion. The year running from May 2007 to May 2008 was the darkest moment in the history of the Pakistani press: 15 journalists were killed in mysterious circumstances, 357 were arrested or abducted, later to be released (an intimidation measure), 123 were assaulted or injured and 154 were threatened or harassed.[148] This unleashing of violence—which seriously qualifies the Musharraf regime's liberal attitude toward the press—only came to an end with the return of a civilian government in 2008.

In his address to the New York Bar Association in November 2008, when the Pakistani lawyers' movement was about to be revived, Iftikhar Chaudhry paid a vibrant tribute to the media in his country:

The (Pakistani) media has also played a remarkable role, and in a country where nothing is free or independent, they have carved a place for themselves in history. There is no doubt about the fact that the media has attained the status of a fourth

---

[146] Cited in Adnan Rehmat, "Murder and Mayhem: The Worst Year Ever for Pakistani Media", *Intermedia*, 3 May 2008, p. 5. http://www.pakistanpressfoundation.org/data/uploaded/worst%20yr%20pak%20media.pdf (verified February 4, 2015).

[147] Which designated in this case all those that published or broadcast "any material that is likely to jeopardise or be prejudicial to the ideology of Pakistan or the sovereignty, integrity or security of Pakistan, or any material that is likely to incite violence or hatred or create inter-faith disorder or be prejudicial to maintenance of law and order". Cited in ibid.

[148] Ibid., p. 2. See chapter 5 of this publication for the list of victims.

pillar of the state, and in the case of Pakistan, it has proved to be both powerful as well as bold and courageous.[149]

This statement indicates that the opposition force the chief justice embodied saw its strength multiplied tenfold by support from another. In fact, the Pakistani media in the 2007–10 period became a fifth estate (or a fourth estate if the parliament and executive are taken together, an approach that since 2008 is justified). President Musharraf had once again tried to divide and conquer. His regime "tried to establish closer links with the Dawn media group in the face of increasingly vociferous attacks from the Jang-Geo media group",[150] but the limits of this approach quickly became apparent: press outlets with the slightest concern for their credibility could no longer stand back during a time of unrelenting protest against the government.

The media's rise in power in the public space can first be explained by technical reasons. Diversification had made state control increasingly difficult, though far from impossible.

Over time, Pakistani press organs not only maintained their circulation (*Daily Jang* was the frontrunner, according to its management, with an Urdu readership of 300,000) but also saw it increase. In 1971, 41 publications were registered with the All Pakistan Newspapers Society. Today there are 262.[151] New titles have been added to those mentioned above, such as the Dawn Group monthly *Herald* (1969), the daily *The Muslim* (1979), the weekly *Friday Times* (1989), the monthly *Newsline* (1989), the dailies *The News* (1991), *Daily Express* (1998), *Daily Times* (2002), and *The Express Tribune* (2010).

Above all, the traditional printed press, which only reaches a small segment of the population—15 million Pakistanis read newspapers which have a total print run of 3 million copies—has been supplemented by the audiovisual media. In 1995 the first FM radio (FM 100) began broadcasting. There are now dozens of them, and even more if local networks are taken into account.[152] More significantly, the state put an end to the Pakistan TeleVision (PTV) monopoly in 2002, at a time when Pakistanis had learned to circum-

---

[149] Iftikhar Muhammad Chaudhry, "Pakistan: Independent Judiciary Vital For Democracy", 17 November 2008. See http://www.hrsolidarity.net/mainfile.php/2008vol18no04/2664/ (Accessed on September 15, 2013).

[150] Mohammad Waseem, "Judging democracy", op. cit., p. 27.

[151] See http://www.apns.com.pk/about_us/index.php (Accessed on September 15, 2013).

[152] See http://en.wikipedia.org/wiki/List_of_radio_channels_in_Pakistan (Accessed on September 15, 2013).

vent their single channel by using parabolic antennas. Zee TV, the Indian TV station started 20 years before, thus enjoyed a wide Pakistani audience. The country has 85 television channels today, in particular with many talk shows that devote considerable discussion to politics. While 15 million Pakistanis read the papers, 90 million have access to television.

All the major media groups are present in both the printed press and the electronic media today. The leader remains the Jang Group, its flagships being *Daily Jang* in Urdu and *The News* in English, not forgetting the monthly *Newsline*. But since 2003, it has become most famous for Geo TV. In second place is still Dawn, which publishes the daily newspaper of the same name, *Herald*, and also the Dawn News television channel. The third is none other than the "old" Nawa-i-Waqt ("Time"), which publishes *Nawa-e-Waqt* in Urdu, *The Nation* in English and is developing its own television station, Waqt TV. Next comes the Express Group owned by the Lakhani family and the Daily Times Group that belonged to the late Salman Taseer.

In addition to the diversification offered by the broadcasting and electronic media era, the printed press has gone on the Internet, giving it an international audience. One of the titles, *Viewpoint*, a leftist newspaper that former *Pakistan Times* editor-in-chief Mazhar Ali Khan had revived from 1975 until his death in 1993, now only exists on line (it moreover mainly publishes Pakistanis in exile).[153] Along with the Internet—used by 20 million Pakistanis today, in other words more than the readership of the printed press—mobile telephones, numbering 80 million in 2008, are also used to relay information.[154]

Although the diversification of media has made the Pakistani press more difficult to control, all governments have made such attempts—including the PPP-led government that came to power in 2008. Even if the Musharraf's reprobate ordinances were repealed and Geo TV was finally permitted to broadcast from Pakistan in 2008, the following year the government forbade it from broadcasting its coverage of the "long march" of lawyers and other Zardari opponents. Beyond that, the new government reformed the PEMRA rules in a direction that was highly unfavourable to the private

---

[153] Mohammad Taqi, "Mazhar Ali Khan's journey from PPL to Viewpoint". See http://www.viewpointonline.net/Old/fullstory.php?t=Mazhar%20Ali%20Khan%20:%20from%20Progressive%20Papers%20to%20Viewpoint&f=full-4-may-21.php&y=2010&m=may (Accessed on September 15, 2013).

[154] On this subject, see Shafique, Frazana and Mahmood Khalid, "Indicators of the Emerging Information Society in Pakistan", *Information Development*, no. 24, 2008, pp. 66–78.

media, as it included no representatives from that side on its board. The Pakistani executive had Geo TV suspended once again in August 2010 after a shoe was thrown and struck Zardari—a humiliating gesture—during his European tour. But this measure was short-lived and Geo TV has demonstrated admirable consistency in its criticism of the PPP-led government, which was all the more damaging as it is the most watched television station in Pakistan.

However, journalists did not spare the security establishment, a much more sensitive target—and paid the price for their audacity. The GEO TV anchor Hamid Mir, who hosts "Capital Talk", a very popular program since 2002, criticised—or let his guests criticise—the army's role in Balochistan, for instance. He was shot at in Karachi in April 2014 but survived this attack that he and his brother, Amir Mir, another journalist, attributed to the ISI and even named the DG ISI, Lt Gen Zaheerul Islam. After their public statements were made or echoed on Geo TV, the Pakistan Electronic Media Regulatory Authority (PEMRA), suspended the channel for 15 days and imposed it a fine of Rs. 10 miilion. After these 15 days, the channel remained non accessible in parts of Pakistan, especially in the cantonment areas.[155]

The influence the army exerted on the media was also obvious during the 2014 movement of Imran Khan's PTI and Tahir ul Qadri's PAT. Neha Ansari, who worked as a senior sub-editor and shift-in-charge at the *Express Tribune*'s national desk in Karachi revealed soon after the peak of the movement in August that

During this time, the owners of Pakistani media powerhouses—namely ARY News, the Express Media Group, and Dunya News—received instructions from the military establishment to support the 'dissenting' leaders and their sit-ins. The military was using the media to add muscle and might to the anti-government movement in an attempt to cut Prime Minister Nawaz Sharif down to size. At the Express Media Group, anything related to Khan and Qadri were inexorably the lead stories on the front page or the hourly news bulletin. I witnessed polls showing support for Sharif being censored, while news stories on the misconduct of the protesters, along with any evidence that support among the protestors for Khan and Qadri was dwindling, were axed.[156]

---

[155] "Journalist Hamid Mir injured in gun attack in Karachi", *Dawn*, 19 April 2014 (http://www.dawn.com/news/1100972/journalist-hamid-mir-injured-in-gun-attack-in-karachi) and "Hamid Mir defiant, still holds ISI responsible for attack", *Dawn*, 24 April 2014 (http://www.dawn.com/news/1102056/hamid-mir-defiant-still-holds-isi-responsible-for-attack).

[156] Neha Ansari, "Not Fit to Print: An Insider Account of Pakistani Censorship",

The year 2014 was not only marked by the Khan/Qadri movement, it was also the year when Pakistan became the country where the largest number of journalists—14—were killed according to the Brussels-based International Federation of Journalists.[157] It then ranked 158 out of 180 countries in the 2014 World Press Freedom Index.[158]

*

For a long time, the government, whether civil or military, has kept the printed press in check by using three complementary levers: it could threaten a press outlet with tax inspection, lower its newsprint quota and modify the amount of advertising it purchased. The first lever has been relatively compromised by the return of the rule of law, the second by the dematerialisation of the media used—particularly for the electronic media—and as for the third, it is practically no longer a threat, as economic liberalisation has made the press dependent on a multitude of private advertisers.[159]

In short, the Pakistani media seems more powerful than before in the context of a certain return to the rule of law, due to the increase in distribution channels, greater financial independence and the power of images. But this observation requires a dual qualification. First, the media is not cut off from the establishment. This is evident from the corruption cases that the Supreme Court revealed in April 2013, when the Court published a list of 282 journalists who had received 177 millions rupees from the government (another list of 155 names has also been made public).[160] But there is more to say about the relationship between the media and the political system.

Foreign Policy, 20 November 2014 (http://foreignpolicy.com/2014/11/20/not-fit-to-print-an-insider-account-of-pakistani-censorship/).

[157] "Pakistan and Syria loom large in violence which killed 118 journalists ad media staff in 2014, says IFJ", 31 December 2014 (http://ifj-safety.org/en/contents/pakistan-and-syria-loom-large-in-violence-which-killed-118-journalists-and-media-staff-in-2014-says-ifj).

[158] Reporters without borders, *World Press Freedom Index 2014*, (http://rsf.org/index2014/en-index2014.php).

[159] Siraj, Ayed Abdul, "Critical Analysis of Press Freedom in Pakistan ", *Journal Media and Communication Studies*, vol. 1(3), September, 2009, pp. 43–47. Available at: http://www.academicjournals.org/jmcs/PDF/pdf2009/august/Siraj.pdf (Accessed on September 15, 2013).

[160] "Secret funds case: list of 282 journalists made public", *The Express Tribune*, 22 April 2013. See http://tribune.com.pk/story/538900/secret-funds-case-list-of-282-journalists-to-be-made-public-today/ (Accessed on September 15, 2013).

The porosity of boundaries between the information world and political circles, even the army, is in fact fairly consequential, as a few emblematic examples suggest.

The most famous one is probably Mahmoud Haroon, the owner of the Dawn group who joined the Muslim League in 1942, became mayor of Karachi in 1954, and at first rallied behind Ayub Khan but later took his distance from him. In conflict with Z.A. Bhutto, he went to London in self-imposed exile in the 1970s and returned to politics under Zia in 1979. He was Zia's Minister of the Interior and then Minister of Defence under Ghulam Ishaq Khan, another indication that this press magnate was appreciated by the military. He became Governor of Sindh after Benazir Bhutto was dismissed from the prime ministership in 1990, but was reappointed to the same position by her in 1944, a sign that, like other personalities of the Pakistani establishment (like S.S. Pirzada or Sartaj Aziz), this man was acceptable to all the sectors of the political system.[161]

While Haroon was a newspaper owner, certain journalists have also related to the political milieu in a similar way—before leaving their profession and joining politics for good (almost). The career of Hussain Haqqani, whose role in "Memogate" was mentioned in chapter 5, offers an illustration of this profile. A journalist from 1980 to 1988, in particular with the *Far Eastern Economic Review*, he was first involved in the creation of the IJI, thus working both for the ISI and the PML. Nawaz Sharif later made him his spokesman before naming him ambassador to Sri Lanka (1993–5), after which he went over to the side of Benazir Bhutto, who also made him her spokesman. Finally, Zardari appointed him ambassador to the United States. Meanwhile, he pursued a career of political analyst in American think tanks and universities, as well as essayist and editorialist in the Pakistani and international press. His wife, a former television producer, was elected to the Senate for the PPP in 2008, before becoming "media advisor" for Zardari.

Sherry Rehman has followed a comparable itinerary. She was editor-in-chief of the *Herald* for ten years, from 1988 to 1998. She joined the PPP, was elected to the Assembly in 2002 and became information minister in 2008. She resigned from the cabinet in 2010 in protest over the restrictions on press freedom mentioned above, but went over to the Zardari camp in 2012 when he named her ambassador to the United States, succeeding Haqqani.

---

[161] See his obituary in *Dawn*, 7 November 2008, available at: http://archives.dawn. com/2008/11/07/top17.htm.

She resigned in 2013, after the victory of the PML(N), a clear indication that she was a political appointee.

Mushahid Hussain has enjoyed a similar trajectory. Appointed editor-in-chief of a daily that has since folded, *The Muslim*, in 1982 at the age of 29, he joined Nawaz Sharif who made him information minister from 1997 to 1999. Hussain, after being imprisoned by Musharraf, joined his party, the PML (Q), of which he is now secretary-general.

Maleeha Lodhi's career has taken a similar path. After being editor-in-chief of *The Muslim* from 1987 to 1990, she filled the same function at the newspaper she founded in 1990, *The News International* (Jang Group), from 1990 to 1993 and from 1997 to 1999, the interruption being due precisely to her having been named ambassador to the United States by President Leghari from 1994 to 1997. In 1999, she was again appointed to this post, but this time by General Musharraf who afterwards appointed her High Commissioner in Great Britain.

Porosity also exists, though to a lesser degree, between media circles and the security establishment, as the Haqqani and Lodhi cases have already suggested. This porosity sometimes simply reflects the narrowness of the Pakistani elite, such that offspring of the same family will unintentionally end up in various top power positions. The current editor-in-chief of *Dawn*, for instance, Zafar Abbas, is the elder brother not only of two other journalists, but also of Major-General Athar Abbas, who was head of the Inter Services Public Relations, the organisation in charge of the military's public relations, between 2008 and 2012.

Beyond family or political ties linking the media world to the political and military establishment, the latter has plenty of other means at its disposal to exert direct influence over the information world—particularly through its security arm.

Not only are hundreds of websites blocked when they criticise the army, but journalists are assaulted, even murdered, when they do the same. In September 2010, Umar Cheema, a journalist working for *The News International*, was kidnapped and tortured both physically and mentally because of his articles denouncing corruption in the army.[162] This was also the case of Saleem Shahzad after he published an article in the *Asia Times Online* that revealed the role of Al Qaeda in the attack on a military base on

---

[162] Bob Ditez, "The Significance of Umar Cheema's Abduction, 9 September 2010", available at: http://cpj.org/blog/2010/09/the-significance-of-umar-cheemas-abduction.php (Accessed on September 15, 2013).

22 May 2011—and this organisation's infiltration of the army. Shahzad was killed in 2011 at the age of 31. The investigation report remained inconclusive. For Human Rights Watch it illustrated "the ability of the ISI to remain beyond the reach of Pakistan's criminal justice system..."[163] In all, eight journalists were killed in 2011.[164] There were just as many in 2012[165] and an equal number in the first four months of 2013, according to the International Press Institute.[166] According to a report released by the Media Monitoring Cell of the Council of Pakistan Newspaper Editors (CPNE) 11 journalists were killed in 2013 (out of 71 worlwide).[167]

In addition to the (sometimes violent) intimidation exerted by the army, the Islamists have also intensified their coercive methods. Mir Shakilur Rehman, owner of Pakistan's leading press group, Jang, for instance exposed the threats he received from the Pakistani Taliban in 2007. He moreover lodged a complaint, in vain. Strictly political issues are thus tinged with more diffuse issues that could be qualified as societal. One of the Taliban's demands in this case pertained to the reproduction of pictures of women in the Jang Group's publications. Lately, in August 2014, the Tehreek-i-Taliban Pakistan "warned the Pakistani media that if they did not stop criticising the Mujahideen, they will be attacked and 'no crying and sobbing' will prevent the holy warriors from punishing journalists".[168]

---

[163] "ISI beyond reach of justice system: HRW", *The Express Tribune*, 31 January 2012, available at: http://tribune.com.pk/story/329671/isi-beyond-reach-of-justice-system-hrw/ (Accessed on September 15, 2013).

[164] Freedom House is probably the best source to follow the evolution of freedom of speech in Pakistan. See http://www.freedomhouse.org/search/Pakistan?f[0]=field_issues%3A263 (Accessed on September 15, 2013).

[165] Elizabeth Rubin (ed.), Roots of Impunity. Pakistan's Endangered Press and the Perilous Web of Militancy, *Security and Politics*, Committee to Protect Journalists, 2012. Available at: http://cpj.org/reports/CPJ.Pakistan.Roots.of.Impunity.pdf. (Accessed on September 15, 2013).

[166] Sasu Siegelbaum, "Journalists killed in Syria and Pakistan", *International Press Institute*, 28 May 2013, http://www.freemedia.at/home/singleview/article/journalists-killed-in-syria-and-pakistan.html (Accessed on September 15, 2013).

[167] "11 journalists killed in Pakistan in 2013: Report", *The Express Tribune*, 31 December 2013 (http://tribune.com.pk/story/652929/11-journalists-killed-in-pakistan-in-2013-report/).

[168] "Taliban declare war on media", *Dawn*, 6 August 2014 (http://www.dawn.com/news/1123549/taliban-declare-war-on-media).

THE JUDICIARY, THE MEDIA AND THE NGOs

The Opposite of Tocqueville: Democratisation without Civil Society?

Aside from the judiciary and the media, forces standing up to the Pakistani establishment are few and far between. This fact reflects the weakness of civil society—even its failure, to use the words of Akbar S. Zaidi who explains: "One major reason why the military tends to dominate state, society and politics in Pakistan, is because of the failure of civil society in Pakistan. Like other social actors in Pakistan, members of civil society are eager to be co-opted and 'serve' military governments, as has been seen after General Musharraf's coup in 1999".[169]

Indeed, history has shown that the military has managed to secure the services not only of politicians, but bureaucrats (or "technicians"), judges and journalists as well. This phenomenon has given rise to the notion of a Pakistani establishment united by a shared sense of forming an elite and defending interests that go along with it, including in terms of corruption.

For a long time, this dominant group, whose leaders number in the mere hundreds, had only occasionally been confronted with opposition forces. Trade unions were prevented from functioning freely from the very birth of Pakistan.[170] In 1949 the Essential Services Maintenance Act (ESMA) gave the government the power to ban trade unions—or at least limit their role— in all economic sectors it considered essential and made stoppage from paid or unpaid work in these fields a penal offence. Agricultural workers were explicitly banned from unionising. The army takeover in 1958 further toughened this legislation. The 1959 Industrial Disputes Act made concili- ation and arbitration mandatory in the event of a labour dispute before any strike could be considered legal. At the same time, dissemination of com- munist literature was prohibited. As a result of all these measures, in the 1990s, 5.5 per cent of nonagricultural workers and 0.7 per cent of the active population were unionised—trade unions moreover not escaping the influ- ence of ethnic identities that made class solidarity extremely fragile.[171]

Trade union weakness partly explains why in Pakistan, "civil society" is often understood as a synonym for NGO. This sector developed rapidly in the 1980s as a consequence of Zia's dictatorship: "State control over the media, art and culture as well as the purge of universities led many socially

---

[169] Akbar S. Zaidi, *Issues in Pakistan's Economy*, op. cit., p. 512.
[170] Christopher Candland, "Workers' Organizations in Pakistan. Why No Role in Formal Politics?" in Roland J. Herring and Rina Agarwala, *Whatever Happened to Class? Reflections from South Asia*, Delhi, Daanish Books, 2008, pp. 73–90.
[171] This is why the miners' trade unions in rural Sindh are in fact Pathan unions.

committed activists to seek expression by forming or joining advocacy-based 'civil society' or non-governmental organizations".[172] These NGOs were particularly active in defending human rights—and more specifically women's rights,[173] toward which the Women Action Forum has been working since 1981, as well as the fight against child labour, and so on. Pakistani NGOs soon federated at the regional and then national level, through NGO Dialogue, the Advocacy Development Network and the Pakistan NGO Forum which as of 1995 brought together the Punjab NGO Coordination Council, the Sindh NGO Federation, the Balochistan NGO Federation, Sarhad NGOs Ittehad and a Coalition of Rawalpindi/Islamabad NGOs.

The government—whether civilian or military—reacted to this rising influence by implementing mechanisms to channel foreign aid and then by passing the "NGO Act". The second Nawaz Sharif government endorsed the disbanding of 2,500 NGOs by the governments in Punjab, the NWFP and Sindh.[174] A minister in the Punjab government went after NGOs campaigning against the 15th Amendment, accusing them of being enemies of Islam and the state. In fact, NGOs generally face hostility not only from political leaders but also the Islamists.

The best organised and most active human rights NGO is none other than the Human Rights Commission of Pakistan (HRCP), which was founded in 1987 in Lahore but which now has regional offices in Karachi, Peshawar, Quetta, Hyderabad, Multan, Islamabad and Gilgit.[175] In 2005, it had a network of 3,500 members representing the organization in 78 out of 103 districts.[176] This commission relentlessly denounces human rights violations, in particular in its annual report on the human rights situation[177] and ad hoc reports

---

[172] Omar Asghar Khan, "Critical Engagements: NGOs and the State", in Anita M. Weiss and S. Zulfiqar Gilani (eds), *Power and Civil Society in Pakistan*, Karachi, Oxford University Press, 2001, p. 276.

[173] The country had a longstanding tradition in this field, Liaquat Ali Khan's wife, Rana Liaquat Ali, having launched the All-Pakistan Women's Association in 1949. Regarding the defence of women's rights, see Rashida Patel, "Challenges Facing Women in Pakistan", in Joanna Kerr (ed.), *Ours by Right: Women's Rights as Human Rights*, London, Zed Books Ltd., 1993.

[174] Omar Asghar Khan, "Critical Engagements: NGOs and the State", op. cit., p. 281.

[175] See http://www.hrcp-web.org (Accessed on September 15, 2013). See also, The Human Rights Commission of Pakistan, *The State of Human Rights in Pakistan: 1997*, Lahore: Rashid Ahmed Chaudhry, Maktaba Jadeed Press, 1998.

[176] Daanish Mustafa, "(Anti)Social Capital in the Production of an (Un)Civil Society in Pakistan", *Geographical Review*, vol. 95, no. 3, July 2005, p. 341.

[177] See for instance, The Human Rights Commission of Pakistan, *State of Human*

on the most vulnerable groups, such as religious minorities. It has also "cultivated close partnerships with trade and worker unions in Pakistan and has highlighted such diverse issues as unemployment, foreign policy, militarization of civilian organizations, media, health, education, and youth affairs in its widely disseminated annual reports and council meetings statements".[178]

The HRCP brings us back to the key role of lawyers. Indeed, the organisation's leadership includes many lawyers, starting with sisters Hina Jilani and Asma Jehangir—the latter having been president of the Supreme Court Bar Association in 2010–11. This NGO—like so many others—is hard to distinguish from the legal community, which as we have seen constitutes—together with the media—the country's main opposition force.

Another organisation to benefit from the expertise and dedication of former lawyers has asserted itself recently: the Free and Fair Election Network (FAFEN). Born in 2006 from a network of 30 NGOs supported by foreign entities (including the Asia Foundation and the British Council), FAFEN deployed observers in polling booths during the 2008 elections in order to identify any form of irregularity. It then acquired a legal status by forming the Trust for Democratic Education and Accountability. In 2013 it pointed out cases of rigging and registered violence when it occurred. It revealed that "as many as 71,397 irregularities and violations of electoral processes were observed in 38,274 polling stations across 263 National Assembly constituencies on the election day".[179] FAFEN is certainly a useful whistleblower that should lead the Election Commission to mend its ways.[180]

The Election Commission—a Work in Progress

Like India, Pakistan created an Election Commission as early as the 1950s to organiss and supervise the electoral process, including the preparation of the electoral rolls, the screening of nomination papers, the physical

---

Rights in Pakistan: 2011, Lahore, available online at http://hrcp-web.org/publication/book-genre/annual-reports/ (Accessed on September 15, 2013).

[178] Ibid., p. 340.

[179] "Fafen urges immediate political dialogue on electoral reform", *Dawn*, 9 May 2014 (http://www.dawn.com/news/1105247).

[180] Interestingly, the Commission has taken the time to respond to some of the accusations waved by FAFEN after the 2013 elections regarding the fact that in some polling stations the turnout was over 100%—it was due to mistakes of the NGO. See http://ecp.gov.pk/misc/Rebuttal_to_FAFEN.pdf (Accessed on September 15, 2013).

holding of the polls, the counting of ballot papers and the proclamation of election results. Provisions for such a commission were made in the 1956 Constitution but the chaotic political life of the country has naturally affected the Commission at times (there was no Chief Election Commissioner between 1958 and 1962 for instance and out of the twenty-four past chief commissioners, thirteen were considered "permanent" and eleven "acting").[181] Article 219 of the 1973 Constitution tries to guarantee the independence of the Chief Election Commissioner through a sophisticated appointment procedure: the CEC and the four other members of the Commission are appointed for five years after the prime minister and the leader of the opposition in the National Assembly recommend three names to a parliamentary committee consisting of twelve members (half from treasury benches, half from opposition parties) who have been selected by the Speaker of the National Assembly. Besides, the CEC can only be removed through an impeachment procedure in the National Assembly that implies a qualified majority.

It must be noted that the Election Commission of Pakistan (ECP), in contrast to that of India—where bureaucrats have been almost systematically appointed to key positions—has been the preserve of former judges.[182] Out of twenty-two CECs since 1956, eighteen were professional lawyers, including six retired judges. Before the 2013 elections the Commission was made up of retired judges, including former Supreme Court Justice Fakhruddin G. Ibrahim; who had been appointed CEC in July 2012. Below him, Justice (Retd.) Muhammad Roshan Essani represented Sindh, Justice (Retd.) Riaz Kiyani represented Punjab, Justice (Retd.) Fazal-ur-Rehman represented Balochistan and Justice (Retd.) Shahzad Akbar Khan represented Khyber–Pakhtunkwa. Moreover, the Election tribunals in charge of electoral complaints and disputes are also directed by judges who are appointed by the CEC in consultation with the Chief Justice of High Courts.[183]

---

[181] "Chief Election Commissioner Fakhruddin G Ebrahim resigns", *The Express Tribune*, 31 July 2013, available at: http://tribune.com.pk/story/584518/chief-election-commissioner-fakhruddin-g-ebrahim-resigns/ (Accessed on September 15, 2013).

[182] This is not only true at the top level: in KP, in 2013, 158 Returning officers were judicial officers, including District and Session judges (Waseem Ahmad Shah, "Rigging charges against judiciary causing anxiety among officers", *Dawn*, 11 August 2014 (http://www.dawn.com/news/1124575/rigging-charges-against-judiciary-causing-anxiety-among-officers).

[183] See the case of Punjab for instance. See: http://ecp.gov.pk/ViewPressRelease NotificDetail.aspx?ID=2071&TypeID=1 (Accessed on September 15, 2013).

The Election Commission gradually asserted itself with the support of the Supreme Court. In the 1989 case *Election Commission v. Javed Hashmi* the Court had decided that in all election matters, the Election Commission in general and the Election tribunals in particular had exclusive jurisdiction. In February 2012, the 20th amendment further upgraded the Election Commission. Indeed, this institution now has the last word in the designation of the interim prime minister and chief ministers before an election. According to the new rules, the PM and CMs in charge are supposed to vacate their seat two months before voters are called upon to cast their votes and interim governments be formed to expedite the current affairs and are responsible for the day-to-day management of the state.

The prime minister and the leader of the opposition in the outgoing National Assembly at the centre and the chief ministers and the leaders of the opposition in the outgoing provincial assemblies are supposed to appoint the caretaker PM and CMs. According to the 20th amendment:

In case the Prime Minister and the Leader of the Opposition in the outgoing National Assembly do not agree on any person to be appointed as the care-taker Prime Minister, within three days of the dissolution of the National Assembly, they shall forward two nominees each to a Committee to be immediately constituted by the Speaker of the National Assembly, comprising eight members of the outgoing National Assembly, or the Senate, or both, having equal representation from the Treasury and the Opposition, to be nominated by the Prime Minister and the Leader of the Opposition respectively.

The 20th amendment makes the same provisions at the provincial level except that the committee is comprised of six members only. In both cases—at the national and provincial levels—if the committees do not agree within three days, "the names of the nominees shall be referred to the Election Commission of Pakistan for final decision within two days".[184]

In 2013, this is what happened for the post of caretaker prime minister. The Committee could not agree and forwarded four names to the EC, which selected a former judge, Mir Hazar Khan Khoso, who had been the Chief Justice of the Balochistan High Court and then of the Federal Sharia Court.[185]

---

[184] http://www.Pakistani.org/pakistan/constitution/amendments/20amendment. html (Accessed on September 15, 2013).

[185] "Justice (r) Mir Hazar Khan Khoso named interim PM of Pakistan", *The Express Tribune*, 24 March 2013. Available online at: http://tribune.com.pk/story/525608/ justice-r-mir-hazar-khan-khoso-named-interim-pm-of-pakistan/ (Accessed on September 15, 2013). In the provinces the EC did not have to intervene. In KP and in Sindh retired Justices were appointed. In Punjab, Najam Sethi was selected.

The appointments of the interim CMs were less problematic in most of the cases, but in Punjab "the caretaker government, in direct contradiction to the spirit of the 20th amendment, was not strictly neutral". In particular, some appointments in the bureaucracy "were highly questionable".[186]

While the 2013 elections have been hailed as marking the advent of a "New Pakistan" and, indeed, registered a good turnout, controversies regarding the ECP abounded. Certainly, the Commission considerably improved the electoral rolls[187] and played a positive role when it rejected the nomination papers of potential candidates with dubious records, such as Musharraf.[188] But the Returning Officers were accused of submitting the candidates to sometimes very tricky tests of Islamic culture in accordance with article 62 of the Constitution.[189] The ECP has also been accused of not effectively guaranteeing women's right to vote in the Pashtun belt where female turnout was indeed very low.[190] More importantly, the ECP's reputation was marred first by the unleashing of pre-election violence which, as mentioned above, prevented some candidates from campaigning normally and, second, by fraud, including massive rigging—especially in Karachi—shown in videos made with hidden cameras posted on YouTube.

The morale of the ECP was also affected by the way the presidential election was organised. While the ECP had announced that the elections would take place on 6 August 2013, Prime Minister Nawaz Sharif petitioned the Supreme Court to move it up to 30 July 2013. The Supreme Court, in contradiction with the spirit of its decision in the *Election Commission v. Javed*

---

[186] Saeed Shafqat and Maheen Saleem Khosa, *Electoral Politics and Electoral Violence in 2013 Elections: The Case of Punjab*, Lahore, Forman Christian College/Centre for Public Policy and Governance, 2014, p. 59.

[187] The improvement of the electoral rolls was achieved with the help of the National Database and Registration Authority (NADRA) which verified 44 million entries "while the remaining 37 million were removed, on the basis of duplication or unverifiable data". The NADRA included 36 million eligible citizens who did not figure on the electoral rolls which also showed "photographs of voters for the first time" (ibid., p. 61).

[188] But candidates such as Raja Pervaiz Ashraf could run, eventually, after the Returning Officers had first turned down their application.

[189] In 1985 Zia had amended the Constitution to insert a provision that no government has tried to remove since then, which stipulates that the electoral candidates must have "adequate knowledge of Islamic teachings".

[190] In some places, all the parties and/or the candidates agreed not to let women vote (following an old consensual practice). But in others such as Kurran and Bajaur, they not only voted but, for the first time were candidates.

Hashmi case, revised the date, arguing that 6 August would coincide with the end of Ramadan. The day after the election of the new President—Mamnoon Hussain, the PML(N) nominee, won against the PTI's nominee, Wajihuddin Ahmed, another retired justice. Chief Election Commissioner Fakhruddin G. Ibrahim resigned because he considered that the new authorities should appoint a new CEC. This episode is revealing of the institution's fragility. First, it has obviously not freed itself of political considerations (in other countries where the presidents appoint the CEC they complete their terms even when the head of state changes). Second, its authority has been vitiated by the Supreme Court, which clearly remains the main power centre counterbalancing the government. Ebrahim had written a note describing the court's decision to change the date of the presidential election as "an attack on the independence of the ECP", but three of the four other members of the Commission refused to endorse it.[191] In June 2014 the leader of the opposition in the National Assembly, the PPP leader Syed Khurshid Ahmed Shah asked Nawaz Sharif to initiate the process of Chief Election Commission's appointment after almost one year of vacancies.[192] As nothing happened, the Supreme Court had to intervene. It set October 28, November 13 and November 25 as deadlines for the Chief Election Commissioner's appointment. Finally on 4 December 2014, a day ahead of the last Supreme Court's deadline,[193] Justice Sardar Raza was recommended for the post by the parliamentary committee. Raza, whose name had been proposed by the PPP, was then the incumbent Chief Justice of the Federal Sharia Court. As a Supreme Court judge (retired in 2011) he had refused to take oath under the PRO after the 2007 imposition of the emergency.[194]

* * *

The first part of this book explored the sociological dimension of Pakistan's national identity issue. The conclusion was reached that the separatism advocated by Jinnah's Muslim League proceeded to a large extent from the

---

[191] Mubashir Zaidi, "Chief Election Commissioner Fakhruddin G. Ebrahim resigns", *Dawn*, 31 July 2013. See http://dawn.com/news/1033217/chief-election-commissioner-fakhruddin-g-ebrahim-resigns (Accessed on September 15, 2013).

[192] Amir Wasim, "Shah urges Sharif to initiate process for CEC's appointment", *Dawn*, 25 June 2014 (http://www.dawn.com/news/1114984).

[193] The apex court had warned the government that on December 5 it would withdraw Justice Anwar Zaheer Jamali who was officiating as acting CEC.

[194] Ali Akbar, "Justice Sardar Raza Khan named CEC", *Dawn*, 4 Dec. 2014 (http://www.dawn.com/news/1148760/justice-sardar-raza-khan-named-cec).

political quest of elites who combined the occupations of litterati and an aristocratic heritage, but who were about to suffer a drop in status. The aspiration to perpetuate a dominant status played a structuring role in the crystallisation of their Islamic ideology and its political instrumentaliza-tion. After 1947, the Muhajirs, who had supported the League more than any other group; indeed controlled the state they had carved out with Partition and gave it a unitary structure as best as they could. During the 1950s they were largely dislodged from power by the Punjabis, but these new quasi-hegemons continued to centralise power in the framework of a unitary nation-state. This elitist syndrome resulting in the concentration of power found itself disputed from Pakistan's very foundation by ethno-national movements that represented lower-ranking regional and landown-ing elites whose identity repertoire was based on other cultures and especially languages other than Urdu. As a result, national integration has been affected by recurring tensions between the centralising, national establishment and ethno-linguistic centrifugal forces.

The regime question that the second part of this book has just explored can partly be stated in similar terms. Politicians and the army have clashed for decades in Pakistan—and the tension remains palpable today—so much so that the political system does not have the same stability as observed elsewhere in the region. While politicians have been traditionally weak, the army has never managed to remain in power for more than eleven years, due to external factors, but also because of the resilience of democratic forces. Hence another contradiction between two poles that partly overlaps the previous one between the Centre and the provinces.

But the strength of the army has always been such, since the 1950s, that even when the civilians are in office, Pakistan is not a full-fledged democ-racy. Not only civilian governments have never been allowed to exert any authority over the army (or defence policy), to shape the foreign policy of Pakistan and to have an upper hand on the nuclear programme—at least since the 1970s—, but as Christine Fair points out, "When civilians have reversed course on the army's preferred policies, the army has ousted them and has resumed its preferred suite of policies".[195] In 1971, when Mujibur Rahman won the elections, twelve generals objected that if he became Prime Minister he "would adopt a conciliatory attitude towards India, rel-egate Kashmir to the back-burner and direct funds from defence to eco-nomic development of East Pakistan"—in the words of Lt. Gen. (Retd.)

---

[195] C. Christine Fair, *Fighting to the End*, op. cit., p. 23.

Kamal Matinuddin.[196] In 1988, Zia dismissed Prime Minister Junejo after he signed the Geneva Accord to end the Afghan war in spite of Zia's opposition. In 1998–99 (and to a lesser extent in 2014), the army undermined the diplomatic overtures of Nawaz Sharif vis-à-vis India by relaunching hostilities in Kashmir.

The opposition between the army and the civilians needs to be qualified, however. On one hand, civilians have not necessarily been great democrats and on the other, army chiefs have not necessarily been power hungry. Civilians (not only bureaucrats but politicians as well) have allowed themselves to be co-opted by military dictators to the point of blurring the distinction between them and army rulers. Second, the two groups have also converged towards the same political ethos, a repertoire based on an authoritarian form of predation and patrimonialism. Civilians and army personnel have been accused of corruption and nepotism in almost equal proportions in recent years. For the common Pakistani people, the civil and military elites form an establishment that boils down to a few hundred families, the ruling classes being inter-related.

While the proponents of Jinnah's idea of Pakistan—civilians or military— faced ethno-religious movements from the start, the establishment just described and largely made of the same people has had to confront two forces of opposition—although belatedly: the courts and the media. These two circles have long been victims of the submissive attitude of their leaders (starting with several chief justices) and co-optation of the weaker links by the authorities. Repression has naturally fostered such defections, often to the benefit of military governments, but so has the army's prestige among certain sectors of society in a context of security anxiety.[197]

The past decade has witnessed the signs of a paradigm shift. For the first time in Pakistan's history, it was not political leaders but lawyers and judges who, as much in the street as in the courts, brought down a military regime with the support of the media which, despite its tendency to com-

---

[196] Kamal Matinuddin, *Tragedy of Errors. East Pakistan Crisis, 1968–1971*, Lahore, Wajidalis, 1994, p. 156.

[197] This context partly explains the army's popularity in opinion polls, which still should be viewed with caution. The Pew Center's annual poll in 2011 showed that 79% of the respondents had a favourable opinion of the army, while 76% of them also had a favourable opinion of journalists, 60% of clerics, 41% of the courts (ill thought-of at the local level, as discussed), and 20% favourable opinions for the government and 14% for Zardari. See http://www.pewglobal.org/2011/06/21/chapter-2-ratings-of-leaders-and-institutions/ (Accessed on September 15, 2013).

promise, is to a large degree staunchly determined and courageous. But lawyers cannot fill the gap resulting from the absence of political leaders observing a moral code and representing the common people.

Like the national identity issue, the question of regime can thus partly be deciphered using the same interpretation key, the core of the Pakistani syndrome: that of a narrow elite's quest for domination and the reactions it arouses, giving rise to violent conflicts.

The 2013 elections in this regard represented an important step in the democratisation process since, for the first time, an elected parliament has taken over from another one after it completed its term. But they have not resulted in the advent of new forces likely to meet the expectations of the masses, as evident from the budget favouring the rich that Nawaz Sharif managed to push through Parliament just after becoming prime minister—as does the 2014 budget.

Two major tensions forming two root causes of the Pakistani syndrome have thus been identified in the first two parts of this book: the opposition between the centralising national elite and ethno-linguistic movements and the opposition between civil and the military establishments as well as between the civil-military establishment and the two opposition forces that are the judiciary, and the media and, to a lesser extent civil society organisations.

A third contradiction needs now to be studied: that emerging from the role of religion and religious organisations. Not only has the status of Islam in the building of the Pakistani state been debated from the start, but the religious factor has also been used at once for the purposes of domination and rejection of this domination, a process all the more powerful as the organs of civil society capable of channelling social protest have been weak, leaving the field clear for the Islamists to serve a social function.

PART THREE

ISLAM: TERRITORIAL IDEOLOGY
OR POLITICAL RELIGION?

Islam, certainly, is the cornerstone of Pakistan.[1] But it has always had different meanings for the different political actors involved. Sir Syed, even before the idea of Pakistan had taken shape, and then Jinnah, viewed it as an identity marker designating a community whose status was in danger. They thought in terms of "Muslimhood". The *ulema*, distancing themselves from the Muslim League in the 1920s, logically enough emphasised the religious dimension. Theirs was hence a transnational, non-territorial view of Islam.

In 1947, the Muslim League had achieved its goal: the Muslims of the former Raj had a homeland—but the place of Islam in the new state remained a bone of contention. The party, true to Jinnah's ethno-cultural definition, wanted to build a nation of Pakistani citizens where all the communities would have equal rights. The religious leaders and the fundamentalist groups, without advocating a theocracy, rejected the multicultural dimension of this project and argued in favour of an Islamic state.

---

[1] The fact that Islam is considered the cornerstone of Pakistani identity finds echoes in history textbooks which almost systematically present the country as a creation of the Arab conquerors of the early medieval period ("What is the most blatant lie taught through Pakistan history textbooks?", *The Herald*, August 2014, pp. 22–26). On the bias affecting history textbooks in Pakistan, see K.K. Aziz, *The Murder of History. A Critique of History Textbooks Used in Pakistan*, Lahore, Vanguard, 2004.

On top of these domestic tensions surrounding the definition of the regime, the international aspect of the issue grew in importance. Not only does Islam connect the Pakistanis with their coreligionists throughout the world, but Islamists have gradually represented a strategic resource for the Pakistani government (whether civil or military) in the context of its regional policy. First, they could be used against the Pashtun nationalists in Afghanistan. Second, they could prove useful in destabilising India by fomenting violent action, especially in Kashmir.

While the Constitutions of 1956 and 1962 represented compromises rather favourable to those known as the "secularists"—such as Jinnah—things changed in the 1970s. The support Bhutto and later Zia gave the Islamists in Afghanistan went hand in hand with the growing Islamisation of the state. Not only did the 1973 Constitution make Islam the state religion of Pakistan, but its efforts to define who was a Muslim resulted in the exclusion of the Ahmadis from the majority community.

Zia's Islamisation policy would go much further since it impacted almost all areas of life, including law and education. It amplified the rift between Sunnis and Shias, a sectarian divide that was largely overdetermined by the proxy war that Saudi Arabia and Iran were fighting in Pakistan.

Another external factor played a more important role, however: the anti-Soviet jihad of the 1980s that resulted in the inflow of thousands of mujahideen from the Middle East. Among them, the founders of Al Qaeda, who contributed—along with the Pakistani state—to the victory of the Taliban in 1996.

In order to achieve "strategic depth" vis-à-vis India and to "bleed India" in Kashmir, Pakistan, indeed, cultivated close relations with Islamist groups. The attacks of 11 September 2001 and the ensuing second Afghan war did not prompt the government, then in the hands of the army, to radically change its policy. To begin with, it repressed the jihadists associated with Al Qaeda and the Taliban in a limited and selective manner. The Islamists had become too powerful to be attacked head on, especially in the difficult terrain of the tribal areas. Second, the Pakistani army was still counting on Mullah Omar and his troops to help reestablish its influence in Afghanistan and on groups such as Lashkar-e-Taiba to weaken India.

Even if the crackdown was moderate, many Islamist groups—including a new one, the Pakistani Taliban, which resented the government's alliance with the United States in the framework of the "global war on terror"—began to attack the Pakistani state. This escalation of violence, which has also fostered the rise of sectarianism and persecutions against religious minorities, has led Pakistan much closer to the brink of civil war than ethnic strife.

8

FROM JINNAH'S SECULARISM
TO ZIA'S ISLAMISATION POLICY

Despite historians' efforts, Jinnah's original plan for Pakistan still remains difficult to define clearly. But there is little doubt that it included a form of secularism in the sense that a theorist of this "ism" such as Charles Taylor means it. Taylor defines this type of relationship between religion and public space in the following terms: (1) everyone can freely exercise his religion; (2) every religion—whether of the majority or the minority—is considered on equal footing in the public sphere; and (3) "all spiritual families must be heard."[2]

In Jinnah's famous speech of 11 August 1947 before the Constituent Assembly of Pakistan, three days before the official foundation of the new state, he outlined a perspective that was very similar to the one that would prevail in the future Indian republic:

You may belong to any religion or caste or creed that has nothing to do with the business of the state. (...) We are starting with this fundamental principle that we are all citizens and equal citizens of one state (...) Now I think we should keep that in front of us as our ideal and you will find that in course of time Hindus would cease to be Hindus and Muslims would cease to be Muslims, not in the religious sense, because that is the personal faith of each individual, but the political sense as citizens of the state.[3]

[2] Charles Taylor, "The Meaning of Secularism", *The Hedgehog Review*, Fall 2010, vol. 12, no. 3, pp. 23–34.
[3] Cited in Shahid Javed Burki, *Pakistan. Fifty Years of Nationhood*, Boulder, Westview Press, 1999, p. 26.

This speech was followed by an important debate on the design of the Pakistan flag in which the Muslim League leaders argued in favour of their party flag becoming the national flag, whereas the representatives of the minorities objected that it represented "a particular community".[4] They were not heard, Muslim League leaders arguing that the white patch the flag represented the minorities.[5] This incident reflected the tension between those who defended the project of a secular Muslim state (like Jinnah) and those who did not accept the domination of the majority community. But there was another tension between those who advocated a Muslim state and those who wanted an Islamic state.

After Jinnah's death in 1948, debates in the Constituent Assembly on that front proved complicated for Liaquat Ali Khan, and after his assassination in 1951, for those known as "secularists", due to opposition from religious activists in this legislative body and from Islamist parties occupying the public space and the street.[6] The lack of consensus on the role of Islam in building the Pakistani state, very aptly pointed out by Farzana Shaikh,[7] would lead to a more advantageous compromise to the secularists in the 1956 and 1962 Constitutions. The 1973 Constitution was theoretically stamped even more with liberal values. Yet, the Bhutto years marked a paradoxical turning point toward a certain Islamisation of politics—for the purposes of collective mobilisation—that General Zia would pursue radically out of conviction and to legitimise his power.

What Islam, for What Policy? (1947–1969)

The first chapters of this book have shown that the Muslim League's and especially Jinnah's idea of Pakistan was a natural extension of Syed Ahmad Khan's reformism. Islam was less perceived as a religion than as an identity marker characteristic of a minority threatened by the Hindus and identifying with a territory. In this regard it can be viewed as an ethnicisation of the religious factor.

This conception was not shared by the clerics responsible for the foundation of the Jamiat-e-Ulema-e Hind (JUH) and the Caliphate Movement, or by the Jama'at-e-Islami, whose agenda will now be examined.

---

[4] Sadia Saeed, "Desecularisation as an instituted process. National identity and religious difference in Pakistan", *Economic and Political Weekly*, vol. xlviii, no. 50, 14 December 2013, p. 65.

[5] Khaled Ahmed, *Sectarian War*, p. xv. 6 Leonard Binder, *Religion and Politics in Pakistan*, Berkeley and Los Angeles, University of California Press, 1963.

[7] Farzana Shaikh, *Making Sense of Pakistan*, London, Hurst, 2009.

Clerics and Fundamentalists: The Jamiat-e-Ulema and the
Jama'at-e-Islami

For the JUH, Islam could not be reduced to a culture and identified with a
nation-state in the way that the two-nations theory supposed. First of all,
this religion had a transnational dimension rooted in the universal nature
of the *umma* and the solidarity beyond borders that it implied among the
faithful. Second, the political aspect mattered less than the societal aspect,
which presented Islam as the legal regulator of the community: the nation
(*qaum*) was less important than the community (*millat*). But this approach
did not necessarily mean that the future of the Muslims of the Raj was in
India. Although many *ulema*—starting with Azad, education minister under
Nehru from 1947 to his death in 1958—identified with Gandhi's Congress
Party, as its multicultural philosophy was respectful of Muslim Personal
Law, sharia, others were more sceptical toward Indian tolerance and opted
for Pakistan in 1947, even before.

In fact, the split between *ulema* who were hostile to the idea of Pakistan
and those who advocated it occurred in the mid-1940s when those in favour
ended up forming a substantial group. Among them, Shabbir Ahmad Usmani
stood out as a new brand of leader. Born in 1886 in Bijnor (today's Uttar
Pradesh, India), Usmani had received his education at the Deoband seminary
where he became a teacher before directing the Madrassah Fatehpuri in
Delhi and then the Darel Uloom in Dabhel, Surat. He then returned to
Deoband where he taught the *hadith* before presiding over the seminary. A
reputed theologian, he also became a public figure by raising funds intended
to aid Muslims in the Balkans during the war there. He was one of the few
Deobandis to choose the Muslim League and support the creation of Pakistan
in 1944. Shortly thereafter, in 1945–6, he was involved in the split affecting
the Jamiat-Ulema-e-Hind and founded the Jamiat-Ulema-e-Islam.

The Barelwi *ulema*, more numerous but far less well organised than the
Deobandis, followed a similar path. In 1948 they formed the Jamiat-e-Ulema
Pakistan (JUP)[8] headed by Khwaja Qamar ul Din Sialvi, a Sufi leader following the Chishti order who had joined the Muslim League in the 1940s.
(He had even campaigned for the party throughout India for the 1946 elections.) The JUP, even before the JUI, had campaigned as of 1947 for the
creation of an Islamic state in Pakistan.

[8] Ahmad, Mujeeb, *Jam'iyyat 'Ulama-i-Pakistan, 1948–1979*, Volume 12 of Historical
1993 studies (Pakistan) series, Islamabad, National Institute of Historical and
Cultural Research, 1993, p. 59.

The JUI and the JUP differed from Jama'at-e-Islami fundamentalists in that they represented the clerics and their conservative view of society, but the three movements made a tactical and even partly ideological rapprochement after the creation of Pakistan.

The history of the Jama'at-e-Islami (JI) is bound up with the trajectory of Sayed Abul Ala Maududi.[9] Maududi was born in 1903 in Aurangabad (Indian Deccan) and descended from a prestigious Chishti lineage and from Syed Ahmed Khan through his paternal grandmother's family. His father was in fact one of the first students at the Aligarh Muslim University, although for only a short while because his parents withdrew him, deeming the teaching there too progressive, a sign of the attachment to traditions that Maududi would faithfully perpetuate. Maududi's mother was from a Turkish family that had contributed many generals to the Aurangzeb army and the Hyderabad Nizam, connecting him with the glorious aristocratic heritage of the Indian Muslims—a golden age for which he cultivated considerable nostalgia. As a youth, Maududi was acutely conscious of the decline of his family and his community,[10] which did not prevent him from reading western literature and developing a purely Indian nationalist sentiment, to the point of writing a hagiography of the Hindu nationalist leader M. M. Malviya. After the Caliphate Movement—in which he participated as a journalist, his first occupation—Maududi moved to Bhopal where he was highly influenced by the Ahl-i-Hadith. But back in Delhi, he returned to his studies at the Deobandi Fatehpuri madrassah—which according to Vali Nasr appealed to him to the point that he became an *alim* of the seminary.[11] Maududi was more reserved about his training:

I do not have the prerogative to belong to the class of Ulema. I am a man of the middle cadre, who has imbibed something from both systems of education, the new and the old; and has gathered my knowledge by traversing both paths. By virtue of my inner light, I concluded that neither the old school nor the new is totally in the right.[12]

---

[9] Two books by Seyyed Vali Reza Nasr remain the best resources on the subject, *The Vanguard of Islamic Revolution: the Jama'at-i Islami of Pakistan*, London and New York, IB Tauris, 1994 and *Mawdudi and the Making of Islamic Revivalism*, New York, Oxford University Press, 1996.

[10] Seyyed Vali Reza Nasr, *Mawdudi and the Making of Islamic Revivalism*, op. cit., p. 11.

[11] Ibid., p. 18.

[12] Cited in ibid., p. 19.

Maududi, who had learned English through private tutoring, is a typical figure of the intelligentsia, a class of men socialised in their domestic tradition but educated at least in part in the western style, and eager to transcend this opposition by inventing an ideological synthesis. Maududi's thinking would be defined in terms of Islamic fundamentalism, a trend that today has a wealth of different streams but in which he played a pioneer role.

Maududi's Islamic activism crystallised in the 1920s in reaction to the so-called Shuddhi Hindu nationalist movement that aimed to (re)convert both Christians and Muslims to the majority religion. *Shuddhi* (lit. purification) campaigns gave rise to tensions between Hindus and Muslims throughout all of North India where according to Maududi, his community was unable to defend its religion adequately. This prompted him to undertake a scholarly investigation to understand the spirit of holy war, or jihad. This exegesis led him to investigate the golden age of his civilisation, an obligatory phase of all ethnic nationalists (the Hindu nationalists who invented the Vedic golden age were on a similar trajectory at the time).

Maududi was nevertheless tormented by a feeling of collective vulnerability that became all the more acute when in 1930 he settled in Hyderabad, a princely state that looked like one of the last Muslim bastions. Muslim dominance, both from a political and cultural standpoint, survived there under the threat of a Hindu wave that nothing—neither demographics nor a change in the socio-economic balance of power—could stop. He viewed the Nizam's conservatism as suicidal, and so he decided to settle in Punjab—where the Muslims' future seemed more secure—to launch an Islamic revival movement with Iqbal's blessing.

Maududi founded his Daru'l-Islam (land of Islam) movement in 1938 in Pathankot, emphasizing the need for Muslims to organize. His observation of the working of the Tablighi Jamaat in Rajasthan in 1939 during a trip there seems to have influenced him considerably. But in this preparatory phase, he also visited the Aligarh Muslim University and the Nadwat al-Ulama in Lucknow, another sign of his positioning at the crossroads of the so-called modern and traditional currents.

He finally founded the Jama'at-e-Islami in Lahore in 1941. Nasr describes the ideology of this organisation as "fundamentalist" because its plan to defend Muslims rested solely on "the Qur'an, the prophetic traditions, and the legal canon (*fiqh*) of Islam as repositories of divine truth."[13] Maududi's aim was to follow the Prophet not as a spiritual guide but as a guide for the

---

[13] Ibid., p. 61.

collective revival of Muslims throughout the world. In fact, Maududi was a modern in that he invented a new jurisprudence overarching the various schools of law whose quarrels he disregarded. In order to reach the masses, he moreover spoke and wrote only in Urdu.

While he did not promote religious discipline as a road to individual salvation, Maududi based his plan for Muslim renewal on individual will to reform. This is indicated by his definition of a Muslim: "A Muslim is not a Muslim by appellation or birth, but by virtue of abiding by holy law."[14] Muslims should merge "completely into Islam their full personality and entire existence."[15] Like its Hindu nationalist counterpart, the Rashtriya Swayamsevak Sangh, the Jama'at-e-Islami embodied an all-embracing philosophy in that its members were expected to devote themselves to it body and soul. But beyond this task of social-psychological reform—which the RSS contented itself with up until the 1950s—the JI developed a political aim. Maududi in fact surmised from the history of India that in the past Islam only truly flourished when power was in Muslim hands. Such was the condition in which sharia could rule, as well as Islam in general, as it did in the Prophet's Medina which remained his model. It nevertheless had to be adapted to the modern era, which explains the idea of a caliphate in which the sovereign (*emir*) would rule in God's name on earth without having any real margin for initiative. The *emir* would be elected, but he would be the only candidate in the running. As for political freedom, it could only be exercised in a transition phase. Regarding Maududi's views, Nasr writes:

Freedom of political expression was limited because it could have currency only during the formative stages of the Islamic state when, in the absence of the rule of divine law, inconsistencies might persist that required protection of individual rights. After the formative years, dissent in a polity based on divine law could only be construed as apostasy.[16]

According to Maududi, residents of the Islamic state are divided into four categories: male Muslims, female Muslims, *zimmis* (protected subjects who followed a religion recognized by Islam) and the others (for example the Ahmadis). Only the first two groups could be regarded as citizens.[17] Among

---

[14] Cited in ibid., p. 64.
[15] Cited in ibid., p. 68.
[16] Cited in ibid., p. 91.
[17] Jan-Peter Hartung, *A System of Life. Mawdudi and the Ideologisation of Islam*, London, Hurst, 2013, p. 149 and p. 153.

male Muslims, Maududi made a distinction between those who followed the precepts of Islam and those who were only nominally Muslims, and also distinguished between Sunnis (giving preference to those who followed the Hanafi school) and Shias.

Maududi organised the JI along these principles. From the start he attempted to make it the enlightened vanguard of an Islamic revival, drawing both on the sectarian model of Sufi orders and modern Marxist-Leninist type cadre parties.[18] This "holy community" set out to re-Islamise society on the whole through a network of morally upright and exemplary local cadres. Initially set up in Sialkot, the JI moved its headquarters to Pathankot in 1942.

A closely-knit community, the JI was also very isolated in the 1940s. First, religious leaders harshly criticised the liberties it took with tradition. The rector of the Nadwat al-Ulama, Maulana Sayyid Abuu'l-Hasan'Ali Nadwi and a respected Deobandi alim, Muhammad Manzur Nu'mani, accused him of denying Muslims individual choice in matters of faith, which they held to be one of the fundamental tenets of Islam. They also disapproved his emphasis on politics as the main vehicle for religious spirituality.[19]

This conflict naturally arose from the fact that Maududi did not belong to the community of *ulema*, in keeping with his self-styled ideology, and that he claimed to speak in the name of Islam without having any official title. Nasr qualifies Maududi's heterodoxy: "Only those who had faith in the shari'ah; had knowledge of the Qur'an, the prophetic traditions, and other sources of religious law; and were proficient in Arabic would practice ijtihad, and these requirements have limited the extent of the Jama'at's break with the traditional perspective."[20] But he was at odds with the traditional perspective for other reasons, the first being that he had started his own school of law, even if he claimed to belong to the Hanafi school. Beyond that, his doctrine made the *ulema* simply obsolete. As long as he sought to revive the Caliphate, they lost their role as leaders and judges, even as

---

[18] Seyyed Vali Reza Nasr, *The Vanguard of Islamic Revolution: the Jama'at-i Islami of Pakistan*, op. cit., pp. 10–13. Interstingly, the present-day leader of the JI, Munawwar Hasan, began his public career as a student leader in the Marxist student union, the National Students Federation. See "Munawwar Hasan", *Dawn*, 13 May 2013, http://dawn.com/2013/04/05/munawwar-hasan-2/ (Accessed on September 15, 2013).

[19] Seyyed Vali Reza Nasr, *Mawdudi and the Making of Islamic Revivalism*, op. cit., pp. 58–59.

[20] Ibid., p. 107.

custodians of the community. As long as he encouraged the faithful to study the Quran and the *hadith* on their own, the ulema were no longer necessary intermediaries between believers and God.[21] For all these reasons, none of the seventy-five *ulema* whom Maududi had invited to the JI inaugural ceremony in 1941 answered positively. The few who replied only answered to criticize his initiative.[22] Maududi was critical of them in return—contrary to what his invitation suggested. As Nasr notes, he "saw the ulama as unequipped to contend with the problems of the modern world, and he believed they misunderstood Islam."[23] Furthermore, he rejected their support for the Congress, a party which he viewed as working for the Hindus cause. He accused JUH leader Maulana Husain Ahmad Madani of "sacrificing Islam at the altar of his anti-British sentiments".[24]

But Maududi's JI was not for all that an ally of the Muslim League. First of all, its leaders—Jinnah in the forefront—seemed too westernised and not enough in tune with Islamic traditions. In 1945, Maududi issued a *fatwa* "forbidding Muslims to vote for the 'secular' Muslim League."[25] Second, in the 1940s, Maududi still accorded priority to working on society in order to revive Islam not only among Muslims, but throughout all of India.

Some observers have found that Maududi was opposed to the idea of Pakistan as it seemed unsuitable to this long-term goal and also due to the transnational aspect of the *umma*, a community that could not be territorialized in terms of a nation-state (which can be compared to the caliphate-type organization contained in Maududi's notion of an Islamic state).[26] In fact, "the Jama'at did not object to Pakistan but to its creation under the aegis of the League",[27] a party that was unlikely to make the new country an Islamic state.

When Partition came about, Maududi resigned himself to the idea of living in a Pakistan created by Jinnah. While some members of the JI remained in India to form the Jama'at-e-Islami-e-Hind, he opted for Pakistan and deployed the remnants of his organisation there. But Maududi continued to work for a truly Islamic Pakistan. In January and February

---

[21] Ibid., p. 115.

[22] Ibid.

[23] Ibid., p. 116.

[24] Seyyed Vali Reza Nasr, *The Vanguard of Islamic Revolution*, op. cit., p. 104

[25] Ibid., p. 114.

[26] Maududi, Abu al-A'la al-, "Political theory of Islam", in Khurshid Ahmad (ed.), *Islam: Its Meaning and Message*, London, Islamic Council of Europe, 1976.

[27] Seyyed Vali Reza Nasr, *The Vanguard of Islamic Revolution*, op. cit., p. 106.

1948, he gave two lectures at the Law College of Lahore where he laid the foundations for what an Islamic state should be. He then undertook a national tour during which he made overtures to the *ulema*, "hinting of a grand Islamic alliance, a suggestion the Muslim League viewed with considerable concern",[28] all the more so as Maududi sent emissaries to Karachi to contact a number of *ulema* who were Constituent Assembly members.

Maududi sparked one controversy after another regarding the meaning of the idea of Pakistan. Following the April 1948 Indian-Pakistani truce in Kashmir, Maududi thus wrote to Maulana Shabbir Ahmad Usmani stating that any guerrilla operation in Kashmir would be against sharia, as it commands Muslims to honour state obligations. In the letter, which has sometimes been interpreted as a *fatwa*, he argued that Pakistan could not conduct infiltration operations in the name of jihad and that it would be better to resume hostilities openly. The Indians having seized upon his remarks, the government in Karachi accused him of sedition, forcing him to revise his statements and recognize the legitimacy of individual jihad.[29] JI leaders were placed under surveillance by the Pakistani government. In the fall of 1948, twenty-five civil servants who were JI members or sympathizers were dismissed in keeping with a declaration that the JI and the Communist Party were seditious. Maududi himself was imprisoned from October 1948 to late 1949 after he claimed he could not serve the Pakistani state—including in the army—as long as it was not fully Islamic.[30] Such repression only brought the JI closer to the *ulema*, as the history of the making of the Pakistani Constitution shows.[31]

The Constitutional Debate

The making of the Pakistani Constitution was turned into a very delicate exercise due to the conflict between the secularists and the two organizations discussed above, the JUI and the JI.

---

[28] Ibid., p. 119.

[29] Frédéric Grare, *Political Islam in the Indian Subcontinent. The Jamaat-i-Islami*, Delhi, Manohar, 2001, p. 30.

[30] Up until 1977, the JI's constitution banned its members from joining the administration or the army. Marc Gaborieau, "Le néo-fondamentalisme au Pakistan: Maududi et la Jama'at-i-Islami", in Olivier Carré and Paul Dumont, *Radicalismes Islamiques*, Paris, L'Harmattan, 1986, p. 60.

[31] Jan-Peter Hartung points out that "While in jail, Mawdudi saw the necessity of forging a strategic alliance with the *ulama* whom he had earlier despised for systematic reasons" (Jan-Peter Hartung, *A System of Life*, op. cit., p. 227).

Among the former, the most influential was none other than the JUI president, Maulana Shabbir Ahmad Usmani, who had thrown his support behind the Muslim League prior to 1947 and was a member of the Constituent Assembly for this party, but he was to make Liaquat Ali Khan's task particularly difficult. As the most prestigious *alim*—who on top of it had broken up the monopoly enjoyed by the Congress among the *ulema*— he had direct access to Pakistan's leaders, including Liaquat Ali Khan. Now, he had a different conception of what Pakistan should be, which was partly shared, even influenced, by Maududi.

In 1948, while in prison, Maududi had sent two *ulema* to Karachi to meet with Usmani. They were Abdul Jabbar Ghazi and Abdul Ghaffar Hasan. These men, who held important roles in the JI—they replaced Maududi while he was behind bars—"worked diligently to bring the various ulama groups into an alliance and were especially successful in influencing Maulana Usmani..."[32] Usmani thus spoke in favour of establishing "a truly Islamic state" in which religious leaders would have an official role. He asked the Assembly to set up "a committee consisting of eminent ulama and thinkers (...) to prepare a draft (Constitution) and present it to the Assembly."[33] He in particular influenced the drafting of the Objectives Resolution that Prime Minister Liaquat Ali Khan submitted to the Constituent Assembly on 12 March 1949.

This resolution, like the one Nehru introduced before the Indian Constituent Assembly three years before, was intended to frame the debates. It already contained signs of effort to reach a compromise regarding the place of Islam:

1. Sovereignty belongs to Allah alone but He has delegated it to the State of Pakistan through its people for being exercised within the limits prescribed by Him as a sacred trust.
2. The State shall exercise its powers and authority through the chosen representatives of the people.
3. The principles of democracy, freedom, equality, tolerance and social justice, as enunciated by Islam, shall be fully observed.
4. Muslims shall be enabled to order their lives in the individual and collective spheres in accordance with the teaching of Islam as set out in the holy Quran and Sunnah.
5. Adequate provision shall be made for the minorities to freely profess and practice their religions and develop their cultures.

---

[32] Seyyed Vali Reza Nasr, *The Vanguard of Islamic Revolution*, op. cit., p. 124
[33] Leonard Binder, *Religion and Politics in Pakistan*, op. cit., pp. 140–141.

6. Pakistan shall be a federation.
7. Fundamental rights shall be guaranteed.
8. The Judiciary shall be independent.[34]

Unsurprisingly, the more convoluted articles of this blueprint for the Constitution are those regarding the role of religion. Leonard Binder, the eminent specialist of relations between religion and politics in the early years of Pakistan, notes with a hint of irony, "Thus is God sovereign, the people sovereign, parliament sovereign, and the state sovereign in Pakistan. It would indeed be a narrow-minded person who was not satisfied with such a compromise."[35]

Maududi greeted the Objectives Resolution as "a victory for Islam and for the Jama'at."[36] To build a Constitution on this basis was bound to be complicated. The main bone of contention had to do with sharia law: "The ulama desired to enshrine the principle of the supremacy of the shari'a, while the politicians, or most of them, found this principle acceptable so long as it was not clearly defined."[37] The Muslim League leaders could not go against Islam, but they wanted to keep its role vague. In mid-April 1949, the twenty-five men on the Basic Principles Committee in charge of drafting the Constitution decided "to set up a board of experts consisting of reputed Scholars well versed in Ta'limat-i-Islamia (Islamic teachings) to advise on matters arising out of the Objectives Resolution."[38] The committee drew its inspiration from the medieval Islamic theory of the caliphs to emphasize the need to select heads of state endowed with personal qualities. It held that the president had to be a Muslim *de jure*.

The Muslim League leaders resigned themselves to making concessions, convinced that Jinnah's secular views had become untenable. But they tried to "relegate Islam to the sphere of policy rather than law."[39] Hence, Liaquat Ali Khan attempted to counter the clerics by emphasizing the Islamic

---

[34] "Objectives resolution is passed", see http://www.storyofpakistan.com (Accessed on September 15, 2013).

[35] Leonard Binder, *Religion and Politics in Pakistan*, Berkeley and Los Angeles, University of California Press, 1963, p. 149.

[36] Seyyed Vali Reza Nasr, *The Vanguard of Islamic Revolution*, op. cit., p. 124.

[37] Leonard Binder, *Religion and Politics in Pakistan*, op. cit., p. 144.

[38] Ibid., p. 156. Among those who sat on the committee were Maulana Saiyid Suleiman Nadvi, Shibli's successor at the helm of the Nadwat al-Ulama despite his age, who came from Lucknow, and Mufti Muhammad Shafi, Usmani's right-hand man.

[39] Ibid., p. 184.

notion of social justice—and his concept of "Islamic socialism"—and by rejecting the idea of "theocracy".[40]

In the course of this face-off, Maududi strove to bring the JI and the *ulema* closer together. In January 1951, he managed to organize a meeting of thirty-one *ulema* in Karachi under the aegis of Sayyid Suleiman Nadwi, who drew up a list of twenty-two principles to be submitted to the Constituent Assembly for consideration.[41] Maududi was encouraged in his activism by Liaquat Ali Khan's disappearance and his replacement by a prime minister more receptive to the clerics' arguments, Khawaja Nazimuddin.[42] In November 1952, the JI held a "Constitution Week" punctuated with demonstrations, the largest taking place in Karachi. The draft Constitution presented to the Constituent Assembly by the Drafting Committee in December 1952 made numerous concessions to religious activists, which Maududi attributed to JI pressure. As a result, "Maududi now raised the stakes. He demanded that Pakistan be called the 'Islamic Republic of Pakistan,' that the shari'ah be made the supreme law of the land, and that ulama boards be set up to oversee the passage of laws."[43] Vali Nasr draws two separate conclusions from the JI's actions in the 1948–53 period. On one hand, "the Jama'at's propaganda and maneuvering and Mawdudi's untiring campaign for Islamization foiled the attempts both of Muslim Leaguers (...) to extricate Islam from politics and of the government to manipulate Islam for its own ends." On the other, "The Jama'at itself also underwent change during this period. Opposition to the state was supplanted by maneuverings within the state system."[44]

The Anti-Ahmadi Movement—and the Crackdown

Pakistan's rulers, however, tried to regain the upper hand in the case of the Ahmadis. This sect, also known—in a more derogatory mode—as Qadianis, are the followers of Mirza Ghulam Ahmad, a nineteenth-century Punjabi Muslim from the district of Qadian who claimed he was a reincarnation of Muhammad (as well as of Jesus Christ). It rejected the notion of jihad for a more quiestist, but intensely proselytising practice of Islam.[45] Other Muslims,

---

[40] Sadia Saeed, "Desecularisation as an instituted process", op. cit., p. 66.

[41] Seyyed Vali Reza Nasr, *The Vanguard of Islamic Revolution*, p. 127.

[42] Ibid., p. 129.

[43] Ibid. p. 130.

[44] Ibid., p. 131.

[45] Yohann Friedmann, *Prophecy Continuous: Aspects of Ahmadi Religious Thought*

who considered them heretics, attacked the Ahmadis from the start. In 1934, the Ahrars, an Islamic group affiliated with the Congress but with socialist leanings (and no stable ideology in any case) combated them with unprecedented aggressiveness. The Ahrars also demanded the resignation of Sir Zafarullah Khan, a famous Ahmadi, from the Viceroy's Council.

After Partition the offensives intensified. The first anti-Ahmadi campaign took place in Punjab in 1949—again at the Ahrars' initiative—with the objective of excommunicating this community so that they would no longer be considered Muslim. Zafarullah Khan, who had become minister of foreign affairs, remained a priority target. On 18 May 1952, Sayyid Suleiman Nadwi called an *ulema* conference to demand that the Ahmadis be officially declared a "non-Muslim minority" and have Zafarullah Khan expelled from the government.

The Jama'at-e-Islami joined the movement later. Maududi, already reluctant to collaborate with the Ahrars—considered that the Ahmadis would gradually fall in line as the Islamisation policy scored points. But many JI cadres deemed that exploiting the Ahmadi issue would help shore up the party's base in Punjab at a time when the party really only existed among the Muhajirs of Karachi; all the more so as the government of Punjab had already taken up the cause of the anti-Ahmadi demonstrators.

Maududi was also prompted to act by the *ulema*, who criticized his wait-and-see attitude. He could not allow himself to be outdone by them. He thus joined in the agitation—going so far as to demand the resignation of Prime Minister Nazimuddin—and in March 1953 published a caustic pamphlet titled *Qadiyani Masalah* (the Ahmadi problem). Nazimuddin reacted with unexpected vigour. Many *ulema*, Ahrar and JI party cadres, including Maududi, were placed under house arrest or imprisoned. The charge against Maududi is worth mentioning as it reflects the government's multiculturalist—in the vocabulary of South Asia, one would even say secular—aspirations: Maududi was arrested for having "promoting feelings of enmity and hatred between different groups in Pakistan."

The disturbances of 1952–3 put a stop to the rise in power of traditionalists and fundamentalists. First, the governor general, Iskander Mirza, used the argument that the chief minister of Punjab, Daultana, and Prime Minister Nazimuddin had flirted with the religious activists (which was true for the latter down to his last and very belated change of heart) to dismiss them from

---

and Its Medieval Background, Berkeley and Los Angeles, University of California Press, 1989.

office: he imposed martial law in Punjab and replaced the prime minister with the very secular Bogra. Second, the terms of the public debate regarding Pakistan's religious identity were entirely reconsidered.

Mirza set up a court of inquiry to investigate the causes for the anti-Ahmadi agitation. It was presided by Chief Justice Munir. The "Munir Report" presented the religious activists and clerics in a particularly unfavourable light. Underscoring their ignorance, the report concluded that there was no specific "definition of Islam, let alone of an Islamic constitution [...] and that the religious experts were best advised to leave the constitution-making process alone."[46]

In May 1953, Maududi was sentenced to death by a military tribunal. He was suspected of having taken part in disturbances organized by the Indians, which made it possible to cast the crime as high treason. The repression was carried out in the name of religious freedom, a key aspect of secularism.[47] And the ruling elite seized the opportunity to exclude religious leaders from the Constitution drafting committee.

Neither Secularism, nor Theocracy: The 1956 Constitution

Although in the early 1950s the alliance between traditional religious leaders and fundamentalists influenced constitutional debates, the atmosphere had changed by the middle of the decade after the crackdown prompted by the anti-Ahmadis riots. Maududi had spent two years in prison, which finished making him a hero in the eyes of his followers but kept him away from the public stage for some time. His lawyer had appealed the death sentence and in April 1955, even before a new trial could be held, the government released him, but he could no longer influence the constitutional debates the way he had in 1951–3.

The 1956 Constitution, the product of a compromise, made few concessions to the most radical Islamic demands. True, it instituted the Islamic Republic of Pakistan, it stipulated that only a Muslim could be President (but it was possible for the speaker of the National Assembly who would replace him in the event of an interim vacancy not to be), that "no Law would be passed against the teachings of Quran and Sunnah and the existing laws would be made Islamic in character" and that steps would "be

---

[46] Seyyed Vali Reza Nasr, *The Vanguard of Islamic Revolution*, op.cit., p. 138.
[47] On the notion of secularism, see Charles Taylor, "The meaning of secularism", *The Hedgehog Review*, Fall 2010, vol. 12, no. 3, pp. 23–34.

taken to enable the Muslims of Pakistan individually and collectively to order their lives in accordance with the Holy Quran and Sunnah." But neither the Objectives Resolution nor the Talimat-i-Islamia Council recommendations regarding Islamic teaching were taken into account, and furthermore, article 18 of the Constitution guaranteed "freedom to profess, practice and propagate any religion and the right to establish, maintain and manage religious institutions"—reflecting the fact that Islam did not have the status of official religion.

The Islamic Republic of Pakistan, as evident from its official name, was not secular since religious minorities did not enjoy the same rights as the Muslim majority which was supposed to produce the head of state. But it was not a theocracy either, since non-Muslims were allowed to live their religion fully and sharia was not the only law. The status of minorities was difficult to determine, however, as was apparent in the question of separate electorates that had given rise to heated debate between Suhrawardy, when he was chief minister of East Pakistan, and the Jama'at-e-Islami. While Suhrawardy had reservations about the idea, the JI on the other hand viewed a joint electorate, in which Hindu voters could take part in choosing the province's representatives, as a negation of Pakistan's Muslim identity.

The members of the Constituent Assembly took care not to settle the issue. The Constitution left it up to the provinces whether or not to perpetuate the system of separate electorates handed down from the British. When they did not view it as an obstacle to nation-building, Muslim leaders were in favour of it, considering it an expression of the two-nations theory, whereas the Hindus, who in 1951 made up 23 per cent of the population of East Pakistan and nearly 10 per cent of that of Sindh (minus Karachi), were concerned about the political "ghettoisation" such a system would produce.[48] Beyond that, most Christian, Parsi, Sikh and other minority leaders considered that the Pakistani Constitution did not meet one of the foundations of secularism, as it did not place minority voters on an equal footing with the Muslim majority. But the most penalised minority was the Hindus, who remained perceived as a fifth column, and who not only never attained positions of responsibility but who were even victims of rioting as early as 1950 in East Pakistan. They therefore gradually left the country for India.

[48] Keith Callard, *Pakistan. A Political Study*, London, G. Allen and Unwin, 1957, chap. 7. The Hindus also rejected a major clause of this arrangement that sets "caste Hindus" apart from the "untouchables", each having a separate electorate in East Pakistan until 1954.

Ayub Khan, Secularism and Statism—up to a point

After the 1958 military coup Ayub Khan set out to modernise Pakistani Islam. He considered that religion was the only foundation for national unity, but publicly he rose up against the *ulema*'s obscurantism and sought to separate the spiritual from the temporal spheres. He pressured imams in mosques to open up to Western science and tried to get Maududi to quit politics by offering him the presidency of Bahawalpur University, in vain. So Ayub Khan chose the hard line. The JI was banned along with other political parties in 1958, and its assets were confiscated. And although Ayub Khan solicited Maududi's support during the war in 1965, he had him arrested twice, in 1964 and 1967. His regime in fact stood poles apart from the JI's fundamentalist agenda.

Ayub Khan also reformed Muslim practices he believed stood in the way of the country's progress, such as divorce by repudiation of wives and polygamy, which was not particularly prevalent in any case. He promulgated the Muslim Family Laws Ordinance (MFLO) on 15 July 1961 to curb the trend. This law set up an arbitration council responsible for examining all petitions for divorce. It had three months to attempt conciliation between spouses, a procedure that actually conformed to the Islamic tradition of *talaq ahsan*—a tradition that South Asian Muslims had gradually replaced by the *talaq al-bid'a* repudiation of wives, which was performed merely by repeating the *talaq* formula three times. This council was also in charge of obtaining a wife's consent in the event that a man wished to take an additional wife. If a husband failed to submit to the council's decision, he was liable to up to one year in jail. Last, the MFLO enabled children orphaned by mother and father to inherit from their grandparents, whether they were male or female. All these reforms clearly reflected the modernist influence the Aligarh University had had over Ayub Khan in his youth—which he attended before pursuing his studies in England.

Pirs and *Ulema*: The Political Influence of Religious Leaders

Ayub Khan also tried to reduce the influence of religious leaders, the *pirs* and the *ulema*. Unlike the *ulema*, urban legal scholars of the Quran, the more rural *pirs* owed their prestige to the mystic status their disciples (*murid*) attribute to them—as mentioned above.[49] These disciples even con-

---

[49] On what she calls "pirism", see Annemarie Schimmel, *Mystical Dimensions of*

sidered them saints and when they were powerful, often donateed land and money.[50]

Because of these assets—which reinforced their spiritual influence—*pirs* have traditionally been political figures[51] and have sometimes held office. In this capacity, land is their main source of influence, especially under a democratic regime when peasants' votes count. But it was not the only one. *Pirs* guaranteed the local villagers' participation in the *barakah*, as long as they pledged absolute obedience (*itâ'ath*).[52] Not only have political parties—starting with the Muslim League—made use of the *pirs'* influence on voters (particularly in the 1946 elections in Punjab), but *pirs* have also solicited votes from "their" villagers to be elected to assemblies.[53] According to K.K. Aziz: "The *pirs* entered Pakistan in 1947 as if they owned it". While the Muslim League was in office, "the *pirs* were its patron saints" and they gradually "added the mastery of intrigue and proficiency in political cut and thrust to their other qualifications". In parallel, "they had grown new tentacles on their body by marrying into industrial and military families".[54]

The Pir Pagaro was a case in point. He was the hereditary spiritual leader of the Sufi order of Hurs. The last man to bear this title in the colonial era was hanged by the British in 1943 for his political activities—a sign of this religious figure's involvement in worldly affairs. His son was rehabilitated

---

Islam, Chapel Hill, N. C., 1975, p. 22. A *pir* may, for instance, be a descendent of a saint and act as a custodian of the tomb/shrine, or claim the Prophet as an ancestor, or head a madrassah (Quranic school). On the *pirs* in South Asia, see Adrian C. Mayer, "Pir and Murshid", *Middle Eastern Studies*, 3/1967, pp. 160–169, and two chapters of the same edited volume: David Gilmartin, "Shrine, succession, and sources of moral authority", in Barbara Metcalf (ed.), *Moral Conduct and Authority*, Berkeley, California University Press, 1984, pp. 221–240 and Richard Eaton, "The Political and Religious Authority of the Shrine of Baba Farid", in ibid., pp. 333–356.

50 Jamal Malik, *Colonization of Islam. Dissolution of Traditional Institutions in Pakistan*, Delhi, Manohar, 1998, p. 57.

51 However, some families have always abstained from going into politics. This is true of the descendents of Shah Abdul Latif Bhittai, Sachal Sarmast and Lal Shahbaz Qalandar. See Hafeez Tunio, "Sindhi Stories: The Pir's Power, the Syed Sway", *The Express Tribune*, 5 April 2013.

52 Jamal Malik, *Colonization of Islam*, op. cit., p. 58.

53 David Gilmartin, "Religious Leadership and the Pakistan Movement in the Punjab", *Modern Asian Studies*, vol. 13, no. 3, 1979, pp. 485–517.

54 K.K. Aziz, *Religion, land and politics in India*, op. cit., pp. 53–55.

and restored to his "throne" in 1952. He immediately joined the Muslim League.[55] Although his bastion was Sanghar district in Sindh, there were some twenty constituencies under his control in 1955 when his supporters in the Sindh assembly enabled the Chief Minister, M.A. Khuro to get the state government approve the One-Unit scheme.[56] Ayub Khan was justly suspicious of him, but at the end of his rule was unable to prevent him from playing a major role in the opposition, behind Fatima Jinnah.

While there was a particularly high number of *pirs* in politics in Sindh, they were also present in South Punjab, as evident in the situation of Bahawalpur district. Makhdumul Mulk Syed Ghulam Miran Shah, a local *pir* who went into politics to promote the creation of Pakistan during the colonial era, was appointed minister in the former princely state of Bahawalpur. His son Makhdoomzada Syed Hassan Mehmud—a nephew of the Pir Pagaro—took part in the same government before becoming chief minister of the province and then going into national politics, still under the Muslim League label, as member of the Constituent Assembly a later as minister. The size of his estate was estimated to be 15,000 acres and his disciples several thousand.[57]

In her study of Makhdoom Ahmed Mehmood, son of Makhdoomzada Syed Hassan Mehmud and current *pir*, Alix Philippon gathered testimonials illustrating the power that *pirs* have over "their" peasants in the first decade of the 21st century. One of them explained during an election rally held by Ahmed Mehmood's brother-in-law: "We've been voting for the makhdum and his family for forty years and you haven't done a thing for us! But we'll vote for you again this time!"[58] Another says of Ahmed Mehmood,

He is very pious. His grandfather was very pious, his whole family is very pious. He is the bridge between us and Allah (...). We don't believe there are intermediaries with Allah, but as a leader, when he comes into our area, makhdum advises us to say our prayers, to be pious. His first word of advice is to obey Allah, to follow Islamic rules and to live our lives according to Islam. He has never counselled us to do something evil (...) If he asks us something, we have to do everything we can to

---

[55] Ibid., p. 84.

[56] Alix Philippon, *La politique du Pir. Du soufisme ou soufIslamisme: recomposition, modernisation et mobilisation des "confréries" au Pakistan*, PhD dissertation in Political Science, University of Aix-Marseille, 2009, p. 147. This PhD has been published in a book form: *Soufisme et politique au Pakistan. Le mouvement barelwi à l'heure de la "guerre contre le terrorisme*, Paris, Karthala, 2011.

[57] Ibid., p. 148.

[58] Cited in ibid., p. 149.

accomplish it. We cannot disregard his instructions and his advice. Whatever he says, we follow him.[59]

This feeling of allegiance—not unlike that Hindu disciples pay to their gurus—largely explains why religious figures have sought to translate their spiritual authority into worldly power: they merely have to contest an election to have a good chance of winning. It is thus only natural that a modern such as Ayub Khan, convinced of the need to build a security state, would fear that these power centers might undermine his own. In the framework of his battle against the feudal lords, Ayub Khan thus tackled the *pirs* in particular, as well as the *ulema*. In his autobiography, Ayub Khan emphasised "irreconciliable nature of the forces of science and reason and the forces of dogmatism and revivalism which was operating against the unification of the people".[60] Interestingly, he analyses this opposition in terms of an opposition between state and religion:

A sharp cleavage has been created between the State and Religion, and all the old controversies—the temporal versus the spiritual, the secular versus the religious—revived. In more precise terms the essential conflict was between the ulema and the educated classes. [...] The ulema, who in some cases [sic!] were versed in Arabic and had made a special study of religious matters, were regarded as the custodians of Islam. Among them were many who did not hesitate to convert the influence which they exercised over the minds of the people into a political asset. They had gradually built up for themselves a strong political position, opposed to that of the western-educated groups in society.[61]

For Ayub Khan, the terms of the debate were thus clear: as a representative of the state and the educated (i.e. westernized) class, it was his duty to combat the obscurantism of the religious leaders who had gained power due to their influence over the common people.

State Control of Islam

To wage this battle, Ayub Khan relied on Javed Iqbal, son of Muhammad Iqbal (1873–1938), and in particular his book, *The Ideology of Pakistan*, which called for the abolition of shrines and urged modernists to curb the influence of the *pirs* and the *ulema*.[62] Ayub Khan unleashed his fight

---

[59] Cited in ibid., p. 151.
[60] Muhammad Ayub Khan, *Friends Not Masters*, op. cit., p. 219.
[61] Ibid., pp. 219–220.
[62] Javed Iqbal, *The Ideology of Pakistan*, Karachi, 1959.

against the clerics in the name of these values, but also with the aim of bringing potential rivals to heel.

He first sought to reduce the financial autonomy of the *waqf*. These Islamic endowments controlled estates, buildings, schools, mosques, shrines and so on that they had received in donation. As inalienable goods, their ownership could not be transferred. This augmented the influence of the *pirs* who presided over them, and their financial autonomy enabled them to develop networks of Quranic schools. Ayub Khan believed the *pirs* mismanaged the *waqf* properties, claiming they were ignorant or even corrupt. In 1961, he promulgated the West Pakistan Waqf Property Ordinance (1961), enabling him to transfer the most profitable waqf properties to the state.

While the *pirs* were the primary targets of the Waqf Ordinance, Ayub Khan's education policy took the *ulema* to task. He placed a public agency, the Awaqf Department, in charge of designing a curriculum for training ulema, even establishing an "Ulema Akademi" in 1970. The two-year curriculum it offered was intended "to 'enrich' the classical theological syllabus with modern subjects."[63] Ayub Khan also modernised the curriculum of the schools that had come under state supervision. Only one of the members of the committee Ayub entrusted with this revision had been educated in a Quranic school.[64] The committee recommended the inclusion of new subjects such as Euclidean mathematics at the expense of other subjects perceived as archaic. While Urdu was to remain the medium of instruction in primary schools, it was to be replaced by English or Arabic afterwards. Last, "religious education not only included instruction in Koran, Hadith and other traditional subjects but was also concerned with issues of national importance and the propagation of an Islamic nation or even of an Islamic community (*umma*). This meant the transformation of Islam from a theological concept to an ideological one."[65] Indeed, Ayub Khan pursued the path of alternative secularization that Sir Syed and Jinnah had embarked on by promoting Islam as a culture in an ethno-religious nationalistic perspective at the expense of Islam as a belief system.

This outlook induced Ayub Khan to grant religion a less prominent place in his 1962 Constitution than it had had in 1956. He wanted "to renege on the concessions made to the men of religion in 1956",[66] to the point of

---

[63] Jamal Malik, *Colonization of Islam*, op. cit., p. 67.

[64] Ibid., p. 155, note 30.

[65] Ibid., p. 128.

[66] Marc Gaborieau, "Islam et politique", in Christophe Jaffrelot (ed.), *Le Pakistan*, Paris, Fayard, 2000, p. 414.

removing the adjective "Islamic" from the official name of the Republic of Pakistan. But this move created such an uproar that the epithet was restored by an amendment in 1963. Ayub Khan also had included in the new Constitution an Advisory Council of Islamic Ideology "to make recommendations to the Central Government and the Provincial Governments as to means of enabling and encouraging the Muslims of Pakistan to order their lives in all respects in accordance with the principles and concepts of Islam (art. 204 (a))."[67] Still, from two standpoints this Council remained in a fairly pluralist perspective. First, it was supposed to represent the various Muslim schools of thought.[68] Second, two Supreme Court justices or one from the state High Courts had to sit on the Council whose Chairman—the only full timer—had to be a Supreme Court justice. In any case, the president of Pakistan exerted final authority over the council. Ayub Khan made this clear in his autobiography, "There was obviously no place for a supra-body of religious experts exercising a power of veto over the Legislature and the Judiciary."[69]

Ayub Khan's rule thus took one more step in the process of bringing Islam under state control already initiated by Jinnah, a process that Jamal Malik has described as "colonisation". Jinnah had attempted to turn Islam into an ethno-territorial ideology that could be exploited to political ends; under Ayub Khan the nation-state that had emerged out of the plan strove to discipline religion especially to neutralize alternative power centres that it might nourish. State control of traditional institutions such as the *waqf* and the reform of Quranic school curricula tended at once to secularise and marginalise their leaders. This policy served secularism not only by confining religion to certain aspects of the public sphere, but also by recognising religious diversity, thereby acknowledging minorities.

---

[67] The Advisory Council of Islamic Ideology partly emulated a Muslim political construction that Ayub Khan valued highly, the model espoused by Caliph Omar (634–644), who governed alone while occasionally seeking advice from a consultative committee.

[68] This recognition met the expectations of the various schools of Muslim thought which had begun to organise in reaction to the state's intervention in religious affairs. Already in 1955, members of the Ahl-e Hadith school, known for their organizational skills, had created the Markaz-e Jam'iyyat Ahl-e Hadith; in 1959 all the other currents of Islam followed suit: the Deobandis founded the Wafaq al-Madaris al'Arabiyyah, the Barelwis, the Tanzim al-Madaris al'Arabiyyah and the Shias, the Majlis-e Nazarate shi'ah Madaris-e Arabiyyah.

[69] Muhammad Ayub Khan, *Friends not Masters*, op. cit., p. 194.

This evolution was fostered by the dilution of the Jama'at-e-Islami discourse, a process indirectly related to Ayub Khan's policies. In implementing a certain "statisation" of Islam when the JI longed for the Islamisation of the state, Khan had become Maududi's archenemy. The JI therefore went about seeking pragmatic alliances with other opponents. It reached a height in 1963—while Maududi was in prison following another wave of repression—with the JI's joining the Combined Opposition Parties.[70] This alliance backed the candidacy of Fatima Jinnah in 1965. As Nasr writes, this represented for the JI "a monumental doctrinal compromise": "The Jama'at appeared to have abandoned its ideological mainstay and declared itself a political machine through and through, one which recognized no ethical or religious limits to its pragmatism."[71]

While Ayub Khan targeted the JI and initiated the "colonisation of Islam" in Pakistan, he spared the *pirs* to a large extent. He saw them "as important sources of influence which it was prudent for the government to retain and utilize for its own again, rather than to suppress and so turn the pirs and their fanatic followers into enemies".[72] Few major shrines were taken over by the state and he himself "visited the shrines regularly, inaugurated the *urses* (festivals in honour of saints) and granted money for the repair and expansion and maintenance of the shrines".[73] In fact, he was trying to benefit from the prestige of the sacred places *pirs* were in charge of, instead of fighting against it. However, his policy was very different from those of his followers who initiated a process of Islamisation.

Islamisation and the Politics of Legitimation (1969–1988)

From the late 1960s to the end of the 1980s, for a period of twenty years, Pakistan's successive leaders, Yayha Khan, Z.A. Bhutto and Zia, would resort to Islam in order to legitimise their rule, or more prosaically, to form tactical alliances. That these Islamisation policies almost never echoed religious sentiments at all sincere in no way detracts from the impact they had on society. Indeed, they gave Islamist movements more room to manoeuvre than any government or state leader had ever allowed them.

[70] Rafiuddin Ahmed, "Redefining Muslim Identity in South Asia: The Transformation of the Jamaat-i-Islami", in Martin E. Marty and Scott R. Appleby (eds), *Accounting for Fundamentalism*, Chicago, University of Chicago Press, 1984.

[71] Seyyed Vali Reza Nasr, *The Vanguard of Islamic Revolution*, op. cit., p. 41

[72] K.K. Aziz, *Religion, Land and Politics in Pakistan*, op. cit., p. 55?

[73] Ibid., p. 72.

The First Association between Islamists and the Military: Yayha Khan and the JI

Ayub Khan's successor, Yayha Khan, was the first head of state to seek the support of fundamentalists. His aim was to fight against the rising star of Pakistani politics at the time, Z.A. Bhutto, in a context of identity crisis dominated by the Bengal question.[74]

The JI, wracked by internal tensions since it had compromised itself in the eyes of its "purest" leaders by backing Fatima Jinnah, responded favourably to the signals it was receiving from Yayha Khan. On 23 March 1969, his information minister, Nawabzadah Shair Ali Khan, met with Maududi and one of his lieutenants, Mian Tufayl, in Lahore. They both concluded, in Tufayl's words, that Yayha Khan was a "champion of Islam", that the Legal Framework Order in preparation would make Pakistan an Islamic state and that power would eventually fall to the JI.[75]

It mobilised in the service of the regime, particularly through the action of its student wing, Islami Jami'at-i Tulabah (IJT), formed back in December 1947 in Lahore. Maududi had sensed the need for a bridgehead in the academic world to attract and shape an intellectual elite that he could not draw from a network of *madaris* the way the JUI did. Originally conceived as a missionary (*da'wa*) movement, in the 1950s the IJT had soon turned its attention to political activism, drawing inspiration from the Muslim Brotherhood under the influence of an Egyptian member of the brotherhood based in Karachi, Sa'id Ramazan. Acting as the JI's shock troops, the IJT led the charge on Pakistani campuses against leftist student groups.[76] The organisation was also involved in the anti-Ahmadi agitation. But it saw its "hour of glory" in 1969–71 when it deployed its cadres against Bhutto's PPP and Bengali separatists with the government's blessing.

The JI, whose IJT had already became known for its robust cultural policing of Pakistani campuses, honed its techniques of intimidation. In Lahore, posters "warned all poets, writers and other intellectuals to behave or [they would] break their pens, smother their tongues and smash their heads".[77] In March 1969, after the failure of the Round Table Conference, Maududi

---

[74] Yayha Khan used the services of the Jama'at-e-Islami, following the generals' example in Indonesia where Sukarno had just been deposed and the communists decimated, partly with the help of Sarakat-a-Islam.

[75] Seyyed Vali Reza Nasr, *The Vanguard of Islamic Revolution*, op. cit., p. 162.

[76] Ibid., pp. 64–65.

[77] Lal Khan, *Pakistan's Other Story. The 1968–69 Revolution*, op. cit., p. 219.

called on JI members "to form committees in every mohalla to smother the tongue that utters the word socialism."[78] On 28 November 1969, Bhutto was attacked by "an infuriated, brick-throwing crowd of mullahs and youths at Sadiqabad in Rahim Yar Khan District."[79] Following this incident, Bhutto put together a security detail and placed retired Major General Akbar Khan in command.

The JI also tried to counter the PPP on ideological grounds. Following a rally of 200,000 peasants at Toba Tek Singh in 1970, the movement organised a Yaum-e-Shaukat-e-Islam, causing Humreira Iqtidar to surmise that the JI "was increasingly defining itself primarily by opposition to the left."[80] Indeed, in its 20 December 1969 meeting, the party had placed a land reform proposal on its electoral manifesto. While the plan was limited in scope, it indicated a significant change from Maududi's prior refusal of any such reform.[81]

At the same time, the JI also backed the army's crackdown on the movement for Bangladesh, especially after an IJT militant was killed on the Dhaka campus. In April 1971 the head of the JI in East Pakistan met with General Tikka Khan and ensured him of his full support against "enemies of Islam."[82]

This first association between the military and the Islamists resulted in a double fiasco: not only did the Bengalis gain their independence, but the PPP came to power in an election that revealed just how narrow the bases of the JI, the JUI and the JUP were. These three parties did not even garner 14 per cent of the vote in the general election, the JI's score of 6.03 per cent not even amounting to the sum of the other two (3.98 and 3.94 respectively), which was yet another failure for Maududi. In all, the JI only won four seats in the Assembly while the other two parties, whose support base was less dispersed, had seven each. In his disappointment, Maududi turned away from politics and reverted to his original aim, to form a "holy community", and thus handed the movement leadership over to Mian Tufayl in 1972.

Yet, if the early 1970s marked the end of a cycle, it was that of Pakistani attempts to institute a form of secularism for in fact, in an ironic twist of history, Bhutto himself would attempt to exploit Islam to political ends.

---

[78] Cited in ibid., p. 272.

[79] Ibid.

[80] Humeira Iqtidar, *Secularizing Islamists? Jama'at-e-Islami and Jama'at-ud-Da'wa in Urban Pakistan*, New Delhi, Permanent Black, 2011, p. 80.

[81] Ibid., p. 86.

[82] Cited in Seyyed Vali Reza Nasr, *The Vanguard of Islamic Revolution*, op. cit., p. 169.

Z.A. Bhutto's Version of Islamisation

By the late 1960s, Bhutto was peppering his speeches with references to Islam to the point of qualifying his doctrine as "Islamic socialism" (*musawat-e Muhammadi*—Muslim equality in Urdu). This reflected an apparently deep conviction about Islam's supposed affinities with the values of equality and fraternity that the Muslim League under Liaquat Ali Khan had also proclaimed. Bhutto thus declared at a rally in Sherpao (NWFP) on 3 November 1968:

Why socialist parties have not succeeded in India is because Hinduism is against socialism, just as it is against Islam. Hinduism can never tolerate socialism, because the Hindu religion provides for various classes. While socialism has not made any headway in India, it can make tremendous progress in Pakistan because there is little difference between Islam and socialism. I want to say this clearly that in the socioeconomic sector there is no difference between Islam and socialism. Had these two systems been in conflict with each other, I would have given up socialism.[83]

Such language appealed to some, including on the left. Shahid Mahmood Nadeem, who could hardly be suspected of sociocultural conservatism, offers an edifying account: "[In 1968] in West Pakistan Bhutto was becoming a national hero, leading the movement from the front. His Islamic Socialism slogan had become quite popular, especially among the youth. It provided a reasonable and safe compromise and did not force a choice between Islam and Socialism."[84]

If Islam played such an important role in Bhutto's political discourse, it was not merely due to his supposed affinities with the religion. It was also because it was a repertoire that could not be ignored. Islam permeated the culture of the masses that were being called to the polls for the first time in 1970. And Islamist parties indulged in Islamic one-upmanship in the 1970 elections. In light of competition from the JI, JUP and JUI, the PPP adopted a three-part slogan in which Islam took the lead: "Islam is our faith. Democracy is our polity. Socialism is our economy."[85] Besides, Bhutto, who had started to look for "someone who could (theologically) retaliate against JI's diatribes against the PPP", invited a former leader of Maududi's party, Kausar Niazi—who had taken part in the anti-Ahmadi movement of 1953—,

---

[83] Z.A. Bhutto, *Awakening the People. A Collection of Articles, Statements and Speeches*, op. cit., p. 179.

[84] Cited in Lal Khan, *Pakistan's Other Story. The 1968–69 Revolution*, op. cit., p. 193.

[85] Z.A. Bhutto, *Pakistan and the alliances*, Lahore, Pakistan People's Party, 1969.

to join the PPP. Niazi agreed, was nominated in a constituency of Sialkot and became a federal minister of religious affairs in 1974.[86]

Added to these considerations was another matter specific to the PPP. This party, to which the large landowners of Sindh and southern Punjab had rallied, had naturally attracted the potentially large estate-owners that were the *pirs*.[87] Makhdoom Muhammad Zaman Talib-ul Mola of Hala was thus one of the first to be recruited by Z.A. Bhutto. Legend even has it that the PPP was founded in his bastion in 1967. At the head of a very large brother-hood, the Makhdoom was an elected member of the assembly under the PPP label until his son, Amin Fahim, staunchly loyal to the Bhutto family, took his place. Amin Fahim has been elected six times, has taken part in different governments and has catered to the needs of the PPP when Benazir was in exile. The Gilanis of Multan form a similar line. Hamid Raza Gilani, a member of this large political family that was always careful not to put their eggs all in the same political basket, joined the PPP in 1970 and then the Z.A. Bhutto cabinet in 1977. Yousaf Raza Gilani, prime minister from 2008 to 2012, also hails from this family. A member of another family of *pirs* from Multan, the Qureshis, also joined Z.A. Bhutto's PPP. Makhdoom Sajjad Hussain Qureshi switched allegiance from Bhutto to Zia (who named him governor of Punjab in 1985), but his son, Shah Mehmud Qureshi, joined the PPP for a while, becoming minister of foreign affairs in 2008 and then shifted to the PTI as mentioned above. These last two families, incidentally, are related by marriage to the family of the Pir Pagaro.

However, the *pirs*' influence within the PPP and the Islamist parties' one-upmanship do less to explain Z.A. Bhutto's use of the Islamic repertoire than the context created by the 1971 Partition and the birth of Bangladesh. The war lost against the East Bengalis and India heightened the fear of India (that Pakistan no longer surrounded and which wanted to crush it, according to Pakistani general opinion). This new situation made it paradoxically even more essential to resort to Islam: although religion had proven to be too weak a cement in the face of Bengali separatism, Pakistan had no other identity base to rely on in the face of India. Islam was more than ever the foundation of Islamic Republic of Pakistan's

---

[86] Niazi, paradoxically, was opposed to declaring the Ahmadi "non-Muslims" in 1974 (Nadeem F. Paracha, "Ahmadiyya question: Setting Niazi free", *Dawn*, 16 November 2014 (http://www.dawn.com/news/1144671).

[87] This paragraph draws from Sarah Ansari, *Sufi Saints and State Power: The Pirs of Sind, 1843–1947*, Cambridge, Cambridge University Press, 1992, and Alix Philippon, "La politique du Pir", op. cit, p. 140–143.

national identity. While the founding fathers of the Land of the Pure considered the religion as being open to other communities, reference to Islam had now become an essential defence mechanism at a time when an existential anxiety hovered: it was the crucible of national identity and politicians who did not sufficiently draw on it (the notion being very relative) ran the risk of being accused of betraying the nation. As Vali Nasr writes, "the inability of Islam to keep the two halves of the country united had not diminished the appeal of religion either to politicians or the people. Oddly enough it even increased it. The precariousness of Pakistan's unity led Pakistanis to reaffirm their Islamic roots. Even the avowedly secularist and left-of-center People's Party government did not remain immune and talked of 're-Islamising' the country."[88]

Bhutto thus capitalised on Islamic sentiment to rebuild his country's unity and restore the shaken Pakistanis' self-esteem.[89]

After taking office, Bhutto played the Islamic card to pacify the Islamists, starting with the JI. He promised to make sharia the supreme law of the land within nine years. Maududi—who was said to have already convinced Bhutto not to recognize Bangladesh until all Pakistani prisoners had been freed[90]—met with Bhutto in September 1972 and "convinced the Prime Minister of the need to evict leftist elements from the PPP and promised, in exchange, to support Bhutto's draft constitution".[91]

The 1973 Constitution changed the name of the Advisory Council for Islamic Ideology to Council of Islamic Ideology and put it in charge of carrying out this task. More essentially, article 2 made Islam "the State religion of Pakistan." Freedom of expression was subject to restrictions "in the interest of the glory of Islam" (art. 19). Elaborating on previous similar provisions, to which others pertaining to education and taxation, art. 31 read:

(1) Steps shall be taken to enable the Muslims of Pakistan, individually and collectively, to order their lives in accordance with the fundamental principles and

---

[88] Seyyed Vali Reza Nasr, *The Vanguard of Islamic Revolution*, op. cit., p. 171.

[89] The importance of Islam as a national ideology in Bhutto's politics is well illustrated by four lectures he gave on this creed from 1948 to 1976: Z.A. Bhutto, *Thoughts on Some Aspects of Islam* http://www.scribd.com/doc/28835156/Zulfikar-Ali-Bhutto-s-Thoughts-on-Islam (Accessed 16 August 2011).

[90] Ahmad Mumtaz, "Madrassa Education in Pakistan and Bangladesh", in Satu P. Limaye, Robert G. Wirsing and Mohan Malik (eds), *Religious Radicalism and Security in South Asia*, Honolulu (HI), Asia Pacific Centre for Security Studies, 2004, p. 477.

[91] Frédéric Grare, *Political Islam in the Indian Subcontinent*, op. cit., p. 36.

basic concepts of Islam and to provide facilities whereby they may be enabled to understand the meaning of life according to the Holy Qur'an and Sunnah.

(2) The State shall endeavor, as respects the Muslims of Pakistan,

    (a) to make the teaching of the Holy Qur'an and Islamiat compulsory, to encourage and facilitate the learning of Arabic language and to secure correct and exact printing and publishing of the Holy Qur'an;

    (b) to promote unity and the observance of the Islamic moral standards; and

    (c) to secure the proper organization of Zakat, (ushr) (see below), auqaf [plural of waqf] and mosques.

More importantly, art. 260 defined for the first time who was a Muslim and who was not. Among the non-Muslims, in addition to Christians, Hindus, Sikhs, Buddhists and Parsis, there were also the Ahmadis, who considered themselves Muslims but who were thus excommunicated.[92] To drive the point home, a Constitutional amendment in 1974 declared them apostates.[93] This decision was taken under the pressure of a new wave of agitation orchestrated by the JI, particularly by the IJT, its student union, which as a result regained popularity, as shown by its success in student elections on the campuses of Karachi as well as Peshawar. Nasr aptly sums up the situation with a few figures regarding the period starting with the demonstration that took place on 26 June 1974:

The ensuing 102 days produced 8,797 meetings and 147 processions, and despite the arrest of some 834 IJT leaders and workers, the government proved unable to stem the tide. On 7 September 1974, the government capitulated, declaring the Ahmadis a non-Muslim minority.[94]

In so doing, "Bhutto gave full approval to the division between full citizens, Muslims, and non-Muslims, whose constitutional status was thereby lowered to that of second-class citizens."[95] In fact, not only were non-Muslims obliged to vote in separate electorates, but they were also excluded from the seniormost state posts.

This approach was mirrored in foreign policy by the rapprochement with countries of the Arab world, the organisation of the Islamic Summit Conference in Lahore in 1974 being the most spectacular aspect.

---

[92] See http://www.Pakistani.org/pakistan/constitution/part12.ch5.html (Accessed on September 15, 2013).

[93] See http://www.Pakistani.org/pakistan/constitution/amendments/2amendment.html (Accessed on September 15, 2013).

[94] Seyyed Vali Reza Nasr, *The Vanguard of Islamic Revolution*, op. cit., p. 182.

[95] Marc Gaborieau, "Islam and Politics", op. cit., p. 247.

At the same time, however, Bhutto continued to pursue one of Ayub Khan's goals: the subjugation of alternative religious centres of power by the state. In 1971, he brought all the endowments resulting from the nationalisation of *waqf* properties under the authority of the central government. In matters of education, the Bhutto government had the diplomas awarded by Quranic schools recognized by the University Grant Commission (UGC). This commission also formed an equivalence committee and on the basis of its recommendations, the education ministry recognized certificates issued by certain Quranic schools as equivalent to the B.A.[96]

Bhutto thus pursued the process initiated by Ayub Khan of "colonising" or bringing Islam under state control, even bureaucraticising it. His policy contrasted, however, with his predecessor's, in that he implemented an Islamisation policy that reached its height after the 1977 elections. To pacify the JI demonstrators who protested against the massive fraud he had orchestrated, Bhutto announced the systematisation of sharia, whereby alcoholic beverages, dancing and gambling would be prohibited.[97]

Bhutto's fears of the religious parties were partly justified. The JUI had won decent scores in the 1970 regional elections, with 14 per cent and 11 per cent of the vote in the NWFP and Balochistan respectively, where it had formed a government coalition with the NAP. In addition, certain Bhutto opponents—starting with the Muhajirs who were concerned by Sindhi nationalism—backed the JI, in particular from a financial standpoint.[98] In 1977 the JI had won a record number of seats—9, including 2 in Punjab, 3 in the NWFP and 4 in Sindh (1 in Hyderabad and 3 in Karachi)—which put the party in a position to "dominate the PNA",[99] the coalition the JI was part of.

Bhutto, by proclaiming that the sharia was now "the law of the country"[100] in 1977 had laid the groundwork for Zia, whose rule in this domain as in others, differed from the previous regimes more in nature than in degree.

---

[96] Jamal Malik, *Colonization of Islam*, op. cit., p. 129.
[97] Bhutto had already promised that he would replace Sunday with Friday as the day of rest.
[98] Seyyed Vali Reza Nasr, *The Vanguard of Islamic Revolution*, op. cit., p. 58.
[99] Ibid., p. 184.
[100] Marc Gaborieau, "Islam and Politics", op. cit., p. 245.

Zia's Islamisation Policy

The premices of Zia's Islamisation policy were visible even before he took power in 1977. The year before, immediately after he became COAS, he changed the motto of the army, replacing Jinnah's formula, "Faith, Unity, Discipline" with "Iman, Taqwa, Jihad-fi-sibilillah (Faith, Piety, holy war) in the name of god".[101] Christine Fair points out that "under Zia an officer's piety and religious practice became a formal part of his assessment for promotion".[102] Zia's Islamisation policy can probably be partly attributed to his religious temperament[103] (he had longstanding affinities with the JI).[104] He was even the first head of state of Pakistan to attend the Raiwind annual meeting of the Tablighi Jamaat, an organisation of which he helped to expand the "presence among army personnel".[105] Zia's social background should also be taken into account, as he represented a new category of officers from the Punjabi conservative lower middle class. He was a son of Partition, his family having migrated from East Punjab. But beyond that, Zia used Islam in the framework of his political strategy. After coming to power through a military coup, Zia thus sought to legitimate his authority.

This is evident from his efforts to ingratiate himself with the Council of Islamic Ideology (CII) by increasing its numbers (from fifteen to twenty members) and enhancing its prestige—as reflected in the publicity it received from the Urdu-language press. In July 1979, Zia asked the CII to answer an unusual sort of question, whether "the prevailing system of election was un-Islamic."[106] The CII first claimed the question did not come under its purview, but then answered negatively. This displeased Zia, who appointed a new committee that reached the same conclusion, that "Parliamentary system of Government, which was in accordance with Islam, would be more appropriate for Pakistan."[107] But finally, in 1983, the

---

[101] Cited in C. Christine Fair, *Fighting to the End*, op. cit., p. 81.

[102] Ibid., p. 83.

[103] Humorously depicted by Mohammed Hanif in his novel, *A Case of Exploding Mangoes*, op. cit.

[104] In 1976 Zia, as chief of the army staff, gave Maududi's book, *Tafhimu'l-Qur'an* (Understanding the Qur'an) as a prize to officers of the Army Education School who won debates (inspired by the practices of British debating societies). He subsequently proposed to include the book in the examination for promotion of captains and majors. See Seyyed Vali Reza Nasr, *The Vanguard of Islamic Revolution*, op. cit., p. 172.

[105] C. Christine Fair, *Fighting to the End*, op. cit., p. 83.

[106] Cited in Jamal Malik, *Colonization of Islam*, op. cit., p. 40.

[107] Cited in ibid., p. 41.

CII considered that "in the light of the Qur'an and Sunnah elections on the basis of political parties are not valid."[108] Zia took full advantage of "this handsome gift from the CII members"[109] in his relations with the PPP and other groups, using it as an argument to hold the 1985 elections on a non-partisan basis.

The CII went farther, however, returning to the proposal made by the Ta'limat-e Islamia Board of 1951 which had discarded both the parliamentary and the presidential systems. Zia had not expected the CII to go so far, nor did he want it to. That is the paradox of strategies to exploit Islam, another form of which will be examined in the following chapter illustrating the pitfalls of manipulating jihadist groups. Zia, who expressed "his utter disappointment regarding the 'ulama'",[110] had to revert to a policy akin to state control over Islam. But that did not mean that he had reverted to Ayub Khan's brand of "statisation", of course. In fact, Zia's Islamisation policy brought about a profound transformation of the legal, educational and fiscal systems.

Islamisation of the Legal System

Zia's judicial reform gave new weight to an Islamic legal system alongside the existing civil courts and the "special tribunals" set up by the regime and peopled with military staff. In each regular court sharia benches made of three *qazis* (judges administering the sharia) were introduced, whose main mission was to "examine and decide the question whether or not any law or provision of law is repugnant to the injunction of Islam."[111] In the event of the affirmative, the incriminated law became void, although one could make an appeal to the Supreme Court. The sharia benches were reserved for lawyers who were also trained as *ulema*.

---

[108] Cited in ibid.

[109] Ibid.

[110] Ibid., p. 47.

[111] Cited in Anita Weiss, "The historical debate on Islam and the state in South Asia", in Anita Weiss (ed.), *Islamic Reassertion in Pakistan. The Application of Islamic Laws in a Modern State*, Lahore, Vanguard, 1987, p. 11. In fact, the Court fulfilled additional, smaller tasks. In 1985, for instance, it was asked to examine a circular of the Awaqf Department prohibiting its employees from saying "*durud* (request for mercy upon the Prophet and praise) or *salam*, which was regarded as shirk by puritans. The matter ended in a case before the Federal Sharia Court in 1985, but could not be solved for good reasons. The circular was withdrawn," Jamal Malik, *Colonization of Islam*, op. cit., p. 59.

But Zia grew concerned that these "sharia benches" might become power centres on the basis of their Islamic legitimacy. He disbanded them one year after their creation and established instead a Federal Sharia Court whose members had to take an oath of allegiance to the president like any other judge.

Zia used the Federal Sharia Court to pursue Ayub Khan's work of putting Islam under the thumb of the state, as shown in his management of the *waqf* properties. In reaction to the Waqf Property Act, religious organizations had been formed and approached the courts, including the Supreme Court. The CII decided to intervene as well, especially to contest the way some *waqf* properties were subjected to land reform. It condemned the Awaqf Department more than once because, according to its members, "the confiscation of the Waqf by one or more persons or by the State was in contradiction to shari'ah and ought to be revoked."[112] Zia's government referred the issue to the Federal Sharia Court which examined all kinds of *waqf ordinances*. It considered, eventually, that nationalisation of this kind of property was not against the sharia.[113]

The main feature of the judicial reform, which was known as the Nizam-e-Islam (Islamic rule) program, lay in the enforcement of *hudud* punishments. Islamic provisions newly introduced in the penal code provided for new punishments for three types of crime: theft (*saraka*), extra-marital sexual relations (*zina*) including adultery and the consumption of alcohol or drugs (*al-sharab*). The most common punishment was lashing, whose practical implementation was explained in the surprisingly detailed Execution of the Punishment of Whipping Ordinance (1979). But more severe punishments were envisaged for the most serious crimes: amputation of the right hand for theft and stoning to death for *zina* offences for instance.[114]

---

[112] Ibid., p. 65.

[113] The state was all the more willing to fight against the *waqf* holders as it promoted a rigorist Salafist brand of Islam that was opposed to saint worship and the *pirs*, who aroused Zia's distrust also because they still formed local power centres. In the 1977 election, some of them had played a major role. Pir Sial Sharif, for instance, held considerable sway over the voters in the districts of Sargodha and Jhang. Katherine Ewing, "The Politics of Sufism. Redefining the Saints of Pakistan", *Journal of Asian Studies*, vol. XLII, no. 2, Feb. 1983, pp. 251–268.

[114] Lucy Carroll, "Nizam-i-Islam: processes and conflicts in Pakistan's programme of Islamization, with special reference to the position of women", *Journal of Commonwealth and Comparative Politics*, no. 20 (1982), pp. 57–95.

Educational Reforms

Educational reforms partly flowed from judicial reforms insofar as, for instance, a sharia department was set up at Quaid-e-Azam University in 1979 to train Islamic legal specialists. But Zia devoted personal attention to the reorganization of Quranic schools (*dini madaris*, plural of *madrassa*). In September 1978 he commissioned a report on the *dini madaris* of the Sargodha division that he used as a prototype for assessing the situation nationwide. This survey, carried out over a 12-month period, produced a report recommending that modern subjects such as science and technology be added to the curriculum.

Interestingly, the chairman of the National Committee for Dini Madaris in charge of the survey, A. W. J. Halepota, had already been involved in a similar task in 1961. This sign of continuity was highly revealing. Although Zia was in favour of Islamisation when Ayub Khan wanted to promote secularization, Zia continued in his predecessor's footsteps for a good reason: the pursuit of a statist orientation.

The Halepota report recommended not only the inclusion of modern subjects but also more uniformity among *dini madaris* statutes and modes of functioning. They were therefore bound to lose some of their autonomy. Networks of *dini madaris*, including major Deobandi institutions, resisted Zia's policy for this very reason. But the government, which toyed with the idea of establishing a National Institute for Dini Madaris Pakistan, was adamant. It achieved some of its objectives by pursuing the policy of recognizing religious degrees that Bhutto had initiated. Some were thus considered equivalent to BAs and MAs awarded by the University Grants Commission[115] as long as they met accreditation criteria. The Barelwi Tanzim consequently adopted a new curriculum. Some *dini madaris* agreed to play by the new rules because it enabled them to receive part of the *zakat* money in exchange (cf. infra). But modernisation required them to register with the administration in accordance with the Societies Act (1860). Zia was clearly trying to submit the Quranic schools to a clientelistic relationship. As Jamal Malik explains, this policy was supposedly to everyone's advantage:

The President sought the acceptance of his leadership by the Ulama and thus an "Islamic" legitimation of his rule. For the bureaucracy and the colonial sector, formalization of the D[ini] M[adaris] served as a means to bring them under control

---

[115] In 1982 degrees awarded by *dini madaris* were recognized as equivalent to the Masters degree in Islamiyat (Muslim civilisation) and Arabic.

and thus to neutralize them politically. The Ulama, in contrast, aimed at finally escaping their "backwardness" and achieving social recognition without giving up their tradition.[116]

In fact, the *ulema* benefited more from the policy than the administration, which never managed to control the *dini madaris*. Their numbers grew exponentially. It was in any event impossible to subject them to any form of micromanagement (particularly as regards curricula), even if they had to register with the state. These schools continued to enjoy relative financial independence due to the funding they received from abroad (especially from Saudi Arabia). Poor parents who valued religious education were even more prepared to send their children to *dini madaris* now that these tuition-free schools also offered modern subjects.[117]

While in the 1960s the number of *dini madaris* students remained nearly the same in West Pakistan, it increased by 119 per cent between 1971 and 1979 and jumped by 160 per cent in only four years, 1979–83. The growth was particularly dramatic in Sindh, with 53.6 per cent and 354 per cent respectively. But the largest number of students were located in the NWFP (– 8 and + 91 per cent respectively) where the Zia government supported the development of *dini madaris* in order to channel Afghan refugees and train militants likely to resist the Soviets. Punjab, which represented 48 per cent of the total in 1983, showed steadier growth in the 1970s and early 1980s, 56 and 54 per cent respectively.

According to Jamal Malik, between 1978 and 1985, the Deobandi *dini madaris* produced the largest number of Maulanas: 3,530 (52.6 per cent of the total)—compared to 3,179 between 1960 and 1977, then came the Barelwi Dini Madaris with 3,093—compared to 464 (though over a shorter period: 1974–7) and finally the Ahl-i-Hadith *dini madaris* with 1,276. Adding the 299 graduates from Shia seminaries, the *dini madaris* awarded degrees to as many students in 1984–5 as in the 17 years prior to Zia's coup, from 1960–77: 3,601 compared to 3,643.[118]

The expansion of *dini madaris* was fostered by support from abroad. Sunni and Shia institutions were aided by Saudi Arabia and Iran respectively. Iran after Khomeini's revolution in 1979 fought a kind of proxy war for the leadership of the Muslim world. Riyadh especially supported the

---

[116] Jamal Malik, *Colonization of Islam*, op. cit., p. 172.

[117] *Dini madaris* could be tuition-free when teachers' salaries and building maintenance were covered by public or foreign funding.

[118] Jamal Malik, *Colonization of Islam*, op. cit., p. 228.

Table 8.1.: Numbers of students and teachers of Dini Madaris in different years and provinces

Province	1960		1971		1979		1983	
	Students	Teachers	Students	Teachers	Students	Teachers	Students	Teachers
West Pakistan	44,407	1,846	45,238	3,186	99,041	5,005	259,827	7,394
Punjab	24,842	1,053	29,096	2,063	80,879	2,992	124,670	3,549
Sindh	6,218	401	5,431	453	8,344	1,245	37,949	1,080
NWFP	7,897	312	8,423	515	7,749	673	78,439	2,217
Balochistan	519	46	1,207	95	1,814	95	8,083	280
Azad Kashmir	n.a.	n.a.	n.a.	n.a.	n.a.	n.a.	1,644	41
Northern Provinces	763	23	1,083	60	n.a.	n.a.	4,384	125
Islamabad	n.a.	n.a.	n.a.	n.a.	n.a.	n.a.	4,638	133

Source: Jamal Malik, *Colonized Islam*, op. cit., p. 178.

Ahl-i-Hadith schools, which in some cases even employed very well paid Saudi teachers.[119] Iran's influence was especially noticeable in the Gilgit area where teachers also appear to be better paid and students given a more substantial allowance than in other Shia schools.[120]

By 1988 when Zia left the scene, the number of *dini madaris* had increased by some 12,000 units.[121] In retrospect, the growing importance of these schools is probably the most significant aspect of Zia's Islamisation policy.

Tax Reform

In the short term, however, the fiscal dimension of the Islamisation policy made a stronger impact. Payment of the alms tax, *zakat*, as well as its agricultural counterpart, ushr, were traditionally private obligations for Muslims in Pakistan. Together they generally represented 2.5 per cent of annual household savings and served as a sort of wealth tax to be redistributed to the Muslim community's poor.[122]

One of the provisions of the 1973 Constitution already stipulated that these taxes should be collected by the government. But Bhutto had made no move to implement it. In 1979, Zia decided to transform what was considered a personal duty of solidarity into a legal obligation. The "Zakat and 'Ushr Ordinance" was issued in 1980. Its urban component, *zakat*, took effect in 1981, whereas *ushr* did not come into effect until 1983. The system by which these taxes were previously levied was replaced by a specific agency to rationalize the collection and distribution of funds, a process that Malik describes as follows:

On the first day of the fasting month of Ramadan, the Zakat Deducting Agencies (banks, post-offices etc.) by means of deduction at source withdraw 2.5 per cent

---

[119] Ibid., p. 229.

[120] Ibid., p. 261.

[121] Ian Talbot, *Pakistan: A Modern History*, op. cit., p. 279. Another, anonymous, source gives different figures: between 1979 and 1988, 1,151 new *dini madaris* were reportedly registered according to International Crisis Group. See ICG, *Pakistan: Madrassas, Extremism and the Military*, ICG Asia Report, n° 36, 29 July 2002, p. 9. But Vali Nasr, assuming that the number of unregistered *dini madaris* was much higher, estimates that there were 25,000 institutions of that kind at the turn of the 21st century. See Seyyed Vali Reza Nasr, "Islam, the State and the Rise of Sectarian Militancy in Pakistan", op. cit., p. 90.

[122] According to Matthew Nelson, *ushr* traditionally amounted to "a tax of 5 per cent on all agricultural produce" (M. Nelson, *In the Shadow of Shari'ah*, op. cit., p. 156).

from all saving accounts above a certain exemption limit (fixed at Rs. 1,000 in the first year of Zakat deduction, 1980). They transfer the Zakat thus collected to the Central Zakat Fund (CZF). This fund is fed also with proceeds from 'voluntary Zakat' and 'donations' and from funds of other institutions. Following certain criteria, the Zakat is then distributed among the Provincial Zakat Funds (PZFs) and the National Zakat Foundation (NZF). Following prescribed quota, the PZFs turn over funds to the Local Zakat Funds (LZFs) to other institutions, to the needy (mustahqin) and to the National Zakat Foundation.[123]

While *ushr* is distributed in the locality where it was collected, the distribution process of the *zakat* shows a whole bureaucratic pyramid in action. Here again the Islamisation policy reinforced state control over religious institutions. Further evidence of this was the Tehsil/Taluka/Subdivisional and Local Committees (Removal of Chairman and Members) Rule (1981), which allowed the state to dismiss the president of a local *zakat* committee, an institution that was previously independent from the state. In 1981, *Al Zakat*, an influential national monthly publication, boasted that 250,000 persons were involved in the new system of collecting and distributing zakat funds.[124]

The fiscal dimension of Zia's Islamisation policy fostered a rise in sectarianism, a term that in Pakistan denotes the conflict between Sunni and Shia Muslims. As soon as Zia's plans for *zakat* and *ushr* were made public, Shia leaders objected that according to the jurisprudence of their sect, payment of these taxes was a purely individual choice, a decision made according to one's conscience.[125] In reaction to the promulgation of the law, they orchestrated a massive demonstration in Islamabad (see below).[126]

The Alliance between the Military and the Religious Right

If Yayha Khan had laid the groundwork for an unprecedented combination between the military and the religious right, Zia later institutionalised it. In search of partners after his coup, he had turned to Bhutto's opponents.

---

[123] Jamal Malik, *Colonization of Islam*, op. cit., p. 95.

[124] Ibid., p. 96.

[125] For the Shias, non-Sayyids (Sayyids being descendants of the Prophet) are not supposed to give *zakat* (but *khums*) to the Sayyids (*khums* represent one-fifth of the annual savings of a non-Sayyid, half of which should be given to the imam or his representative).

[126] Ann Elizabeth Mayer, "Islamization and Taxation in Pakistan", in Anita Weiss (ed.), op. cit., pp. 62–63.

The PNA was at first hostile to the military overthrow, but soon joined the Zia camp to prevent Bhutto's return—and grab a share of power. The JI was in a prime position at the time. Not only could it take advantage of the two-thirds quota of ministers it was up to the PNA to appoint, but it also provided personnel for the Zia contingent (the remaining third). Thus it received three portfolios on one side (production and industry; petroleum, minerals, water and power; and information and broadcasting) and a fourth (planning) on the other. As Nasr explains, Zia was offering "the Islamist parties a power-sharing arrangement in which the state would act as the senior partner, but the Islamic forces would gain from state patronage."[127]

The JI fully profited from this arrangement at first, as could be seen in its electoral success in the Karachi municipal elections, where the party won 57 out of the 160 seats it contested in September 1979. Maududi was also involved in the Islamisation program Zia had announced, making countless proposals. Zia in response "accorded Mawdudi the status of a senior states-man, sought his advice, and allowed his words to adorn the front pages of the newspapers."[128] But Maududi died in September 1979 and the putschist general was disappointed in the JI's proposals, finding them too abstract: the JI had no convincing solutions for working Islam into the country's economic and political operations.[129] In addition were the problems posed by the IJT. In the late 1970s, Zia used the JI student organization to combat leftwing and PPP influence on university campuses. But the IJT continued to use its strongarm tactics beyond what Zia considered necessary. Some 80 students were killed between 1982 and 1988. The General thus decided to outlaw the IJT in 1984, despite Mian Tufayl's attempt to mediate.[130] The divorce was finalised in 1987 when Qazi Hussain replaced Mian Tufayl at the head of the organisation at a time when the JI accused Zia of catering to the MQM—at the JI's expense—in Karachi. But for ten years, the alliance between the military and the Islamists had prompted an upsurge of Islamist activism, particularly through the jihad in Afghanistan that will be anal-ysed in the following chapter. The JI in particular was able to deepen its strategy of infiltrating the state apparatus. First focusing on the intellectual elite—reflected in the founding of the IJT—it now extended to the army and

---

[127] Seyyed Vali Reza Nasr, *The Vanguard of Islamic Revolution*, p. 188.

[128] Seyyed Vali Reza Nasr, *Mawdudi and the Making of Islamic Revivalism*, op. cit., p. 46.

[129] Seyyed Vali Reza Nasr, *The Vanguard of Islamic Revolution*, p. 194.

[130] Ibid., p. 69.

the administration (the ban on its members joining the civil service was lifted in 1977).

*

Zia's Islamisation policy—unprecedented since the birth of Pakistan—had multiple and sometimes unintentional consequences on Pakistani society. Although Zia's policy was consistent with his religious fervour, even dogmatism, he also pursued it to political ends. By instrumentalising Islam he hoped to gain the legitimacy he was lacking due to the conditions in which he rose to power. That much was evident in the terms of the so-called question asked of Pakistanis in the 1984 referendum. The citizens were to answer if they "endorse[d] the process initiated by General Muhammad Zia-ul-Haq, the President of Pakistan, for bringing the laws of Pakistan in conformity with the injunctions of Islam as laid down in the Holy Quran and Sunnah of the Holy Prophet (PBUH) and for the preservation of the Islamic ideology of Pakistan, for the continuation and consolidation of that process, and for the smooth and orderly transfer of power to the elected representatives of the people." 98.5% of the voters said "Yes". Not only was the ballot marred by several irregularities, but a "No" to Islam was unthinkable.

But Zia did not want religious leaders—whom he despised—to gain too much influence. He therefore pursued the statist agenda that Ayub Khan had initiated. The comparison stops there, however, all the more so as Zia was unable to thwart the clerics' rising influence. While minorities did not suffer from Ayub Khan's policies, they were the collateral victims of laws Zia enacted, as was predictable with the tightening of the Blasphemy Law. The Pakistan Penal Code (PPC) and the Criminal Procedure Code (CPC) were amended in 1980, 1982 and 1986 in such a way that blaspheming the Qur'an and the Prophet were punishable by life imprisonment and by life imprisonment or death respectively.[131] Muslims were supposed to be the

---

[131] Art. 295 B of the PPC stated, "Whoever wilfully defiles, damages or desecrates a copy of the Holy Quran or of an extract therefrom or uses it in any derogatory manner or for any unlawful purpose shall be punishable for imprisonment for life." And art. 295 C stated: "Whoever by words, either spoken or written or by visible representation, or by any imputation, innuendo, or insinuation, directly or indirectly, defiles the sacred name of the Holy Prophet Mohammed (PBUH) shall be punished with death, or imprisonment for life, and shall also be liable to fine."

primary victims of these new provisions, but minorities felt directly targeted by them.

They also experienced the revival of separate electorates as a new form of discrimination. Hindus, Sikhs, Baha'is, Jews and Kalash until then voted with other Pakistanis, and protested against what they deemed a manner of relegating them to the status of second-class citizens (see chapter 10).

* * *

Over the years 1947 to 1988, in the space of about four decades, Pakistan's relationship to Islam underwent considerable changes, yet with a certain degree of continuity.

The constitutional debates between 1947 and 1956 reveal a fundamental disagreement as to the role of Islam in the formation of national identity—a difficulty already discussed in Part One of this book. Two schools with still shifting contours stand in opposition: one, handed down from Jinnah and the Muslim League, viewed Islam as an identity marker compatible with a form of secularism (which therefore respected religious minorities); the other, dominated by clerics, embodied an Islamic vision in which non-Muslims—including the Ahmadis—were bound to become second-class citizens.

Although the 1956 Constitution reflected a search for middle ground, this compromise—coming in the wake of the suppression of the anti-Ahmadi movement—leaned in favour of the secularists. The tendency was further accentuated when Ayub Khan, an "enlightened dictator" hostile to obscurantists, took control. In addition to the many common points between military and civilian leaders identified in the preceding chapters—concluding that both were often part of the same establishment—they share yet another: support for Islamisation by leading figures in both camps. Indeed, in the 1970s it was a civilian—Bhutto[132]—and then through the 1980s, a military ruler—Zia—who led the challenges to secularist gains by making Islam the religion of the state, by declaring the Ahmadis a "non-Muslim minority" and by Islamising the educational, legal and tax system. If Zia's Islamisation policy marked a turning point, the reorientation dates back to Bhutto, further clouding the issue: civilians and the military decidedly cannot be associated with two different categories that could be qualified respectively as liberal-democratic and conservative-authoritarian.

---

[132] Although, as noted above, Yayha Khan was the first Pakistani head of state to join hands with fundamentalists.

The reasons for the change from a regime with the trappings of secularism to one with Islamic characteristics are many. First of all, the Islamic aspect of national identity—although originally defined by Jinnah on a more cultural (and territorial) than religious basis—enabled the ulema and fundamentalists to develop their ideological repertoires—and exploit Islam—in the political sphere legitimately. Although Nehru and Indira Gandhi managed to keep the Hindu nationalists at bay in the name of state secularism in India in the 1950s through the 1970s, in Pakistan secular leaders had only a very slim margin for manoeuvre in this regard. In fact, a party acting as a pressure group such as the Jama'at-e-Islami (and its student wing) indulged in one-upmanship (and entryism in both the army and the university system), such that it helped to shift the focus of political rhetoric by claiming inspiration in the founding values of the Islamic Republic of Pakistan.

Second, the trauma of the 1971 Partition fostered a parallel evolution by exacerbating the reference to Islam as Jinnah intended it—as a structuring reference point for a national identity—in the face of what many Pakistanis perceived as an ever-increasing threat from India. Although the Islam Bhutto made reference to in this context was not the same as Maududi's, he used the same word to tighten the ranks of a wounded and anxious nation, thus fostering the Islamisation described in this chapter—of which the JI was one of the primary vehicles and beneficiaries.

Third, in the late 1970s Zia brought about a change in the situation as much due to his personal inclinations as his need for legitimation, he who had come to power in a still more illegitimate fashion than the previous putschists. But the Islamisation that Zia implemented had two additional elements of complexity. One, it was in line with Ayub Khan's and Bhutto's efforts to bring Islam under state control: Zia did not want to turn the country into a theocracy—all the more as he despised clerics and certain JI leaders, as uncontrollable as those of the IJT; what he was interested in was using Islam. And two, Zia's Islamisation policy can only be understood when replaced in the context of the war in Afghanistan in which Pakistan endeavoured to exploit the strike force of jihadist groups to spread its sphere of influence. It is this external dimension of the relation of Pakistan's ruling elites to Islam that must now be explored, as well as the devastating backlash it has had on Pakistani society, for the notion that the authorities (even military authorities) can control the Islamists has proven to be largely illusory, especially after the war in Afghanistan against the Soviets.

9

JIHADISM, SECTARIANISM AND TALIBANISM

FROM MILITARY/MULLAH COOPERATION TO 9/11

The Islamisation policies conducted over some two decades during the 1969–88 period laid the groundwork for a rise in sectarianism, but also went hand in hand with a new form of jihadism. These two phenomena—sectarianism and jihadism—are at the junction of internal and external dynamics. Sectarianism, which refers to the antagonism between Sunnis and Shias, took root in Zia's Islamisation policy described in the preceding chapter, but it was considerably amplified by the impact of the Iranian revolution on Pakistani Shias and by the reaction of Saudi Arabia, which waged a proxy war against Tehran by backing Sunni movements in Pakistan.

Jihadism, on the other hand is primarily an exogenous movement. Holy war was first fought in Afghanistan in the 1970s–80s and later in Indian Kashmir in the 1980s–90s, where sporadic outbreaks had already occurred since 1947. In both cases, jihadism has brought together Islamists and the military (especially from the ISI). But a serious jihadist backlash occurred in the 2000s, with militants investing the national territory in response to the pro-American turnaround made by the Pakistani authorities after the 11 September 2001 attacks.

Sectarian and jihadist movements, which already displayed obvious affinities, have gradually converged, even merged, particularly in the FATA where they have backed the Pakistani Taliban in their takeover of entire areas from the Pakistani authorities. Beyond these territorial conquests detrimental to state sovereignty, the escalation in violence—both at the microsociological village level and in indiscriminate attacks on urban areas—is jeopardizing the country's national cohesion in ways unseen since 1971.

The Rise of Sectarianism or the Invention of a New Enemy Within

A Legacy of Peaceful Cohabitation

While Sunnis have always dominated South Asian Islam, Shias have traditionally played an important role, and the two main branches of the Muslim religion long maintained peaceful relations.[1] The first Mughal Emperor gave the following advice to his son in his will: "Overlook the difference between the Sunnis and the Shias, otherwise the decrepitude of Islam would inevitably follow".[2] Humayun went even further: after fleeing to Iran once defeated by the Aghan invader Sher Shah Suri, he became a Shia.[3] But, "Mughal tolerance of the Shia became more pronounced under Emperor Jalaluddin Akbar (1542–1605)", whose son, Jehangir married "Nur Jahan, an Iranian lady who actually spread the Shia custom among the masses".[4] Even under Aurangzeb—a Mughal Emperor known for his militant Sunnism—almost one third of the aristocracy and more than half of its senior most functionaries were nevertheless Shias.[5] At the societal level, popular Islam scarcely differentiated between Shiism and Sunnism. The Barelwis of Punjab and Sindh, for instance, used to take part in Moharram ceremonies (but did not practice flagellation and other, more extreme ritual

---

[1] See Muhammad Qasim Zaman, "Sectarianism in Pakistan: the radicalization of Shia and Sunni identities", *Modern Asian Studies*, vol. 32, no. 3, 1998, pp. 687–716 and Seyyed Vali Reza Nasr, "The rise of Sunni Militancy in Pakistan: the Changing Role of Islamism and the Ulamain Society and Politics", *Modern Asian Studies*, vol. 34, no. 1, January 2000, pp. 143–185.

[2] Cited in John F. Standish, *Persia and the Gulf: Retrospect and Prospect*, Saint Martin's Press, 1998, p. 39.

[3] Khaled Ahmed, *Sectarian War. Pakistan's Sunni-Shia Violence and its Links to the Middle East*, Karachi, Oxford University Press, 2013, p. 2.

[4] Ibid.

[5] Juan R.I. Cole, *Roots of North Indian Shi'ism in Iran and Iraq. Religion and State in Awadh*, Berkeley and Los Angeles, University of California Press, 1988, p. 81. For a historical overview, with special references to Hyderabad, see the first chapter of Toby M. Howarth, *The Twelver Shi'a as a Muslim Minority in India*, London and New York, Routledge, 2005.

procedures).[6] One of the most prestigious Sufi orders of South Asia, the Chishtis, did not discriminate at all against the Shias.

During the British Raj, the only place where relations between Shias and Sunnis were strained was in Lucknow, the capital of the former kingdom of Awadh.[7] Tensions developed there in the nineteenth century due competition facing the former Shia ruling dynasty and the aristocracy that remained faithful to it from a rising Sunni bourgeoisie. In 1906, Sunnis took to criticizing Shia rituals, saying that they were heterodox innovations, and began to practice *Madh-e sahaba* (a procession conducted on the occasion of the Prophet's birthday) as a show of strength.[8] Rioting ensued, such that the Shias created the Shia Conference, an organisation that was renamed Shia Political Conference in 1909. Despite its new name, this institution did not articulate specific political demands, except a separate count of the Shias in the census.[9] (This is how the figure of 4 per cent—probably much lower than the actual percentage—was established by the Census Office after it acceded to the Shias' demand.) In the mid-1930s, the Shia Political Conference merged into the Congress Party. Without there being an apparent causal relationship, that was precisely when a new outbreak of rioting occurred, continuing into the early 1940s.[10] But the division between Shias and Sunnis remained a local issue and never affected the cohesion of the Muslim League.

After the creation of Pakistan, relations between Shias and Sunnis remained peaceful up until the 1970s.[11] In fact, the distinction was generally irrelevant:

---

[6] See Vernon Schubel, *Religious Performance in Contemporary Islam. Shi'i Devotional Rituals in South Asia*, Columbia, University of South Carolina Press, 1993, pp. 160–161.

[7] The other city with a significant Shia minority, Hyderabad, did not experience such tensions.

[8] Keith Hjortshoj, "Shi'i Identity and the Significance of Muharram in Lucknow, India", in Martin Kramer (ed.), *Shi'ism, Resistance and Revolution*, Boulder, Westview Press, 1987.

[9] Mushir ul Hasan, "Traditional Rites and Contested Meanings: Sectarian Strife in Colonial Lucknow", in Violette Graff (ed.), *Lucknow, Memories of a City*, Delhi, Oxford University Press, 1997, pp. 114–135.

[10] Mushir ul Hasan, *Islam, Communities and the Nation. Muslim Identities in South Asia and Beyond*, Dhaka, The University Press, 1988, p. 341 ff.

[11] Andreas Rieck, "The Struggle for Equal Rights as a Minority: Shia Communal Organizations in Pakistan, 1948–1968", in Rainer Brunner and Werner Ende (eds), *The Twelver Shia in Modern Times*, Leiden, Brill, 2000, pp. 268–283.

There was intermarriage between the two communities and no one minded if the spouses continued to differ in their beliefs and rutuals. Only in moments of curiosity did the Sunnis refer to the 'strange' practices of the Shia: their *kalma* (Muslim catechism) was different from the *kalmia* of the Sunnis, their timings of *namaz* was different, they observed the month of fasting according to timings that differed to Sunni timings, and they went to different mosques and followed different rituals of burial of the dead. This curiosity was not flecked with any suspicion or misgiving.[12]

Mariam Abou Zahab points out that it was even improper to ask someone whether he belonged to one group or the other.[13] Jinnah himself converted to Shiism according to his secretary, Syed Sharifuddin Pirzada, after his original Ismaili community objected to the fact that two of his sisters married Sunnis.[14] According to Vali Nasr, Khawaja Nazimuddin (who became Governor General of Pakistan after Jinnah's death) and Liaquat Ali Khan were also Shia.[15] In the 1950s–60s, two unelected heads of state—Iskander Mirza (1956–8) and Yahya Khan (1969–70)—were Shia. Another Commander-in-Chief, Musa Khan, was a Shia who decided to be buried in Mashhad, in Iran. And while the Bhutto family has kept its religious affiliation virtually a state secret, some people suspect that they are Shias. Z.A. Bhutto's father, Sir Shah nawaz Bhutto was "a renowned Shia politician" according to Hassan Abbas[16] and his wife was Iranian. Another interesting clue: there are "many references to Shiism in the representation of Benazir's martyrdom".[17] Vali Nasr points out that the colour of the PPP's flag, black, red, green are those of Shiism.[18]

The Pakistani Shias nevertheless organized separately. Shia landlords (mostly from South Punjab) and *ulema*—sometimes after having left the Congress party just before Partition to support the Muslim League—met in Lahore in March 1948 to form the All Parties Shia Conference (APSC). More militant Shias reacted by creating a rival organisation quick to up the ante

[12] Khaled Ahmed, *Sectarian War*, op. cit., p. 4.
[13] "Entretien avec Mariam Abou Zahab. L'Islamisme combattant au Pakistan: un état des lieux", *Hérodote*, no. 139, 2010, p. 90.
[14] Khaled Ahmed, *Sectarian War*, op. cit., p. 8.
[15] Vali Nasr, *The Shia Revival. How Conflicts within Islam Shape the Future*, New York, W.W. Norton & Company, 2006, p. 88.
[16] Hasan Abbas, *Shiism and Sectarian Conflict in* Pakistan, Occasional Paper Series, West Point, Combating Terrorism Center, 2010, p. 23
[17] Michel Boivin and Remy Delage, "Benazir en odeur de sainteté. Naissance d'un lieu de culte au Pakistan", *Archives de sciences sociales des religions*, no. 151, July/September 2010, p. 199.
[18] Vali Nasr, *The Shia Revival*, op. cit.

on its forerunner, asking for political rights for their community. Their organization, the Idara-e Tahaffuz-e Hoquq-e Shia (ITHS—Organisation for the defence of Shias' rights) was founded also in 1948. Both groups were dominated by Punjabi landlords who patronized *zakirs* (clerics) and both groups concentrated on educational and ritual issues such as the introduction of a separate *Islamiyat* (Muslim civilisation) curriculum for Shia students (as was the case in the Raj) and the recognition of the *azadari* (public ceremonies commemorating the martyrs of Karbala). These demands to a large extent went unheeded (a separate *Islamiyat* curriculum was not introduced as an optional course in the Punjab until 1954).

In 1963, Shias were victims of Sunni attacks of an unprecedented magnitude in Theri, a small town near Khairpur (Sindh), and then in Lahore. Hassan Abbas points out that "The anti-Shia violence of 1963 had a major impact on Shia thinking and, consequently, on the community's organizational politics. In the wake of the violence, the ITHS and the APSC lost significant support due to a perception that their activities had not produced more security for the community". An All Pakistan Shia Ulema Convention took place in Karachi in 1964 and designated Syed Muhammad Dihlawi as its leader. In 1966 Dilhawi started the Shia Demands Committee which requested the state to guarantee freedom and security for *azadari* funeral processions, separate religious instructions for Shias in public schools and self administration of Shia trusts, shrines and property being part of *awaqf*.[19]

In 1968 Ayub Khan bowed to these demands—despite the opposition of Sunni organizations—but the president was to resign from his post a few months later and his successor, Yayha Khan (even though a Shia) would prove a greater ally to Sunni activists such as the Jama'at-e-Islami, as we have seen.

Crystallisation of Political Sectarianism

Politicization of the Pakistani Shias gained momentum in the late 1970s– early 1980s in the wake of the Iranian revolution under the influence of Ayatollah Khomeini. Khomeini had left Iran in 1964 and settled down in Najaf in 1965 where he was sought out by young Shia clerics from Iran, Lebanon, Afghanistan and Pakistan.[20] In 1972 Pakistani students founded

---

[19] Hassan Abbas, *Shiism and Sectarian Conflict in* Pakistan, op. cit., pp. 22–23.
[20] Chibli Mallat, *The Renewal of Islamic Law. Muhammad Baqer as-Sadr, Najaf and the Shi'i International*, New York, Columbia University Press, 1993.

the Imamia Students' Organisation (ISO, Shia Student Organisation).[21] They focused on religious and social issues (including aid for poor students) to such an extent that the older generations of clerics looked at them as leftists, but they paved the way for political agitation that crystallized after the Iranian revolution.

After Khomeini took power in Iran in 1979, Pakistan was one of his targets in his endeavour to export the Iranian revolution. Tehran for instance distributed scholarships to Shia students who were invited to study at educational institutions in Qom. There, young Pakistanis met co-religionists from the rest of the Middle East. Iranian cultural centres also multiplied in Pakistan. More importantly, as Mariam Abou Zahab writes, "The Iranian revolution inspired Pakistani Shias and contributed to their politicization."[22] The replacement of old *zakirs* by new ones trained in Iran contributed to this "complete change in the Shia community."[23]

The Iranian revolution definitely had a strong impact on the Pakistani Shias, but before that, Zia's Islamisation policy was even more directly responsible for the crystallization of Shia political mobilization, in particular his efforts to introduce Hanafi Sunni laws and his reform of *zakat* mentioned above, which was at odds with the Jafari school of Islamic jurisprudence followed by the Shias. The Tehrik-e Nifaz-e Fiqh Jaafriya (TNJF—Movement for the implementation of Shia jurisprudence) was created in April 1979 in reaction to Zia's policy by Mufti Jaafar Hussain with the support of the ISO which became the youth wing of the organisation. It orchestrated agitation campaigns, including "a two-day siege of Islamabad by Shia demonstrators from across Pakistan on 5 July 1980, which openly defied the martial law ban on public gatherings, and virtually shut down the government."[24] There is no doubt that the Iranian revolution had galvanized Pakistani Shias at that time. One of their leaders, Allama Arif Hussain al-Hussaini, a young Iran-educated cleric who was Khomeini's *vakil* (representative) in Pakistan, emulated his style with a certain degree of success. But the key factor in the mobilization clearly came from within.

---

[21] Mariam Abou Zahab, "The Politicization of the Shia Community in Pakistan in the 1970s and 1980s", in Alessandro Monsutti, Silvia Naef and Farian Sabahi (eds), *The Other Shiites*, Berne, Peter Lang, 2007.

[22] Mariam Abou Zahab, "The Regional Dimension of Sectarian Conflicts in Pakistan", in Christophe Jaffrelot (ed.), *Pakistan. Nationalism without a Nation?* London, Zed Books, 2004, p. 115.

[23] Ibid., p. 116.

[24] Seyyed Vali Reza Nasr, "Islam, the State and the Rise of Sectarian Militancy in Pakistan", in ibid., p. 88.

The TNFJ asked for the recognition of Shia law by the courts, the formation of Shia Waqf Boards and separate Islamic studies courses for Shia students. Zia, eventually made concessions in 1980 in each of these domains in what is known as the "Islamabad Pact". On 27 April 1981 the Ministry of Finance exempted Shias from the taxes. But the "Pact" was "not implemented fully till 1985"[25]—when there were new demonstrations to put pressure on Zia. The rallies were peaceful in Lahore and Peshawar but turned violent in Quetta where 20 Shia demonstrators were killed by the police.[26] Other concessions were counterproductive. For instance, "throughout the 1980s Shia Generals held prominent positions in the military, albeit none were placed in charge of sensitive operations."[27] This tactic aroused opposition among Sunni activists who were highly disturbed by the Iranian revolution and who consequently were prepared to receive support from Saudi Arabia, a country that now was competing with Iran for leadership of the Muslim world. In the early 1980s, Saudi Arabia was playing an increasingly important role in Pakistan politics and society. First, it had become deeply involved in the anti-Soviet jihad which had been launched from the NWFP—and as Khaled Ahmed pointed out "Jihad and sectarianism intermingled in Pakistan (...) Because jihad was exclusively Deobandi and Ahl-e-Hadith, both schools traditionally anti-Shia...".[28] Besides, Saudi Arabia had encouraged Pakistan in the early 1980s to proclaim the edict of *zakat*. Maruf Dualibi, "the Arab scholar who was sent to Pakistan by Saudi Arabia to impose the anti-Shia laws that Pakistan was averse to enforcing",[29] was the one who "framed" the 1980 Zakat and Ushr Ordinance. King Faisal even "gave Zia the 'seed money' to start the *zakat* system in Pakistan with the condition that a part of it go to the Wahhabi party", the Ahl-e-Hadith.[30] Subsequently, in the late 1980s, Pakistan "succumbed to the Saudi persuasion by ousting the Iran-

---

[25] Muhammad Amir Rana, "Evolution of militant groups in Pakistan (4)", *Conflict and Peace Studies*, vol. 6, no. 1, January–June 2014, p. 117.

[26] Ibid.

[27] Seyyed Vali Reza Nasr, "Islam, the State and the Rise of Sectarian Militancy in Pakistan", p. 89.

[28] Khaled Ahmed, *Sectarian War*, op. cit., p. 114.

[29] Khaled Ahmed, "Can the Taliban be far behind?" *The Indian Express*, 21 March 2014 (http://indianexpress.com/article/opinion/columns/can-the-taliban-be-far-behind/). Khaled Ahmed's interpretation of history here should be qualified because Pakistan was certainly not as passive as it is suggested in this account.

[30] Khaled Ahmed, *Sectarian War.*, p. 29.

based Shia jihadi outfits in the Afghan government-in-exile formed in Peshawar".[31]

Sipaha-e-Sahaba Pakistan (SSP—the Army of the Companions of the Prophets) was formed in this context in 1985,[32] with the support of Zia after he had a "bad meeting" with Khomeini.[33] The SSP grew out of the Deobandi-oriented Jamiat-e-Ulema-e-Islam (JUI) and enjoyed state support.[34] Zia himself was keen to use Sunni militants to resist Shia mobilization and contain Iranian influence in Pakistan.[35] The SSP's primary goal was to have the Shias declared non-Muslim, just as the Ahmadis had been. It is therefore no surprise that many of its leaders had taken part in the 1974 anti-Ahmadi movement. In 1986 three *fatwa* apostatising the Shias were issued by the Darul Uloom Binori Town, the Jamia Ashrafia and the Haqqania.[36]

Shias radicalised around the same time. In 1983, the death of Mufti Jaafar Hussain enabled Allama Arif Hussain al-Hussaini to take over the TNFJ. This Pashtun from the Turi (Shia) tribe of Kurram (FATA)—Khomeini's *vakil* in Pakistan—according to Hassan Abbas, "can be considered the architect of Shia radicalism in Pakistan".[37] He transformed the TNFJ into a political party in 1987. Sectarian violence took on new forms around that time: riots (such as in Lahore in 1987) and targeted killings. The principal leaders were assassinated one after another in the late 1980s-early 1990s: in 1987, Ehsan Elahi Zaheer, the Ahl-e-Hadith author of *Shias and Shiaism. Their genesis and evolution* was killed; the following year came the turn of Allama Arif Hussain, reportedly with the complicity of the ISI and Zia's entourage;[38] in 1990, Haq Nawaz Jhangvi, founder of the SSP, was

---

[31] Ibid., p. 105.

[32] It grew out of the Anjuman Sipah-e-Sahaba created the year before.

[33] Khaled Ahmed, *Sectarian War*, op. cit., p. 95.

[34] Mariam Abou Zahab, "The SSP. Herald of Militant Sunni Islam in Pakistan", in Laurent Gayer and Christophe Jaffrelot (eds), *Armed Militias of South Asia. Fundamentalists, Maoists and Separatists*, New York, Columbia University Press, 2009, pp. 160–161.

[35] In 2012, a former Director General of the Federal Investigation Agency, Tariq Khosa declared before the Senate Committee on Defense and Defense Production that in 1980 already, General Zia had asked the police of Jhang to release Haq Nawaz Jhangvi, who was to be the founder of the SSP, after his arrest because of anti-Shia provocations (http://www.senate.gov.pk/uploads/documents/13650922 65_822.pdf).

[36] Khaled Ahmed, *Sectarian War*, op. cit., p. 105.

[37] Hassan Abbas, *Shiism and Sectarian Conflict in* Pakistan, op. cit., p. 35.

[38] Mariam Abou Zahab, "The SSP. Herald of Militant Sunni Islam in Pakistan", op. cit., p. 169.

shot dead, probably by a Sunni rival, but the SSP accused the Shias and in retaliation killed the Iranian consul general in Lahore.[39]

The successor of Hussaini, Allama Sajid Naqvi, was more moderate. His party stopped contesting elections and entered into an electoral alliance with the PPP in 1988. Naqvi also rechristened it Tehrik-e Jafria Pakistan (TJP—Movement of Pakistani Shias) in 1993, "deftly removing from its name the word *nifaz*, which in Urdu means 'implementation'", in order "to appear less provocative to Sunnis...".[40] But the TJP thereby alienated the most radical members of the party.

They established the Sipah-e Mohammad Pakistan (SMP—Army of Mohammed) in 1993.[41] On the Sunni side, an extremist faction of the SSP founded the Lashkar-e-Jhangvi (The Army of Jhangvi, named for SSP's founder) one year later.[42] The SSP—like the TJP—had taken advantage of the democratic opening following the death of Zia to take part in elections. In 1990, it won its first seat. But it indulged in more radical activities too under the LeJ label. There was a division of labour between the two which was intended to retain the façade of respectability the SSP, as a political party, was longing for. But in fact the "SSP, in conjunction with the LeJ, morphed into a powerful criminal syndicate, hate group, political party, and terror organization".[43]

LeJ activists were already in contact with the Taliban whose "militant Deobandism" they shared and with Al Qaeda leaders, to whom the LeJ provided "access to Pakistan's urban areas, particularly in Punjab".[44] In return, the Taliban provided the LeJ with "a safe haven from which to operate; and Al-Qaeda leaders and operatives offer[ed] LeJ militants expert training as well as grand strategy and broader narrative to anchor their militancy".[45] This is evident from the organisation's list of "Objectives and Goals". The first four are:

---

[39] Arif Rafiq, *Sunni Deobandi-Shi'i Sectarian Violence in Pakistan*, Middle East Institute, December 2014, p. 18.(http://www.mei.edu/sites/default/files/publications/Arif%20Rafiq%20report.pdf).

[40] Hassan Abbas, *Shiism and Sectarian Conflict in* Pakistan, op. cit., p. 37.

[41] Ibid.

[42] The symmetry of these two splits needs to be qualified according to Khaled Ahmed. For him, "the SMP-TJP 'unannounced' break was genuine while the SSP-Lashkar-e-Jhangvi 'announced' break was not" (Khaled Ahmed, *Sectarian War*, op. cit., p. 142).

[43] Arif Rafiq, *Sunni Deobandi-Shi'i Sectarian Violence in Pakistan*, op. cit., p. 20.

[44] Ibid., p. 28.

[45] Ibid.

1) Struggle for the establishment of Islamic Shariah government in Pakistan and the entire world and removing all obstacles toward it.
2) Declare Shiʻa a non-Muslim minority.
3) Kill every person who blasphemes or insults the Prophet Muhammad (peace be upon him), the Prophet Muhammad's pure wives, companions, the Qur'an, and the religion of Islam.
4) Kill every journalist, businessman, lawyer, bureaucrat, doctor, engineer, or professor who misuses his social position to tarnish the beliefs of Muslims or engage in any way in the preaching or publishing against the Islamic creed and beliefs.[46]

The driving force behind the LeJ was Riaz Basra, a Punjabi trained in Sargodha and Lahore *dini madaris* before going off to fight the Soviets in the Harakat-ul Mujahideen and joining the SSP in 1985.[47] As of 1995, the LeJ no longer limited their targets to Shia political leaders but began targeting individual members of the opposite community: doctors, civil servants and even army officers were the main victims of this evolution. But from 1997 onwards, the organisation has used less discriminating methods, resorting to the perpetration of mass crimes that aim not only to decapitate the rival organization but terrorise the other: bombs explode outside a mosque after the Friday prayer, suicide bombers decimate a procession or a family celebration, each time killing dozens (see table 9.1).

Table 9.1: Sectarian Violence in Pakistan: 1989–2013

Year	Incidents	Killed	Wounded
1989	67	18	102
1990	274	32	328
1991	180	47	263
1992	135	58	261
1993	90	39	247
1994	162	73	326
1995	88	59	189
1996	80	86	168
1997	103	193	219
1998	188	157	231
1999	103	86	189
2000	109	149	n.a.
2001	154	261	495

(table contd.)

[46] Cited in ibid. p. 29.
[47] Khaled Ahmed, *Sectarian War*, op. cit., p. 123.

(*table contd.*)

2002	63	121	257
2003	22	102	103
2004	19	187	619
2005	62	160	354
2006	38	201	349
2007	341	441	630
2008	97	306	505
2009	106 (152)	190 (446)	398 (587)
2010	57 (152)	509 (663)	1170 (1 569)
2011	30 (139)	203 (397)	297 (626)
2012	173 (213)	507 (563)	577 (900)
2013	128 (220)	525 (687)	914 (1,319)
Total	2,869	4,710	9,191

Sources: http://www.satp.org/satporgtp/countries/pakistan/database/sect-killing. htm and, in parentheses, *Pakistan Security Report—2013*, Islamabad, Pak Institute for Peace Studies, 2014, p. 24.

Up until the mid-1990s, there were more incidents labelled sectarian than casualties resulting from such violence. Since that time the tendency has been reversed, reaching a height in 2010 with 57 attacks killing 509 people (in 1989, 67 incidents were responsible for the death of 18 people, see table 9.1). Other sources give different figures, as evident from the 2013 report of the Pak Institute for Peace Studies (PIPS) (see also the web site of the Shaheed Foundation, www.shaheedfoundation.org). The Interior Ministry has also produced statistics occasionally. In April 2014, it informed the senators that sectarian violence had been responsible of the death of 2,090 people in five years.[48]

The breakdown for these figures community-wise is not always available, but the death toll on the Shia side is notably higher, not only because minorities generally fare the worst (as shown by the Muslim situation in India), but also because Sunni movements quickly joined forces with jihadists and have learned from their rather summary modus operandi.[49] In 2013,

[48] Irfan Ghauri, "Sectarian violence: over 2,000 people killed in 5 years, Interior Ministry tells Senate", *The Express Tribune*, 24 April 2014 (http://tribune.com.pk/ story/699421/sectarian-violence-over-2000-people-killed-in-5-years-says-interior-ministry/).

[49] Frédéric Grare, "The Evolution of Sectarian Conflicts in Pakistan and the Ever-Changing Face of Islamic Violence", *South Asia: Journal of South Asian Studies*, (Routledge), vol. 30, no. 1, April 2007, p. 138.

according to the PIPS, out of 658 casualties, 471 were Shias and 99 Sunnis.[50] No place was completely spared. Even in the garrison city that is Rawalpindi, 13 attempted targeted killings were registered in the first eleven months of 2014 (seven people died).[51]

Arif Rafiq points out that, according to his data, sectarian violence increased after 2007. He partly explains this phenomenon by the attitude of the politicians who had taken over from Musharraf, and more especially the PML (N) whose leading family, the Sharif brothers, started to rule Punjab again around that time. Their attitude vis-à-vis the SSP had always been quite ambivalent. In 1990, the SSP was already part of the IJI electoral alliance led by Nawaz Sharif. But in the 1990s the PPP also partnered with the SSP, which had not yet indulged in mass violence. In the 2000s, protecting the SSP (rechristened Ahl-e-Sunnat Wal Jama'at after its ban in 2002) as did the PML(N), especially in Punjab, has different implications, given the reputation for violence and the growing influence this movement had acquired. The PLM(N) attitude resulted from three considerations. First, the SSP has built a real "vote bank" in the province and the PML(N) relied partly on it to win seats in this stronghold (the 2010 by election in Jhang was a case in point).[52] Second, the PML(N) government tried to buy peace in the Punjab by accommodating the SSP. For instance, in 2011, Malik Ishaq, the co-founder of the LeJ who had already spent fourteen years in jail, was "released as part of a deal between Shahbaz Sharif's provincial government in Punjab and the SSP/ASWJ, aimed at bolstering the ruling party and sparing the province from jihadi violence engulfing the country".[53] Last but not least, the PML(N)—which had distanced itself from the Sunni militants during the 2013 elections "backtracked from its tougher approach towards the SSP/ASWJ, likely due to its perceived dependence on the group for talks with the TTP and for maintaining relative peace in Punjab".[54] Indeed, the government of Nawaz Sharif tried to initiate peace talks for six months in 2013–14 and relied on SSP/ASWJ leaders such as its president, Ahmed Ludhianvi, to do so—unsuccessfully.

---

[50] *Pakistan Security Report—2013*, Islamabad, Pak Institute for Peace Studies, 2014, p. 25.

[51] Mohammad Asghar, "Target killings rise in Rawalpindi as sectarian hatred is fanned", *Dawn*, 15 November 2014 (http://www.dawn.com/news/1144577).

[52] Arif Rafiq, *Sunni Deobandi-Shi'i Sectarian Violence in Pakistan*, op. cit., p. 38.

[53] Ibid., p. 34.

[54] Ibid., p. 40.

However, Punjab is not the only province where Sunni militant groups have made inroads in the 2000s. Similar developments have taken place in Balochistan and Karachi. Arif Rafiq points out that in Balochistan, "the SSP/ASWJ and LeJ have a local infrastructure that consists of ethnic Baluch militants",[55] including Usman Kurd, their Quetta-based leader. Their main targets are naturally the Hazaras, who—as mentioned above—came from Afghanistan and are easy to identify because of their Asian features. Like in Punjab, socio-economic rivalries played a role in their case as well. Having invested in education more than the other communities, Hazaras hold a sizeable share of government jobs and are major shareholders in small business in Quetta. By targeting them, the LeJ received the support of other Sunnis who competed with the Hazaras and benefited from the way were intimidated and even terrorised. Thousands of Hazaras have left mixed neighbourhoods or even Quetta and Balochistan after selling the properties they had outside their enclaves.[56] Hazaras victims of sectarian attacks accuse the paramilitary Frontier Corps (and even the army sometimes) of joining hands with the LeJ (or, at least, of not repressing this groups' activists) because of their common worlview and also because the authorities relied on Sunni militants against Baloch nationalists.[57] Other analysts, including Tariq Khosa, the former head of the FIA, claim on the contrary that, Baloch nationalists and the Sunni militants having a common enemy—the state—the LeJ has "developed a nexus with BLA and other militant outfits in the province to cause systematic mayhem".[58] Whatever the reason, sectarian violence has dramatically increased in Balochistan in the 2010s. In two years, the average annual number of "deaths in suspected or confirmed anti-Shia attacks" almost doubled between 2011 and 2013.[59]

In Karachi sectarian violence has also surged, partly because the 2009 military operations in Swat and South Waziristan have resulted "in a massive flow of displaced persons, including some militants, from these areas into Karachi".[60] The number of deaths in suspected or confirmed Sunni Deobandi-Shia violence increased from 52 in 2010 and 77 in 2011 to 212 in

---

[55] Ibid., p. 45.

[56] Ibid., p. 57.

[57] Ibid., p. 49.

[58] Tariq Khosa, "Baluchistan at the Edge of Precipice, Slipping into Chaos," *The News*, 7 October 2011, http://www.thenews.com.pk/Todays-News-6–71385-Baluchistan-atthe-edge-of-precipice-slipping-into-chaos.

[59] Arif Rafiq, *Sunni Deobandi-Shi'i Sectarian Violence in Pakistan*, op. cit., p. 44.

[60] Ibid., p. 78.

2012 and 283 in 2013.[61] These figures reflect a "new wave of anti-Shi'a terror attacks (which) effectively began on December 28, 2009, when a suicide bomber detonated his explosive vest at a Shi'a procession commemorating the holy day of Ashura".[62] Forty-three people died in the blast. In addition to targeted killings, these attacks were directed towards small communities that had been spared so far (including the Dawoodi Bohras and the Aga Khanis) and Shia enclaves such as Ancholi, Jaffer-e-Tayyar in Malir and Old Rizvia in Golimar. These enclaves resulted from a ghettoization process which was intended to make Shias safer where they were in larger numbers, but which also made them easier targets.[63]

Apart from the recent escalation of violence, sectarianism—partly because of the attempts of the PML(N) to mainstream the SSP/ASWJ—has become a part of everyday life in Pakistan—as evident from the pervasiveness of anti-Shia graffiti on the walls of some Pakistani cities.[64] While the Sunni/Shia distinction had little significance in the early decades of post-independence Pakistan, today it has became a structuring feature of its identity—or rather identity crisis. No one talks about it in public—except declared activists—for the topic is politically incorrect: after all, the "Land of the Pure" was founded to provide all Muslims without distinction with a homeland. But there is deep-seated uneasiness. Khaled Ahmed points out that a "war of names" is now at work: "In earlier times such Shia names as Naqvi, Jafri and Rizvi aroused no curiosity; now there is a tension in the air the moments these names are mentioned". At the same time, "extremist Sunnis have begun to name their sons Muawiyya, the man who contested the caliphate of Ali and whose son Yazid got Imam Husayn martyred".[65]

According to Matthew Nelson, "throughout Pakistan, religious and sectarian differences of opinion had come to resemble something like the proverbial 'elephant in the living room'".[66] Nelson concludes from his 800 or so interviews on religious education in Pakistan that "difference itself

---

[61] Ibid., p. 77.

[62] Ibid., p. 79.

[63] Ibid., pp. 81–83.

[64] Muhammad Asif, "Sectarian ideological warfare through graffiti", *Conflict and Peace Studies*, vol. 6, no. 1, January–June 2014, p. 88.

[65] Khaled Ahmed, *Sectarian War*, op. cit., p. xxv.

[66] Matthew J. Nelson, "Dealing with Difference: Religious Education and the Challenge of Democracy in Pakistan", *Modern Asian Studies*, vol. 43, no. 3, 2009, p. 801.

was the thing that most of [his] respondents had been taught to regard as undesirable, unacceptable and, at some level, 'un-Islamic'",[67] but a large majority of them did not want a Shia teacher for their children if they were Sunnis, considered that there should be only one style of *namaz* and justified this stand in the most simple way: because Sunnis were in a majority. Nelson found that his respondents "were less concerned about the finer points of religious doctrine, ritual practice or religious sectarian boundaries than they were about essentialized (political) majorities."[68]

In fact, Nasr convincingly argues that "sectarianism is a form of religiopolitical nationalism" and an "ethnic discourse of power".[69] Power, indeed, is the key variable explaining the crystallization of Shia as well as Sunni sectarian movements. Already in Lucknow in the early 20th century, Shia/Sunni tensions reflected a power struggle between the former Shia rulers and a rising Sunni middle class.[70] This configuration runs parallel to the conflict during the same period between the Hindu middle class and a waning Muslim aristocracy that eventually gave rise to the Muslim League and the demand for Pakistan.

A similar dynamic explains the resurgence of sectarianism since the 1980s. Sunnis felt threatened—arguably excessively—by Shia mobilisation in the wake of the Iranian revolution, viewing its Pakistani followers as a sort of fifth column. Against this national backdrop, oppositions crystallised in places where the local context was fertile, in other words where Sunnis felt particular resentment toward age-old Shia domination.[71] Jhang district in Punjab is a case in point. After Partition, Shia landlords employed Sunni refugees who had left India with next to nothing as tenant farmers. As Sunnis improved their level of education and became more urbanized, they emancipated themselves from their old masters and demanded their place in the sun, including a share of power. Thus in 1992, SSP leader Azam Tariq won the Jhang seat in the National Assembly, an unprecedented achievement for a previously marginal political force, all the more as he

[67] Ibid., p. 604.
[68] Ibid., p. 607.
[69] Seyyed Vali Reza Nasr, "Islam, the State and the Rise of Sectarian Militancy in Pakistan", op. cit., p. 87 and 86.
[70] Imtiaz Ahmed, "The Sunni-Shia Dispute in Lucknow", in Milton Israel and N.K. Wagle (eds), *Islamic Society and Culture: Essays in Honour of Professor Aziz Ahmad*, Delhi, Manohar, 1983, pp. 335–350.
[71] Mohammad Waseem, "Sectarian Conflict in Pakistan" in K.M. De Silva (ed.), *Conflict and Violence in South Asia*, Kandy, ICES, 2001, pp. 19–89.

was reelected in 1993. He lost his seat in 1997, but Jhang remains an SSP stronghold due to Sunni resentment toward Shia dominance.[72]

While power relations largely explain the "metamorphosis from religious schism into political conflict around mobilization of communal identity"[73] on the Sunni side, among Shias this metamorphosis has remained incomplete. To achieve such a transformation, a community needs to believe in the relevance of the political fight. It is a self-defeating perspective for the Shias. Not only can they not hope to win many seats in Parliament on the strength of their numbers alone, but in the mid 1990s they also lost Iran's financial backing, something Mariam Abou Zahab attributes partly to the fact that it was seen as "counterproductive" and to the fear of "a backlash of Sunni militancy fuelled by Pakistani Sunni extremists in Iranian Baluchistan".[74] However, in 2011, Karachi's Crime Investigation Department (CID), on the basis of the confessions of arrested Shia activists, "alleged that up to 200 SMP militants received training from Iran".[75]

The Iranian support declining, the Shias have lately explored three alternative routes:

1) Regarding the use of violence: during the 1990s Shia militants have massively resorted to terrorism through the SMP which "was involved in 250 acts of terrorism between 1993 and 2001".[76] But this strategy is on the decline because it has been affected by faction fights and has resulted in Sunni retaliation operations: the chief of the SMP, Maulana Yazdani, was assassinated in 1996 by his rivals—who were arrested by the police; security-service crackdowns, including one on the SMP's headquarters in Thokar Niaz Beg (in the suburb of Lahore), have also decimated the organisation.[77] In 2001, Musharraf banned the SMP and

---

[72] Mariam Abou Zahab, "The Sunni-Shia Conflict in Jhang (Pakistan)" in Imtiaz Ahmad and Helmut Reifield (eds), *Lived Islam in South Asia. Adaptation, Accommodation and Conflict*, Delhi: Social Science Press, 2004. pp. 135–148.

[73] Seyyed Vali Reza Nasr, "Islam", op. cit., p. 86.

[74] M. Abou Zahab, "The Regional Dimension of Sectarian Conflicts in Pakistan", op. cit., p. 117. Today Iran seems to encourage the training of transnational Shia elites on its own soil.

[75] Tariq Habib, "200 Iranian-trained Sipah-e Muhammad Activists Hunting Down ASWJ Workers," *Pakistan Today*, 26 May 2011, http://www.pakistantoday.com.pk/2011/05/26/city/karachi/%E2%80%98200-iraniantrained-sipah-e-muhammad-activists-hunting-down-aswj-workers%E2%80%99/.

[76] Khaled Ahmed, *Sectarian War*, op. cit., p. 143.

[77] Hassan Abbas, *Shiism and Sectarian Conflict in* Pakistan, op. cit., p. 38.

the LeJ, which both re-appeared immediately under different names, respectively Tehrik-e-Islami Pakistan (TIP—Movement of Islam Pakistan) and Millat-e-Islamia Pakistan (MIP—Nation of Islam Pakistan).

In Karachi, a Shia activist told Arif Rafiq: "The intent to retaliate is there, but the resources are not".[78] Which does not mean that SMP militants have stopped resorting to targeted killings aiming at Sunni activists, in Karachi as elsewhere. But instead of retaliating against terrorist attacks by using the same techniques, some Shia communities among the more vulnerable ones tend to demonstrate peacefully in order to put pressure on the state apparatus which should protect them. In Balochistan, the Hazaras protested against the bombing of a bus full of pilgrims in Matsung by organising a sit-in and by refusing to bury their dead in January 2014.[79]

2) In the domain of party politics: they have sought to bargain for electoral support among the mainstream parties. The PPP has been their principal partner, but they have achieved little thanks to that party—which has not always been a very reliable protector. In 1993, in Punjab, the PPP formed a coalition with the SSP—probably "to deny the PML an opportunity to partner with the party".[80] Those who still believed in the possibility of a Shia political agenda formed the TIP (ex-SMP) and joined the Muttahida Majlis-e-Amal (MMA—United Action Front) in 2002. In 2008, after the division of the MMA, no Shia party contested the election. But the year after, former ISO leaders and Shia clerics who considered that the TJP leadership was too "quietist and self-serving" started the Majlis-e-Wahdat-e-Muslimeen (MWM) which won one seat in the Baloch state assembly in 2013—and which was "considered the major Shia party in Pakistan" in 2014.[81] While the MWM emerged in the FATA in reaction to the rise of the TTP, it is "now establishing itself in Karachi and elsewhere—especially Jhang", in conjunction with the Shia *ulema* who are well represented among the party leaders.[82] In Karachi—where

[78] Arif Rafiq, *Sunni Deobandi-Shi'i Sectarian Violence in Pakistan*, op. cit., p. 86.

[79] "Hazaras refuse to bury Matsung blast victims", *The Express Tribune*, 26 January 2014 (http://tribune.com.pk/story/662310/hazaras-refuse-to-bury-mastung-blast-victims/).

[80] Arif Rafiq, *Sunni Deobandi-Shi'i Sectarian Violence in Pakistan*, op. cit., p. 26.

[81] Muhammad Amir Rana, "Evolution of militant groups in Pakistan (4)", op. cit., p. 122.

[82] Mohammad Waseem and Mariam Mufti, *Political Parties in Pakistan*, op. cit., p. 83.

the MWM fielded fourteen National and Sindh Assembly candidates in 2013–, it seems that the MQM has "been losing support from some of Karachi's Shias to the rising MWM".[83]

3) At the societal level, they tend to regroup in towns and cities where they thought they would be less vulnerable. But this process of ghettoization, according to Khaled Ahmed, has made them "easy to kill"[84] even in places like Karachi where the MQM may nevertheless offer the Shias protection.[85] Some Shias have also tended to find refuge in religiosity, a process that is nourished by "a deep-seated feeling of fatalism".[86] That was the route the TNFJ faction, which split from the Hussaini-led group in 1983, followed already. Those who have taken it have turned their back on politics to cultivate rituals in a more emotive fashion than in Iran where the republic's official Shiism has discontinued flagellation, for instance.

All things considered, the rise in sectarianism since the 1970s has introduced a vertical split in Pakistani society that probably represents one of the biggest challenges to national cohesion today. Especially since, besides peripheral groups like the Hazaras of Balochistan[87] and the Shias of Gilgit-Baltistan[88] (where sectarian violence began in 1988),[89] one of the most severely affected areas is the core province of Punjab, as will be seen in greater detail in the next chapter.

From One Jihad to Another: From Afghanistan to Kashmir and Back

Along with "sectarian" groups, jihadist movements have also experienced a spectacular development since the 1980s, first in Afghanistan and later in

[83] Arif Rafiq, *Sunni Deobandi-Shi'i Sectarian Violence in Pakistan*, op. cit., p. 89.

[84] Khaled Ahmed, *Sectarian War*, op. cit., p. xxiii.

[85] In fact, the MQM(A) is probably the only party that continues to harbour a large number of Shias without even recognizing sectarian differences, understandably because Muhajirs cannot afford to be divided along such lines. But Shia Muhajir leaders are now targeted in Karachi by the Pakistani Taliban.

[86] Arif Rafiq, *Sunni Deobandi-Shi'i Sectarian Violence in Pakistan*, op. cit., p. 89.

[87] Muhammad Yunas, "The Systematic Extermination of Hazaras", *Dawn*, 21 February 2013. See http://dawn.com/news/787677/the-systematic-extermination-of-hazaras (Accessed on September 15, 2013).

[88] Shujat Hussain Mesam, "Eyewitness Accounts of Shia Genocide in Gilgit and Chilas", 6 April 2012. Available at: http://criticalppp.com/archives/75456 (Accessed on September 15, 2013).

[89] On sectarianism in Gilgit Baltistan, see Khaled Ahmed, *Sectarian War*, op. cit., pp. 189–192.

Indian Kashmir. The intensification of relations between both official and unofficial Pakistani actors and Afghan Islamists predates the 1979 Soviet invasion. The process began in the early 1970s under Z.A. Bhutto—who clearly must be considered the first politician to have played the Islamist card, not only on the domestic political scene but also along Pakistan's borders. While Bhutto devoted considerable energy to the Kashmir dispute, it was in his Afghanistan policy that he took initiatives that have had far-reaching consequences.

Part One of this book discussed the extent to which Pashtun irredentism posed a problem for the Pakistani authorities. In the early 1970s, the men governing Kabul not only stoked this ideology but also made overtures to Moscow that irritated Islamabad and Washington. In 1973 Sardar Muhammad Daoud deposed his cousin Zahir Shah to promote at once Pashtun nationalism and rapprochement with the USSR—which the Afghan state had already initiated.[90] Z.A. Bhutto was all the more worried about Daoud's expansionist aims as according to a Pakistani source the Afghan head of state had begun helping Baloch rebels in their war against Islamabad in 1973–4. Bhutto thus sent the Commandant of the Frontier Corps based in Peshawar, Major General Naseerullah Babar (who became interior minister under Benazir in 1993–6 and architect of her Afghan policy) to identify Afghan opponents to the regime in Kabul that his government could help. Babar enlisted the aid of Brigadier Aslam Bodla and Major Aftab Sherpao—who headed the NWFP government on two occasions, in 1988–90 and in 1994–6, after being invited by Z.A. Bhutto to leave the army and join the PPP. These two men threw their support behind Islamist opponents to the regime in Kabul. Imtiaz Gul recounts "In early 1974, Pakistan's embassy in Kabul received a list of 1,331 Afghan nationals and their families from a colonel with the ISI, with instructions for monthly payments to be made to the Afghans."[91] In September 1974, Babar summoned an ISI agent, Amir Sultan Amir, better known by his nom de guerre

---

[90] In the wake of a crisis in Afghan-Pakistan relations in 1949–50, the government in Karachi had put Afghanistan under an embargo that forced Kabul to turn to Moscow: the Soviets granted the Afghans a barter agreement (oil for wool and cotton), before becoming its largest source of aid (in 1968, Afghanistan received 550 million dollars in aid from the USSR compared to 250 million from the United States). See John Griffiths, *Afghanistan: Key To A Continent*, Boulder, Westview Press, 1981, p. 142.

[91] Imtiaz Gul, *The Most Dangerous Place. Pakistan's Lawless Frontier*, New York, Viking, 2010, p. 2.

"Colonel Imam", to Peshawar to train some of these youths in guerrilla warfare.[92]

Among them were young Islamists who would make names for themselves: Burhanuddin Rabbani, (who in 1972 with the help of the Pakistani Jama'at-e-Islami created an almost eponymous movement, the Jamiat-e-Islami Afghanistan) and two of his fellow students at Kabul University, Gulbuddin Hekmatyar and Ahmed Shah Massoud, as well as Younus Khalis and Rasool Sayyaf. All of them were "selected for commando training at Cherat", the military base where the Pakistani special forces were already trained, 50 km southeast of Peshawar. The JI also participated in training Hekmatyar, Massoud and others through Qazi Hussein Ahmad—a Pakistani Pashtun who would become the movement's emir.[93]

In 1976, Hekmatyar broke away from the Jami'at-e-Islami Afghanistan to form Hezb-e-Islami as a reaction to what he considered heel-dragging on Rabbani's part. Rabbani, like his mentor, Maududi—was loath to resort to violence, while Hekmatyar did not share the same qualms. Whether they advocated the use of violence or not, these men were recommended by the Pakistanis to the Americans who at the time were seeking to counter Moscow's growing influence in Afghanistan through a wide variety of tactics. In May 1978 Babar thus sent Hekmatyar and Rabbani to American diplomats posted in Islamabad[94]—but the ISI was already impressed by Hekmatyar's activism.[95]

The Pursuit of "Strategic Depth" and the Anti-Soviet Jihad: A New Political and Social Course

Although contacts between Pakistanis and Afghan Islamists had begun under Bhutto, it was naturally under Zia that they took on a new dimension and reached such proportions as to upset the entire regional balance.

The Pakistan Army had sought to secure "strategic depth" in Afghanistan in the face of India since Ayub Khan.[96] To achieve this, shortly after the

---

[92] Carey Schofield, *Inside the Pakistan Army*, London, Biteback Publishing, 2011, p. 59.

[93] Mariam Abou Zahab and Olivier Roy, *Islamic Networks. The Afghan-Pakistani Connection*, London, Hurst, 2003, p. 27.

[94] Imtiaz Gul, *The Most Dangerous Place*, op. cit., p. 3.

[95] Husain Haqqani, *Pakistan. Between Mosque and Military*, Washington DC, Carnegie, 2005, p. 174.

[96] Ayub Khan was in fact the first to mention this concept. See A. Pande, *Explaining*

December 1979 Soviet invasion, the ISI was prepared to use Afghan Islamists. This policy—Zia's brainchild—was orchestrated by Lieutenant General Akhter Abdur Rehman, whom Zia had appointed chief of the ISI in 1979 and who remained in this post until 1987. This man, who "was not a radical Islamist, but a staunch Muslim nationalist",[97] began by relying on Afghan mujahideen who had mobilised right after the Soviet invasion.

The Pakistanis, so as to better control these "resistance fighters", only recognised seven groups of mujahideen that were urged to organise if they hoped to receive foreign (especially American) aid flowing through Pakistan.[98] In addition to Rabbani's Jamiat-e-Islami and Hekmatyar's Hezb, which had the Pakistanis' favour, there was also Ittehad-e-Islami (the Islamic Union) led by the Wahabite Abdur Rab Rasool Sayyaf (backed by the Saudis), the Hezb faction led by a Pashtun cleric, Yunus Khalis—who had broken ties with Hekmatyar in 1979—Pir Sayed Gailani's National Islamic Front for Afghanistan,[99] Mojaddedi's Afghanistan National Liberation Front and Mohammadi's Revolutionary Islamic Movement to be reckoned with. These seven parties formed the Islamic Unity of Afghanistan Mujahideen in 1985 in Peshawar, its headquarters.

By the end of 1980, there were 1 million Afghan refugees living in camps within the Pakistan border and nearly 2.4 million one year later. In 1988, there were 3.2 million.[100] Although these camps were run by the UNHCR, they provided a virtually inexhaustible recruitment pool for ISI-sponsored mujahideen. As Frédéric Grare writes, by the early 1980s, "It was without a doubt the ISI's strict control over the conveyance and delivery of weap-

---

Pakistan's Foreign Policy, op. cit., p. 61. But another former general, Asghar Khan, made it more explicit. In 1969 he defined it plainly: "Depth is distance, and distance provides time to a defensive system to react". See Asghar Khan, *Pakistan at the Cross-Roads*, op. cit., p. 9.

[97] Zahid Hussain, *Frontline Pakistan. The Struggle with Militant Islam*, New York, Columbia University Press, 2007, p. 16.

[98] Regarding Pakistani efforts to federate the Afghan resistance, see Gilles Dorronsoro, *Revolution Unending*, London, Hurst, 2005, pp. 144–147.

[99] Descending from the founder of the Qadri Sufi order, Pir Gailani—whose father had come from Baghdad in 1905 to settle in Afghanistan—was a respected religious figure among the Pashtuns. His wife came from the royal family of Afghanistan.

[100] Frédéric Grare, *Le Pakistan face au conflit afghan (1979–1985). Au tournant de la guerre froide*, Paris, L'Harmattan, 1997, p. 62 and p. 89 (note 4).

ons to the resistance that gave Pakistan its most direct influence over the course of the war."[101]

Beyond the Afghan mujahideen, the Pakistanis equipped Islamists who came from all over the world. In 1989, Hamid Gul, then chief of the ISI,[102] boasted about how his organisation had channelled Islamists from a large number of Muslim countries: "We are fighting a jihad and this is the first Islamic brigade in the modern era."[103] This policy—which resulted in the recruitment of Arab, Uzbek, Maghreban, African and other militants—was implemented as of 1983 with the aid of Saudi Arabia and the United States. Prince Turki, the Saudi intelligence minister, played a key role in implementing this plan to "transfer Islamic volunteers to Afghanistan."[104] The plan naturally had Washington's support. In 1986 CIA chief William Casey even secured permission from the United States Congress that year to deliver Stinger missile launchers to the Afghan resistance.

The ISI relied on the JI, which had gained a share of power under Zia, to carry out its strategy. The JI—which claimed the first martyr in the Afghan jihad[105]—was not linked with a tight *dini madaris* network like the JUI, nor did it have a stronghold in the Pashtun areas (its main bases were in Karachi and Punjab). But it took the opportunity of jihad in Afghanistan to set up a large number of *dini madaris* (41 of its total 107 schools) along the Afghan-Pakistani border "to aid and host the refugees"—and especially mujahideen.[106] In the early 1980s, this party often had the task of welcoming and orienting newcomers before arming them, partly thanks to funds from Saudi Arabia, which had vowed to match U.S. aid to the Afghan cause. As Olivier Roy writes, the operation had the trappings of "a joint venture

---

[101] Ibid. p. 104.

[102] Born in 1936, Gul was a Punjabi army officer whose career accelerated thanks to Zia, his patron, who appointed him DGISI in 1987—at a critical moment for Afghanistan.

[103] Cited in Ahmed Rashid, *Taliban. Militant Islam, Oil and Fundamentalism in Central Asia*, New Haven, Yale University Press, 2010, op. cit. p. 129

[104] Mariam Abou-Zahab and Olivier Roy, *Islamic Networks*. op. cit., p. 14. See also Steve Coll's meticulous reconstruction of events in *Ghost Wars. The Secret History of the CIA, Afghanistan, and Bin Laden from the Soviet Invasion to September 10, 2001*, New York, Penguin, 2004, p. 79 ff.

[105] Posted at the entrance to his headquarters in Mansoora (Lahore) is the list of hundreds of martyrs of the Afghan and Kashmiri jihads, including this student's, Imaran Shaheed (*Pakistan: Madrasas, Extremism and the Military*, International Crisis Group, ICG Asia Report no. 36 (29 July 2002), pp. 11–12).

[106] Ibid., p. 12.

between the Saudis, the Muslim Brotherhood and the Jama'at-e-Islami, put together by the ISI."[107]

Ahmed Rashid estimates that "Between 1982 and 1992 some 35,000 Muslim radicals from 43 Islamic countries in the Middle East, North and East Africa, Central Asia and the Far East would pass their baptism under fire with the Afghan mujahideen. Tens of thousands more foreign Muslim radicals came to study in the hundreds of new madrassas that Zia's military government began to fund in Pakistan and along the foreign border."[108]

Among the prominent Arab names the ISI had recruited was Abdul Rasul Sayyaf, the Afghan scholar sent by the Saudis to preach Wahhabism; Abdullah Azzam, a Jordano-Palestinian who had come to Afghanistan in 1979 and had founded a jihadist organisation in 1984 called Makhtab al Khidmat (or Services Office) and one of his former students, Osama bin Laden, whom he had met at the university in Jeddah and who had "visited Afghanistan in 1981" for the first time.[109] The ISI particularly appreciated Bin Laden's presence as, although he was not of royal blood, he was close enough to the ruling family to indicate that Saudi involvement was not limited to sending merely foot soldiers or funds—albeit substantial, and which Bin Laden would further supplement thanks to the fortune his father had amassed in contracts to renovate Medina and Mecca.[110] Established in Peshawar in 1982, Bin Laden—together with the CIA—contributed in the mid-1980s to the construction of roads, tunnels[111] and underground depots for use by the resistance in Khost, where he also set up his first training camp for jihadists. After Azzam's violent and mysterious death in 1989, Bin Laden took over the head of his organisation and later founded Al Qaeda.

The alliance of foreign, Afghan and Pakistani mujahideen together with military and financial backing from the United States and Saudi Arabia enabled the ISI to complete the first phase of its plan in 1989, after ten years of war, which was to drive out the Soviets and ensure "strategic depth" in

---

[107] Olivier Roy, *Afghanistan, from Holy War to Civil War*, Princeton, Princeton University Press, 1995.

[108] Ahmed Rashid, *Taliban*, op. cit., p. 130.

[109] Muhammad Amir Rana and Rohan Gunaratna, *Al-Qaeda Fights Back. Inside Pakistani Tribal Areas*, Islamabad, Pak Institute for Peace Studies, 2008, p. 12.

[110] Ahmed Rashid, *Taliban*, op. cit., p. 131.

[111] Colonel Imam, whom Zia again sent to Afghanistan in 1983, says he met Bin Laden in the field in 1986, recounting that "He'd brought money, and was building jeepable tracks and tunnels". Cited in Carey Schofield, *Inside the Pakistani Army*, op. cit., p. 64.

Afghanistan. This objective implied, however, installing a friendly government in Kabul. The Pakistan Army's main protegé, Gulbuddin Hekmatyar, proved to be ineffective, forcing Islamabad to explore other avenues. The search was first conducted by Asad Durrani's successor at the head of the ISI—Durrani had been DGISI in 1990–92—General Javed Nasir, who turned out to be as well disposed toward the Islamists as Hamid Gul.[112] But it was finally his replacement, Javed Ashraf Qazi, DGISI in 1993–5, who opted for the Taliban. These "students" had often grown up in refugee camps on the Pakistan side and were later trained in Deobandi *dini madaris* run by the JUI. The Haqqania madrassah in Akhora Khatak, on the road from Islamabad to Peshawar is worthy of special mention. Founded in 1947 by Maulana Abdul Haq, it expanded considerably under the auspices of his son, Samiul Haq who "served in Zia's Majlis-e-Shura and aggressively campaigned in support of Islamic legislation such as the Hudood Ordinances, Qisas and Diyat laws, and anti Ahmadi legislation".[113] In the 1970s, it had the capacity to board some 1500 students. A number of Mullah Omar's lieutenants studied there.[114] In 1985, 60 per cent of the madrassah students were Afghan.[115]

In the fall of 1994, the Benazir Bhutto government—starting with her interior minister, General Naseerullah Babar—sided with the Taliban[116] following a mediation made by JUI leader Fazlur Rehman, who was part of the ruling coalition and then chairman of the Standing Committee for

---

[112] Nasir, who also shipped weapons to the Bosnians, had been appointed by Nawaz Sharif, whose taste for adventurism has already been discussed. He was dismissed by the interim prime minister, Moeen Qureshi, after Sharif left office in 1993. See Zahid Hussain, *Frontline Pakistan*, op. cit., p. 27.

[113] Mohammad Waseem and Mariam Mufti, *Political Parties in Pakistan*, op. cit., p. 79.

[114] Ahmed Rashid, *Taliban*, p. 91. After the Taliban took over, Samiul Haq remained in contact with Mullah Omar, helping him both by recruiting Pakistani youth and by acting as an intermediary with the outside world.

[115] Zahid Hussain, *Frontline Pakistan*, op. cit., p. 81. The school was shut down in 1997 to enable its students to join the Taliban effort to take Mazar-i-Sharif.

[116] The pace of this rapprochement as well as those who advocated it is debated. According to Imtiaz Gul, Benazir Bhutto hesitated to go forward until March 1996. The decision to support Mullah Omar's troops was allegedly not made until they had established their rule over Kandahar and Unocal, the American company interested in building a gas pipeline between Turkmenistan and Pakistan, had confirmed its plans. See Imtiaz Gul, *The Unholy Nexus: Pak-Afghan Relations under the Taliban*, Lahore, Vanguard Books, 2002.

Foreign Affairs at the National Assembly.[117] Joshua White partly attributes the resilient affinities between the JUI and the PPP to the fact that the socialist discourse of the later echoed "the populism and anti-imperialism of the pre-Partition Jamiat Ulema movements".[118] Once again there were no clear boundaries: civilians in the PPP took part in decisions developed jointly with the military and Islamic leaders. The ISI, particularly through Colonel Imam who had been appointed consul in Herat, armed, trained and coordinated the Taliban who thus acquired the wherewithal to take over southern Afghanistan.[119] Kandahar was one of the first cities to fall. This Pashtun stronghold—where Mullah Omar established his headquarters— soon became the nerve centre of Taliban power. As of December 1994, 12,000 "Afghan and Pakistani students (from JUI seminaries) had joined the Taliban in Kandahar."[120]

Less than two years later, the Taliban took Kabul, again with help from the ISI—particularly from Colonel Imam, Consul General in Herat until 2001 and Hamid Gul, who "supervised the training of commandos".[121] Many other Pakistani officers supported the Taliban in their conquest of power, to such an extent that in 2001, after the American offensive had begun in Afghanistan, Pakistan had to send a plane to Kunduz to exfiltrate its officers fighting alongside the Taliban and Al Qaeda combatants.

Ousted from the Afghan capital, Commander Massoud and his Northern Alliance fell back on the Tajik enclave of Panshir where the war lasted until his death. But as of 1996 the Taliban controlled Afghanistan with the aid of Pakistan, one of the three countries together with Saudi Arabia and the United Arab Emirates to have recognized their government. And Bin Laden returned—probably from Sudan—to Afghanistan and settled there with the support of the ISI in September 1996.[122] This was a turning point, as Mariam Abou Zahab and Olivier Roy explain:

The encounter between Bin Laden and the Taliban changed the rules. The Taliban entrusted to Bin Laden control of the non-Pakistani militants, while the Pakistani

---

[117] Ahmed Rashid, *Taliban*, op. cit., p. 27.

[118] Joshua White, *Pakistan's Islamst Frontier: Islamic Politics and and U.S. Policy in North-West Frontier*, Arlington (VA), Centre on Faith & International Affairs, 2008, p. 28.

[119] After the fall of Kandahar, Babar privately described the Taliban as "our boys" (in any case the ISI's). See ibid., p. 29.

[120] Ibid., p. 29.

[121] Mariam Abou Zahab and Olivier Roy, *Islamic Networks. The Afghan-Pakistani Connection*, op. cit., p. 56.

[122] Ibid., p. 16.

organisations, especially the Harakat ul-Mujahidin [see infra] took control of a number of training camps in the province of Paktia. (...) During this period Bin Laden brought the Arabs under his control and isolated them from the Afghan population. The leaders were installed in what amounted to residential complexes near Kandahar and Jalalabad, while the ordinary fighters were grouped together in cantonments in Kabul and Kunduz. At the same time a third echelon was established, made up of militants from Western countries who were being trained to return home and carry out terrorist activities.[123]

Taliban presence in Kabul held a number of advantages in the eyes of the Pakistani military-Islamist coalition. For the military—and the civilian rulers—it offered a guarantee of "strategic depth", a notion appropriated by COAS Aslam Beg who, in August 1988, "first talked about this doctrine to his formation commanders and officers at the Rawalpindi garrison".[124] Islamabad thus maintained its military assistance to the Taliban fighting against the Northern Alliance until it fell in 2001, as well as considerable aid in cash and kind. In 1997–8, for instance, "Pakistan provided the Taliban with an estimated US $30 million in aid. This included 600,000 tons of wheat, diesel, petroleum and kerosene fuel which was partly paid for by Saudi Arabia, arms and ammunition, aerial bombs, maintenance and spare parts for its Soviet-era military equipment such as tanks and heavy artillery, repairs and maintenance of the Taliban's airforce and airport operations, road building, electricity supply in Kandahar and salaries."[125] By 1997, "experts estimated the personnel strength of the Taliban to be 50,000 fighters and 40,000 trained reservists and at their disposition 300 tanks, A[rmoured] P[ersonnel] C[arriers], cannons, a squadron of MIG fighter planes and sufficient hand-held weapons with ammunitons". Hein Kiessling points out that such a military apparatus could function only because "the ISI and the Pakistan Army stood helpfully on the sidelines".[126]

Although the ISI remained in contact with the mujahideen groups it had helped during the jihad against the Soviets, this policy was conducted by the Benazir government—particularly by Babar—who wanted to take the matter out of ISI hands. Babar thus created a cell for trade development between Pakistan and Afghanistan within the Interior Ministry and was

---

[123] Mariam Abou Zahab and Olivier Roy, *Islamic Networks. The Afghan-Pakistani Connection*, op. cit., pp. 48–49.

[124] Ashish Shukla, "Pakistan's quest for strategic depth. Regional security implications", *Himalayan and Central Asian* Studies, vol. 15, n° 3, July–September 2011, p. 86.

[125] Ahmed Rashid, *Taliban*, op. cit., p. 184

[126] Hein Kiessling, *Faith, Unity, Discipline: the ISI of Pakistan*, op. cit.

responsible for extending his country's telephone grid to Afghanistan, which could be reached at the price of a domestic call.[127]

For Pakistani Islamists, especially those linked with the JUI,[128] the Taliban takeover was an ideological victory as well as a logistic one. The new government in Kabul in fact provided a doubly useful rear base. First, Afghanistan offered a safe haven for sectarian groups such as Lashkar-e-Jhangvi (LeJ),[129] involved in attacks against the Shias and therefore wanted by the police. Second, Afghanistan under the Taliban was rich in training camps where jihadist groups could train members for the other jihad, the one in Kashmir. The Pakistanis added to the extant infrastructure as "the ISI moved its training facilities for Kashmiri mujahideen into Afghanistan, where anti-American terrorists and Kashmiri jihadists trained together."[130] This is how the Harakat ul-Ansar group (see below) wound up managing Hekmatyar's former Hezb camp in Paktia in 1996—which provided a sanctuary for LJ militants.[131]

India, Land of Jihad

After the (re)conquest of Afghanistan, Pakistani jihadist movements turned their efforts to Indian Kashmir—still with the aid of the ISI and the Pakistan Army. One general involved in this strategy to "bleed India" by infiltrating jihadists into its despised neighbour explained to Ahmed Rashid the predominant rationale in the 1990s in very simple terms: "It kept 700,000 Indian troops and paramilitary forces in Kashmir at very low cost to Pakistan; at the same time, it ensured that the Indian Army could not threaten Pakistan, created enormous expenditures for India, and kept it bogged down in military and political terms."[132]

In 1989, Pakistani jihadists and their ISI sponsors began exploiting the mobilisation of Kashmiri separatist groups which, owing to errors

---

[127] Ahmed Rashid, *Taliban*, op. cit., pp. 184–185.

[128] The JI, on the other hand, had backed Hekmatyar's Hezb.

[129] This group would use Hekmatyar's former Salman ul-Farsi Hezb camp in Paktia, renamed "Amir Moawiya" after the Taliban broke with Hekmatyar. Mariam Abou Zahab and Olivier Roy, *Islamic Networks. The Afghan-Pakistani Connection*, op. cit., pp. 48–49.

[130] Husain Haqqani, *Pakistan: Between Mosque and Military*, op. cit., p. 243.

[131] Mariam Abou Zahab and Olivier Roy, *Islamic Networks. The Afghan-Pakistani Connection*, op. cit., p. 49.

[132] Ahmed Rashid, *Pakistan on the Brink. The Future of Pakistan, Afghanistan and the West*, London, Allen Lane, 2012, p. 56

made by New Delhi,[133] were regaining popularity. Their call to boycott the November 1989 general elections was widely heeded, as voter turnout was no more than 6 per cent in Jammu and Kashmir.[134]

As in Afghanistan, this jihad was conducted jointly by the ISI and Islamists—who had often earned their first stripes in the war against the Soviets in Afghanistan. The main jihadist organisations active in Indian Kashmir were the Harakat groups and Lashkar-e-Taiba.[135]

Harakat ul-Jihad-i-Islami/ul-Mujahideen/Al-Ansar

This movement grew out of the JUI Deobandi *dini madaris*, and more especially out of the Binori Town seminary. This religious complex known today by the name of Jamia Uloom ul Islamia in Binori Town (a merchant neighbourhood of Karachi), was founded in 1953 by a Deobandi cleric for whom it was named: Maulana Muhammad Yousuf Binori (1908–77).[136] This maulana was very involved in the anti-Ahmadi movement. He was later appointed to the Council of Islamic Ideology by Zia. During the jihad in Afghanistan his madrassah became a bastion of resistance to the Soviets. It would appear that Mufti Nizamuddin Shamzai—who directed the institution at the time—was even behind the first meeting between Mullah Omar and Osama bin Laden in Binori Town.[137] Although in 1996 nine of the

---

[133] The Indian government suspected Kashmiri political leaders (starting with National Conference members) of harbouring pro-Pakistani sympathies to such an extent that they could not bring themselves to allow them to administer Jammu and Kashmir like other provinces in the Indian Union and even went so far as to rig regional elections.

[134] Christophe Jaffrelot and Jasmine Zérinini, "La question du Cachemire. Après le 11 September et la nouvelle donne au Jammu-et-Cachemire", *Occasional Papers*, Institut d'études et de sécurité de l'Union européenne, no. 43, March 2003. Available online at: http://www.iss.europa.eu/uploads/media/occ43.pdf (Accessed on September 15, 2013).

[135] Other groups played a role in the jihadist activities that developed in Kasmir in the 1980s-90s. As early as 1988, Jalaluddin Haqqani declared in a conference held in Gujrat (Punjab) by the Harakat-ul Jihad al-Islami: "Brothers: know that we will not lay down our arms once Afghanistan becomes free. We will fight and help Muslims in India and Kashmir to get their freedom from the Hindus..." (Cited in Vahid Brown and Don Rassler, *Fountainhead of Jihad, The Haqqani Nexus, 1973–2012*, London, Hurst, 2013, p. 92).

[136] See http://www.banuri.edu.pk/en/Establishment-of-Jamiah (Accessed on September 15, 2013).

[137] See John K. Cooley, *Unholy Wars: Afghanistan, America and International Terrorism*, London, Pluto Press, 1999.

members of the Taliban government had been trained at Haqqania, three had been trained in Binori Town.[138]

As early as February 1980, Binori Town sent students to fight against the Soviets in Afghanistan—via Peshawar where they created the Jamiat ul-Ansar (League of Partisans), which in 1988 spawned the Harakat ul-Jihad-i-Islami (HuJI), a jihadist movement formed to fight against the Soviets in Afghanistan.[139] One of its leaders trained in Binori Town, Qari Saifullah Akhtar, who was born in South Waziristan according to Khaled Ahmed[140] and in Chishtian (Bahawalnagar district, Punjab) according to Muhammad Amir Rana and Rohan Gunaratna, had developed "close links with ISI and Pakistani military establishment".[141] (In 1995 he was to be involved in the attempted coup d'état against Benazir Bhutto fomented by four Pakistan Army officers, including Major General Zaheer, head of the ISI cell in Delhi.[142] He then served the Taliban regime as "military advisor to Mullah Omar").[143] The HuJI established its first camp in Wana, and then another one

---

[138] "The Great Banuri Town Seminary", available online at: http://www.sunniforum.com/forum/showthread.php?10176-Binori-Town-Ulema (Accessed on September 15, 2013).

[139] See Mariam Abou Zahab and Olivier Roy, *Islamic Networks. The Afghan-Pakistani Connection*, op. cit., p. 27.

[140] Khaled Ahmed, *Sectarian War*, op. cit., p. 134.

[141] Muhammad Amir Rana and Rohan Gunaratna, *Al-Qaeda Fights Back*, op. cit., p. 85.

[142] See Wilson John, "Harakat-ul Jihad al-Islami', in Wilson John and Swati Parashar (eds), *Terrorism in Southeast Asia: Implications for South Asia*, New Delhi, Observer Research Foundation/Pearson Education, 2005, p. 81.

[143] Muhammad Amir Rana, "Evolution of Militant Groups in Pakistan (III)", *Conflict & Peace Studies*, vol. 5, no. 1, January–June 2013, p. 103. Qari was probably too close to the Pakistani "deep state" to be produced before a court of law—inspite of the fact that he was arrested several times. Muhammad Amir Rana, who has interviewed him, points out that "Saifullah Akhtar remains a mysterious figure in Pakistan's political and jihad account. He is considered among the founders of jihad in Pakistan, who was among the first batches of Pakistani mujahideen in Afghanistan. His name was mentioned with regard to the 1995 attempted military coup case, but was then dropped from that case. Besides serving as the military advisor to Mullah Omar during the Taliban regime in Afghanistan and helping Mullah Omar escape after US forces attacked Kandahar in 2001, Saifullah was the first Pakistani jihad leader arrested abroad (he was captured in Dubai in 2004) and handed over to Pakistan in August 2004 by the United Arab Emirates government. He was released in 2006 and arrested again in February 2008 in connection with the October 2007 blast in Karachi that targeted former

in Kurram Agency, before developing two others in Afganistan, in the provinces of Paktia and Khost.[144] In the mid-1980s, Qari took over from Maulana Irshad and became leader of the HuJI which held its first annual congregation in Chechawatni (Punjab). Qari seized this opportunity to spell out its programme which aimed to "free the Muslims of the world from the clutches of occupation and slavery in the east and the west and eventually establish a united Muslim power in the world".[145] However, two HuJI cadres—alumni of the madrassah of Jamia Khair ul-Aloom (Multan)—Maulana Fazlur Rehman Khalil (who had subsequently joined the madrassah of Binori Town) and Maulana Massod Alvi disapproved of the extension of the HuJI agenda and wanted to remain focused on the Afghan jihad. They formed a new organisation, the Harakat-ul Mujahideen which remained in close contact with the ISI,[146] and fought in Afghanistan "under the leadership of Jalaluddin Haqqani"[147] (see the section on the Haqqani network below). Khalil continued to recruit most of his combatants in Karachi—in Binori Town especially—before turning to the breeding ground offered by the Red Mosque (which will be dealt with in the next chapter).[148] With the support of Maulana Abdul Haq, the principal of the Jamia Haqqania, Khalil—who had up to 3,000 fighters coming from all over Pakistan—established his first camp in Miran Shah, the administrative headquarters of North Waziristan, where the Haqqani network had also its base.[149] In the late 1980s, the HuM "played a vital role in the conquest of Khost".[150]

After the Soviet withdrawal from Afghanistan, Khalil's action focused on Indian Kashmir, and it is for those jihadist operations that the Harakat groups became known, whatever the faction involved. Indeed, this move-

---

Prime Minister Benazir Bhutto's convoy when she had returned to Pakistan following an eight-year self-imposed exile". (Ibid., p. 107).

[144] Muhammad Amir Rana, "Evolution of Militant Groups in Pakistan (II)", *Conflict & Peace Studies*, vol. 4, no. 3, July–September 2011, p. 106.

[145] Cited in ibid., p. 108.

[146] Imtiaz Gul, *The Most Dangerous Place*, op. cit., p. 250.

[147] Muhammad Amir Rana, "Evolution of Militant Groups in Pakistan (II)", op. cit., p. 110.

[148] Syed Saleem Shahzad, *Beyond Bin Laden and 9/11*, New York, Palgrave, 2011 p. 160.

[149] Muhammad Amir Rana and Rohan Gunaratna, *Al-Qaeda Fights Back*, op. cit., p. 23.

[150] Muhammad Amir Rana, "Evolution of Militant Groups in Pakistan (II)", op. cit., p. 110.

ment has gone through a variety of incarnations. In 1993 HuJI and HuM, again merged to form the Harakat-ul-Ansar, still under Khalil's leadership. The new organisation remained close to Al Qaeda. This became plain in 1998 when the United States missile strike on the Al Qaeda training camp in response to attacks on their embassies in Dar-es-Salam and Nairobi claimed nine of Khalil's partisans among the twenty-five dead.[151]

One of the Harakat leaders who was "instrumental in getting Harakat-ul Mujahideen and Harakat ul-Jihad-i-Islami to merge"[152] was Maulana Masood Azhar. A native of Bahawalpur (South Punjab), born into a family connected to the Ahrar movement, he was also trained in Binori Town where a recruiting agent from Harakat-ul-Ansar sought him out. He thus also began his jihadist career in the Afghanistan province of Khost, but with a Sunni militant overtone since he was "devoted to Maulana Haq Nawaz Jhangvi",[153] the founder of the SSP. Like so many others, he went to Indian Kashmir after the Soviet withdrawal from Afghanistan. He was captured there in 1994 by the Indian Army, which already held prisoner two other of the movement's leaders in Kashmir, Nasrullah Mansur Langrayal and Sajjad Afghani. The Harakat-ul-Ansar (HuA) and the ISI went to great lengths to liberate these men. The movement's preferred technique was to kidnap foreign tourists to use them as bargaining chips. Thus the HuA sent one of its British members of Pakistani origin, Ahmed Omar Saeed Shaikh, then a student at the London School of Economics, to Delhi to kidnap Western tourists.[154] He fulfilled his mission, but the police managed to arrest him and free his prisoners. In 1995, more kidnappings took place. One of the abducted tourists escaped, but four others were executed, the authorities in Delhi not having yielded to what they considered blackmail.[155]

In 1997, the United States suspected the movement of working hand in glove with Al Qaeda and put it on the State Department list of terrorist organisations.[156] The group thus reverted to its former name, Harakat-ul

---

[151] Imtiaz Gul, *The Most Dangerous Place*, op. cit., p. 250.

[152] Khaled Ahmed, *Sectarian war*, op. cit., p. 133.

[153] Ibid., p. 134.

[154] The son of a rich Pakistani merchant who immigrated to England, Sheikh apparently went over to Islamism in 1992 during the war in Bosnia.

[155] "Security Council Committee pursuant to resolutions 1267 (1999) and 1989 (2011) concerning Al-Qaida and associated individuals and entities," United Nations, October 10, 2011. See http://www.un.org/sc/committees/1267/NSQE00801E.shtml (Accessed on September 15, 2013).

[156] "Harkat-ul-Mujahideen", available at: http://www.satp.org/satporgtp/countries/

Mujahideen. Up until the early 2000s, the HuM remained one of the most active jihadist movements in Indian Kashmir.[157] In 1999 it claimed to have killed 1,825 Indian soldiers (including 43 officers) in that one year alone. It also admitted to losing 96 combatants.[158] At the time, the movement was still using the Rishkor camp in the suburbs of Kabul to train its militants.[159]

One of the Harakat leaders who has been an active jihadist in Jammu and Kashmir in the 1990s, Ilyas Kashmiri, who hailed from PoK/Azad Kashmir, had a particularly interesting trajectory. To begin with he belonged to one of the Pakistani army's elite corps, the Special Service Group (SSG). He was "deputed by Pakistan army to train the Afghan Mujahideen fighting against the Russian army in [the] mid-1980s".[160] As an Harakat-ul Mujahideen cadre, he worked first as an instructor in a training camp near Miramshah (North Waziristan). After being "asked by Pakistani establishment to work with Kashmiri militants",[161] he joined the Kashmir chapter of the Harakatul Jihad-e-Islam in 1991 but eventually created his own movement, the 313 Brigade. He multiplied guerrilla operations across the LoC in the 1990s (the Indian army arrested him, but he escaped from jail two years later and immediatey "became a legend"[162] in Pakistan. Musharraf himself, as COAS, gave him "a cash award of rupees one lakh"[163] for one of his operations. Ilyas Kashmiri built a training camp in Kotli (PoK/Azad Kashmir)—that Corps Commander, Rawalpindi, Lt Gen Mehmood Ahmed, visited at least once. According to Hamid Mir, Kashmiri's "honeymoon with the Pakistan Army generals was over after the creation of Jaish-e-Muhammad. Gen. Mehmood wanted Ilyas Kashmiri to join JeM and accept Maulana Masood Azhar as his leader but the one eyed militant refused to do so".[164] After 9/11

---

india/states/jandk/terrorist_outfits/harkatul_mujahideen.htm (Accessed on September 15, 2013).

[157] "Emergence of Harkat-ul-Mujahideen", *The Express Tribune*, 25 June 2011. See http://tribune.com.pk/story/196001/emergence-of-harkat-ul-mujahideen/ (Accessed on September 15, 2013).

[158] Imtiaz Gul, *The Most Dangerous Place*, op. cit., p. 250.

[159] Ibid., p. 251.

[160] Hamid Mir, "How an ex-Army commando became a terrorist", *The News*, 20 September 2009 (http://www.thenews.com.pk/TodaysPrintDetail.aspx?ID=2 4626&Cat=13&dt=9/19/2009).

[161] Ibid.

[162] Ibid.

[163] Ibid.

[164] Ibid.

Kashmiri apparently turned his guns to Musharraf and his regime in reaction to the way Pakistan had become a partner of the US in the global war on terror. He was arrested after an attack on Gen. Musharraf in December 2003. Released three years later, he went to North Waziristan after the Lal Masjid episode, reorganised his Brigade 313 and joined forces with the Taliban.[165]

The career of Ilysa Kashmiri is revealing of the relations which existed between the Pakistani army and jihadists—who sometimes, as in his case, came directly from its ranks. But this relation has been even deeper and more lasting in the case of the Lashkar-e-Taiba.

Lashkar-e-Taiba, between Jihad and *Dawa*

The LeT is the main jihadist movement tied to the Ahl-e-Hadith school of thought.[166] Aside from this specific feature, which should not be overemphasised,[167] the LeT is typical of jihadist movements that came together in the war against the Soviets in Afghanistan before focusing their efforts on Kashmir—even India in general. The movement was born in the Afghan province of Kinaur and that may be where its proponents first met Bin Laden, their allegiance to Ahl-e-Hadith possibly creating particular affinities with the Saudi militant. The fact remains that Bin Laden addressed the annual LeT conventions by telephone three times, in 1995, 1996 and 1997.[168]

The architects of LeT represented the two complementary facets of Pakistani Islamism. In fact, it was a joint venture that grew out of a connection between Zakiur Rehman Lakhvi, who had created an armed Ahl-e-

---

[165] Ilyas Kashmiri was allegedly killed in a drone strike in 2009 or 2010 (Muhammad Amir Rana, "Evolution of Militant Groups in Pakistan (III)", op. cit., p. 108).

[166] The Ahl-e-Hadith had started a political movement just before the creation of the LeT, the Markazi Jamiat Ahl-e-Hadith (MJAH), which was quite active by 1986. In 2002 it took part in the MMA coalition. See Mariam Abou Zahab, "Salafism in Pakistan: The Ahl-e Hadith Movement", in Roel Meijer (ed.), *Global Salafism: Islam's New Religious Movement*, London, Hurst, 2009, p. 131.

[167] Especially since the LeT attracted from the start many Deobandi and Barelwi militants for two good reasons: first because the Ahl-e-Hadith represented only 10% of the Pakistanis and second, because the LeT was at odds with the sect's *ulema*, many of whom were opposed to the use of violence in the context of jihad (See Christine Fair, "Lashkar-e-Tayiba and the Pakistani State", *Survival*, vol. 53, no. 4, August–Sept. 2011, p. 35).

[168] Mariam Abou Zahab and Olivier Roy, *Islamic Networks. The Afghan-Pakistani Connection*, op. cit., p. 60.

Hadith movement in 1984, and two instructors at the University of Engineering and Technology in Lahore, Hafiz Saeed and Zafar Iqbal, who had founded the Jama'at-ul-Dawa (Organisation for Propagation of the Faith). These two movements converged in 1986 to form the Markaz al-Dawa-Wal-Irshad (MDI), with the aim of coordinating Ahl-e-Hadith groups. Saeed, who had been a student of Azzam in Saudi Arabia,[169] due to the prestige of his rank of *alim*, was made head of the movement. The MDI officially created its armed wing, the LeT, in 1990 under Saeed's leadership—now *emir* of both the LeT and MDI—while Lakhvi remained in charge of armed operations. There is little doubt that from the start Saeed had the strongest personality of the three men. He maintained that Kashmir was "the gateway to the liberation of Indian Muslims". He considered that in India as elsewhere, "Jihad will continue until Islam becomes the dominant religion."[170] According to Zahid Hussain, "The horrors of the partition of India in 1947, which uprooted his family from their home in Simla, left a huge imprint on Hafiz Saeed's personality."[171] His radicalism was also bolstered by his studies at the King Abdul Aziz Islamic University in Ryad where he also taught.

When the war in Afghanistan was over, the organisation purposely split up its activities between the MDI and the LeT. Faster and more radically than other mujahideen organisations, the group soon turned its sights against India, which became its almost exclusive target.[172] In 1993–5, its action even concentrated solely on Indian Kashmir.[173] There it set itself apart in two ways. First, its militants demonstrated relatively more discipline and restraint than the other combatants: they lived off the local population less and committed less rape of Indian Kashmir women than other groups. Second, in Kashmir as elsewhere, the LeT did not resort to suicide attacks but rather a new form of violence, fidayeen missions, which Tankel describes:

The aim of Lashkar's fidayeen attacks was not for the fighters to be martyred right away, but to inflict as much damage as possible on the enemy in order to inspire

---

[169] Khaled Ahmed, *Sectarian War*, op. cit., p. 285.

[170] Zahid Hussain, *Frontline Pakistan*, op. cit., p. 53.

[171] Ibid.

[172] Saeed Shafqat, "From Official Islam to Islamism: The Rise of Dawat-ul-Irshad and Lashkar-e-Taiba", in Christophe Jaffrelot (ed.), *Pakistan: Nationalism without a Nation?*, New York, Zed Books, 2002, pp. 131–47.

[173] Yoginder Sikand, "The Islamist militancy in Kashmir: The Case of the Lashkar-e-Taiba", in Aparna Rao and alii (eds), *The Practice of War: Production, Reproduction and Communication of Armed Violence*, New York, Berghahn Books, 2007, pp. 215–38.

fear in others. These battles often lasted many hours and sometimes more than a day, which at times led security forces to employ heavy firepower that destroyed their own installations [infiltrated by fidayeens].[174]

The fear this technique is supposed to instil is not the sole rationale for this terrorist tactic.[175] It also came about in connection with the debate surrounding suicide attacks, which are just as likely to inspire terror: according to some scholars and theologians, Islam forbids voluntary death. The perpetrator of a *fidayeen* attack can terrorise without necessarily facing death, even though those who escape such fate generally return to combat and repeat the exercise until they achieve martyrdom.[176] Between mid-1999 and 2002, the LeT perpetrated fifty-five fidayeen attacks in India. This period marked a major transition. The 22 December 2000 attack on Red Fort in Delhi, the former seat of Mughal power converted into barracks, illustrated the LeT's intention to bring jihad beyond Kashmir into the rest of India.[177] In fact, in November 2000 Saeed gave a speech indicating his aims went well beyond Kashmir:

Jihad is not about Kashmir only. About fifteen years ago people might have found it ridiculous if someone had told them about the disintegration of the USSR. Today I announce the break up of India, inshallah. We will not rest until the whole (of) India is dissolved into Pakistan.[178]

---

[174] Stephen Tankel, *Storming the World Stage: The Story of Lashkar-e-Taiba*, Hurst, London, 2011, p. 63.

[175] On the terrorist techniques of Islamist groups, see Amélie Blom, Laetitia Bucaille and Luis Martinez (eds), *The Enigma of Islamist Violence*, London, Hurst, 2007; Faisal Devji, *Landscapes of the Jihad: Militancy, Morality, Modernity*, Ithaca, Cornell University Press, 2005, and *The Terrorist in Search of Humanity: Militant Islam and Global Politics*, New York, Columbia University Press, 2008.

[176] Regarding the role of martyrdom in the organisation, see Mariam Abou Zahab, "'I Shall Be Waiting for You at the Door of Paradise': The Pakistani Martyrs of the Lashkar-e-Taiba (Army of the Pure)", in Aparna Rao (ed.), *The Practice of War*, op. cit., pp. 133–158.

[177] Mariam Abou Zahab and Olivier Roy point out that a re-enactment of this attack "was organised on the occasion of the Id al-Adha (the Feast of the Sacrifice) in Lahore's largest sports stadium with no reaction from the authorities, though all political assemblies were banned". See Mariam Abou Zahab and Olivier Roy, *Islamic Networks. The Afghan-Pakistani Connection*, op. cit., p. 35, note 4.

[178] Cited in Imtiaz Gul, *The Most Dangerous Place*, op. cit., p. 255. He also declared, "Our jihad will continue until Islam becomes the dominant religion (...) Kashmir is no more than the gateway to India, and we shall strive also for the liberation

The Pakistani authorities backed the jihadists active in Indian Kashmir with a different perspective than the one governing their policy in Afghanistan. The army was less interested in (re)conquering territory that New Delhi had the wherewithal to defend than to "bleed India" (to use the standard expression) without being in the front line: after losing three wars (or almost), it seemed wiser to outsource what was now a low-intensity conflict to the Islamists. This strategy was concocted by the ISI, which had gained considerable influence owing to the latest war in Afghanistan. Tankel provides ample proof of such collusion between the military apparatus and Islamist paramilitaries with whom officials deny any relation. Cultivating the art of "plausible denials" (to use another standard expression), the Pakistan Army will always deny remote-controlling jihadists operations in Indian Kashmir. Yet, the ISI has never ceased training, funding and arming "paramilitary" troops, to use yet another particularly apt expression in the case of LeT militants. Until the early 2000s, with ISI support, this organisation maintained three camps in Pakistani Kashmir. The largest of them, near Muzaffarabad, trained 500 mujahideen per month.[179] In all, the movement had at its disposal between 100,000 and 300,000 youths who had undergone such military training.[180]

Of all jihad organisations, the LeT has probably provided the most loyal and enduring services. Although the Harakat-ul-Mujahideen and the Harakat-ul-Ansar were sponsored by the ISI in turn, only to escape its control, the LeT has remained a close ally of the military establishment. The constancy of this relationship is likely explained by the LeT's obsession with India, which resonates with that of the Pakistan Army. Furthermore, many LeT members come from military families, an organic link explained by the overlap of the main LeT and army recruitment areas in Punjab. Some officers also leave the army to join the LeT where they serve as excellent trainers, thereby creating another organic link.

The protection the LeT enjoys within the state apparatus (and particularly the ISI) no doubt accounts for its exceptional resilience, but this is also due to the foundation provided by its polymorphic nature: while giving it formidable striking power, jihad is only one aspect of its action. The other

---

of the 200 million Indian Muslims", cited in Mariam Abou Zahab and Olivier Roy, *Islamic Networks. The Afghan-Pakistani Connection*, op. cit., p. 35.

[179] Mariam Abou Zahab and Olivier Roy, *Islamic Networks. The Afghan-Pakistani Connection*, op. cit., p. 39.

[180] Ibid., p. 39.

is *dawa*, Islamisation through preaching or example. These two sides of the same coin are consubstantial with LeT. They appeared together from its very inception and are embodied in two of its founding principles. The organisation thus has a number of departments that indicate the scope of its field of action: *dawa*, education, the construction of mosques and *dini madaris*, media, publishing, social work, etc. The emphasis on education is particularly noteworthy: 127 schools educate 15,000 pupils in both religious and scientific subjects. Zafar Iqbal—head of this department—suggests that the source of inspiration for LeT's work in education is none other than the archetypal Western Other, Christians:

Christians have set up high quality schools in order to wean Muslim children from Islam. These schools teach Christianity even to Muslim children. Christians are thus successful in their mission. We are setting up Islamic institutions along the lines of Christian missionary schools.[181]

This acknowledgement reflects the mimetic nature of the LeT whose social welfare strategy, beyond its educational activities, is reminiscent of Christian missionary social work as well as that carried out by Hindu nationalists. Like the latter, the LeT owes much of its popularity to the mobilisation of its members in the event of natural disasters. The 2005 earthquake in Kashmir and the 2010 floods gave LeT activists the opportunity to bask in the light of service to the masses. That the LeT is a mass organisation embedded in the fabric of Pakistani or in any event Punjabi society is clear in the numbers attracted by the annual Dawat wal Irshad conventions where 100,000 flocked to Muridke for a period of three days. The organisation had also set up a dense network of 2,000 offices throughout the country.[182]

Mariam Abou Zahab and Olivier Roy explain the appeal of LeT on the basis of societal considerations: "Under-achieving groups compensate for their inferiority in terms of power and privilege by adopting an ostentatious religiosity, and especially through the prestige which comes from participating in the jihad in Kashmir; this in turn reflects on all the family members of a combatant and even more on those of a martyr."[183] Moreover, LeT training camps offer young recruits experiences from which they return home not only psychologically but also physically "transformed.

[181] Cited in Stephen Tankel, *Storming the World Stage*, op. cit., p. 73.
[182] Mariam Abou Zahab and Olivier Roy, *Islamic Networks. The Afghan-Pakistani Connection*, op. cit., pp. 36–37.
[183] Ibid., p. 38.

They kept their hair long, ceased to shave their beards, and wore their trousers short above their ankles. They also abandoned their own names and took the surname of a companion of the Prophet or a hero of the early days of Islam."[184]

Exemplarity is at the heart of the Muridke project, named for a town located some twenty miles from Lahore where the LeT has built a counter-society putting Islamic precepts into practice down to the letter over some 15 acres, which includes a model farm. This community purports to be the prototype of the ideal town in a virtually millennialist perspective. Saeed himself sees it as a long-term process: "We do not believe in revolutionary change in Pakistan; rather we want a gradual reform through dawa."[185] This method is not unlike that used by the Rashtriya Swayamsevak Sangh (National Volunteers Association), spearhead of the Hindu nationalist movement in India, which also has a millennialist outlook.[186] The LeT in short combines violent action and long-term bottom-up re-Islamisation. The Pakistan Army has thus taken the risk of backing a group whose agenda is not limited to jihad, focusing on how it could be used against India. The Kargil episode offers a textbook case of this cooperation between jihadists and the military.

The Year 1999, a High Point in Military/Islamist Cooperation

According to a retired Pakistani officer, Brig. Shaukat Qadir, in November 1998 COAS Musharraf and a handful of other generals[187] conceived a plan to infiltrate Jammu and Kashmir near the town of Kargil, taking advantage of the India's winter troop withdrawal. On the basis of her fieldwork, Christine Fair came to the conclusion that "the army was seeking to redeem itself (and

---

[184] Ibid., p. 39.

[185] Cited in Stephen Tankel, *Storming the World Stage*, op. cit., p. 43.

[186] In fashioning its counter-strategy the RSS also drew inspiration from others it believed were threats to the Hindus—not only Christians but especially Muslims. The reader interested in the comparison can see Christophe Jaffrelot, *The Hindu Nationalist Movement and Indian Politics in India*, London, Hurst, 1993, chap. 1.

[187] Shaukat Qadir, "An analysis of the Kargil crisis, 1999", *RUSI Journal*, April 2002. According to C. Christine Fair, "The Kargil operation's origins can be traced to Lt. Gen. Mahmud Ahmed, the Commander of 10 Corps, who in November 1998 asked the chief of general staff, Lt. Gen. Muhammad Aziz, to secure him a meeting with Musharraf (...). The two men sought Musharraf's permission to execute a plan to seize and occupy terrain in the Kargil-Dras sectors in Indian-administered Kashmir" (C. Christine Fair, *Fighting to the End*, op. cit., p. 150).

also to punish India) for the 1971 defeat, India's occupation of the Siachen glacier, and India's periodic shelling of the Neelum Valley road and other 'provocations' along the LOC".[188] But Musharraf probably also saw in this operation a good means to undermine the peace talks that Nawaz Sharif and A.B. Vajpayee had initiated. It seems that the "rest of the army was not notified of the operation until March 1999" and that "Sharif was not formally briefed until April".[189] The campaign involved deploying some thousand Northern Light Infantry men—to which were added four times as many rearguard soldiers in charge of logistics—and a few Islamists.[190]

The most plausible interpretation for this infiltration is that the Pakistani army, by initiating hostilities, hoped to put on the international agenda an issue that New Delhi wanted to keep under bilateral negotiations.[191] For the ISI it was not only a matter of penetrating territory under India's control, thereby running the risk of triggering a clash, but also of taking over strategic points for the most part overhanging the road from Srinagar to Leh (in the Ladakh) and the Siachen glacier. The most extensive infiltration took place on the Kargil plateau where hundreds of men built solid bunkers at the top of impregnable cliffs about 10 miles beyond the Line of Control.

The Indian Army did not discover the infiltrators until May 1999 but instantly accused Pakistan. Islamabad immediately shrugged off responsibility by claiming to know nothing about the operation. India sent in troops and attacked, while demonstrating a certain degree of restraint—its fighter planes did not, for instance, fly over Pakistani territory. The offensive caused hundreds of casualties in both camps, including among Pakistani soldiers, but India retook the summits occupied by the infiltrators one by one, reclaiming the last peak, Khalubar (5,287 m), on 2 July.

The "Kargil war" did not come to an end, however, until after Nawaz Sharif met with Bill Clinton in Washington on 4 July and was enjoined to withdraw his troops.[192] The decision to heed the United States admonition

---

[188] Ibid., p. 151.

[189] Ibid., pp. 151–152.

[190] Shaukat Qadir, "An analysis of the Kargil crisis, 1999", op. cit..

[191] This theory is expounded in Praveen Swami, *The Kargil War*, New Delhi, LeftWord Books, 1999, pp. 33–34.

[192] The Pakistani prime minister's responsibility has not been formally established, the country's policy toward Kashmir having to that extent come under the control of the ISI and the army. See Amélie Blom, "The 'Multi-vocal State': The Policy of Pakistan on Kashmir", in Amélie Blom, Leaticia Bucaille, Luis Martinez (eds), *The Enigma of Islamist Violence*, op. cit., pp. 283–309.

was highly resented by the Pakistani military, starting with General Musharraf, who is widely believed to have conceived the Kargil operation. The dispute further deteriorated relations between the two men at a time when Musharraf was already concerned about Sharif's receptivity to American pressure regarding complete cessation of Pakistan's nuclear tests.

At the end of 1999, another episode illustrated the intensity of relations between the ISI and the jihadists: the hijacking of flight IC 814. The Indian Airlines craft left Kathmandu for New Delhi on 24 December 1999. It was diverted by Pakistani Islamists demanding that the Indian government release two jihadists: Masood Azhar and Ahmed Omar Saeed Shaikh, two former Harakat-ul-Mujahideen leaders. Both had been captured in India five years before. The plane landed in Kandahar where the hijackers were visibly well treated by the Taliban. The Indian government gave in to their demands after they slit a passenger's throat. Mullah Wakil Ahmed Muttawakil, then foreign affairs minister in Kabul, later revealed that "the hijackers were taking instructions from Pakistani officials present at the airport."[193] In fact, as soon as he was freed, Masood Azhar was back in Pakistan where he founded a new jihadist movement, Jaish-e-Mohammed, which became one of the jihadist groups the ISI used in Kashmir and elsewhere. As for Omar Saeed Shaikh, he was implicated in the murder of Daniel Pearl some two years later.[194]

In 1999, little doubt remained as to cooperation between the military (especially the ISI) and jihadists in Pakistan.

The Taliban: the Price of "Friendship"

Pakistan's relations with the Taliban regime grew complicated over time. In the second half of the 1990s, Islamabad could pride itself in having achieved a degree of "strategic depth" in Afghanistan, but the other goal the Pakistani government pursued had not been achieved. By backing the Afghan Islamists starting in the 1970s under Bhutto, the Pakistanis had in fact hoped to counter Pashtun nationalism. The outcome, however, was very different. The Taliban had developed an Islamic variant of this ideology, drawing as much on the Pashtunwali code as from sharia law, and, more importantly, Pasistani

---

[193] Zahid Hussain, *Frontline Pakistan*, op. cit., p. 63.
[194] Robert San Anson, "The journalist and the terrorist", *Vanity Fair*, August 2002 (http://www.fromthewilderness.com/timeline/2002/vanityfair0802.html).

officials were bitterly disappointed when the Taliban refused to recognize the Durand Line as the international border.[195]

The cost of Pakistan's Afghan policy was not limited to financial support. In addition, there was a considerable loss of customs revenue. In 1950, Kabul and Karachi had signed the Afghan Transit Trade agreement that aimed to open up Afghanistan by enabling the country to be provisioned through Pakistani ports and cross the Land of the Pure without paying customs duties. Predictably, surplus merchandise soon made its way illegally back into Pakistan—where it cost less than from a merchant who had had to pay duty. The black market had little financial impact until the 1990s, at which time it took on huge proportions with the end of a war in which those involved had already regularly taken the Kabul-Peshawar-Karachi route. The fleet of trucks crossing the Afghan-Pakistani border ferrying duty-free merchandise crossed right back over carrying loads almost as large to provision the black market, costing the Pakistani an estimated 30 per cent drop in customs revenue. The loss was calculated at 3.5 billion rupees in 1992–3, 11 billion in 1993–4 and 30 billion in 1997–8.[196] Such trafficking would not have been possible without corrupt customs officers and other officials at the border who turned a blind eye in exchange for bribes.

This went along with another smuggling activity. Revenue from drug trafficking had helped finance the Afghan resistance during the war, but once it was over, it had a debilitating effect on Pakistani society. A detailed United Nations report indicated that between 1990 and 1994 opium production more than doubled, going from 1.5 to 3.4 million tons, and subsequently continued to grow. Helmand province on the border with Pakistan accounted for more than 40 per cent of the total in 2002.[197] Due to this geographic factor, combined with many others including the Pakistani establishment's greed, contraband increasingly took routes southeast.[198] Drug smuggling not only fed organised crime and corruption in Pakistan:

---

[195] Zahid Hussain, *Frontline Pakistan*, op. cit., p. 30.

[196] Ahmed Rashid, *Taliban*, op. cit., p. 191.

[197] Office on Drugs and Crime, *The Opium Economy in Afghanistan*, New York, UN, 2003. See http://www.unodc.org//pdf/publications/afg_opium_economy_www. pdf, p. 6. (Accessed on September 15, 2013).

[198] "In the 1990s, trafficking routes became increasingly diversified and a larger number of ethnic groups participated. Improved border control between Pakistan and Iran resulted in some heroin being smuggled from Pakistan to Europe by air or in container, often organized by Pakistani groups living in Europe (e.g. U.K.)". Ibid., p. 53.

it also had a debilitating effect on consumers. The number of users steadily increased from 50,000 in 1980 to 8.1 million in 2011.[199]

Moreover, the Taliban gradually emancipated themselves from Pakistan's influence. Ahmed Rashid dates the start of this process to 1997, considering that it coincided with the handover of foreign mujahideen training camp management to Al Qaeda. The jihadists were changing sponsors. The ISI had been outclassed, particularly for financial reasons, by Bin Laden's networks, which were far better endowed. For Pakistan, the consequences of this shift were decisive:

> In these camps, Kashmiri and Pakistani extremists mixed with young militants from all over the Muslim world and from Europe, just as an earlier generation had done in the 1980s in Afghanistan. Al Qaeda's indoctrination had an enormous impact on them: some embraced the idea of global jihad, joined Al Qaeda and went on to provide it with skills and facilities.[200]

In the late 1990s, the Pakistani security establishment had every reason to be worried about the newfound independence of a jihadist trend it had largely helped to cultivate. In 2001, the Bamiyan Buddhas crisis cast it in the spotlight. In February of that year, the Taliban regime decided to demolish these monumental works of art. Pierre Lafrance, UNESCO's envoy to the site, attested to Pakistani efforts—even by Samiul Haq, Mullah Omar's former mentor—to convince the Taliban to cancel their plans, but in vain.[201]

Lastly, Sunnis sectarian groups such as Lashkar-e-Jhangvi were now using Afghanistan as a rear base they could fall back on after carrying out attacks in Pakistan. They thus escaped the police despite exhortations from the Pakistani authorities, who were unable to reason with the Taliban. Ahmed Rashid concluded from this accumulation of adverse factors that "Pakistan, rather than being the master of the Taliban, was instead becoming its victim."[202]

In his autobiography, Abdul Salam Zaeff, the Taliban ambassador to Islamabad in 2000–01, shows just how structurally delicate Afghan-

---

[199] Rahib Raza, "Day against drug abuse: more than 8.1 m addicts in Pakistan now", *The Tribune*, 26 June 2011. See http://tribune.com.pk/story/196455/day-against-drug-abuse-more-than-8-1-m-addicts-in-pakistan-now/ (Accessed on September 15, 2013).

[200] Ahmed Rashid, *Pakistan on the Brink*, op. cit., p. 49.

[201] Pierre Lafrance, "Comment les bouddhas de Bamyan n'ont pas été sauvés", *Critique internationale*, no. 12, July 2001, p. 19.

[202] Ahmed Rashid, *Taliban*, op. cit., p. 186.

Pakistani relations were, even after the rise of Mullah Omar, due to clashes between national sovereignties, even nationalisms. Considering the relationship from a historic viewpoint, he writes, "The wolf and sheep may drink water from the same stream, but since the start of the jihad the ISI extended its roots deep into Afghanistan like a cancer puts down its roots in the human body; every ruler of Afghanistan complained about it, but none could get rid of it."[203] As the Taliban's ambassador to Pakistan, Zaeff in fact had more trouble with the ISI than with any other Pakistani institution. Eager to increase his country's autonomy without breaking with its Pakistani sponsor, he explains that he had to steer a course between two dangers: "In my dealing with them (the ISI) I tried to be not so sweet that I would be eaten whole, and not so bitter that I would be spat out."[204] In an attempt to increase his margin for manoeuvre, Zaeff went so far as to tell the United States ambassador in Islamabad, who systematically went through the Pakistani authorities to deliver his messages, that he would do better to be in direct contact with him for one simple reason: "Pakistan is never an honest mediator and will control and manipulate any talk they mediate or participate in."[205]

Even though Pakistan's relations with the Taliban were thus more strained than many observers have imagined, the ISI and the Pakistani army in general supported them till the end in their fight against Massoud's Northern Alliance. The breaking point came only after 11 September 2001 when the United States urged Islamabad to decide where its loyalties lay.

The 11 September 2001 Attacks: A Watershed Moment

In the wake of the 11 September 2001 attacks, the Bush administration quickly deemed it could not conduct its operations in Afghanistan to dismantle Bin Laden's networks and put an end to the Taliban regime without Pakistan, not only because it occupied a key geopolitical position but also due to information it was likely to possess regarding the Islamist movement. On 13 September, Deputy Secretary of State Richard Armitage, meeting with Pakistani ambassador to the United States and the head of the ISI during their visit to Washington, conveyed a list of seven demands:

– To stop al Qaeda operatives at its border and end all logistical support for Bin Laden;

---

[203] Abdu Salam Zaeef, *My Life with the Taliban*, London, Hurst, 2010, p. 123.
[204] Ibid., p. 105.
[205] Cited in ibid., p. 109.

- To give the United States blanket overflight and landing rights for all necessary military and intelligence operations;
- To provide the United States with intelligence information;
- To provide territorial access to U.S. and allied military intelligence and other personnel to conduct operations against Al Qaeda;
- To continue to publicly condemn the terrorist acts;
- To cut off all shipments of fuel to the Taliban and stop recruits from going to Afghanistan; and,
- If the evidence implicated Bin Laden and al Qaeda and the Taliban continued to harbour them, to break relations with the Taliban government.[206]

In his memoirs, Musharraf confessed that he had to demonstrate great strength of conviction to bring his ministers and the Pakistan army Corps Commanders around to his decision to agree to these demands.[207] He saw it as an opportunity to bring Pakistan back into the concert of nations, to have sanctions lifted and thereby be eligible once again for foreign aid. He probably also believed at the time that cooperating with the United States in its fight against "Islamic terrorism" would not necessarily force him to alter his policy of support for the Taliban and cooperation with jihadist movements in Kashmir. In any event, there were not many alternatives: if the United States could not make a deal with the Pakistanis, they would turn to the Indians who had already offered their services. Washington took an even harsher stance—Armitage reportedly threatened to bring the Land of the Pure "back to the Stone Age"[208]—at a time when the failure of Pakistan's economy[209] and the diplomatic isolation it suffered from left it very little margin for manoeuvre.

Islamabad thus ended up agreeing to United States terms, and the diplomatic dividends for Pakistan's good behaviour did not take long to materialise. The British and Dutch prime ministers, the German chancellor, the Turkish president, the U.S. Secretary of State and his counterpart for Defence, foreign affairs ministers from France, Germany and Saudi Arabia as well as many others all made visits to Islamabad. Musharraf himself

---

[206] *The 9/11 Commission Report*, New York, W.W. Norton and Co, p. 331.

[207] Pervez Musharraf, *In the Line of Fire*, op. cit., p. 206. John R. Schmidt indicates that United States demands were scaled back at the Pakistanis' request, but only slightly. John R. Schmidt, *The Unraveling. Pakistan in the Age of Jihad*, New York, Farrar, Straus and Giroux, 2011, p. 124.

[208] Pervez Musharraf, *In the Line of Fire*, op. cit., p. 201.

[209] In 2000, service the debt accounted for 45% of budget expenditure (and 63% of revenue) and was valued at 293% of Pakistan's annual foreign currency intake, whereas the IMF sets the "sustainable" amount at 150%.

toured capitals including Tehran, Istanbul, Paris and London. He also visited New York, where the UN gave him an opportunity to address the General Assembly. The president-general had his moment of glory on 12 November 2001 when he stood beside George W. Bush. The joint communiqué at the end of this official visit stressed the strong friendship uniting the United States and Pakistan "for the past fifty years."[210]

At every stage in Pakistan's re-entry into the international community, Musharraf reiterated the cost of the Afghan crisis for his country, emphasising the fact that this burden had a major humanitarian component due to the inundation of refugees. The HCR estimated in mid-October 2001 that 2,000 Afghan refugees crossed the border each day. In response to Musharraf's speech, the wealthiest partners of the anti-terrorist coalition did not withhold their financial support: a good fifteen debts were renegotiated within the Clubs of Paris and London; bilateral aid immediately exceeded a billion dollars. The United States took the lead with 673 million dollars. In addition to its 50 million euros in aid, the European Union made trade concessions for textile exports: customs duties on these products (60 per cent of Pakistan's exports to the European Union) were removed and the import quota was raised to 15 per cent. The IMF granted Pakistan the advantages of the Poverty Reduction and Growth Facility together with a loan of 1.3 billion dollars. The World Bank loaned 300 million dollars. Altogether, adding up direct aid, economic support and trade facilities, Pakistan picked up 6 billion dollars in three months.

This assistance was granted with no strings attached, either in terms of structural reform or democratisation. All the sanctions Washington had imposed on Pakistan were soon lifted. The first to go were those pertaining to nuclear proliferation imposed by the Symington (1976), Glenn (1977), Pressler (1990) and Glenn (1998) amendments. The sanctions incurred by the military coup were also reconsidered after a military delegation from the Pentagon visited Islamabad and a hasty debate was conducted in the Senate, after which the United States was more or less obliged to issue Pakistan a certificate of democracy. The lifting of sanctions soon enabled Islamabad not only to secure loans from the United States but also to send soldiers there for training, something that had been impossible since 1990.[211]

---

[210] Christophe Jaffrelot, "Le Pakistan et l'Inde 'à qui perd gagne'", *Critique internationale*, January 2002, no. 14, pp. 12–19.

[211] During his visit to Islamabad in October 2001, Secretary of State Colin Powell moreover assured Musharraf that the United States wished to resume military

The Pakistani establishment hoped this return to the international fold would be compatible with the pursuit of its policy in Afghanistan, albeit in a necessarily different form. Musharraf and his army of course did not expect to maintain the same privileged relations with the Taliban, but some officers intended to maintain Afghan partners, as was apparent in the continuing convoys of foodstuffs, fuel and possibly weapons across the border to provision Mullah Omar's followers. In particular, Musharraf himself intended to place "moderate Taliban" in a national unity government so that it would escape control of Pakistan's enemy—the Northern Alliance—which was mainly of Tajik allegiance and allied to India.

The United States long gave the impression of being receptive to this demand and that they would hold the partisans of the late Commander Massoud at bay. This was probably its intention until the Taliban resistance prompted them to rely more on the Northern Alliance.[212] On 12 November, President Bush, in the presence of Musharraf, during their famous meeting in New York, asked Northern Alliance forces not to enter Kabul, even if that meant circumventing the Afghan capital in their reconquest of the country. But the following day, the city fell into the Alliance's hands, and Pakistani television viewers soon saw United States Special Forces on the ground instructing combatants in strategic matters. Pakistan was all the more displeased as the United States did not bolster Islamabad's efforts to bring about a Pashtun alternative to the Taliban, as the Americans seemed to believe the latter's fate was sealed. They thus ignored Pir Sayed Gailani, in whom Islamabad had placed great store.[213] It was as if the United States, despite its friendly statements to Musharraf, distrusted him immensely.[214]

---

cooperation, probably viewing it as a means in the long run to divert officers from the Islamist temptation.

[212] Yunas Samad, *The Pakistan-US Conundrum*, London, Hurst, 2011, p. 33.

[213] Pir Sayed Gailani, whose role during the fight against the Soviets has been mentioned above, had settled in Peshawar where he founded the National Islamic Front of Afghanistan. He sought to form a Pashtun alternative to the Taliban with Pakistani support in October 2001 by creating the Association for Peace and National Unity in Afghanistan. In this framework he held a meeting in Peshawar on 24 and 25 October 2001 bringing together 1,500 Pashtun delegates among whom many were Afghan tribal chiefs. Not only did the Pakistani authorities allow them in, but they even supplied an official vehicle.

[214] See Ahmed Rashid's excellent analysis, "Post-Taliban Order is a Source of Concern for Pakistan", 25 Oct. 2001. See www.eurasianet.org (Accessed on September 15, 2013).

In a sense, the Pakistanis had met their masters in the art of doublespeak, unless—as is likely—the decision to take Kabul was more in line with the Pentagon's strategy, as it needed a military victory at any price, than in keeping with Secretary of State Colin Powell's, who was more inclined to follow Pakistan's wishes. Whatever the truth of the matter, the Pakistanis viewed the capture of Kabul as an American betrayal.

With the fall of the Taliban, Pakistan lost its precious "strategic depth" in Afghanistan, its rear base that was intended to give it more weight in its dealings with India. This defeat marked the failure of Pakistan's strategy in the region as initiated by Zia and then pursued by his successors. Relations between Islamabad and Kabul had indeed become strained since the Taliban had partly come under the influence of Al Qaeda, but they remained valuable allies. Islamabad was all the more distressed by the Taliban's fall as it placed Kabul in the hands of its enemy, the forces of the late Commander Massoud. Since the Northern Alliance had New Delhi's backing, Pakistan was even likely to develop an encirclement syndrome.

The long process of setting up new institutions in Afghanistan initiated with the Bonn Conference basically ratified this new balance of power. Pakistan had no very reliable or very powerful allies among the delegations at the bargaining table in Bonn, as only Pir Sayed Gailani's group defended pro-Pakistani positions. In the interim authority set up at the conference, Gailani's Peshawar group finally obtained only three ministerial posts out of the twenty-nine. The Pashtuns, whom Islamabad viewed as its staunchest supporters, were not even in the majority. Although they were represented by President Hamid Karzai, he is no friend of Pakistan. His father, a Taliban opponent, had been murdered on orders from Kabul at the time when the Afghan regime was close to Islamabad. India, on the other hand, had allies in this government, starting with Foreign Affairs Minister Dr. Abdullah, whose family lived in exile in Delhi.

While the 11 September attacks thus brought Pakistan back into the United States' good graces, which implied returning to diplomatic favour and financial support, the price was a break with the policy Zia had launched in the 1970s. When the American air strikes began in Afghanistan on 7 October 2001, pressure from Washington forced Musharraf to oust the figures from his junta who had most closely collaborated with the Taliban, despite the support these men had given his takeover: General Usmani and General Mehmood (then head of the ISI) left the president's entourage whereas General Mohammed Aziz Khan, another close associate of Musharraf suspected of Islamist sympathies, was promoted to the largely honorary rank of chairman of the Joint Chiefs of Staff Committee. During his last visit to the Taliban ambassador, Zaeff, in Islamabad, General Mehmood had trouble holding back his tears after uttering these words:

We know that you are aware of what will happen in the near future and we also know that you believe that Pakistan will join the international community and America against Afghanistan (...) We want to assure you that you will not be alone in this Jihad against America. We will be with you.[215]

These remarks were the harbinger of a most ambivalent policy.

Musharraf and the Islamists: A Selective Break

Prior to 11 September 2001, there was already a certain awareness of the dangers to national cohesion posed by the rising power of the Islamists in some Pakistani circles. Nawaz Sharif had for instance made up his mind to go after some sectarian groups. In 1997, they had acquired so much influence that many judges refused to handle their cases out of fear of reprisal.[216] The Sharif government particularly set its sights on the Lashkar-e-Jhangvi. In retaliation, this movement perpetrated an attack on Nawaz Sharif in January 1999 that he only narrowly escaped. He was ousted from power a few months later without having pursued his goal.

The Limits to "Moderate Islam" according to Musharraf

After deposing Sharif, Musharraf in turn worried about the turmoil caused by sectarian violence in the country. In fact, between his coup d'état on 12 October 1999 and August 2001, sectarian clashes resulted in 220 deaths and 2000 injuries in the course of 83 riots and attacks in 30 towns. As evident from table 9.1., the year 2001 registered a record number of deaths due to sectarianism, 261. Most seriously affected were the Federally Administered Tribal Agencies (FATA), followed by Karachi. These outbreaks of violence were fomented primarily by Lashkar-e-Jhangvi (LeJ) and the Sipah-e-Sahaba Pakistan (SSP). The Musharraf government decided to take repressive measures after the February 2001 execution of an SSP militant sentenced to death for assassinating the Iranian consul general in 1990 sparked a new outbreak of violence from his comrades-in-arms. In this incident of anti-Shia

---

[215] Abdul Salam Zaeff, *My Life with the Taliban*, op. cit., p. 147.

[216] Supreme Court Chief Justice Sajjad Ali Shah, had asked for a list of these judges. See Zahid Hussain, *Frontline Pakistan*, op. cit., p. 97.

retaliation, eight people were killed in an attack using heavy artillery. On 14 August, Musharraf decided to ban the LeJ and for good measure the Shia movement Sipah-e-Muhammad Pakistan as well. But at the same time he authorised the release of SSP leader Azam Tariq, who had been jailed in the February disturbances, an indication that Musharraf was unwilling to risk head-on confrontation with the Sunni party.

Also in the summer of 2001, a controversy came to a head around the question of *dini madaris*, perceived as the breeding ground of jihadism, especially due to the number of foreign and particularly Arab students they accommodated, estimated at around 30,000 (half of them Afghans in 2002—see table 9.2).

Table 9.2: Profile of madrassah education in Pakistan (Year not specified)

Number of secondary and higher Dini Madaris	6,000
Senior and graduate level Dini Madaris	4,335
Deobandi Dini Madaris	2,333
Barelwi Dini Madaris	1,625
Ahl-e-Hadith Dini Madaris	224
Shia Dini Madaris	163
Number of all students	604,421
Local students (Pakistani)	586,604
Foreign students	17,817
Afghan students	16,598

Source: Adapted from Mumtaz Ahmad, "Madrassa Education in Pakistan and Bangladesh" in S. P. Limaye, R. Wirsing, and M. Malik (eds.), *Religious Radicalism and Security in South Asia*, Honolulu, Asia Pacific Centre for Security Studies, 2004 (http://www.apcss.org/Publications/Edited%20Volumes/ReligiousRadicalism/ReligiousRadicalismandSecurityinSouthAsia.pdf).

On 18 August 2001, Musharraf decided to promulgate a law framing the activity of these schools and integrating them into the public education system. Not only would they be forced to adopt a standard curriculum, but they would also have to declare their sources of funding to the state in order to identify the origin of foreign financing. The senior *dini madaris* staff and all the Islamist groups in general immediately rejected this decision, which largely remained a dead letter, as Musharraf did not enforce the measure: another indication of his reluctance to confront the Islamist movement. Musharraf himself admitted that he was moving slowly with the *dini madaris* reform. He thus told the *Financial Times* in March 2001:

There are about 10,000 of them [dini madaris] and there are about 1 million poor students getting free board and lodging. These madrassahs are doing a welfare service to the poor. The negative side is that most of them are only teaching religion, so my belief is that we need to carry out reforms to reinforce their strengths and eliminate their weaknesses.[217]

In fact, the reform of the *dini madaris* in 2002 under the "Madrassa Registration Ordinance" (MRO) took a paradoxical turn. Musharraf considered that Pakistan needed more Quranic schools and so was prepared to allocate them 5.7 billion rupees so they could register, submit the names of foreign students enrolled for administrative authorisation and include English, Urdu, science and mathematics in their curriculum. But they increased considerably in number without their curriculum really changing.[218] The number of Deobandi *dini madaris* thus rose from 10,430 to 13,500 (according to a different source from that of table 9.2, making comparison with 2002 difficult).[219]

Musharraf was equally careful in his handling of the Islamists over the controversy surrounding the Blasphemy Law. Since Zia, as mentioned above, the law stipulated that blasphemy could be punishable by death. In April 2000, Musharraf agreed to demands made by Christians to reform the law so that charges of blasphemy had to be substantiated by a deputy commissioner before the police could be called in, usually by clerics or Islamists. Islamist movements were roused into action and Musharraf had to backtrack. They hailed this retreat as a victory to chalk up alongside another one six months earlier, in December 1999, when the Supreme Court had declared interest-bearing loans (riba) "non-Islamic".

At the request of Islamist parties, Musharraf also promulgated in 2000 an amendment to the Provisional Constitutional Order that had served as Pakistan's Constitution since 14 October 1999. The amendment reactivated the provisions regarding Islam in the 1973 Constitution that had been suspended along with the Constitution since his military takeover. Articles

---

[217] Interview in *Financial Times Survey*, 6 March 2001.

[218] The difficulty researchers encounter when it comes to calculating the number of *dini madaris* and their enrolment is made clear in the article by Andrabi, Tahir, Jishnu Das, Asim Ijaz Khwaja, and Tristan Zajonc, "Religious School Enrollment in Pakistan: A Look at the Data", *Comparative Education Review*, vol. 50, no. 3 (2006), pp. 446–477. Available at: http://www.jstor.org/stable/pdfplus/10.1086/503885.pdf?acceptTC=true (Accessed on September 15, 2013).

[219] Farhang Morady and Ismail Siriner (eds), *Globalisation, Religion & Development*, London, International Journal of Politics & Economics Publication, 2011.

203A and 203J regarding the Federal Sharia Court instituted by Zia as well as articles 260(a) and 260(b) defining "Muslims" and "Non-Muslims" thus came back into effect.

Musharraf's ambivalent attitude toward the Islamists was partly a reflection of his own deep personal ambiguity. On one hand, Musharraf—who grew up in Turkey—claimed to be a Kemalist and a proponent of "moderate Islam", not only because he shared Ataturk's modernising approach of wanting to transform "the sick man of Europe"—a diagnosis easily transposable to Pakistan within South Asia—but also because he saw himself from the outset as a defender of a praetorian state, even against Islamists who disturbed the peace. To promote this "moderate Islam",[220] he emphasised Pakistan's Sufi heritage, even creating the National Council for the Promotion of Sufism in 2006, which Farzana Shaikh aptly described as a "gimmick conceived by a military regime anxious to bolster its legitimacy by playing to a liberal lobby at home and abroad."[221]

On the other hand, this man, whom the Jama'at-e-Islami allegedly recommended to Zia in the 1980s, was a longstanding ally of the Islamists, even of Sunni militants. Not only did Zia supposedly entrust him with the task of recruiting and training mujahideen to wage war against the Soviets in Afghanistan, but he also proved his worth in putting down a Shia uprising in Gilgit in 1988 during which his men demonstrated remarkable cruelty.[222] Eleven years later during the Kargil war in Indian Kashmir, the army he led collaborated with the Islamists. This collusion was even more obvious in December 1999, when Maulana Masood Azhar, liberated in circumstances mentioned above, founded Jaish-e-Mohammad with ISI support. This institution was then headed by one of Musharraf's close associates, General Mehmood—who was among the officers who had helped him seize power in October 1999.[223]

Apart from their common interests in Kashmir, the Islamists served as Musharraf's allies against political parties. Musharraf allowed the Islamists to occupy the streets while demonstrations organised by the Pakistan

---

[220] Regarding this expression, see Khurshid Ahmad, "Explaining Musharraf's "Enlightened Moderation"", *Current Affairs*, February 2005, no. 126, pp. 18–26.

[221] Farzana Shaikh, "Will Sufi Islam Save Pakistan?" in Shahzad Bashir and Robert D. Crews (eds), *Under the Drones. Modern Lives in the Afghanistan-Pakistan Borderlands*, Cambridge (Mass.), Harvard University Press, 2012, pp. 174–175.

[222] Mikhaïl Beletski, "Pervez Moucharraf: un itinéraire trouble", Moskovie Novosti, reproduced in *Courrier international*, no. 576, 21 November 2001, p. 42.

[223] Rohan Gunaratne, "Terror unlimited", *Frontline*, 12 October 2001, p. 28.

People's Party or the Pakistan Muslim League (Nawaz) were crushed. The tone was set on 3 November 1999 when Musharraf authorised Lashkar-e-Taiba to hold a rally in Lahore attended by about a half-million followers. A similar show of strength took place in spring 2001 with the Aalmi Deoband Conference organised by Maulana Fazlur Rehman, JUI leader, in the NWFP: again there were 500,000 people in attendance, a sign that the Islamists were well and truly part of the public scene, with Musharraf's blessing. Rahman used the opportunity to reiterate his support for the Taliban and their leader Mullah Omar, who addressed the audience via a recorded message.[224]

Musharraf took a harder line toward some Islamists a few weeks before 11 September, after a resurgence of sectarian violence. He thus promulgated the Anti-Terrorism Amendment Ordinance, 2001 which included measures against jihadist organisations such as Jaish-e-Mohammad and Lashkar-e-Taiba, whose offices were shut down. Such operations, however, were mainly confined to Karachi. The situation did not truly begin to change, however, until the war in Afghanistan in autumn 2001, which marked the beginning of Musharraf's break with certain Islamist groups and correlatively the end of the partnership between the army and jihadist paramilitaries in Afghanistan and Kashmir.

After 11 September: A Selective but True Break

With the first American strikes in Afghanistan on 7 October 2001, Musharraf sought to offer the United States guarantees by placing under house arrest the most anti-American leaders, such as Maulana Fazlur Rehman, head of the Jamiat Ulema-i-Islam, and Qazi Hussain Ahmed, the Jama'at-e-Islami leader arrested on 5 November 2001.

He went no further, however. With the Pakistani Islamists reeling from the shock of the Taliban's fall, conditions were favourable for a government

---

[224] One of the main Islamist groups, Qazi Hussain Ahmad's Jama'at-e-Islami, was highly critical of Musharraf's Kemalist style and along with tradesmen, took the lead in the protests against the tax inspections decided in 2000, but it was very isolated among the Islamist movement. Other parties such as the JUI did not answer Qazi Hussain Ahmed's calls for an anti-government action campaign in late 2000. They had realised that while combating traditional political parties was one of Musharraf's priorities, he treated the Islamists with kid gloves, even viewing them as allies against the PPP, the MQM and the Muslim League, those the military and the Islamists called the "politicians".

clampdown.[225] But Musharraf settled for targeting the sectarian groups he had already begun to tackle, only adding to the list Al Qaeda, the Americans' priority. The sectarian groups were fairly easy targets once they had lost their sanctuary in Afghanistan. In 2002, the main Lashkar-e-Jhangvi leaders—Riaz Basra (the founder), Asif Ramji and Akram Lahori—were killed, sometimes in extrajudicial executions organised after the men had been arrested in order to avoid a trial.

But Al Qaeda leaders also began to fall that same year. An estimated 3,000 combatants for Bin Laden were believed to be in Afghanistan at the start of the Western offensive. Although some of them merely went through Pakistan en route for the Middle East, most of them stayed. Non-Arabs (whether Uzbeks or Sudanese) mainly remained in the tribal areas, while Arabs (and of course Pakistanis) who could take advantage of urban anonymity found refuge in cities. Many of them were nevertheless captured. Abu Zubaida, who was born in Saudi Arabia to Palestinian parents, then raised in the Gaza Strip where he joined Hamas, later becoming a follower of Bin Laden who made him Al Qaeda's head of operations in 1996,[226] was the first to be taken in March 2002 in Faisalabad. The Yemeni Ramzi Bin al-Sibh, head of Al Qaeda's military wing and associated with Mohammed Atta (who flew one of the planes on 11 September) in Hamburg, was arrested in Karachi in September 2002. Khalid Shaikh Mohammed, who masterminded 11 September, was arrested in February 2003 in Rawalpindi, in the house of a JI activist, and his two sons in Karachi a few months later. Abu Fara al-Libi, who had replaced Khalid Shaikh Mohammed as head of external operations after his arrest, was captured in May 2003.

Under heavy pressure from the United States, even more since the 13 December 2001 attack in New Delhi (cf. infra), Musharraf delivered his famous "address to the nation" on 12 January 2002. The speech was actually aimed primarily at the outside world and in particular the United States. Under cover of returning to the sources of Pakistani ideology as expressed by Jinnah, he railed against the rise of intolerance and fundamentalism. He spoke in the Kemalist tones he had already employed in his attacks on sectarian movements in 2000 and 2001, saying for example, "Sectarian ter-

---

[225] The Americans urged Musharraf to finish them off once and for all. CIA head George Tenet went to Islamabad in early December 2001 to encourage him to do this and even identified the most dangerous figures he wanted placed under close surveillance.

[226] He had coordinated the attack on the USS Cole in October 2000.

rorism has been going on for years. Everyone of us is fed up of it. It is becoming unbearable. Our peace-loving people are keen to get rid of the Kalashnikov and weapon culture. [...] Do we want Pakistan to become a theocratic state? Do we believe that religious education alone is enough for governance or do we want Pakistan to emerge as a progressive and dynamic Islamic welfare state?"[227] Naturally there were ulterior motives behind this speech. The Islamists had ended up forming "a state within the state", defying the government's authority, to use Musharraf's own words, and this was the threat he intended to act against. On this point he went so far as to say, "We are capable of meeting external danger. We have to safeguard ourselves against internal dangers." Beyond reference to threats weighing on the domestic sphere, the other essential point of his speech referred to foreign affairs when Musharraf said: "I would request that we should stop interfering in the affairs of others."

This combination of internal and external concerns explains the measures Musharraf announced on 12 January 2002: all *dini madaris*—as well as all their foreign students—had to be registered with the authorities by 23 March; persons implicated in terrorist acts and sectarian violence would be tried by "speedy trial courts"; above all, the Jaish-e-Mohammed, Lashkar-e-Taiba, Sipah-e-Sahaba Pakistan, Tehrik-e-Jafria Pakistan and Tanzim Nifaz-e-Shariat Mohammadi were banned. Militants of these movements were immediately subject to legal proceedings: according to Interior Ministry officials, 1,900 activists were arrested within four days and 600 establishments shut down. Right away trials were scheduled. But this apparent hard line was a mere façade. The movements banned on 12 January 2002 reappeared under new names (which will not be used in this book so as to avoid confusion)[228] and none of the trials announced were held. LeT and Jaish leaders continued to conduct their business openly and expound their propaganda after more or less time spent under house arrest. It is true that the courts made it easy for them as mentioned in chapter 7.[229]

---

[227] "General Pervez Musharraf's address to the nation, January 12, 2002". See http://www.satp.org/satporgtp/countries/pakistan/document/papers/2002Jan12.htm (Accessed on September 15, 2013).

[228] Jaish-e-Mohammad was renamed Tehrik-e-Khudamul Islam (Movement of the Servants of Islam), Harakat-ul-Mujhideen the Jamiat-ul-Ansar (Party of Hosts), Sipah-i-Sahaba the Millat-e-Islamia (Islamic Fraternity), etc.

[229] Incidentally, in India, the judiciary also took decisions in favour of the Hindu nationalist organisations that had been banned after the demolition of the Babri Masjid in 1992.

Aside from the Pakistani authorities' display of determination in the fight against the LJ—the perfect "scapegoat"[230]—and Al Qaeda, the remainder of their Islamist crackdown was stamped with great ambivalence. Three movements were clearly spared—the Afghan Taliban, the Haqqani network and the jihadists—notwithstanding Musharraf's speech.

In reaction to the rise to power of Hamid Karzai, who gradually developed a new Afghan-Indian partnership, Islamabad continued to bank on the Taliban to eventually regain a foothold in Afghanistan. The wait was bound to be a long one given that NATO had deployed tens of thousands of soldiers. The Pakistani establishment nevertheless came to the aid of the Taliban leaders. Already in 2003, there were several indications that the ISI was helping the Taliban regain military ground in Afghanistan. Their logistics and military operations suggested that they were receiving expert training.[231] In a report to President Obama in 2009, General McChrystal, Commander of the International Security Assistance Force (ISAF) in Afghanistan, deemed that Taliban leaders—starting with Mullah Omar—were holding Shura (council) meetings in Quetta to coordinate their offensives against NATO on the other side of the Durand Line.[232] This hypothesis was corroborated in a report by Matt Waldman who after conducting a dozen or so interviews with Taliban leaders in 2010 concluded that the ISI was represented within this Shura and thus took part in attacks on NATO forces.[233] The authorities in Islamabad immediately denounced this report, going so far as to deny the very existence of a Taliban Shura. But shortly prior to that, in 2009, the defence minister himself, Ahmad Mukhtar,

---

[230] Musharraf's government attributed most of the Islamist violence to the LeJ, sparing other groups with which Pakistan's security establishment had stronger relations. Mariam Abou Zahab, "Pashtun and Punjabi Taliban: The Jihadi-Sectarian Nexus", in Jeevan Deol and Zaheer Kazmi (eds), *Contextualising Jihadi Thought*, London, Hurst, 2012, p. 373.

[231] See Antonio Giustozzi, *Koran, Kalashnikov and Laptop*, London, Hurst, 2007 and Antonio Giustozzi, (ed.), *Decoding the New Taliban: Insights from the Afghan Field*, London, Hurst, 2009.

[232] James Mazol, "The Quetta Shura Taliban: an overlooked problem", *International Affairs Review*, 23 November 2009. See http://www.iar-gwu.org/node/106 (Accessed on September 15, 2013).

[233] Matt Waldman, "The Sun in the Sky: The Relationship between Pakistan's ISI and Afghan Insurgents", *LSE Crisis States Discussion Papers*, 2010, pp. 5–8. See http://www.foreignpolicy.com/files/fp_uploaded_documents/100613_201061385 31279734lse-isi-taliban.pdf (Accessed on September 15, 2013).

acknowledged[234] the existence of this Shura, claiming that police operations had neutralised the threat it posed. These operations actually began in 2010.

The Resilience of the Haqqani Network

Of all the Taliban submovements, the Haqqani network is probably the oldest (at least on the Pakistani side), the best organised (even the most effective) and the one which in the FATA has remained the most consistently in close contact with the ISI.[235] Its founder, Jalaluddin Haqqani, born in 1939 and hailing from Shrana (the headquarters of Paktika, in eastern Afghanistan, very close to Pakistan) is a pure product of the famous madrassah in Akhora Khattak, the Dar-ul-Uloom Haqqania where he became a "Maulana".[236] But given his taste for action, Jalaluddin was above all one of the mujahideen that the ISI had spotted and then would train in the 1970s—along with Hekmatyar, Rabbani and Massoud—to combat the ruler of Kabul, Daoud.[237] That was the time—between 1973 and 1975—when he "shifted his base of operations to North Waziristan".[238] During the anti-Soviet jihad, he was one of the most active commanders around Khost—near Miran Shah—and one of those who received the most backing from the CIA, the ISI and Saudi Arabia. The ISI and the CIA "supplied the Haqqanis with at least 12,000 tons of war material every year during the 1980s...".[239] Haqqani probably did also the best job of channelling the flow of Arab combatants streaming in as of the early 1980s. This paved the way for fund-raising. Steve Coll writes,

Celebrated as a kind of noble savage by slack-bellied preachers in Saudi Arabia's wealthy urban mosques, Haqqani became a militant folk hero to Wahhabi activists. He operated fund-raising offices in the Persian Gulf and hosted young Arab jihad volunteers in his tribal territory. In part because of Haqqani's patronage, the border

[234] "Quetta Shura no longer poses threat: Ahmad Mukhtar", *Dawn*, 11 December 2009.

[235] Jeffrey Dressler, "The Haqqani Network: A Foreign Terrorist Organization", *Backgrounder*, Institute for the Study of War, 5 September 2012.

[236] Vahid Brown and Don Rassler, *Fountainhead of Jihad*, op. cit., p. 28.

[237] Thomas Ruttig, "The Haqqani Network as an Autonomous Entity" in Antonio Giustozzi (ed.) *Decoding the New Taliban: Insights from the Afghan Field*, London, Hurst, 2009, p. 64.

[238] Vahid Brown and Don Rassler, *Fountainhead of Jihad*, op. cit., p. 46.

[239] Ibid., p. 6.

regions nearest Pakistan became increasingly the province of interlocking networks of Pakistani intelligence officers, Arab volunteers, and Wahhabi madrassas.[240]

In the area of Khost, he worked together with Bin Laden, building a maze of underground caves and tunnels to store vast stocks of ammunition and fuel.[241] They built together the camp of Zhawara Valley, the first major camp for both Al Qaeda and the Haqqani network. Vahid Brown and Don Rassler point out that both, "in other words, evolved together, and they have remained intertwined throughout their history".[242] But Bin Laden was not the only Arab with whom Jalaluddin Haqqani worked in Pakistan. In fact, a major characteristic of his network lays in his sense of extraversion which helped him to get support, not only from the CIA, but also, even before the anti-Soviet jihad, from the Gulf. Jalaluddin Haqqani had already started recruiting foreign fighters in this region a few months before the Soviet invasion, while the situation in Afghanistan was deteriorating.[243] As a result, five years before Al Qaeda started bringing Arabs for jihad, the Haqqani network was the main recruiting and training agency for the foreign mujahideens. Before he looked for fighters, J. Haqqani had sent a group of local *ulema* to tour the Gulf to solicit financial support.[244] Most of the money was to come from the Saudis.[245] The Haqqani network has continued to welcome foreign fighters, even after the anti-Soviet jihad was over. While the largest number of fighters—Saudis, Kuwaitis, Jordanians, Palestinians, Algerians, Tunisians, Syrians, Lybians, Qataris...—arrived in 1989–91[246] by then, however, the foreigners who had started to come in large numbers were not only Arabs, but Kashmiris, Uighurs, Chechens and, even more importantly, Uzbeks—who were to form the Islamic Movement of Uzbekistan in the mid-1990s under Yuldashev.[247]

While claiming to be a member of Hezb-ul Mujahideen (Yunis Khalis faction), Jalaluddin jealously maintained his independence, even after the Taliban victory. In fact, "Haqqanis explicitly demanded regional autonomy in return for recognizing the Taliban", with one priority in mind: to protect

---

[240] Steve Coll, *Ghost Wars. The Secret History of the CIA, Afghanistan, and Bin Laden from the Soviet Invasion to September 10 2001*, op. cit., p. 157.

[241] Thomas Ruttig, "The Haqqani Network as an Autonomous Entity", op. cit., p. 85

[242] Vahid Brown and Don Rassler, *Fountainhead of Jihad*, op. cit., p. 8.

[243] Ibid., p. 60.

[244] Ibid. 64.

[245] Ibid., p. 68.

[246] Ibid., p. 82.

[247] Ibid., pp. 94–97.

their economic interests.[248] When the Taliban seized power in 1996, Jalaluddin Haqqani was not part of the first circle of Mullah Omar's lieutenants and retained a degree of autonomy. He was appointed minister of tribal and border affairs, which did not require his full presence in Kabul, allowing him to consolidate his base at the Pakistani border, in Loya Paktia especially (this region is made of Paktia, Paktika, Khost and a fraction of Logar and Ghazni).

The ISI continued to back him in this endeavour, which made up for the drop in resources he experienced once the Americans had withdrawn from the area. If the capacity of Jalaluddin Haqqani to reach out supporters out of Afganistan and Pakistan—his extroversion—is its first characteristic, the second lies in his capacity to retain a close association with the ISI. This connection began in the early 1970s, as mentioned above, when the ISI decided to train and arm Afghan Islamists at war with Daoud, the Pashtun nationalist. But at that time, ISI's main contacts were Hekmatyar and Rabbani. Gradually, J. Haqqani took over from them. He was first upgraded during the anti-Soviet jihad when the Pakistani army helped him conduct battles strategically and supplied arms to the Zhawara base.[249] Gretchen Peters attests to this on the strength of documents seized by the Americans in 2002 after their conquest of Afghanistan. Exchanges of faxes between Jalaluddin and ISI cadres show that during the war against the Soviets the intelligence agency supplied the Haqqani network in all manner of weapons, food and money.[250] Regarding style, Peters points out, "Jalaluddin, in both his tone and language, appears to be conciliatory and subordinate",[251] particularly in his battlefield reports (the Haqqani network seems to have been particularly well versed in the use of Stinger missiles). ISI support continued after the war, but the Haqqani network diversified its resources.

---

[248] Ibid., p. 104.

[249] Ibid., p. 153. According to Brown and Rassler, "The Zhawara base was the first major training center inside the borders of Afghanistan, and it grew over the first half of the 1980s to include a hospital, a hotel for visitors, a machine workshop, a garage, a mosque, numerous caves for storing arms, and the *Voice of Afghanistan*, the first Afghan mujahidin radio station, which from 1984 on issued three da ily hour-and-a-half broadcasts in Pashto, Dari, Uzbek, and Russian" (ibid., p. 67).

[250] Gretchen Peters, *Haqqani Network Financing: the Evolution of an Industry*, Harmony Program, The Combating Terrorism Center at West Point, July 2012, p. 17.

[251] Ibid.

Aside from collecting virtually a revolutionary tax from local merchants, as well as outright extortion, it took advantage of the booming drug trade and explored avenues for funding that offered it contacts in the Arab countries and the Persian Gulf. Among the UEA states, Abu Dhabi is probably the most supportive. As early as 1991, President Shaikh Zayed "accorded Jalaluddin Haqqani a personal state reception".[252]

When the anti-Soviet jihad was over, the Haqqani network helped the ISI with some of the groups based in Afghanistan, including Taliban and Al Qaeda, which had appreciated Jalaluddin Haqqani's efforts to bring the different factions of mujahideens together in the early 1990s—unsuccessfully. Jalaluddin Haqqani acted therefore "as a diplomatic liaison".[253] In exchange, the Haqqani network could rule over North Waziristan, a situation that was to continue after the "global war on terror" was launched.[254]

In September 2001, in anticipation of the war to come, Mullah Omar appointed Jalaluddin Haqqani to head the military resistance.[255] After the Taliban regime was brought down, the Haqqani network gave refuge to Al Qaeda leaders and Arabs fleeing Afghanistan in its stronghold of North Waziristan.

The ISI pursued its relations with the Haqqani network after the Karzai government was formed. For the Pakistan Army, it was a particularly useful resource to combat India's presence in Afghanistan. In fact, "Elements of the ISI are believed to have supported new Taliban and Haqqani network camps as early as 2004".[256] This support implied training in military techniques such as attacks, ambushes and use of improvised explosive devices. These allegations are particularly important given the fact that the Haqqani network is widely held responsible for the two attacks on the Indian embassy in Kabul that took place in July 2008 (forty-one people were killed) and in October 2009 (seventeen were killed).

But the Haqqani network has largely broken free from a sponsor that in fact was never exclusive, particularly from a financial standpoint.[257] In addition to money from the Gulf, extortion of funds from kidnappings for ransom and the proceeds of drug smuggling, the Haqqani network paradoxically benefitted from the arrival of the Americans and more generally

[252] Vahid Brown and Don Rassler, *Fountainhead of Jihad*, op. cit., p. 110.

[253] Ibid., p. 159.

[254] Ibid., p. 167.

[255] Thomas Ruttig, "The Haqqani Network as an Autonomous Entity", op. cit., p. 66.

[256] Vahid Brown and Don Rassler, *Fountainhead of Jihad*, op. cit., p. 175.

[257] Gretchen Peters, *Haqqani Network Financing*, op. cit.

NATO troops in the regions for two reasons. First, it managed to collect a tax from trucks crossing the Durand Line (which otherwise would be attacked). Second, it collected on a number of development contracts, including highway construction, financed by international aid. Not to mention sometimes bloody bank robberies such as the attack on the Kabul Bank branch in Jalalabad that left 38 people dead.

In addition to these illicit doings are more licit activities, such as a network of eighty *dini madaris* (spanning southern Afghanistan and North and South Waziristan), hospitals, service stations, a trucking firm with 200 semi-trailers, real estate holdings in Kabul, Gardez, Khost, Miran Shah, Peshawar, Kohat, Rawalpindi, Karachi, Abu Dhabi and Dubai.[258] The Haqqani network is a little economic empire with countless transnational ramifications.

This organization is destined to survive its founder. Jalaluddin suffered a stroke in 2005 that left him incapacitated, but his immediate family, already involved in the network, immediately took over. The three sons of his Afghan wife—his second wife is from the United Arab Emirates—have long held key complementary posts. Following his father, Sirajuddin was made responsible for coordinating the network's operations from Miran Shah, as well as relations with the Quetta Shura and business strategy. At the more concrete level, Badruddin—whose mother was an Arab—was based in North Waziristan and in charge of armed operations until he was killed in a drone strike in August 2012. Nasiruddin—who was mysterously killed in November 2013 in Islamabad—handled financial operations for the group, which he managed from a more central location in Pakistan, making frequent visits from there to the Gulf countries. Jalaluddin's brother Khalil takes care of fundraising. In the end, the Haqqani network has become a vast enterprise straddling the line between armed struggle and organised crime.

While the relationship between the Haqqanis and the ISI is complex and often fraught with more tension than outsiders imagine,[259] this network has been spared by the Pakistani army so far.

* * *

The Pakistani state has been largely responsible for the development of sectarianism, jihadism and the Taliban movement. The first of these phe-

---

[258] Ibid., p. 57 and Vahid Brown and Don Rassler, *Fountainhead of Jihad*, op. cit., p. 131.

[259] Gretchen Peters, *Haqqani Network Financing: the Evolution of an Industry*, op. cit., p. 38.

nomena no doubt flows from the support post-Khomeini Iran gave Pakistani Shia groups and from Saudi backing for Sunni groups. But General Zia also helped the latter and fostered the crystallisation of sectarian conflicts through an Islamisation policy that was virtually one of "Sunnisation". Promotion of jihadism by the Pakistani state—and even more by the state within a state that the ISI has become—has its roots in the Pakistani establishment's obsession with India. After the defeat of 1971— and the second Partition resulting from it—both military and civil leaders, convinced of the Pakistan Army's inferiority to India's, sought to buttress its strength in the face of its larger neighbour by arming jihadist movements in Afghanistan (to acquire "strategic depth") and in Kashmir (to "bleed India"). As for the Talibanisation of Afghanistan, it falls in line with this same thinking in that Islamabad believed Mullah Omar's troops were bound to be reliable and lasting allies, giving the Pakistan Army a rear base with respect to India.

This strategy proved its limits as of the late 1990s. The infiltration of armed combatants near Kargil in 1999 forced Pakistan into a humiliating retreat and the 11 September 2001 attacks brought an end to the strategic depth gained in Afghanistan. Beyond that, the tolerance the state long showed certain Sunni groups exacerbated sectarian violence, forcing the authorities to take action, with more or less conviction, in the late 1990s.

The United States also forced the Pakistanis to crack down on the Islamists, in a different manner, after 11 September 2001. Islamabad went about this selectively for tactical considerations. The army continued to perceive the Afghan Taliban, the Haqqani network and a jihadist group such as the LeT as an asset in Afghanistan and in the face of India. The refusal to tackle head on groups the establishment basically sympathised with has enabled these organisations to acquire such power that today they can defy the state and create the conditions of a low intensity civil war.

10

TOWARD CIVIL WAR?

THE STATE VS. (SOME) ISLAMISTS, THE ISLAMISTS
VS. THE MINORITIES

From Zia to Musharraf the Pakistani state fostered the rise of Islamist movements that today constitute an unprecedented political and social force. This tendency has developed especially in the Pashtun area (from the FATA to the NWFP—renamed Khyber–Pakhtunkhwa in 2010) and in Punjab owing to the jihad wars carried out in Afghanistan and Kashmir. The anti-Soviet jihad, a nearly ten-year war, and then militant combat alongside the Taliban have had a profound impact on Pakistani society. Not only have these events given militant Islam a second wind, but they have also raised the status of its advocates, starting with the jihadists, including second-rank mullahs whose mosques and *dini madaris* have experienced a considerable boom. By implication, an entire social order—albeit an extremely inegalitarian one—has been challenged. Islamists have in some cases managed to take root in the social fabric not only as heralds of Islam but also as dispensers of justice committed to sharia law and social work. After the Taliban took over in Afghanistan, Pakistani Islamist groups benefited from a new rear base. And Pashtuns were overrepresented among the almost 100,000 Pakistanis trained in Afghan camps run by Al Qaeda.[1]

---

[1] Khaled Ahmed, *Sectarian War*, op. cit., p. 290.

Since the mid-2000s, the pervasiveness of the jihadist phenomenon has been at once the cause and consequence of the atmosphere of civil war (and sometimes more) tearing apart Pakistan. Goaded by its allies, especially the United States, the state has become conscious of the danger and tackled a growing number of Islamist groups. But due to their social embeddedness (particularly in Pashtun areas and even more so in the FATA) and more broadly speaking, their sense of organisation (in many regards military), these groups have proven to be fearsome adversaries. In many towns and villages—in the FATA of course, but in Punjab as well—the Islamists lay down the law, making the life of minorities increasingly difficult.

The Islamists, a Social and Political Force

The Islamists vs. the Establishment, or the Roots of a Popular Following

The social welfare strategy deployed by a number of Islamist movements— mentioned in the preceding chapter with regard to the Lashkar-e-Taiba—is not enough to explain their embeddedness in society. It also owes much to their ability to resort to a revolutionary rhetoric. This is partly an unintended consequence of the policy of Islamisation and support for jihad movements that the Pakistani authorities have conducted since Zia, which has indirectly upset the social order in many provinces. The Afghan jihad of the 1980s contributed especially to this process by giving clerics a status and a room for manoeuvre against the ruling elite that they had never before enjoyed. Until then, both the civil and military elites readily held them in supreme contempt, and the wealthy (the business community in towns and the feudal families in the country) hardly had any more respect for them. As of the 1980s, they gained prominence because Zia—who paradoxically did not hold the clerics in high esteem either—needed them to bolster his own legitimacy and, more importantly, wanted to use them against the Soviets. They distinguished themselves in this fight, falling as martyrs in the holy war covered in newfound glory. Then, the state showed them unprecedented marks of respect, also encouraging the founding of new *dini madaris*, particularly in Pashtun areas, to supply the jihad with cannon fodder.

Dini Madaris and Social Change

The expansion of Deobandi *dini madaris* has been particularly spectacular. Only Shia schools have experienced more dramatic growth.

Table 10.1: Change in the number of Dini Madaris, by denomination, between 1988 and 2002

Deobandi		Barelwi		Ahl-e-Hadith		Shia		Jamat-e Islami		Total	
1988	2002	1988	2002	1988	2002	1988	2002	1988	2002	1988	2002
1,779	7,000	717	1,585	161	376	47	419	97*	500	2,801	9,880

* In 1988, this figure came under the more general heading "Other", but it was public knowledge that the JI Din Madari made up most of this category.
Source: Tariq Rahman, "The Madrassa and the State of Pakistan", *Himal South Asian*, February 2004. (http://www.himalmag.com/component/content/article/1712-the-madrassa-and-the-state-of-pakistan.html).

The phenomenon is not confined to the Pashtun areas. In fact, the rise in the number of *dini madaris* was greater in Punjab than in the NWFP between 1988 and 2000, as table 10.2 below shows.

Table 10.2: Change in the number of Dini Madaris by province from 1947 to 2000

Province/Area	1947	1960	1980	1988	2000
Punjab	121	195	1,012	1,320	3,153
NWFP	59	87	426	678	1,281
Sindh	21	87	380	291	905
Balochistan	28	70	135	347	692
Azad Kashmir	4	8	29	76	151
Islamabad	–	1	27	47	94
Northern Areas	12	16	47	102	185
FATA	–	–	–	–	300
Total	245	464	2,056	2,861	6,741

Source: Adapted from Christine C. Fair, *The Madrassah Challenge: Militancy and Religious Education in Pakistan*, Washington, DC, United States Institute of Peace Press, 2008. (http://home.comcast.net/~christine_fair/pubs/Madrassah918_1As.pdf)

Correlatively, Punjab also has the highest number of students in *dini madaris*. According to the Pakistan Human Rights Commission, based in Lahore, in March 2002 there were 250,000 such students in this province out of a total of 600,000.[2]

[2] Suba Chandran, "Madrassas in Pakistan" *IPCS Issue Brief*, September 2003. See: http://www.ipcs.org/pdf_file/issue/2032153432IB11-SubaChandran-MadrassasIn-Pak.pdf (Accessed on September 15, 2013).

Syed Tauqir Hussain Shah, on the basis of a detailed study of *dini madaris* in South Punjab, sees this as a major macro-sociological and political shift:

Historically the Feudal leadership has been playing the role of a broker between state and the poor citizens. And they have been extremely dishonest and inefficient brokers. The poor people had to beg the local feudals (who had political power also) for getting small favours or personal grievances redressed by local administration and police. These feudals were impossible to access; if after months of begging and at time forced and unpaid labour a poor person managed to get an audience with a local feudal, at best he would scribble a non decipherable recommendatory letter to local administration or police. It was unimaginable for the local feudal political leader to accompany a poor person to government office or call up an official.

While suffering the debouched feudal and corrupt and inefficient state functionary, the poor, and faceless people saw the rise of religious leaders. They silently observed that this local manager of Madrassah, who at times may even be an outsider from NWFP or Baluchistan, or another district, is commanding immense influence with local state functionaries, particularly police and administration.

Moreover he was always available to help, readily accompanying people to police stations and local offices; he was neither charging people for this service nor treating them in a demeaning manner. Moreover it is seen that he is more effective than the feudal political leadership.

The state functionaries were particularly receptive and obliging to religious/sectarian leaders, thus adding to their mass appeal. The particular disposition of administrative machinery towards religious leaders, specially those belonging to militant radical deobandi groups has been a post-Afghan Jihad phenomenon. Since these leaders belonged to groups who were "Strategic Partners" of the government and the west led by the United States, the administrative functionaries extended patronage to these groups accordingly. This phenomenon brought a sea change in the social standing of Madrassah and its graduates. It began to symbolize a revolution against oppressive feudal and social set up [sic].[3]

Jihad appears to be a major factor of social change in that it has undercut ancestral hierarchies. The author could have added that the *dini madaris'* prestige has also benefited from the recent recognition of the degrees they offer. In any event Shah ascribes the growing attractiveness of *dini madaris* in the 1990s to their newfound "social power" more than to poverty among peasant families and their religious fervour. In the *tehsil* of Bahawalpur District in South Punjab where he carried out his survey, it was between 1991

---

[3] Syed Tauqir Hussain Shah, *Madrassahs in Pakistan: A Threat to Enlightened and Moderate Pakistan?* Budapest, Open Society Institute, 2006, pp. 33–34. Available online at: http://www.policy.hu/news/Shah-PS/22 (Accessed on September 15, 2013).

and 1995 that *dini madaris* experienced their most robust growth. The reason the author puts forward for this boom—the jihadists' "social power"—also partly explains why the Deobandis were the first to experience this expansion. In 2004, out of 26,030 *dini madaris* students, 13,332 (51 per cent) were Deobandi followers, compared to 11,045 Barelwis (1,366 Ahl-e-Hadith and 287 Ahl Tashi—that is, Shias). By way of comparison, public schools drew only about twice as many (55,892).[4] These figures should be regarded with caution as they do not take into account private schools that are not *dini madaris* or chilcren who are not enrolled in school.

The TNSM and the "FM Mullah", An Islamic Revolutionary Movement

As of the 1980s, the Islamists' revolutionary potential was particularly obvious in the Pashtun areas where their participation in the anti-Soviet jihad lent the *mullahs* considerable prestige at the expense of traditional notables, especially tribal chiefs who had been associated with Pashtun nationalism from the time of Abdul Ghaffar Khan. An illustration of this process can be found in the trajectory of the leaders of Tehrik-e-Nifaz-e-Shariat-e-Mohammadi (TNSM—Movement for the Enforcement of Islamic Law), a movement that denounced the Pakistani judicial system as un-Islamic.

The rise of TNSM is inseparable from features of the land where it originated, Malakand Division, which was formed by the grouping of three former princely states—Swat, Chitral and Dir—which had previously retained some of their autonomy, and especially their own laws until 1969.[5] The dominants of yesteryear—the *khans* and the *maliks*—protested against losing their powers of law enforcement and justice after rules specific to the Provincially Administrated Tribal Areas (PATA) were introduced. Two judicial systems began to coexist within this framework: offences against the state (including the armed forces) came under the administration's jurisdiction, while the others were decided by a traditional *jirga* through which *khans* and *maliks* tried to reassert their authority. The Supreme

---

[4] Ibid., pp. 16–17.

[5] Swat, due to the open-mindedness of its sovereign, was fairly modern, at least in terms of access to education and health care, while the other two lagged behind from these two standpoints. Lubna Abid Ali and Naveed Iqbal Khan, "The Rise of Tehreek-e-Nifaz-e-Shariat-e-Mohammadi in Malakand Division, NWFP: A Case Study of the Process of 'State Inversion'," *Pakistan Vision*, vol. 11, no. 1, p. 90. Available online at: http://pu.edu.pk/images/journal/studies/PDF-FILES/Artical %20No-5.pdf (Accessed on September 15, 2013).

Court put an end to the latter in 1994, deeming it unconstitutional but the way the local notables defended their privileges was strongly resented by the plebeians.

In Malakand Division, the crucible of Islamism was the Jama'at-e-Islami. The first militants who joined the anti-Soviet jihad came the student union of this party, the Islami Jamiat Talaba, which prepared the ground for the TNSM.[6] This organisation was founded in 1989 by Maulana Sufi Mohammad, a Wahhabi and native of Dir who had backed Hekmatyar's Hezb-e-Islami during the anti-Soviet jihad. He was a member of the Jama'at-e-Islami until 1981—at which time he broke with the party, deciding that the game of electoral politics was not worthwhile (although he had once participated in it as a local elected official). In 1989, he established the TNSM, which launched its first agitation for the application of sharia in 1991. His influence rose after the Supreme Court decision of 1994 that "deprived the executive authorities and local Khans, Maliks and other influential people of their judicial powers. Therefore, they conspired with the local religious leaders to launch a movement for Shariah."[7] Furthermore, PATA regulations made the regional assembly a rather toothless institution, compared to the authority vested in the governor, appointed by the president and answerable to him.

In November 1994, the TNSM staged an armed operation enabling it to take control of several administrative buildings to force the government to promulgate the Sharia Regulation, making sharia the primary source of law. Some 25,000 persons took part in this agitation,[8] in particular former combatants in Afghanistan trained in guerrilla warfare,[9] prompting Chief Minister Sherpao to make substantial concessions.

Sufi Mohammad remained in government custody for only a short period of time, and by November 1994 senior government functionaries sent him official letters addressed to "Honorable Maulana Sufi Mohammad bin Hasan Mahmud," updating him about government directives to enforce Sharia law and requesting his cooperation. Immediate official instructions were then

[6] Muhammad Amir Rana and Rohan Gunaratna, *Al-Qaeda Fights Back*, op. cit., p. 35.

[7] Ibid., p. 94.

[8] Ibid., p. 100

[9] Hassan Abbas, "The black-turbaned brigade: the rise of the TNSM in Pakistan", *The Jamestown Foundation*, 14 April 2006. See http://web.archive.org/web/2007 0930192222/http://jamestown.org/news_details.php?news_id=209 (Accessed on September 15, 2013).

issued to establish religious courts. TNSM's supporters, also started to tell men to grow beards. In short, Talibanization began to take place.[10]

In September–October 2001, TNSM marshalled 10,000 militants behind Sufi Mohammad to aid the Taliban as they sustained the Western (and Northern Alliance) military attacks. Eyewitness testimonies recall that "most people were farmers, labourers and unemployed" from the districts of Swat, Lower and Upper Dir, Malakand and Buner. These poorly armed foot soldiers and 300 vehicles crossed the Ghakhi Pass (Bajaur Agency) and came under a hail of bombs on their way to Kunar.[11] Most of them died on the battlefield, but Sufi Mohammad managed to return to Pakistan where he was arrested and sentenced to three years in prison for leading his men into such unequal combat. The TNSM was banned.

The movement continued to function nevertheless under the leadership of his son-in-law, Mullah Fazlullah, who was released after seventeen months and who appeared as one of the Taliban after fighting with them in Afghanistan. Fazlullah was a "cable car operator and part-time guest-room attendant at Fizza Ghat near his native village Mam Dheri"[12] in the Swat valley. He became popular after he began to broadcast his sermons by radio from Swat. These sermons, delivered in a quietist tone, gained an enormous following, to the point where the *mullah* became known as "Mullah Radio". Fazlullah's popularity, during what Muhammad Feyyaz called the "first phase" of his activities, resulted from two factors. First, his speeches targeted the landed aristocracy which had deprived the peasants of their land during the princely era in 1917. Their descendents "were among the first to join Taliban ranks to reclaim their lands from Khans".[13] Second, "Fazlullah cleverly aimed his radio propaganda at women, motivating them in every speech and sermon to send their sons, husbands and brothers for jihad".[14] Here, Fazlullah appeared revolutionary in social and cultural terms since he "used his radio sermons to oppose social taboos discriminating against women availing their legal rights to inheritance, *mehr* (amount of money paid by the groom to the bride), divorce".[15] Women

[10] Ibid.

[11] Irfan Haider, "After jihad: Abandoned...", *Dawn*, 4 August 2014 (http://www.dawn.com/news/1122605).

[12] Muhammad Feyyaz, "Political Economy of Tehrik-i-Taliban Swat", *Conflict and Peace Studies*, vol. 4, no. 3, July–September 2011, p. 43.

[13] Ibid., p. 43.

[14] Ibid., p. 44.

[15] Ibid., p. 43.

appreciated these speeches, as evident from the extent of gold jewelry they donated for the building of his seminary.

Fazlullah was one of the first to have used radio broadcasts to convey his message and build his influence. But many other "FM Mullahs"[16] would follow his lead. Their ascension represented a challenge to the established order, marked by even more pronounced inequalities in the region neighbouring the PATA, the FATA.

The FATA, a Laboratory for Insurgency?

The Federally Administered Tribal Areas (FATA) comprise some of the most destitute and least integrated regions of Pakistan,[17] which has contributed to making them a hotbed of Islamist insurrection. The figures for a few socio-economic indicators illustrate the scope of the problem: its literacy rate is 17.42 per cent, compared to the national average of 43.92 per cent; only 43 per cent of the people have access to drinking water and there is only one doctor for every 7,670 inhabitants.[18] Regarding their national integration, the FATA are the result of an arrangement dating back to British rule in the nineteenth century when five administrative entities were established along the Afghan border, South Waziristan, North Waziristan, Kurram, Khyber and Malakand. These geographic units were designed to act as a buffer with Afghanistan, as Russia's expansion southward in the Great Game had set off several wars. These areas were inhabited by Pashtun tribes forming a society in many ways comparable to that found in the adjacent region to the east, which was to become North West Frontier Province in 1901.

The area's villages were governed by *khans* or *maliks*, chiefs of the main clans, who deliberated in tribal assemblies known as *jirgas*. The relations of these holders of worldly power with the clerics were ambiguous. Examining their situation in the colonial era, Sana Haroon points out that "In an equitable exchange of support, *mullas* confirmed *maliki* authority and the institutional integrity of the *jirga* while the *maliks* legitimised the *mulla*'s

---

[16] This expression refers to the use made by many of these mullahs after Musharraf liberalised the airwaves in the early 2000s (Sonya Fatah, "FM Mullahs", *Columbia Journalism Review*, vol. 45, no. 2, July/August 2006, pp. 16–17.

[17] Carlos Setas, "The Semi-Autonomous Tribal Areas of Pakistan", *Himalayan and Central Asian Studies*, vol. 15, n° 3, July–September 2011, pp. 105–119.

[18] Syed Manzar Abbas Zaidi, "Understanding FATA", *Conflict and Peace Studies*, vol. 3, n° 4, October–December 2010, p. 118.

directives."[19] These directives naturally drew on sharia law and were generally compatible with Pashtunwali, the unwritten Pashtun code of honour. But Sana Haroon admits, "tensions often arise where the application of religious precept by the *mulla* and the cultural practices preferred by the community could not be reconciled."[20] The *mullah* and the *malik* in fact were somewhat in competition, even if the *mullah* often arbitrated between rival maliks, and some *mullah* travelled throughout the tribal area to settle disputes. On the strength of their spiritual authority, the *mullah* could muster troops by raising private armies or *lashkar*—just as *maliks* had their own militias. This was accepted practice to enforce payment of a fine, to physically punish a wayward Muslim and to resist the British.[21] Such armed operations were qualified as jihad.

The British never managed to establish any real control over the tribal areas bordering Afghanistan, facing sporadic revolts leading at times to murder or the abduction of a "white man" (*gora*)—to which they retaliated with increasingly disproportionate means—being unable to manage it from an administrative standpoint, if only to collect taxes and put down uprisings. The first of these took place in 1914 when the head of a Deoband seminary, Maulana Mahmudul Hasan, decided to fight the British from the tribal area that had—already!—then been chosen "for its state of non-administration".[22] The Jamiat-e-Mujahidin, which led this war with the mullahs' backing, campaigned in the name of a "Yaghistan" that supposedly corresponded to the tribal area.

The western flank of this territory was marked out by Mortimer Durand in 1893, a very problematic "border". Not only was it disputed by the tribes straddling the line,[23] but tribes located to the East also continued to swear allegiance to the Afghan rulers. In 1947, the Pashtuns in the tribal areas were divided between a sense of ethnic belonging making them lean toward Afghanistan and a religious identity that encouraged them to iden-

---

[19] Sana Haroon, *Frontier of Faith—Islam in the Indo-Afghan Borderland*, London, Hurst, 2007, p. 67.

[20] Ibid., p. 69.

[21] Ibid., pp. 86–87.

[22] Ibid., p. 93.

[23] On these population movements partly due to the transhumance of pastoralists, see the fictionalised memoirs of Jamil Ahmad, who after joining the Pakistani Civil Service in 1954 was posted to the FATA and started to write his famous book in the 1970s. See Jamil Ahmad, *The Wandering Falcon*, New York, Riverhead Books, 2011.

tify with the idea of Pakistan that was materialising. When the local tribes heard reports of the crimes against Muslims committed by the Hindus in Punjab and elsewhere at the time of Partition, they attacked Sikh and Gurkha convoys leaving the area.[24] In October 1947, "some thousands of Mahsuds, Mohmands and Afridis, moved into Kashmir to liberate it from the Hindus",[25] eliciting thanks from Jinnah for the tribes' support.[26] But at the same time, the Faqir of Ipi's militia in North Waziristan, which the British had already bombarded from the air in the 1930s,[27] continued to fight, no longer against the infidels but against supra-regional tutelage. For while they may have been Muslims, the tribes in the area jealously guarded their autonomy, or otherwise looked to Kabul.

In response to this demand for independence, the Karachi government continued along the British path: it relied on local leaders, the *maliks*, to whom they granted an annual stipend of one million rupees and considerable autonomy. Orakzai, Mohmand and Bajaur were added to the areas mentioned above to make up the Federally Administered Tribal Areas. The British had resigned themselves to leaving the tribals in this area great autonomy, allowing them as of 1901 to govern themselves by their codes and *jirgas* within the limits of a procedure called Frontier Crimes Regulation. This series of administrative and judicial regulations were based on a principle of collective responsibility that was fairly consistent with the idea of tribal self-government: since the tribes managed public affairs, if a crime was committed, they could be held collectively responsible and punished. The Pakistani government aligned its policy with this perspective.

Ayub Khan, who had commanded a brigade in Mir Ali (North Waziristan) at the start of his career in 1947, made no secret about it: "My policy is clear: we will not intrude upon their areas unless they ask us, and when they do ask we will develop their territories, but not buy individuals."[28] Like in the time of the British, this principle of "indirect rule" was based on cooperation

---

[24] Sana Haroon, *Frontier of Faith*, op. cit., p. 179.

[25] Ibid., p. 180.

[26] Ibid., p. 182.

[27] Siddiqui A. R. "Faqir of Ipi's Cross Border Nexus", see http://www.khyber.org/articles/2005/Faqir_of_Ipis_Cross_Border_Nex.shtml (Accessed on September 15, 2013) and Hauner, Milan (Jan., 1981) "One Man against the Empire: The Faqir of Ipi and the British in Central Asia on the Eve of and during the Second World War", see http://www.khyber.org/publications/021–025/faqiripi.shtml (Accessed on September 15, 2013).

[28] Ayub Khan, *Friends, not Masters*, op. cit., p. 34.

between the maliks and the bureaucrats, two administrative corps that for lack of any popular representation wielded considerable power.

As their name implies, the FATA come directly under the authority of Pakistan's president who delegates power to the NWFP governor to oversee the administration. But at the level of each agency, power lies mainly in the hands of the Political Agent (PA—of which neither the name nor perimeter of action have changed since the British) who enjoys extensive authority under the Frontier Crimes Regulation which also remained in effect after 1947. According to this body of laws, the PA, a bureaucrat appointed by the governor, can punish any tribe as he sees fit. He can notably imprison whomever he likes for three years without having to offer justification.[29] The PA and the Frontier Corps—a border police force usually led by an army Major General—rely on the maliks and their own militias, the Khassadars. The maliks are usually appointed by the Pakistani president himself, while holders of *lungi* (at the head of subclans) are named by the governor.

Imtiaz Gul, an expert on the FATA, believes that "The main reason for the popularity of successive Islamist movements in the tribal areas stems from the draconian system of the FCR (...) the search for a fair justice system and the craving for equal citizenship has come to be synonymous with sharia."[30] Many Islamist groups in fact claim a role of dispensers of justice, not only because they redress the wrongs done to the downtrodden, but also as they combat inequalities.

In the 1980s, Islamist movements began to prosper in the tribal areas in a context of the anti-Soviet jihad, while "Deobandi Islam never really had a foothold in FATA until the Afghan jihad started".[31] Despite efforts on the part of Pakistani authorities to prevent Afghan refugee camps from being set up in the FATA—an area over which they had little control—104 of the 278 refugee tented villages in the Pashtun areas were in the FATA in 1988.[32] The attraction of a border that had always been porous explains this natural inclination: by virtue of the Easement Rights Regulation, at times up to 40,000 people crossed the Durand Line daily at Torkham (Khyber), one of the border crossing points.[33] As of 1984, with the partial withdrawal of Soviet troops, many mujahideen were even able to circulate between their

[29] Imtiaz Gul, *The Most Dangerous Place. Pakistan's Lawless Frontier*, op. cit., p. 45.
[30] Ibid., p. 53.
[31] Syed Manzar Abbas Zaidi, "Understanding FATA", op. cit., p. 119.
[32] Nancy Duprée, "Demographic Reporting on Afghan Refugees in Pakistan", *Modern Asian Studies*, vol. 22, no. 4, October 1988, p. 846.
[33] Imtiaz Gul, *The Most Dangerous Place. Pakistan's Lawless Frontier*, op. cit., p. 52.

old and their new residences.[34] Thus a sort of osmosis was created, closely meshing the tribal areas and the Afghan jihad, a form of integration first reflected in the development of new *dini madaris*. Sheikh Jamiur Rahman, a native of Kunar, thus reportedly not only set up camp in Bajaur, but 250 *dini madaris* throughout the FATA as well.[35] Pakistani jihadist groups also set up their headquarters and/or their training camps in Wana (South Waziristan) and in Mir Ali (North Waziristan) and on the Afghan side, in Khost, where Al Qaeda had its base in the late 1980s.

A segment of the FATA youth was thus drawn into the jihad in the 1980s and then over the course of the following decade. The case of Nek Muhammad offers an interesting illustration. As one journalist from the daily newspaper *Dawn* wrote upon his death in 2004, "If there is one man operating in the South Waziristan Agency who is truly the child of the tumultuous 1980s, it is Nek Mohammad."[36] The man came from a poor family of Kalusha (Wana), received some education in a JUI *madrassah*, the Jamia Darul Uloom Waziristan, prior to trying his hand at trading—unsuccessfully.[37] He was recruited by a *mullah* of Wana to join the Taliban in the mid-1990s. One of his fellow Wazir tribesmen explains his brilliant military career by his feats of arms, especially in Kargha (10 km west of Kabul where he had set up his base): "He started off as a footsoldier but the tremendous self-respect that drove his actions catapulted him to a middle-level position in the Taliban military hierarchy, commanding 3,000 men at one time (...) The only time he abandoned his trenches without an argument (with his superiors) was in November 2001 when the US and Northern Alliance troops descended on Bagram and the Taliban melted into the countryside."[38] As of 1998, Nek Mohammed was at the helm of a "regiment" of Wazir tribe fellows in Bagram, not far from Kabul.[39]

Returning to Kalosha (South Waziristan) with a fleet of six all-terrain pickups, Nek was someone to be reckoned with. But the retreat of Arab Al Qaeda fighters to his territory brought him even more money in exchange

---

[34] Nancy Duprée, "Demographic Reporting on Afghan Refugees in Pakistan", op. cit., p. 848.

[35] Sana Haroon, *Frontier of Faith*, op. cit., p. 204.

[36] M. Ilyas Khan, "Profile of Nek Mohammad", *Dawn*, 19 June 2004.

[37] Mariam Abou Zahab, "Frontières dans la tourmente: la talibanisation des zones tribales", *Outre-Terre. Revue de géopolitique*, no. 24, 2010, p. 351.

[38] Cited in M. Ilyas Khan, "Profile of Nek Mohammad", op. cit.

[39] Claudio Franco, "The Tehrik-e-Taliban Pakistan", in Antonio Giustozzi (ed.), *Decoding the New Taliban: Insights from the Afghan Field*, op. cit., p. 277.

for protection. In 2003, he possessed a fleet of forty-four vehicles, some of them bullet-proof.[40] These details may seem trivial, but they indicate a social ascension in a society that was highly inegalitarian. For those kept at the bottom of the social hierarchy by local elites (*khans* and *maliks*) and an inequitable judicial system perpetuated by the state, the jihad of the 1980s marked a turning point by offering new perspectives of individual mobility. Beyond the individual, Nek Mohammad had an impact on the area at a time when the social dynamics were conducive to change, as Syed Saleem Shahzad explains:

The old fiefdoms of the tribal elders started to collapse. Young men in their teens and twenties were organized by Nek Muhammad to challenge the old order. Within months, the centuries-old tribal structure had melted. The younger generation was calling the shots. Their insubordination knew no bounds. Tribal elders and senior Muslim clerics lost their grip. The traditional tribal dynamic had literally changed overnight. The younger militants were not ready to tolerate the presence of any-body who might rival them. The tribal chiefs were either killed or fled to the cities. Their fiefdoms fell into the hands of this new generation, who were totally commit-ted to Al-Qaeda.[41]

Syed Saleem Shahzad probably exaggerates the suddenness of a process that was in gestation, even already in operation, since the jihad against the Soviets. He recognises this himself when he reports that 600,000 youths had been part of the jihad since 1979, that 100,000 Pakistanis belonged to jihad-ist organisations and that one million of them had been trained in a *madrassah*.[42] But there is no doubt that the retreat of Al-Qaeda to the FATA in 2001 (discussed in the following section) hastened the process. Before gauging its impact, it should be pointed out that even starting in the 1990s, along with Nek Mohammad there were many cadres from the jihad who acted as much as vigilantes as combatants for Islam. The case of Mangal Bagh is one of the most interesting ones. A journalist from *The News* describes him as a poor, even coarse man, but noble:

Commander Mangal Bagh is a slightly-built and bearded man aged about 35. He confessed being illiterate even though he is able to read Urdu newspapers and applications made by people seeking his intervention and help in almost every matter. He did study for some years in a madrassa and is, therefore, able to quote from the Quran and Ahadith to make his point. He is articulate and his nightly 9 pm speeches on his illegal FM radio channel are eagerly listened to by people in

---

[40] M. Ilyas Khan, "Profile of Nek Mohammad", *Dawn*, 19 June 2004.
[41] Syed Saleem Shahzad, *Inside Al-Qaeda and the Taliban*, op. cit., p. 6.
[42] Ibid., p. 8.

Bara to keep themselves abreast about his decisions and policies. Listeners pointed out that he speaks like a learned man and can go on for long (...) His humble origins have made him anti-feudal and pro-people. He loses no opportunity to criticise the Maliks, the hereditary tribal elders who are traditionally pro-establishment and receive all the benefits doled out by the government. He is keen to highlight the plight of the ordinary tribesmen and motivated to solve the problems confronting the common man. If he has his way, he would like to rob the rich to pay the poor like a modern-day Robin Hood. That explains the reason for young men, mostly jobless, to flock to his banner and make up bulk of his Lashkar-i-Islam outfit. One heard stories galore as to how Mangal Bagh punished rich Maliks and other tribesmen violating the tribal and Lashkar-i-Islam's code of conduct by ordering them to host feast of rice cooked with meat to feed the whole tribe.[43]

From the Afridi tribe, Mangal Bagh's itinerary is fairly typical of the social upward mobility of Islamists recognized as Robin Hoods. He worked first as a taxi driver and now claims that he has 120,000 men under his orders. He took part in the jihad against the Soviets in Afghanistan as a young man, returning home in 1989 after the occupiers had left. What is more unusual is that he began by joining the ranks of the ANP, the Pashtun nationalist party that professed secularism, before joining Lashkar-e-Islam, of which he took the lead after the departure of its founder, Mufti Munir Shakir. But there remains a difference: contrary to most other movements, this Lashkar was not pro-Taliban to begin with. Mangal Bagh did not wish to fight the Pakistan Army in his own country and did not object to its presence in his stronghold in Bara.[44]

The Islamist sphere that has developed since the 1980s–90s both in Punjab and the Pashtun areas owing to the succession of conflicts in Afghanistan where its cadres earn their stripes thus owes its popularity not only to the prestige of the jihadists but to their social role as well. They embody the rising influence of heretofore dominated groups, fighting against status inequalities—but they also act as vigilantes, an issue that will be discussed further on. This set of variables largely explains the mass organization aspect that the network of *dini madaris* has acquired, especially those of the Deobandi school.

---

[43] Rahimullah Yusufzai, "The man from Bara", *The News*, 11 May 2008. See http://jang.com.pk/thenews/may2008-weekly/nos-11–05–2008/dia.htm (Accessed on September 15, 2013).

[44] Things changed in April 2013 when the Pakistani army attacked Mangah Bagh, who has since become the TTP's representative in Khyber Agency.

Islamist Connections: Jihadists, Sectarians, Taliban All Fighting the Same Battle

The power of the Islamist sphere also derives from the fact that many of the organisations, sometimes representing distinct sensibilities within it, wind up converging. During the 1980s and 1990s, this process fostered the constitution of a new political force that is far more homogenous than it seems. The distinction frequently made, even in the specialised literature, between sectarian movements and jihadists for instance needs to be put in perspective. Thus, Jaish-e-Muhammad, the SSP and Lashkar-e-Jhangvi are "the three wings of the same party",[45] as evident from the fact that Jaish had anti-Shia activities as early as 2000, when it was founded.

These groups grew out of the same matrix, the JUI, which was the crucible for the Taliban and the SSP, especially one of the *dini madaris*, the Binori Town *madrassah* mentioned earlier. Its chancellor, Shamzai, who sat on the JUI Shura (governing council), was also the sponsor of the Harakat movement. When Masood Azhar—having returned from India—broke off with Fazlur Rehman Khalil to form the Jaish-e-Mohammed, Shamzai immediately followed him.[46] The Binori Town *madrassah* and other such breeding grounds for Islamists who would later wind up in sectarian or jihadist organisations provided a common foundation for groups that hence continue to have considerable affinities.

The Al Rasheed Trust played a similar role in the area of financing. Founded by another Binori Town dignitary, Maulana Mufti Rasheed Ahmad, this trust raised funds throughout Pakistan and abroad (particularly in the Persian Gulf) to help Islamist groups and the Taliban government, to which it reportedly gave 20 million rupees.[47] Beyond that, the trust is also believed to have contributed financial support to the Harakat movement, the Jaish and the LeT.[48]

---

[45] Mariam Abou Zahab, "Pashtun and Punjabi Taliban: The Jihadi-Sectarian Nexus", op. cit., p. 370.

[46] Shamzai, who formulated 2000 *fatwas* in his lifetime, issued one against the Soviet invasion of Afghanistan and another against the American armed operation against the Taliban in 2001. He was assassinated in 2004, at a time when Musharraf—whose coup he had backed—was taking part in the "global war on terror" with a certain zeal but also selectively, as we have seen. See http://www.globaljihad.net/view_page.asp?id=1448 (Accessed on September 15, 2013).

[47] See http://www.satp.org/satporgtp/countries/pakistan/terroristoutfits/al-rashid_trust.htm (Accessed on September 15, 2013).

[48] Ibid.

Aside from the crucibles for cementing militants from various ideological horizons (sectarian or jihadist) that are Deobandi *dini madaris* in Pashtun areas as well in Karachi, the experience of Afghanistan also played a major role. The battlefield brought together around a single cause young Pakistanis who were often from very different backgrounds. The sociology of non-Afghan prisoners captured by Commander Massoud's forces prior to 2001 is highly instructive in this regard. Of the 109 Pakistanis (out of a total of 113), 60 per cent were between 21 and 25 years of age, only 48 per cent were students of religion—the others having a profession (7 per cent taught in a *madrassah*), only 33 were Pashtuns, 28 were Punjabis, 17 were "Urdu speakers" (probably Muhajirs), 15 Sindhis and 11 Baloch, and only 43 per cent had received their training in a *madrassah*. Moreover, 51 of them claimed allegiance to the Harakat movement, 48 to the JUI, and the other 4 said they sympathised with the PML(N), a party that was supposedly against unconstitutional methods.[49]

The Afghan experience naturally unified sectarians and jihadists when the Hazaras, who are Shias, from the Mazar-e-Sharif region, became targets for the Taliban. 8,000 were reportedly massacred. The militant Sunni group Lashkar-e-Jhangvi also developed linkages with the Taliban and their Al Qaeda guests when its thugs sought sanctuary there after each terrorist act they perpetrated in Pakistan. Dawood Badani, for instance, an LJ member responsible for anti-Shia attacks in Quetta, took advantage of protection from Al Qaeda leader Khalid Sheikh Mohammed, one of his close relatives.[50]

The history of the Khost camp is enlightening as regards this symbiosis. SSP and Taliban cadres trained there when the camp was run by Al Qaeda. The Taliban later took over its management, finally handing it over to the Harkat-ul-Ansar faction led by jihadist chief Fazlur Rehman Khalil—himself a product of the JUI.[51] The history of this camp is enough to show the linkages between sectarians, jihadists and Talibans, as well as the role of incubator played by JUI.

Sectarian and jihadist groups had already become familiar with one another in the FATA as well. While most sectarian movements originated in Punjab, some Pashtuns developed Sunni militant movements in the

---

[49] Julie Sirrs, "The Taliban's International Ambitions", *The Middle East Quarterly*, Summer 2001, pp. 61–71. See http://www.meforum.org/486/the-talibans-international-ambitions. (Accessed on September 15, 2013).

[50] Zahid Hussain, *Frontline Pakistan*, op. cit., p. 91.

[51] Ahmed Rashid, *Taliban*, op. cit., p. 92.

FATA—sometimes under the influence of the former[52]—even before mili-tants chased from the rest of Pakistan took refuge there. In Orakzai and Kurram, where the proportion of Shias was higher than average, sectarian clashes took place before the ideology of sectarianism crystallised in Pakistan. In Kurram, Turi tribes (Shias) and Bangash as well as Mangal tribes (Sunnis) have fought against each other several times since the 1930s. But tensions increased during the Afghan anti-Soviet jihad, especially after Shia and Sunni militant groups got organised Pakistan. Mariam Abou Zahab points out that "Afghan refugees introduced a militant brand of Sunni ideology at a time when the Shia of Parachinar (Kurram's capital) under the leadership of Allama Arif Hussain al-Hussaini were being radi-calized by the Iranian revolution".[53] Al-Hussaini became a national figure after he took over the TNJF in 1983, as mentioned above. Fearing the grow-ing influence of Khomeini in Pakistan, General Zia, in 1986, "allowed" Sunni mujahideen from the Hezb-e-Islami of Hekmatyar and some mem-bers of the JI to kill hundreds of Shias in the Kurram Agency.[54] This Agency remained a hotbed of sectarian politics when the TNJF and the SSP gained momentum. Azam Tariq, the SSP leader who had been elected MNA from Jhang in 1992 and who had been assassinated in 2003 "was as popular in Kurram as he was across Punjab", according to some press reports.[55]

Subsequently, Qari Hussain Mehsud, head of the TTP suicide squads in the late 2000s, helped to establish the SSP in the FATA. He had studied for four years in a Deobandi madrassah in Jhang, Jamia Farooqia, before joining the SSP there, one of its bastions.[56] In 2008, Qari Hussain's cousin, Hakimullah Mehsud—who took over for Baitullah at the head of the TTP (Tehrik-e-Taliban Pakistan—see below) in 2009—was made the organization's com-mander for the area covering the Khyber, Orakzai and Kurram agencies. He would be behind a wave of particularly bloody sectarian attacks.

The retreat of Lashkar-e-Jhangvi militants to the FATA after 2003 natu-rally aggravated Sunni sectarianism. In 2003, two attempts were made on

---

[52] For instance, the SSP and the Jaish had established Dini Madaris in the region of Kohat-Hangu as early as the 1990s. Mariam Abou Zahab, "Pashtun and Punjabi Taliban", op. cit., p. 374.

[53] Mariam Abou Zahab, *Unholy Nexus: Talibanism and Sectarianism in Pakistan's 'Tribal Areas*, Paris, CERI-Sciences po/CNRS, June 2009, p. 2. http://www.scienc-espo.fr/ceri/sites/sciencespo.fr.ceri/files/art_mz.pdf.

[54] Khaled Ahmed, *Sectarian War*, op. cit., p. 182.

[55] Cited in Arif Rafiq, *Sunni Deobandi-Shi'i Sectarian Violence in Pakistan*, op. cit., p. 61.

[56] Imtiaz Gul, *The Most Dangerous Place*, op. cit., p. 228.

President Musharraf's life, from which he narrowly escaped on both occasions. The trail of the investigation each time led to the LeJ, and its cadres were consequently hunted down with renewed determination. Many of them, along with SSP leaders, took refuge in the tribal areas. While the army hunted down some SSP and LeJ activists who had found a safe haven in the FATA, it seems that it spared (and even helped) others because these Sunni activists could help the Pakistani military of clearing the Kurram Agency from Shias in order to use this "Agency as an alternative entry point for North Waziristan-based militants into Afghanistan"—where they fought against the NATO forces as well as the Indian presence. Activists from the Haqqani network were the main potential beneficiaries from this strategy. After the Obama administration intensified the drone strikes on North Waziristan in 2010, this strategy was also intended to offer another safe haven to this network.[57] The other explanation for making sense of the pervasiveness of Sunni militants in Kurram is sheer military incompetence. Whatever the reason, the absence of effective repression of the Sunni militants partly accounts for the large number of casualties of sectarianism—1,500–3,000 people—in Kurram.[58]

While Sunni activists retreated to FATA in the early 2000s from the opposite bank of the Indus, Al Qaeda had already done the same at least two years earlier, but this time from Afghanistan—which was to have a much heavier impact on the area.

The Impact of Al Qaeda's Retreat to FATA

After the fall of the Taliban regime in Afghanistan, Al Qaeda retreated to FATA, more particularly to North Waziristan, which had become the stronghold of the Haqqani network in which Bin Laden and Al-Zawahiri had the utmost confidence. South Waziristan, which offered direct access to the Afghan province of Helmand, would be more the Afghan Taliban's turf. These two provinces became strongholds of the Islamists, whose rise in power owed much to Al Qaeda's support. As Imtiaz Gul explains, Al Qaeda brought two things into FATA: "money, which they showered on people they trusted to host them despite warnings by officials, and ideas of Muslim fraternity and Islamic ideology, which appealed to the emotional tribesmen."[59]

---

[57] Arif Rafiq, *Sunni Deobandi-Shi'i Sectarian Violence in Pakistan*, op. cit., pp. 66–67.

[58] Ibid., p. 64.

[59] Imtiaz Gul, *The Most Dangerous Place*, op. cit., p. 12.

Al Qaeda, whose fighting power relied on some 2,000 foreign combatants—including a large Uzbek contingent[60]—first attempted to recruit and train young local Pashtuns. To this end, it created two organisations, Jaishul al-Qiba al-Jihadi al-Siri al-Alami (Secret Army of International Jihad) and Jundullah (Army of God), which "succeeded in training and disseminating the requisite dose of militant ideology and military discipline to a generation of new Jihadis."[61] Nek Mohammad was not the least of the recruits to be trained between 2002 and 2005 before shifting into action. Syed Saleem Shahzad estimates the number of troops trained and coordinated by Al Qaeda In North Waziristan to be around 27,000 combatants (including 12,000 "locals", 10,000 jihadists from cities and towns in Pakistan, 3,000 Afghans and 2,000 foreigners—Uzbeks, Arabs, Chechens, Uighurs, etc.), while in South Waziristan there were thought to be some 13,000—for a total of 40,000 strong.

Aside from its numbers, this strike force acquired new techniques. The use of improvised explosive devices (IEDs), generally made using chemical fertilizers, was not the least of them. These weapons, the result of "technology transfer" from the Iraqi resistance, did much to dissuade Pakistani soldiers from patrolling the two Waziristans where mined tracks have claimed a number of lives among the military.[62] Another technique—imported from Iraq—was suicide attacks, previously unknown in the area.[63] The number of suicide attacks jumped from 6 in 2006 (they had been even in smaller numbers before) to 60 in 2007, 63 in 2008 and 86 in 2009.[64] Between

---

[60] The presence of a large Uzbek contingent in the FATA is the result of the retreat into the area by members of the Islamic Movement of Turkestan (renamed Islamic Movement of Uzbekistan in 2001). This movement, whose activists were run out by Karimov in Uzbekistan, had found refuge in Afghanistan in the 1990s. In 1996, it set up headquarters in Kunduz. In 2001, Tahir Yuldashev took control of the IMU.

[61] Syed Saleem Shahzad, *Inside Al-Qaeda*, op. cit., p. 26.

[62] Ibid., p. 28.

[63] One of the links between Iraq and Pakistan has been Abu Musab al-Zarkawi who had come to Peshawar in 1989 and had been sent to fight the anti-Soviet jihad in Miranshah and Khost (Khaled Ahmed, *Sectarian War*, op. cit., p. 147). According to Hassan Abbas "A group of Iraqi insurgent leaders even met the Afghan Taliban in FATA in late 2005 and taught them lessons from the Iraq theatre" (Hassan Abbas, *The Taliban revival Violence and extremism on the Pakistan—Afghanistan frontier*, New Haven, Yale University Press, 2014, p. 117).

[64] Khuram Iqbal, "Evolution of Suicide Terrorism in Pakistan and Counter-Strategies", *Conflict and Peace Studies*, vol. 3, no. 1, January–March, 2010, p. 55.

2002 and July 2010, 3,719 people died in 257 such attacks.[65] According to Syed Saleem Shahzad, a squad of 450 suicide attackers (including 70 women)[66] were recruited in Pakistan and trained in the Kunar valley.[67]

These techniques and the targeted killing of tribal chiefs mentioned above have enabled Islamists to take control of the two Waziristans and proclaim Islamic states. The judicial apparatus has been replaced by sharia courts and a culture police enforces a ban on music, rigorous observance of prayers, the forced veiling of women and bearding of men, and so on. Furthermore, schools for girls have fairly systematically been targets for destruction.

Until the mid-2000s, the main objective of the Islamists within FATA was nevertheless the fight against foreign troops occupying Afghanistan. Such was the justification behind the offensive against NATO forces in the spring of 2006 in Helmand province. Within a few weeks or months, the Taliban retook control of entire areas in southern Afghanistan, including in the area around Kandahar. The Americans then understood the scale of the forces defying them, and that their rear base—even the nerve centre—was in the FATA in Pakistan, and in Balochistan (where there are large numbers of Pashtuns).

The State's Double Game in Pashtun Areas—and the Islamists' Measured Response

Negotiate with the Islamists

The United States has put pressure on Pakistan since 2001 for it to deploy troops in FATA—but without much energy until the spring 2006 offensive and Dick Cheney's visit to Islamabad in February 2007.

Until 2007, the Pakistan Army had thus settled for carrying out limited operations in these areas. Indeed in 2002, it had launched Operation Meezan, a bolder feat than it might seem at first, as it involved "entering FATA for the first time since the country's independence in 1947."[68] Some

---

[65] Akbar Nasir Khan, "Analyzing Suicide Attacks in Pakistan", *Conflict and Peace Studies*, vol. 3, no. 4, October–December 2010, p. 141.

[66] Imtiaz Gul points out, however, that the first suicide bombing perpetrated by a woman came much later, in December 2007, in the wave of attacks following the storming of the Red Mosque. Imtiaz Gul, *The Most Dangerous Place*, op. cit., p. 137.

[67] Syed Saleem Shahzad, *Inside Al-Qaeda*, op. cit., p. 31.

[68] Hassan Abbas, "An Assessment of Pakistan's Peace Agreements with Militants in Waziristan (2004–2008)", in Daveed Gartenstein-Ross and Clifford D. May

24,000 soldiers were deployed there. The initial operation turned out to be insufficient, and so a second one, code named "Kalusha" (named after a village of South Waziristan), was organised in March 2004. It also failed, and the losses made army officers aware "that the problem was far more serious than they had thought."[69] In April 2004 another operation in South Waziristan, apparently named, "Hammer and Anvil", was even more counterproductive. The deployment of troops in areas which used to ignore the state and be self-ruled alienated the locals, especially after the Shakai attack.[70] Not only were the local tribes hostile to these incursions and uncooperative, but the Islamist groups turned out to be well equipped against an army poorly trained in counterinsurgency methods and whose indiscriminate bombings further infuriated the civilian populations. Last, many Pakistani soldiers (especially Pashtuns) refused to fight their fellow citizens. Although the matter remains a closely guarded secret, reliable testimonials give account of mutinies leading to court-martials.[71] A number of officers preferred early retirement to fighting such a war.

The army finally preferred to negotiate with the Islamists. They found bargaining partners among the Wazirs, who saw the opportunity to finally settle an old score with their local rivals, the Mehsuds. The Wazirs and the Mehsuds, the two most important tribes of both Waziristans, are locked in age-old rivalry.[72] Due to their numbers (they made up two-thirds of the population at the time), the Mehsuds had received the lion's share of public funds under the British Raj. The privilege had continued after independence even though the demographic balance had shifted with the emigration of large numbers of Mehsuds, to Karachi for the most part—where their physical qualities often landed them jobs in the army and the police, but also in the construction business.[73] The state thus "bought" peace with the Wazirs in exchange for favours. The 2004 agreement was signed with Nek Muhammad in Shakai, South Waziristan. During the signing ceremony "he

---

(eds), *The Afghanistan-Pakistan Theater. Militant Islam, Security and Stability*, Washington D.C., FDD Press, 2010, p. 9.

[69] Imtiaz Gul, *The Most Dangerous Place*, op. cit., p. 24.

[70] Muhammad Amir Rana and Rohan Gunaratna, *Al-Qaeda Fights Back*, op. cit., p. 69.

[71] This fragmentary information was gleaned from interviews with former senior officials in the Pakistani administration in April 2012.

[72] Hassan Abbas, *The Taliban Revival*, op. cit., p. 107.

[73] I thank Mariam Abou Zahab for these details.

was publicly guarlanded by the 11th-Corps Commander, Lieutenant General Safdar Hussain. This event was heavily covered by Pakistan's media, helping Mohammad gain widespread legitimacy".[74] According to the terms of the agreement, in exchange for Nek Mohammad's commitment to refrain from attacking NATO troops in Afghanistan the Pakistani government released 163 prisoners, granted financial compensation to the victims of military operations and pledged to leave the foreign mujahideen alone as long as they registered with the administration. This particular clause was mainly intended for the Uzbeks, whose numbers and ferocity particularly irritated the government. Due to lack of compliance (the clause was indeed extremely naive), military operations resumed in June 2004. But they soon resulted in new rounds of talks, leading to another agreement signed in February 2005, this time by Baitullah Mehsud (see below) who had succeeded Nek Muhammed, killed in 2004, as head of what were soon to become known as the Pakistani Taliban.

The year 2004 marks the resurgence (or, in some places, emergence) of the Islamist guerrillas in South Waziristan, due partly to the way Al Qaeda had regrouped and started to recruit and train local volunteers thanks to its huge financial resources. But it was also due to the negative effect of the military operations mentioned above and the assassination of Nek Mohammad. Hassan Abbas points out that he immediately "became a hero in the eyes of the local populace; and although he was killed after he backed out of the deal, he created a new model of defiance for young radicals of the area. The recent history of FATA had witnessed many fighters, but hardly anyone had challenged Pakistan's military: in this sense Nek Mohammad had set a precedent".[75]

Nek Mohammad was not killed by the Pakistanis but by an American drone strike. In the mid-2000s, the United States began to grow impatient, even worrying about the Pakistan Army's propensity to negotiate truces that finally strengthened the Islamists in Pashtun areas. As a result, they decided to act alone, primarily via drone strikes which in fact the Pakistan Army had authorised. Aware that the Pakistan Army did not envision attacking them head on, the Islamists preferred two types of response: one taking the foreign route (as the increasing number of attacks in India attest), the other the political path (as shown by the creation of the MMA—with Musharraf's help in fact—which governed the NWFP from 2002 to 2007).

---

[74] C. Christine Fair, *Fight to the End*, op. cit., p. 246.
[75] Hassan Abbas, *The Taliban revival*, op. cit., p. 110.

The Islamist Response

Create Diversion

To begin with, jihadist movements would start carrying out spectacular attacks in India. On 1 October 2001, the Jammu and Kashmir assembly in Srinagar was the victim of a bombing that killed thirty-eight. No group claimed responsibility, but the technique used bore the signature of either Jaish-e-Mohammed or Lashkar-e-Taiba. A few weeks later, the 13 December attack in Delhi claimed fewer lives (fifteen in all), but had a far greater impact because its target was the parliament in New Delhi, which was infiltrated by five militants. They gained access to the premises using an official car armed with explosives and grenades as well as assault rifles while several ministers were debating in the assembly. Security services prevented the attackers from hitting the government members, no doubt their initial target, but the fact that fedayeen could stage such an operation proved to the stunned Indian population that they could strike at the very highest offices of the state. The Indian government accused Lashkar-e-Taiba, Jaish-e-Mohammed and the ISI of acting in concert.[76]

The attack in Srinagar prompted the Indian government to urge the Americans with even greater firmness than in the past to place Islamist groups active in Kashmir such as Lashkar-e-Taiba and Jaish-e-Mohammed on the State Department's list of foreign terrorist organisations compiled in the aftermath of 11 September. Till then, only Harkat-ul-Mujahideen had been blacklisted by the United States under its previous name, Harkat-ul Ansar, in 1997. The United States agreed to consider the demand, but still took its time. On 1 November, the Justice Department recommended that the State Department put Lashkar-e-Taiba and Jaish-e-Mohammed on the list of terrorist groups.

After the 13 December attack, New Delhi arraigned Islamabad before the world, criticising the Pakistani authorities for its involvement in the operation. The Indian government demanded the extradition of twenty terrorists, including Masood Azhar (leader of Jaish-e-Mohammed), Syed Salahuddin (head of Hezbul Mujahideen), and a number of their lieutenants, the perpetrators of the December 1999 plane hijacking, as well as gangsters New

---

[76] According to the authorities in New Delhi, the leader of the fedayeen was one of the hijackers of an Indian Airlines flight in December 1999. Pakistani involvement was confirmed, according to these same authorities, by the make of the explosives (Wah Nobel)—the detonator having been found on site.

Delhi claimed had been involved in attacks in Bombay in 1993, such as Dawood Ibrahim and Sikh separatists that Pakistan allegedly backed at the height of the struggle for Khalistan in the 1990s in Punjab. Islamabad replied that Pakistan's involvement in the 13 December attack had yet to be proven and that in any event none of the twenty people accused by New Delhi was in the country. This outright refusal prompted India to engage in a test of strength. India's Defence Minister, George Fernandes, announced an unprecedented troop deployment—even greater than in 1971—along the Pakistani border. On 26 December he also stated that Indian missiles were disposed in battle array. The following day India reported that mortar fire had killed twenty-three soldiers among the Pakistanis and that nineteen bunkers had been destroyed on the other side of the Line of Control. On 11 January, the Indian Chief of Army Staff, General Padmanabhan, declared there was "scope for a limited conventional war" with Pakistan if Islamabad did not abandon "terrorism as an instrument of state policy", remarks that were all the more noteworthy as the Indian military rarely speaks out in public, even less in such bellicose terms. It was in this extremely tense situation that the United States formally added Lashkar-e-Taiba and Jaish-e-Mohammed to the list of terrorist organisations. It now contained the names of five movements based in Pakistan, no other country being as "well" represented on this list of thirty-nine names.

In response, Pakistan amassed a considerable number of soldiers on its eastern border—probably more than 200,000. This was precisely the intended goal of the jihadist groups behind the 13 December attacks in Delhi. This deployment was to the detriment of what the Americans had requested in order to monitor the western border that victims of Operation Enduring Freedom fleeing Afghanistan were attempting to cross. The Islamists thus managed to trick the Pakistan Army by creating a diversion, enabling thousands of combatants to fall back on FATA and beyond. This tactic would be repeated in 2008 with the Mumbai attacks (see below).

Political Mobilisation

In the early 2000s the second Islamist reaction to Musharraf's gradual and selective turnaround against them was political. In the late 1990s, the Islamic parties were in total disarray.[77] The number of their members in the

---

[77] Amélie Blom, "Les partis islamistes à la recherche d'un second souffle", in Christophe Jaffrelot (ed.), *Le Pakistan, carrefour de tensions régionales*, op. cit., p. 99.

National Assembly had dropped from nine in 1993 to two in 1997 (both of them had been elected under the JUI label, the JI not even having the courage to field any candidates). In 2001, in the face of adversity, the Islamic parties joined forces in a way they never had before. In the wake of Operation Enduring Freedom, they first united within the Defence of Afghanistan Council, soon renamed the Defence of Afghanistan and Pakistan Council. The organization was founded in November 2001 by former ISI officials (such as Hamid Gul) and politicians (such as Sheikh Rasheed Ahmed) Islamist parties such as Maulana Samiul-Haq's JUI (S), the JI, the JUP and jihadist organisations like the LeT.[78]

In 2002, with the perspective of general elections coming into focus, the organisations that were already members of the Council, the JI, the JUI (this time Fazlur Rehman's faction—the JUI (F)) and the JUP formed the core of a broader coalition also bringing in Shia (the TJP) and Ahl-e-Hadith (the Jamiat Ahl-e-Hadith) political forces. The banding together of parties that had been on the wane in the 1990s only became possible due to Musharraf's efforts to engineer a rapprochement among rival organisations. He entrusted this operation to the ISI.[79] Musharraf helped the Islamic parties at the time of the 2002 elections by declaring *dini madaris* degrees as equivalent of a standard BA degree, the minimum requirement to contest.

What Musharraf stood to gain from such a rapprochement was far from obvious, given the direction the United States pressured him into taking in 2001. But Afrasiyab Khattak, the former chairman of the Pakistan's Human Rights Commission convincingly argues that Musharraf promoted the MMA because "Without the threat of religious extremism, the military would have lost its utility for western powers"[80]—which were supporting Pakistan financially in the framework of the Global War on Terror. Musharraf was also counting on the Islamic parties to act as a counterweight against his real enemies at the time: the PPP and the PML(N). The fact that the Islamic parties played along with Musharraf demonstrates the resilience of the relationship between the army and religious leaders in politics.

The Muttahida Majlis-e-Amal (MMA—United Action Committee), the coalition formed by these parties, performed remarkably at the polls, taking Musharraf by surprise. Even though the MMA only garnered 11.6 per cent

[78] See its official website: http://www.difaepakistan.com/about-us.html (Accessed on September 15, 2013).

[79] Zahid Hussain, *Frontline Pakistan*, op. cit., p. 175.

[80] Hassan Abbas, *The Taliban revival*, op. cit., p. 101.

of the vote, support for the coalition was so concentrated geographically that the percentage of votes cast—comparable to that won by the JUI/JUP and JI in 1970—handed it sixty-three seats in the National Assembly and enabled it to govern the NWFP and Balochistan as well, as part of a coalition. Musharraf, as noted in chapter 6, could count on the MMA to come to his aid in parliament. Fazlur Rehman was indeed a peculiar opposition leader, as shown by the passage of the Seventeenth Amendment authorising Musharraf to remain in uniform in 2004.

But the MMA's success in the NWFP enabled it to conduct an Islamisation policy that no party in Pakistan had ever before attempted and demonstrated just how radical it had become, even though this inclination was rooted more in anti-Americanism than in religion. In July 2005, the NWFP provincial assembly passed a Hisba ("accountability") law. This law prohibited dancing and music playing, and set up a watchdog body to ensure that the Muslims in the province adhered to prayers, did not engage in commerce during Friday prayers and that unrelated men and women did not appear in public together. According to the law, decisions made by the man in charge of this culture police, the *mohatasib* (litt. the one who holds others accountable)—reminiscent of the ministry of vice and virtue in the Taliban government in the years 1996–2001—could not be challenged by the courts. He also had the power to monitor the way the media dealt with Islam. The Supreme Court declared the law unconstitutional,[81] but the infringements on personal freedoms that it advocated reflected a worldview that was translated in everyday government practice by repeated hindrances to NGO activity, for instance, particularly when they worked to improve the condition of women.

Beyond that, the MMA put an end to co-educational schools in the NWFP and closed down a number of movie theatres. The chief minister, Akram Khan Durrani, had to let his beard grow—a practice that was strongly advised for men in the province.

The Rise of Extremes

While in the 2001–7 period Musharraf had broken off only with certain Islamist groups, primarily Al Qaeda, sectarian groups and the Pashtun movement to which the TSNM belonged, the years 2007–10 represented a watershed by which to gauge the force of Islamist groups.

---

[81] Ibid., p. 182.

Lal Masjid 2007: The Social Undercurrents of a "Religious" Crisis

In 2007, the Red Mosque (Lal Masjid) crisis not only hastened the divorce between Musharraf and the Islamists, but also highlighted the social dimension of the conflict between them.[82]

The Red Mosque in Islamabad dates practically to the construction of Pakistan's capital, as it was built in 1965. The following year, a Deobandi *alim*, Maulana Muhammad Abdullah, was made its head. The mosque subsequently played a major role in Zia's Islamisation strategy: it was a centre of anti-Shia propaganda and for promoting the anti-Soviet jihad in the 1980s. During the following decade, the Abdullah family maintained close ties with jihadists active in Indian Kashmir.[83] Members of the army and the ISI—its headquarters being located nearby—frequented the Lal Masjid, and conservative well-to-do families in Islamabad sent their children, especially their daughters, to its adjoining schools.

Following Muhammad Abdullah's mysterious and violent death, his two sons took over the *madrassah* attached to the mosque, Jamia Fareedia, Abdul Aziz, the elder, becoming the rector, and his younger brother, Ghazi, the deputy rector. This seminary, built in 1984 at the height of the Islamisation policy and the anti-Soviet jihad, had about 2,000 students enrolled in 2007. Its twin institution for women, Jamia Hafsa, run by Abdul Aziz's wife, was even larger, as it had 3,500 students. Both were affiliated with the federation of Deobandi *dini madaris* and operated in the sphere of Al Qaeda for which the Red Mosque Rouge had become a "powerhouse" according to Syed Saleem Shahzad.[84] In fact, a veteran of Bin Laden's movement, Sheikh Essa—a member of the Muslim Brotherhood who is said to have taken part in the assassination of Anwar Sadat and had spent years in Egyptian prisons for that reason before travelling to Afghanistan in 1986—attempted to rally Maulana Abdul Aziz to his cause.[85] He finally managed to do so in 2004, at which time Aziz issued a *fatwa* criticising the

---

[82] The following section draws on Amélie Blom's remarkable analysis, "Changing Religious Leadership in Contemporary Pakistan: The Case of the Red Mosque", in Marta Bolognani & Stephen M. Lyon (eds.), *Pakistan and Its Diaspora. Multidisciplinary Approaches*, New York: Palgrave Macmillan, 2011, pp. 135–168.

[83] The Red Mosque seems in particular to have supplied the Harakat-ul Mujahideen movement with young jihadists. Syed Saleem Shahzad, *Inside Al-Qaeda*, op. cit., p. 160.

[84] Ibid., p. 43.

[85] Ibid., p. 160.

anti-Islamic nature of the Pakistan Army for shooting at Muslims at the United States' request.

In January 2007, the city government of Islamabad informed eighty-four mosques and *dini madaris*, including Jamia Hafsa, that they had to implement Musharraf's reform of Quranic schools. The city authorities also had an illegal neighbouring mosque demolished. Jamia Hafsa put up resistance and marshalled its forces into cultural policing. Jamia Fareedia did the same. Students patrolled the city streets to force video and music stores to shut down and burned their wares in public. The students also fought against moral "degradation", vowing to close down all the city's brothels. A woman suspected of prostitution was kidnapped until she admitted publicly, wearing a *burqa*, that she ran a house of ill repute. In April, the Abdullah brothers set up a sharia court that began dealing with vice crimes, among others. This activity received considerable media publicity. In June, the movement came to a climax with the abduction of four police officers and Chinese citizens accused of prostitution.

Musharraf declared at that point that Al Qaeda militants were hiding out in the Red Mosque.[86] Transformed virtually into a fortified camp, the mosque was put under siege for a week, after which some 700 students surrendered.[87] But 400 diehards remained within and about one hundred were killed in the final assault, which ended in a bloodbath. This outcome is indicative of the extent of the divorce between Musharraf and some of the most important Islamist groups.

Beyond that, the episode is revealing of the social undercurrents of the conflict between the Pakistani establishment and the Islamists. The Abdullah brothers' discourse, in fact, was rooted in class struggle even before the crisis, and even more so as it unfolded, faithfully mirroring the

---

[86] Before reaching that point, Musharraf had called on one of Abdul Aziz's acquaintances, Ejaz-ul-Haq, who was minister of religious affairs and son of Zia-ul-Haq, who had visited Maulana Abdullah frequently. Then Musharraf resorted in vain to asking Abdul Aziz's mentor, Mufti Taqi Usmani, to intervene. He came from Karachi to speak to him, but in the face of his obstinacy repudiated him (yet another sign of the emancipation of the new mullahs from the authority of traditional *ulema*). In the end, Musharraf asked the leader of the banned Harakat-ul-Mujahideen, Maulana Fazlur Rehman Khalil, to mediate (ibid., p. 163).

[87] A "Lal Masjid Report" was completed in 2013 by a one-man commission of inquiry, Justice Shahzado Sheikh of the Federal Sharia Court, which was appointed by the Supreme Court in order to identify the causes of the tragedy and to establish responsibilities.

sociology of their madrassah: 80 per cent of Jamia Fareedia students came from small towns in the Pashtun area and all were of humble origin. As Amélie Blom writes, "These ill-integrated youngsters, often nicknamed *pindoos* (village bumpkins) by the locals, had initiated their own battle against Islamabad (literally "the abode of Islam"), perceived as a new Sodom".[88] In an interview with a western journalist, Ghazi acts as the spokesman of a revolutionary agenda:

> We don't care if Musharraf remains or not—we don't want to change the face, we want to change the system... The system has failed; it is not working. The same people keep coming from the same families to rule the country, and they exploit everyone in Pakistan. We want abolish this system; an Islamic system should be enforced. There comes a point when people stand up, when they rise up against the system.[89]

The entire movement falls within a repertoire of opposition to the establishment, even to Islamic party leaders perceived as having betrayed the cause of the Muslim people. When the mosque reopened on 27 July, demonstrators shouted at them: "Where were you when our sisters and mothers were brutally slaughtered? We won't let you offer your prayers here, go to London and do your political meetings!" The Abdullah brothers professed to be above politics in a quest for justice through sacrifice against all manner of dominators. Ghazi thus declared: "We want this system changed; it works only to the advantage of the elite; it has nothing for the common man. What we are doing, or hope to do, is simply to raise our voice against this system and the injustices it perpetrates and perpetuates". The fact that the Abdullah brothers had set up a sharia court illustrates this rationale in a country where the poor have virtually no access to the legal system.

Responses from the Pashtun Areas

In response to the events at the Red Mosque, the TNSM would regain the initiative in the Swat Valley, and Islamist leaders in FATA would found the Pakistani Taliban movement, the Tehrik-e-Taliban Pakistan (TTP). These two reactions are not at all disconnected but rather enmeshed, if only because TNSM is part of the TTP.

---

[88] Amélie Blom, "Changing Religious Leadership in Contemporary Pakistan", op. cit.

[89] Cited in Faisal Devji, "Red Mosque", in Shahzad Bashir and Robert D. Crews (eds), *Under the Drones*, op. cit., p. 157.

The TTP: An Islamist Confederation out to Conquer Power

Syed Saleem Shahzad points out that the Red Mosque incident was a turning point for Al Qaeda. When its "*shura* met in North Waziristan to discuss future strategy, it was agreed that the time had arrived when Pakistan's alliance with the United States was so cogent that sporadic, stand-alone tactics against it would not work (...) Osama bin Laden installed Abdul Hameed, aka Abu Obaida al-Misri, as the *imama-e-khuruj* (the leader of revolt) for Pakistan."[90] This revolt first took the form of intensified guerrilla warfare. On 2 September 2007, Baitullah Mehsud ambushed 247 Pakistanis, including several officers, and to add to their humiliation, which struck the entire country's imagination, they were forced to praise the rebellion over the BBC. Checkpoints were attacked by various means, including suicide bombings. In the space of three weeks, 65 soldiers had been killed or captured. The army then sent combat helicopters and fighter planes to Mir Ali (North Waziristan). The fighting, on an unprecedented scale, left 257 dead in four days (including 175 Islamists and 47 soldiers).[91]

These developments not only aggravated the Islamists, who did not wish to fight against the Pakistani authorities, but also and especially those most for whom the liberation of Afghanistan was a priority. This was especially the case for Afghan Taliban under Mullah Omar and Mullah Nazir, a former Hekmatyar lieutenant well established in South Waziristan who was worried about the influence of Uzbek combatants and their international agenda—including their targeting of the Pakistani state. Indeed, their leader, Tahir Yuldashev, had publicly declared war on Pakistan, making the fight against NATO a secondary objective. Tribal allegiance partly explained Nazir's attitude: a Wazir like Nek Mohammad, he was more inclined to negotiate with the state to gain advantages over which his clan had fought with the Mehsuds for decades. The Pakistan Army sought to bolster Nazir against Baitullah Mehsud, who was protecting the Uzbeks. Nazir has twice been the target of suicide attacks, both probably ordered by Baitullah Mehsud. Having escaped, he finally started his own Taliban movement once he had rid South Waziristan of the Uzbeks, who took shelter in North Waziristan in the spring of 2007.[92] It is in this context that Al

---

[90] Syed Saleem Shahzad, *Inside Al-Qaeda*, op. cit., pp. 46–47.

[91] Ibid., p. 49.

[92] Not all the Waziri leaders, however, were hostile to the Uzbeks. Haji Omar, who took over for Nek Mohammad, viewed them with favour. But he was in the minority and had to fall back on North Waziristan. In addition to Nazir, Khanan

Qaeda allegedly advocated the creation of a new movement, the Tehrik-e-Taliban Pakistan (TTP), to defuse two likely sources of tension: first, by forming this organisation—already on the cards[93]—Al Qaeda federated under Baitullah Mehsud's authority chiefs whose rivalry was likely to worsen; second, by creating a Pakistani Taliban movement, the organisation freed B. Mehsud and his partisans from the influence of Mullah Omar, who was nevertheless invited to give his blessing.[94]

Baitullah Mehsud, "a semi literate imam in a village mosque",[95] had joined the Haqqani network in the mid-1990s to fight in Afghanistan along the Taliban.[96] In 2004, Mullah Omar chose B. Mehsud to succeed Nek Mohammad as representative of the Taliban movement in South Waziristan with the basic mission of launching attacks on NATO forces in Afghanistan from FATA. Mehsud had followed the same strategy toward Islamabad as his predecessor, alternately negotiating with the Pakistan Army and breaking off talks. The agreement reached in 2004 stipulated that the Islamists would cease to attack Pakistani state officials and back foreign combatants, in exchange for which the Pakistani government pledged not to take action against Mehsud and his supporters for past acts. Mehsud violated this accord in August 2007 "in reaction to increased patrols by Pakistan's army" in South Waziristan".[97] A similar agreement had been made in North Waziristan in 2006 and broken in 2007.

The Red Mosque incident would alter B. Mehsud's priorities. He turned his weapons against the Pakistani state and to this end organised the TTP under the auspices of Al Qaeda. Its five-point program, as summarized by Hassan Abbas, read as follows:

Wazir was also against the Uzbeks. Imtiaz Gul, *The Most Dangerous Place*, op. cit., pp. 230–231.

[93] The start of the Pakistani Taliban movement seems to date from 2006. The movement is said to have been founded by Abdullah Mehsud, leader of the tribe by the same name in South Waziristan who while fighting alongside the Afghan Taliban was arrested in 2001 and detained in Guantanamo. But Abdullah was killed the same year and the TTP did not get off the ground until 2007 under the leadership of Baitullah Mehsud. Franco, Claudio, "The Tehrik-e-Taliban Pakistan", in Antonio Giustozzi (ed.), *Decoding the New Taliban: Insights from the Afghan Field*, London, Hurst, 2009.

[94] Syed Saleem Shahzad, *Inside Al-Qaeda*, op. cit., p. 55.

[95] Hassan Abbas, *The Taliban revival*, op. cit., p. 111.

[96] Vahid Brown and Don Rassler, *Fountainhead of Jihad*, op. cit., p. 108.

[97] Hassan Abbas, "An assessment", op. cit., p. 12.

- Enforce Islamic law;
- Unite against NATO forces in Afghanistan and wage a defensive Jihad against Pakistani forces;
- Abolish checkpoints in FATA and end military operations in Swat and North Waziristan;
- No more negotiations with the government on any future peace deals;
- Release Lal Masjid cleric Abdul Aziz.[98]

The organization was basically a federation bringing together Sunni militants such as Qadri Hussain Mehsud (representing the SSP in South Waziristan) and chiefs of various armed groups in FATA. According to Imtiaz Gul "The TTP [was] essentially a conglomerate of about two dozen commanders from various FATA areas; its central consultative forum is a large shura comprised of representatives from all seven tribal regions, with the chief commander from respective regions designated as deputy *emir*."[99]

Among these is Mulla Nazir Ahmed, who as noted previously had opposed Baitullah Mehsud on the matter of Uzbek combatants before signing up his Tehrik-e-Taliban (TT) with the TTP in 2009 in order to close ranks in reaction to the government crackdown. Another of Baitullah Mehsud's lieutenants was none other than Hafiz Gul Bahadur, the North Waziristan warlord who also had dissented—partly because of the old rivalry between Wazirs and Mehsuds, partly because the Pakistani army had wooed him, playing on this rivalry, partly because Wazirs resented the role of the Uzbeks in the TTP—but then fell back in line in 2009.[100] As for Kurram Agency—north of the northernmost part of Waziristan—its specificity (as mentioned above) lay in its strong Shia presence which prompted a particularly violent attack on the part of Qari Hussain Mehsud, the TTP representative in the area.[101] In the wake of the Red Mosque incident,

---

[98] Hassan Abbas, *The Taliban Revival*, op. cit., p. 152.
[99] Imtiaz Gul, *The Most Dangerous Place*, op. cit., p. 41.
[100] For a complete list of B. Mehsud's lieutenants by tribal area, see "Who is Who in the Pakistani Taliban: A Sampling of Insurgent Personalities in Seven Operational Zones in Pakistan's Federally Administered Tribal Area (FATA) and North Western Frontier Province", Naval Postgraduate School, available at: http://www.nps.edu/Programs/CCS/Docs/Pakistan/Pakistan_Taliban_Bios.pdf (Accessed on September 15, 2013).
[101] Mariam Abou Zahab, "Sectarianism in Pakistan's Kurram Tribal Agency", op. cit., and Imtiaz Ali, "Shiite-Sunni Strife Paralyzes Life in Pakistan's Kurram Tribal Agency", in Hassan Abbas (ed.), *Pakistan's Troubled Frontier*, Washington DC, The Jamestown Foundation, 2009.

havoc was wreaked throughout the region, the Shias being targeted by the TTP. Clashes not only prevented security forces from intervening, but also led to one of the largest population displacements since Partition. A truce was signed on 9 June 2008 following talks between Sunni and Shia leaders, but the TTP continued to block access to the Agency by closing off roads, and a low-intensity insurgency has taken hold in the area.[102]

Like other movements, such as the one led by Mangal Bagh, who persisted in his refusal to join B. Mehsud's organisation until 2013—the TTP made itself known for a certain ability to dispense swift (even expedient) justice, including to the detriment of the powerful. Once again this is the case of a movement of which the social dimension is at least as important as the religious aspect. This fact is further reinforced by the (class) struggle that TTP cadres and local tribal leaders, the *maliks*, engaged in and which the state seeks to use to fight against the Islamists. Whether they raise militias (*lashkar*) with the army's help or they act as informers, many of them would be targets for the TTP. For instance, in November 2008, a suicide attack decimated an assembly of elders, killing more than 20 in Bajaur. The previous month, in the same district, eight others had been beheaded to set an example.[103] Among the victims of this murderous campaign were also *maliks* who were current or former elected members of parliament, such as Malik Faridullah Khan in South Waziristan.[104]

Another point in common among the Taliban commanders in all Pashtun areas—including outside FATA, of course—is the targeted killing of ANP leaders. The TTP has reportedly killed a total of 500 members of this party in recent years, and issued threats to ANP members to quit the party if they wanted to remain safe and sound.[105] In Swat alone, 200 party workers were killed.[106] Relatives are sometimes prevented from attending

---

[102] "Conflict in Kurram", *The Express Tribune*, 18 July 2011. See http://tribune.com. pk/story/212285/conflict-in-kurram/ (Accessed on September 15, 2013).

[103] Imtiaz Gul, *The Most Dangerous Place*, op. cit., p. 86.

[104] Baitullah Mehsud also had rivals executed that the Pakistan Army was seeking to organise within his own tribe and camp, such as Qari Zainuddin. See Chris Harnisch, "Qadri Zaiuddin Mehsud Assassination and Biography", *Critical Threats*, 24 June 2009—http://www.criticalthreats.org/pakistan/qari-zainuddin-mehsud-assassination-and-biography) (Accessed on September 15, 2013).

[105] Javed Mahmood, "TTP warns ANP workers to quit party", *Central Asia Online*, 26 July 2012. Available at: http://centralasiaonline.com/en_GB/articles/caii/features/pakistan/main/2012/07/26/feature-01?mobile=true (Accessed on September 15, 2013).

[106] Javed Aziz Khan, "ANP leadership remains on hit list of terrorists", *The News*

the funeral of their loved ones due to measures of intimidation.[107] This atmosphere has prompted survivors to flee to Peshawar or Karachi, and even Dubai.

Among the victims was the son of ANP leader Mian Iftikhar Hussain in 2010 and veteran party member Bashir Bilour.[108]

Escalation and Alienation

In addition to unleashing terror in the FATA, the TTP increased attacks outside the area to punish Islamabad for its actions (particularly the raid on the Red Mosque) or to dissuade it from undertaking others. In September 2007, B. Mehsud claimed an incredibly bold attack near Pakistan Army headquarters in Rawalpindi (25 dead, including a colonel). A few months later he was accused of perpetrating the attack that cost Benazir Bhutto her life.[109] However, most of the attacks fomented by the TTP have taken place in the neighbouring province of the NWFP.[110] A suicide bombing for instance took a dozen lives and left about one hundred injured in a mosque frequented by the military in Nowshera (Dera Ismail Khan district) in June 2009.[111]

Kayani, the COAS, finally concluded that "[Beitullah Mehsud] has a hand in virtually every terrorist attack in Pakistan."[112] In fact, the Pakistani authorities attributed to him the death of 1,200 individuals—including Benazir Bhutto, which he has always denied.[113] Capturing him thus became a priority. He was finally killed in a drone strike on 5 August 2009. But it

---

International, 18 January 2010. See http://www.khyberwatch.com/forums/showthread.php?8151-ANP-leadership-remains-on-hit-list-of-terrorists&s=260 3898ade057c68e87b8d2a4a3cbea7 (Accessed on September 15, 2013).

[107] Imtiaz Gul, *The Most Dangerous Place,* op. cit., p. 120.

[108] His brother Ghulam Ahmad Bilour, another senior ANP leader, escaped the same fate after he campaigned against a film that the Taliban considered hostile to Islam. "Ghulam Ahmad Bilour", *Dawn,* 1 May 2013.

[109] Omar Waraich and Saeed Shah, "Pakistani army hit as suicide bombers kill 25", *The Independent,* 4 Sept. 2007.

[110] Claudio Franco, "The Tehrik-e-Taliban Pakistan", op. cit, p. 283.

[111] See http://alertpak.wordpress.com/2009/06/15/friday-prayers-in-nowshera-hit-by-blast/

[112] Ismail Khan, "Mehsuds Watch Bid to Isolate Baitullah from Fence," *Dawn News Online,* 16 June 2009. Available at: http://beta.dawn.com/news/471750/mehsuds-watch-bid-to-isolate-baitullah-from-the-fence (Accessed on September 15, 2013).

[113] Declan Walsh, "Pakistani Army Ordered to Find 'Root of All Evil' Taleban Chief," *The Guardian,* 16 June 2009, International Section.

wasn't long before he was replaced by Hakimullah Mehsud, age 29, a TTP commander who until then operated in Orakzai Agency—"the birthplace of the Pakistani Taliban"[114] where Shias were evicted from the best land and obliged to pay *jizya*, a tax levied on non-Muslims in the Mughal Empire. He had opened a new front in 2008 by trying to block NATO supply lines. Khyber Pass in fact sustained so many attacks that for a time the Pakistan Army was unable to ensure security there.

The escalation of violence under the aegis of the TTP in the second half of the last decade is evident from the data collected by the Pakistan Institute for Peace Studies (PIPS). This institute has inventoried 254 violent episodes (leaving 216 dead) in 2005, 675 in 2006 and 1,503 (a 129 per cent increase) in 2007, the year the Red Mosque was stormed, in which the death toll rose to 3,348. In 2008, the overall figure again rose by 43 per cent with 2,610 violent incidents claiming a record number of lives: 8,297. The worst was yet to come: in 2009, there were 3,816 acts of violence all forms combined, killing nearly twice as many: 12,632.

Of all the types of violence inventoried by PIPS, what the Institute qualifies as "terrorist" is by far the most frequent. This catchall category warrants closer examination to understand better what it holds. The PIPS did the breakdown only for 2008 and 2009, shown in table 10.4.

Table 10.3 below helps to gauge the variety in the modes action used by armed groups, which are mainly Islamist. The range was expanded, as we have seen, by contacts between Pashtun tribes and Al Qaeda experts in the field. The introduction of suicide bombings, heretofore unheard of in the area, is evidence of this.[115] Imtiaz Gul provides similar figures, with the added advantage of describing a longer statistical series: in 2006, he listed 6 suicide attacks, in 2007, 56, in 2008, 613and in 2009, 87.[116] The 63 suicide attacks in 2008 caused 967 deaths, nearly one-third of all victims of terrorism.[117]

The geographic distribution of the violence shows a concentration of Islamist groups in Pashtun areas, these being the most affected, year after year, whether it is the NWFP (now Khyber–Pakhtunkhwa) or FATA.

---

[114] Mariam Abou Zahab, "Pashtun and Punjabi Taliban: The Jihadi-Sectarian Nexus", op. cit, p. 379.

[115] It was not until 19 December 2009 that a substantial number of clerics, as request by the ministry of religious affairs, gathered their courage to criticize suicide bombings as being contrary to Islam.

[116] Imtiaz Gul, *The Most Dangerous Place*, op. cit., p. 129.

[117] *Pakistan Security Report 2008*, Islamabad, Pak Institute for Peace Studies, 2008, p. 3.

Table 10.3.: Forms of Political Violence in Pakistan from 2008 to 2013

Nature of Attacks	2008			2009			2010			2011			2012			2013		
	No.	Killed	Injured	No.	Killed	Injured	No.	Killed	Injured	No.	Killed	Injured	No.	Killed	Injured	No.	Killed	Injured
Terrorist attacks	2,148	2,267	4,558	2,586	3,021	7,334	2,113	2,913	5,824	1,966	2,391	4,389	1 577	2 050	3 822	1,717	2,451	5,438
Operational attacks	–	3,182	2267	596	6,329	3,181	260	2,631	1,495	144	1,046	384	109	960	469	90	673	252
Clashes between security forces/militants	95	655	557	209	1,163	780	369	2,007	877	301	1,668	642	115	705	490	105	515	263
(Ethno)political violence	88	162	419	130	210	370	233	660	966	265	698	532	183	288	182	224	283	223
Sectarian and/or inter-tribal clashes	191	1,336	1,662	217	1,209	787	214	766	685	150	486	430	213	100	156	28	75	243
Border clashes	55	395	207	78	700	363	69	65	53	84	261	206	79	326	227	103	59	165
Drone attacks	33	300					135	961	383	75	557	153	45	336	67	31	204	37
Total	2,610	8,297	9,670	3,816	12,632	12,815	3,393	10,003	10,283	2,985	7,107	6,736	2,321	4,765	5,413	2,555*	4,725*	6,932*

* These totals are superior to the sum of the figure above because PIPS, in the course of time has started to take into account new crimes (including abduction and inter-militant clashes) which are not taken into consideration in this table.

Sources: Pakistan Security Report for 2008, 2009, 2010, 2011, 2012 and 2013, Islamabad, PIPS (accessible at www.san-pips.com).

Table 10.4: Forms of Terrorist Violence in 2008 and 2009

Tactic	Number of Incidents in 2008 and 2009	
Suicide attacks	63	87
Rocket attacks	381	422
Beheadings	46	49
Remote-controlled bombs	112	189
Kidnappings	116	174
Landmines	110	111
Shootings	451	568
Sabotage/Fire	116	89
Improvised explosive devices (IEDs)	373	355
Targeted killings	26	82
Bomb blasts	298	341
Hand grenades	82	219
Total	2,174	2,586

Source: *Pakistan Security Report 2009*, Islamabad, Pak Institute for Peace Studies, 2009, p. 5.

New operational methods alone, such as suicide bombings and anti-personnel mines, do not explain the scale of the violence. It also stems from the growing sophistication of materials used. During the military operation carried out in Bajaur in 2009, the army found evidence of the use of Stella and Milan missiles, which had destroyed two tanks.[118] Such weapons cost millions of dollars. In 2008, NWFP governor Owais Ahmed Ghani estimated that Baitullah Mehsud spent 2.5–3 billion rupees (31–37 million dollars) annually in procuring weapons and vehicles, paying wages for his troops and helping the families of those killed.[119] But suicide bombing itself is costly. Brigadier Abu Bakr Amin Bajwa, who contributed to the military operation that took place in South Waziristan in 2009 came to the conclusion that it "takes about three months to prepare a suicide bomber" and that the total expenditure on preparing him was Rs 450,000—"out of which Rs 150,000 was paid to the family of the bomber and the remaining Rs 300,000 (…) on other miscellaneous expenditures, including the traners' fee".[120]

---

[118] Imtiaz Gul, *The Most Dangerous Place*, op. cit., p. 187.

[119] Iqbal Khattak, "Mehsud spending up to Rs 3bn on militancy annually: Ghani", *Daily Times*, 30 May 2008. Available at: http://www.dailytimes.com.pk/default. asp?page=2008%5C05%5C30%5Cstory_30-5-2008_pg7_6 (Accessed on September 15, 2013).

[120] Brigadier Abu Bakr Amin Bajwa, *Inside Waziristan, Journey from War to Peace—*

Table: 10.5: Geographic Location of Terrorist Attacks

Year	2008			2009			2010			2011			2012			2013		
Province/Area	Frequency	Killed	Injured	Frequency	Killed	Injured	Frequency	Killed	Injured	Frequency	Killed	Injured	Frequency	Killed	Injured	Frequency	Killed	Injured
FATA	385	619	392	559	1046	644	1433	904	720	675	612	1190	388	631	1 032	499	706	1,745
NWFP/K-P	1009	982	1735	3616	1439	1137	1832	836	459	512	820	1684	456	401	1 081	293	425	932
Punjab	35	219	621	1342	420	46	897	309	62	30	116	378	17	75	1 095	38	47	142
Balochistan	692	296	807	1070	386	792	1117	600	737	640	710	853	474	631	1 032	487	727	1,577
Sindh (excluding Karachi)	n.a.	n.a.	n.a.	7	3	6	30	5	18	21	5	32	28	17	45	34	31	123
Karachi	n.a.	n.a.	n.a.	155	65	24	436	233	93	58	115	224	187	272	352	356	492	908
Gilgit Baltistan	n.a.	n.a.	n.a.	19	13	5	16	7	13	26	9	24	26	22	33	5	16	5
Azad Kashmir	4	3	10	93	17	5	28	4	5	0	0	0	0	0	0	1	2	1
Islamabad	9	119	n.a.	72	30	10	35	15	6	4	4	4	1	1	0	4	5	5
Total	2,134	2,237	3,556	6,933	3,419	2,669	5,824	2,913	2,113	1,966	2,391	4,389	1 577	2 050	3 822	1,717	2,451	5,438

Sources: *Pakistan Security Report* for 2008, 2009, 2010, 2011, 2012 and 2013, Islamabad, PIPS (accessible at www.san-pips.com).

The first source of TTP funding is naturally narcotics, as Afghanistan supplies 95 per cent of the world's opium. But added to that are donations from Saudi Arabia and the Gulf countries, timber smuggling, ransom from kidnappings, government allocation of funds earmarked for development (whether or not from abroad) in the framework of various negotiations (including those leading to the release of soldiers captured by the TTP).[121]

Not only have the Pashtun areas been the hardest hit by terrorist violence; they are also where the Islamists have conquered territory and subjected the population to a new Taliban-like regime. These developments have not only had a lasting effect in FATA, as discussed above, but also in a more unstable manner in the districts of Swat and Buner where the TNSM has made significant inroads.

The "fighting mullah", which the population viewed as dispensers of justice and Robin Hood figures, gradually alienated Pashtun society, which was not only antagonised by the presence of foreigners (Arabs, Uzbeks, etc.) but suffered from the Taliban's oppressive rigorism and extortion. Even Mangal Bagh, who did not join the TTP until 2013, adhered to the Taliban's puritan agenda to the point of forming a culture police aiming to "promote virtue and prevent vice".[122] The author of a portrait of Mangal Bagh adds:

Bagh considers himself justified in adopting a coercive attitude towards the enforcement of sharia. He orders men to don religious caps and women to wear shuttlecock burqas, the black veil that envelops the entire female form in a heavy covering, leaving barely discernible outlets for the eyes. It is the prevalent form of women's garb in FATA under Bagh.

In the second week of June 2005, Lashkar-e-Islam forced markets to close down, announced formation of an Islamic government, banned interest banking, and warned of strict punishment for infractions. It was reportedly announced that a murderer would pay a fine equivalent to roughly $6,000; the fine for having a dish antenna was $600; and failure to pray five times a day would cost $6. No woman was to be allowed in market areas without one of her blood relatives. CD shops were closed down. Music of any kind is not tolerated. Television is ordained by Bagh's illegal FM radio transmissions as un-Islamic. Beards are to be grown compulsorily. Shopkeepers in Bara pay a monthly fee to Lashkar-e-Islam that they used

---

Insight into the Taliban Movement and an Account of Protecting People from Terrorists, Lahore, Vanguard, 2013, p. 49.

[121] Ibid., p. 51.

[122] Cited in Iqbal Khattak, "Mehsud spending up to Rs 3bn on militancy annually: Ghani", op. cit..

to give to a bazaar committee for security in the large markets; Bagh claims to fill that role Bagh has set up Qazi courts for the dispensation of justice. The people come to him for ready and speedily granted justice, unfortunately a rare commodity in the area. Yet, amputation of hands as a punishment of theft is being practiced, and there have been reports of beheadings.[123]

The TTP was worse still, especially because it made a speciality of demolishing schools, but not only that: like many insurrectionist movements, it has lived off the country. When Brigadier Abu Bakr Amin Bajwa, who was posted in South Waziristan in 2009, "tried to find out the reasons why the youngsters join the ranks of the Taliban", he came to the conclusion that on one hand "Maliks/notables send one of their children for their own protection as he would act as an informer for them" and that on the other hand, "poor and unemployed youngsters, who do not have anything to earn for their livelihood, join them, as free food and better lifestyle along with authority is a quite attractive bargain for them".[124] The importance of these material factors partly explains the criminalisation of the TTP which extorted money from the locals in many different ways. Mangal Bagh—who had quickly dilapidated his image of a Robin Hood—indulged in this criminalisation process, too.[125] While abduction for ransom targeted mostly the rich, other forms of taxation by the Taliban affected more ordinary citizens. As Hassan Abbas points out "The crimes, of course, damaged their public standing, but the TTP had no plans to contest an election any time soon...".[126] The transformation of the modus operandi—and the image—of the Taliban was especially obvious after the TNSM's conquest of the Swat and Bajaur Valleys in 2008.

The TNSM Conquest of the Swat Valley, Bajaur—and Buner

Since its exploits in the 1990s, the TNSM pursued its career with the blessing of all political parties which, with the approaching 2002 elections, had attempted to share the popularity that its feats in the name of Islam had

---

[123] Syed Manzar Abbas Zaidi, "A profile of Mangal Bagh", *The Long War Journal*, Nov. 2008. See http://www.longwarjournal.org/multimedia/Mangal-Bagh-Profile.pdf (Accessed on September 15, 2013).

[124] Brigadier Abu Bakr Amin Bajwa, *Inside Waziristan*, op. cit., p. 47.

[125] Michael Fredholm, "Kashmir, Afghanistan, India and beyond. A taxonomy of Islamic extremism and terrorism in Pakistan", *Himalayan and Central Asian Studies*, vol. 15, no. 3, July–September 2011, p. 52.

[126] Hassan Abbas, *The Taliban Revival*, op. cit., p. 153.

brought it, particularly in the Swat Valley. But the TNSM only threw its backing behind Islamic parties affiliated with the MMA—which returned the favour. The rescue operations undertaken by movement in the wake of the 2005 earthquake further polished its image. But the situation was already changing with the rise of Fazlullah in 2005 and what Muhammad Feyyaz call the "second phase" of the movement. By 2006, the TNSM—which, by then, was sometimes called Tehrik-i-Taliban Swat (TTS)—"began to use every possible means to generate money, procure weapons and ammunitions and pay salaries to what was now a much larger network".[127] Indeed, by then, "Besides TNSM militants, many other elements also joined the TTS fold; these included gangs of car-lifters, the timber mafia, farmers who had disputes with Khans, loan defaulters, smugglers and many other criminal elements".[128]

In 2007, after the storming of the Red Mosque, the TNSM struck an alliance with the TTP and launched a new offensive. In late October, 4,500 TNSM combatants took control of some sixty villages in the Swat Valley which they subjected to cultural policing operations and expedient sharia courts. The army's response—a deployment of 25,000 men—forced the TNSM to enter into negotiations in which Sufi Mohammad participated—while leaving the leadership in charge of his son-in-law. The ceasefire agreement stipulated that sharia would now be the source of law.

The TNSM went back on the offensive in 2008. Its troops took control of the valley in an unspeakable wave of violence: in January 2009, there were 1,200 civilians killed, 170 schools destroyed and a vice squad along with its sharia courts went into operation: girls were prevented from attending school (their schools were the first to be demolished), women were no longer to appear in public, men had to grow beards. As a result, 500,000 of the some 1.7 million inhabitants fled the valley toward the south.[129] A local resident, Zubar Torwali, points out that the Tablighi Jamaat "was

---

[127] Muhammad Feyyaz, "The Political Economy of Tehrik-i-Taliban Swat", op. cit., p. 49.

[128] Ibid., p. 48.

[129] Shaheen Buneri, "Pakistan falters against Taliban in Swat Valley", *World Politics Review*, 26 January 2009. See http://www.worldpoliticsreview.com/articles/3207/pakistan-falters-against-taliban-in-swat-valley (Accessed on September 15, 2013). According to another estimate, 1 million people fled from Swat, 183 schools were "blown up" and 80,000 girls were deprived from access to education (K. Warikoo, "Religious extremism and terrorism in Pakistan and its implications", *Himalayan and Central Asian Studies*, vol. 15, no. 3, July–September 2011, p. 8).

behind the Swat Taliban gaining many young men as supporters" during their conquest.[130]

Shahzad explains the extreme violence of this conquest by the backstage role played by Al-Qaeda. Its leaders had sent one of their Pakistani recruits, Bin Yameen, a veteran from Afghanistan reported to have spent seven years in the Northern Alliance's jails and who had joined Jaish-e-Mohammed. In the wake of attempts on Musharraf's life in 2003, he was arrested in his home in Peshawar in 2004 and held in ISI custody for two and a half years, where he was subject to extensive physical and mental torture.[131] Once released, he was summoned by Al Qaeda to North Waziristan:

Bin Yameen was given money and Uzbek and Arab fighters to set up his own *maaskar* (training camp). His first task was essentially simple. He was to hijack the Tehrik-e-Nifaz-e-Shariat-e-Mohammadi (TNSM) founded by Maulana Sufi Mohammad, after whose detention it was controlled by Fazlullah.[132]

Qari Hussain Mehsud joined Bin Yameen in this operation. The two men had taken control of the TNSM in early 2008 and carried out the violence described above as well as other heinous acts such as the murder of a Barelwi leader, Pir Samiullah, whom the government had armed and charged with raising a militia. In late 2008, the Swat Valley was virtually under the complete control of TTP representatives.

The ISI then decided to release Sufi Muhammad to hammer out a ceasefire agreement with him. In February 2009, the government (dominated by the ANP Pashtun nationalists since 2008) and the militants agreed to a truce according to which sharia became law in Malakand Division (to which the Swat Valley belonged) in exchange for an end to the violence. But Bin Yameen was instructed to break the agreement and reopen the front in Swat at a time when Pakistani troops were about to conduct an offensive in South Waziristan. In April the TNSM thus violated the agreement it had only just signed, on the pretence that the government did not allow the TNSM to appoint the judges of sharia courts. The ISI again turned to Sufi Mohammad who had become hostage to the TTP to the point of no longer answering his

[130] Zubar Torwali, "My life in Swat—under the Taliban", *The Express Tribune*, 23 September 2013 (http://tribune.com.pk/story/608149/my-life-in-swat-under-the-taliban/).
[131] Syed Saleem Shahzad, *Inside Al Qaeda*, op. cit., p. 168.
[132] Ibid., p. 169.

telephone and reading a speech written for him in which he in particular demanded that all judges withdraw and be replaced by Islamic courts.[133]

The movement then further extended its control over the Swat Valley to the districts of Lower Dir, Shangla and especially Buner, about 65 miles (100 km) from Islamabad. Apart from its usual methods, of which women and girls were the principal victims, they stepped up punitive executions, hanging their opponents from trees and at traffic circles as an example. This campaign caused nearly 4.5 million people to flee[134] and prompted the army to launch an assault. This military action was apparently due to the fact that, while "Pakistanis remained opposed to the army undertaking offensives against Pakistan's own militants" until April 2009, "public opinion dramatically changed course after the Taliban reneged on the sharia-for-peace deal and overran Buner".[135] The military operation officially left 168 dead and 454 injured among security forces between 27 April and 30 June 2009, but 1,635 Islamists were killed and only 254 injured and taken prisoner, an indication of the operation's brutality.[136] The army had deployed 150,000 troops and used attack helicopters and fighter planes to crush their resistance.[137] The scale of the damage prevented many refugees from returning to their devastated towns and villages. Pakistan was experiencing for the first time a civil war some 100 miles (130 km) from its capital, without managing to break the back of the TNSM, as Fazlullah found sanctuary in Afghanistan, and more precisely in the Kunar and Nuristan areas from where he conducted raids inside Pakistan.[138]

*

The Islamists combating the establishment that have been analysed in this chapter, whether they are the Abdullah brothers of the Red Mosque or Pashtun leaders of the TTP (Nek Muhammad, Baitullah and Hakimullah Mehsud) or the TNSM (Sufi Muhammad and Fazlullah), are all representative of a new charismatic figure Amélie Blom portrays as the "fighting mullah". Certainly, as she clearly states, militarization of the religious in certain areas such as the Pashtun belt dates back to the colonial era when

---

[133] Ibid., p. 174.

[134] Noor ul Haq (ed.), *The Operation Rah-eRast*, Islamabad, IPRI, 2009. See http://www.ipripak.org/factfiles/ff111.pdf (Accessed on September 15, 2013).

[135] C. Christine Fair, *Fighting to the End*, op. cit., p. 248.

[136] Noor ul Haq (ed.), *The Operation Rah-eRast*, op. cit., pp. 154–157.

[137] Ibid., p. 24.

[138] Hassan Abbas, *The Taliban revival*, op. cit., p. 207.

mullahs took up arms to resist the British. But their combat aimed only to protect their territory from outside influence, especially in terms of moral behaviour. Today, the "fighting mullahs" carry a message of revolution that they promote effectively owing to a new sense of organisation: "to the qualities of a fighting jihadi, the modern 'fighting mullahs' add the skill of a 'tribal entrepreneur', raising funds by welcoming 'guests', that is foreign militants, and who also mobilize a younger generation, belonging to poor and marginalized strata or to minor tribal clans, motivated by challenging the traditional patterns of domination".[139]

Mariam Abou Zahab has shown in detail that in South Waziristan the process of Talibanisation has resulted from social conflicts. It enabled local *mullahs* with a plebeian background to dislodge the *maliks*—either because of their charisma, or by eliminating them physically.[140] On the other hand, competition between Taliban groups is overdetermined by tribal rivalries not only between the Mehsuds and the Wazirs but also, within tribal groups, between *kashars* (the underprivileged youth of dominated lineages) and *mashars* (the elders of the traditionally dominant clans).[141] This approach highlights a class element usually neglected by other analysts—but that has been systematically traced throughout this entire book.

The social underpinnings of Islamism are what lend the phenomenon its strength today. Pakistan was created by an elite anxious to preserve its status first by eluding the influence of the Hindu majority in India, and later that of the masses in Pakistan. The civil-military establishment ruled supreme for 60 years—from 1947 to 2007—by crushing or betraying social movements and preventing the development of civil society. Today civil society really only exists at the local level through Islamic networks, the Dini Madaris being the most visible aspect. Since 11 September 2001, due to American pressure, these networks—which owed their expansion in the 1980s–90s to army sponsorship—are privileged targets. Their counteroffensive thus feeds as much on defence of Islam as on mass resentment in the name of justice.

In FATA this conflict has led to an outright insurgency. In Islamabad, the Red Mosque episode demonstrated the striking power that a "fighting mul-

---

[139] Amélie Blom, "Changing Religious Leadership in Contemporary Pakistan: The Case of the Red Mosque", op. cit.

[140] See the section called "Jihad as a Means of Social Empowerment" in Mariam Abou Zahab, "Kashars against Mashars. Jihad and Social Change in the FATA", in Benjamin D. Hopkins and Magnus Marsden (eds), *Beyond Swat*, op. cit., p. 59.

[141] Ibid., p. 52.

lah" could mobilise (*ghazi* is moreover the title given to those who, unlike martyrs, return from the jihad). In Punjab, the conflict is much lower in intensity, but the rise of sectarian groups has placed the state on the defensive in a new perspective.

The Army: Accomplice and/or Out of Its Depth?

The question raised by the situation evoked above naturally pertains to the army's role. Its low-key action till the end of the 2000s suggests that it did not throw all its energy into battle, and when it did, it was under pressure from the United States. The state of affairs is of such intricate complexity that the topic requires highly nuanced treatment.

Islamist Sympathies—within the Army, and among Civilians

The infiltration of the Pakistani army by Islamists or officers' sympathies vis-à-vis Islamists are obviously not very well documented. The only conspiracy associating army officers and Islamists that has been publicly acknowledged was the one that targeted Benazir Bhutto in 1995. The "plan was radical, it included the murder of PM Benazir Bhutto, Army Chief Waheed Kakar and some generals, the goal was the establishment of a Pakistan-Afghan caliphate".[142] One of the Islamists involved, Qari Saifullah Akhtar, was a key figure of the Pakistani Jihadi nebula, but on the army side, the highest-ranking officer involved was Major General Zaheer ul-Islam Abbasi, who, as a brigadier, had been the ISI-based military attaché in New Delhi. After the plot was discovered, Abbasi and his accomplices were arrested and condemned by a military court to several years of detention. But they were prematurely released after Musharraf took over in 1999. Qari himself spent only five months in jail in 1995 and probably retained some of his ISI contacts, as mentioned above. In her posthumously published book, Benazir Bhutto maintained that he was involved in the attempt on her life in Karachi in October 2007. After she was killed, the Musharraf regime had no other choice but to detain him. However, he was free again after three months in June 2008, not only because the ISI still "kept faith" in him, according to Owen Bennett-Jones, but because he was also protected by politicians. Indeed, the man "formally responsible for his release, the Punjab Home Minister, Rana Sanaullah, told reporters in Lahore that Akhtar 'can-

---

[142] Hein Kiessling, *Faith, Unity, Discipline: the ISI of Pakistan,* op. cit.

not be termed terrorist'".[143] The role of Sanaullah, whose affinities with Sunni sectarian groups will be studied below, suggests that army men and (ex-)ISI officers are not the only ones who collaborate with Islamists. Such a conclusion could already be drawn from the support of a civilian government to the Afghan Taliban in 1994 since "the dubious honour of being their midwife and godfather goes to PM Benazir Bhutto, her husband Asif Zardari and her Minister of Interior Naseerullah Babar".[144]

In fact, civilians, ex-officers and Islamists sometimes form an explicit alliance. The Defense of Pakistan Council is a case in point since the organization founded in November 2001 was relaunched ten years later in November 2011 in reaction to the killing of twenty-four Pakistani soldiers by a NATO aircraft in Salala near the Durand Line. This Council chaired by Maulana Samiul-Haq, the JUI (S) leader, includes former ISI officials (such as Hamid Gul) and politicians (such as Sheikh Rasheed), leaders of Islamic parties such as the JI and the JUP as well as jihadists (including leaders of the Jama'at-ud Dawa, the new name of the LeT).

The presence of members of the Tablighi Jamaat at the top of the military hierarchy has been another sign of infiltrations of the army by Islamist ideas. But, again, civilians were partly responsible for their rise to power. In 1992, for instance, Nawaz Sharif, after becoming Prime Minister for the first time appointed "a born again" Tablighi as DG ISI, Javed Nasir—the Pakistani army's first bearded general.[145] The same man became a security advisor to Sharif in 1997 when he returned to power. The religious inclination of Nasir was well in tune with Sharif's plans of amending the Pakistani Constitution in order to make the sharia the highest law in the country—a change that would have transformed him into the *Amir-ul Monimeen*, the leader of the faithful.[146] Indeed, the bill—passed by a two-thirds majority in the National Assembly in October 1998—"empowered the Prime Minister to enforce what he thought was right and to prohibit what he considered was wrong in Islam and Shariah, irrespective of what the Constitution or any judgement of the court said".[147] But this amendment was never passed

---

[143] Owen Bennett-Jones, "Questions concerning the murder of Benazir Bhutto", *London Review of Books*, vol. 34, no. 23, 6 December 2012, (http://www.lrb.co.uk/v34/n23/owen-bennett-jones/questions-concerning-the-murder-of-benazir-bhutto).

[144] Hein Kiessling, *Faith, Unity, Discipline: the ISI of Pakistan*, op. cit.

[145] Ibid., p. 51.

[146] Ibid., p. 70.

[147] M. Ziauddin, "Nawaz Sharif's Shariat bill", *The Express Tribune*, 5 March 2013 (http://tribune.com.pk/story/516152/nawaz-sharifs-shariat-bill/).

by the Senate—because of opposition from the MQM among others—and the episode exposes the Islamic tendencies of some civilians as much as those of some military officers.

Military officers have also occasionally expressed ideological sympathies for Islamists in their individual capacity. Hamid Gul is a case in point. Even after he ceased to be DG ISI, in the early 1990s, while he had been transferred to the post of Corps Commander in Multan, he "continued to enjoy a high reputation among the Afghan mujahideen leaders. Many of them came to Multan and reported on the situation in the neighbouring country. Additionally, numerous Pakistani politicians sought his advice: for many of them Gul was still a powerful and influential man".[148] This is an interesting case because after retiring from the army, Gul continued to support Islamic causes. He travelled to Bosnia and "assisted in the training in the HuM camps" and another former DG ISI, Durrani, while he was Ambassador in Germany "coordinated, from Bonn, young Muslims from the Ummah for the Bosnia assignment".[149]

Another DG ISI, Mahmood Ahmed, showed sympathies for the Islamists ten years after Gul, not only for ideological reasons, but also because of religious affinities. Ahmed had been appointed DG ISI by Musharraf immediately after the 1999 coup (to which he had contributed). He then became a "born again Muslim" and actively criticized army officers who "were not good Muslims".[150] After 9/11, the profile of Ahmed became very problematic. He was sent by Musharraf to Mullah Omar to ask the Taliban chief to extradite Bin Laden, as demanded by the US. But in his discussion with Omar, he "advised against it",[151] and Musharraf had to send him into retirement.

Other individual trajectories suggest that soldiers' sympathies for the Islamists—and more precisely for Jaish-e-Mohammad and Lashkar-e-Taiba[152]—might have become more widespread after 9/11. The story of

---

[148] Hein Kiessling, *Faith, Unity, Discipline: the ISI of Pakistan*, op. cit.

[149] Ibid., p. 62.

[150] Ibid., p. 91.

[151] Ibid., p. 92.

[152] The relative porosity between the ISI and the LeT was candidly admitted by David Coleman Headley (formerly Daood Gilani) during his trial for his involvement in the 2008 Mumbai attack. The son of a Pakistani diplomat and an American woman (with whom he lived in the US as a young man) Headley had begun his adult life as as drug smuggler (and an informant of the Drug Enforcement Administration) before joining the LeT in the early 2000s—whose leaders asked him to adopt his mother's name. When he was arrested with one of his colleagues, they were "brought to a man named Major Ali. They told him

Captain Khurram revealed by Syed Saleem Shahzad is a case in point. Unlike Hamid Gul or other former officers, he was not a personality who publicly defended the Islamist cause but a sort of double agent clandestinely providing his experience of soldiering to jihadist groups. Captain Khurram was assault commander of a unit in the Pakistan Army's Special Service Group (SSG), an elite commando, when the 11 September 2001 attacks occurred. In an email message to Shahzad he recounts that as a consequence of the event, he was "struck by the Jihadi waves and joined Lashkar-e-Taiba in Kashmir."[153] His elder brother, Major Haroon, who had taken part in the Kargil operation in 1999, did likewise after taking early retirement.[154] This decision may be partly explained by their family's Salafist loyalties and their Kashmiri origins, but the American offensive in the fall of 2001 in Afghanistan was the real catalyst for this turn to jihadism. As in the case of Mohsin Hamid's "reluctant fundamentalist",[155] the promotion of Islam as religion is here a less determining factor in the choice of a career in the jihad than defending a country, albeit a Muslim one. Another major, Abdul Rahman, joined the two brothers. But they were disappointed in the LeT, according to Khurram, due to "the extreme hypocrisy, luxuries, and evils of these so called mujahideen leaders."[156] Khurram

---

that they were working for Laskar, and explained Headley's US passport and recent name-change. Major Ali was 'very pleased', and asked Headley if he would mind working for the ISI as well. Headley told him that he would not mind" (Liz Mermin, "The art of the deal", *The Caravan*, July 2011, p. 33). It seemed that Headley had two ISI handlers, including Sajid Mir, an LeT cadre who had gone to the same high school as himself (a clear indication of their common, elitist social background) and a mysterious Major Iqbal, possibly one of the persons "associated" with the ISI who had been "associated" with the Mumbai attack according to General Ahmed Shuja Pasha, the then DG ISI, in the late 2000s. Speaking to American officials in Washington, Pasha made clear that such an association was "different from authority, direction and control" (Bob Woodward, *Obama's Wars*, New York, Simon & Schuster, 2010, pp. 46–47).

[153] Syed Saleem Shahzad, *Inside Al-Qaeda*, op. cit., p. 82.

[154] Headley, during his trial, mentioned a man with a similar trajectory, "a former major who had left the Pakistani army because he refused to fight against the Taliban" and who joined the LeT (Liz Mermin, "The art of the deal", op. cit., p. 33).

[155] The title of another work of fiction truer than reality. Mohsin Hamid, *The Reluctant Fundamentalist*, Boston/New York, A Mariner Book, Houghton Mifflin Harcourt, 2008.

[156] Cited in Syed Saleem Shahzad, *Inside Al-Qaeda*, op. cit. p. 83.

and Rahman thus joined the jihad in Afghanistan where Khurram would die "as a martyr" in 2007.

After his brother's death, Major Haroon reactivated his contacts within the LeT better to serve the jihadist cause. He journeyed frequently to North Waziristan, using his military past to impress the LeT and to mix with his former comrades. Shahzad thus reports that during his travels, "When night fell, he stayed in army messes in the countryside. Being an ex-army officer he was allowed this facility. He always kept his army revolver on him with lots of bullets in case he was obstructed at any checkpoint, but his imposing bearing and unmistakable military accent in both English and Urdu always prevented this from happening."[157] By mixing with the military, Major Haroon was better able to spy on the army than anyone else. This is how he reached the conviction that some Pakistani military were about to give in to American pressure to the point of lastingly damaging national sovereignty. He thus concocted a plan "to make a horrible example of them to deter others from joining the United States". He set his sights on a retired officer, an easier though no less appropriate target: Rtd. Major General Ameer Faisal Alvi had commanded SSG operations in Angoor Ada in October 2003, during an operation that targeted Bin Laden himself. The operation did not achieve its goal but eight Al Qaeda cadres were killed (including Abdur Rehman Khadar, a Canadian-born Egyptian, and Hassan Maksum, a Uighur considered by the Chinese to be a "top terrorist").[158] Major Haroon murdered Alvi with his army revolver on 19 November 2008, thus showing officers still serving—he hoped—that one day they would also retire and could very well suffer the same fate. Ilyas Kashmiri was allegedly behind this crime and paid Haroon 150,000 rupees to carry it out.[159]

Major Haroon then went back to his former LeT comrades, especially commander Abu Hamza, to suggest a plan that the ISI had conceived but was in the process of discarding: an attack on symbolic locations in Mumbai. Major Rahman was involved, as he had often visited Mumbai and had brought back photographs of the targets in question. Hamza presented the plan to Zakiur Rahman Lakhvi, who approved it. It is probably around

---

[157] Ibid., p. 92.

[158] "Al Qaeda suspect identified", available online at: http://www.theage.com.au/articles/2004/01/25/1074965420892.html (Accessed on September 15, 2013).

[159] This suspicion emerged belatedly. See Amir Mir, "Who killed Gen. Alvi?" *The News*, 20 November 2008. Available at: http://www.thenews.com.pk/Todays PrintDetail.aspx?ID=18472&Cat=13&dt=11/20/2008 (Accessed on September 15, 2013).

that time that Headley was sent to Mumbai "to conduct surveillance".[160] What followed were the 26 November 2008 attacks, by which their master-minds intended to provoke a war between India and Pakistan, thereby shifting the priority for military operations away from the Pashtun areas— such as after the December 2001 attack on the Indian Parliament. India did not go to war but mustered thousands of soldiers at the Pakistani border, forcing Islamabad to withdraw troops from the western front, giving the Islamist groups there new room to manoeuvre.

The Aggiornamento of the Pakistani Military?

Although the story of Major Haroon and his army confederates (including his brother) suggests that some officers are influenced by Islamist sympa-thies,[161] the case of his victim, Alvi, indicates that many soldiers were prepared to combat Islamism—after they realised what was at stake in purely pragmatic terms. Indeed, the main reason why the Pakistani army supported Islamists had little to do with ideology: the jihadists were sup-posed to help Pakistaan "to bleed India" and to give the country some "strategic depth" in Afghanistan. When the price to pay for these worldly objectives became too expensive, Rawalpindi started to change tack.

The Pakistan Army gradually began to selectively crack down in the tribal areas, engaging its troops under growing pressure from the United States, which applied with the carrot and stick approach. On one hand, US intelligence services were well enough established in the area to denounce ISI cooperation with the Islamists.[162] On the other, the carrot involved increasingly convincing financial arguments. American aid had in fact

---

[160] Liz Mermin, "The art of the deal", op. cit., p. 34.

[161] On this whole question, see C. Christine Fair, "Has the Pakistan Army Islamized? What the Data Suggest", Mortara Center for International Studies, Edmund A. Walsh School of Foreign Service, Georgetown University, *Working Paper*, 2011–13, 7 September 2011. In the mid-1990s, four officers, including two colo-nels, had devised plans to dislodge Benazir Bhutto from power and declare Pakistan a "Sunni state". While the conspiracy is evidence of the popularity of Islamist ideas among certain mid-ranking officers, a legacy of the Zia years, it was a contained and isolated case.

[162] As Imtiaz Gul writes, "While old contacts with organizations such as Hezbul Mujahideen, Harakatul Mujahideen, and Lashkar-e-Taiba may be intact, the microscopic surveillance by the CIA and FBI, through an elaborate chain of contacts, restricts the ISI from conducting business the way it did until 2004". (Imtiaz Gul, *The Most Dangerous Place*, op. cit., p. 171).

reached unprecedented heights in the mid-2000s, the main component being security-related (see table 10.6):

The Pakistan Army was all the more sensitive to the financial argument used by the Americans as this windfall finally enabled it to procure military equipment that could rival with India's.[163]

General Musharraf's strategy changed course in the mid-2000s. He purged the ISI, no longer settling for replacing overtly visible chiefs at the top, but also going further down the hierarchy. Colonel Imam thus fell out of favour.[164] Musharraf gradually learned lessons from operations carried out in the tribal areas. The Kazha Punga offensive had clearly demonstrated the need to strengthen the Special Services Group (SSG), the elite commando with which Musharraf himself had trained. Musharraf thus created the SSG Special Operations Task Force (SOTF) and required the head of the SSG to be a two-star general. In August 2003, Major General Amir Faisal Alvi, whose tragic end was related above, was appointed to this post. A few months later, on 2 October 2003, he conducted the operation in Angoor Ada mentioned above. Alvi had been eager to improve his organization's cooperation with Western security forces (particularly British special forces).[165] But Alvi had to face opposition within the army, which allegedly forced him into early retirement in 2005. He was murdered three years later.

After Musharraf was replaced as COAS by former ISI head General Kayani (one of the last senior Pakistani officers to have been partly trained in the United States in the 1960s), the Pakistan Army proved more determined in its fight against Islamism—up to a point. Major Haroon was arrested in February 2009 and six months later—though there is not necessarily a relationship of cause and effect—Interior Minister Malik Rehman stated on television, "officers of the rank of major in the intelligence agencies with links with the Taliban and Al Qaeda had been arrested because they wanted to target army generals."[166] The army stepped up operations

---

[163] For further detail see Christophe Jaffrelot, "La relation Pakistan-Etats-Unis: un patron et son client au bord de la rupture?" *Les Etudes du CERI*, no. 187, September 2012.

[164] Imtiaz Gul, *The Most Dangerous Place*, op. cit., p. 175. Colonel Imam was kidnapped in March 2010 by the Pakistani Taliban while travelling for the umpteenth time in the tribal area and his murder was made public in a video (also showing Hakimullah Mehsud) in February 2011. Carey Schofield, *Inside the Pakistan Army*, London, Biteback Publishing, 2011, p. 67.

[165] Ibid., p. 189.

[166] "Second Editorial: Ilyas Kashmiri's death", *Daily Times*, 18 September 2009. See

Table 10.6.: American Aid to Pakistan (2002–2013), in millions of dollars

Accounts	2002	2003	2004	2005	2006	2007	2008	2009	2010	2011	2012	2013
Security-related disbursement totals	1,346	1,505	818	1,313	1,260	1,127	1,536	1,674	2,735	2,395	1,537	1,195
Non-security related totals	654	274	296	388	539	576	507	1,366	1,769	1,277	1,067	353
(% of total)	32.7	15.4	26.6	22.8	30	33.8	24.8	44,9	39,2	35,6	40,9	22,8
Total	2,000	1,779	1,114	1,701	1,800	1,703	2,043	3,040	4,504	3,581	2,604	1,548

Source: Adapted from K. Alan Kronstadt, Pakistan-U.S. Relations, op. cit., p. 94 and K. Alan Kronstadt, "Direct Overt U.S. Aid and Military Reimbursements to Pakistan, FY2002–FY2015", (http://www.fas.org/sgp/crs/row/pakaid.pdf)

in the Pashtun areas. 211 of them reportedly took place from 2007 to 2010, involving 150,000 of its 550,000 soldiers. Losses were heavy, estimated at around 2,300, including three generals, five brigadiers and seventy-three intelligence agents.[167] Operations in Swat and Bajaur Valleys alone cost the lives of 400 soldiers.[168]

Some of the territory that had been lost was won back through this engagement. The army regained a footing in Kurram Agency, for instance. There are probably several explanations for this change in strategy. First, the army became aware of the challenge the entire Islamist sphere (including what it heretofore considered as "good Islamists") posed to its authority and Pakistan's territorial integrity.[169] Second, public opinion had evolved, as much in FATA—where the Islamists' Robin Hood image had been seriously tarnished by the oppressive and violent methods mentioned above— as in the rest of the country, particularly after the bloody "conquest" of the Swat Valley: the army now had backing for its military operations against groups no longer perceived as mujahideen out to liberate Afghanistan as was often the case before, but as aggressors challenging a lifestyle and culture associated with modernity and national identity respectively.

While the Swat operation prepared the ground for larger deployments of troops, the Pakistani army has not intervened in the FATA in an equally decisive manner. It has constantly been reluctant to do so, despite American pressure, not only because this area is where the Haqqani network is located, but also because of the substantial consequences such an attack would entail. First, the Pakistan Army is afraid of sustaining unbearable losses, or even of failing in its mission. Second, it fears threats of suicide attacks in retaliation.

---

http://www.dailytimes.com.pk/default.asp?page=2009\09\18\story_18-9-2009_pg3_1 (Accessed on September 15, 2013).

167 Imtiaz Gul, *The Most Dangerous Place*, op. cit., p. 213.

168 Ibid., p. 127.

169 Ibid., p. 215. This is the conclusion some analysts have drawn from the inclusion of a new chapter on "non conventional war" in the 2013 edition of the famous "green book" spelling out the military doctrine of the Pakistani army. See http://beta.dawn.com/news/775781/pakistan-army-sees-internal-threats-as-greatest-security-risk and http://tribune.com.pk/story/488362/new-doctrine-army-identifies-homegrownmilitancy-as-biggest-threat/. (Accessed on September 15, 2013). But it does not mean that Indian is not the priority target of the Pakistani army any more ("Pakistan Army to Preempt India's "Cold Start Doctrine"", *The Express Tribune*, 16 June 2013. See http://tribune.com.pk/story/564136/pakistan-army-topreempt-indias-cold-start-doctrine (Accessed on September 15, 2013).

Such is the conclusion reached by observers of the series of attacks in 2009 that aimed to dissuade the army from carrying out the operation it had planned in South Waziristan. The upsurge in terrorist violence had gone as far as Punjab, even reaching the summits of military leadership, as we will see in the following section, indicating the Islamists striking power. As long as the violence was concentrated on the other side of the Indus River, the country's nerve centres from Lahore to Islamabad as well as public opinion showed little concern.[170]

In 2009, however, the army did launch an operation in South Waziristan, Operation Rah-e-Nijat. 30,000 troops were deployed against 15,000 combatants, including 1,500 foreign fighters (two thirds of them Uzbeks). By the end of the year the army had regained its control over South Waziristan and killed, officially, 500 Taliban and 200 Uzbeks.[171] One of the military officers who implemented it, Brigadier Abu Bakr Amin Bajwa, reported that the army seized "tons of ammunition", including anti-aircraft ammunition of 12.7 mm and 14.5 mm and anti-aircraft guns as well as rocket launchers.[172] But he admitted that few terrorists were caught or killed: they were "on the run", either in Afghanistan or in North Waziristan—the heart of the matter in the FATA.

The Pakistani Army and Drones

As a result of the shortcomings of such operations and the casualties (direct or collateral) they entailed, the army preferred to refrain from deploying ground troops beyond a certain point and partly left the matter in American hands without specifically saying so. It was in this context that the United States decided to use massive drone strikes, a technique Brigadier Abu Bakr Amin Bajwa approved of with some qualifications:

Drone flights definitely do cause a scare amongst the Taliban and locals alike, and keep the fence sitters away from the Taliban, ths further isolating them. In view of the numerous issues related to Pakistan's sovereignty and territorial integrity, it would be more prudent if this technology is given to Pakistan by our war ally, the USA, and we engage targets ourselves in our own territory.[173]

[170] I am grateful to Mariam Abou Zahab for this insight.

[171] Hein Kiessling, *Faith, Unity, Discipline: the ISI of Pakistan*, op. cit.

[172] Brigadier Abu Bakr Amin Bajwa, *Inside Waziristan. Journey from war to peace— Insight into the Taliban movement and an account of protecing people from terrorists*, Lahore, Vanguard, 2013, p. 126.

[173] Ibid., 115.

The Pakistani authorities have cultivated ambiguity with regard to drones. While the army could not officially approve a flagrant violation of the country's sovereignty, it was unofficially happy, it seems, to leave what it deemed a worthwhile job—at least in part—to others. Till 2010, the "drones were deployed in Pakistani territory, the ISI provided the coordinates of the target and the CIA deployed the drones".[174] Hassan Abbas points out that "drone strikes were regularly coordinated with the Pakistani military authorities until 2010, and during the early phase (2004–7) even 5–7 days' notice was given by either side for the other to monitor the target and mutually decide whether to go for it or not. Within military units operating in the tribal area, drone attacks were generally seen in a positive light".[175] In a diplomatic cable made public by Wikileaks in May 2009, the American ambassador to Pakistan, Anne Patterson, told the State Department that the United States had "created Intelligence Fusion cells with embedded US Special Forces with both SSG and Frontier Corps (Bala Hisar, Peshawar) with the Rover equipment ready to deploy. Through these embeds, we are assisting the Pakistanis collect and coordinate existing intelligence assets."[176] This information was in particular intended to localise Islamist leaders that would later be the aim of targeted killings. In another cable in September 2009, Ambassador Patterson indicated, "Pakistan has begun to accept intelligence, surveillance, and reconnaissance support from the US military for COIN [counterinsurrection] operations". "Intelligence fusion centers" had also been set up "at the headquarters of Frontier Corps and 11th Corps". The purpose of intelligence sharing was, among other things, to plan targeted drone strikes wanted by the Pakistanis. Another cable made public by Wikileaks indicated that already in January 2008 Kayani had asked the United States for drone coverage in South Waziristan where his troops were carrying out operations. According to Alan Kronstadt, a specialist on South Asia at the Congressional Research Service, in April 2008, three Predator drones were said to be "deployed at a secret Pakistani airbase and can be operated by

---

[174] Hein Kiessling, *Faith, Unity, Discipline: the ISI of Pakistan*, op. cit.

[175] Hassan Abbas, *The Taliban revival*, op. cit., p. 160.

[176] Hasan Zaidi, "Army Chief Wanted more Drone Support", 20 May 2011. See http://x.dawn.com/2011/05/20/army-chief-wanted-more-drone-support/ (Accessed on September 15, 2013). See also "Government official urged follow-up drone strikes", *Dawn*, 20 May 2011. See http://www.dawn.com/2011/05/20/government-official-urged-follow-up-drone-strikes.html.

the U.S. Central Intelligence Agency without specific permission from the Islamabad government."[177]

The New American Foundation estimates that the number of drone strikes went from 9 in the 2004–7 period to 33 in 2008, 52 in 2009, 122 in 2010, and then fell to 73 in 2011, 48 in 2012 and 27 in 2013. The number of casualties tallied was 94 in 2006, 63 in 2007, 298 in 2008, 549 in 2009, 849 in 2010, 517 in 2011, 306 in 2012 and 153 in 2013. According to the Foundation's analysis, posted on its website in October 2014, the 379 strikes reported in the press in northwest Pakistan since 2004 killed between 2,141 and 3,510 persons, among whom anywhere from 1,684 to 2,869 were described as militant Islamists in reliable press reports (the main source of the Foundation) and from 457 to 641 either civilians or "unknown".[178] In 2013 the real fatality rate of non-militants (innocent collateral victims) since 2004 was thus probably about one-fifth but techniques have improved and therefore it is thought to be closer to 9 per cent today (if the figures regarding the "civilians" and the "unknown" are bracketed together).[179] Since 2010, attacks have concentrated on North Waziristan where Islamists have gathered in the wake of operations against South Waziristan. The number of strikes in this area rose from 22 in 2009 to 104 in 2010.[180] Other sources present different data, such as the London-based Bureau of Investigative Journalism, which said in February 2015 that only 714 people out of the 2,426 to 3,926 persons killed by the 410 drone attacks in Pakistan from 2004 to February 2015 have been identified.[181]

This technique in combating Islamists has been criticised for many reasons. First because decimating the movement leadership deprives the Pakistani state of possible interlocutors for negotiation. Second, by causing collateral (and other) victims, it nurtures terrorist inclinations among those who have lost a family member or a friend.[182] Third, it has affected the sovereignty of the Pakistani state.

---

[177] K. Alan Kronstadt, *Pakistan-U.S. Relations*, op. cit., p. 22.

[178] http://securitydata.newamerica.net/drones/pakistan/analysis (Accessed on October 6, 2014).

[179] Peter Bergen and Katherine Tiedeman, "The Year of the Drone", New American Foundation. Counterterrorism Strategy Initiative. See http://counterterrorism.newamerica.net/drones. (Accessed 10 August 2013).

[180] Eric Schmitt, "Pakistan's failure to hit militant sanctuary has positive side for the US", *The New York Times*, 17 January 2011.

[181] http://www.thebureauinvestigates.com/namingthedead/?lang=en (Accessed on 10 October 2014).

[182] Hassan Abbas, *The Taliban revival*, op. cit., p. 202.

The North Waziristan operation: from talks to Zarb-e-Azb, a paradigmatic shift?

In 2013, drone attacks became a major issue in the context of the election campaign. Imran Khan, as mentioned above, tried to mobilise the voters against these strikes by arguing that they violated the country's sovereignty. After his party, the PTI, came second in the general elections and formed a ruling coalition with the JI in KP, he exhorted the new prime minister, Nawaz Sharif, to initiate talks with the Taliban. He still maintained, in March 2014, that the TTP wanted only "to get out of America's war", and not to impose the sharia by force.[183] The PTI was not the only party following this line. On 9 September 2013, an All Parties Conference called upon Nawaz Sharif "to initiate the dialogue with all stake holders forthwith and for this purpose, authorize it to take all necessary steps as it may deem fit, including development of an appropriate mechanism and identification of interlocutors".[184] Nawaz Sharif himself was keen to promote peace, not only because it would help him to relaunch the economy, but also because it would improve his popularity, especially if resulting in an emancipation of Pakistan from American influence. He made a gesture in this direction by releasing Mullah Abdul Ghani Baradar, the Afghan Taliban's second in command, in October 2013—in response to an old demand of Hamid Karzai who considered that the reconciliation process that Kabul tried to promote implied the liberation of some of the Taliban leaders from the Pakistani jails.

To identify the right interlocutors was not an easy task—as the failure of the talks initiated soon before by the US in Doha with Afghan Taliban had just shown. But the Sharif government could exploit the rift among the TTP. Here, the killing of organisation leader, Hakimullah Mehsud, by a drone on 1 November 2013 was a blessing in disguise. This strike took place one day before a peace delegation was to travel to North Waziristan—where Mehsud had been killed—to initiate talks.[185] All kinds of party lead-

---

[183] Saqib Nasir, "TTP only want to get out of US war, not impose sharia by force: Imran Khan", *The Express Tribune*, 27 March 2014 (http://tribune.com.pk/story/687926/ttp-only-want-to-get-out-of-us-war-not-impose-sharia-by-force-imran-khan/).

[184] "Resolution of the All Parties Conference on Sept 9, 2013", *Dawn*, 9 Sept. 2013 (http://www.dawn.com/news/1041675).

[185] Ismail Sheikh, "Drone strike US atempt to sabotage peace process with Taliban, decry politicians", *The Express Tribune*, 1 November 2013 (http://tribune.com.pk/story/625919/drone-strike-us-attempt-to-sabotage-peace-process-with-taliban-shireen-mazari/).

ers accused the US of sabotaging the negotiations. The Interior Minister, Chaudhry Nisar Khan called this targeted killing "murder of peace".[186] But the death of H. Mehsud somewhat destabilised the TTP. While Khan Said Sajna, a South Waziristan-based Taliban leader, was supposed to take over from him, eventually Fazlullah prevailed. For the first time, a man from neither South Waziristan nor North Waziristan was at the helm of the Pakistani Taliban.

Two Wazir leaders, Maulvi Nazir Ahmed Nazir and Hafiz Gul Bahadur—respectively from South and North Waziristan—had already distanced themselves from the TTP. In 2006, Gul Bahadur had signed a peace accord with the government. That had been short-lived, but he had maintained "good relations with the Pakistan ISI",[187] his main interlocutor. Bahadur and Nazir "loved the regular 'honorarium' and the occasional armaments they received from the ISI for their services; and they shared a special distate for Uzbek and other foreign militants who were enjoying sanctuary in North Waziristan",[188] as mentioned above. While Wazir had traditionally been easier to engage for the Pakistan state, the Mehsuds started to be less problematic after the rivalry between Sajna, a Mehsud leader, and Fazlullah intensified—and resulted finally in the former leaving the TTP.[189] Mariam Abou Zahab points out that "Mehsud militants who were dominant in the organizational structure and policy-making of the TTP could not accept Fazlullah as the emir and the majority of them chose Khan Said (alias Sajna) as their leader".[190]

While the southern front of the FATA seemed safer, the Sharif government, in March 2014, initiated talks with the TTP via teams of negotiators. The government committee consisted of former ambassador Rustam Shah Mohmand, Additional Chief Secretary Fata Arbab Arif, Secretary Ports and

---

[186] "Peace talks: Nisar terms Friday's drone strike 'murder of peace'", *The Express Tribune*, 2 November 2013, (http://tribune.com.pk/story/626216/peace-talks-nisar-terms-firdays-drone-strike-murder-of-peace/).

[187] Hassan Abbas, *The Taliban revival*, op. cit., p. 114.

[188] Ibid., p. 155.

[189] Ismail Khan, "With militants in disarray, is it time for action?", *Dawn*, 11 June 2014 (http://www.dawn.com/news/1111958) and Zulfiqar Ali, "After the split: TTP faction says ready to negotiate with government", *The Express Tribune*, 2 June 2014 (http://tribune.com.pk/story/716370/after-the-split-ttp-faction-says-ready-to-negotiate-with-government/).

[190] Mariam Abou Zahab, "Turmoil in the Frontier", in Christophe Jaffrelot (ed.), *Pakistan at the Crossroads. Domestic Dynamics and External Pressures*, New York, Columbia University Press, (forthcoming).

Shipping Habibullah Khattak and Additional Secretary to the Prime Minister, Fawad Hasan Fawad and former ISI official, Rtd. Major Mohammad Amir. The TTP representatives included Maulana Samiul Haq, the leader of the JUI (S),[191] Prof. Ibrahim, a Jama'at-e-Islami leader and JUI (S) spokeperson Maulana Yousuf Shah. In February, the TTP *shura* (headed by Fazlullah) had finalised a 15-point list of demands that included the introduction of sharia law courts, Islamisation of the education system and the replacement of the democratic system of governance by an Islamic one.[192] The government negotiators made clear that the talks would have to take place within the parameters of the Constitution. On 13 March 2014, the second group went to North Waziristan to report to the TTP *shura* which reasserted its stand. This dialogue of the deaf went on for weeks, nobody wanting to break off talks or be accused of being responsible for such a break.

However, the situation deteriorated in the field and the army became more and mote impatient. In September 2013, Kayani had declared: "While it is understandable to give peace a chance through a political process, no one should have any misgivings that we would let terrorists coerce us into accepting their terms".[193] Kayani was most reluctant to accept TTP's demands regarding the withdrawal of the army from the FATA and the liberation of Taliban prisoners. His successor, Raheel Sharif, an expert in counterinsurgency who took over in December 2013, was even more determined.

The negotiations derailed after the TTP multiplied operations which suggested that either they were not interested in peace talks or that some of

---

[191] There are many indications of the proximity between the JUI (S) and the TTP. One of the party's former MNA, Shah Abdul Aziz, who had defeated Imran Khan in the 2002 elections from Karak district and who had been arrested because of his alleged involvement in the murder case of a Polish engineer declared to the police that he belonged to the TTP and that Baitullah Mehsud, the former TTP chief, was a martyr on TV after being released on bail in late 2009 (https://lubpak.com/archives/1394). In June 2009, Aziz had been arrested while allegedly "carrying a letter of Baitullah Mehsud addressing to a former high profile ISI general, known for his strong pro-Taliban views..." (Rauf Klasra, "Karak-ex MNA carrying Baitullah letter", *The News*, 28 June 2009 (http://www.khyberwatch.com/forums/showthread.php?7215-Karak-ex-MNA-arrested-carrying-Baitullah-Letter)).

[192] Zahir Shah Sherazi, "TTP finalises 15 point draft for talks", *Dawn*, 10 February 2014 (http://www.dawn.com/news/1085920).

[193] Kamran Yousaf, "Quest for peace: Fitting rejoinder to Taliban dictates", *The Express Tribune*, 17 September 2013 (http://tribune.com.pk/story/605353/quest-for-peace-fitting-rejoinder-to-taliban-dictates/).

their faction leaders wanted to sabotage them. In September 2013, the killing of Maj. Gen. Sanaullah, the General Officer Commanding for Malakand Division and Lt. Col. Tauseef Ahmed, while they were traveling near the Afghan border in Upper Dir district was a shock for the army. Then, in January 2014, twenty security personnel were killed and thirty others injured when an explosion targeted a convoy near Razmak Gate in Bannu (K-P). One month later, Omar Khalid Khorasani, the leader of the TTP in Mohamand Agency (who broke from the TTP to create his own organisation around the same time) announced the beheading of twenty-three troops he had kidnapped two years before.[194] Still more importantly, in June, twelve people were killed in the assault on Jinnah International Airport in Karachi after four to five terrorists managed to reach the runway, heavily armed (one of them had a 7 mm rifle and a rocket-propelled grenade), a clear indication of accomplices within the airport.[195] The TTP claimed responsibility for all these attacks.

In this context, the army intensified its strikes. In January 2014, Pakistan Air Force jets and helicopters multiplied the bombing of suspected hideouts in North Waziristan (and, to a lesser extent, in the Khyber and Orakzai agencies). According to press reports, dozens of militants were killed, including Uzbeks.[196] In March 2014, Interior Minister Chaudhry Nisar Khan took pains to clarify that the army was only conducting "precision strikes"[197] and Nawaz

---

[194] Bil Roggio, "Taliban splinter group Jamaat-ul-Ahrar forms in northwestern Pakistan", *The Long War Journal*, 26 August 2014 (http://www.longwarjournal.org/archives/2014/08/taliban_splinter_gro.php).

[195] Faraz Khan, Saad Hasan and Sohail Khattak, "Terror in Karachi: airport under siege", *The Express Tribune*, 9 June 2014 (http://tribune.com.pk/story/719307/terror-in-karachi-airport-under-siege/).

[196] Kamran Yousaf, "North Waziristan: TTP shura leader, master trainer killed in air strike, say officials", *The Express Tribune*, 23 January 2014 (http://tribune.com.pk/story/662242/north-waziristan-ttp-shura-leader-master-trainer-killed-in-air-strikes-say-officials/), "Military offensive: Over 50 militants killed in Waziristan, Khyber air blitzes", *The Express Tribune*, 22 January 2014 (http://tribune.com.pk/story/661806/military-offensive-over-50-militants-killed-in-waziristan-khyber–air-blitzes/), "40 militant killed in North Waziristan aerial bombing", *The Express Tribune*, 20 February, 2014, "Helicopter shelling kills six militants in Hangu", *Dawn*, 22 February 2014 (http://www.juancole.com/news/the-dawn/2014/02/helicopter-shelling-militants), "Bombing in North Waziristan leaves 60 dead", *The Express Tribune*, 21 May 2014 (http://tribune.com.pk/story/711140/bombing-in-north-waziristan-leaves-30-militants-dead/).

[197] Khanwar Ghumman, "Targeted strikes under way, not operation: Nisar", *Dawn*, 1 March 2014 (http://www.dawn.com/news/1090229).

Sharif reaffirmed that his government was serious about peace talks when he met a delegation of the All Pakistan Ulema Council,[198] but the fate of the peace negotiations was sealed even before the attack of the Karachi airport, which convinced the government to give them up and allowed the military to unleash the North Waziristan operation that it had already prepared.

The Pakistani army had been under pressure from the US to deploy troops in North Waziristan for years. It apparently decided to launch such deployment in early 2014 and had to wait for the civilians to exhaust the possibility of peace talks before implementing its plans. The chronology of events suggests that this operation was the brain child of the new COAS, Raheel Sharif, who had taken over in late 2013. Immediately after it began, former DG IPSR Maj. Gen. Athar Abbas and former Prime Minister Gilani in fact declared separately that Kayani had been responsible for postponing any military operation in North Waziristan.[199] Hinting at a paradigmatic shift, Muhammad Ali Ehsan pointed out that Musharraf and Kayani "believed in the 'sacred doctrine of strategic depth' that possibly was the reason that tied their hands behind their backs as the army continued fighting a 'stalemated war' that was being characterised more by 'firefighting acts' than any military actions of substance. General Raheel Sharif, from the outset, vouched to respond to every terrorist act with a military action".[200]

The North Waziristan operation that officially began on 15 June 2014 was given the name of Zarb-e-Azb (the name of the sword that Prophet Mohammad used in the battles of Badr ad Uhud). It was massive, primarily because of the huge number of internally displaced persons (IDPs) that it generated. By the first week of July, 800,000 people had left their homes and

[198] "Govt serious about peace talks, Nawaz tells Ulema Council", *The Express Tribune*, 13 March 2014 (http://tribune.com.pk/story/682340/govt-serious-about-peace-talks-nawaz-tells-ulema-council/).

[199] The former DG Inter-Services Public Relations, Maj. Gen. (Rtd.) Athar Abbas declared that Kayani delayed any significant military operation in North Waziristan in order to spare the Haqqani network, inter alia ("'Kayani was reluctant to launch N Waziristan operation'", *Dawn*, 30 June 2014, (http://tribune.com.pk/story/729162/kayani-was-reluctant-to-launch-n-waziristan-operation-three-years-ago/). See also Hafeez Tunio, "Gilani says decision to launch N Waziristan operation was reserved by Kayani", *The Express Tribune*, 12 July 2014 (http://tribune.com.pk/story/734223/pml-n-should-honour-musharraf-resignation-deal-says-gilani/).

[200] Muhammad Ali Ehsan, "The importance of the North Waziristan operation", *The Express Tribune*, 24 June 2014 (http://tribune.com.pk/story/725982/the-importance-of-the-north-waziristan-operation/).

migrated to KP[201] and two weeks later the 1 million mark was crossed.[202] Given these humanitarian collateral casualties, it was even more important for the army to mobilise society behind the operation. It was legitimised by the Sunni Ulema Board which declared that it was a jihad[203] and the army claimed that it had "the support of the entire nation".[204] By early September, the army announced that 910 terrorists had been killed (whereas 82 soldiers had died), that dozens of hideouts and 27 explosives and arms-making factories had been destroyed and that the towns of Miramshah, Mirali, Dattakhel, Boya and Dogan had returned to the control of the state.[205] The army claimed that the Haqqani network had not been spared,[206] but admitted that its cadre had crossed over to Afghanistan.[207] In fact, most of the Islamists had done the same except, probably, foreigners (mostly Uzbeks) who could not benefit from the same tribal solidarity in Afghanistan. Kunar in particular, became a very attractive place—it was already where Fazlullah had fled in 2010, probably in order to join al-Zawahiri, the Al Qaeda leader.[208] Pakistan kept asking Kabul to seal the border and to extradite Islamist leaders like Fazlullah, but in response the Afghan government demanded that Islamabad take action against the Haqqani network and free Taliban who could contribute to the national reconciliation. Ironically, Afghanistan has become for the TTP the same kind of safe haven as the

---

[201] Zahir Shah Sherazi, "North Waziristan IDPs figure reaches 800,000", *Dawn*, 8 July 2014 (http://www.dawn.com/news/1117879).

[202] Azam Khan, "1 million IDPs and counting", *The Express Tribune*, 23 July 2014 (http://tribune.com.pk/story/739664/1-million-idps-and-counting/).

[203] "Fatwa declared Zarb-i-Azb a jihad", *Dawn*, 23 June 2014 (http://www.dawn.com/news/1114565).

[204] Capt. Kanwal Kiani, "Operation Zarb-e-Azb. Nation's war", *Hilal*, July 2014, p. 19.

[205] "Army says 910 'terrorists', 82 soldiers killed in North Waziristan", *Dawn*, 3 September 2014 (http://www.dawn.com/news/1129619).

[206] Zahir Shah Sherazi and Mateen Haider, "Haqqani network also target of N Waziristan operation: ISPR", *Dawn*, 26 June 2014 (http://www.dawn.com/news/1115240).

[207] Tahir Khan, "Kabul trip: Haqqani threat neutralised, Islamabad assures Washington", *The Express Tribune*, 23 July 2014 (http://tribune.com.pk/story/739645/kabul-trip-haqqani-threat-neutralised-islamabad-assures-washington/).

[208] Kunar was already the place from where Omar Khalid Khorasani had announced the beheading of 23 Pakistani soldiers in February 2014 (Khaled Ahmed, "Unchecked in Kunar", *The Express Tribune*, 3 September 2014 (http://indianexpress.com/article/opinion/columns/unchecked-in-kunar/).

FATA and Quetta used to be for Al Qaeda and the Afghan Taliban—and the situation will probably not improve in 2015 after the withdrawal of more NATO forces.[209]

While the Pakistani army might have initiated a paradigmatic shift and has regained control over the territory of North Waziristan (and most of the FATA), the resilience of those who have crossed over to Afghanistan will probably maintain a climate of civil war in the Pashtun belt, even if the new Afghan president, Ashraf Ghani, seemed prepared to collaborate with the Pakistani authorities soon after his election in September 2014. On 6 December he handed over Latif Mehsud, a close aide of former TTP chief Hakimullah Mehsud.

Besides the North Waziristan operation and some signs of anti-terrorist cooperation between Kabul and Islamabad, the Islamists were weakened in 2014 by the development of tensions, a process Sajna and Fazlullah had initiated in 2013. This process was not only due to tribal solidarities and hostilities, but also to external factors and tactical differences. First, some groups left the TTP—which had always been a loose federation anyway—when Fazlullah and the government agreed on a month-long cease-fire in the context of the ongoing peace talks. Ahrar ul Hind, that split from the Punjabi Taliban (which had already broken with the TTP Punjab leader Muawiya when he had engaged in peace talks) refused to observe the truce. Similarly, "Mohmand militants led by Abdul Wali (alias Omar Khalid Khorasani) left the TTP in August 2014 to form Jamaat-ul-Ahrar and announced their support for Lashkar-e-Islam of Mangal Bagh, a group active in Khyber Agency and which is not part of the TTP"[210]—in spite of the fact that the TTP claimed that both organisations had joined hands.[211] Second, the influence of Daesh (or the Islamic State in Iraq and Syria) divided the TTP.[212] In November 2014, six commanders of the organisation announced their allegiance to Daesh leader Abu Bakar Al-Baghdadi, including the spokesman of the organisation, Shahidullah Shahid, the TTP chief in Orakzai Agency, Saeed Khan, the TTP chief of Kurram Agency, Daulat

---

[209] Rahimullah Yusufzai, "Fight to the finish", *Newsline*, July 2014, p. 19.

[210] Mariam Abou Zahab, "Turmoil in the Frontier", op. cit.

[211] Zahir Shah Sherazi, "TTP joins hands with Lashkar-e-Islam in Khyber", *Dawn*, 7 November 2014 (http://www.dawn.com/news/1142908).

[212] On Daesh in Pakistan, see Hassan Abbas, *Policy Brief: ISIS eyes influence in Pakistan—Focus, Fears & Future Prospects*, Islamabad, Jinnah Institute, 23 December 2014 (http://jinnah-institute.org/policy-brief-isis-eyes-influence-in-pakistan-focus-fears-future-prospects-2/).

Khan, the TTP chief of Khyber Agency, Fateh Gul Zaman, the TTP chief of Peshawar, Mufti Hassan and the TTP chief of Hangu, Khalid Mansoor. Graffiti supporting Daesh and the flags of the organization appeared in different cities of Pakistan.[213] The TTP, whose leaders made clear that Mullah Omar remained their chief, sacked Shahid and appointed a new spokeperson, Muhammad Khorasani. But emissaries of Daesh had apparently been sent to Balochistan and had been in contact with Sunni militants from Lashkar-e-Jhangvi and such relations will probably have some impact.

The tensions within the TTP and the army crackdown on the Islamists after the beginning of the North Waziristan operation so far have not resulted in any decline in terrorism, on the contrary. First, competition between splinter groups has found expression in escalation. In November 2014, Jundullah and Jama'a—ul-Ahrar claimed responsibility for the Wagah attack that killed 60 people near the border with India.[214] Second, violence reached new paroxystic levels in reaction to the North Waziristan operation. On 16 December 2014, half a dozen of TTP terrorists entered an Army Public School in Peshawar and killed 145 people, including 132 children and teenagers. The TTP claimed responsibility for this attack. Its spokeperson said—like after the Wagah attack—that it was in retaliation to the North Waziristan operation.[215]

Despite the Pakistani army's fight against the TTP and attempt to regain the upper hand on the national territory, its ambivalence vis-à-vis some Islamist groups has not been dispelled.

First, the Bin Laden raid, in May 2011 raised many questions that the report of the Abbottabad (Osama bin Laden) Commission has not resolved. The leaked 336-page classified report revealed by Al Jazeera in July 2013[216] documented the movements of Bin Laden in Pakistan—including his visits

[213] "IS visits militants in Balochistan: Jundullah spokesman", *Dawn*, 12 November 2014 (http://www.dawn.com/news/1143997).

[214] Wasim Riaz, "TTP splinter groups claim Wagah attack; 60 dead", *Dawn*, 3 November 2014 (http://www.dawn.com/news/1142006/ttp-splinter-groups-claim-wagah-attack-60-dead) and Ismail Khan, "Wagah attack: Ahrar claim of responsibility appears more credible", *Dawn*, 4 November 2014 (http://www.dawn.com/news/1142307).

[215] Tahir Khan, "TTP claim responsibility for Peshawar school attack", *The Express Tribune*, 16 December 2014 (http://tribune.com.pk/story/807574/ttp-claim-responsibility-for-peshawar-school-attack/).

[216] http://www.aljazeera.com/indepth/spotlight/binladenfiles/2013/07/2013781439 27822246.html

to South Waziristan and the district of Swat before establishing that he settled down in 2005 in Abottabad, a town that is home of the Military Academy and where many retired officers live. While the Commission admitted that "Connivance, collaboration and cooperation at some levels cannot be entirely discounted", the Commission emphasized more "the collective incompetence and negligence, at the very least, of the security and intelligence community in the Abbottabad area".

However, the intelligence community at stake was probably not only local. In October 2011, former DG ISI Ziauddin Batt declared that Osama bin Laden had been kept, by order of Gen. Musharraf, in an Intelligence Bureau of Pakistan safe house by Brigadier Ijaz Shah who allegedly ran a special ISI desk at the time with no other task than taking care of Bin Laden.[217] Brig. Ijaz Shah, who was one of the four persons Benazir Bhutto named in her 2007 letter to Musharraf as the most likely to have her killed, had been an ISI operator before becoming the Director of the Intelligence Bureau from 2004–8. In the ISI, he had been "responsible", according to Khaled Ahmed, for hiding Omar Saeed Sheikh, the murderer of Daniel Pearl.[218] Issues like the Bin Laden stay in Pakistan, the murder of Daniel Pearl and Benazir Bhutto's assassination probably hark back to all the shades of the "deep state"'s relation to Islamists.

Second, the army has not cut off ties with all Islamic groups. The ongoing relationship between the army and the LeT is largely explained by this organization's attitude. Some of the movement's cadres, who had to put a damper on their action in Kashmir due to American pressure relayed by the ISI as of 2001, merely returned to the place where the organization got its start, Afghanistan, where it continued to fight against India in a proxy war. By redeploying in this way, the LeT managed to defuse the anger of its militants who were irked by its leaders' indulgence toward Musharraf, a President-cum-US-lackey. The LeT then went back to attacking India to demonstrate its ability to do harm and preserve its reputation as spearhead of the Pakistani jihad by launching the November 2008 operation against Mumbai, one of the most spectacular acts in the history of terrorism that

---

[217] Carlotta Gall, who investigated the Bin Laden story for years, has reached the same conclusion (Carlotta Gall, "What Pakistan knew about Bin Laden", *The New York Times*, 19 March 2014 (http://www.nytimes.com/2014/03/23/magazine/what-pakistan-knew-about-bin-laden.html?_r=0).

[218] Khaled Ahmed, "No terrorists here", *Indian Express*, 6 April 2014 (http://indian-express.com/article/opinion/columns/no-terrorists-here/).

resulted in the death of 173 persons:[219] ten heavily armed men arrived in Mumbai by sea where they machine-gunned the central train station and a restaurant popular with Western tourists before taking dozens of hostages in a Jewish centre and two luxury hotels, executing the non-Muslims among them. The only survivor among the ten militants, Kasab, immediately told the Indian investigators that he belonged to the LeT. Such an action reinforced the organisation's status as leader of the Pakistani jihad and could not be condemned by the ISI, a likely accomplice—at least not to the point of prompting a significant crackdown despite American pressure. On the contrary, the "ISI added fuel to these suspicions. As soon as the first pictures of the terrorists surfaced around the world, they tried to erase the traces. The ISI appeared in Kasab's village Faridkot, in the Okara district in Punjab and threatened the neighbours to silence. Kasab's parents disappeared from the village".[220]

As long as the LeT does not attack Pakistan, the army is likely to protect the movement in order to use it again. When Shahbaz questioned Major Haroon about the affinities between the military and the LeT, he explained it at once by the army's Punjabi base, shared with the LeT—"The Pakistani army is culturally Punjabi"—and the legitimism of the Ahl-e-Hadith: "in this school of thought *khuruj* (revolt) is not allowed. In other words, LeT is a pro-establishment group."[221] Christine Fair, relying on a 2004 manifesto of the LeT, *Hum Kyon Jihad Kar Rahen Hein?* (Why Are We Waging Jihad?), makes a converging point. While the manifesto admits that the Pakistani government "supports the *kafirs*", it also concedes that it is "cooperating" with the LeT and that, in any case, Muslims are brothers and the organisation should not target them.[222]

While Zia-ur-Rehman Lakhvi, the LeT supreme commander for Kashmir and chief operations in India has been incarcerated since the Mumbai attack, "he continues to guide the organization" from behind the bars.[223] The judiciary has not put the LeT to the book either. In May 2010, the Islamabad High Court "ruled that there was not enough evidence against Hafiz Saeed in the Mumbai case and acquitted the LeT leader".[224] In spite of the $10 million

[219] Lata Jagtiani, *Mumbai Terror Attacks*, New Delhi, Rupa, 2009.

[220] Hein Kiessling, *Faith, Unity, Discipline: the ISI of Pakistan*, op. cit.

[221] Cited in Syed Saleem Shahzad, *Inside Al-Qaeda*, op. cit., p. 102.

[222] C. Christine Fair, *Fighting to the End*, op. cit., p. 256.

[223] Ibid., p. 253.

[224] Hein Kiessling, *Faith, Unity, Discipline: the ISI of Pakistan*, op. cit.

bounty offered for Saeed by the US, he continues to live in his Lahore house and to hold meetings—like Masood Azhar, incidentally.[225]

Punjab, New Land of Conquest?

Punjab, the key province of Pakistan, has traditionally been one of the most conservative regions of the country, as evident from its attachment to the sharia. According to a 2009 survey comparing Punjab, Sindh and Balochistan, 49 per cent of the Punjabis, 20 per cent of the Sindhis and 17 per cent of the Balochs wanted sharia "to play a much larger role than present" in the state.[226] Moreover, Punjab has been the birthplace of most of the Islamic and Islamist organisations, including the Jama'at-e-Islami and the LeT. The increasing militancy of Punjabi Islamists has found expression in the convergence of sectarian groups, jihadist movements and the Taliban, as the recent upsurge in violence indicates.

This rapprochement was precipitated, as mentioned above, by Musharraf's policy after 9/11. The closing down of jihadi camps in Azad Kashmir and elsewhere pushed militants towards the FATA, where the Islamists who were to form the TTP welcome them, not only because of ideological affinities, but for logistical reasons. Eager to sustain terror campaigns in Islamabad and Lahore—probably the power centres which matter the most—the Pashtun jihadists needed the expertise of Punjab-based militants. They also needed additional supporters to contain foreign fighters when the problem arose. And therefore about "2,000 militants from southern and northern Punjab Province had moved to South Waziristan even before the TTP was launched to help out Maulvi Nazir's campaign against the Uzbeks; and more followed in theur footsteps".[227] The fact that so many Islamists could move to the Pashtun area is a reflection of their strength in Punjab, and in the Lahore Division in particular.

This Division has a record number of Islamist headquarters. It is home to the historic Jama'at-e-Islami headquarters in Mansoora (Lahore), those of

---

[225] "Masood Azhar's address to rally in Muzaffarabad draws Indian ire", *The Indian Express*, 22 February 2014 (http://tribune.com.pk/story/674624/masood-azhars-address-to-rally-in-muzaffarabad-draws-indian-ire/).

[226] C.Christine Fair, *Fighting to the End*, op. cit., p. 272 Unless otherwise specified, this regional study is based on information provided in Mujahid Hussain, *Punjabi Taliban. Driving Extremism in Pakistan*, New Delhi, Pentagon Security International, 2012.

[227] Hassan Abbas, *The Taliban revival*, op. cit., p. 156.

LeT in the "model town" of Muridke and those of Tablighi Jamaat in Raiwind (a neighbouring town where the movement's annual congregation draws as many as one million people). In addition are famous *dini madaris* such as the Jamaia Asharfia Deobandi seminary, as well as Shia centres such as Begum Khot, where a holy figure, Bawa Sada Hussain, resides. Regarding the Shias, Thokar Niaz Beg, in the suburbs of Lahore, was chosen in the 1990s by Sipah-e-Muhammad leader Ghulam Raza Naqvi (originally from Jhang) to serve as headquarters for his organization.[228]

Bahawalpur Division has almost as many hot spots. Rahim Yar Khan district (of which Lashkar-e-Jhangvi commander Malik Ishaq is a native) is home to the Deobandi *madrassah* Makhzanul-Uloom, established in 1944, which became a hotbed of anti-Shiism under the leadership of Maulana Darhwasti, its rector until his death in 1994 (upon which he was replaced by his son). But most of all, the city of Bahawalpur is headquarters to the Jaish-e-Mohammad. Its founder, Masood Azhar, is a native of the city and still lives there, more or less under house arrest since 2000.

Faisalabad Division, and within it Jhang district, is known for being the stronghold of Sunni sectarianism where the SSP and the LeJ operate scores of seminaries and other centres, including training camps.[229] Many leaders within this Sunni strand hail from there, starting with Haq Nawaz Jhangvi and Amjad Farooqi. Farooqi, who comes from a remote village in Toba Tek Singh district, has been implicated in an impressive list of operations, from the murder of Daniel Pearl to the December 2003 attempt on Musharraf's life, and including attacks on Protestant churches in Islamabad and Bahawalpur.[230] But Faislabad Division is also the LeT's stronghold, this organization claiming "that a majority of their 'martyrs' hailed from Faisalabad."[231] Gujranwala district is where another jihadist movement was born, the Harkat-ul-Mujahideen, which was a pioneer in the "holy war" in Kashmir.

The deep embeddedness of Islamist groups in Punjab partly explains why the province has offered several safe havens for Al Qaeda cadres that fled Afghanistan after 11 September 2001: Abu Zubaida was arrested in

---

[228] Ian Talbot, "Understanding Religious Violence in Contemporary Pakistan: Themes and Theories", in Ravinder Kaur (ed.), *Religion, Violence and Political Mobilisation in South Asia*, New Delhi, Sage, 2005, p. 154.

[229] Mujahid Hussain, *Punjabi Taliban. Driving Extremism in Pakistan*, New Delhi, Pentagon Security International, 2012, p. 49.

[230] Ibid., p. 57.

[231] Ibid., p. 60. Some villages and towns in the district have cemeteries reserved for them.

Faisalabad in a house arranged for by an LeT member;[232] Abu Khalfan, one of the mains suspects in the attacks in Nairobi and Dar-es-Salam, was arrested in 2004 in Gujranwala with his Uzbek wife.

The density of Islamist networks in Punjab also explains the high number of attacks intended to punish the authorities for its pro-American turn-around after 11 September and/or to dissuade them from continuing along this path. The attacks, which mainly targeted the army and the police force, turned out to be almost as deadly as the usual sectarian (anti-Ahmadi, anti-Shia and anti-Sufi attacks), which remain very high. In 2007–2009, 24 attacks killed 376 policemen and soldiers whereas in 2008–2010, ten attacks killed 283 people (mostly Shias).[233]

The last decade has seen the intensification of attacks on security forces in Punjab as of 2007 (in the wake of the Red Mosque incident), reaching a height in 2009 when Islamist groups were determined to dissuade Islamabad (and Rawalpindi) from launching the offensive in South Waziristan, and then punished them for it. In 2007, suicide bombers virtually targeted only vehicles (mainly buses) transporting soldiers and police officers, whereas in 2008 and even more in 2009, the ISI and army buildings were targeted. The Navy War College was hit on 4 March 2008 and one week later it was the Federal Investigation Authority in Lahore. Ensuing attacks targeted the Pakistan Ordnance Factories in Wah Cantonment—employing between 25,000 to 30,000 people in arms production (21 August 2008), a Frontier Constabulary checkpoint in Islamabad (4 April 2009), and especially the army headquarters in Rawalpindi (10 October 2009) and the ISI office in Multan (8 December 2009). All told, in 2009, there was an average of one attack per month in the province, the death toll among police officers and soldiers rising from 122 in 2007 to nearly 150 in 2009.

In 2010, Islamist groups abandoned their chosen targets of the year before due to the fairly little harm caused by the operation in South Waziristan, returning their attention to their traditional enemies, the Shias and the Ahmadis. (In 2013, out of the thirty-eight terrorist attacks which took place in Punjab, fifteen were sectarian in nature).[234] But they broadened their perimeter of action to the Barelwis and more generally to Sufi holy sites. The TTP thus claimed the 1 July 2010 attack on Data Darbar, the shrine of saint Gunj Bakhsh in Lahore. On 25 October, a similar attack perpetrated

---

[232] Zahid Hussain, *Frontline Pakistan*, op. cit., p. 127.

[233] Mujahid Hussain, *Punjabi Taliban*, op.cit., pp. 194–211.

[234] *Pakistan Security Report—2013*, op. cit., p. 21.

against the shrine of Baba Fareed Ganj Shakar in Pakpatan (Sahiwal Division) added to the year's toll.

The targeting of the Barelwis is not new in the Punjab, where this school of thought is in a majority but traditionally not well organised. Khaled Ahmed points out that "the sectarian Sunni clergy always regarded their fellow Sunnis of the Barelwi school of thought as renegades because of their sympathetic attitude towards the Shia".[235] Barelwis organised first in Karachi—as evident from the electoral performances of their party, the JUP, in the city in the 1970s. In 1990, the Sunni Tehreek was set up there by a Guajarati Memon, Salim Qadri (a former member of the JUP) in reaction to the growing influence of the Deobandis and the Ahl-e-Hadith. Qadri was killed in 2001 by SSP attackers[236]—probably because of his campaign to reclaim mosques which, he alleged, were originally Barelwi.[237] The organisation was again targeted in 2006 when the successor of Salim Qadri, Abbas Wadri, was assassinated in Karachi. But it continued to grow in Karachi under the aegis of Sarwat Ejaz Qadri with the support of Gujarati Memons.[238] In Punjab, however, the largest Barelwi organisations are the the Sunni Ittehad Council, a federation of Barelwi institutions and the Dawat-e-Islami (a.k.a. the Green Turbans)—another Karachi-based organisation founded in 1981—of Maulana Ilyas Qadri, the former Punjab President of the JUP youth wing.[239]

Whether targeting the military or the Barelwis, the Islamists in Punjab managed to kill several hundred of them each year between 2008 and 2010. By spreading terror, they very probably induced the Pakistan Army to defer operations it had finally made up its mind to carry out in FATA under US pressure.

The strength of Islamist groups in Punjab also affected minorities through these recurrent attacks and the climate of fear they provoke. It is equally reflected in a certain routinisation of persecution of the Shias.

Mujahid Hussain relates an instructive account of the village of Aadiwal, in a district nevertheless less subject to sectarianism than others, Sialkot. There, 109 families lived on good terms: seventy-seven were Muslim

---

[235] Khald Ahmed, *Sectarian War*, op. cit., p. 151.

[236] Ibid., p. 155.

[237] Ibid.

[238] Mohammad Waseem and Mariam Mufti, *Political Parties in Pakistan*, op. cit., p. 81.

[239] Musa Khan Jalalzai, *Punjabi Taliban. Extremism, Talibanisation and the Fight for Saraikistan*, Karachi, Royal Book Company, 2013, p. 59 and p. 85.

(including sixty Barelwis and seventeen Shias), twenty-three Hindu, eight Christian and one Ahmadi. Even Partition had not chased out the Hindus. There was only one mosque in the vicinity. The minorities did not have their own places of worship, but everyone respected their religious calendars. On 5 February 1992, in the course of Kashmir Solidarity Day celebrations,[240] Jama'at-e-Islami militants from Sialkot came to attack the Hindu families. The rest of the villagers came to their defence. But another attack was launched on them in December in retaliation for the demolition of the Ayodhya mosque in India. Commuting into the city to work became difficult. One night two Hindu girls were abducted. Three days later they were found to have been converted to Islam by force and married off. The jihadist militants (Hussain does not name the organisation) celebrated their triumph boisterously in the village. One girl committed suicide, the other went to Peshawar with her husband. The eighteen remaining Hindu families moved to Jalandhar, in Indian Punjab. The Ahmadi family met with a similar fate. When the paterfamilias, a retired schoolteacher, died, a jihadist organisation (which again Hussain does not name) informed his family that his body could not be interred in the cemetery because it was reserved for Muslims. The family left with the coffin and moved to Rabwa, headquarters of the Ahmadi community. As for the Christians, they were first distressed by trials for "blasphemy" on the rise in the neighbouring district of Gujranwala. When local organisations, which Hussain still does not name, demonstrated outside the village demanding that the guilty parties be sentenced to death, six of the eight Christian families left the village, where there are now three mosques, an indication of the influence the city finally had on local Muslims.[241]

While the story of Aadiwal is not a common one, it is not unique either. Similar mechanisms have been observed elsewhere, including in India: the pernicious impact urban militants can have on rural areas that had always been syncretic; the desire to avenge one's own who are persecuted in neighbouring countries—in this case India—by attacking a minority which on the other side of the border exercises oppression and, finally, migration—to the neighbour country or to urban areas where minorities seek security by forming ghettos having a sort of critical mass. Where Hussain's

---

[240] Since 1990, the 5th of February is the day when Pakistanis celebrate their solidarity with the Indian Kashmiris and protest against the occupation of the province by India. The idea of this Kashmir Solidarity Day was first suggested by the then chief of the JI, Qazi Hussain Ahmed.

[241] Mujahid Hussain, *Punjabi Taliban*, op. cit., pp. 68–72.

narrative differs from other such accounts, is in the anonymity he grants the assailants, not even mentioning the name of the organisations responsible for violence, except in one case, out of fear of reprisals. He in fact hints that not everything can be talked about:

In our society we have often observed that after a crackdown against any criminal gang or individual there was a great type [hype?] about their real or alleged assets but nothing was ever brought to the limelight after a ban on any extremist outfit or the arrest of its mighty activists. The main reason is the fear that chills the spines of "impartial and dauntless media" before breaking any news about these groups.[242]

The Islamist groups of Punjab have gained some coherence over the course of time, so much so that people now speak of the "Punjabi Taliban" to designate this group[243] which is now represented in the TTP *shura*.[244] These new or neo-Taliban have become so powerful that not only do journalists fear them, but political parties have given up the idea of taking them to task, and even attempt to take advantage of their influence as much in terms of coercion as in force of persuasion. The PML(N) offers a good example of this attitude. In the late 1990s, while advocating sharia, Nawaz Sharif had tackled sectarian groups, as we have seen. Returning from exile ten years later with his brother—chief minister of Punjab—his behaviour was entirely different. In 2008, while sectarian movements had been subject to crackdowns under Musharraf for several years already, they turned to the PML(N) for a certain degree of political protection in exchange for electoral support. The party played along according to a complex reckoning, as mentioned above. One of the agents of this rapprochement was none other than Rana Sanaullah, a former PPP elected official who joined the PML(N).[245] In his bastion of Faisalabad, Rana represents the Rajputs and the Deobandi school against his rival, the Jat Barelwi leader Sahibzada Fazil-e-Karim, who himself went over from the JUP to the JUI (F). Rana Sanaullah's tactic involved bringing in to the party former SSP and Lashkar-e-Jhangvi cadres to cope with his adversaries more effectively. Sardar Zulfiqar Khosa—at the time PML(N) president for Punjab—did the same in Dera Ghazi Khan. Once elected, Rana Sanaullah was appointed

---

242 Ibid., p. 31.

243 Hassan Abbas, "Defining the Punjabi Taliban Network", *CTC Sentinel*, vol. 2, no. 4, April 2009.

244 Mariam Abou Zahab, "Pashtun and Punjabi Taliban", op. cit, p. 381.

245 See http://dawn.com/2012/01/13/rana-sanaullah/ (Accessed on September 15, 2013).

Law minister in the government of Punjab and it was in this capacity that he was able to repay his debt toward the Sunni sectarian militants who had helped him get elected. SSP leader Muhammad Ahmed Ludhianvi moreover declared that in the 2008 elections his movement had procured "armed support" for dozens of PML(N) candidates and that most of them had been elected.[246] Having been made minister, not only did Rana Sanaullah protect Sunni sectarian militants after a spate of attacks that should have led to far more intensive legal action, but he also showed devotion to SSP heroes. Thus in February 2010 he paid his respects at the tombs of Maulana Haq Nawaz Jhangvi and Azam Tariq.[247] Re-elected in 2013, Sanaullah was re-appointed in his cabinet by Shahbaz Sharif who, in addition to Law, gave him the Local Government portfolio—a source of additional leverage. He resigned from the government in 2014 for another reason.

The moves of the PML(N) leaders partly reflects Nawaz Sharif's affinities with conservative, even militant, Sunnism, as can be seen in his family ties with the Tablighi Jamaat (his father was close enough to one of the organization's major figures, Muhammad Rafiq Tarar, to have him appointed Pakistan's president in 1998). Mariam Abou Zahab moreover considers that "the SSP is the new ally of the PML(N) in Punjab".[248] But all the parties more or less indulge in the same practices. In the 1993–6 period, Manzoor Wattoo, a Punjabi leader who easily switched allegiances—moving from the PML(Junejo) to the PML (Q) and then to the PPP in the space of fifteen years as mentioned above—led coalition governments in Lahore among which there were many sympathisers with Sunni sectarian groups.[249] After the 2008 elections, Mujahid Hussain considered that "163 members of the Punjab Assembly are directly involved in material support and aid of extremist religious organisations, jihadist outfits and sectarian groups because they also had sought the support from these powerful and well-armed outfits during their election campaign of 2008 on the promise of return the favour if they got elected to the assembly."[250]

Such transactions mainly dealt with supplying sectarian and jihadist groups with arms. Punjabi elected officials granted them thousands of permits enabling them legally to acquire real arsenals. The younger brother of PPP Interior Minister Rahman Malik took part in this exchange of favours

[246] Cited in Mujahid Hussain, *Punjabi Taliban*, op. cit., 149.

[247] Khaled Ahmed, "Foreword", in ibid., p. xi.

[248] Mariam Abou Zahab, "Pashtun and Punjabi Taliban", op. cit, p. 382.

[249] Mujahid Hussain, *Punjabi Taliban*, op. cit., p. 103.

[250] Ibid., p. 149.

with his elder's blessing, apparently.[251] Beyond that, Shia politicians admitted that they could not win elections without the backing of militant Sunni groups and also turned to their underlings in the same terms. This was the case for instance of Riaz Pirzada, elected under the PML(Q) label in Bahawalpur in 2008, even though his father had been killed by the SSP. Even though Azam Tariq had been arrested for this murder, "Riaz Pirzada woke up to the reality and won the elections of February [2008] by getting support from the extremist Deobandi outfit Jaish-e-Mohammed."[252] Pirzada subsequently joined the PML(N) in 2012, was re-elected in 2013 and became a federal minister.

Punjabi politicians may have more or less consciously been banking on the fact that Sunni sectarian groups would be absorbed into politics, as was customary of the Pakistani establishment for the past 60 years. But nothing is less certain, and it can be just as well assumed that these groups take advantage of the weaknesses of their opponents to strengthen their positions without at all losing sight of their most radical objectives. Already, the influence they have acquired has resulted in the loss of elementary social guarantees that minorities used to enjoy in Punjab and elsewhere.

Minorities under Attack

Minorities have always suffered from some form of discrimination in Pakistan, despite the Liaquat Ali Khan-Jawaharlal Nehru Pact (or Delhi Pact) of 1950 that enjoined the states of India and Pakistan to guarantee all their citizens the same rights (including safety). As early as 1949, the elected representative of minorities to the Constituent Assembly of Pakistan protested against the Islamic dimension of the Objectives Resolution.[253] They then were obliged to accept a system of separate electorates that they opposed.[254] It was

---

[251] Ibid., pp. 154–155.

[252] Ibid., p. 150.

[253] Sri Chandra Chattopadhyay, a Hindu representative from East Bengal then declared: "I have been passing sleeples nights pondering what shall I now tell my people whom I have so long been advising to stick to the land of the birth? And on the top of this all, by this Resolution you condemn them to a perpetual state of inferiority" (Cited in Amina Jillani, "Singling out the minorities", *The Express Tribune*, 4 October 2014, (http://tribune.com.pk/story/613530/singling-out-the-minorities/)).

[254] Rasul Bakhsh Rais, "Islamic Radicalism and Minorities in Pakistan", in Satu P. Limaye, Mohan Malik and Robert G. Wirsing (eds), *Religious Radicalism and Security in South Asia*, Honolulu, Asia-Pacific Center for Security Studies, 2004, p. 451

the Muslim majority in West Pakistan who had asked for this system in an endeavour to pursue the two-nation theory. It was intended to protect them from the Hindus (who were often seen as India's fifth column) and more importantly to negate the notion of equality among all Pakistani citizens that Jinnah had mentioned in his famous August 11, 1948 speech. Minorities, however, wanted to abolish this legacy of the Raj in order to become full-fledged citizens of their state. The main political leaders in East Bengal supported their demand, partly because of their political culture, and partly because of the sheer numbers of Hindus in their province, who might be called on to vote one day, hopefully for them. The 1956 Constitution, as mentioned above, allowed the two wings of the state to decide whether or not they wished to continue with separate electorates. West Pakistan chose to maintain the system; East Pakistan did not.

Ayub Khan, true to his patriotic credentials, introduced the idea of a single collegium in the 1962 Constitution. The 1973 Constitution also maintained this system and even introduced reserved seats for minorities: six in the National Assembly, five in the Punjab assembly, two in the Sindh assembly, two in the Balochistan assembly and one in the NWFP assembly. Bhutto also made it a point to appoint a representative for minorities in his cabinet. Zia claimed to go further by increasing the number of reserved seats in the National Assembly from five to ten. But he made the act of voting very complicated for the minorities by drawing huge constituencies for them. More importantly, in 1985, he reintroduced separate electorates. One collegium was made up of Muslims, another of Christians, a third for Hindus, a fourth for Sikhs, Buddhists and Parsis, and a fifth one for the Ahmadis.[255] This system remained in place throughout the democratisation phase from 1988 to 1999, and for the local elections of 2000. Musharraf abolished most of the separate electorates in 2002.

The situation of minorities of Pakistan is especially precarious because of their small numbers. According to the 1998 census, the most recent, minorities represented about 8 per cent of the Pakistani population at the time. The three largest groups were the Christians (1.9 per cent), the Hindus (1.2 per cent) and the Ahmadis.[256] A more recent estimate put the proportion of Hindus at 1.6 per cent, Christians 1.59 per cent (to which 0.25 per cent

---

[255] Naeem Shakir, "Pakistan: Joint Electorates—A Democratic Ethos", *Human Rights Solidarity*, 17 August 2001. See http://www.hrsolidarity.net/mainfile.php/2000vol 10no09/706/.

[256] For a more complete picture, see Iftikhar H. Malik, *Religious Minorities in Pakistan*, Minorities Rights Group International, 2002.

Dalits should be added), Ahmadis 0.25 per cent and 0.007 others (Sikhs, Parsis, Bahais and Kalash). The government formed in March 2008 worked toward improving the conditions of these groups. A ministry of "Minority Affairs" was created.[257] A Christian, Shahbaz Bhatti, was placed in charge. He officialized the celebration of ten religious holidays observed by minorities, introduced a minority quota of 5 per cent in the national and state civil services and set up a hotline for members of a minority to call if they were victims of violence.[258] Two years later, the Eighteenth Amendment reserved ten seats for minorities in the National Assembly and four in the Senate, one per province. Regional assemblies were given a similar setup.[259] These initiatives have, however, not been enough to reverse the trend of harsh treatment—not only because the quotas remained unfulfilled.[260]

Ahmadis, Powerless in the Face of Persecution

The intensification of minority persecution in Pakistan has been in step with the decline in legal protection these groups traditionally enjoyed. The Ahmadis are a case in point, for although the judges have asserted their independence in the face of those in power, they have almost given up defending the rights of this class of citizen.

In the 1950s–60s, the courts took a liberal attitude toward religious matters. One might recall that the Munir Commission appointed after the anti-Ahmadi agitation had deemed it impossible to define who was a Muslim and who was not. Until the 1970s the judges had protected the Ahmadis against their critics. After the Second Amendment to the Constitution was passed in 1974 denying them the status of Muslim, Islamist groups put pressure on the Ahmadis to ban them from calling their place of worship a "mosque" and disallow them from publicly calling their congregation to

---

[257] Following passage of the 18th Amendment, this ministry was renamed Ministry of National Harmony in 2011 and its initial attributions were mostly delegated to the provincial governments.

[258] United Nations High Commissioner for Refugees, *UNHCR Eligibility Guidelines for Assessing the International Protection Needs of Members of Religious Minorities from Pakistan*, UNHCR, 14 May 2012, p. 4.

[259] Minorities have 3 reserved seats in Khyber–Pakhtunkhwa province, 8 in Punjab, 9 in Sindh and 3 in Balochistan. Minorities also have at least one seat in each municipal and district council.

[260] Rana Tanweer, "Implementing the minority quota", *The Express Tribune*, 5 June 2014 (http://tribune.com.pk/story/717196/implementing-the-minority-quota/).

prayer by reciting the *azaan*. The matter was brought before the Dera Ghazi Khan district court, which ruled in favour of the Ahmadis' critics. Ahmadis appealed the judgment before the Lahore High Court in the *Abdur Rahman Mobashir v. Amir Ali Shah* case in 1978. In his judgment, Justice Hussain overturned the verdict of the Dera Ghazi Khan court and defended the Ahmadis' freedom of worship such that they were able to go on with their ritual practices.

Things changed in 1984 when Zia promulgated an ordinance citing all the Ahmadis' denominations: the "Anti-Islamic Activities of the Qadiani Group, Lahori Group and Ahmadis (Prohibition and Punishment) Ordinance" forbade them from using Arabic words traditionally reserved for the Prophet, his disciples and his wives, from referring to their places of worship as mosques and from reciting the *azaan*. The Ahmadis Rahman took the matter before the Federal Sharia Court in 1985 in the *Mujibur Rehman v. Federal Government of Pakistan* case. Their case was dismissed in circumstances that attest to the judiciary's loss of independence under Zia, recalling that he alone appointed the justices of the Federal Sharia Court. In 1985, Justice Hussain—whom Zia had made chief of this court—had prepared a judgment in favour of the Ahmadis. Zia found out about it before the verdict was handed down and dismissed Chief Justice Hussain, replacing him with a man who decided against the Ahmadis' case.[261]

The community then appealed the case before the Supreme Court in 1993, disputing the constitutionality of the 1984 ordinance in the *Zaheeruddin v. The State* case. They held that the ordinance contravened the clauses of the Constitution that guaranteed religious freedom. The Supreme Court once again ruled against them by virtue of sharia, which for the first time was invoked to restrict a constitutional right.[262] Chief Justice Chaudhry considered that "By using Muslim words and epithets, Ahmadis defiled Islam and deceived ordinary people as to their true identity and it was the duty of an Islamic state to protect words associated with Islam."[263] He even went so

---

[261] Sadia Saeed, "The Nation and Its Heretics: Courts, State Authority and Minority Rights in Pakistan", p. 22. See http://web.law.columbia.edu/sites/default/.../Nation%26Heretics_SAEED.pdf (Accessed on September 15, 2013).

[262] The complete judgement is available on http://www.irshad.org/exposed/legal/pkcort93.php. (Accessed on September 15, 2013). The interested reader can find a detailed analysis of the judgement in an article by Tayyab Mahmud, "Freedom of religion and religious minorities in Pakistan", *Fordham International Law Journal*, vol. 19, no. 1, 1995.

[263] Sadia Saeed, "The Nation and Its Heretics", op. cit., p. 25.

far as to describe the Ahmadis as "a threat to the Muslim Ummah and to the socio-political organization of their society which is based on Islam."[264] This discourse is very revealing of the feelings of insecurity that the Ahmadis create among Pakistani Muslims—for the simple reason that in a country that is supposed to be the homeland of South Asian Muslims, Islam can only be defined in the manner that suits the majority (and not the way followers of a new Prophet define it).

The Ahmadis' lawyers whom Sadia Saeed has interviewed recount that the 1993 trial took place in an extremely tense atmosphere. The courtroom was full of activists from both sides, but clearly of unequal strength. One of the lawyers—Fakhruddin G. Ebrahim, a Bohra who was to become Chief Election Commissioner, and had agreed to defend the Ahmadis—whereas many of his colleagues had declined the "offer"—recalls that "Judges were throughout on the defensive (...) They were afraid... afraid of being called pro-Ahmadi."[265]

The judges' abdication and the politicisation of the judicial apparatus brought down one of the last dikes protecting the Ahmadis, who would become targets of ever-increasing persecution. Out of the 1,060 people accused of blasphemy between 1986 and 2010, 479 were Ahmadis and 476 Muslims.[266]

In 2002, the Ahmadis were the only minority not to benefit from the abolition of the system of separate electorates that Musharraf implemented through the Conduct of General Elections Order that he promulgated on 27 February. He even felt it necessary to issue another ordinance on 17 June that explained that the status of the Ahmadis would remain the same and that, if one of them was suspected to have cast his vote in the general (i.e. Muslim) collegium, he would have to sign a declaration within the following fifteen days reaffirming the "absolute and unqualified finality of the Prophethood of Muhammad", which would have come in contradiction with the Ahmadi creed.[267]

The Ahmadis were further stigmatised by the government's decision to have religious affiliation marked on ID cards and passports. To have

---

[264] Ibid., p. 26.

[265] Cited in ibid., p. 28

[266] Jinnah Institute, *A Question of Faith. A Report on the Status of Religious Minorities in Pakistan*, Islamabad, 2011, p. 40. See http://jinnah-institute.org/images/stories/jinnah_minority_report.pdf (Accessed on September 15, 2013).

[267] See http://www.thepersecution.org/50years/jointelec.html. (Accessed on September 15, 2013).

"Muslim" on one's ID, one had to sign a declaration denying the prophet-hood of the Ahmadi movement's founder. Most Ahmadis did not easily resign themselves to doing this, even though this sign of official recognition made their identification easier.

Ahmadis are increasingly victims of violence. On 28 May 2010, armed men attacked two places of worship in Lahore, one in Garhi Shahu, the other in Model Town. The attacks left 96 dead. They were buried in Rabwa, in the same cemetery as Dr. Abdul Salaam, Nobel Prize for physics in 1979, who had left Pakistan to flee persecution, but who was interred in Rabwa and whose tomb was desecrated.[268] But moral violence can cause as much harm as physical violence. In 2013, the Ahmadis were involuntarily the focus of one of the pre-electoral controversies when Fazlur Rehman, the JUI(F) leader, accused Imran Khan of being in favour of abolishing the constitutional amendment declaring the Ahmadi non-Muslims. Imran Khan vehemently denied such intention.[269]

In August 2014, a Canada-based doctor, Qamar Ali Mehdi, who had come to Rabwa to pray at the grave of his parents, was killed without any reason.[270] A few days before, twenty-eight Ahmadi families had had to leave Racecourse Road in Gujranwala after their houses were torched over the alleged blasphemous Facebook post by a teenage boy.[271] They probably went to Rabwa. The Gujranwalla episode is revealing of the new attitude of the police, as Rabia Mehmood points out:

"When clerics and anti-Ahmadi individuals who are trying to intimidate local Ahmadis fail, they go to the police and file a ciomplaint. Then, a group of policemen go to the administration of the Ahmadi community, and ask them to do whatever it is the clerics want to do. The community says, the act demanded by the clerics is against their faith, so the authorities get pro-active and for the sake of maintaining peace in the area, actually commit the hurtful acts which the bigoted clergy were

---

[268] Jinnah Institute, *A Question of Faith*, op. cit., p. 34. See http://jinnah-institute. org/images/stories/jinnah_minority_report.pdf (Accessed on September 15, 2013).

[269] Nabeel Jafri, "No Place for Ahmadis in Imran Khan's Naya Pakistan", *The Express Tribune*, 3 May 2013. See http://blogs.tribune.com.pk/story/17157/no-place-forahmadis-in-imran-khans-naya-pakistan/. (Accessed on September 15, 2013).

[270] Muhammad Hassan Miraj, "Murder in Rabwah", *Dawn*, 28 May 2014 (http://www.dawn.com/news/1108902).

[271] Nasir Jamal, "Footprints: no space for Ahmadis", *Dawn*, 1 August 2014 (http://www.dawn.com/news/1122504) and Mirza Iqbal, "Ahmadis on the run: fearing death in People's Colony", *Dawn*, 18 August 2014 (http://www.dawn.com/news/1123873).

threatening to do themselves. (...) Over the last few years, there has been an increase in the number of incidents where the police goes to the Ahmadi community, asking them to 'co-operate', and further, acts on covering the *Kalima* with a black sheet from the place of worship's facades, demolishing the minarets of the community's place of worship, removing scriptures from their shops or just the word 'Muslim' from their gravestones or scratching away the name of a Pakistani citizen from his shop name-plate because it resembles a Muslim name, like Muhammad Ali".[272]

The Blasphemy Law, Christians and Others

Christians have been more recent victims of radical Islamist movements. Like other minorities, they have been represented at the pinnacle of the state by renowned figures such as the famous Chief Justice, A. R. Cornelius.[273] While most of those who belonged to the middle class did not suffer from their religious identity, those who did not—and more precisely the large proportion of Dalit Christians—have been increasingly subjected to different forms of harassment and persecution. Forced conversion and marriage of Christian girls have been increasingly commonplace, for instance.[274] But legal cases due to alleged blasphemy have been even more dramatic. Between 1986 and 2010, accusations of blasphemy were made against 180 Christians. Many of these accusations have not been followed through with legal proceedings, judges having dismissed the case for lack of evidence. But verdicts sometimes only come after months and even years of proceedings, and many of the people arrested are subject to abuse while in prison—and even die there (in some cases following torture), when they are not murdered upon their release by extremists who take the law in their own hands.

According to the Centre for Research and Security Studies and "the data on the blasphemy cases, 59 persons have been extrajudicially murdered in

---

[272] Rabia Mehmood, "Ahmadis, seared to the wall", *Dawn*, 30 July 2014 (http://www.dawn.com/news/1122333).

[273] A.R. Cornelius was an influential figure who defended the Christians of Pakistan until his death in 1991. See Ralph Braibanti, *Chief Justice Cornelius of Pakistan: An Analysis With Letters and Speeches*, Karachi, Oxford University Press, 1999.

[274] Movement for Solidarity and Peace, *Forced Marriages & Forced Conversions in the Christian Community of Pakistan*, 2014 (http://d3n8a8pro7vhmx.cloudfront.net/msp/pages/162/attachments/original/1396724215/MSP_Report_-_Forced_Marriages_and_Conversions_of_Christian_Women_in_Pakistan.pdf?1396724 215).

the country since 1990".[275] Half of the victims belong to the minorities and the districts of Gujranwala and Lahore are particularly affected. Christians, are overrepresented among them.[276] Christian churches have protested vigorously against the law. The Catholic bishop of Faisalabad, Father John Joseph, killed himself in 1998 in protest against the law after he had attempted in vain to find a lawyer to defend a young Christian man accused of blasphemy.

In 2010, Christians were once again the focus of the controversy. In a village of Punjab, a Christian farmhand, Aasia Bibi, was accused of blasphemy by Muslim fellow female labourers after a dispute: Aasia Bibi (probably a Scheduled Caste member), having drunk water from one of these women's cups, the women apparently refused to drink after her, which gave rise to a remark about Muslims by the Christian woman, prompting the accusation of blasphemy. The local court in Nankana Sahib district sentenced her to death on 8 November 2010. President Zardari asked his government to review the case. The verdict was found to be unsound and a presidential pardon was sought. But on 29 November the Lahore High Court came out against granting a pardon, claiming it was premature. Zardari kept a low profile, but some of his close associates campaigned in favour of Aasia Bibi and for a reform of the blasphemy law. Two of these supporters were Sherry Rehman, former information and broadcasting minister, and Salman Taseer, governor of Punjab. A businessman and media entrepreneur—he owned the *Daily Times*— Taseer had been active in politics since the late 1960s when he joined Z.A. Bhutto's PPP. A close ally of Benazir, he was elected for the PPP in 1988, but then lost all the elections in the 1990s. In 2008, Zardari appointed him governor of Punjab. Two years later, he publicly took Aasia Bibi's defense, drawing the wrath of orthodox clerics and costing him his life. As mentioned in Chapter 7, on 4 January 2011, one of his bodyguards, Malik Mumtaz Qadri, shot him twenty-seven times as he was going to his car after a lunch in Islamabad. His murderer, an adept of the Sunni Tehreek movement, was part of a commando unit trained by the Punjabi security apparatus, the Elite Punjab Police. Radical movements applauded his act—as did many members of the legal community. It was no easier to find a judge who would agree to

---

[275] "Blatant misuse of blasphemy law", Centre for Research & Security Studies, 29 September 2014 (http://crss.pk/story/blatant-misuse-of-blasphemy-law/).

[276] See the specific case studies made by the Jinnah Institute, Jinnah Institute, *A Question of Faith*, p. 41. Available at http://jinnah-institute.org/images/stories/jinnah_minority_report.pdf. (Accessed on September 15, 2013).

hear the case than it was to find a cleric who would perform Taseer's funeral rites. But his murderer was finally sentenced to death on 1 October 2011. It remains to be seen whether the sentence will be carried out. For the moment, "Mumtaz Qadri rules in prison", as evident from the fact that he persuaded one of his guards to kill another inmate, a blasphemy convict called Mohammad Asghar.[277] The trajectory of Malik Mumtaz Qadri suggests that the same kind of radicalisation that was in evidence among the Deobandis and the Ahl-e-Hadith is now affecting the Barelwis.

The other regime dignitary who lost his life was none other than Shahbaz Bhatti. Pakistan's first minister for minority affairs. As a student Bhatti founded the Christian Liberation Front in 1985. Then in 2002 he participated in forming the All Pakistan Minorities Alliance, a movement he chaired. Bhatti had received death threats since 2009 and more frequently after taking up Aasia Bibi's cause. He was assassinated on 2 March 2011 when thugs from the TTP (to believe later claims) stormed his vehicle. His brother took his place in the cabinet before migrating to Italy because of death threats on his life. The trial of Bhatti's murderer may never take place because the witness also faces death threats.[278]

In May 2014, Rashid Rehman, an advocate from Multan who had been harassed because he represented a man accused of commiting blasphemy using his Facebook account was shot dead.[279] Six months later, a Christian couple working in a brick kiln were accused of desecrating a copy of the Holy Quran and killed by an enraged mob in a small town 60 km way from Lahore.[280]

Persecution of Christians does not only take the form of such individual killings. In March 2013 the Christian Saint Joseph colony was for instance attacked in Lahore. In September 2013, a double suicide bombing at the All Saints Church in Peshawar killed 127 people. Two groups, the TTP and Jundullah claimed responsibility for the attack.[281]

277 Rafia Zakaria, "Mumtaz Qadri, Prison King", *Dawn*, 1 November 2014 (http://www.dawn.com/news/1141574).

278 "Extremist threats hamper Shahbaz Bhatti's murder trial", *Dawn*, 9 February 2014 (http://www.dawn.com/news/1085703).

279 Owais Jafri and Asad Kharal, "Human rights lawyer Rashid Rehman shot dead", *The Express Tribune*, 8 May 2014 (http://tribune.com.pk/story/705659/human-rights-lawyer-rashid-rehman-shot-dead/).

280 "Christian couple beaten to death for 'desecrating Quran': police", *Dawn*, 6 November 2014 (http://www.dawn.com/news/1142386).

281 Ismail Khan, "Wagah attack", op. cit.,

In October 2014 the Lahore High Court confirmed the death sentence of Aasia Bibi.[282] Her advocates filed an appeal in the Supreme Court in November of that year.[283]

The Departure of the Last Hindus, Partition's Final Act?

After Partition few Hindus remained in West Pakistan (compared to East Pakistan). They are mainly concentrated in towns in Sindh[284] where their safety was long ensured. Some of them even managed to rise to positions of prestige, such as Rana Bhagwandas, who sat on the Supreme Court and even served as interim chief justice in 2005, 2006 and 2007.

The situation of Hindus in Pakistan deteriorated parallel with that of Muslims in India in keeping with a finely tuned dialectic. The violence the Muslims of India were subjected to in the 1980s–90s—reaching a height with the demolition of the Ayodhya mosque in 1992 and the aftermath of this incident—gave rise to anti-Hindu retaliation in Pakistan where temples were destroyed, especially in Karachi and Lahore. Beyond that, the persecution of Hindus increasingly took the route of kidnappings, whether for ransom or not. The priest of the Kali Mata temple in Kalat (Balochistan) was for instance abducted on 21 December 2010 at the age of 82. No trace of him has ever been found.

But the most frequent modus operandi involves kidnapping young Hindu girls who are forced to convert and marry. In 2011–12, the Hindu Council of Karachi estimated there had been 15 to 20 such cases per month in the Sindh capital alone.[285] In 2012, the Hindu Council took the case of three abductions before the Supreme Court, which was able to locate the three young women and allowed them to choose their own future. All three chose to remain with their husbands, being fully aware that reintegrating their original community and even their families would be highly compli-

---

282 Asad Jamal, "A berry-picker's trial", *Herald*, 22 December 2014 (http://herald. dawn.com/2014/12/22/a-berry-pickers-trial.html).

283 "On death row for blasphemy, Aasia Bibi makes final appeal to SC", *Dawn*, 24 November 2014 (http://www.dawn.com/news/1146577).

284 The 1998 census indicated that about 250–300,000 Hindus lived in the cities of Hyderabad, Badin, Sanghar, Mirpurkhas, Umerkhot and Tharparkar where they accounted for between 12 and 47% of the population.

285 United Nations High Commissioner for Refugees, *UNHCR Eligibility Guidelines*, op. cit., p. 32, note 225. The figure was confirmed by the Lahore Human Rights Commission.

cated. The abduction of Hindu women and the subsequent forced marriages are made easier, according to the community leaders, by the fact that the Hindu marriages are not registered—hence their demand for a Hindu Marriage Act.[286]

These developments led to renewed migration of Hindus to India. In March 2011, Ram Singh Sodho, a member of the Sindh provincial assembly led the way, soon followed by hundreds of families. In 2014, more than 100 families were leaving Pakistan each month, according to Hindu rights groups.[287] Ramesh Kumar Vankwani, a Hindu MNA, declared in late 2014 that over 5,000 Hindus were migrating from Sindh every year.[288] Eager to curb a mass exodus, Pakistani authorities demanded a written pledge from Hindus crossing the border to undertake pilgrimages in India that they would not seek asylum. Many of them nevertheless remained in India— where Dalits are not necessarily as well received as others.[289] The small number of Sikhs (about 30,000) living in Pakistan may take the same route given the persecution they suffer.[290] In August 2014, the killing of Jagmohan Singh took 600 of them to the streets of Peshawar.[291]

* * *

The place of Islam in Pakistan has never been the subject of consensus. While Jinnah, in the footsteps of Sir Syed and Iqbal, viewed Islam as a territorialisable identity marker of a community discriminated against by the British and the Hindus, the Islamists—whether *ulema* or Maududi-style fundamentalists—emphasised its purely religious dimensions. After 1947, Jinnah and Liaquat Ali Khan, true to their notion of "Muslimhood" in

[286] Shazia Hasan, "Hindu community irked by 'forced conversion'", *Dawn*, 17 February 2014 (http://www.dawn.com/news/1087469).

[287] "Hindus, other minorities in Pakistan face surge of violence", *The Express Tribune*, 21 May 2014 (http://tribune.com.pk/story/704806/hindus-other-minorities-in-pakistan-face-surge-of-violence/).

[288] Manesh Kumar, "'Leave your faith or leave the country'", *Dawn*, 10 November 2014 (http://www.dawn.com/news/1143524).

[289] See, for example, "Pakistani Hindus arrive with horror tales", *Hindustan Times*, 10 August 2012.

[290] Regarding the problem of religious minorities in Pakistani society in general, see *International Religious Reform Report for 2011*, United States Department of State, 2011. See http://www.state.gov/j/drl/rls/irf/2011/sca/192933.htm (Accessed on September 15, 2013).

[291] "Minorities under siege", *The Express Tribune*, 8 August 2014 (http://tribune.com.pk/story/745655/minorities-under-siege/).

which Islam was an ideology more than a creed, promoted a multicultural, secular nation-state in which minorities would be recognized as full-fledged citizens, whereas the *ulema* and the Jama'at-e-Islami advocated an Islamic state.

Secular leaders—be they civilians or military—seized the "opportunity" of the 1953 anti-Ahmadi movement to put down the Islamists and marginalise their leaders in the course of constitutional debates. As a result, the 1956 Constitution, although it made important concessions to Islamists, guaranteed citizenship rights for minorities. The 1962 Constitution did the same. So did the one promulgated in 1973 at first, but the amendment in 1974 declaring the Ahmadis "non-Muslims" was part of a larger questioning of the regime's secular nature—already apparent in the way Islam was made the state religion.

Z. A. Bhutto, who is usually remembered as a progressive leader, was responsible for this paradoxical evolution. First, he was under the pressure of fundamentalists demonstrating in the street. Second, he found affinities between Islam and socialism. Third, he was keen to instrumentalise Islam in the political realm for his own electoral prospects and for the good of the country at a time when after the 1971 war, Pakistanis needed to rally around a common identity. On top of it, Bhutto's use of Islam was not only part of his domestic agenda. He also cashed in on this repertoire to support Afghan Islamist leaders who could help him destabilise the Pastun nationalists who ruled in Kabul.

Systematic Islamisation policies, however, were not implemented until Zia came to power. This "soldier of Islam" also exploited religion to legitimate the position he had usurped. But he went farther than that, possibly because of his conservative religious temperament, by submitting all areas of social and political life—law, education, taxation and so on—to Islamic rules and principles. Since this policy largely amounted to a form of "Sunnisation" that the Shias resented, the Zia years precipitated the crystallisation of sectarian movements. This new line of division, however, was accentuated by foreign actors, Iran and Saudi Arabia, which have been fighting a proxy war in Pakistan since the 1980s. Sectarianism today poses an existential threat to Pakistan—as it vertically divides a nation supposedly built on Islam—in the most violent way. In 2012, for instance, Lashkar-e-Jhangvi was held responsible for 128 attacks, mostly in Balochistan and Karachi.[292] Zia's policy also destabilised Pakistani society by allowing *dini*

---

[292] *Pakistan Security Report 2012*, op. cit., p. 11. These figures are consistent with

madaris to multiply, particularly in the Pashtun belt where they were intended to train anti-Soviet jihadis, and by lending newfound respectability to *mullahs* who have asserted themselves at the expense of traditional notables, in the NWFP and the FATA especially.

The groups of Islamists that emerged in the 1980s began to be used by the state after the Soviet withdrawal. In Afghanistan, they helped the ISI install the Talibans in Kabul to achieve "strategic depth", and in Kashmir they contributed to "bleeding India". But some emancipated themselves to some extent, moving closer to Al Qaeda whose fight against the United States from 1998 on and even more so after 11 September 2001 had huge consequences for Pakistan. The country then lost its strategic depth in Afghanistan and watched helplessly as New Delhi developed ties with Kabul. Pakistan was also prompted to review its strategy in another major theatre of operation, Kashmir, where it had been active through well-oiled cooperation between the regular army and Islamist groups ranging from the Taliban to Jaish-i-Mohammed and Lashkar-e-Taiba, as evident from the Kargil war.

It was obliged to pull back, but the state has not resigned easily to fighting groups that the army in general and the ISI in particular probably intended to use again once NATO troops were withdrawn from Afghanistan. Although the state's repressive measures have spared some of these partners (the LeT and the Haqqani network), they have infuriated Islamist groups, especially after the Red Mosque episode in 2007, which showed that Pakistan could go very far indeed in its partnership with the United States in its "global war on terror". The TTP, well entrenched in the FATA, has reacted by attacking the Pakistani state with such vigour that for five years now Pakistan has been experiencing a form of low intensity civil war, especially in areas where Islamist actions are compounded with ethnic strife, such as in Balochistan and Karachi.

In some place, the insurrectional nature of the Islamist upsurge reflects the movement's popularity among the Pakistani masses. The common people may indeed perceive the Islamists as an alternative to oppression by the establishment. Islamists not only benefit from a certain religious aura (especially when they cultivate martyrdom and anti-Americanism), but they have

those of the Movement for Solidarity and Peace's 2014 report in which one could read that the "most conservative estimates" of forced marriages and conversions of minor Hindu girls "put the number of victims at 300 a year" (MPC, *Report on Forced Marriages & Forced Conversions*, op. cit., p. 2).

also promoted social work and popular justice. If Islamism is perceived by some as an agent of social change, it is largely because of this long-standing dimension of the Pakistani syndrome: the radical elitism of Pakistan's rulers, be they feudals, businessmen, bureaucrats or military officers.

The Islamists' revolutionary potential has been weakened, however, by their own methods. The Pakistani people have gradually rejected the criminal techniques and the cultural policing of fundamentalists who prohibit music and prevent girls from attending school. The most militant groups have tended to turn away from their social aims to pursue an endless quest for religious purification by targeting scapegoats such as Shias and non-Muslim minorities. This is most obvious in Punjab where sectarian groups, instead of combating the dominant parties, have been increasingly patronized by them, especially the PML(N). As a result, in this key province (and elsewhere), Ahmadis, Christians, Hindus and to some degree Shias, are being targeted to such an extent that Jinnah's plan for a multicultural Pakistan is more in jeopardy than ever.

This dream nevertheless shows some signs of resilience. Nawaz Sharif, when forming his government in 2013, made it a point to give a Christian, Kamran Michael, a portfolio that was more substantial than any his predecessors had received: Ports and Shipping. At the same time, Sharif endorsed the appointment of Maulana Muhammad Khan Sherani as chairman of the Council of Islamic Ideology by Asif Zardari. This JUI (F) senator has indulged in reactionary decisions that have prompted protests from the women's rights NGO, Aurat Foundation (led by Justice (Rtd) Nasira Javid Iqbal—the daughter-in-law of Muhammad Iqbal). In September 2013 the CII ruled that DNA tests were not acceptable as primary evidence in rape cases and in March 2014, it has declared section 6 of the Muslim Family Law Ordinance (1961) as violative of the sharia. This section—which is not implemented—decrees that a husband needs the permission of his first wife if he wants to marry a second time. The CII also considers child marriages as Islamic.[293] The very fact that the authors of such rulings have been appointed by leaders of mainstream parties reflect the traditional ambivalence of these parties. While in Part Two of this book we have seen that civilians were not necessarily democrats, in this part we have observed that since Z.A. Bhutto's era, politi-

[293] "CII rules out DNA as primary evidence in rape cases", *Dawn*, 23 September 2013 (http://www.dawn.com/news/1044879, "CII: pushing Pakistan back to the caves", *Dawn*, 13 March 2014 (http://www.dawn.com/news/1092893) and Waseem Ahmad Shah, "View from courtroom: bill related to child mariages generates heated debate", *Dawn*, 31 March 2014 (http://www.dawn.com/news/1096802).

cians belonging to the PPP and (even more obviously) to the PML(N) have used Islam and Islamists (including sectarian) tactically in the region as well as as domestically. The PTI has followed the same orientation, as evident from Imran Khan's speeches and the coalition he formed in KP with the Jama'at-e-Islami—whose leader Munawar Hassan declared in January 2014 that Bin Laden was still "alive in people's heart".[294]

Naturally, the liberals are also more discrete because of intimidation measures. Besides the case of the journalists mentioned above, lawyers are at the receiving end. In 2013 the judge who sentenced the murderer of Salman Taseer, Qadri, "left the country in fear"—before the PTI demanded Qadri's liberation ...—and the prosecutor in the Benazir Bhutto assassination case, Chaudhry Zulfiqar was murdered.[295]

[294] Saqib Nasir, "Osama bin Laden still alive in people's hearts: JI Chief", *The Express Tribune*, 28 January 2014 (http://tribune.com.pk/story/664425/osama-bin-laden-still-alive-in-peoples-hearts-ji-chief/).

[295] Halima Mansoor, "Naya Pakistan, where Salmaan Taseer's murderer is a hero", *The Express Tribune*, 20 June 2013 (http://blogs.tribune.com.pk/story/17814/naya-pakistan-where-salman-taseers-murderer-is-a-hero/) and Mubashir Zaidi, "Al Qaeda activist arrested in murder of Benazir case prosecutor", *Dawn*, 14 June 2013 (http://www.dawn.com/news/1018011).

CONCLUSION

Pakistan's trajectory finally seems to be far more complex than most of the simplistic approaches tend to acknowledge. The country is no more doomed to break apart than it is destined to be dominated by the military. Its history has been marked by a succession of authoritarian phases under army rule alternating with processes of democratisation in which the rule of law has demonstrated remarkable resilience. While some ethnic groups—the Baloch and the Mohajirs following in suit with the Bengalis—have developed strong ethno-nationalist movements inclined toward separatism or political autonomy, others—the Sindhis, and to some extent the Pashtuns—have joined the Punjabis in a move toward true national integration. So much so that Pakistan in the 2000s seems less vulnerable to centrifugal forces than it was in the 1970s. From the standpoint of both its national identity and its regime, Pakistan in fact seems to move between two finally well-identified poles, as shown by the virtually ritualistic nature of military overthrows.[1] The country's cyclical shifts from one political regime to another and the recurrence of ethnic conflict nonetheless reflect chronic instability, a challenge more acute today as the Islamists are increasingly contesting Jinnah's ideology of "Muslimhood". This book has sought the key to this instability in the history and sociology of Pakistan, and the movement leading to its foundation.

---

[1] This has given rise to the theory that Pakistan cultivates a "stability paradox," an idea that however soon shows its limits. Ashutosh Misra and Michael E. Clarke (eds), *Pakistan's Stability Paradox. Domestic, Regional and International Dimensions*, London, Routledge, 2012.

One Syndrome, Three Contradictions

The Pakistani syndrome, defined in the introduction by multisectoral instability, is articulated around three types of tension: between the project for
a unitary nation-state and provinces with a strong ethnic identity; between
an authoritarian political culture and democratic forces; and between competing conceptions of Islam. A different section of the present volume has
been devoted to each of these three sources of tension. To understand how
they fit together like three sides of a triangle, the sources of the movement
for Pakistan had to be re-examined. The movement took root in separatist
demands borne by the Urdu-speaking elite of Northern India, scions of the
Mughal Empire threatened with a decline in their status due to the rise of
the Hindu majority in the last quarter of the nineteenth century. This
Muslim group embodied socio-political interests as well as a patrician culture, even a sense of entitlement by virtue of which they refused to be
subjected to a common regime, and especially the law of numbers. These
characteristics reflected the ardour with which the group defended its
interests, but can also be explained by its erstwhile status, its upper caste
ethos and its belief in the moral superiority of its Islam. It was all the less
inclined toward democracy as Muslims were a minority in Northern India.
This political culture and the mobilisation it generated to defend the interests of the community under the leadership of Syed Ahmad Khan starting
the 1880s went along with a modernisation effort through education spearheaded by the Aligarh College. But already in the early twentieth century,
Sir Syed's backers—most of them trained at Aligarh—turned their efforts to
politics by founding the Muslim League. The party developed a separatist
agenda in the sense that it petitioned the British rulers for a separate electorate—which was granted in 1906—to protect it from the Hindu majority
at a time when the Raj was undergoing democratisation.

M.A. Jinnah took the League a step further by demanding a separate
territory for Indian Muslims. The demand for Pakistan was problematic
right from the start. The men behind the project came from provinces in
which Muslims were a minority, whereas in the provinces Jinnah designated as those that should form Pakistan as of 1940, Muslims were a majority—that was precisely the reason why he, Iqbal and others before him, had
selected them. But they were not the League's strongholds, not only
because Muslims did not feel threatened by Hindus there, but also because
they maintained socio-economic relations with Hindus (and Sikhs) based
on a class logic over and above any ethno-religious agenda. Jinnah was not

able to win over the Muslim leaders in these provinces—Punjab, Bengal and Sindh—until the mid-1940s on the [strength of his promise to preserve considerable autonomy for their province(s] and because of their fear that the Hindu-dominated Congress Party was about to take over for British rule in New Delhi.

In 1947, tension immediately crystallised between the provinces identified with ethnic groups that rallied behind Jinnah's political project in the final hour and the centralist shape he gave Pakistan in the name of a unitary definition of the nation-state in which Urdu was established alongside Islam as a vehicle for national integration. This contradiction would result in yet another partition—of East Bengal this time—and would remain the source of recurrent conflicts everywhere else except, naturally,[in Punjab, as the Punjabis had identified with the Pakistani state all the better to dominate it.]The dialectic between the Centre and the provinces has often led to an exacerbation of ethnic conflicts due to the[poor sense of compromise characteristic of the central government] quick to justify its unitary reflex by pointing to the threat of India. Without denying the truth of this threat—or at least the Pakistanis' subjective perception of it, especially after 1971—it is virtually certain that members of the civilian and military establishment alike exploited it to bring the population around to their cause and subsume internal ethnic divisions by taking a united stand against a common external enemy.[2]

The authoritarianism of the ruling elites is at the crux of the second area of instability eating away at Pakistan: its political regime. This instability is inferred from the succession of periods of democratisation, coups d'état and the various Constitutions. But it would be an error to stop at appearances and consider that the pendulum thus swings from military dictatorship to a respectable form of parliamentarianism at regular intervals. In fact, no elected prime minister has ever fully played by the rules of the democratic game for his or her entire term, either because the army prevented them from doing so by (like Benazir Bhutto and Nawaz Sharif during his first term) or because they did not have the inclination. Whether it was Z.A. Bhutto or Nawaz Sharif in his second term, all of them tried either to stuff ballot boxes or to enlist the judiciary into their service.[The weakness of this democratic culture dates back to Jinnah who, perpetuating the British viceregal mode of governance, justified his

[2] This logic is at the heart of the notion of "nationalism without a nation" (Christophe Jaffrelot (ed.), *Pakistan: Nationalism Without a Nation?* op. cit.).

emphasis on discipline to the detriment of civil liberties by the sheer scale of the task at hand: to build a country from the bottom up in the shadow of the Indian threat.]

But while the fear of India is not merely a pretence, the authoritarianism of the ruling elites also proceeds from sociological factors. Since 1947 and even before then, the[political personnel has been recruited mainly among the traditional rural notables,]whether the large landowners of Punjab, the *waderos* in Sindh, the *khans* in Pashtun areas or the *sardars* of Balochistan. All of them embody a strongly hierarchical social ethos and dominate clientelistic relationships that put "their" peasant voters under obligation to them. This profoundly conservative system has managed to endure for lack of any serious land reform, which was compromised precisely by the political weight of feudal lords. A similar pattern emerged among urban notables after the PML(N) became the mouthpiece for the Punjabi business community, the PML(Q) being more the representative for agrarian interests, a role the PPP continues to fulfil in Sindh and southern Punjab.

It seems that many members of the civilian elites primarily went into politics to defend their own interests. This moreover explains the collusive transactions they cultivate with the military, thereby exposing the limits of their sense of democracy—a reasoning that should however be tempered somewhat, as even the Bhutto family has known prison and death. But even though Punjabi leaders from Nawaz Sharif to Chaudhry Shujaat Hussain have carried such collaboration with the military further than anyone else, it should be remembered that Z. A. Bhutto began his career as minister under Mirza and later served under Ayub Khan. Such blurring of the boundaries between civil and military reflects the existence of a civil-military establishment whose primary goal is to perpetuate its dominant status in both the political and socio-economic sphere. The military's acquired taste for such endeavours is moreover evidenced by their new commercial and industrial activities and the scale of corruption in their midst—even if politicians remain the champions of personal enrichment. The convergence of civil and military authorities within an establishment comprising some 2,000 families offers a key to the interpretation of the country's stability paradox:[whether political parties or the army are in power, it is the interests of one and the same class that are protected[3]]—as shown by the persistently low tax burden, the absence of land reform and

---

[3] This analysis naturally allows for an exception: Z. A. Bhutto's policy to control the business community that resulted in widespread nationalisations.

the continuously high level of military expenditure.[4] Today, as long as the army remains in charge of the state's policy regarding Afghanistan, India and the nuclear programme, it prefers to be in a position to exert power without political responsibility.

The collusion and transactions between the civilians and the military continue to go on whereas mass poverty remains the rule: the poorest 20 per cent scarcely have a larger share of the national revenue in 1993–4 than they did in 1963–4: 9.2 per cent as opposed to 6.4 per cent.[5]

[Pakistan's less privileged classes have, however, never completely resigned themselves to this state of affairs.]In the 1950s-60s, they supported, leftist forces that defended socialist ideas in elections, when held, and otherwise in the street. The finest example of political and social mobilisation remains the movement of 1968–9. The judiciary has also sought to counterbalance civil and military governments, including in the street in 2007, though without emerging as a force in the service of the common man. In fact, the people have been without a recognized spokesman since the PPP watered down its programme in the early 1970s.

The marginalisation of leftwing forces, which commenced with the banning of the Communist Party in 1954, in fact went hand in hand with the establishment's assertion of its social ascendancy. Even if power changes hands as governments and regimes follow in succession the public policies implemented have always favoured a slim elite. This dimension of the Pakistani syndrome intersects with the previous one. Centralisation of power is congruent with the concentration of not only political power but also economic and social power. And these two sources of tension reflect the domination of elite groups that have inherited their status from their noble ancestors or in the case of nouveaux riches, who have modelled their ethos after them and have assumed their interests.

This political economy is a factor aggravating the third Pakistani contradiction, which pertains to the place of Islam. The lack of a consensus regarding the role of Islam in the plan for Pakistan is the repercussion of a contradiction that can be traced back to the last third of the nineteenth century when on one hand the Aligarh movement defined the community it wished to defend on the basis of a culture rooted in a territory—that of Urdu-speaking Muslims in Northern India—whereas on the other hand, the

---

[4] Nawaz Sharif increased them by 10% immediately after taking power in 2013.

[5] Muhammad Abdul Qader, *Pakistan. Social and Cultural Transformations in a Muslim Nation*, London, Routledge, 2006, p. 8.

Deoband seminar took the path of a return to the sources of Islam that could only mean the *umma* as a whole. This conflict persisted in the colonial twentieth century, as Jinnah adopted Sir Syed's territorial conception in his demand for a nation-state, while the *ulema* from Deoband and other seminaries backed the Congress Party in exchange for recognition of the Muslim *millet*'s autonomy.

Partition further sharpened this opposition. The Muslim League went down the road of a certain multiculturalism given that, in keeping with the ideal spelled out by Jinnah, religious minorities were to have the same rights as other citizens, whereas the *ulema* and the Jama'at-e-Islami fundamentalists demanded the establishment of an Islamic state and/or lapsed into potentially borderless Islamism. The compromises crafted by each of the three Constitutions all leaned in favour of the first option. But in practice this line was deviated from as of 1974, the year in which the Ahmadis were declared non-Muslims, and even more so under Zia due to his wholesale Islamisation policy.

Starting in the 1980s, Pakistan was confronted with a contradiction between an ideological legacy using Islam to define a cultural community ("Muslimhood"), which, although dominant, was not exclusive, and another that asserted the need for the majority to prevail, at the expense of minorities relegated to second-class citizens. The growing affirmation of the latter posture would not have been such a considerable factor of destabilisation if it had not resulted in the persecution of microscopic minorities such as the Ahmadis, the Hindus and the Christians. But the quest for Islamic purity and more prosaically the formulation of public policies intended to serve Islamisation, exacerbated a division between Sunni and Shia Muslims with ominous implications.

This sectarian conflict probably represents a more serious existential threat to Pakistan's unity than any other. It in fact has the potential to divide the country vertically, whereas most of the other dividing lines, most of them along ethnic bases, are confined to a region and do not affect Punjab. This major source of instability lies at the intersection of internal and external dynamics. Indeed, on top of Zia's Islamisation policy—which can also be qualified as "Sunnisation"—has also come the proxy war that Iran and Saudi Arabia have been waging in Pakistan since the 1980s, an additional explanation for the rise of sectarianism.

But the risks of destabilisation that the various forms of Islamism pose to Pakistan also arise from another phenomenon blending internal and external factors, and that is jihadism. Here again, national policies spawned these problems, even though they only took on considerable importance due to regional contexts. Pakistan's leaders were for instance the first to fly to the aid of Afghan Islamists, viewing them as useful to combat Pashtun nationalism in the 1970s. This policy, instigated by Z.A. Bhutto, was pursued and systematised by Zia in the wake of the Soviet invasion of Afghanistan and the Afghan mujahideen falling back on Pakistan.

Similarly, Zia and his successors, from Benazir Bhutto to Musharraf and including Nawaz Sharif, later used jihadists returning from Afghanistan after the Soviet withdrawal to "bleed India" in Kashmir—going so far as to trigger an armed conflict in Kargil. Although this more or less low-intensity conflict was orchestrated by the ISI, the civil and military officials at best left them a free hand. In the 1990s, jihadist groups and militant Sunni organisations thus thrived and joined forces, particularly in Afghanistan, after the victory of the Taliban—which Pakistan largely set up in power.

This policy met with a spectacular backlash after 11 September 2001 and the fall of the Taliban. Pakistan, which had been the crucible for groups active in Afghanistan—including Al Qaeda—was naturally used as their fallback position. But it became their target, and the base for a new movement, the Pakistani Taliban, once Musharraf undertook to crack down on his erstwhile partners under pressure from the United States. The spread of terrorist violence throughout the country has been accompanied by the formation of pockets of civil war, especially in the FATA.

The Pakistani generals' adventurist policies in their search for allies against India and the Pashtun nationalists from Afghanistan are not, however, the only explanation for the scale of the Islamist phenomenon. It also flows from the observation drawn from the previous contradiction: monopolisation of social power by a slim elite, the widening of inequalities and the absence of leftist forces have all contributed in their own ways to the Islamists' popularity. In the eyes of the common people, they can appear to offer an alternative to an oppressive establishment, all the more since the best organized Islamist groups, such as Lashkar-e-Taiba, are involved in social welfare activities and rescue operations such as those following the 2005 earthquake and the 2010 floods. Beyond that, a number of fighting *mullahs*—those from the Red Mosque down to the Pakistani Taliban— expound a revolutionary rhetoric that is sometimes acted upon: in the FATA, Islamists have killed a number of feudal landlords, their direct competitors, and meted out summary justice which for a while was a factor in their popularity, together with the dominant parameter: their hostility to the American "occupation" of Afghanistan.

The third dimension of the Pakistani syndrome, which today has taken the shape of militant Islamism, is thus connected to the second—the harshness of societal hierarchies—partly reducing a problem of identity to a socio-political issue. This was moreover the conclusion reached in the analysis of the original tension between the Centre and the provinces, the exacerbation of ethnic centrifugal forces owing much to the hunger for power of an establishment that defends a unitary definition of "its" nation-state. This interpretation, partly founded on a political economy analysis, should not mask the role of symbols—by protecting their interests, the elites are also defending their symbolic status or prestige—or emotions: the fear of India is of course partly exploited by the establishment to justify considerable military expenditure and the quashing of opponents, but it is also a reality that dates back to Partition and is reactivated every now and then, from one war to the next.

The plebeian and anti-establishment nature of the Islamists should nevertheless be qualified. Not only are their violent methods and their cultural policing resented by followers of popular Islam throughout the country, but some of them, including sectarian groups in Punjab, have joined hands with mainstream parties, including the PML(N), articulating the interests of dominant groups. Whether such moves are purely tactical or if instead major Islamist organisations such as the SSP and the LeT have truly turned away from their social agenda to focus on their fight against Shias and minorities remains to be seen.

The Fourth Dimension: Elites Backed by External Support

[If the three dimensions of the Pakistani syndrome dealt with in this volume and summarized in the preceding pages form a system, they must still be viewed in their regional as well as international context to be fully understandable.)

In all countries, the political sphere is situated at the interface of internal and external dynamics. This interaction has even given rise to a subset of international relations theories.[6] But in Pakistan, this phenomenon has taken on such a scale that the international environment should be regarded as forming a full-fledged component of domestic policy. The influence of this external element on Pakistan can first be explained by the

[6] Marcel Merle can probably be considered the trailbreaker in this regard. See his book *Sociologie des relations internationales*, Paris, Dalloz, 1974.

feeling of vulnerability Pakistani elites have toward India—and its Afghan partner at the time of independence in 1947. As a result, as Khalid Bin Sayeed pointed out in 1964, in matters of foreign policy, "Almost every action of Pakistan can be interpreted as being motivated by fear of India."[7] An editorial published in *Dawn* in 1963 explains in this regard, "If the main concern of the Christian West is the containment of Chinese communism, the main concern of Muslim Pakistan is the containment of militarist and militant Hinduism."[8]

Pakistan from its very creation in 1947 situated itself precisely at the intersection of these two preoccupations by offering the United States its services. Eisenhower seized upon this offer at the start of the Korean War in 1952.[9] This collaboration offers a textbook case of clientelism.[10] Beginning in the 1950s, Washington decided to rely on the "Land of the Pure" to better contain communism in Asia by getting Pakistan—which had become a member of CENTO and SEATO—to agree to the installation of an air force base for its U2 spy planes; in exchange, Pakistan turned American support to its advantage in keeping with two roots of its syndrome: the fear of India and the preservation of its elites' status.

To allay its fear of India, the United States sold increasingly sophisticated weapons to Pakistan. To help its elites maintain their status, the Americans gave the country such aid that it could do without any true fiscal policy to achieve modernization. Ayub Khan candidly admitted as much when he dealt with the topic in his memoirs:

Development presupposes resources, and in our social conditions and our scheme of values these resources cannot all be generated or mobilized through regimentation. Therefore we have to look for external assistance to build up the social overheads and provide the initial capital investment. This necessitates our having good relations with the United States and other western powers who are in the position to help us economically. Now any assistance creates certain liabilities; we have to

---

[7] Khalid Bin Sayeed, "Pakistan's Foreign Policy: An Analysis of Pakistan's Fears and Interests," *Asian Survey*, vol. 4, no. 3, 1965, p. 747.

[8] Cited in Aparna Pande, *Explaining Pakistan's Foreign Policy*, London, Routledge, 2011, p. 24.

[9] Regarding relations between Pakistan and the United States from Truman to George W. Bush, see Dennis Kux, *The United States and Pakistan, 1947–2000. Disenchanted Allies*, Baltimore and London, The Johns Hopkins University Press, 2001.

[10] For further details, see Christophe Jaffrelot, "La relation Pakistan-Etats-Unis: un patron et son client au bord de la rupture?," *Les Etudes du CERI*, no. 187, September 2012.

ensure that we do not incur such liabilities as would compromise or damage our national interests.[11]

Already in the 1960s, Ayub Khan thus outlined the contours of the fourth dimension of the Pakistani syndrome: the country's development would not be financed through taxes, which the rich would refuse to pay and compelling them was out of the question. Instead, it would be funded by foreign aid, and American assistance would have to be sought.[12] This approach, however, made Pakistan run the risk of compromising its sovereignty.

For many years, Pakistan-US relations would be perceived as mutually beneficial. As Akbar Zaidi explains, "By 1964, overall aid and assistance to Pakistan was around 5 percent of its GDP and was arguably critical in spurring Pakistani industrialization and development, with GDP growth rates rising to as much as 7 percent per annum."[13] The war of 1965, which provoked American sanctions, was followed by a decline, later reversed by the war against the Soviets in Afghanistan during which the United States funded Pakistan for ten years. While military aid could be counted in hundreds of millions of dollars to the great delight of the army in general and Zia in particular, civilian assistance also resumed its upward curve, soaring from 57 million dollars in 1981 to 302 million in 1985 and 351 million in 1990.[14] The 1990s saw another downhill slide due to Pakistan's nuclear proliferation activities and Islamabad's ties with the Taliban, two reasons that prompted Washington to impose new sanctions on Islamabad. But the 11 September attacks brought the two countries back to forms of cooperation comparable to those of the 1980s, this time with Afghanistan the theatre of a war against terrorism. To help Pakistan fight it, and especially to persuade it to do so, the United States once again offered the country a military windfall as well as considerable civilian assistance; between a quarter and a third of the nearly twenty billion dollars Washington paid Islamabad from 2001 to 2011 was earmarked for development.[15]

---

[11] Muhammad Ayub Khan, *Friends not Masters*, op. cit., p. 138.

[12] In the early 1960s the tax-to-GDP ratio was below 10% and more than 70% of the total resources available to spend in Pakistan were external funds. (Ilhan Niaz, *The Culture of Power and Governance of Pakistan*, op. cit., p. 214).

[13] S. Akbar Zaidi, "Who Benefits from US Aid to Pakistan?" *Economic and Political Weekly*, vol. 46, no. 32, 2011.

[14] Abdul Sattar, *Pakistan Foreign Policy, 1947–2009*, Karachi, Oxford University Press, 2010, p. 186.

[15] K. Alan Kronstadt, *Pakistan-U.S. Relations*, op. cit., p. 94 and K. Alan Kronstadt,

CONCLUSION

The clientelistic relationship between Pakistan and the United States is fraught with contradictions.[16] First of all, it spares the state from having to implement a fiscal policy that would enable transfers from the richest to the poorest segments of the population and to finance such elementary public services as education. In so doing, it perpetuates the most debilitating aspects of the social contradiction discussed above.[17] Second, it imposes on the country a loss of sovereignty that is difficult to accept. As long as the United States continues to pay, it will obtain concessions from Pakistan that erode its sovereignty, such as access to the nation's territory to step up drone strikes. The US armed forces occasionally enter Pakistani territory without permission, as during the raid on Osama bin Laden on 2 May 2011.

This infringement on the state's sovereignty, which follows on decades of a clientelistic relationship, is the cause of a huge deficit of self-esteem. One Pakistani intellectual thus admitted in 2010, "We acknowledge to ourselves privately that Pakistan is a client state of the U.S. But on the other hand, the U.S. is acting against Muslim interests globally. A sort of self-loathing came about."[18]

This feeling is at the root of staunch anti-Americanism and hence of demonstrations unequalled in scale in the Muslim world whenever a Protestant fundamentalist burns a copy of the Quran in the depths of Texas or when a film showing disrespect for Islam is shown in the United States.

"Direct Overt U.S. Aid and Military Reimbursements to Pakistan, FY2002–FY2011." See http://www.fas.org/sgp/crs/row/pakaid.pdf. (Accessed on September 15, 2013).

[16] For a detailed analysis, see C. Jaffrelot, "The US-Pakistan Relations under Obama: Resilience of Clientelism?", in C. Jaffrelot (ed.), *Pakistan at the Crossroads. Domestic Dynamics and External Pressures*, New York, Columbia University Press (forthcoming).

[17] This dependence is bound to increase. In 2013, the budget Nawaz Sharif had passed in parliament relied on a 1.37% increase in foreign assistance, raising this budget line to 5.7 billion dollars, or 13% of the fiscal revenue. Shahbaz Rana, "Govt Fails in Reducing Reliance on Foreign Assistance", *The Express Tribune*, 14 June 2013. See http://tribune.com.pk/story/562958/govt-fails-reducing-reliance-on-foreign-assistance/ (Accessed on September 15, 2013) and Ferya Ilyas, "If I'm Taxing the Rich, People Should Support Me: Ishaq Dar", ibid., 13 June 2013, available at: http://tribune.com.pk/story/562727/if-im-taxing-the-rich-people-should-support-me-ishaq-dar (Accessed on September 15, 2013).

[18] Cited in Sabrina Tavernise, "US Is a Top Villain in Pakistan's Conspiracy Talk," *The New York Times*, 25 May 2010 (http://www.nytimes.com/2010/05/26/world/asia/26pstan.html?pagewanted=all).

More recently, this rejection of Uncle Sam has fostered the rise of the party led by Imran Khan, who in particular has campaigned against drone strikes in the FATA.[19]

Pakistan will be less indispensable to Washington once the withdrawal of American troops from Afghanistan is complete. The United States will then accelerate the reduction in financial assistance that it provides to the country, a process already underway. If China and Saudi Arabia do not take over this role, which they are unlikely to do given the amounts involved, Islamabad will have to undertake tax reform that might reverse the course it has been confined to by the fourth dimension of the Pakistani syndrome.[20]

[19] Regarding the appeal of Imran Khan's anti-American rhetoric, see Madiha R. Tahir, "What Pakistan sees in Imran Khan," *The Caravan*, vol. 4, no. 1, January 2012, pp. 32–45.

[20] Alternatively, Pakistan will have to rely more on the remittances that overseas workers send home (but the amount already jumped from $ 1.5 bn in 2001 to almost $ 15 bn in 2013) and on the IMF (but debt servicing already represent $ 2 bn every year). For a detailed analysis, see Saim Saeed and Khurram Siddiqui, "The Express Tribune explains foreign debt", *The Express Tribune*, 24 December 2014 (http://labs.tribune.com.pk/foreign-debt/).

AFTER 16 DECEMBER 2014

WHAT "POST-PESHAWAR" PAKISTAN?

On 16 December 2014, nine gunmen attacked an Army Public School in Peshawar after entering it disguised in uniforms of the Frontier Corps. They went directly to the auditorium and opened fire on the children as well as the staff. Teachers and the principal were burnt alive in front of the pupils. Most of the children who were targeted were shot in the head. A total of 150 people were killed, including 134 children, ten schoolteachers and three soldiers. The nine gunmen, who were all killed once the Special Services Group intervened, were members of the TTP, which claimed responsibility for the attack.[1] The organisation spokesperson, Muhammad Omar Khorasani, declared: "we targeted the school because the Army targets our families", a clear indication that the attack was designed as an act of revenge for the North Waziristan operation.

Instead of weakening the army and dissuading it from fighting the Islamists, the trauma that this attack has caused for Pakistan has strengthened the military and its determination to take on at least some militants. First, the loss of so many sons of army personnel has created an emotional urge for solidarity with an institution whose soldiers and officers were not only fighting on the ground, but were now suffering as fathers. Second, in a war-like atmosphere of this kind, the army appeared more than before as the saviour. Ayesha Siddiqa pointed out that "The political class in general

---

[1] The TTP has targeted children previously, including Malala Yousafzai in 2012. She was to win the Peace Nobel Prize in 2014 along with Gandhian activist Kailash Satyarthi.

will have to understand the fact that the popular political narrative has been re-defined and no longer favours them. Ultimately, it is the military which saved the people, the first one to execute terrorists and the sole guarantor of security".[2] Third, the army showed a great sense of decisiveness, as evident from COAS Raheel Sharif's trip to Kabul on December 17 to persuade the Afghan authorities to help the Pakistani army take on Fazlullah, the TTP chief who supposedly operates from Afghanistan. Certainly, Nawaz Sharif displayed a degree of firmness as well by lifting the moratorium on capital punishment, but the first two executions, on December 20, were those of Dr Usman (who had taken part in the attack against the GHQ in 2009) and that of Arshad Mehmood (who had participated in the assassination attempt against Musharraf in 2003). The five executions that followed on December 22 and 31 were also of militants who had been involved in attacks against the former COAS turned President of Pakistan, as if those who deserved to be killed first were those who had targeted the army.

Fourth, the reaction of the government and the parliament has reinforced the army. On December 24, a National Action Plan was shaped by representatives of the whole nation, indeed, including all the parties with elected members in Parliament—even those from the PTI which seized this opportunity to suspend its six-month agitation—and the army. Among the 20 points of the NAP figured "Zero tolerance for militancy in Punjab", a province where the PML(N) had been accused of complacency; the commitment that "Execution of convicted terrorists will continue" and the "Establishment of special trial courts for two years for speedy trial of terror suspects".[3]

Certainly, something had to be done to fight terrorism and punish the guilty men more effectively. In Sindh, for instance, in addition to the existing 18 Anti-Terrorist Courts, in 2013, the government had given 15 sessions court in Karachi the additional task of acting as Anti-Terrorist Courts and of trying the cases falling within the purview of the Anti-Terrorist Act (1997). But in one year, only 798 cases out of 2,700 had been disposed of and 543 accused had been acquitted. Hence a very low conviction rate (32%).[4]

---

[2] Ayesha Siddiqa, "Return of nationalism", *The Express Tribune*, 25 Dec. 2014 (http://tribune.com.pk/story/811741/return-of-nationalism/).

[3] For the complete list see Abdul Manan, "Fight against terrorism: Defining moment", *The Express Tribune*, 25 Dec. 2014 (http://tribune.com.pk/story/811947/fight-against-terrorism-defining-moment/).

[4] Ishaq Tanoli, "Eight of Sindh's 33 ATCs acquitted all the suspects they tried in 15

Such dysfunction of the rule of law was generally attributed to the judiciary, but the problems often arose from poor investigation by the police and the absence of witness (and lawyer) protection by the security apparatus. The government's fear of reprisals needs to be factored in, too. The judges have sentenced to death about 8,000 criminals who are now on death row—a world record—but the PPP government had decided a moratorium on executions in 2008 and Nawaz Sharif upheld it until the Peshawar tragedy.

After this tragedy, the limitations of the judicial process, instead of resulting in a reform, led the All-Parties Conference that produced the 20-point NAP to hand the terrorism cases over to military courts. Certainly, dissenting voices were heard among Islamic parties—especially the JUI(F)[5]—and within the PPP and the PTI. But opponents argued mostly (sometimes only) against the need to amend the Constitution to do so.[6] PPP senator Aitzaz Ahsan, for instance, supported recourse to military courts in terrorism-related cases, but considered that it could be achieved "through a simple amendment to the law, instead of amending the constitution".[7]

However, the military was adamant: it wanted this transfer of judicial power (which nullified an important aspect of the separation of powers) to be protected as much as possible from a Supreme Court ruling. Indeed, in the past, the Court has struck down similar laws on the grounds that they violated the Constitution. The political class offered them this huge concession

---

months", *Dawn*, 6 January 2015 (http://www.dawn.com/news/1155170). In some cases, even the prosecutors were inhibited by fear, as in the case of Salman Taseer's murderer (Malik Asad, "Govt lawyers not ready to prosecute Mumtaz Qadri", *Dawn*, 25 January 2015 (http://www.dawn.com/news/11593). In that particular case, a special judge of the ATC who convicted Qadri fled the country because of threats to his life. Similarly, the ATC of Islamabad granted bail to Zakiur Rehman Lakhvi in December 2014 because of legal loopholes affecting his trial—primarily the fact that in six years, only 50 witnesses had been examined.

[5] Fazlur Rehman was clearly apprehensive that the military courts should be "used to target religious seminaries and institutions" (Raza Bangash, "Fazl mobilising religious parties to protest against military courts law", *Dawn*, 7 January 2015, (http://www.dawn.com/news/1155499).

[6] The JUI(F) was also against the tenth item regarding "Registration and regulation of Madrassas".

[7] "PTI, PPP rethink support for military courts", *Dawn*, 31 December 2014 (http://www.dawn.com/news/1154114). See also "PPP lawmaker's unhappy over leadership's decision on military courts", *Dawn*, 6 January 2015 (http://www.dawn.com/news/1155195).

on a platter. In that sense, the post-Peshawar scenario has allowed the army to continue to assert its power at the expense of the civilians—to such an extend that, according to Zahid Hussain, "Even the term 'soft coup' may not be an appropriate one."[8] However, after the Peshawar tragedy, civil society organisations mobilised in a rather unprecedented manner. In Islamabad, demonstrators protested before the Red Mosque after its main cleric, Maulana Abdul Aziz, declared that he would not condemn the killing of the children of Peshawar and that he would not consider them as martyrs. A case was filed against him on December 19, and on December 26 the district court of Islamabad issued a non-bailable warrant for his arrest on the charge of threatening the demonstrators who camped for a few days before the mosque. But "police officers said they were finding it hard to implement the orders in the case of Abdul Aziz, and feared that his detention under the Maintenance of Public Order (MPO) may create a law and order situation".[9]

In fact, police had already registered 22 cases against him before and after the Red Mosque affair in 2007. None of them materialised mainly because "witnesses either changed their testimony or never appeared in court".[10] Their attitude was largely due to fear. Hardly anything has changed after Peshawar, except that the cleric delivered his sermons over the phone, using the microphone of the Red Mosque, which is run by the government.[11]

Besides Abdul Aziz, other Islamists have been spared. The Haqqani network and Jamaatud Dawa[12] are cases in point. In January 2015, the US administration welcomed Pakistan's decision to ban them, but the government of Islamabad had made no such announcement. It merely indicated that these organisations had been designated as terrorist organisations by the UN and Pakistan, as a UN country "is under obligations to proscribe the entities and individuals that are listed".[13] Except that the Haqqani network

8. Zahid Hussain, "Down a slippery slope", *Dawn*, 22 January 2015 (http://www.dawn.com/news/1158315).

9. Munawer Azeem, "Police 'reluctant' to execute warrants for Lal Masjid cleric's arrest", *Dawn*, 27 Dec. 2014 (http://www.dawn.com/news/1153394).

10. Ibid..

11. Ikram Junaidi, "Maulana Aziz delivers another Friday sermon over the phone", *Dawn*, 24 January 2015 (http://www.dawn.com/news/1159105).

12. JuD is the name of the mother organisation of the LeT, which was used by the LeT too—because it was less controversial—after the LeT was designated as a terrorist organisation by the US in 2001 and even more after the LeT was banned in Pakistan in 2002.

13. Cited in Baqir Sajjad Syed and Iftikhar A. Khan, "Confusion over status of JuD, Haqqani network", *Dawn*, 23 January 2015 (http://www.dawn.com/news/1158809).

and the JuD and its chief Hafiz Saeed were "listed" by the UN respectively in 2012 and 2008 and this has made hardly any difference in Pakistan. In December 2014, the organisation, for the first time since the 1980s, held its annual *ijtema* (congregation) in Punjab. Saeed addressed a crowd of 400,000 people.[14] Asked five weeks later about the "ban" that the US had announced, Saeed declared that it was "nothing new": "It has been going on over the past six years".[15]

On December 24, 2014, one week after the Peshawar tragedy, in a televised address, Prime Minister Sharif declared, "A line has been drawn. On one side are coward terrorists and on the other side stands the whole nation". He also stated, "The Peshawar atrocity has changed Pakistan". Is this new Pakistan different from the "Naya Pakistan" promoted during the 2013 election? Or is it a "new" new Pakistan? Only the future will tell, but while the army is pursuing the North Waziristan operation with unprecedented determination, it is also acquiring more and more power at the expense of the democratisation process—and "good Islamists", including the LeT, still have a strong presence in the public sphere.

[14] Amjad Mahmood, "Footprints: JuD's show of strength", *Dawn*, 7 December 2014 (http://www.dawn.com/news/1149307).
[15] Cited in "Hafiz Saeed unmoved by talk of ban on JuD", *Dawn* 25 January 2015 (http://www.dawn.com/news/1159338).

GLOSSARY

ahmadis	members from a heterodox Muslim sect founded by Mirza Ghulam Ahmad in 1899. Ahmad presented himself as a prophet and was acknowledged as such by his disciples, in contradiction with the Muslim dogma according to which Muhammad is the last prophet.
anjuman	meeting, assembly.
Arya Samaj	Hindu revivalist movement born in 1875 in Punjab.
Ashraf	lit. "nobles"; generic term designating all Muslims of foreign origin in India—Arabs, Turks and Afghans–, who, with high caste converts form a social category that is superior to the *Ajlaf*, the low caste converts.
awqaf	plural for waqf (see waqf).
baraka	divine flow transmitted by Muslim saints; by extension, blessing and luck.
Barelwis	adepts of a Sunni movement that appeared in the 1880s in North India in reaction to Deobandi school. Barelwis are a majority in Pakistan and their singularity rests in the importance they give to worshipping saints and in their particular devotion to the Prophet.
Biharis	name given to Urdu-speaking Muslims from East Pakistan, later Bangladesh, who mostly belong to families that left Bihar during Partition.
biradari or *biraderi*	lit. "fraternity"; endogamous unit descending from a common ancestor—clan, community or sub-caste.

GLOSSARY

Bohra	Muslim group from Indian Gujarat, mostly Ismaili Shias from the Musta'li branch.
dargah	lit. "door", "threshold"; holy place, and more precisely sanctuary of a Muslim saint.
da'wah	lit. "invitation" to accept Islam. The word refers to various forms of proselytism and predication.
Deobandis	adepts of a socio-religious reforms movement deriving from the madrassah created in 1867 in the city of Deoband. Deobandis are part of the first Muslim fundamentalists in South Asia.
dini madaris	religious schools (plural for madrassah).
fatwa	traditionally, judgement given by a qualified jurisconsult of Muslim law. Islamist movements have also started issuing fatwas.
fiqh	lit. "understanding"; Muslim law, jurisprudence.
hadith	oral Islamic tradition reporting the Prophet's words and doings.
hajj	pilgrimage to Mecca.
hijra	lit. "migration"; Hegira or migration of the Prophet from Mecca to Medina in 622. This migration marks the official start of the Islamic religion.
hudud	plural for hadd, lit. "limit". The word refers to a punishment meted out in Muslim law for certain violations of divine law (theft, alcohol consumption, fornication...)
ijma	lit. "consensus"; the third source of Muslim law after the Quran and Sunnah. Generally it refers to a consensus among ulema.
ijtihad	the use of human reason, for example to interpret a rule of sharia law.
islamiyat	lit. "Islamity"; name given in Pakistan to the religious curriculum taught since Zulfikar Ali Bhutto's regime.
jat	large intermediary caste of farmers in Punjab.
jazirat al-Arab	the Arabian peninsula.
jirga	assembly of tribal chiefs, mostly among Pashtuns.
jotedar	small landowner, or even rich tenant farmer, in Bengal.
kafir	unbeliever, infidel.

Karbala (battle of)	a battle that took place in Karbala (today's Iraq) in 680 between the troops of Husain and caliph Yazid. Husain (Muhammad's grandson, son of Ali and Fatima) lost his life during the battle. The mausoleum built in his memory has become one of the principal places of Shia pilgrimage.
khan	name generally given by Pathans to designate the leader of a clan or tribe. It is also a very common surname in the Indian subcontinent in other communities as well.
Khoja	Muslim group from Indian Gujarat, mostly Ismaili Shias of the Nizari branch.
lashkar	army, militia, military camp.
Makhdum	title used for a pir.
malik	title used by Pashtun tribes to refer to the leader of a clan.
millat	lit. "religious community". In the Indian context, a Muslim community within the Indian nation.
Muhajir	Muslim of Indian origin having permanently migrated to Pakistan following Partition.
murîd	a Sufi disciple.
namaz	canonical prayer.
Pir	spiritual master in a Sufi brotherhood; Muslim saint, living or dead, who can perform miracles.
qaum	Any subdivision of the universal Muslim community; in British India and during the movement for the creation of Pakistan, *qaum* refers to the community opposed to Hindus and considered as a nation by the Muslim League.
qazi	judge in charge of enforcing Islamic law.
qisas	private retaliation for a murder or mutilation, consisting of inflicting the same damage on the guilty party.
raj	state, and more particularly its power of control. If capitalized, the word refers to the British Empire in India: the British Raj.
Rajput	caste of warriors belonging to the second order (Kshatriya) in the caste hierarchy.
riba	loan with interests, usury.

sajjada nashin	lit. "the one sitting on a prayer mat"; guardian of a Sufi sanctuary.
sardar	Persian title for commander, tribal chief—mostly in Balochistan.
sharia	Muslim law made up of norms and injunctions from the Quran and Sunnah.
Shudras	fourth order in the caste hierarchy. Below high castes, in particular because of their impurity, shudras are mainly farmers, livestock breeders and craftsmen.
Sipahi	soldier, law enforcement agent.
Sunnah	the Prophet's good custom, a code of proper conduct for Muslims. It is recorded in the traditions (hadith) passed on by the Prophet's companions. Sunnah is the second source of Muslim law after the Quran.
tahsildar	head of a local administrative subdivision of the state in the Indian subcontinent since the Mughal Empire.
taliban	plural for taleb; students of theology trained in seminars or dini madaris.
taluqdar	large landowners in Awadh.
tanzim	organization, federation.
ulema	plural for alim, doctor in Muslim law.
Umma	universal Muslim community, by opposition to national communities (qaum and millat).
ushr	lit. "tithe"; religious tax on harvest, generally 10%.
waderos	big land owners of Sindh.
waqf	results generally from donations. A waqf is a Muslim religious endowment or inalienable property dedicated to Allah the income from which goes to fund religious or charitable institutions.
zakat	lit. "purification"; compulsory alms for all Muslims, corresponding to 2.5% of annual income.
zamindar	representative of the Mughal Empire in charge of collecting property taxes for a given area. The term has come to mean more generally large landowner.

LIST OF ACRONYMS

ANP	Awami National Party
APMSO	All Pakistan Mohajir Students Organization
APNEC	All Pakistan Newspapers Employees Confederation
APNS	All Pakistan Newspapers Society
APP	Associated Press of Pakistan
APWA	All Pakistan Women's Association
ATC	Anti-terrorist Court
AZO	Al Zulfikar Organization
BLA	Balochistan Liberation Army
BNA	Baloch National Alliance
BNM	Baloch National Movement
BNP	Baloch National Party
BNR&R	Bureau of National Research and Reconstruction
BPLF	Baluch People's Liberation Front
BRA	Baloch Republican Army
BSO	Baloch Students Organization
CII	Council of Islamic Ideology
CMLA	Chief Martial Law Administrator
CNDS	Committee for Defence and National Security
COAS	Chief of Army Staff
COS	Chief of Staff
CSS	Central Superior Service
CZF	Central Zakat Fund
DCC	Defence Committee of the Cabinet
DGMO	Director General of Military Operations
DM	dini madaris

DPR	Defence of Pakistan Rules
EBDO	Elective Bodies Disqualification Order
ESMA	Essential Services Maintenance Act
FAFEN	Free and Fair Election Network
FATA	Federally Administered Tribal Areas
FF	Fauji Foundation
FIA	Federal Investigation Agency
FLL	Federative Legislative List
HRCP	Human Rights Commission of Pakistan
HuJI	Harakat-ul-Jihad-e-Islami
HuM	Harakat-ul-Mujahideen
IJI	Islami Jamhoori Ittehad
IJT	Islami Jamiat-e-Tulaba
ISI	Inter-Services Intelligence
ISO	Imamia Student's Organization
ITHS	Idara-e Tahaffuz-e Hoquq-e Shia
JCSC	Joint Chiefs of Staff Committee
JI	Jama'at-e-Islami
JUH	Jamiat-e-Ulama-e-Hind
JUI	Jamiat-Ulema-e-Islam
JUI(F)	Jamiat-e-Ulema-e-Islam (Fazlur Rehman)
JUI(S)	Jamiat-e-Ulema-e-Islam (Sami ul-Haq))
JUP	Jamiat-e-Ulema Pakistan
JWP	Jamhoori Watan Party
K-P	Khyber-Pakhtunkhwa
KSP	Krishak Sramik Party
LeJ	Lashkar-e-Jhangvi
LeL	Lashkar-e-Islam
LeT	Lashkar-e-Taiba
LZF	Local Zakat Funds
MDI	Markaz al-Dawa-wal-Irshad
MFLO	Muslim Family Laws Ordinance
MIT	Muhajir Ittehad Tehrik
MKP	Mazdoor Kisan Party
MMA	Muttahida Majlis-e-Amal
MQM	Mohajir Qaumi Mahaz, and subsequently Muttehida Qaumi Mahaz
MQM(A)	MQM Altaf
MQM (Haqiqi)	MQM 'authentic'

MRD	Movement for the Restauration of Democracy
MRO	Madrassa Registration Ordinance
NAB	National Accountability Bureau
NADRA	National Database and Registration Authority
NAP	National Awami Party
NDP	National Democratic Party
NFC	National Finance Commission
NPP	National People's Party
NRO	National Reconciliation Ordinance
NSC	National Security Council
NSF	National Students Federation
NUP	National United Party
NZF	National Zakat Foundation
PATA	Provincially Administered Tribal Areas
PCO	Provisional Constitutional Order
PDA	People's Democratic Alliance
PEMRA	Pakistan Electronic Media Regulatory Agency
PFUJ	Pakistan Federal Union of Journalists
PILDAT	Pakistan Institute of Legislative Development and Transparency
PIPS	Pakistan Institute of Peace Studies
PkMAP	Pakhtunkhwa Milli Awami Party
PML	Pakistan Muslim League
PML(F)	Pakistan Muslim League (Functional)
PML(N)	Pakistan Muslim League (Nawaz)
PML(Q)	Pakistan Muslim League (Qaïd-e-Azam)
PML (Pagaro)	see PML(F)
PNA	Pakistan National Alliance
PONM	Pakistan Oppressed National Minorities
PPI	Punjabi Pakhtoon Ittehad
PPL	Progressive Papers Ltd
PPP	Pakistan People's Party
PPPP	Pakistan People's Party Parliamentarians
PRODA	Public and Representative Office (Disqualification) Act
PTI	Pakistan Tehrik-e-Insaf
PZF	Provincial Zakat Funds
RCO	Revival of Constitution of 1973 Order
RSS	Rashtriya Swayamsevak Sangh
SJC	Supreme Judicial Council

LIST OF ACRONYMS

SMC	Summary Military Courts
SMP	Sipah-e Muhammad Pakistan
SOTF	Special Operations Task Force
SPCCR	Special Parliamentary Committee on Constitutional Reforms
SSG	Special Services Group
SSP	Sipah-e-Sahaba Pakistan
TJP	Tehrik-e Jafria Pakistan
TNJF	Tehrik-e Nifaz-e Fiqh Jaafriya
TNSM	Tehrik-e-Nifaz-e-Shariat-e-Muhammadi
TT	Tehrik-e-taliban
TTP	Tehrik-e-taliban Pakistan
UGC	University Grants Commission
UP	United Provinces, then Uttar Pradesh

BIBLIOGRAPHY

Abou Zahab Mariam and Roy Olivier, *Islamist Networks. The Afghan-Pakistan Connection*, London, Hurst, 2006.

Ahmed Feroz, *Ethnicity and Politics in Pakistan*, Karachi, Oxford University Press, 1998.

Akbar Zaidi S., *Issues in Pakistan's Economy*, Karachi, Oxford University Press, 2005.

Binder Leonard, *Religion and Politics in Pakistan*, Berkeley, University of California Press, 1962.

Burki Shahid Javed, *Pakistan. Fifty Years of Nationhood*, Boulder, Westview Press, 1999.

Cohen Stephen P., *The Pakistani Army*, Karachi, Oxford University Press, 1998.

Gaborieau M., *Un autre islam. Inde, Pakistan, Bangladesh*, Paris, Albin Michel, 2007.

Gayer Laurent, *Karachi. Ordered Disorder and the Struggle for the City*, London, Hurst, 2013.

Grare Frédéric, *Le Pakistan face au conflit afghan (1979–1985). Au tournant de la guerre froide*, Paris, L'Harmattan, 1997.

Grare Frédéric, *Political Islam in the Indian Subcontinent. The Jamaati-Islami*, Delhi, Manohar, 2001.

Gul Imtiaz, *The Most Dangerous Place. Pakistan's Lawless Frontier*, London, Penguin Books, 2010.

Haqqani Hussain, *Pakistan. Between Mosque and Military*, Washington DC, Carnegie, 2005.

Hasan Mushirul, *Nationalism and Communal Politics in India, 1916–1928*, New Delhi, Manohar, 1991.

Hussain Zahid, *Frontline Pakistan. The Struggle with Militant Islam*, New York, Columbia University Press, 2008.

Jaffrelot Christophe (ed.), *Le Pakistan, carrefour de tensions régionales*, Bruxelles, Complexe, 2002.

——, *A History of Pakistan and its origins*, London, Anthem Press, 2004

——, *Pakistan. Nationalism without a Nation?*, London/New York, Zed Books, 2002.

Jalal Ayesha, *The Sole Spokesman. Jinnah, the Muslim League and the Demand for Pakistan*, Cambridge, Cambridge University Press, 1985.

BIBLIOGRAPHY

———, *The State of Martial Rule. The Origins of Pakistan's Political Economy of Defence*, Cambridge, Cambridge University Press, 1990.

Kazimi M.R. (ed.), *M.A. Jinnah. Views and Reviews*, Karachi, Oxford University Press, 2005.

Kennedy Charles H., *Bureaucracy in Pakistan*, Karachi, Oxford University Press, 1987.

Khan Lal, *Pakistan's Other Story. The 1968–69 Revolution*, Lahore, The Struggle Publications, 2010.

Lelyveld David, *Aligarh's First Generation. Muslim Solidarity in British India*, Princeton, Princeton University Press, 1978.

Malik I.H., *State and Civil Society in Pakistan*, Londres, MacMillan, 1997.

Malik Jamal, *Colonization of Islam. Dissolution of Traditional Institutions in Pakistan*, Delhi, Manohar, 1998.

McGrath Allen, *The Destruction of Pakistan's Democracy*, Karachi, Oxford University Press, 1998.

Nasr Seyyed Vali Reza, *Mawdudi and the Making of Islamic Revivalism*, New York, Oxford University Press, 1996.

———, *The Vanguard of Islamic Revolution: The Jama'ati Islami of Pakistan*, Berkeley, University of California Press, 1994.

Nawaz Shuja, *Crossed Swords. Pakistan, Its Army and the Wars Within*, New York, Oxford University Press, 2008.

Newberg Paula, *Judging the State. Courts and Constitutional Politics in Pakistan*, Cambridge, Cambridge University Press, 1995.

Niazi Zamir, *The Press in Chains*, Karachi, Karachi Press Club, 1986.

Oldenburg Philip, *India, Pakistan and Democracy. Solving the Puzzle of Divergent Paths*, London & New York, Routledge, 2010.

Rahman Tariq, *Language and Politics in Pakistan*, Karachi, Oxford University Press, 1998.

Rashid Ahmed, *Descent into Chaos. The U.S. and the disaster in Pakistan, Afghanistan, and Central Asia*, London, Pengin, 2008.

———, *Pakistan on the Brink. The Future of Pakistan, Afghanistan and the West*, London, Allen Lane, 2012.

———, *Taliban. Militant Islam, Oil and Fundamentalism in Central Asia*, New Haven, Yale University Press, 2010.

Rizvi Hasan-Askari, *Military, State and Society in Pakistan*, London, Macmillan, 2000.

Robinson Francis, *Separatism among Indian Muslims*, Cambridge, Cambridge University Press, 1974.

Samad Yunus, *A Nation in Turmoil. Nationalism and Ethnicity in Pakistan, 1937–1958*, New Delhi, Sage, 1989.

Sayeed Khalid B., *The Political System of Pakistan*, Boston, Houghton Mifflin, 1967.

Shaikh Farzana, *Community and Consensus in Islam. Muslim Representation in Colonial India, 1860–1947 [1989]*, Delhi, Imprint One, 2012.

———, *Making Sense of Pakistan*, Londres, Hurst, 2009.

Siddiqa Ayesha, *Military Inc. Inside Pakistan's Military Economy*, Londres, Pluto Press, 2007.

BIBLIOGRAPHY

Sisson Richard and Rose Leo E., *War and Secession. Pakistan, India and the Creation of Bangladesh*, Berkeley and Los Angeles, University of California Press, 1990.

Talbot Ian, *Pakistan. A Modern History*, London, Hurst, 1999.

———, *Pakistan. A New History*, London, Hurst, 2012.

Tankel Stephen, *Storming the World Stage: The Story of Lashkar-e-Taiba*, London, Hurst, 2011.

Waseem Mohammad, *Politics and the State in Pakistan*, Islamabad, National Institute of Historical and Cultural Research, 1994.

Wolpert Stanley, *Zulfi Bhutto of Pakistan. His Life and Times*, New York, Oxford University Press, 1993.

INDEX

INDEX

INDEX

INDEX

INDEX

INDEX

INDEX

INDEX

INDEX